BizTalk Server 2002 Design and Implementation

XIN CHEN

BizTalk Server 2002 Design and Implementation
Copyright ©2003 by Xin Chen

ISBN (pbk): 1-59059-034-1

Technical Reviewer: Gordon Mackie
Editorial Directors: Dan Appleman, Gary Cornell, Jason Gilmore, Simon Hayes, Karen Watterson, John Zukowski
Managing Editor: Grace Wong
Project Manager: Sofia Marchant
Development Editor: Andy Carroll
Copy Editor: Ami Knox
Compositor: Impressions Book and Journal Services, Inc.
Indexer: Nancy Guenther
Cover Designer: Kurt Krames
Production Manager: Kari Brooks
Manufacturing Manager: Tom Debolski
Marketing Manager: Stephanie Rodriguez

Distributed to the book trade in the United States by Springer-Verlag New York, Inc., 175 Fifth Avenue, New York, NY, 10010 and outside the United States by Springer-Verlag GmbH & Co. KG, Tiergartenstr. 17, 69112 Heidelberg, Germany.

In the United States, phone 1-800-SPRINGER, email orders@springer-ny.com, or visit http://www.springer-ny.com. Outside the United States, fax +49 6221 345229, email orders@springer.de, or visit http://www.springer.de.

For information on translations, please contact Apress directly at 2560 Ninth Street, Suite 219, Berkeley, CA 94710. Phone 510-549-5930, fax 510-549-5939, email info@apress.com, or visit http://www.apress.com.

The source code for this book is available to readers at http://www.apress.com in the Downloads section.

For my father

Contents at a Glance

Contents

Appendix B BizTalk Server API Reference 645

Foreword

CREATING A COMPANY is a wonderfully precarious endeavor. In spearheading this effort, I had a mix of emotions: pride and excitement matched with fear; wide-eyed naivete anchored with plenty of lessons learned. All of the challenges of turning an idea into tangible results, however, pale in comparison to breathing life into a nascent company while the world around you falls into chaos. This was the reality that we faced when we launched i-Deal LLC, a provider of new issue technologies to the global financial marketplace, in late August of 2001. We had worked through most of 2001, starting development, securing partners and funding, and trying to keep morale up while my staff sat shoulder to shoulder at card tables, pushing each other toward success. Less than a month later, all of our hard work almost ended on September 11, 2001, when we watched the World Trade Center burst into flames from our office window on Fulton Street and Broadway.

Life was uncertain after that. We didn't know whether our founding partners, Merrill Lynch, Salomon Smith Barney, Thomson Financial, and Microsoft, would pull the plug, given most had suffered such devastating losses and had so much aftershock to deal with. To their credit, they kept our dream alive and gave us the chance we needed to develop our platform and test the commercial waters with our software. Even more credit is to be given to the dozen of employees and consultants, Xin Chen being one of them, who came back to work across the street from Ground Zero every day to finish the job that they started. We worked side by side, supported one another, and immersed ourselves in our work, trying to erase images of madness and shards of a once mighty edifice.

Today our company is alive and well, almost 180 strong, and back on track to meet the challenge of delivering the world's only global new-issue platform that supports equities, fixed income, and municipal offerings. Delivering on such a wide and complex mandate is a tall order. First and foremost, our clients are the brokerage firms whose bread and butter is the new issue business. It is their crown jewel, so nothing but the best, most efficient solution would be sufficient to meet their heavy global demands. Second, as a business that is an ASP, we have to give our clients the comfort that their information is secure, yet readily accessible to only authenticated users. Third, we had to have the ability to map their proprietary business processing to our internal business processes and make the integration and data exchange seamless. The new issue business, by nature, involves a "syndicate" that needs to collaborate in order to execute a transaction. Whether the requirement is pure data exchange or system-to-system interoperability, data exchange needs to be robust, flexible, secure, and redundant. We chose BizTalk Server to meet this business need.

Xin was one of the key developers who utilized BizTalk Server to enable our clients to map large feeds of standing data and historical information, and he paved the way for what ultimately became our straight-through-processing solution. BizTalk Server and BizTalk Orchestration allow i-Deal to react to our clients' diverse business needs and processing requirements. It allows our company to easily deploy and manage integrated solutions, which is the lifeblood for an ASP business model with a client base of financial institutions. Xin was instrumental in delivering our solution—his discovery and thoughtful leadership allowed us to simplify many tasks that are typically complex and time consuming, thus minimizing project risks.

When Xin contacted me about writing the foreword for his book, the first thought that came to mind was, "When did he find the time to write a book? He was always working!" Then I thought about it further and it was clear that he had always been consumed by the adventure of learning and teaching, and it all made perfect sense. His dedication to his craft has always been unquestioned and unequaled. His ability to break down a problem set into manageable tasks and deliver an easily understood solution has always been his strength. The reader of this book will find more of the same.

Frank LaQuinta
Chief Technology Officer
i-Deal LLC
New York City, New York
September 18, 2002

About the Foreword Writer

Frank LaQuinta is a financial services technology veteran with over 18 years of experience. Frank has been i-Deal's chief technology officer from the company's inception. In addition to having the responsibility for i-Deal's technology strategy and vision, Frank oversees the day-to-day development and implementation of the firm's core initiatives.

Previously, Frank led technology product management and development for e-syndicate activity at Merrill Lynch's Direct Markets (MLX) institutional e-commerce group. In addition, he was responsible for building the original suite of new issuance technology that is the framework of i-Deal's platform.

Frank earned his BBA and MBA in information systems from Pace University.

About the Author

 **Xin Chen** is a solution development consultant at Avanade (a joint venture between Microsoft and Accenture). His professional career has been focused on Web and B2B application development with Microsoft technology from the old DNA days to the developments of .NET today. Chen is very proud that he designed and built the very first BizTalk Server application for the U.S. financial industry, a chance that comes only once a lifetime. He is also a contributing author of *BizTalk Server: The Complete Reference*. Xin Chen holds MCSD, MCSE, and MCDBA certifications. He earned his MS in statistics from Columbia University.

About the Technical Reviewer

Gordon Mackie works as a senior developer consultant for The Mandelbrot Set (now part of Charteris plc). He has worked with Visual Basic from the early days, mostly at the coalface as a contract programmer for various banks and large corporations, but also as a trainer and consultant. He recently spent 8 months working at Microsoft on .NET projects. Gordon can be reached at gordon.mackie@charteris.com.

Acknowledgments

I FIRST THOUGHT about writing a BizTalk Server book when I rolled off a project at i-Deal where I was helping to build a BizTalk Server application. I've seen what BizTalk Server offers firsthand and have come to appreciate it. I've also seen many people reject BizTalk Server based on their lack of knowledge about the product. That's when I decided to write a book to tell the story of what I learned about BizTalk Server.

BizTalk Server introduced many new concepts for building an application compared to other server products out there. I felt that the traditional "manual-style" writing wouldn't deliver these concepts efficiently, since many of BizTalk Server's features and their applications are rather difficult to grasp at first glance. The book would be much more comprehensible if I could talk about these features in a context that allowed readers to come to understand not only each aspect of BizTalk Server but also how they all fit together in the overall picture. So I came up with a fictitious story of two characters and a project to make learning BizTalk Server an enjoyable experience.

Writing a book is a long process and requires great dedication. However, it has never entered my mind that it's tiresome work. I guess that perception is due to a familiar influence. My father wrote several books when I was still in elementary school. He was always writing and rarely played with me. In the mind of a 6-year-old child, that seemed like it was so much fun. Many years later, I found myself doing the exact same thing. That's just one more instance of something you find out later in life that confirms your parents are always right.

In process of bringing this book to you, many people have spent a considerable amount of effort. I want to thank Karen Watterson for her unreserved support and dedication to my book; Andy Carroll for a great job editing my book to make it more enjoyable to read; Gordon Mackie for helping ensure the technical accuracy of each chapter and providing a number of great ideas that I have included in the book; Sofia Marchant for ensuring an effective collaboration among author, editors, and reviewers during the whole process; and Ami Knox, Kari Brooks, and many other Apress professionals for working hard together to make this book possible. I also want to give special thanks to Frank LaQuinta for writing such a wonderful and resonating foreword and for providing me an invaluable opportunity from which my experiences in BizTalk Server originated, and Ralph Foster, a good friend and admirable colleague, for mentoring me on BizTalk Server and many other technologies of personal interest.

CHAPTER 1

Introduction to BizTalk Server 2002

THIS CHAPTER COVERS the following topics:

- What BizTalk Server is and does

- The main BizTalk Server tools

- New features in BizTalk Server 2002

This book is about BizTalk Server 2002 and how you can take advantage of its features to solve problems associated with integrating business processes from multiple sources. In this chapter, you'll get the chance to explore BizTalk Server and how you can use it for both enterprise integration within an organization and creating business-to-business (B2B) solutions.

What Is BizTalk Server?

In simple terms, BizTalk Server is a server platform that provides solutions for business processes integration. The rather slippery term "business processes integration" (which, I'm happy to say, doesn't seem to be widely "acronymized" yet) refers to integrating different business processes so that they operate in collaboration to provide services. There are three major areas you need to consider when developing a business integration solution:

- Enterprise application integration (EAI)

- Business-to-business (B2B) implementation

- Business processing automation (BPA)

Before plunging into BizTalk Server per se, let's pause to see how you can use it and why you would want to.

EAI

I don't think there's a company on earth today that only uses a single application. Most organizations, from small office/home office (SOHO) to small and medium-sized business (SMB) to the world's largest global conglomerates use dozens if not hundreds—even thousands—of different applications. And it's not uncommon for these applications to basically be "stovepipe" applications—applications that were designed in relative isolation from other applications or business processes, often using proprietary data formats.

The result is a set of applications that need to talk to each other in order to provide certain services, but that speak different languages. Problems such as incompatible data formats and incompatible communication protocols make application integration within an enterprise a veritable nightmare—one that increases exponentially in complexity as more applications are added into the solution (see Figure 1-1).

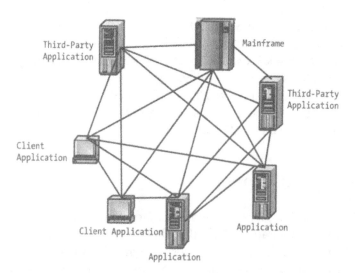

Figure 1-1. The complexity increases as more applications participate in business processes.

Imagine, for example, a situation where one application supports only method calls over Distributed COM (DCOM, an aging protocol used by Windows applications to call other COM components on the remote host), while another application that it tries to communicate with only supports Hypertext Transfer Protocol (HTTP, a protocol commonly used to transmit data across the Internet). To enable such incompatible applications to talk to each other, you would have to create point-to-point communications between each application involved in the business processes, and create customized programs to resolve the incompatible communications among these applications. Besides the massive development efforts that make the application integration difficult, the number of individual links required between applications would also make the management of these applications a job no one wants, except perhaps programmers in search of lifetime job security.

B2B

Like EAI, B2B is also about integrating business processes, but in this case between different organizations. Consider a classic online purchase. Let's assume that when a customer submits an order to a retailer's Web site, the retailer's Web site generates a purchase order and sends it to the manufacturer. The manufacturer's system then checks its warehouse for this product. If the product is in stock, a confirmation is generated and sent to the retailer. The retailer then passes the confirmation to the customer to notify him or her that the order is being processed.

From the customer's point of view, his or her order represents a single process, but in our simple example, there are actually two organizations involved in completing this order. Both retailer and manufacturer must have integrated their business processes and order purchasing processes to complete the transaction.

Figure 1-2 illustrates a typical B2B scenario in which one organization conducts business with a number of external business partners.

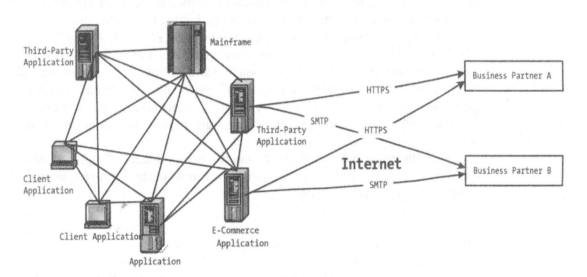

Figure 1-2. A typical B2B environment

In addition to the technical challenges people face in an EAI scenario, B2B implementations also have to deal with Security (yes, uppercase *S*). When data flies back and forth over the Internet between different organizations, you must take extra care to ensure that the transmitted data remains private to the organizations that conduct business together. And you have to not only ensure that the data is secured, but also that it reaches its intended destination and no others. All these things must be considered when building B2B applications.

(In case you're wondering whether all enterprises participating in B2B have to use Microsoft's BizTalk Servers, the answer is a resounding "No." One of BizTalk's many features is that it's based on the Web's newest lingua franca, XML.)

BPA

In either the EAI or B2B scenario, the overall process must control and orchestrate the tasks of disparate applications that work together to provide an integrated business process. BPA can be thought of as a control center for the participating applications either within the organization or between organizations.

Why Use BizTalk Server?

Tools, no matter whether they are hardware or software, are created to solve some specific problems. BizTalk Server is no exception. It is a tool built to solve the problems that commonly exist in the areas of B2B, EAI, and BPA. BizTalk Server provides the integration solutions outlined in the previous sections with its two major components: BizTalk Messaging and BizTalk Orchestration. BizTalk Messaging provides the ability to route data between different and independent applications within an organization or between organizations. BizTalk Orchestration provides the ability to automate disparate business processes that span different applications and organizations.

We'll dig down into the details of these two components in Chapter 3. For now, let's take a brief look at how BizTalk Server could facilitate and enhance operations in EAI, B2B, and BPA.

BizTalk Server in an EAI Scenario

As you can see in Figure 1-3, in its capacity as message broker, BizTalk Server can help reduce the integration complexity an organization faces (compare with Figure 1-1).

Figure 1-3. An EAI scenario with BizTalk Server

By implementing BizTalk Server as message broker to route data between applications, individual applications no longer need to establish multiple connections with different applications and support various data formats. Instead, each application only needs to communicate with BizTalk Server using the application's native data format and communication protocol. BizTalk Messaging, one of the BizTalk Server services, takes care of interapplication messaging and supports many types of communication protocols including HTTP, Simple Mail Transfer Protocol (SMTP), and Microsoft Message Queue (MSMQ), and multiple data formats such as Extensible Markup Language (XML), Electronic Data Interchange (EDI), and so on. BizTalk Messaging converts the data formats and protocols to ensure the applications can send and receive data to and from other applications within the enterprise.

BizTalk Server in a B2B Scenario

BizTalk Server can produce similar benefits in a B2B scenario. Besides the ability to convert data between different formats and support numerous communication protocols, BizTalk Server also comes with built-in security features that ensure the data is transmitted between different organizations over the Internet securely.

Figure 1-4 shows BizTalk Server acting as a message broker for internal applications as well as being a gateway to applications in external organizations (compare with Figure 1-2).

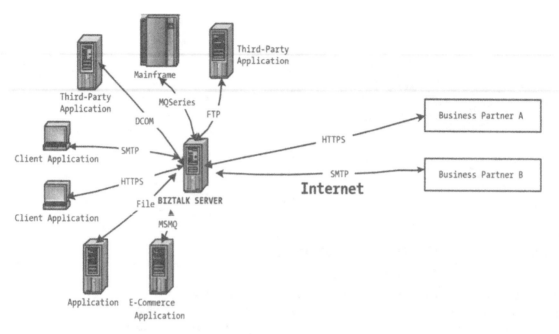

Figure 1-4. A B2B scenario with BizTalk Server

In a B2B scenario, BizTalk Server not only facilitates business process integration by routing data between applications within the organization, it also facilitates business process integration that extends to external organizations.

BizTalk Server in a BPA Scenario

BizTalk Orchestration, which is another important component of BizTalk Server, is what you use to achieve business process automation. BizTalk Orchestration allows organizations to coordinate and manage their business processes across multiple applications and organizations.

BizTalk Orchestration comes with a graphic design tool called BizTalk Orchestration Designer, shown in Figure 1-5, which allows you to create workflows that consist of a series of business processes in a user-friendly interface. BizTalk Orchestration Designer is built on top of Microsoft's Visio, so its user interface looks very similar to that of Visio. As a matter of fact, BizTalk Orchestration needs Visio 2000 or higher on the machine to run. The business processes in the workflow can then be associated with different applications both within the organization and in other organizations. BizTalk Orchestration can automate this series of business processes by orchestrating how data flows into and out of business processes and how each business process responds to the data.

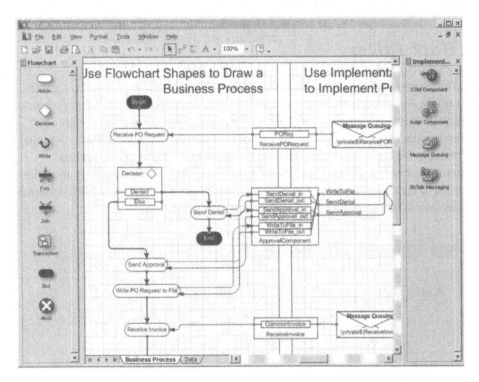

Figure 1-5. The BizTalk Orchestration Designer interface

With BizTalk Orchestration, you can define a series of business processes to provide certain business services. For example, in a B2B order processing scenario, a number of disparate business processes would be involved in processing a purchase order. Those business processes could be for receiving a purchase order, receiving an invoice, and sending a payment. Each of these business processes may be performed by a different application in a different organization. With BizTalk Orchestration Designer, you can create a workflow to automate these processes by connecting each of the business processes and applications together as shown in Figure 1-5. (You'll see how it's done in Chapter 3.)

BizTalk Server comes with a set of feature-rich tools that you can use to develop a BizTalk solution for business process integration. I'll give a quick overview on these tools next.

BizTalk Server Quick Overview

As you've seen, BizTalk's Messaging and Orchestration components serve as its foundation. However, BizTalk Server is more than Messaging and Orchestration. It also comes with a handful of tools and utilities you'll use to build your integration solutions. Here's a quick overview of these tools.

BizTalk Editor

BizTalk Server technology is built around the idea of XML. In fact, XML is used as BizTalk Server's internal data format, and it is central to BizTalk Server's functionality, so it isn't surprising BizTalk Server comes with a set of tools that deal directly with XML. BizTalk Editor is one of these tools. BizTalk Editor allows you to define a BizTalk schema in a GUI environment (see Figure 1-6). BizTalk schemas are based on the XML-Data Reduced (XDR) schema, which is an earlier version of an XML schema created by Microsoft before the current XML Schema Definition (XSD) became a W3C recommendation.

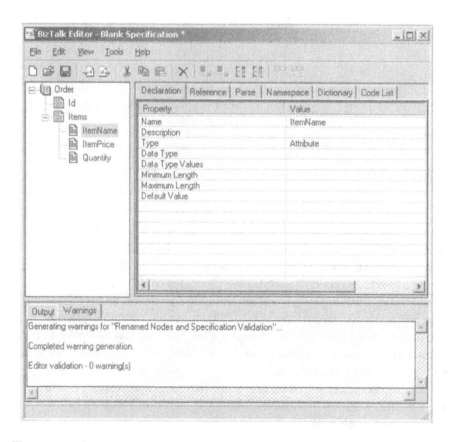

Figure 1-6. The BizTalk Editor interface

BizTalk Editor doesn't just create schemas for XML documents; it also allows you to create schemas for flat file documents, X12 documents (X12 is an EDI standard set by Accredited Standards Committee X12), EDI documents, and other types of documents as long as you have the document parser for that type of document. (For example, you need an HIPAA parser to process an HIPAA document, HIPAA being a document standard that is used by the healthcare industry.) BizTalk comes with four document parsers out of the box: XML, X12, EDI, and flat file. After you create a schema, you can save it to a file location or to Web Distributed Authoring and Versioning (WebDAV), which allows you to retrieve the file through the HTTP protocol. I'll show you how to create an XML schema from scratch in Chapter 3, where I'll discuss BizTalk Editor in more detail.

BizTalk Mapper

BizTalk Mapper is a very important tool that allows you to transform data from one schema to another. It uses Extensible Stylesheet Language Transformations (XSLT) technology to perform the actual data transformation.

To convert an XML document from one schema to another schema, you must first create XSLT codes. Anyone who has done some Web development using XSLT knows how much effort goes into converting a small amount of XML data to HTML (HTML being a special Web page version of XML). BizTalk Mapper offers a drag-and-drop interface for creating XSLT, which is an attractive alternative to handcrafting it. Figure 1-7 shows one XSLT file I wouldn't want to create by hand.

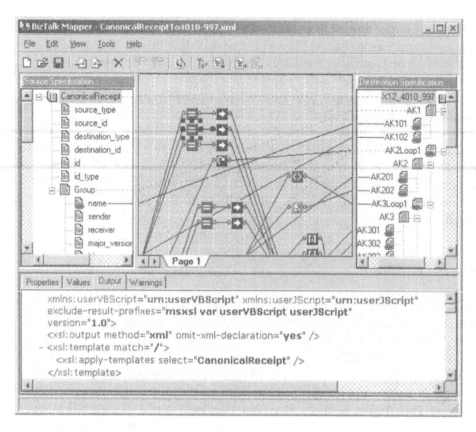

Figure 1-7. BizTalk Mapper in action

Figure 1-7 shows an XML document in the top-left panel and an X12 document on the right. The lines that connect elements in the XML document with elements in the X12 document indicate that data from the elements in the XML document should be plugged into the elements in the X12 document. The colorful icons in the middle panel are called *functoids,* and they allow you to manipulate the data before it is plugged into the second document. (BizTalk ships with many useful functoids for mathematical calculation and string manipulation, and you can also write your own scripts using VBScript or JavaScript to modify the data before it is plugged into the other document.)

The code in the bottom half of the window is the XSLT code generated by the drag-and-drop interface above it. BizTalk Mapper also allows you to specify a document to be transformed, and Mapper will then output the mapped document so that you can verify that all the links are correct. It's easier to debug the mapping than to follow all the tangled lines to ensure the data transformation is correct.

BizTalk Messaging Manager

BizTalk Server's Messaging Manager is one of those tools BizTalk developers typically spend a lot of time looking at because it's where messaging configuration takes place (see Figure 1-8). Messaging Manager will help you configure data providers and data consumers, and establish how data is transmitted from one party to another and how the tasks are performed while data is flowing through the system. Messaging Manager also provides a browser UI, which means you can use it remotely as a Web application.

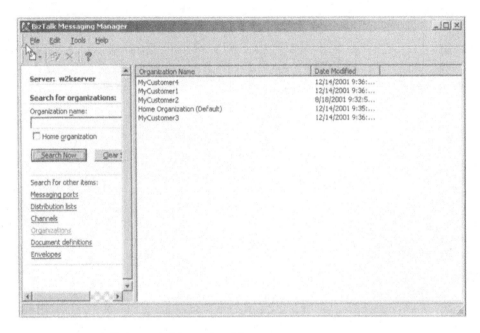

Figure 1-8. BizTalk Server's Messaging Manager

In the left panel of Figure 1-8, you can see six items in the list, with Organizations selected. On the right, you can see the entries for the selected item. There's a lot more to be said about Messaging Manager, and in Chapter 3 I'll demonstrate how to use it to configure a number of routes though which data will be transferred.

BizTalk Orchestration Designer

BizTalk Server's Orchestration Designer is where you'll define the workflow for your business processes (see Figure 1-9). Powerful as it is, bear in mind that

BizTalk Orchestration isn't a complete programming language (although many features of BizTalk Server can be extended programmatically, as you'll see in Chapter 11). It can handle loops and simple if-then-else statements, but it's not designed to handle complex logic. You can't, for example, create variables inside an orchestration. BizTalk Orchestration is designed to let business analysts or programmers combine different business processes to perform a task.

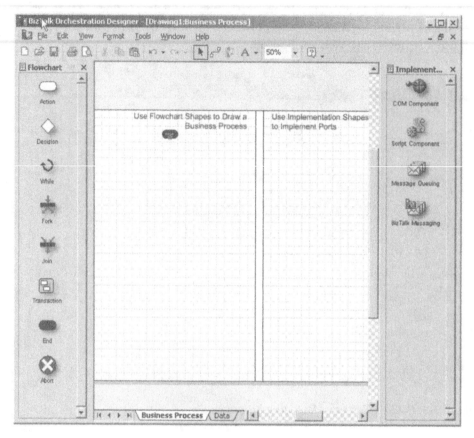

Figure 1-9. BizTalk Orchestration Designer

Figure 1-9 shows flowchart shapes and implementation shapes in the far left and right panels, respectively. BizTalk Orchestration currently supports four types of implementation shapes:

- *COM Component:* This gives BizTalk Orchestration the ability to send data to a COM component as input.

- *Script Component:* This is similar to the COM Component except instead of using a COM DLL, it uses a Windows Scripting Component (WSC) file.

- *Message Queuing:* This represents a MSMQ store, both local MSMQ and remote MSMQ. Orchestration can send the data to a message queue on a local machine or on a remote server by attaching this shape to it.

- *BizTalk Messaging:* This shape allows BizTalk to bring data into an orchestration or to retrieve data from an orchestration. It is a bidirectional link between BizTalk Messaging and BizTalk Orchestration.

Got you curious? Rest assured that I'll dig deep into BizTalk Orchestration in Chapters 3 and 4.

BizTalk Server Administration

BizTalk Server Administration is another program you're likely to spend quite a bit of time with. It allows you to configure BizTalk Server properties, such as the database connection property, SMTP host, HTTP proxy setting, and so on. Figure 1-10 shows the BizTalk Server Administration interface. BizTalk Server Administration can also be accessed through an MMC console snap-in.

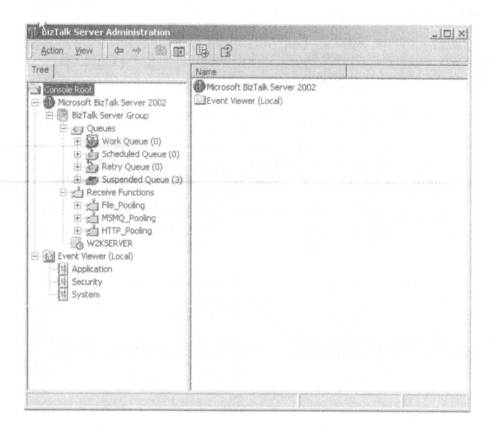

Figure 1-10. The BizTalk Server Administration interface

In the left panel in Figure 1-10, you can see a node called BizTalk Server Group with three nodes below it: Queues, Receive Functions, and W2KSERVER (the local system's name in this example).

The Event Viewer shown in the left panel of the console is similar to the Event Viewer found under Administrative Tools on the Program menu of the Start button, and it provides a handy way for you to see what the current events are without opening another window.

Queues

The Queues node is not related to Microsoft Message Queuing (MSMQ) as the name implies. It refers to BizTalk Queues, which are really a bunch of database tables used to store messages that are passing through BizTalk Server. There are four queues:

- The *work queue* holds all the messages that are waiting to be processed or are being processed.

- The *scheduled queue* holds all the messages that are scheduled to be processed at a specific time. For instance, there may be some large messages that you only want to process at night, so when that kind of message arrives, BizTalk Server will put it into a scheduled queue so that it can be picked up at night for processing.

- The *retry queue* holds messages that are having problems reaching their destination. For instance, if a trading partner's Web site just goes down, a message that is being sent will be put in this queue to be resubmitted at a later time. If the Web site is still down at that later time, the message will be moved to the suspended queue.

- The *suspended queue* holds messages that, for one reason or another, can't be processed. The reasons for messages not being processed are many. An invalid XML message or a message with an invalid schema will be put into this queue. By checking this queue, you can identify problems in your BizTalk system.

Receive Functions

Before BizTalk Server can perform its work, the document has to somehow get into BizTalk Server. Receive Functions provide one of two ways a document can be submitted to BizTalk Server. The second way is through the use of the BizTalk Interchange component, which I'll cover in Chapter 3.

BizTalk Server Administration has the following three types of Receive Functions:

- The *File Receive Function* defines a file location, either local or remote, that BizTalk Server constantly watches for arriving files. When new files arrive, BizTalk Server will read the data and save it into BizTalk Server's work queue (a database table that holds all the incoming data), and then remove the file. Data providers send their data as files to this location and expect them to be picked up by BizTalk Server for processing.

- The *MSMQ Receive Function* uses the same concept as the File Receive Function, except it reads data stored in MSMQ rather than a file location. After BizTalk reads the data, it is removed from MSMQ.

- The *HTTP Receive Function* is a bit different from the other two because, although the file receive and MSMQ Receive Functions both watch a location, file, or queue for incoming data, the HTTP Receive Function doesn't watch any kind of location. It simply consists of an ISAPI file called BizTalkHttpReceive.dll that is exposed through a Web directory. When data is posted to this file through the virtual Web directory, BizTalkHttpReceive.dll will accept the data in HTTP POST and bring it to BizTalk Server's work queue or save the data to a file location. Although the technology behind the HTTP Receive Function is different from the other two, it offers the same end result—an entry point for external data providers to get their data into BizTalk Server. (You'll get a look at this topic in detail in Chapter 9, so don't worry if this brief explanation has left you puzzled.)

BizTalk Member Server

The third node in Figure 1-10 (below the Receive Functions node) sports a computer icon with a green arrow in it that indicates the status of BizTalk Server—whether or not it's running. In Figure 1-10, this node is labeled W2KSERVER, which is my BizTalk Server, but the Administration Console will display multiple icons (BizTalk Servers) if you've set up a BizTalk Server group. If one BizTalk Server fails in a server group, the other BizTalk Servers will pick up the load and continue the service without interruption. This is a great way to provide both fault tolerance and load balancing. I'll discuss BizTalk Server groups in detail in Chapter13.

BizTalk SEED Wizard

BizTalk's SEED Wizard, shown in Figure 1-11, is a tool that can help you quickly set up all the components necessary to start sending documents from one organization to another. It is only useful when both organizations are using BizTalk Server. This wizard has many screens, and you'll see it in action in Chapter 9.

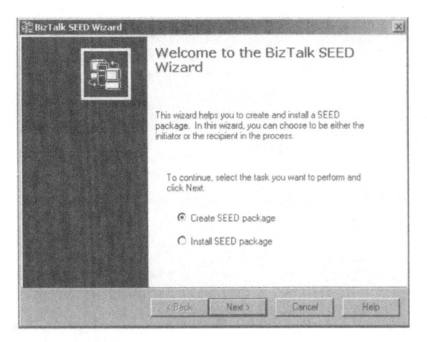

Figure 1-11. BizTalk SEED Wizard

BizTalk Document Tracking

BizTalk Document Tracking gives you the ability to track every document passing through BizTalk Server. Don't worry—you can also turn off the tracking for certain types of documents if you want to. By default, however, BizTalk Server saves *every* document that passes though it to its tracking database. This tracking database can be queried through the BizTalk Document Tracking Web application to find out exactly what documents come in at what hours of which days. It's clearly very handy when you need to track down a specific document, or when, for legal reasons, you need to maintain an audit trail. Figure 1-12 shows the BizTalk Document Tracking Web application.

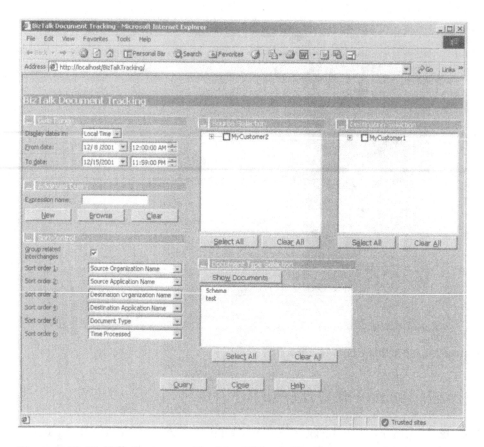

Figure 1-12. BizTalk Document Tracking Web application

With the BizTalk Document Tracking Web application, you can search for a specific document type from one specific organization to another, as shown in Figure 1-12. Clicking the Query button at the bottom of the window should result in a list of documents that fit the criteria, as shown in Figure 1-13. You can see the content of the documents by clicking the Notepad icon.

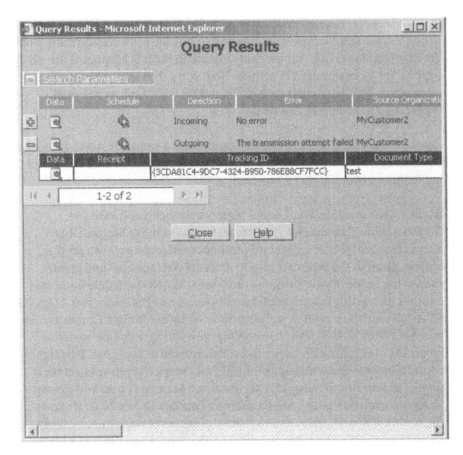

Figure 1-13. Results of a tracking query

New Features in BizTalk Server 2002

So far, this chapter has provided an overview of some of the features and tools in
BizTalk Server. In case you're familiar with BizTalk Server 2000, you may be interested in knowing what's new:

- *BizTalk Editor:* An XSD schema can be exported from a BizTalk schema
  using this editor. You still can't import an XSD schema in this version, but
  being able to export means you don't need to handcraft the conversion
  yourself.

- *BizTalk Mapper:* You can now test a mapping of an instance of a document within the BizTalk Mapper, enabling you to quickly see what the output of the mapping looks like. Another new feature in BizTalk Mapper is the .NET support for its customized functoids. Now you can create your own functoids using .NET languages such as C# and VB.NET. And, as you might expect, you'll see how in this book.

- *Receive Function:* The HTTP Receive function is a welcome new addition to BizTalk Server 2002. It contains a high-performance ISAPI DLL for accepting data sent over the HTTP protocol.

- *BizTalk Orchestration:* Web service support has been enhanced in Orchestration. This enables your orchestration to make Simple Object Access Protocol (SOAP, a standard protocol used to access Web service objects through the Internet) calls to external Web services and greatly extend the scope of your business processes. XLANG Schedule pooling is another interesting feature added to this version of BizTalk Server. (XLANG Schedules are the workflow scripts produced by the BizTalk Orchestration process.) With XLANG Schedule pooling, you can specify how many instances of certain schedules can be instantiated at one time. This significantly increases the scalability of the XLANG service when your server is unable to handle too many XLANG instances at once. A new and cleaner XLANG correlation is also now available in BizTalk Server 2002. It allows the multiple XLANG instances to share the same message queue during a correlation. (We'll be talking about XLANG correlation more in later chapters.)

- *Integrated Security for BizTalk Server's database:* Unlike the earlier version, BizTalk Server now supports the Windows Authentication mode for databases used by BizTalk Server. (Windows Authentication mode allows a user to connect to SQL Server through a Microsoft Windows NT 4.0 or Windows 2000 user account.) In the previous version, only Mixed mode was supported. (Mixed mode allows users to connect to an instance of SQL Server using either Windows Authentication or SQL Server Authentication.)

- *Database management:* Some new stored procedures and SQL Agent Jobs have been added to maintain the Document Tracking and XLANG databases.

- *SEED:* The SEED Wizard has been added to this version to provide faster ways for business partners to set up the necessary BizTalk Messaging configurations so they can quickly start sending documents for processing.

- *Deployment with Application Center:* Now that BizTalk Server has been integrated with Application Center (Microsoft's deployment and management tool for high-availability Web applications built on the Microsoft Windows 2000 operating system), the deployment of the BizTalk Server application can be replicated and synchronized among different environments, thereby simplifying deployment.

- *MOM package:* A Microsoft Operations Manager (MOM) package comes with BizTalk Server 2002. (MOM is a Microsoft software product that provides event and performance management for the Windows 2000 Server family of operating systems and .NET Enterprise Server applications.) This package contains many useful predefined event processing rules, alerts, and performance monitors that are ready to run (assuming you own MOM). By enabling this package, you can centralize the management for all your BizTalk Servers from a single console, and set up customized actions to be taken when certain events or alerts fire on the BizTalk Server. It provides a great amount of information on what's happening on each BizTalk Server.

Summary

In this chapter, you have learned the basic concepts of BizTalk Server 2002. You've looked at various business-process scenarios, both within and between organisations and their trading partners, and learned a few three-letter acronyms (TLAs) along the way. I've shown you the needs and problems associated with these scenarios and have begun to introduce the various aspects of BizTalk Server that will help meet these needs and solve these problems. You've also taken a brief look at BizTalk Server tools and new features that I'll discuss in detail in later chapters. The next chapter will cover the installation of BizTalk Server 2002.

CHAPTER 2

BizTalk Server 2002 Installation

THIS CHAPTER COVERS the following topics:

- Hardware and software requirements for BizTalk Server 2002

- Installing BizTalk Server 2002

- Managing BizTalk Server databases

To successfully install BizTalk Server 2002, your system must meet some minimum requirements, both in terms of hardware and software. BizTalk Server can't work alone—its operations depend on a suite of software programs, such as IIS, SQL Server, and MSMQ, so you should verify that these are installed properly before installing BizTalk Server.

The most important advice I can give anyone who's getting ready to install BizTalk Server is to stop and think and plan first. Don't let Microsoft's automated installation routine make all the decisions for you—you may live to regret it. For starters, are you installing a development installation, or one that you plan to morph into a production version? What user account do you plan to use to run BizTalk Server services? What are the database implications you need to consider? These are the kinds of issues I'll be discussing in this chapter, and, frankly, I recommend you at least look through the topics I cover here—even if you have already installed BizTalk Server and it is up and running.

BizTalk Server System Requirements

Before you install the BizTalk Server software, you should know something about the various editions available. There are three editions of BizTalk Server: Enterprise Edition, Standard Edition, and Developer Edition. To find out how much each will cost you, see the BizTalk Server Web site at http://www.microsoft.com/BizTalk.

The Enterprise Edition supports the integration of unlimited internal applications and trading partners. It also supports multiple processors and BizTalk Server groups (multiple BizTalk Servers processing documents as a group—see Chapter 13 for a detailed discussion). The Enterprise Edition is most suitable for large organizations or electronic trading hubs.

The Standard Edition is designed for small to medium-sized organizations where transaction volume is small. The Standard Edition provides support for integrating up to five internal applications with up to five external trading partners. This edition doesn't support multiple processors or BizTalk Server groups.

The Developer Edition provides all the tools and features in the Enterprise Edition, but it is designed for BizTalk developers who develop and test BizTalk Server solutions in the development environment and should not be used in the production environment.

BizTalk Server system requirements consist of both hardware and software requirements. Let's look at the hardware requirements first.

Hardware Requirements

The faster the better, the more the merrier. Make sure your system meets the following minimum requirements:

- 400 MHz or higher Intel Pentium–compatible CPU

- 256MB of RAM

- 6GB of hard disk space (6GB is the minimum recommended by Microsoft. The actual installation requires less disk space than 6GB. Perhaps Microsoft wants to make sure you have enough room to install more of their software.)

- CD-ROM drive

- Network adapter card

- VGA or Super VGA monitor (note that you'll need at least 16MB of graphic memory if you plan to play Quake II on BizTalk Server)

- Microsoft mouse or a compatible pointing device

Let's be honest, folks—these are the *minimum* requirements. The complete installation of BizTalk Server requires 90MB of free hard disk space, plus the disk space for the BizTalk Server databases, namely, BizTalk Messaging database,

BizTalk Tracking database, BizTalk Share Queue database, and BizTalk Orchestration Persistence database. In a production environment, these databases would be hosted on a *remote* database server. You should watch the available free space on such a database server because the BizTalk Tracking and Orchestration Persistence databases can grow very large quickly—make sure you have enough disk space on the server. Later in this chapter, you'll learn a couple of ways to help manage these two databases so that their size won't get out of control.

Also, in terms of physical memory, the more the better. This is especially true for BizTalk Server because it uses an XML DOM parser to handle the validation and mapping of XML documents.

DOM, which stands for Document Object Model, provides a standardized way to access and manipulate the information stored in XML documents. The DOM parser loads a whole XML document into system memory before it can start processing it; if a BizTalk Server doesn't have adequate physical memory to load the document, it will incur heavy disk operation, which will slow down the system dramatically. The system performance under such conditions is usually unacceptable. When a document is small, you can probably get away with less physical memory on the server, since BizTalk Server will free up memory by unloading the documents from memory when it finishes with them. However, if a 7MB or 8MB document is submitted to the BizTalk Server, the server's physical memory would be occupied until the whole document is completely validated and mapped, which may take quite some time even with the fastest processor. In such a case, you should try to chop the large document into many smaller pieces and process them one by one.

Software Requirements

The software requirements for BizTalk Server are as follows:

- Microsoft Windows 2000 Server or Professional with Service Pack 2 (SP2) and NT File System (NTFS, the recommended file system for the Windows 2000 system). BizTalk Server can be installed on both Windows 2000 Professional and Server. Keep in mind that the limit of ten simultaneous connections on the Professional version also applies to the HTTP connections as well. If you're running BizTalk Server on Windows 2000 Professional, and many people try to post documents to your Web server at once, some of them won't get through.

- Microsoft SQL Server 7.0 with SP3 or SQL Server 2000 SP1.

- Internet Information Server (IIS) 5.0 or higher. BizTalk Server uses Web Distributed Authoring and Versioning (WebDAV) to retrieve and save document schema definitions to and from the BizTalk Messaging database. WebDAV uses HTTP as its transport protocol. All the document schema definitions are stored as files under a virtual directory, and WebDAV accesses these files by making HTTP requests. This requires IIS to be up and running. To install IIS if it is not already installed, open Control Panel and select Add/Remove Programs. Click the Add/Remove Windows Component button on the left panel, and a new window opens, as shown in Figure 2-1. Check the Internet Information Services (IIS) option, and click Next to install it.

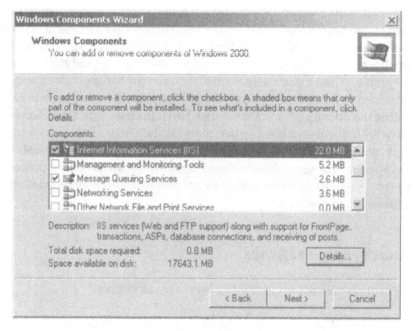

Figure 2-1. Installing IIS on BizTalk Server

- Microsoft Message Queue (MSMQ) 2.0 or higher. BizTalk Server uses MSMQ as one of its transport protocols and as an internal data buffer for transmitting data between BizTalk Messaging and BizTalk Orchestration. To install MSMQ, follow the same procedure as described for installing IIS in the previous point, but check the Message Queuing Services option instead of the Internet Information Services (IIS) option.

NOTE *When asked whether you want to install a dependent queue or an independent queue during the installation of MSMQ, you should select the independent queue option, which has its own local queue store. The dependent queue contains only a set of MSMQ APIs and doesn't have the local queue store. BizTalk Server requires a local queue store on the system.*

- World Wide Web Publishing Service is required for the BizTalk Messaging Manager to run. You can enable the service and make it start automatically through the Service Console under Administrative Tools.

- You'll need Application Center 2000 with SP1 if you want to use the BizTalk Server deployment feature.

- You'll need Microsoft Operations Manager (MOM) if you want to use the BizTalk MOM package that comes with BizTalk Server 2002.

- Microsoft XML Parser (MSXML, a set of objects that allow developers to process the XML document programmatically) version 3 with SP1 is required, and it is part of the installation of BizTalk Server 2002, so no additional attention is required. However, if you need to have both MSXML version 3 and MSXML version 4 installed on the system, you must first uninstall MSXML version 4, install BizTalk Server 2002, and then reinstall MSXML version 4.

- Visio 2002 Standard Edition or higher is required to enable the BizTalk Orchestration Designer.

Installing BizTalk Server 2002

Now that you know the hardware and software requirements, let me show you how to install your first BizTalk Server 2002.

NOTE *The following procedure is for installing BizTalk Server 2002 on a system that doesn't have an earlier version of BizTalk Server installed. If an earlier version is present on the system, you can upgrade it to BizTalk Server 2002, but configuration settings for BizTalk Server 2000 Services and COM+ packages will be lost when you upgrade to BizTalk Server 2002. This is because the BizTalk Server database schemas have changed in BizTalk Server 2002. Unfortunately, there is no easy way to back up the data if the database schemas have changed. If you don't want to lose all the old settings from the earlier version of BizTalk Server, you'll have to write down all the important information, such as your BizTalk Server configuration, before you perform the upgrade, and reproduce these settings after the server is upgraded. Backing up the databases won't solve the problem, since data records in the two versions of BizTalk Server are not compatible. User beware: The backward compatibility for BizTalk Server is not very pleasant, at least for now.*

To install BizTalk Server 2002 on your computer, log on as a member of Local Administrators and execute Setup.exe from the BizTalk Server 2002 CD-ROM. You should see the screen shown in Figure 2-2.

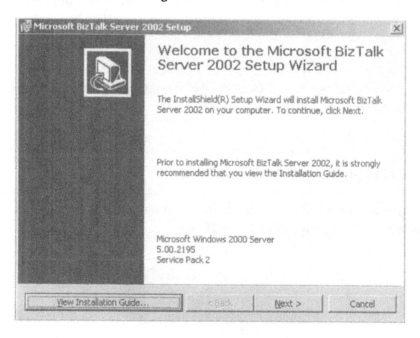

Figure 2-2. BizTalk Server 2002 Welcome screen

Click Next to proceed, until you reach the Destination Folder window shown in Figure 2-3.

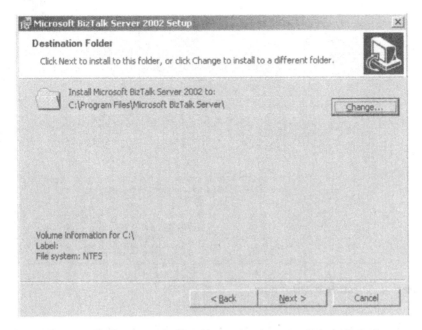

Figure 2-3. Specifying the location where BizTalk Server is installed

The location where BizTalk Server is installed is very important, and it needs to be synchronized with the deployment script, which I'll cover in Chapter 9. For now, you can change the location to whatever drive you prefer, and then click Next to move to the Setup Type window, shown in Figure 2-4.

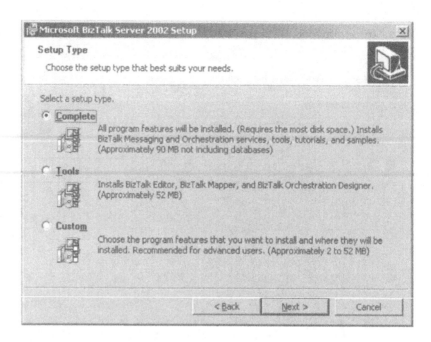

Figure 2-4. Selecting a setup type

In the window shown in Figure 2-4, you can select which setup type you want on your system. The Complete setup installs everything in BizTalk Server, including the BizTalk Server sample and SDK. The Tool setup installs only the client tools such as BizTalk Editor, BizTalk Mapper, BizTalk Orchestration Designer, and so on, but it won't install the BizTalk Server engine, which processes the document. The Custom setup allows you to selectively include and exclude features. For example, if you wanted to install everything except the documentation, you would need to choose this option.

For now, select Complete setup because you'll be exploring many of the features in BizTalk Server in upcoming chapters. If you are installing in a production environment, you can choose Custom setup and omit the tools and samples that are not needed in that environment. Click Next to continue to the window shown in Figure 2-5.

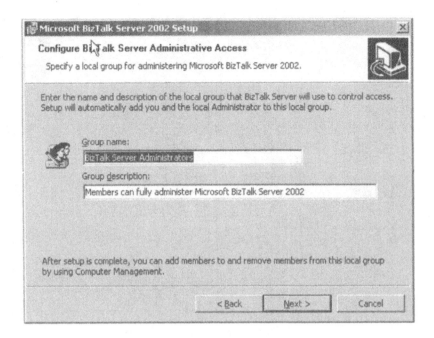

Figure 2-5. Configuring BizTalk Server administrative access

In the window shown in Figure 2-5, BizTalk Server will attempt to create a local Windows user group that has administrative rights on BizTalk Server tools, such as BizTalk Messaging Manager and BizTalk Server Administration. You want to leave the group name with its default value, as I'll refer to this BizTalk Server Administrators group throughout the book. Click Next to continue to the window shown in Figure 2-6.

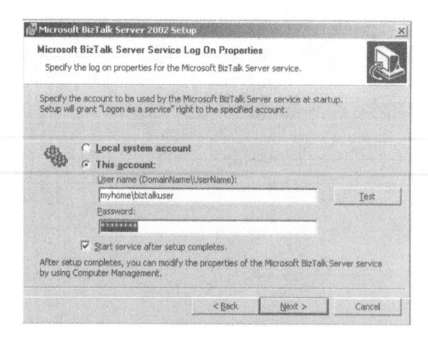

Figure 2-6. Configuring the logon account for the BizTalk Server service

The window in Figure 2-6 is where you specify the user account that will be used to run the BizTalk Server service. You have two options: You can run BizTalk Server under a local system account, which has most of the administrative rights on the local machine, or you can run BizTalk Server under a domain user account.

If you use the local system account and a remote SQL Server to host BizTalk Server databases, you *must* explicitly add the local system account of this machine to the SQL Server's logon users accounts and grant this account full control for all the BizTalk Server databases on the SQL Server, because SQL Server doesn't recognize other machines' local system accounts by default. There are other reasons for not running the BizTalk Server service under a local system account, and I'll cover this issue in more detail in Chapter 12.

NOTE   *For more information on SQL Server, see* SQL Server: Common Problems, Tested Solutions *by Neil Pike (Apress).*

For now, choose a domain account—in my case, I set up a user called biztalkuser in the myhome domain (as shown in Figure 2-6). Additional steps are required to make this user account eligible to run the BizTalk Server service—you'll learn more about this in Chapter 12.

> **NOTE** *If you aren't running the system in a domain environment, you can select the Local system account option or specify a local account. You certainly don't have to use a domain user. It is, however, an important strategic decision that I'll discuss in more depth in Chapter 12. If, for example, you're just installing BizTalk Server for development purposes, the local account may be an acceptable choice. If you want to install BizTalk Server on your own development box or a laptop so you can carry it around with you, you should install both SQL Server and BizTalk Server on the same computer and configure the BizTalk Server service to run under the local system administrator account.*

Click Next, and the BizTalk Server installer will start copying files. Once it has finished, you'll see the window shown in Figure 2-7. This is where you'll set up the BizTalk Server databases, four of them in total.

Figure 2-7. Configuring the BizTalk Messaging database

Click Next to proceed to the next window (shown in Figure 2-8), which is where you'll specify which database server and database name you want to use for the BizTalk Messaging database.

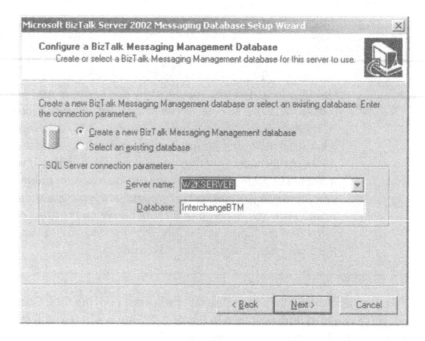

Figure 2-8. Configuring database information for the BizTalk Messaging database

NOTE *If you're upgrading from a previous version of BizTalk Server (such as BizTalk Server 2000) and have accepted the warning message about upgrading, you'll not see these Database Setup Wizard screens, and the installation will overwrite the existing four databases. Make sure you back up your old BizTalk Server databases before upgrading.*

In Figure 2-8, I am creating a new database for BizTalk Messaging, since this is a fresh installation of BizTalk Server 2002. However, if you have uninstalled BizTalk Server 2002, the databases that were created by the previous installation are not removed automatically. Those databases stay with SQL Server until you manually remove them. If you are installing BizTalk Server 2002 and wish to use the databases from a previous installation, select the Select an existing database option in this window.

Under the SQL Server connection parameters section in Figure 2-8, you must provide a SQL Server name and a name for the BizTalk Messaging database. The SQL Server can be local or remote, and you must use a NetBIOS name to reference the SQL Server. For example, if the server name is W2KSERVER, you must use W2KSERVER as the server name, not W2KSERVER.myhome.com. If the SQL Server contains multiple instances (this feature only exists in SQL Server 2000 and higher), you must specify the server name in the format ServerName\InstanceName (for example, W2KSERVER\Instance1). I recommend you leave all database names at their defaults—a number of stored procedures reference the database name in their code, and you must change the code to reflect the new name if you don't choose the default.

Click Next to continue. A number of dialog boxes will follow, showing you the progress of the installation of the database. If the database is created without error, you should see the window in Figure 2-9, where you can specify the BizTalk Server Group property.

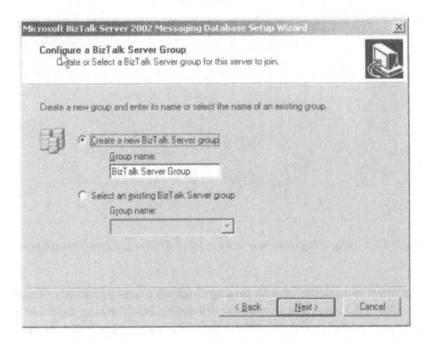

Figure 2-9. Configuring the BizTalk Server Group property

The BizTalk Server group is a very important concept for developing scalable and fault-tolerant BizTalk Server applications. To fully take advantage of this feature, at least two or more BizTalk Servers need to work together to form a group. BizTalk Servers are considered to be in the same group if they share the same

BizTalk Messaging database, BizTalk Tracking database, and BizTalk Shared Queue database on the same SQL Server.

When installing the very first BizTalk Server, the installer will ask you to create a new BizTalk Server group. If other BizTalk Servers already exist on the network, you can either create a new BizTalk Server group or join an existing BizTalk Server group. Because this is the first BizTalk Server on my network, I must choose to create a new BizTalk Server group (as shown in Figure 2-9).

Click Next to proceed to the window shown in Figure 2-10. It looks similar to the one you saw in Figure 2-8 for setting up the BizTalk Messaging database.

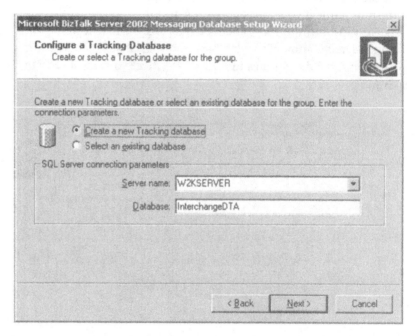

Figure 2-10. Configuring database information for the BizTalk Tracking database

As when you selected the Messaging database server previously, you can choose the SQL Server that should contain the BizTalk Tracking database. You don't have to put all the BizTalk Server databases onto a single SQL Server. In fact, it is a good practice to put the Tracking database on a separate SQL Server for performance reasons. I'll discuss a number of design issues that involve different database configurations in Chapter 13. For now, you can use the same SQL Server for all the BizTalk Server databases.

Click Next to continue to the window shown in Figure 2-11. This is where you specify the database information for yet another BizTalk Server database, the

Shared Queue database. Again, choose the Create a new Shared Queue database option using the same SQL Server, and click Next to continue.

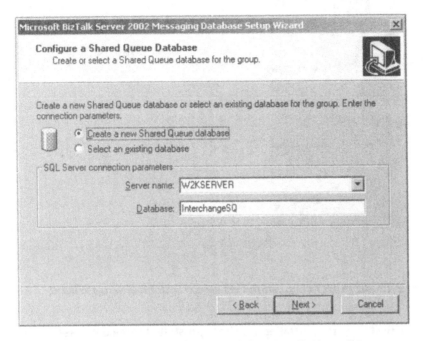

Figure 2-11. Configuring database information for BizTalk Shared Queue

After clicking Next a couple of times, you'll come to the window shown in Figure 2-12.

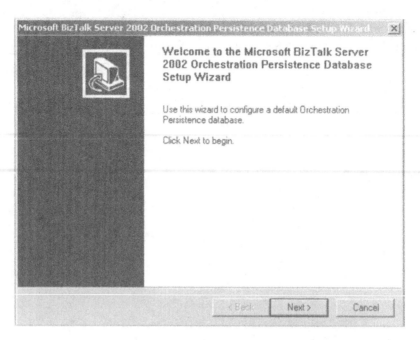

Figure 2-12. BizTalk Orchestration Persistence Database Setup Wizard

The BizTalk Server installer has already installed three databases at this point: BizTalk Messaging database, BizTalk Tracking database, and BizTalk Shared Queue database. BizTalk Server will now install the last database, the Orchestration Persistence database, which is responsible for storing and retrieving the orchestration state information to and from the database for the duration of a BizTalk orchestration instance. Click Next to get to the window shown in Figure 2-13.

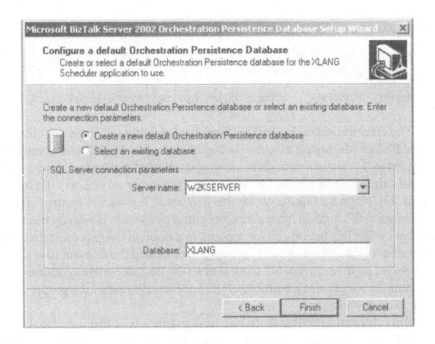

Figure 2-13. Configuring database information for the Orchestration Persistence database

The Orchestration Persistence database is different from the other three. This database doesn't have to be shared in a BizTalk Server group situation. In other words, if you have three BizTalk Servers within a server group, each server within the group can have its own Orchestration Persistence database installed locally. The reason for this is that the BizTalk orchestration instance is machine affiliated, which means the server that starts the orchestration instance is the only server that can process this orchestration instance. Unlike the other three BizTalk Server databases, which require all the BizTalk Servers involved to share the data stored in these databases, the Orchestration Persistence database contains data that is only meaningful to one BizTalk Server. For now, use the same SQL Server that is used by the other databases, and click Finish.

You have just installed BizTalk Server 2002. Let's do a quick check to make sure everything is installed properly. First, look for the Application Event Viewer under Administrative Tools. Normally, the Application Event log will tell you if anything in BizTalk Server went wrong. If you followed the installation as described, you should be getting the following error:

```
An error occurred in BizTalk Server.

Details:
----------------
[0x80040e4d] BizTalk Server failed to initialize a connection to database:
"InterchangeBTM"
on server: "W2KSERVER".  :'Login failed for user 'MYHOME\BizTalkuser'.'
```

The error indicates that BizTalk Server's Messaging service is not able to talk to the BizTalk Messaging database using the myhome\BizTalkuser account. This is expected if you use a domain account instead of a local system account or a local administrator account to run the BizTalk Server service, as I did in Figure 2-6. When BizTalk Server creates databases, it gives full control of these databases to the built-in Administrators group by default. However, when you change the BizTalk Server service account to a domain user account that is not a member of this Administrators group, you must add the domain user to the SQL Server login and grant full control of all the BizTalk Server databases to it. If this domain user is also a member of the built-in Administrators group, you don't have to do anything.

You can grant full control of a database to a new user through the SQL Server Login Properties window shown in Figure 2-14. On the Server Roles tab, select System administrator as the role for the new user. On the Database Access tab, give the new user permission for a specific database by checking the checkbox next to the database name. For detailed instructions on how to grant a user access privilege to a database, refer to SQL Server's *Books Online* online help file (installed with SQL Server by default, but also available online as part of the MSDN Library).

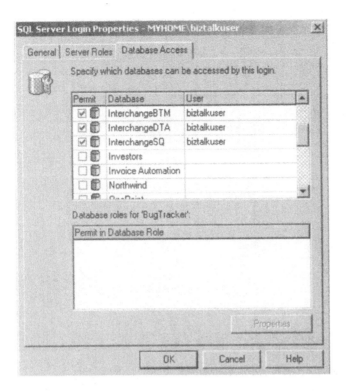

Figure 2-14. Granting a user database access control

You'll also need to grant Log on locally, Log on as service, and Act as part of operating system rights to this domain user account (in my case, MYHOME\BizTalkuser). This is done through Local Security Settings under Administrative Tools. For details on these settings, refer to Chapter 12.

After modifying these settings as necessary, you are ready to run some BizTalk Server tools to see if the BizTalk Server is up and running. Open BizTalk Server Administration, and you should see the window shown in Figure 2-15.

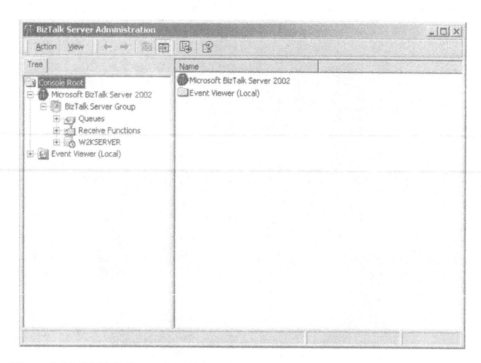

Figure 2-15. BizTalk Server Administration

If you can see the nodes Queues and Receive Functions, and the node labeled with your BizTalk Server name under the BizTalk Server Group, it means your BizTalk Server is able to talk to its databases. Notice the green arrow next to the BizTalk Server name (W2KSERVER in this case)—it indicates the status of the BizTalk Messaging service on W2KSERVER. A green arrow means the service is running, a red square means the service is stopped, and a red X over the icon means the BizTalk Server is unable to talk to its databases.

If you see the red X, the first place you can look for more information is the Event Viewer, which will show error information associated with BizTalk Server. You would normally get some insight into why the BizTalk Server can't start, or why there is a failed connection between BizTalk Server and its database server. For detailed information on installation problems, refer to the *BizTalk Server Installation Guide*.

Post-Installation Configuration

Earlier in this chapter, I mentioned that the BizTalk Tracking database and the Orchestration Persistence database can grow very large very quickly. BizTalk Server 2002 comes with a number of stored procedures that can help you manage these two databases.

Under the [BizTalk Server installation directory]\setup folder resides a file called BTS_Tracking_Archive_Purge_Script.sql. By default, this SQL script is not installed during the BizTalk Server installation, but you can install it manually using SQL Server's Query Analyzer. This script contains stored procedures and SQL statements that allow you to create SQL jobs that either periodically purge the data in the Tracking database or that archive the tracking data to a different server before purging it. By enabling these SQL jobs, the Tracking database won't grow out of control.

There are also a number of stored procedures installed as part of BizTalk Server 2002 that can help you manage the Orchestration Persistence database. The database administrator can delete the data records associated with completed XLANG orchestrations by running these stored procedures. You can also activate a preconfigured SQL job to execute these stored procedures automatically at scheduled times to achieve the same result.

Summary

In this chapter, I showed you BizTalk Server installation requirements and procedures, and you should now have BizTalk Server 2002 successfully installed. In the next chapter, you'll learn a great deal about BizTalk Server 2002 while working on a BizTalk Server project.

CHAPTER 3

Planning a BizTalk
Server Solution

IN THE NEXT FEW CHAPTERS, you get the opportunity to look at the details of BizTalk
Server as I walk you through developing a B2B project. This chapter will introduce the project, which features a retired mutual fund manager who sees an
opportunity to start his own online business. You'll see how you can use BizTalk
Server 2002 to build this B2B solution.

Bob's Plan

Bob worked for 30 years as a mutual fund manager, and now that he has retired,
he's thinking of creating a B2B company to provide services to financial institutions.

What Bob has in mind is an application service provider (ASP, a general
industry term, not to be confused with Microsoft's Active Server Pages technology, whose acronym is also ASP) for small to medium-sized mutual fund companies. Over the years, Bob has seen many of his friends and colleagues start
their own mutual fund companies—often with three or four business partners
who are experts at analyzing the market and picking stocks. They don't know
much about the computer systems that make the mutual fund companies work.
Bob's idea is to provide those services.

Many systems and applications are involved in running a mutual fund company. There are systems to provide customer service, to submit the buy and sell
orders to traders, to process all the transactions that occur during the day, to generate all the financial reports, and so on. All these systems run behind the scenes,
though, and fund managers usually don't know much about them. However,
when fund managers start running their own companies, they realize that this is
a critical part of the business. Bob knows strong interest exists among these small
and medium-sized mutual fund companies to contract out most of the internal
operations and computing processes, such as customer management and transaction processes, so that the companies can focus on analyzing and picking
stocks.

Bob has read a number of articles on ASP and considers it a good model for what he wants to do. Figure 3-1 shows what he thinks his service provider should look like. There will be two types of "users" of Bob's application: mutual fund companies and individual investors who hold accounts with the mutual fund companies (i.e., the mutual fund companies' customers). A B2B integration engine will form the core, with other components providing interfaces and functionality to the various systems and parties involved.

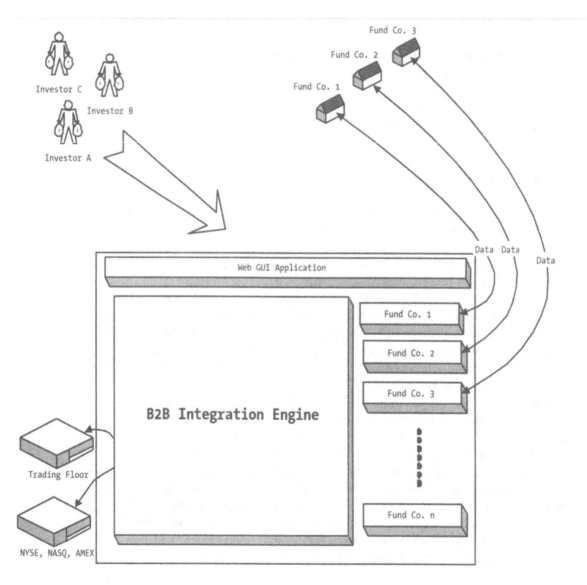

Figure 3-1. Bob's idea of a mutual fund service provider

In Bob's ideal application, the mutual fund companies will interact with the B2B integration engine, which will need to be able to perform many tasks that commonly are done by a mutual fund company. When mutual fund companies want to use the facilities offered by Bob's new system, they will open an account with Bob's company. Bob's application will then allow these mutual fund companies to add their own customers and other information to the system. Bob's application will also allow the mutual fund companies to place trades. When the trades are processed, the mutual fund companies will receive confirmation. Bob's application will also generate customer and trade reports for each of the mutual fund companies.

The individual investors will be customers of one or more of these mutual fund companies. Since the mutual fund companies will be using Bob's application, Bob's application will contain their customer information and will be able to provide a Web interface allowing individual investors to check their portfolios and modify their accounts. Bob's application will record the changes each investor makes and will send the information to the appropriate mutual fund company.

Bob has brainstormed these high-level requirements, and after talking to some mutual fund companies he's received some encouragement—a number of mutual fund companies are interested in the concept and are willing to give it a try when the application is ready. His former employer is also thinking about contracting out many operations because the company's existing system can't handle the tremendous business growth it's experiencing.

So the challenge is to build a prototype quickly in order to demonstrate the application to venture capitalists. Bob has heard that a couple of big financial firms are thinking along the same lines. Getting his service to market quickly will be very important if he is to get any money from the venture capitalists and survive in this highly competitive market. Bob wants to focus on the B2B integration engine first because it is important to get several mutual fund companies on board. The Web GUI application will consist of a number of dynamic pages that will retrieve and modify data from the database, and it will be built last.

Not wanting to waste any time, Bob gets his developer Mike involved. Early one Monday morning, while he and Mike are sitting at the coffee table in their office chatting, Bob shows Mike the high-level diagram for the mutual fund ASP, and then tells him, "I've been talking to the venture capitalists. They're giving us 30 days to come up with a working prototype of the ASP; otherwise funding is out of question. I've told them it won't be a problem.

"I've talked to friends at some mutual fund companies, and they're willing to give us a try," Bob continued. "They can start sending us data over the Internet as soon as we tell them what kind of data we're expecting. My former employer is one of the largest mutual fund firms in the world, and they are also interested in our ASP. They have their own flat file document schema, though, and they won't modify their system just for us, so we have to make sure our system is compatible with their data. My former employer is our biggest potential customer, and we have to do what we can to win that account."

Mike makes notes as Bob continues. "I want to have two major functions in our prototype application. I want it to allow the mutual fund companies to add their customers to our system. This is the first step in providing a complete customer management service. The second major function is to process trades for the mutual fund companies. We'll update the records in our transaction database so that mutual fund companies can view the transactions through our Web application when we build that. When the trade is executed, our application should notify the client of the transaction's status and also send the final trade price. I also want to store the final transaction status to our database as well. Because this information is confidential, I want the data to be transmitted between us and the mutual fund companies securely over the Internet."

"How about it, Mike? Think we can do it in one month?" Bob asks excitedly.

"That's an awful lot to do," Mike responds. "Don't you think we should hire a couple more people?"

Bob shakes his head. "Not unless I sell the house and car, and move my family out onto the street. Also, I almost forgot," he adds, "I promised the mutual fund firms that our application will be very scalable and fault tolerant. We need to keep that in mind."

Mike's To-Do List

Mike's next action is to begin brainstorming a solution. He comes up with a list of things that will be needed to meet Bob's requirements. Here's the list:

- Develop an Internet entry point for the documents coming from the mutual fund companies.

- Develop a program to validate XML documents (from the mutual fund companies) against their schemas to ensure the data is structured correctly. Most of the mutual fund companies will submit data in XML documents.

- Develop XSLT to transform the various schemas into a standard schema so that the processing component doesn't need to support multiple schemas.

- Write a customized program to convert flat file documents into XML documents so that the business component can read and process them. (At least one important client will be sending data in flat file format.)

- Develop a component to handle customer management. This component will need to take the mutual fund companies' customer data input and do three things: insert or update the customer information in the database, send an e-mail to the individual investors to notify them that their account is being processed, and send a response document that reports to the appropriate mutual fund firm on the status of the transaction. Should an error occur during this process, the system administrator will have to be notified. Allow for adding features in the future, such as personalization data in the database.

- Develop another component to handle the trade requests from the mutual fund company. This component will take a client trade order as input and perform at least four actions: Store the trade order in the database and set its status as "processing"; pass the data to a prebuilt component for the trade execution; set the status of the transaction to "complete" once the execution has completed; and finally send a response document containing the transaction's status information back to the mutual fund company. Room must also be left in this component for future changes to the way trades are executed. In the future, a different component might be called, or more components may be added to provide additional services.

- Create a component that will send the response document back to the mutual fund companies through HTTPS and SMTP. The program must support mutual authentication, meaning that both the ASP system and the mutual fund company must identify themselves with digital certificates before the transmission begins.

- Develop a data table that keeps track of the values of variables needed at runtime to process the document. These variables may be the schema used to validate the document at runtime, the XSLT file used at runtime, parameter values for the business components (perhaps response documents for each mutual fund company should be sent to different URLs), and so on.

- Make the entire application scalable and fault tolerant.

- Ensure the application is relatively bug free and ready in one month.

Fortunately, Mike has helpful friends like me who can advise him on difficult projects like this one. I know that BizTalk Server will enable Mike to build the three applications for Bob within the target deadline of a single month. Let's have a look at how. . . .

A BizTalk Server Solution

BizTalk Server 2002 contains two technologies—BizTalk Messaging and BizTalk Orchestration—and in many situations, a BizTalk Server solution consists of a combination of both. Bob wants an ASP system that will be able to interact with mutual fund companies. Figure 3-2 shows a high-level view of a BizTalk Server solution.

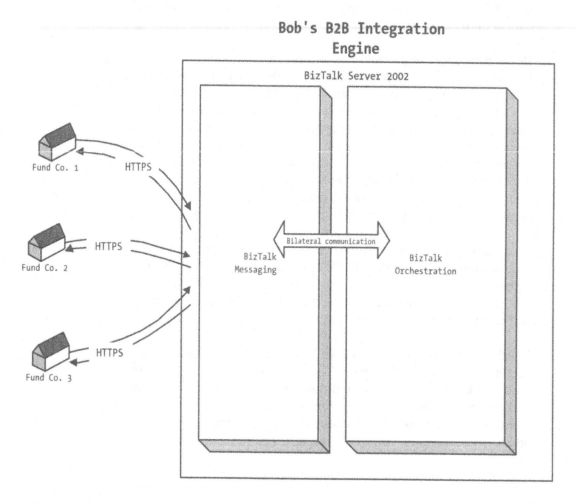

Figure 3-2. Architecture of an ASP application using BizTalk Server 2002

Bob's ASP application needs to do two things to provide its services to mutual fund companies. First, it must be able to receive documents from each mutual fund company that uses its services, and send documents back to those companies. Second, it must be able to process these documents using some business components. After all, Bob's ASP application must perform some real service for its clients, such as storing customer accounts in a database or buying or selling stocks.

One way the mutual fund companies and Bob's ASP application can communicate is by exchanging data over the Internet. BizTalk Messaging can facilitate this communication through a number of Internet protocols, such as HTTP, HTTPS, SMTP, and so on. BizTalk Messaging can also perform other operations, such as transforming schemas and encrypting and decrypting documents.

However, BizTalk Messaging can't help execute any business logic on these documents, such as calling a customized component to process the incoming document. (There are exceptions to this general rule, such as AIC, or Application Integration component, but don't worry about them for now. I'll discuss this in depth in Chapter 10.) In Bob's ASP application, customized components will be needed to add new customers and to execute the buy and sell orders from the mutual fund companies. BizTalk Messaging's primary task is to receive data and transfer data from one location to another—jobs involving business logic need to be delegated to BizTalk Orchestration.

BizTalk Orchestration provides workflow facilities that can perform a series of business processes, and it's possible to add or change the business logic in the workflow with little effort. For Bob's application, BizTalk Orchestration can perform the tasks needed to add a customer to the database or to make a trade. BizTalk Orchestration is also tightly integrated with BizTalk Messaging, meaning that Orchestration and Messaging can easily send documents to each other. BizTalk Messaging can forward the documents it receives from the mutual fund companies to BizTalk Orchestration for processing. BizTalk Orchestration can process the documents and generate the responses. The responses can then be returned to BizTalk Messaging, which will forward them to the mutual fund companies.

With BizTalk Server accepting data, processing it, and returning data to the clients, the resulting application is just like an extension of the clients' own systems. With its ability to receive, process, and transfer business documents, BizTalk Server provides all the necessary functionality for Bob's ASP application to service its mutual fund companies.

You now have a basic idea of how BizTalk Server 2002 can help build the B2B ASP application. You still have to learn how to implement it and turn the nice drawings into code. Let's look at Bob's requirements and see how BizTalk Server can solve each of these concrete problems. Here is a tidied-up version of the to-do list for the project:

- *Data entry point:* A data entry point for the application, where documents submitted by mutual fund companies will be received.

- *Non-XML document parser:* A parser to convert non-XML documents, such as flat text documents, into XML documents, which will be used as the document format for internal applications.

- *XML validation:* A tool to validate documents from the mutual fund companies to make sure they contain the data in the format that your applications expect.

- *XML transformation:* XSLT that will convert the incoming document to a common document specification that your applications can understand.

- *Data exit point:* A data exit point from which the documents will be sent back to the mutual fund companies over the Internet. This data exit point needs to support HTTP, HTTPS, and SMTP.

- *Workflows:* Two programs or workflows that contain a number of tasks. The programs or workflows must be flexible enough to allow for future expansion and modification.

- *Document routing and processing:* A document routing system to keep track of where specific documents came from, where they will be going, and what processes should happen in between.

- *Application cluster:* An application cluster to ensure that the service continues if one of the servers goes down.

In order to build this mutual fund ASP, these elements need to be created. You can code them yourself or, even better, let BizTalk Server 2002 do all the dirty work.

The BizTalk Server Solution in Detail

Let's take a closer look and see whether the subsystems of BizTalk Server can provide solutions for the requirements in this project's to-do list. As you can see in Figure 3-3, many subsystems combine to form both BizTalk Messaging and BizTalk Orchestration.

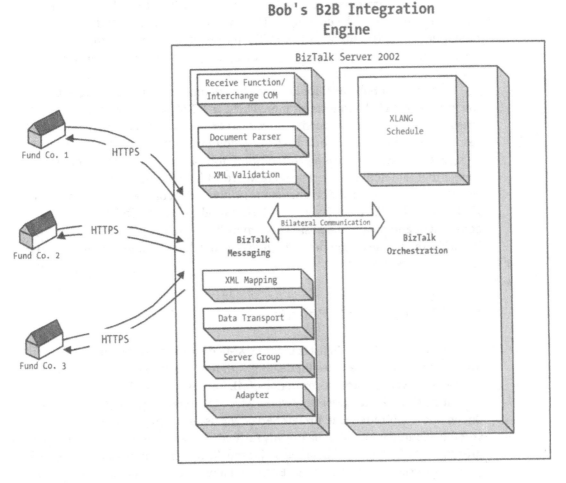

Figure 3-3. Subsystems of BizTalk Messaging and Orchestration

Data Entry Point

The Receive Function/Interchange COM subsystem can serve as your entry point in Bob's ASP application. BizTalk Server can get the data into its system in two ways: through Receive Functions and via BizTalk Interchange.

A Receive Function can be set up to watch for arriving documents at either a file location or a message queue. When a document arrives at the location, this Receive Function will read the document, copy the document to its internal work queue (a database table), and delete the document from where it arrived. This ensures that the document is read only once. The document will stay in the work queue until it's picked up for processing.

One of the parameters of a method call to the BizTalk Interchange component is the content of the document. Thus, when the BizTalk Interchange component is called, BizTalk will save the passed-in document to the work queue. The document will then be picked up for processing later as it would be with the Receive Function.

In the case of Bob's ASP application, the documents will be coming in through the Internet as HTTP requests (or more likely, as HTTPS requests—for security reasons). Because the documents arrive neither as a file nor as a queue message, using a Receive Function alone as an entry point won't be adequate. However, using BizTalk Interchange is a good solution. You can set up an Active Server Page (remember that Active Server Pages are Microsoft's Web programming technology) to accept the documents the mutual fund companies post through HTTP(S). Within the page, you can make COM calls to the BizTalk Interchange component and pass in the posted document as one of the parameters. The BizTalk Interchange component will then save the document into its work queue for later processing.

Non-XML Document Parser

The next item on the to-do list is the non-XML document parser. BizTalk Messaging has many features for dealing with XML documents, including the ability to convert documents from non-XML formats into XML format.

Internally, BizTalk Server only works with XML documents, so if a non-XML document is submitted to it, BizTalk Server will use its document parsers to convert the document into XML before any further processing. After the document is processed, BizTalk Server can also convert the XML document back to its original format using document serializers. Figure 3-4 illustrates this document conversion.

BizTalk Server comes with four types of document parsers and serializers:

- XML

- EDI

- X12

- Flat text

You can also write your own parser and serializer to use on BizTalk Server. Creating customized document parsers is beyond the scope of this book, but if you are interested in the subject, you can check the Microsoft BizTalk Server Web site (`http://www.microsoft.com/biztalk`) for more information.

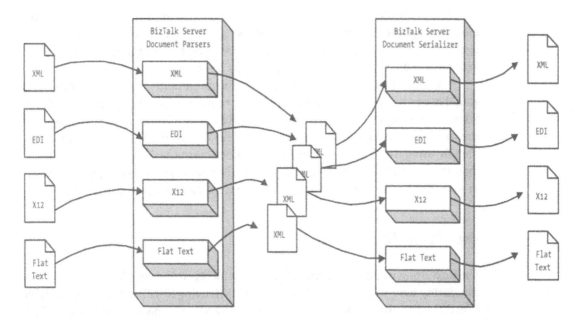

Figure 3-4. With BizTalk Server document parsers, documents of different formats can be converted into XML and then back to their native formats.

When a document arrives at BizTalk Server, BizTalk Messaging will identify the document format, and if it isn't already XML, it will select the appropriate document parser to convert the document into XML. After the document has been processed, BizTalk Server will generate a response document for the original sender; by default this document will be in XML format. If the original sender is expecting a document in a different format (for example, if the client's system only supports EDI or flat text files), the BizTalk Server document serializers will be called to convert the XML document to whatever format the client is expecting.

With BizTalk Server's document parsers and serializers, you no longer need to handcraft your own programs to convert documents to various formats.

XML Validation

A document's schema is the data structure of a document. It basically tells the user of the document what information is stored where inside the document. There are a number of schemas being used today, such as W3C's XSD schema, the XDR schema, and BizTalk's schema, which is based on XDR and is used exclusively inside BizTalk Server.

Each document that arrives at BizTalk Server will eventually be fed into some kind of program or component for processing, and by validating the document against its schema when the document arrives, you can eliminate the need to validate the document inside your programs or components.

Bob's ASP application needs to validate the documents that are sent to it. What would happen if a sell order came in and the number of shares was not specified? Would you really want to wait until it reached the trade component to discover that mistake? Fortunately, BizTalk Server 2002 is bundled with a schema validation feature. By using this feature, you can validate documents as the very first step after they arrive at the BizTalk Server; if a document contains incorrect tags or the data in some fields isn't in a valid range, the document can be rejected immediately.

XML Transformation

The next thing to do is transform the XML, which is done with XSLT. You may be wondering why you need to transform the XML using XSLT. The documents have already been converted from other formats to XML, so now everything is XML, right? What else needs to be done?

Yes, the documents are all now in XML, but they don't necessarily use the same XML schema. The XSLT is like an interpreter. It translates the XML in different schema into XML in a common schema so that the applications can understand the XML data.

Creating XSLT to translate XML documents into a different schema isn't an easy undertaking, especially when the documents are complicated. The good news is that BizTalk Server 2002 comes with a GUI tool called BizTalk Mapper that allows you to generate the XSLT file through a graphic interface. BizTalk Messaging then uses the generated XSLT file at runtime to transform the XML documents from one schema to another, as shown in Figure 3-5.

Data Exit Point

When Bob's application has finished with the document and all the processes are done, it will send some type of response document back to the client. This response document may contain confirmation information or an error message about what happened during processing. Besides the response document, the application may also send other documents it generates, such as portfolio information or the customer's monthly statements.

The only connection Bob's application has with the external mutual fund company is through the Internet, so you need to establish an exit point through which documents can be sent to the mutual fund companies. It isn't particularly difficult to create a program to send an e-mail message or to make an HTTP post.

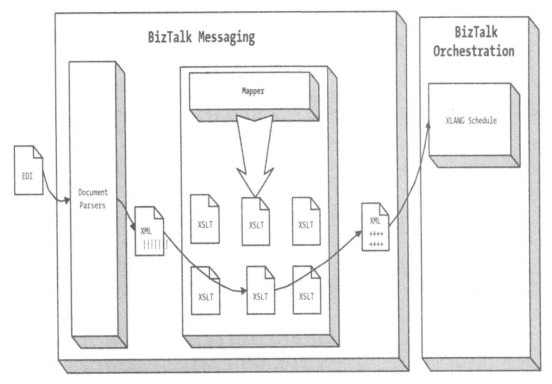

Figure 3-5. BizTalk Server's Mapper, coupled with XSLT, is a very powerful feature for converting documents into different schemas.

However, HTTP and e-mail aren't secure ways of sending data, since data isn't encrypted when using either method. Most companies today use HTTPS (i.e., the secure form of HTTP) when transferring data over the Internet. However, to cre-ate a program to send data using HTTPS normally involves a lot of coding effort. Wouldn't it be great if BizTalk Server handled these all these communications, both secured and unsecured, for you?

Well, BizTalk Server's transport subsystem will do just that. It supports many transport protocols. Besides SMTP, HTTP, and HTTPS (with both server authentication and mutual authentication), it also supports MSMQ, File, AIC (Application Integration Component), and BizTalk XLANG Schedule. Figure 3-6 illustrates how BizTalk Messaging can provide an exit point for Bob's application.

As you can see, BizTalk Messaging supports many protocols for sending documents to both internal and external receivers. BizTalk Messaging can send a document as an e-mail or HTTPS post. It can also send the document to differ-ent applications and servers within an organization, such as a message queue or network file drive. If you create an orchestration (i.e., a workflow) to process the document, BizTalk Messaging can start that orchestration when the document arrives.

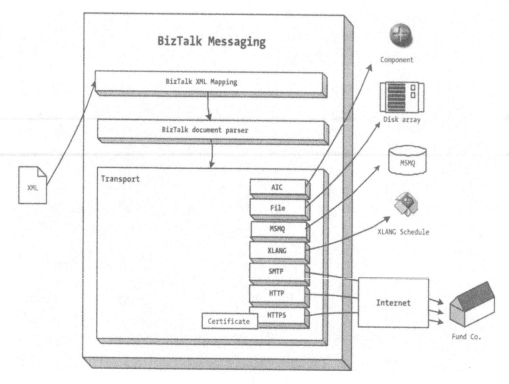

Figure 3-6. BizTalk Messaging supports many protocols that can be used to send documents to external parties.

BizTalk Messaging also allows you to plug in a customized AIC to send a document using protocols that aren't included in BizTalk Server. For instance, if you want to send a document using FTP, you would have to create a customized component that is capable of sending documents over FTP, since FTP support isn't included as part of BizTalk Server. You can also code your own AIC to perform tasks when BizTalk Messaging passes the document to it. You will learn how to create an AIC in Chapter 11.

AICs greatly increase your system's extensibility and its ability to integrate with both Microsoft and non-Microsoft systems. For instance, Microsoft produces an AIC that allows you to send a document to IBM's MQSeries server (a message queue server that provides message queuing solutions in most non-Microsoft environments).

Many software companies are building their businesses around BizTalk Server AICs. If you want to integrate BizTalk Server with some well-known system, someone has probably already created an AIC for it and is willing to sell it to you. As I write this, several hundred BizTalk Server adapters are available from third-party vendors. (An adapter normally contains AICs and a set of tools to accelerate the development effort involved in integrating BizTalk Server with other systems.)

Workflows

BizTalk Orchestration will take on the job of creating the two workflows to handle customer management and trade processing.

Document Routing and Processing

As a document flows through BizTalk Server, you need to have some kind of system that keeps track of what should be done with it and where it should go next. The processes in a B2B application can be very complex, especially when many organizations and document types are involved. Having a document process management model that is flexible and easy to understand and maintain is critical to the success of the application.

BizTalk Server 2002 comes with its own model to manage the routing of the documents and the processes involved at each step. It also comes with a graphical tool called BizTalk Messaging Manager to help BizTalk Server administrators control these processes. With BizTalk Messaging Manager, BizTalk Server administrators can define how each document is passed through BizTalk Server and what processes are performed on each document. BizTalk Messaging Manager stores these rules in the BizTalk Messaging database, and uses them to provide the processing information at runtime. Figure 3-7 illustrates the relationship between the BizTalk Messaging Manager, the BizTalk Messaging service, and the BizTalk Messaging database.

Application Cluster

The last item on the to-do list is to find a way to provide the clustering capability for the application. *Clustering* is when you have two or more identical systems working together to provide a common service. If one system fails for any reason, the other system or systems will continue providing the service. Clustering provides fault tolerance for critical business applications.

In some contexts, clustering can also provide load-balancing for your applications. When all the systems are up and running, the processing load on each system will be a fraction of the total workload for the whole cluster. This makes the application more scalable because more systems can be added to the cluster to lighten the load on each individual system.

Clustering can be implemented in many different ways and with many different technologies. In BizTalk Server 2002, you can use the BizTalk Server group to provide the clustering service. Figure 3-8 shows a simple BizTalk Server group with two member servers.

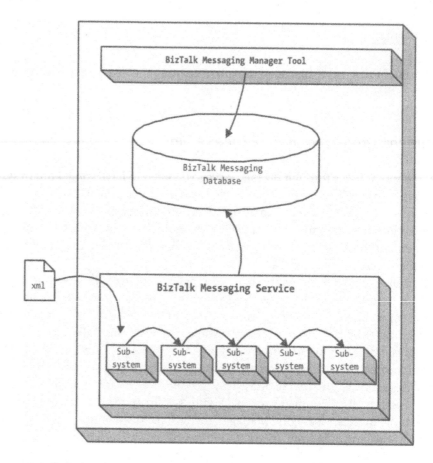

Figure 3-7. Relationship of the BizTalk Messaging database to the BizTalk Messaging Service and the BizTalk Messaging Manager tool

When at least two BizTalk Servers share the same rules on how to process the documents and have access to the same documents waiting to be processed, these two BizTalk Servers have formed a BizTalk Server group. In order to better understand BizTalk Server groups, let's first take a look at where the processing rules and incoming documents are saved in the system.

There are four types of persistent data that BizTalk Server needs to access at runtime to process the documents that clients have submitted. These four types of persistent data are in four BizTalk Server databases:

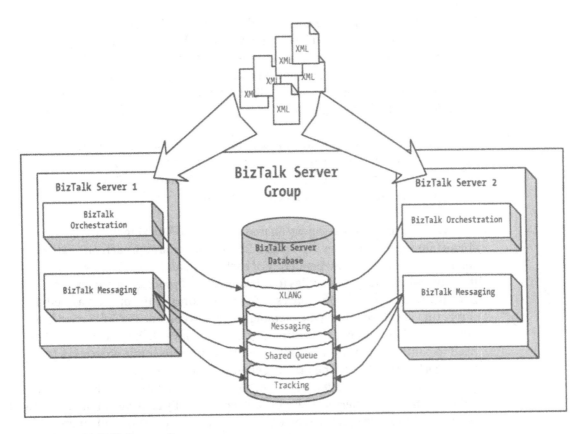

Figure 3-8. BizTalk Server Group

- *XLANG, or Orchestration Persistence database (default name—XLANG):*
  This database stores an orchestration instance's state information, such as
  information about the current transactional status of a particular instance,
  and state information of the *dehydrated* orchestration instance, which will
  be used later to *rehydrate* that particular instance. (Don't worry too much
  about these references to dehydration and rehydration—I'll describe these
  concepts in later chapters.) A shared XLANG database is optional in
  a BizTalk Server group—each member server can have its own separate
  XLANG database.

- *BizTalk Messaging database (default name—InterchangeBTM):* This stores
  all the management information that is needed to process the documents
  at runtime, such as what schema the documents are validated against,
  what XSLT file will be used to map the XML documents, which orchestration will be instantiated to process the document, and so on. A shared
  BizTalk Messaging database is required for a BizTalk Server group.

- *BizTalk Shared Queue database (default name—InterchangeSQ):* This stores all the documents that have been picked up by BizTalk Messaging through either a Receive Function or an Interchange submission, and that are waiting to be processed. This database is the first stop when documents arrive at the BizTalk Server. A shared BizTalk Shared Queue database is required for a BizTalk Server group.

- *BizTalk Tracking database (default name—InterchangeDTA):* BizTalk Server can be configured to log every single incoming and outgoing document and store the information in this database. A shared BizTalk Tracking database is required for a BizTalk Server group.

When the BizTalk Messaging, Shared Queue, and Tracking databases are shared among the member servers in a BizTalk Server group, each one of the servers can then work independently of each other, and all of them will use the same configuration and rules for picking up and processing documents. Because every member server in a server group stores all the data on a database server that is shared among the member servers, when one BizTalk Server goes down, the other member servers in the group still have all the information they need to continue their work. A BizTalk Server group can continue to serve its clients as long as at least one BizTalk Server is up and running.

However, there is a catch. Even when you can eliminate the single point of failure at the BizTalk Server level, you still haven't really achieved fault tolerance until you cluster the database server, which can be a single point of failure. Microsoft SQL Server, which BizTalk Server requires, supports database clustering, and I'll discuss SQL Server database clustering in Chapter 13.

Summary

You've looked at BizTalk Messaging and BizTalk Orchestration and seen how you can use them to solve specific problems, such as validating and transforming documents. After comparing the challenges on Mike's to-do list with what BizTalk Server 2002 can do, it's clear that you can use the features of BizTalk Server to solve the many common tasks involved in Bob's ASP application. In the next chapter, I'll show you how to implement Bob's ASP application with BizTalk Server.

CHAPTER 4

Starting with BizTalk Messaging

BY DAY THREE, Mike is willing to give BizTalk Server 2002 a shot. The question on his mind is, "Where should we start? It seems there are so many things going on in a BizTalk Server—what is the first thing we need to do that makes the most sense?"

Document Specification

The main purpose of B2B applications is exchanging documents, and Bob's ASP application is no exception. The application will receive documents from business partners, process the information, and send documents back.

Specifying documents is a good place to start when developing a BizTalk Server application. Based on Bob's business requirements, his ASP application should provide customer-management service for the mutual fund companies, thereby allowing them to add and remove their own investors, and to buy and sell funds for their investors' accounts.

Here is an XML document that Mike has decided to use for the mutual fund companies' customer-management process. The mutual fund companies will send this document to Bob's ASP application for processing. When the process is completed, a document with the same structure will be sent back to the original sender.

```
<FundInvestors>
    <FundCompany>Henry Fonda Inc.</FundCompany>
    <Investors>
        <Investor>
            <InvestorName >Fernando Rey</InvestorName >
            <Action>OpenAccount</Action>
            <InvestorInfo>
                <email>frey@frenchconnection.com</email>
                <phone>212-555-1515</phone>
                <ssn>111111111</ssn>
                <balance>5000</balance>
```

```
                    </InvestorInfo>
                    <Status description=""/>
              </Investor>
              <Investor>
                    <InvestorName >Toshiro Mifune</InvestorName >
                    <Action>OpenAccount</Action>
                    <InvestorInfo>
                        <email>tmifune@highandlow.com</email>
                        <phone>212-555-1516</phone>
                        <ssn>222222222</ssn>
                        <balance>6000</balance>
                    </InvestorInfo>
                    <Status description=""/>
              </Investor>
              <Investor>
                    <InvestorName>Gene Hackman</InvestorName >
                    <Action>Trade</Action>
                    <Funds>
                        <Fund name="Fonda International Income Fund" _
transaction="buy" quantity="100" price="15.6"/>


                        <Fund name="Fonda International Growth Fund" _
transaction="buy" quantity="100" price="26"/>


                        <Fund name="Fonda US Treasury Fund" _
transaction="sell" quantity="200" price="12"/>
                    </Funds>
                    <Status description=""/>
              </Investor>
          </Investors>
</FundInvestors>
```

This XML document contains XML elements and XML attributes. (You may recognize the names of the actors from some of my favorite movies: *12 Angry Men, The French Connection,* and *High and Low.*) The <FundCompany> node contains information about which mutual fund company sent this document; Bob's ASP application will deal with many mutual fund companies, and it therefore needs to identify which company the document came from. The <Investors> node contains one or more <Investor> nodes, which in turn contain the detail information for each of the mutual fund company's investor transactions. Under each <Investor> node reside many subnodes: <InvestorName> identifies who the investor is; <Action> identifies what type of action is associated with the investor, and this node can have many possible values, such as OpenAccount, Trade, and so on; and <Funds> contains many subnodes to describe each fund the investor wants to buy or sell.

In order for BizTalk Server to work with this type of document, you must first create a BizTalk Server schema that defines this particular document structure. To do so, you can use a handy tool called BizTalk Editor, which I'll show you next.

The best way to learn how to use BizTalk Editor is to use it, so let's create the FundInvestors document specification.

Creating a New Document Specification

To begin, select Start ➤ Programs ➤ BizTalk Server 2002, and then select BizTalk Editor to open the editor window. From the menu of BizTalk Editor, select File ➤ New, since you are creating a document specification from scratch. A new window comes up, as shown in Figure 4-1.

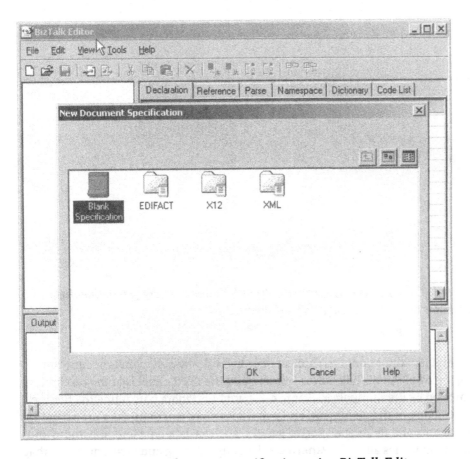

Figure 4-1. Creating a new document specification using BizTalk Editor

Select the Blank Specification document in the New Document Specification window. The other three choices in the window are templates for industry standard and vertical document specifications. You don't want to use a standard template since in this case you want your document to be highly customized and specific only to your system. Click OK to open a new, blank specification (see Figure 4-2).

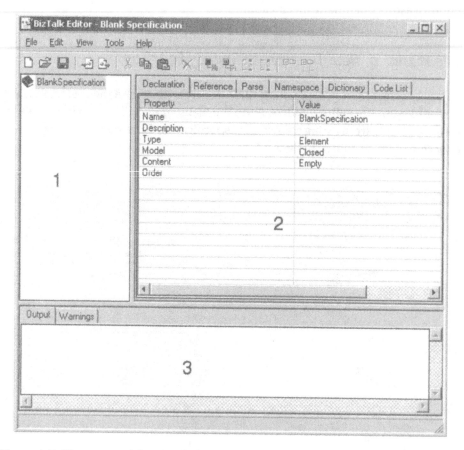

Figure 4-2. The upper-right panel of BizTalk Editor is where you define the attributes of the document and its elements.

BizTalk Editor contains three panels: two side-by-side panels occupy the major part of the BizTalk Editor window, and the third panel is at the bottom. As indicated by the numbers in Figure 4-2, panel 1 is where you define the hierarchical structure of the document, and panel 2 is where you define the properties for the records and fields specified in panel 1, such as data type and maximum and minimum values allowed. Panel 3 displays any warning and error messages that exist in the schema when you compile it. BizTalk Editor also can generate a

sample instance of the document and in this case displays the content of the
document in panel 3 (you will see this later).

Records and Fields

The first thing you need to know is the difference between the terms *record* and
field as they are used in BizTalk Editor. Right-click one of the nodes in the specification, and a menu like the one shown in Figure 4-3 will pop up. You can add either
a new record or a new field to the document structure from this pop-up menu.

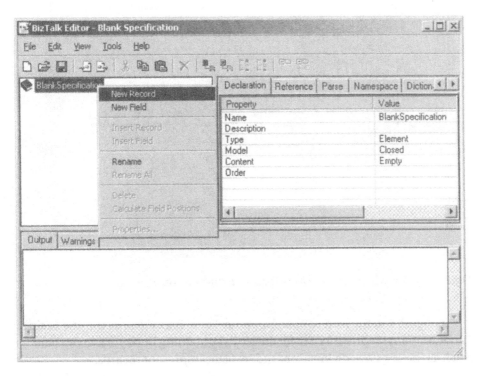

Figure 4-3. Creating a new record or field

In BizTalk Editor, records and fields don't represent the elements and attributes that you find in an XML document. (Well they do, but not in the fashion
that you might initially expect, and certainly not on a one-to-one basis). A BizTalk
Editor *record* is an element that can contain child elements. A *field*, which can be
either an element or an attribute, contains only a literal value. (I'll explain *elements* and *attributes* shortly.) The only time you would create a field is when you
want an attribute or an element to contain only a literal value. In the example

XML document presented earlier, FundCompany is a field, since it can only contain the textual name of the fund company. FundInvestors, Investors, and Investor are records, since they all contain child elements.

Figure 4-4 shows how this document should appear when correctly defined in the BizTalk Editor.

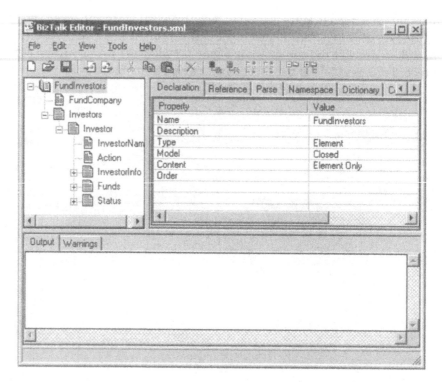

Figure 4-4. FundInvestors document specification in BizTalk Editor

In Figure 4-4, the icon containing vertical blue bars (such as the one beside FundCompany) represents a field; the icons containing horizontal green bars (such as the ones beside Investors and Investor) represent records.

Configuring Document Properties

The second panel of the BizTalk Editor window has several tabs. There are a set of properties pages (shown in Figure 4-5) for each record and field defined in the document that can be used to set various properties. I'll first describe each of the tabs and then show you how to set the document specifications for the ASP application.

In each of the tabs, the properties that are available and the values they can be set to will vary, depending on whether a record or field is selected and what type of document standard specification you are creating. Often you will be warned when changing a value—for example, when changing a type from Element to Attribute or vice versa—that doing so will affect other settings and might result in the loss of information.

The majority of the commonly used property settings are located on the Declaration tab, shown in Figure 4-5.

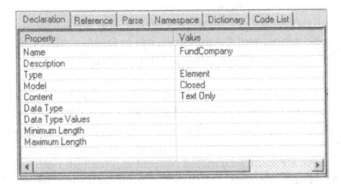

Figure 4-5. Configuring document properties on the Declaration tab

Following is a list of important property settings for attributes and elements that you should be aware of when creating a document specification:

- *Name:* This is the name of the record or field. In Figure 4-5, I've changed the name from the default BlankSpecification to the desired record name—FundCompany.

- *Description:* This allows you to add a longer, more informative description for the record or field.

- *Type:* You can choose whether the selected item should be rendered in an XML document based on this specification, as an XML element or attribute. The difference between an element and an attribute in an XML document is that an attribute describes a particular element. This is best explained with an example: In the following XML string, "Fund" is of type element and "name", "transaction", "quantity", and "price" are of type attribute.

```
<Fund name="Fonda International Income Fund" transaction="buy" quantity="100" _
price="15.6"/>
```

The document root record must be of type element.

- *Model:* This property allows you to change the degree of compliance of a document instance to its schema. When the model is set to Closed, the document must be compliant with its specification; no child records or fields that are not defined in the specification can exist in the document. When the model is set to Open, the document is considered to be valid even if it has some undefined child records or fields. If some unexpected records and fields may exist in the document, and this isn't a problem, just set the model property of the parent record to Open, so that the BizTalk Server XML engine won't complain about the document.

- *Content:* The value for this property varies depending on whether the field is an attribute or element. If the field is an attribute, Text Only is the only Content property option, since it can't contain elements. However, if the field is an element, you have two options for this property: Element Only and Mixed. An element with mixed content can contain both textual information and child elements, like the following <Book> record, which contains both text and the <Subject> element:

```
<Book>This book is about <Subject>BizTalk Server 2002</Subject></Book>
```

- *Data Type:* This property only applies to a field, and it specifies the data type of the text content of an element or attribute. This property doesn't apply to records whose Content property is Element Only.

- *Data Type Values:* This property only applies to fields and allows you to specify enumerated values. *Enumerated values* are the values that are valid for that particular field. For example, in this FundInvestors document, you want the values of the Action field under Investor to be restricted to either OpenAccount, CloseAccount, or Trade. To enforce this, you would specify the Data Type Values property for the Action field to be "OpenAccount CloseAccount Trade" (with the values being separated by a space). Note that when you want to specify an enumeration, you must set the Data Type property of the field to Enumeration; otherwise you will not be able to edit this field.

- *Maximum Length and Minimum Length:* These properties indicate the maximum number and minimum number of characters the field can contain if the field has a data type of string, number, binary (Base64) or binary (Hex).

- *Order:* The Order property will appear if the element is a record (as opposed to a field). There are three possible values this property can have: Many, One, or Sequence. When the Order property's value is Many, this record's child records may appear in any order. When the value is One, one and only one of the record's child records or fields can appear. When the Order property's value is Sequence, all the child elements or attributes must appear in the listed order. Sequence is the default value.

The next tab in the BizTalk Editor window is the Reference tab, shown in Figure 4-6.

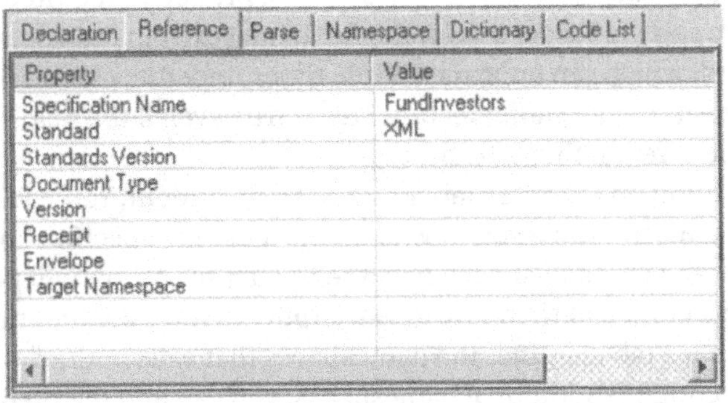

Figure 4-6. Configuring the document properties on the Reference tab

Figure 4-6 shows the Reference tab of the root record, which contains some special properties. The most important property here is the Standard property, which specifies which document parser you want to use to parse this document. There are four values for this property: XML, X12, EDIFACT, and CUSTOM. If you want to specify that the document should be a flat text file, you would select the CUSTOM option, and change its text to "FlatFile"—this would tell BizTalk Messaging to parse it using the flat text file parser. In the case of Bob's application, you are defining an XML document specification, so you can select XML for the Standard property.

NOTE *You can rename CUSTOM to FlatFile because the flat file parser is part of BizTalk Server. If you need to parse documents other than the standard four types (XML, X12, EDIFACT, FlatFile), you must provide your own parser for BizTalk Server to use before it can successfully parse your document.*

The Reference tab of a nonroot record contains only two properties: Minimum Occurrences and Maximum Occurrences. Setting Minimum Occurrences to 1 ensures that the record must appear in the document at least once. Setting the Maximum Occurrences to an asterisk (*) allows infinite appearances of that record in the document. Setting both properties to 1 ensures that the record will appear once and only once.

The Reference tab for a field contains only one property: Required. By setting the Required property to Yes for a field, the field must exist in the document. Unlike the record, which can appear multiple times under its parent, the field can appear only once under its parent record. This is true even if the field has had its type set to Element rather than Attribute.

There is nothing on the Parse tab for an XML document. You will see properties on this tab when I show you how to create a flat file specification in Chapter 7. This tab is used to specify how the document parser will parse a non-XML document, and therefore doesn't apply to XML documents.

The Namespace tab identifies the namespaces that exist in the document. If your document contains additional namespaces, you can add the prefixes and the URLs of those namespaces on this tab. Namespaces can be used to avoid clashes of identically named records or fields within a document specification.

The Dictionary tab contains many important properties that BizTalk Messaging uses at runtime to decide how to route the document. I'll discuss the self-routing concept and configure this tab later in this chapter.

The Code List tab is used only by X12 or EDIFACT documents. X12 and EDIFACT documents include special codes to represent each data field.

Creating the FundInvestors Document Specification

Now you need to put all this information to work and create Bob's FundInvestors document specification. Figure 4-7 shows the completed specification.

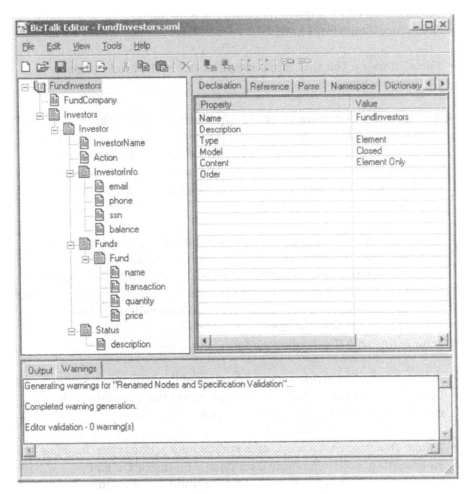

Figure 4-7. The complete specification for the FundInvestors document

What you need to do is set the properties based on the business requirements—this way the specification will be able to identify any invalid documents.
Following are the elements and attributes in the FundInvestors specification and
the properties that need to be defined for each. In the following list, the property
name is enclosed in square brackets; for example, [Reference\Standard]=XML
means that the value of the Standard property under the References tab should
be set to XML. You can now start adding the following records and attributes to
the empty document specification:

- *FundInvestors:* This is the root node of the document, [Reference\Standard] = XML.

- *FundCompany:* This field represents the name of the fund company. [Reference\Required] = Yes.

- *Investors:* This record encapsulates information for one or more individual investors. [Reference\Minimum Occurrence] = 1, [Reference\Maximum Occurrence] = 1. These settings ensure that the Investors record appears exactly once in the document, because you want your specification to allow just one collection of investors containing one or more investor records.

- *Investor:* This record contains the detail information on what action is to be taken for an individual investor. Since this is a required record, you must set [Reference\Minimum Occurrence] = 1, [Reference\Maximum Occurrence]= *. This ensures that the Investor record appears once or more times in the document. You also need to make sure all subnodes in this record are arranged in the exact order defined in BizTalk Editor—you can achieve this with [Declaration\Order] = Sequence.

- *InvestorName:* This field contains the name of the investor. [Reference\Required] = Yes. This setting ensures that the name of the investor appears under the Investor record.

- *Action:* This field contains one of the predefined action types. To define an enumeration, set [Declaration\Data Type] = Enumeration and [Declaration\Data Type Values] = "OpenAccount CloseAccount Trade". The values are space delimited. If a value itself contains a space, use double quotes around the value.

- *InvestorInfo:* This record contains information about the investor. Because this record is not required, you set [Reference\Minimum Occurrence] = 0, [Reference\Maximum Occurrence] = 1.

- *email, phone, ssn, balance:* These are required fields when the InvestorInfo record is present. Set [Reference/Required] = Yes.

- *Funds:* This record contains information on the funds the investor buys or sells. [Reference\Minimum Occurrence] = 0, [Reference\Maximum Occurrence] = 1. This record is not required because it is only used when investors are making a trade; it may not apply to an investor who is opening or closing an account.

- *Fund:* This record contains the detail information about the transaction that occurs on each fund. This record should not contain any child record, so you need to set [Declaration\Content] = Text Only. Because an investor can buy or sell multiple funds at once, you must set [Reference\Minimum Occurrence] = 1, [Reference\Maximum Occurrence] = *.

- *name, transaction, quantity, and price:* These are attributes under the Fund record. Set [Declaration\Type] = Attribute and [References\Required]="Yes".

- *Status:* This record contains information about the state of the process for the document. A client may or may not supply this record in his or her document—it's your application's responsibility to provide the content for this record. Set [Reference\Minimum Occurrence] = 0, [Reference\Maximum Occurrence]= 1, which specifies that the record is not required. [Declaration\Content] = Text Only ensures that there won't be a child record under Status.

- *Description:* This field contains a detailed description of the status. [Reference\Required] = No.

Once these fields and records have been defined in BizTalk Editor, you've created the document specification for the FundInvestors, and you're ready to save the document specification. But before you save it, you may want to test whether the document specification as defined is really what you want, and whether you made any errors.

Validating a Document Specification

You have three tools available to help you to check your work. These allow you to check the internal consistency of your specification, check it against a sample document that it should match for structure and format, and if you don't have a sample to check against, generate a sample document from the specification to see if it matches your expectations.

Validating the specification just checks that it's internally consistent and that none of the settings in one part of the document conflict with others in another—a record set as Text Only when it has child records would fail this consistency check, for example. Use F5 to validate a document specification, or select the option from the Tools menu.

BizTalk Editor comes with a very handy validation tool to validate documents against document specifications. You can use this tool to test the FundInvestors document specification against the sample document you just created to check whether the document complies with the specification. If it doesn't, then you have an error in the document specification (assume the sample document is correct).

To test the document against the specification, open the document specification in BizTalk Editor and select Validate Instance from the Tools menu, as shown in Figure 4-8.

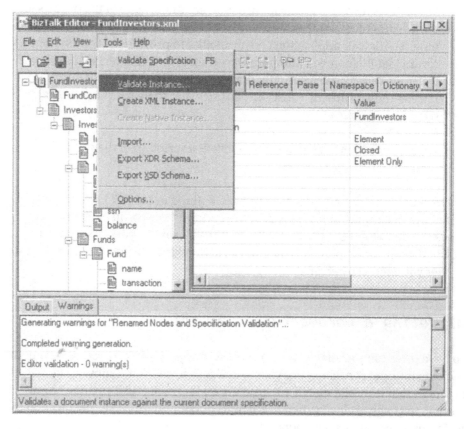

Figure 4-8. Checking the compliance between the document instance and its document specification

A window will pop up, asking you to provide a file. In this case, you would select the FundInvestors document you created earlier. If the document is compliant with the specification, then the Warnings windows at the bottom of the BizTalk Editor window will display the message "The document instance validation succeeded"; otherwise, the Warnings window will show an error description and the position in the document instance where this error occurs. For example, if I created the FundCompany fields in the specification, but no FundCompany field exists in the document instance, the Warnings window would output the following:

```
The XML document has failed validation for the following reason:
Element content is invalid according to the DTD/Schema.
Expecting: FundCompany.
Line:3, Position:13
    <Investors>
```

The other thing you can do to validate your specification is to create a sample instance of your XML document. This option is available from the Tools menu directly under the Validate Instance option. Through this option you can create an output document, which you can save to disk, that will have the structure defined in the specification with placeholder values for the content. You can then look at this in a browser or any other program that lets you load and view XML to check it.

Saving and Distributing a Document Specification

After checking that the specification you created is exactly what you want it to be, you are ready to store the specification in the WebDAV, which is basically a virtual directory on IIS. You must save the document specification using WebDAV in order for BizTalk Server to retrieve it.

To save the specification to WebDAV, select Store to WebDAV in the File menu. Give it a filename of FundInvestors—it doesn't have to match the name of the root of the document, but using the same name is simpler.

If you've been following along to this point, you've now created your first document specification, or BizTalk schema. You'll expect your clients to submit documents that are compliant with the specification, so you need to provide your clients with a copy of the document specification so they can construct their documents accordingly. How do you send them this information?

The document specification you have just created in BizTalk Editor is in a BizTalk schema, which is a proprietary Microsoft technology. Most businesses today expect document specifications in XML Schema Definition language (XSD), which is a format recommended by W3C and is becoming an industry standard for defining document structures. BizTalk Server 2002 has a feature that allows you to automatically convert your document specification to an XSD standard schema.

To generate XSD from a BizTalk schema, open the document specification (BizTalk schema) you want to export in the XML editor. On the menu bar, select Tools ➤ Export XSD Schema. You can then save the exported XSD schema to a file and send it to your clients. The clients can then construct their documents based on this XSD schema. You can also generate an XML Data Reduced (XDR) schema of your specification, if necessary, by selecting Tools ➤ Export XDR schema.

Ports and Channels

Now that you've got the document specification created, what is the next step? The ultimate goal is to get this FundInvestors document into your system so it can be processed. That means you need to create a destination at your end to which clients can send the FundInvestors document. Therefore, the second step in building Bob's ASP application is to define a destination for the document. This leads us to the topic of BizTalk Messaging Manager.

When a document arrives at BizTalk Server, it is processed through some sort of "BizTalk Magic," and will then reach one of the destinations shown in Figure 4-9.

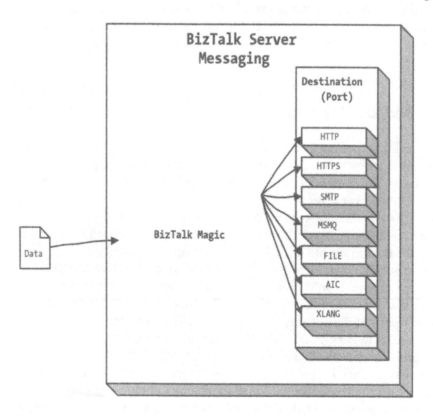

Figure 4-9. BizTalk Server destinations (ports)

In Bob's ASP application, the FundInvestors document will eventually be processed by an XLANG Schedule (created with BizTalk Orchestration Designer), which is one of the possible destinations in BizTalk Server. BizTalk Server refers to these destinations as *ports*—locations where documents can be loaded and unloaded. The first thing to do is create a port.

Creating a Messaging Port

To define (or create) a port, open BizTalk Messaging Manager (shown in Figure 4-10).

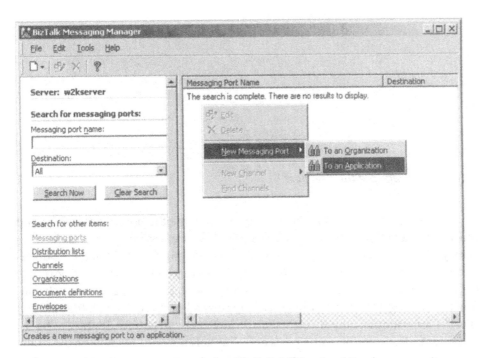

Figure 4-10. Creating a new port using BizTalk Messaging Manager

You'll see from the left panel that BizTalk Messaging Manager is able to work with more than ports, but for now make sure that Messaging Ports is selected, and the first column in the right panel displays Messaging Port Name. (If not, select Messaging Ports and click the Search Now button.)

In the right panel, right-click an empty place, and from the pop-up menu, select New Messaging Port, and then select To an Application (the other choice is To an Organization, which I'll cover in Chapter 6). The New Messaging Port window will open, as shown in Figure 4-11.

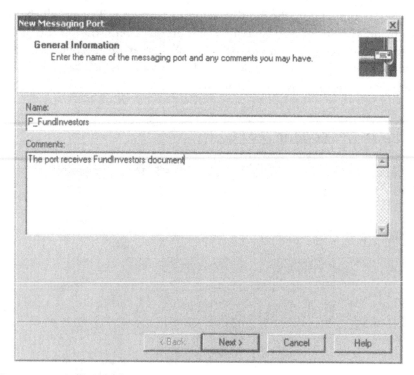

Figure 4-11. Defining the new port

This General Information page is where you name the port. It's always a good practice to have some convention for naming things in BizTalk Server. In this case, you can see I start the port name with "P" for "port". I also include the document name as part of the port name so that I know by its name that this port is the one that deals with the FundInvestors document. (Another alternative, if you don't mind longer names for things, is to append all port names with the suffix "Port"—for example, FundInvestorsPort. Whichever you choose, it's best to be consistent.) The way you name ports and channels may not seem like a big deal at first, but as you define more ports and channels, you will be glad to be able to identify their purposes by their names. Click Next to proceed to the Destination Application page, shown in Figure 4-12.

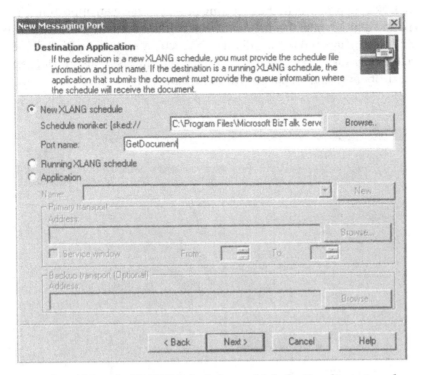

Figure 4-12. Specifying the XLANG Schedule to which the FundInvestors document will be passed by BizTalk Messaging

Lots of text boxes and radio buttons appear in this window, but don't be intimidated—using this window is really quite simple. You just need to tell BizTalk Server which BizTalk XLANG Schedule will be used to process the FundInvestors document. I haven't discussed BizTalk Orchestration yet or created any XLANG Schedules, so for now just make up a name. Select the New XLANG Schedule radio button, and type the name and location for a future XLANG Schedule of file type .skx, for example **C:\Program Files\Microsoft BizTalk Server\XLANG Scheduler\FundInvestors.skx,** and type **GetDocument** next to the Port Name text box.

NOTE   *This Port Name setting has nothing to do with the BizTalk Messaging port—it is just a technical term used in an XLANG Schedule. The fact that it is also called "port" has caused much confusion to many developers.*

Click Next to proceed. In the following page, you have an opportunity to encrypt and digitally sign the document as it comes out of the port. We'll revisit this window in Chapter 6 where I discuss the security features in BizTalk Messaging. For now, just accept the default values and click Next again. The next page is the Security Information page, shown in Figure 4-13.

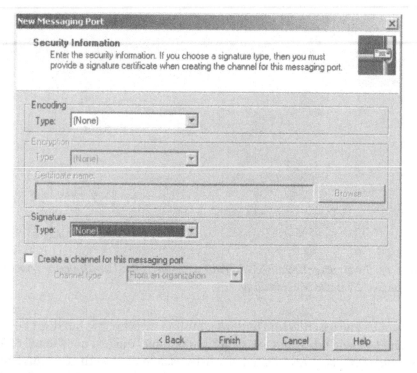

Figure 4-13. Finishing creating the new port

Before you click the Finish button, uncheck the Create a Channel for This Messaging Port checkbox. You need to learn a bit more about messaging channels before you create one. Click Finish to create the new port.

Understanding Messaging Channels

So, what are messaging channels, and what do they do in BizTalk Server 2002? A good analogy for the channel is a map. Suppose I want to go from New York City to visit my father in Atlanta—I log on to http://maps.yahoo.com, and type the starting address and the destination address in the appropriate text boxes, and search for the driving directions. Yahoo's map portal will tell me which roads to take to get to my father's place. Those roads already exist, and Yahoo's map portal knows how to pick the roads that are the most convenient for traveling.

BizTalk Messaging provides a similar function through messaging channels. When a document arrives at BizTalk Server, BizTalk Server needs to know the source of the document (who sent it) and the destination of the document (who will get it), along with the type of the document, in order to route the document to the right location. The route the document will take as it passes through BizTalk Server is called the *channel*. A number of processes will take place in the channel, such as document mapping and data decryption. Different processes may be involved in different channels.

Figure 4-14 shows the relationship between channels and ports in BizTalk Server Messaging. As you can see, a port can have many channels associated with it, but a channel can only associate with one port. Each channel has one end connected to a source, and the other end to a port, and carries a specific type of document.

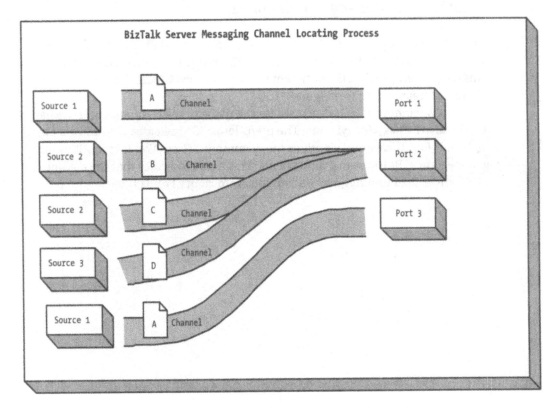

Figure 4-14. BizTalk Server requires three criteria to locate a channel for a document: source, destination, and document type.

Every channel defined in BizTalk Server is associated with these three criteria: a source organization, a destination organization, and a document. When a document arrives at BizTalk Server from a client, it must identify itself with these three pieces of information. A document can provide this information to BizTalk Messaging Server in three ways, and I'll cover them in the next section.

For now, let's assume BizTalk Server has received these three pieces of information from the incoming document—BizTalk Messaging will then try to find an existing channel whose criteria matches those three pieces of information. If BizTalk Messaging is able to find a match, it will feed the document into the channel, and the document will come out at the other end where the port is waiting for it. If BizTalk Messaging is unable to find a channel based on those three criteria, it will raise an error saying it can't find a channel for the document, and the error will appear under the application log of Event Viewer; the document will be sent to the suspend queue.

Creating a Messaging Channel

Let's create a channel and see how the three criteria are defined. Open BizTalk Messaging Manager, and locate the P_FundInvestors port you created earlier in this chapter. Right-click the port name and select New Channel, and then select From an Organization (see Figure 4-15).

A new window pops up and asks for the name of the channel. Enter the name **C_FundInvestors_HenryFonda**. The prefix letter "C" indicates that this is a channel, and "FundInvestors" identifies the document. "HenryFonda" identifies the source, one of Bob's mutual fund clients. This name indicates that the channel will handle the FundInvestors documents from Henry Fonda Inc.

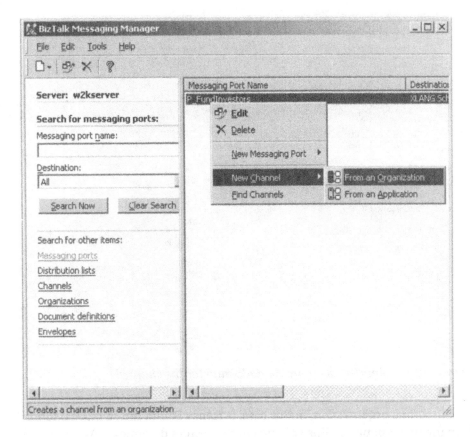

Figure 4-15. Creating a channel for a port using BizTalk Messaging Manager

Another important point is that this channel is automatically attached to the P_FundInvestors port, since you created this channel by right-clicking that port and selecting New Channel. This associates the new channel with that port.

After naming the channel, click Next to go to the Source Organization window, which is described in the next section.

Setting Up the Messaging Organization

BizTalk Server requires that you identify a source organization for each channel. This information is defined in the Source Organization window (shown in Figure 4-16).

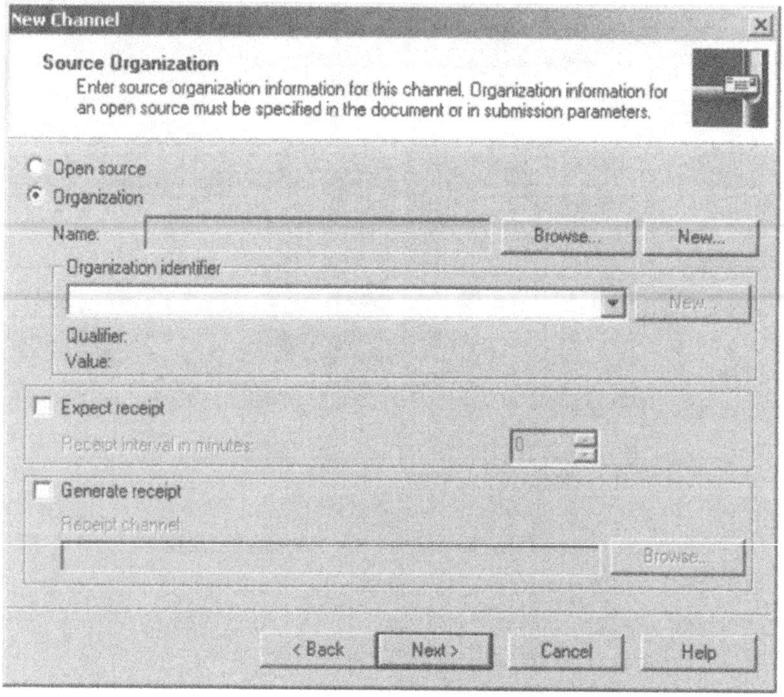

Figure 4-16. Configuring the source organization for the channel

The source organization, in this case, is Henry Fonda Inc., a mutual fund company that will be sending you the FundInvestors document. Two radio buttons appear at the top of the window shown in Figure 4-16: Open source and Organization. I'll cover the Open sources option later; for now, select the Organization option, and click the Browse button next to the Name field.

A new window pops up and asks you to select an organization. You'll find that there is only one organization in the window, SEED test Organization, which was created by default when you installed BizTalk Server. Henry Fonda Inc. is nowhere to be found. This is because you haven't yet defined that organization. Click the Cancel button to exit this window and return to the Source Organization window.

Click the New button next to the Browse button to create a new organization. A New Organization window opens, as shown in Figure 4-17.

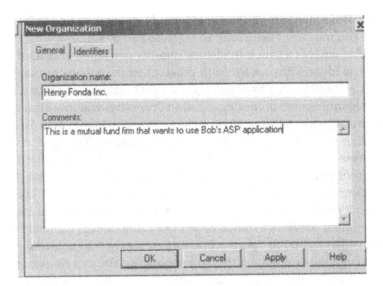

Figure 4-17. Creating an new organization to represent Henry Fonda Inc.

Type a name and any comments for Henry Fonda Inc. on the General tab. Then switch to the Identifiers tab. The Identifiers tab, shown in Figure 4-18, lets you identify an organization by more than one name-value pair.

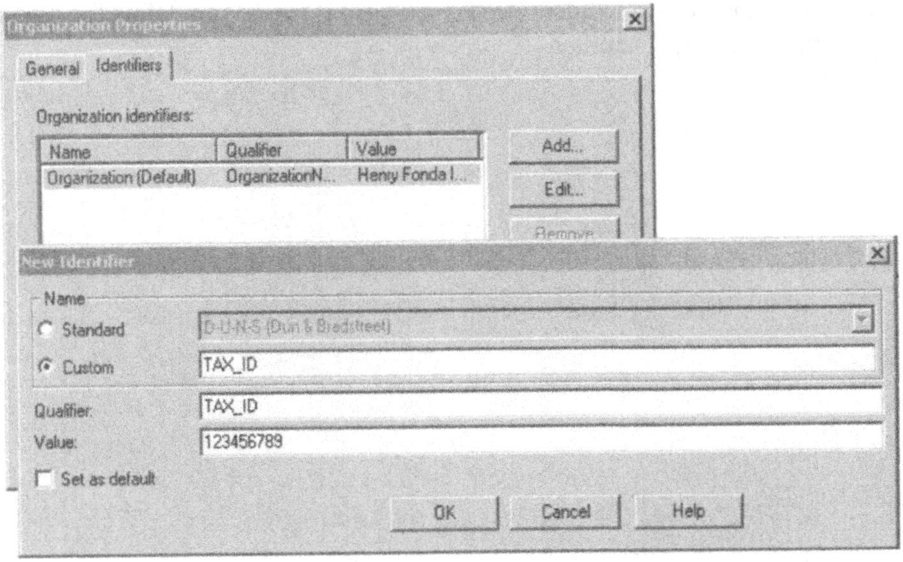

Figure 4-18. Identifying an organization with multiple name-value pairs

In some situations you won't want to identify an organization by its name. Sometimes you may want to identify an organization by some type of ID or standard identifier, such as a Dun & Bradstreet number or a federal tax ID. If Bob's clients want to identify themselves with values other than their company names, you can certainly allow that by entering these other values in the Identifiers tab.

On the Identifiers tab of the Organization Properties window, click the Add button, and a New Identifier window opens as shown in Figure 4-18. You can now define another name-value pair to represent Henry Fonda Inc.

With these multiple identifiers, BizTalk Server can identify that a document is coming from Henry Fonda Inc. when the document's source is either "OrganizationName = Henry Fonda Inc" or "TAX_ID = 123456789". The names of these two identifiers (OrganizationName and TAX_ID) are called *qualifiers*.

If a document provides a source value of XYZ, but doesn't explicitly state what the qualifier is, BizTalk Server will assume it means "OrganizationName = XYZ", since OrganizationName is the default qualifier. You can change the default qualifier by checking the Set as default checkbox in the New Identifier window.

Click OK until you get back to the Source Organization window (shown in Figure 4-16). Then click Next to proceed to the Inbound Document window, which is described in the next section.

Choosing the Messaging Document Specification

The Inbound Document window (see Figure 4-19) is where you define the type of document the channel handles.

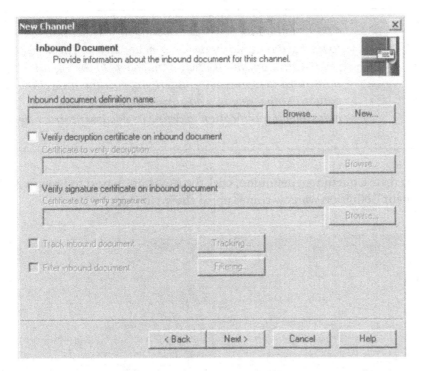

Figure 4-19. Configuring what kind of documents will pass into the channel

In the Inbound Document window, you specify the document type, which is the third criterion BizTalk Server uses to locate a channel for the document. To specify a document type, click the Browse button. A new window pops up, but you'll find that at this point there is no item to select—you must first define a document definition for the FundInvestors specification. Click Cancel to return. (You may be wondering what happened to the specification you created earlier with BizTalk Editor. You saved it to the BizTalk repository using WebDAV, didn't you? The answer is that all you have done is create an XML schema and save it where BizTalk Server can find it. You must also create a document definition in BizTalk Messaging so that BizTalk Messaging can link this document type to the concrete XML schema specification.)

> **NOTE**   *In BizTalk Server, the document specification refers to the file that contains the document schema. The document definition, on the other hand, refers to the logical name used to represent its underlying document specification. In other words, a document definition uses a document specification to define its document structure.*

To create a document definition, click the New button next to Browse. A New Document Definition window comes up, as shown in Figure 4-20.

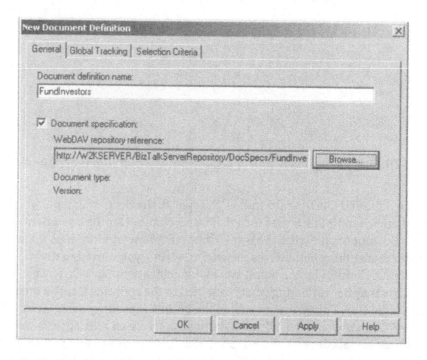

Figure 4-20. Creating a document definition and associating it with a document specification

You can enter a document definition name—the name doesn't have to be the same as the document specification name. Then check the Document Specification checkbox and click Browse to select a file. A new window will open, pointing to BizTalk Server's document repository folder, which is by default located under [BizTalk Installation Directory]\BizTalkServerRepository\DocSpecs. Notice that the reference uses HTTP as its protocol; this is how WebDAV receives files in BizTalk Server.

I'll talk more about the Global Tracking tab when I demonstrate document tracking in Chapter 9. The Selection Criteria tab is used only by EDI or X12 documents, so I won't be discussing it further.

NOTE *You can create a document definition without associating it with a document specification by unchecking the Document Specification checkbox, but BizTalk Server will not be able to validate the document or map it to another schema, since it has no information about the structure of the document. This is useful in situations where you don't want to validate and map the document.*

After setting the values on the General tab, click OK to save the document definition and return to the Inbound Document window shown in Figure 4-19. Besides providing an inbound document name, you can also specify in this window whether you want to verify the digital signature and decrypt the document. I'll bring up these items again in Chapter 6. For Bob's ASP application, leave these two checkboxes unchecked. I'll also discuss the Tracking inbound document option in Chapter 9 .

Click Next to proceed to the Outbound Document window, shown in Figure 4-21. In this window, you specify what document will be coming out of this channel. Click the Browse button and select the FundInvestors document definition, which you just created. Then click OK to return to the Outbound Document window.

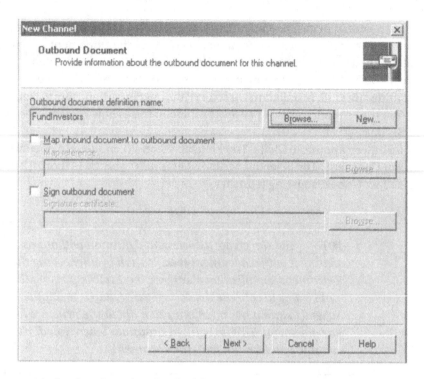

Figure 4-21. Configuring what kind of documents will pass out of the channel

If you had chosen a document definition that was different from the inbound document, you would also have to provide a map file for the document transformation. You can still provide a map file, even though the inbound document and outbound document are the same—mapping can be used to change the data in the document while leaving the data structure untouched. You can also sign the outbound document with a certificate. In this case, leave the checkboxes in the Outbound Document window unchecked, and click Next to proceed. You'll learn more about document mapping in Chapter 7.

The next window is the Document Logging window, shown in Figure 4-22. Here you have an opportunity to log the document in your tracking database. You can specify the logging options for both inbound and outbound documents, and selectively log documents based on the channels through which the documents pass.

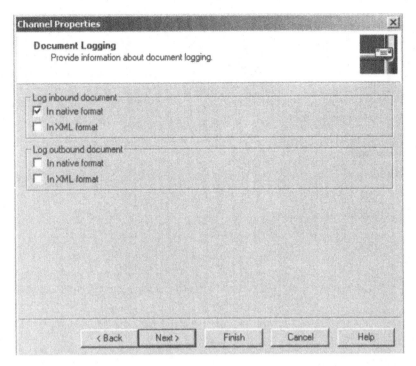

Figure 4-22. Configuring the logging property for the document passing through this channel

We'll explore the logging feature in Chapter 9; for now, accept the default values and click Finish to create the channel.

Reviewing the Channel Setup

You have just created a channel, so let's examine the three criteria this channel is associated with.

You know the source organization is Henry Fonda Inc., and the document type for the channel is the same as the inbound document, which is FundInvestors, but what is the destination organization? You have associated the channel with a port, but what organization is that port considered to be?

A good way to check the destination organization for a port is through BizTalk Messaging Manager. To search on a port, click the Messaging Ports link in the left panel, then type in the name of the messaging port, and click the Search Now button. (This search method applies to all items in the list at the bottom of the left panel, by the way.) The result is shown in the right panel (see Figure 4-23).

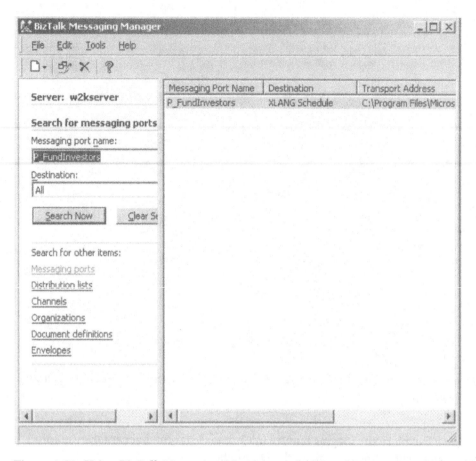

Figure 4-23. Using BizTalk Messaging Manager to find out the properties for port, channel, etc.

As you can see in Figure 4-23, the Destination for port P_FundInvestors, which is the port your newly created channel attaches to, is XLANG Schedule. A destination port of XLANG Schedule means that the destination organization for that port is Home Organization, which represents the organization this BizTalk Server is currently a part of. Simply put, Home Organization is your organization. It may seem odd at first, but it makes perfect sense. When a document arrives at your BizTalk Server from a client, it is coming from another organization to your organization, Home Organization.

Here is a summary of the values for the channel C_FundInvestors_HenryFonda:

- *Source organization:* Henry Fonda Inc.

- *Document definition:* FundInvestors

- *Destination organization:* Home Organization

Data Entry Points

With the channel created, C_FundInvestors_HenryFonda is ready to take on any document that meets the three criteria of source organization, document definition, and destination organization. So how can a document tell BizTalk Server that it is a FundInvestors document and that it comes from Henry Fonda Inc. and goes to Home Organization?

There are three ways to do this: the Interchange submit method, the Receive Functions, and the self-routing document. Because you should be familiar with the Interchange submit method and Receive Functions from earlier chapters, I'll cover them first, then I'll explain the self-routing document, a very important concept in BizTalk Server.

BizTalk Interchange Submit Method and Receive Function

One of the ways to present the source, destination, and document type information to BizTalk Server is through the parameters of an Interchange submit call. When clients use Interchange components to submit data to BizTalk Server, they can provide the source and destination organizations by specifying them in the parameters Source Qualifier, Source ID, Destination Qualifier, and Destination ID.

Source Qualifier and Destination Qualifier indicate the type of identification the Source ID and Destination ID represent. The qualifier can be an organization name or tax ID, and in the example the ID would be "HenryFonda Inc." or "123456789," respectively. By default, the Source Qualifier and Destination Qualifier are "Organization Name" if they are not explicitly specified.

BizTalk Server can figure out the document type by examining the document root. If there is a predefined document definition on BizTalk Server that has the same document root as the submitted document, then this document is considered to be the type of that predefined document definition. You can also provide the document type name as the parameter of the method call so that BizTalk Server doesn't have to figure it out on its own. For example, you can submit a document that goes through the C_FundInvestors_HenryFonda channel with following code:

```
dim oInterchange
dim data
'set data equal to the complete document content
data="<FundInvestors><. . . . ></FundInvestors>"
set oInterchange = CreateObject("BizTalk.Interchange")
oInterchange.submit 1,data,,"OrganizationName","Henry Fonda _
  Inc.","OrganizationName","Home Organization"
```

The second way to get the source, destination, and document information to BizTalk Server is through the property settings of Receive Functions. When a Receive Function is used to retrieve the data and bring it into BizTalk Server, the source organization and destination organization can be specified on the Receive Function's advanced properties page. All the documents picked up by this Receive Function would then carry this source and destination.

To configure the source and destination on a Receive Function, open the BizTalk Server Administration console, and select a Receive Function in the console. Right-click the Receive Function, and a new pop-up menu comes up as shown in Figure 4-24.

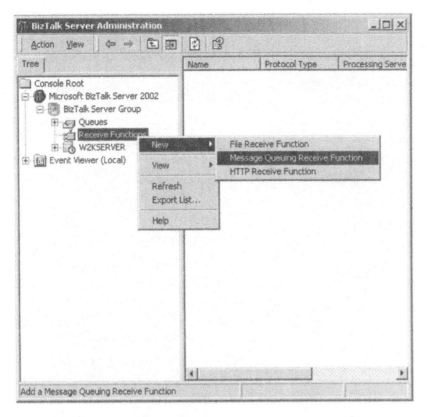

Figure 4-24. Creating a new Receive Function

Upon selecting New ➢ Message Queuing Receive Function to create
a Receive Function for the message queue, a new window comes up as shown in
Figure 4-25.

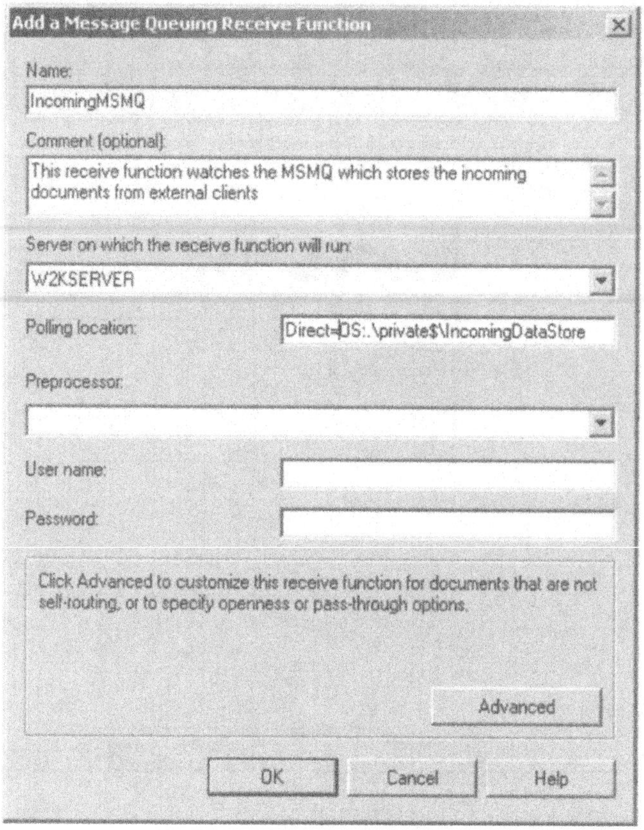

Figure 4-25. Properties page of the Receive Function

On this window, you need to provide a Receive Function name and the polling location. The polling location is the place where this Receive Function watches and pulls out any document as it arrives and sends it to the BizTalk Server's work queue. Another set of properties is associated with the routing information for the Receive Function. You can configure these by clicking the Advanced button on the lower part of window shown in Figure 4-25.

Click the Advanced button to open the Advanced Receive Function Options window of the Receive Function, as shown in Figure 4-26.

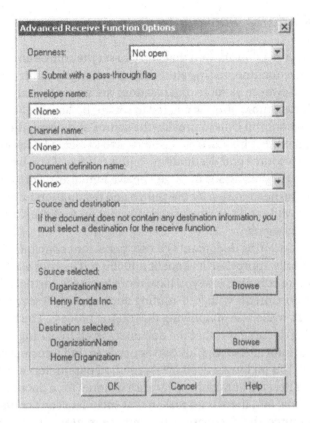

Figure 4-26. Setting the source and destination information for a Receive Function

In the bottom half of the window shown in Figure 4-26, you can specify the source and destination information for this Receive Function. These options are null by default, but you can click the Browse button next to each item and select both the organization qualifier and the identifier value. For example, with the settings shown in Figure 4-26, every document that is picked up by this Receive Function would be considered a document that comes from Henry Fonda Inc. and goes to Home Organization.

Self-Routing Documents

The previous section showed that you can set the source and destination information for a document using either an Interchange submit call or a Receive Function. However, as more organizations are set up to exchange data with BizTalk Server, more effort is needed to set up the Receive Function or Interchange submit calls to provide the source and destination information of the document. For instance, you would have to create 20 Receive Functions, each with its own source and destination configurations, if you wanted to exchange data with 20 organizations through Receive Functions. Fortunately, you can eliminate the need to specify the source and destination information for the document while still providing such information to BizTalk Server by using *self-routing documents*.

The self-routing document is a very important concept in BizTalk Server. You might not fully appreciate its benefit initially, but as your applications grow bigger and more complex, and you have more business partners that you need to exchange documents with, self-routing documents will save you a lot of development effort, while also simplifying the routing process. The idea behind the self-routing document is that the document itself (meaning its content) will provide all the information BizTalk Server needs to find a correct channel for the document. You no longer need messy method parameters and tedious configurations of Receive Functions to locate a channel for a document. A document contains data, and there is no reason that such data can't contain information about its source and destination. It's simply a matter of telling BizTalk Server where to find such information inside a document using what are known as *dictionary properties*.

When you create a document specification, you can set the dictionary properties for the document using the BizTalk Editor tab I glossed over in the earlier discussion of document specifications—the Dictionary tab, shown in Figure 4-27. As you can see, these dictionary properties are similar to the properties that appear on the Receive Function, and they enable you to express the source and destination information to BizTalk Server within a document.

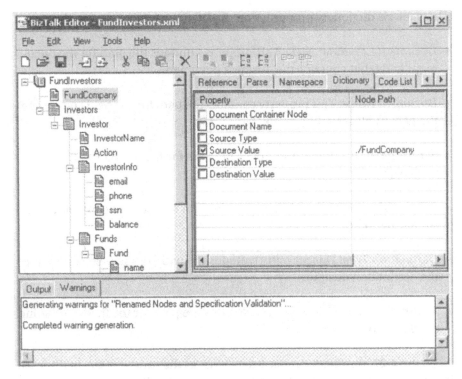

Figure 4-27. Configuring the dictionary properties for a document in BizTalk Editor

To set the values for a dictionary property, first locate and then select the field that contains the textual value in the left panel, and then check the checkbox next to the appropriate dictionary property in the right panel while the focus is still on the field. BizTalk Editor will automatically add the XPath expression for the field. (XPath is a comprehensive language used for navigating through the hierarchy of an XML document.)

NOTE   *With the exception of the Document Container Node property, you must choose a field instead of a record when setting values for these dictionary properties, because BizTalk Server expects to retrieve the textual value embedded in those fields. As you move around from Record node to Field node and back, you will notice that the checkboxes are enabled and disabled appropriately to enforce this.*

There are six dictionary properties on the Dictionary tab:

- *Document Container Node:* This property contains the path for the document node that contains the business document.

- *Document Name:* This property contains the path for the field containing the document definition name.

- *Source Type:* This property contains the path for the field containing the source qualifier.

- *Source Value:* This property contains the path for the field containing the source identifier.

- *Destination Type:* This property contains the path for the field containing the destination qualifier.

- *Destination Value:* This property contains the path for the field containing the destination value.

In Figure 4-27, the FundCompany field is set as the source value. In this case, I didn't set the dictionary property for the source type, so its source type will be OrganizationName since that is the default value. You can leave the Document Name property blank, since BizTalk Server will figure it out by examining the document root.

What about the destination type and destination values? You could set the dictionary properties if you had fields containing destination information in your document, but you don't have any fields in the document for such information. There are two solutions for this problem. The first one is obvious—you can add more fields in the document for the destination information, and then set the dictionary properties accordingly. The second choice is to provide the missing information by specifying the additional properties settings on the Receive Function, or by using the additional parameter value if the Interchange submit call is used to submit the document.

So what happens if a document's dictionary properties and the Receive Function properties (or Interchange submit call's parameters) contain conflicting information? Which information will be used by BizTalk Server to locate a channel? The answer is that the settings in the Receive Function or the parameters of the Interchange submit call always override the corresponding information in the document's dictionary properties.

For example, if a document field has configured as the source value in its dictionary property "XYZ company", but the Receive Function used to pick up this document has its source value configured as "ABC company" on its advanced properties page, BizTalk Server will defer to the Receive Function and consider this document to be sent from ABC company. The same rule applies to the Interchange submit call—the parameters of the method call override the values in the document's dictionary properties.

On the other hand, when the document dictionary properties and the Receive Function (or Interchange submit call) provide information that doesn't overlap, the information from both sources will be used by BizTalk Server to find a channel. For instance, in the FundInvestors document, the source type is defined in the document dictionary property, but no value is presented for source type, destination type, or destination value. You can provide the missing information by setting it in the advanced properties page of the Receive Function, as shown in Figure 4-28.

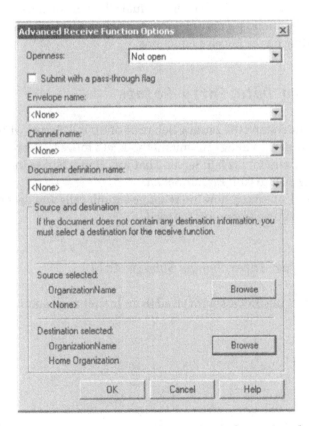

Figure 4-28. Configuring the source and destination information that is absent in the document

In the Source and Destination section of the properties page in Figure 4-28, the source value is <None>, which means the source value will be provided by the document. Because values are provided for the destination on the Receive Function, the destination for the document will always be Home Organization no matter what values are presented in the document. With information specified inside the document and configured on the Receive Function (or Interchange submit method), BizTalk Server will have enough information to find the correct channel for the document.

Hard-coding the destination value on the Receive Function or Interchange submit call is perfectly all right in most cases. If your BizTalk application allows clients to submit documents, then every document arriving at your BizTalk Server will have your organization as its destination. The only situation in which this might not be appropriate is if you want to allow clients to send a document to another of your clients through your BizTalk Server—in this case hard-coding the destination information may not be cost effective, since you would have to set up the Receive Function for each individual client. In such a situation, you can provide both source and destination information inside the document and avoid hard-coding on the Receive Functions.

Implementing Data Entry Points

Now that you understand the routing behavior of BizTalk Server with the Receive Functions and the Interchange submit method, let's move to the next step and set up the entry point for BizTalk Server. That way Henry Fonda Inc. can actually send something over to your BizTalk Server.

Let's first look at exactly how Interchange submit calls and Receive Functions work, and then set up entry points for each.

Entry Point for Interchange Submit Call

Figure 4-29 shows the processes involved in an Interchange submit call.

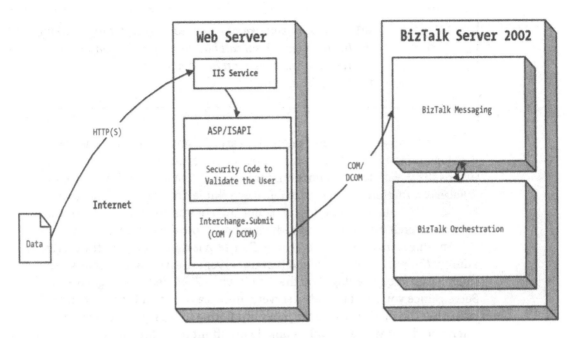

Figure 4-29. Sending a document through an Interchange submit call

When a client posts a document to an ASP page or ISAPI program on your Web server using HTTP(S), the ASP page or ISAPI on the Web server is responsible for submitting the document to BizTalk Server. If BizTalk Server and the Web server are on two separate servers, a proxy for the Interchange component needs to be deployed on the Web server with BizTalk Server configured as its target.

Within the ASP page or ISAPI program, code should be added to verify the sender of the document for security purposes (which you'll learn more about in Chapter 12). After you verify the sender, you can submit the document to BizTalk Server by calling the Interchange.Submit() method. You can also generate the parameters for this method at runtime to change the routing behavior of the document.

NOTE *You must make sure the user account that is making the Interchange submit call has access permission to the Interchange component on BizTalk Server in order for the call to be successful.*

The Interchange.Submit() method is very straightforward and easy to develop and implement. However, for better performance, Microsoft recommends the use of Receive Functions for bringing data into BizTalk Server. A Receive Function is designed to receive multiple documents from a target location at a time, and it performs significantly better under heavy loads than does an Interchange submit call, which submits one document at a time.

Another benefit of using a Receive Function is that it removes the server affinity. When the Web server and BizTalk Server are on separate servers, the Interchange proxy deployed on the Web server will be tied to a single BizTalk Server, since you must provide a server name as a target for the proxy. In the event that the BizTalk Server the proxy is pointing to fails, your service will be interrupted. Some clients will be unable to submit their documents even if other BizTalk Servers are up and running in your BizTalk Server group. The BizTalk Server group only guarantees uninterrupted service for the documents that are already in its work queue. There is little a BizTalk Server group can do if a document is unable to reach the work queue in the first place.

Technology like Component Load Balancing (CLB) in Application Center can provide a solution for this server affinity problem by load balancing the Interchange submit calls across the member servers in a BizTalk Server group. However, making your application work with Application Center may involve a significant amount of effort. (In Chapter 13, I'll talk about HTTP Receive Functions—which are not really Receive Functions as such, but rather customized ISAPI programs that provide a great alternative to Component Load Balancing.)

Entry Point for Receive Functions

To take advantage of the high performance that Receive Functions offer in BizTalk Server, let's take a look at the design shown in Figure 4-30.

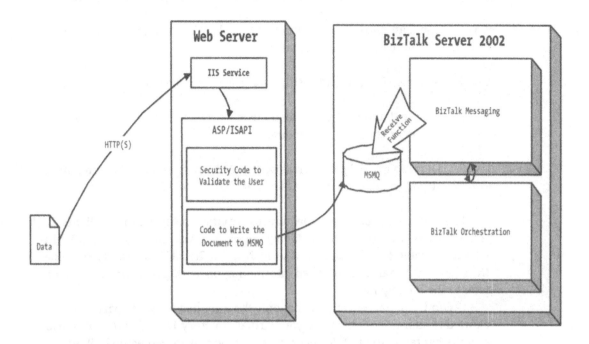

Figure 4-30. Sending a document to BizTalk Server using a Receive Function

In Figure 4-30, the Web server receives an HTTP(S) post from clients over the Internet, but instead of making an Interchange submit call, the ASP page or ISAPI sends the document to a message queue. Receive Functions watch for any documents arriving at the queue and pull them into BizTalk Server as soon as they arrive. The MSMQ can be located on either the BizTalk Server or, for the purpose of fault tolerance, on a clustered MSMQ server that is watched by Receive Functions from multiple servers in a BizTalk Server group.

With Receive Functions and a centralized message queue or file location, you can eliminate the server affinity problem you saw in the Interchange submit method. There is a problem associated with this design involving transactional reads from the message queue—you'll learn more about this problem in Chapter 13.

Implementing an Entry Point for Interchange Submit Call

To implement an entry point for Bob's ASP application using an Interchange submit call, there are three major steps:

1. Set up a virtual directory that is accessible to the clients.

2. Ensure that only the intended business partners are allowed to submit documents to that virtual directory.

3. Develop an ASP page to receive the HTTP post and call the Interchange submit method to submit the posted data to the BizTalk Server.

First, you must set up a virtual directory that is accessible to the clients. To do this, open the Internet Services Manager under the Administrative tools. Right-click the default Web directory and select New ➤ Virtual Directory. Then follow the on-screen wizard. For detailed information on setting up a virtual directory, refer to the IIS help file.

Second, you need to ensure that only the intended business partners are allowed to submit documents to your virtual directory. Digital certificates, user security contexts, and COM+ security need to be considered when building a secure B2B application with BizTalk Server. In Chapter 12, you'll have a chance to look at these issues in detail. For now, let's just focus on how to get the document into BizTalk Server.

Ignoring for a moment what I've just said, let's make sure anyone can access the BizTalk Interchange component in Component Service by turning off the security checking for the component. To do so, open the Component Service console under Administrative Tools and locate BizTalk Server Interchange Application in the console. Then open the component's properties page, and make sure the "Enforce access checks for this application" checkbox is unchecked as shown in Figure 4-31. This checkbox is unchecked by default. (The properties page for BizTalk Server Interchange Application is not editable by default. To edit its value, you must first uncheck the "Disable deletion" and "Disable changes" checkboxes on the Advanced tab of the properties page.)

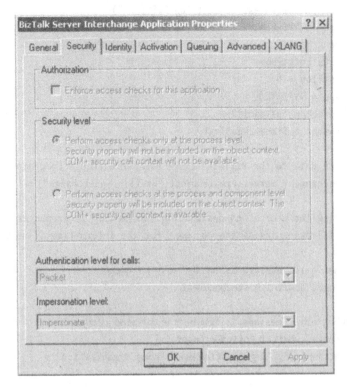

Figure 4-31. Verifying the security properties of BizTalk Server Interchange Application under the Component Service

Third, you need to develop an ASP page to receive the HTTP post and call the Interchange submit method to submit the posted data to the BizTalk Server. Here is a typical example of the code you would use to achieve this. This code is from the file FundInvestorsPost.asp (which is available from the Downloads section of the Apress Web site [http://www.apress.com]):

```
<%
    Const TYPE_BINARY = 1
    Const TYPE_TEXT = 2
    Dim account
    Dim stream
    Dim PostedDocument
    Dim EntityBody
    Dim position
    Dim oInterchange
    'code to extract the data from HTTP Post.
    EntityBody=Request.BinaryRead(Request.TotalBytes)
```

```
Set Stream = Server.CreateObject("AdoDB.Stream")
Stream.Type = TYPE_BINARY
stream.Open
Stream.Write EntityBody
Stream.Position = 0
Stream.Type = TYPE_TEXT
Stream.Charset = "us-ascii"
PostedDocument = Stream.ReadText


'submit the data to the BizTalk Server with Interchange component
set oInterchange = Server.CreateObject("Biztalk.Interchange")

'by omitting the source and destination information in parameters, BizTalk
'Server is looking inside the document for the information it needs.

'check what error message is on the suspend queue.
oInterchange.submit 1,PostedDocument

'check what error message is now on the suspend queue?
'oInterchange.submit 1,PostedDocument,, _
"OrganizationName",,"OrganizationName","Home Organization"

set oInterchange=nothing
set stream=nothing
Response.Status="200 OK"
%>
```

In the preceding code, ASP's Request.BinaryRead method reads the whole posted document as binary data. Then the Stream object in the ADODB object converts the binary code into ASCII data by setting the Charset property, which does all the decoding. Then Stream.ReadText returns a string that contains the entire document posted by the client.

You are now ready to make the Interchange submit call to BizTalk Server. Use the following code to submit the document:

```
oInterchange.submit 1,PostedDocument
```

In the next section, you'll substitute the preceding line with the following one and take a look at what difference it makes:

```
oInterchange.submit 1,PostedDocument,,
"OrganizationName",,"OrganizationName","Home Organization"
```

Testing the Entry Point

To test the entry point, you need a client program that can post a document to
a URL and display a response code to indicate whether the HTTP post is successful. This client program will come in handy when doing testing, and it can be
easily created using Visual Basic and the XMLHTTP class (a class containing
methods that allow you to easily open an HTTP connection and post data to the
URL). Figure 4-32 shows such a client program; the source code is located on
the Downloads section of the Apress Web site (`http://www.apress.com`).

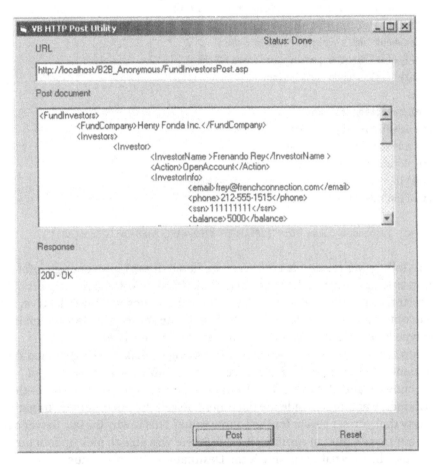

Figure 4-32. Posting a document to a URL with a homemade HTTP post utility

This HTTP post utility client uses a text box for document input, and a text
box for the HTTP response. As you can see in Figure 4-32, after I posted the sample FundInvestors document you saw earlier in the chapter, I received a "200-OK"

code, which means no error occurred on the ASP page, and the submit call was successful.

Now, let's take a look at the application log in the Event Viewer to see how far the document went. As you'll see, there is a BizTalk Server error in the event view:

```
An error occurred in BizTalk Server.

 Details:
 ------------------------------------------------
 [0x0133] At least one of the fields necessary to
 select a channel is missing. Verify that
 your document and envelopes extract the
 proper fields for the parser, or specify the
 necessary fields upon submission.

 Channel selection fields:
 Source identifier type: "OrganizationName"
 Source identifier value: "Henry Fonda Inc."
 Source document name: "FundInvestors"
 Destination identifier type: "OrganizationName"
 Destination identifier value: ""

 [0x1730] Suspended Queue ID: "{28FAEC1F-42F2-43FC-84E8-BACD2C60AC30}"
```

BizTalk Server raises this type of error when it doesn't have enough information to locate a channel for the document. If you look at the name pairs of the source and destination information, you'll see the values that BizTalk Server was able to obtain from this submission. By default, the source and destination identifier type is OrganizationName, even if they are not specified.

As you can see from the message shown here, BizTalk Server identified the document as a FundInvestors document by examining the root element of the document, and also identified "Henry Fonda Inc." as its source value—this information was stored inside the document. Recall the document dictionary property that you set earlier for the source value? This is why BizTalk Server can figure out these values at runtime. BizTalk Server was able to pick up four out of five fields. The only value missing is the Destination identifier value.

Now let's see what happens if you use the other line of code in the FundInvestorPost.asp to submit the document:

```
oInterchange.submit  1, _ PostedDocument,,
"OrganizationName",,"OrganizationName","Home Organization"
```

NOTE   *We don't have to add an "OrganizationName"
parameter, since this is a default value.*

Submit the document again with the HTTP post utility client, and you will
get another error, as follows. The good news is that it is a different error:

```
An error occurred in BizTalk Server.

 Details:
 --------------------------------------------------
 [0x8004500c] The XLANG schedule file is not valid.
 "0x800C0005" error occurred while trying to load the following URL: "file:
 //C:\Program Files\Microsoft BizTalk Server\XLANG Scheduler\FundInvestors.skx".
  [0x0159] The server encountered a transport error while processing the
 messaging
 port "P_FundInvestors", which uses a transport component with a ProgID of
 "BizTalk.BPOActivation.1".

 [0x012b] A transmission attempt failed.
```

This error indicates that BizTalk Server is unable to load "file://C:\Program
Files\Microsoft BizTalk Server\XLANG Scheduler\FundInvestors.skx". This file is
the XLANG Schedule that you intend to use to process the document. You haven't
created this file (you entered a filename during the port configuration, but you
haven't yet created the file with Orchestration Designer), so this error is good
news—it means the document is done with BizTalk Messaging and is ready to be
passed on to BizTalk Orchestration for further processing.

Implementing an Entry Point for a Receive Function

Before moving on to the topic of BizTalk Orchestration, let's look at how to create
an entry point for a Receive Function, instead of for the Interchange submit
method. There are three things you need to do:

1.   Create a transactional message queue.

2. Modify the ASP page so that it sends the posted document to a message queue instead of calling the Interchange submit method.

3. Set up a Receive Function to watch the message queue you created and configure the destination information that is missing in the document.

To set up a message queue, open the Computer Management window under Administrative Tools. The Message Queue node is located under the Service and Application node.

To add a private transactional message queue, right-click the Private Queue folder under the Message Queue node and select New ➤ Private Queue. A dialog box opens, as shown in Figure 4-33, and you can type a name for the queue and check the Transactional checkbox to make this a transactional queue.

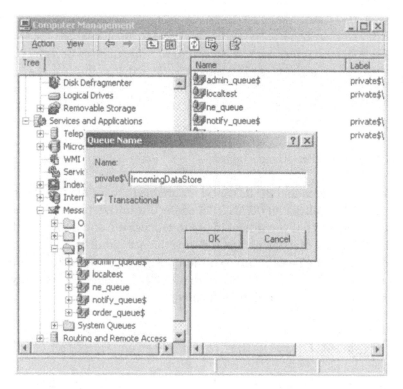

Figure 4-33. Creating a transactional local private queue with the Computer Management console

During the development stage, it is a good idea to enable the journal for this message queue. MSMQ will save a copy of all the messages that arrive at the queue to its journal message folder if the message journal is enabled, so you can find out whether the message has been picked up, or whether it has not arrived at the queue at all, by checking the journal message folder. Journal properties can be set on the properties page of the message queue.

Next, you can use the ASP page (FundInvestorsPost.asp) from the Interchange submit call section, and just modify it for the Receive Function. The following code is in the FundInvestorsPost_MSMQ.asp file (which is available from the Downloads section of the Apress Web site [http://www.apress.com]):

```
<%
    Const TYPE_BINARY = 1
    Const TYPE_TEXT = 2
    Const MQ_SEND_ACCESS = 2
    Const MQ_DENY_NONE = 0
    Const MQ_SINGLE_MESSAGE = 3
    Dim account
    Dim stream
    Dim PostedDocument
    Dim EntityBody
    Dim position
    Dim oInterchange

    'code to extract the data from HTTP Post.
    EntityBody=Request.BinaryRead(Request.TotalBytes)
    Set Stream = Server.CreateObject("AdoDB.Stream")
    Stream.Type = TYPE_BINARY
    stream.Open
    Stream.Write EntityBody
    Stream.Position = 0
    Stream.Type = Const TYPE_TEXT
    Stream.Charset = "us-ascii"
    PostedDocument = PostedDocument & Stream.ReadText

'Send the document to a message queue in a transactional send
    Dim queue
    Dim queueinfo
    Dim queuemsg
    set queueinfo = Server.CreateObject("MSMQ.MSMQQueueInfo")
    set queuemsg = Server.CreateObject("MSMQ.MSMQMessage")
    'set the formatname for the queue
    queueinfo.FormatName="Direct=OS:.\private$\IncomingDataStore"
```

```
set queue=queueinfo.open ( MQ_SEND_ACCESS, MQ_DENY_NONE)
'set up a queue message
queuemsg.Label = "Incoming Document for Bob"
queuemsg.Body = PostedDocument

'send a message in to the queue a single message transaction.

queuemsg.Send queue, MQ_SINGLE_MESSAGE

set stream = nothing
set queue = nothing
set queueinfo = nothing
set queuemsg = nothing
Response.Status="200 OK"
%>
```

The preceding code first receives the document posted from the client and then sends the document to a predefined message queue instead of making an Interchange submit call. When this ASP page completes, the client document will be at the message queue, waiting to be picked up.

Next, you need to create a Receive Function to retrieve the document from the message queue. To create a Receive Function, select Start ➤ Programs ➤ Microsoft BizTalk Server 2002, and open BizTalk Server Administration under BizTalk Server group. Right-click Receive Functions and select New ➤ Message Queuing Receive Function, as shown in Figure 4-34.

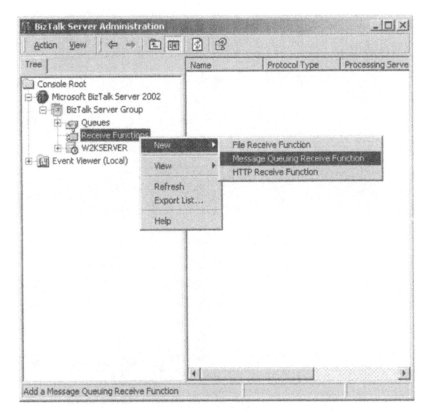

Figure 4-34. Adding a new Message Queuing Receive Function

An Add a Message Queuing Receive Function window will open, containing two sets of properties you can configure for a Receive Function. You can see the first set in Figure 4-35.

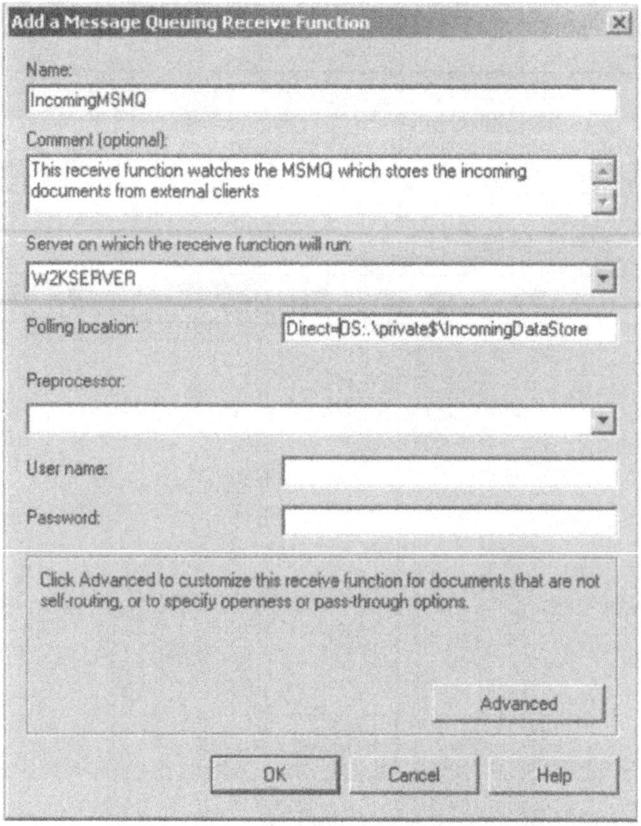

Figure 4-35. Setting the general properties for a Message Queuing Receive Function

There are a couple of things to notice in the window shown in Figure 4-35. First, the drop-down list for "Server on which the Receive Function will run" indicates which server will execute this Receive Function. In a single server scenario, this setting has little meaning, since only one machine can execute this Receive Function. However, in a server group environment, where more than one BizTalk Server is involved, you can delegate the Receive Function to any one of the member servers in the group by selecting the server name in this drop-down list.

Second, the polling location is the location that the Receive Function will watch for incoming documents. In case of a message queue Receive Function, you need to specify the name of the message queue in the format of "Direct = OS:<servername>\<queuename>". You can also use the IP address instead, such as "Direct=TCP:<ip address>\<queuename>".

The Receive Function is run under the user account that runs the BizTalk Messaging service; however, if this account doesn't have access to the message queue, you can always provide a separate user name and password that you want the Receive Function to use to access the targeted message queue at runtime.

The second set of properties defines how the documents are routed when they are picked up by the Receive Function. Click the Advanced button in the window shown in Figure 4-35 and a new window will open, as shown in Figure 4-36.

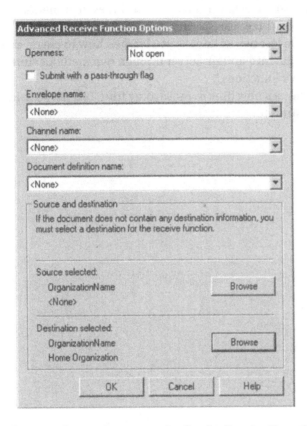

Figure 4-36. Configuring the routing properties for the Receive Function

If you compare the properties on this window with the parameters of the Interchange submit method, you will find that they correspond to each other perfectly. In many ways, the Receive Function is a graphical version of the Interchange submit method.

You can click the Browse button under the source and destination sections to select the source and destination for this Receive Function. This setting will produce the same result as the parameter values you set on the Interchange submit call earlier.

Click OK to save your changes.

Now it is time to test the Receive Function. Post the document to FundInvestorsPost_MSMQ.asp. The result should be as you expect—a message that indicates the error for loading the invalid XLANG Schedule.

Summary

You've learned quite a bit in this chapter. You now know how to create and configure messaging channels, ports, and organizations using BizTalk Messaging Manager. You also know how BizTalk Server routes documents to their destinations, based on three search criteria.

Through the last two examples, you learned how to create an entry point for a document to get into BizTalk Server through two methods: Interchange submit calls and Receive Functions.

After all this, it's now time to move away from BizTalk Messaging and look at BizTalk Orchestration.

CHAPTER 5

Implementing BizTalk Orchestration

IN THE LAST CHAPTER, you learned how to receive a document from a customer and transfer it from one place to the next. With the power of BizTalk Server Receive Functions and messaging channels and ports, moving data within and between organizations is greatly simplified.

Unlike the stock market where a lot of money is made simply by transferring paper—stock certificates—from one hand to the next, most businesses must do some real work to survive. The real work for BizTalk Server is the document processing.

In this chapter, we'll look at how BizTalk Server processes the documents using BizTalk Orchestration. I'll first show you how BizTalk Orchestration processes the documents, and later I'll show you how to create a BizTalk Orchestration from scratch to manage the document processes required by Bob's ASP application.

Designing Business Processes

The first question you may have about BizTalk Orchestration is what a *business process* is. We hear this kind of marketing lingo from technology companies on a daily basis, along with the other big terms, such as strategic decisions, enterprise solutions, collaborative business relationships, and so on. Communication could be enhanced significantly if these terms were prohibited by law.

A *business process* is a *task*, in my dictionary. Anything you do in the course of business can be labeled a business process. Receiving and processing a customer order or creating and issuing an invoice can be a business process. Extracting meaningful data from a document and performing other tasks, such as persisting it to database tables, passing it to business objects, or forwarding it to different external business partners, can also be a business process or a collection of business processes, depending on your point of view. BizTalk Orchestration can help you design and implement these business processes.

The first step is to come up with a logical design for the business process you are trying to build. BizTalk Orchestration Designer allows you to design your business processes in a flowchart-like environment that is surprisingly similar to a logic design diagram. To open BizTalk Orchestration Designer, select Start ➤ Programs ➤ Microsoft BizTalk Server 2002 ➤ BizTalk Orchestration Designer. Figure 5-1 shows the BizTalk Orchestration Designer.

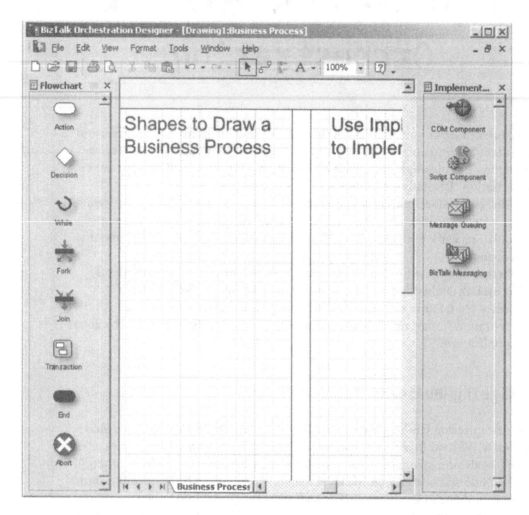

Figure 5-1. The BizTalk Orchestration Designer interface

The Orchestration Designer window consists of two green panels on either side, with white design space in the middle. The left panel is the Flowchart panel, and it contains shapes, labeled "Action", "Decision", etc., that you'll use to create the logic design of the business processes you want to build. The right panel is the Implementation panel, and it contains shapes, labeled "COM Component", "Script Component", etc., that you'll use to implement the business processes.

To create a business process, you drag and drop the shapes from either side panel and arrange them in the design space in the middle.

Workflows

BizTalk Orchestration Designer allows you to model the logic design of your business processes in a drag-and-drop environment. You can simply drag the Action shape from the flowchart panel and drop it onto the design space. Each Action shape represents a building block of the overall business process.

For example, if you want to design a business process for having lunch, you would add four Action shapes to the left side of the design space and name them "Go to restaurant", "Order food", "Wait for food", and "Eat". You can then connect these actions together to accomplish the tasks of having lunch. Actions that are connected in this serial manner are referred as a *workflow* in BizTalk Server. A workflow integrates multiple tasks into a single process flow and makes automating multiple business processes and tasks possible. The workflow will encapsulate all the steps needed to complete a business process.

When processing a document in BizTalk Server, many individual tasks may be involved. You can use BizTalk Orchestration Designer to define a workflow for the process, such as the one shown in Figure 5-2. In this example, multiple business processes or tasks are combined to process a document.

The workflow shown in Figure 5-2 indicates the work that needs to be done to process the document, but this is merely a logic design. You would still need to *implement* each task within the workflow.

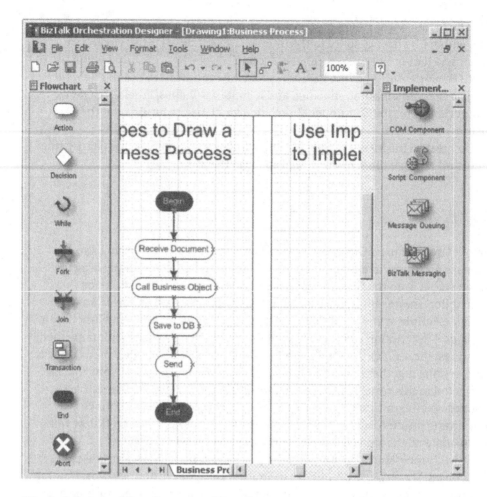

Figure 5-2. A workflow for processing a document

You might ask, "Why am I using BizTalk Orchestration Designer to create a workflow? I can easily do that using regular Visio, or other software tools." So far you have only seen a fancy tool that draws nice pictures. You can't really appreciate the power of BizTalk Orchestration until you understand what the implementation shapes on the right panel can do and how they can work together with the flowchart shapes to create a business process that is "ready to run."

Implementing Business Processes

The biggest difference between BizTalk Orchestration Designer and other software tools that model the business processes is that BizTalk Orchestration Designer allows you to create an executable called an *XLANG Schedule*, which I'll cover shortly.

After you have designed a workflow, the next step is to implement it. Normally, you would hand the workflow diagram to a development team, which would implement it. The implementation would involve several developers, and each implementation component, wherever it was located, would be hooked up together at the end to produce the desired result.

You would also need to document the relationship between the implementation and its logic design so that people can understand how the system works. The end result of the separate documentation of individual components is that it becomes very difficult to get a good overall idea of how the system is built. This also results in problems maintaining and modifying the system when the people who originally built the system have left the organization.

BizTalk Orchestration takes another approach to this problem. It integrates separated business processes and their implementations in a workflow. In this one place, you can define your business processes and how these processes are actually implemented. Business analysts can create a workflow using BizTalk Orchestration Designer and then hand it off to the development team, which will define how each step, or Action shape, of the workflow is implemented, and they do this in the same workflow.

The end result is a BizTalk Orchestration file for a workflow that contains both the analyst's design and developer's implementation. This single file, known as an XLANG Schedule, can be compiled using BizTalk Orchestration Designer into an "executable workflow." You can then deploy this XLANG Schedule to the BizTalk Server, which executes your workflow at runtime using its XLANG engine.

BizTalk Orchestration Designer not only allows you to create a workflow that integrates separate business processes in one place, but it also documents how these separate business processes are implemented. People can now look at this one file to understand, maintain, and modify an existing system. This becomes more important and beneficial as the number of different and complex processes involved in the system increases.

Figure 5-3 shows a workflow in BizTalk Orchestration Designer. In this workflow, both the logic design and implementation are completed.

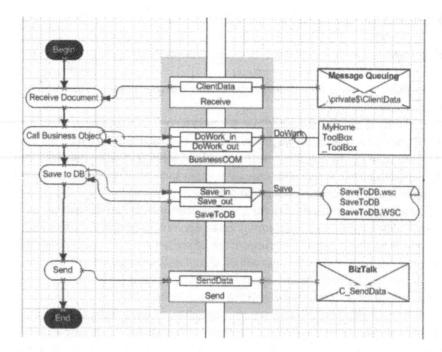

Figure 5-3. A complete workflow in BizTalk Orchestration Designer

Compared to the workflow shown earlier in Figure 5-2, the workflow in Figure 5-3 contains two new sets of items. These are the implementation shapes on the far right and the *ports* in the shaded area in the middle (the shading has been added just for clarification).

The implementation shapes on the right side represent how each step in the logic design on the left side will actually be done. For example, the workflow in Figure 5-3 indicates that the Receive Document action is performed by retrieving data from the message queue. Call Business Object is performed by calling the DoWork function in the MyHome.Toolbox component. The Save to DB action is performed by a scripting component (.wsc) called SaveToDB. The last action, Send, is performed by sending data to the BizTalk Messaging Service through the C_SendData messaging channel.

To add an implementation shape to the workflow, you simply drag and drop the implementation shape from the right panel (shown in Figure 5-2) onto the page, and a configuration wizard will take you through the steps from there. I will cover the configuration wizard in the "Implementing the Processes with Implementation Shapes" section of the chapter where I'll show you how to actually create a workflow, step by step.

NOTE *You can associate multiple Action shapes with one implementation shape, but there can only be one implementation shape for each Action shape.*

After you have added the implementation shapes, you also have to connect the implementation shapes to the corresponding Action shapes. To connect an implementation shape with an Action shape, you drag a link out from the edge of the implementation shape, and drop it onto the Action shape. A configuration wizard window will pop up immediately, and the wizard will ask you to provide the workflow information for the type of data flowing from shape to shape.

Executing Business Processes

After you complete the workflow, you need to make the workflow *executable*. BizTalk Server comes with a COM+ application called XLANG Scheduler, which is the XLANG engine used to execute workflows you have created through BizTalk Orchestration.

When you complete the workflow within BizTalk Orchestration, you need to save it as an .skv file. This is a Visio file that contains the visual representation of your workflow, such as the one shown in Figure 5-3. However, BizTalk Server's XLANG engine can't directly process this .skv file. BizTalk Server can only process the workflow when it is converted to XLANG language, which is a language that describes the logical sequencing of business processes, as well as the implementation of the business processes. XLANG language is expressed in XML format.

To convert a workflow into something BizTalk Server can execute, you need to compile the .skv file into an .skx file, which is actually an XML document written in XLANG language that represents the workflow described in the .skv file. You create an .skx file by loading an .skv file into the Orchestration Designer, and selecting File ➤ Make XLANG [filename].skx from the menus, as shown in Figure 5-4.

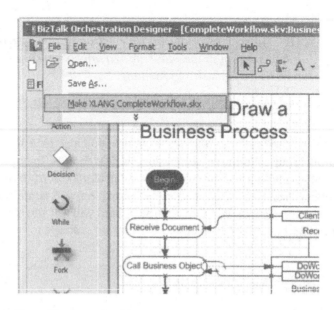

Figure 5-4. Compiling an .skv file

Once you have a compiled a workflow file (an .skx file), there are several ways you can execute the workflow. You'll see one method later in the chapter in the "Testing the Workflow" section, and you'll also learn about other ways to run a workflow in Chapter 11.

Enough with the theory. You can learn BizTalk Orchestration best by actually creating a workflow from scratch and seeing it work. We'll continue to follow Bob's journey as he builds his ASP application, and we'll use it as a starting point for our exploration of BizTalk Server.

Bob's Business Processes

Let's recap Bob's requirements for processing the FundInvestors document in BizTalk Orchestration. These are the business processes for Bob's ASP:

- Receive a document from a client.

- Send an e-mail to any new individual investors who are opening an account with the client.

- Update the customer management data for any transactions on existing accounts. Add new investors to the customer management database.

- Report any errors during execution of the FundInvestorsCOM component to the system administrator.

- If the document is processed without errors, send the response document back to the client.

Building a Workflow from Scratch

Creating a workflow in BizTalk Orchestration designer involves four major steps:

1. Modeling the processes with flowchart shapes.

2. Implementing the processes with implementation shapes. This step includes using the BizTalk Messaging Binding Wizard and XML Communication Wizard.

3. Specifying the data flow on the data page.

4. Compiling the workflow.

Let's look at these steps in turn.

Step 1: Modeling the Processes with Flowchart Shapes

After Mike gets these business requirements from Bob, Mike starts documenting the requirements as he does in every project. He opens Visio and starts diagramming the business processes flowchart. "Why not document the process flowchart in BizTalk Orchestration?" Bob suggests.

Indeed, with BizTalk Orchestration, you can have your business process's logical design and technical implementation side by side—what better way to document your application is there? Mike opens BizTalk Orchestration and starts building a design diagram for the business processes based on Bob's requirements (see Figure 5-5).

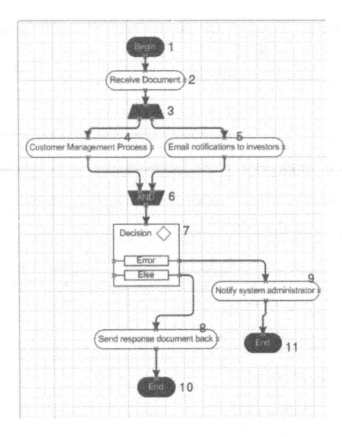

Figure 5-5. Logical design diagram created in BizTalk Orchestration Designer

To draw a design diagram representing business processes, you need to use the shapes from the Flowchart panel on the left side of BizTalk Orchestration Designer. There are total of nine flowchart shapes, and they are described in Table 5-1.

Table 5-1. The Flowchart Shapes Used in BizTalk Orchestration Designer

SHAPE	NAME	DESCRIPTION
Begin	Begin	This is where execution begins. In any given flowchart, there will be one and only one Begin shape.
	Action	An Action shape indicates some kind of process is taking place, such as sending and receiving messages from BizTalk Messaging, instantiating a COM component, sending a message to a message queue, etc.
	Decision	The Decision shape lets you define if-then-else logic in the flowchart. With the Decision shape, your orchestration can decide at runtime which branch of action to take.
	While	The While shape gives you the ability to define a loop and execute a group of actions as long as the condition is true.
	Fork	The Fork shape allows you to branch the current flow into multiple concurrent flows. This gives the schedule the ability to execute more than one action at a time.
	Join	The Join shape joins the multiple flows created by the Fork shape, and merges them into a single branch or flow again.
	Transaction	The Transaction shape lets you define the transaction around actions. I'll discuss transactions in Chapter 10.
	End	The End shape indicates the end of the schedule or workflow.
	Abort	The Abort shape terminates the enclosing transaction. It also terminates the schedule if no corrective actions are defined.

Now, let's see what each shape does in the flowchart shown in Figure 5-5 (I have numbered each shape in that figure for reference purposes):

1. This is the Begin shape, which indicates the start of the schedule.

2. The Receive Document action indicates the receipt of a document from BizTalk Messaging.

3. This is a Fork shape, which will start the two actions below it simultaneously.

4. The Customer Management Process action will send the document to the customer management program for processing.

5. The Email notifications to investors action will send an e-mail to investors who are opening an account.

6. The Join shape will merge the flows in steps 4 and 5 back into one flow again.

7. The Decision shape will check whether there has been an error processing the document. Different actions are taken based on the result of the Decision shape.

8. This action, which sends the response document back to the original sender, will take place if no error occurred.

9. This action, which notifies the system administrator that something went wrong, will take place if an error occurred.

10. This End shape indicates the successful completion of the schedule.

11. This End shape indicates the unsuccessful completion of the schedule.

After completing the flowchart part of the orchestration, you must now associate all the Action shapes in the flowchart shown in Figure 5-5 with implementation shapes from the right side of the Orchestration Designer.

After you create a workflow to represent the business processes, as shown in Figure 5-5, it is time to define how you want to implement each action. This leads you to the second step.

Step 2: Implementing the Processes with Implementation Shapes

Before you learn how to connect the implementation shapes to the flowchart, let's look at what these implementation shapes do—see Table 5-2.

Table 5-2. The Implementation Shapes Used in BizTalk Orchestration Designer

SHAPE	NAME	DESCRIPTION
	COM Component	This shape represents any COM component, either local or remote. With this shape, you can both send and receive messages to and from COM components within the orchestration.
	Scripting Component	This shape is very similar to the COM Component shape, except that this shape represents a Windows Scripting Components (WSC) file.
	Message Queuing	This shape allows you to send messages to and receive them from a message queue within the orchestration.
	BizTalk Messaging	This shape represents the BizTalk Messaging service. With this shape you can send messages to and retrieve them from BizTalk Messaging within the orchestration.

To better understand these implementation shapes, let's look at them in action. First, though, you need to understand the concept of a *port* in an orchestration. Every Action shape in the flowchart needs to be linked to an implementation shape through a *port*. A port in BizTalk Orchestration is a connection between the logical flowchart and the physical implementation.

Configuring the Implementation Shape for the Receive Document Action

First, let's connect the Receive Document action in Figure 5-5 to a BizTalk Messaging implementation shape—the FundInvestors document will flow from BizTalk Messaging to the orchestration. When you drag a link from the BizTalk Messaging shape in the Implementation panel and attach it to the right side of a port in the design space, the BizTalk Messaging Binding Wizard will appear (see Figure 5-6).

Figure 5-6. The BizTalk Messaging Binding Wizard will connect the BizTalk Messaging implementation shape to an Action shape.

In this wizard window, you must give the port a name. The port name can't be random. Every port is an entry point into the schedule, to be used by external sources—external programs can use them to feed data into a schedule. In order to send the data to the right location (the right shape in the flowchart), you must know which port connects to a particular shape on the flowchart. (Later you'll see some examples of how to feed data into a schedule programmatically.)

In this case, BizTalk Messaging is the program that is feeding the data into the orchestration, so the port name you define inside the orchestration must match the port name property of the BizTalk Messaging port. Remember the messaging port you created in Chapter 4 to instantiate this XLANG Schedule? (See Figure 5-7.)

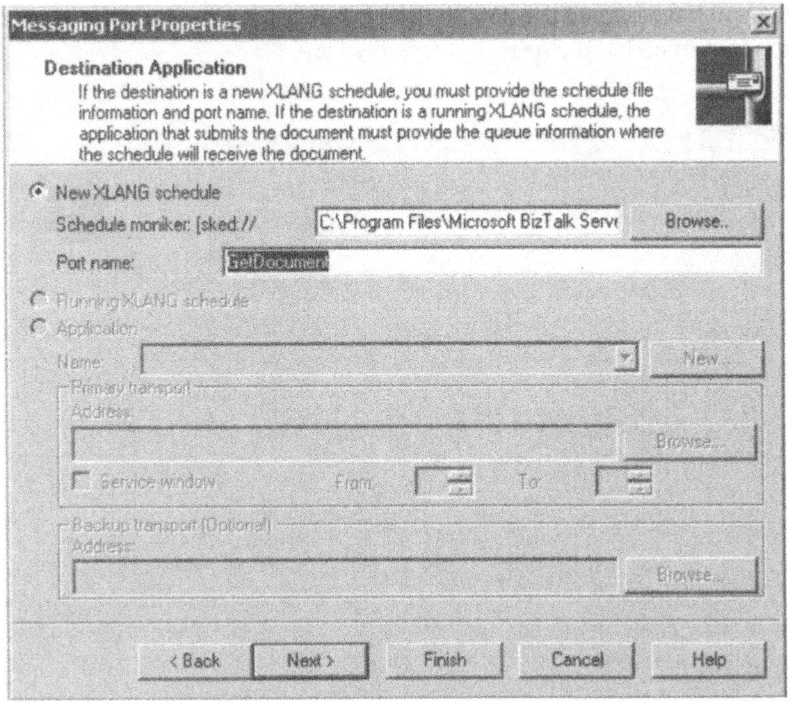

Figure 5-7. The Messaging Port created in Chapter 4 using BizTalk Messaging Manager

Figure 5-7. The Messaging Port created in Chapter 4 using BizTalk Messaging Manager

The port name highlighted in Figure 5-7 is the port that BizTalk Messaging uses as an entry point to feed the document to the orchestration. The port can have any name as long as the same name is used for both the BizTalk Messaging port and the connected port in BizTalk Orchestration.

NOTE   *One of the things I found most confusing when I started using BizTalk Server is the term "port" in BizTalk Orchestration. I thought it had some relationship with the messaging port created in BizTalk Messaging Manager. But in fact, the term "port" in Orchestration doesn't refer to the messaging ports at all. The fact that these two items are both labeled "port" makes it easy to confuse them. In an attempt to avoid this sort of confusion, I will refer to the ports created in BizTalk Orchestration as "orchestration ports" from now on, although this isn't a term used by Microsoft.*

Once you have named the port in the BizTalk Messaging Binding Wizard, click Next to proceed to the next step (see Figure 5-8).

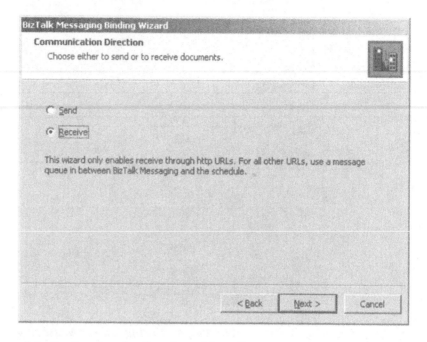

Figure 5-8. Configuring the direction of data flow

The next wizard window asks whether the Action shape is sending the data to the implementation shape, or receiving the data from the implementation shape. In this case (see Figure 5-8), it is asking whether the Receive Document action is sending data to BizTalk Messaging or is receiving the data from BizTalk Messaging. Select Receive and click Next.

If you don't understand the description next to the radio button in the next wizard window (see Figure 5-9), don't worry about it. This window lets you specify the activation of the schedule. If you select Yes, the schedule is instantiated when a message arrives at the GetDocument port from BizTalk Messaging. This is what you want to do because it allows you to start this schedule whenever messages come to P_FundInvestors. If you select No, the schedule must be run some other way—this option is commonly used when you already have a running schedule that is sending data to BizTalk Messaging or expecting some data from BizTalk Messaging. In that situation, you don't need to instantiate another new schedule. Select Yes and click Finish.

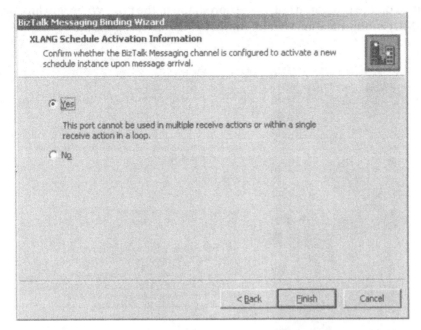

Figure 5-9. Configuring the activation properties of the schedule

The orchestration now looks like what you see in Figure 5-10.

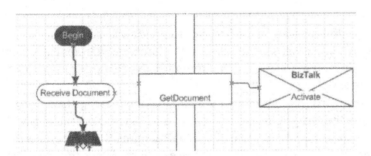

Figure 5-10. The BizTalk Messaging implementation shape has been linked to the GetDocument orchestration port.

Configuring the Port for the Receive Document Action

You have connected the BizTalk Messaging implementation shape to the orchestration port, but your job isn't done until you also connect the Receive Document Action shape to the port so that the Action shape and implementation shape are linked together. You can use the connector tool (whose icon has two linked squares) on the toolbar to link the Action shape to the port. When you link them, the XML Communication Wizard, shown in Figure 5-11, pops up.

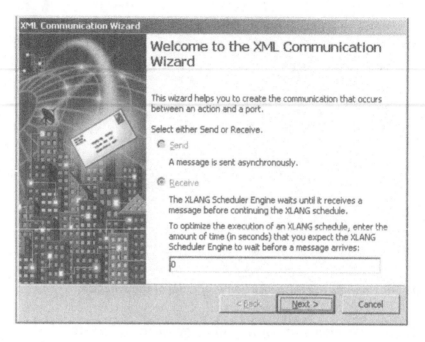

Figure 5-11. XML Communication Wizard

The only editable value in the first wizard window is the amount of time BizTalk Orchestration waits for the message before it dehydrates the schedule. I'll discuss dehydration in Chapter 10, but for now leave this value as 0, and click Next to continue.

The next wizard window asks for the name of the message (see Figure 5-12). Whenever you link an Action shape to a port, a message is passed between them. This wizard window is where you define a logical name that represents that physical message so that any subsequent processes can reference this message by this name. This message name can be any name, but keep in mind that this message name represents the document that flows through this port.

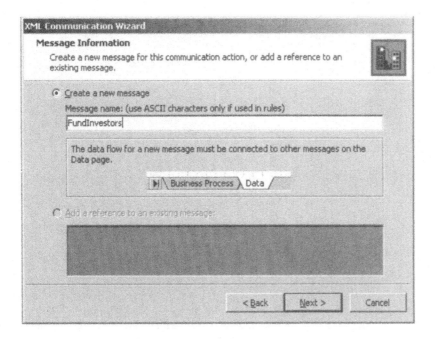

Figure 5-12. Naming the new message

The Add a reference to an existing message radio button is inactive in Figure 5-12 because no message has been created yet. If there are already messages defined in the schedule, you could select an existing message to represent the document flowing through this port.

Click Next to proceed to the XML Translation Information window, and leave the default setting as is.

Click Next to proceed to the next wizard window, which asks for the message type (see Figure 5-13).

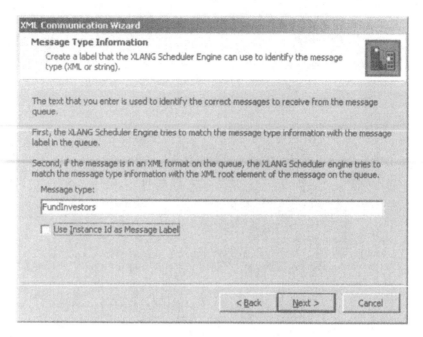

Figure 5-13. Specifying the message types that are received from BizTalk Messaging

The wizard describes two ways in which the correct message can be identified in the message queue: by message label or by XML root element. In this case, we want the second scenario to work, so the Message Type value should be the same as the root element of the FundInvestor document, which is FundInvestors. Leave the Use Instance UD as Message Label checkbox blank—I'll cover that when I discuss the orchestration correlation. Click Next to proceed to the next wizard window (see Figure 5-14).

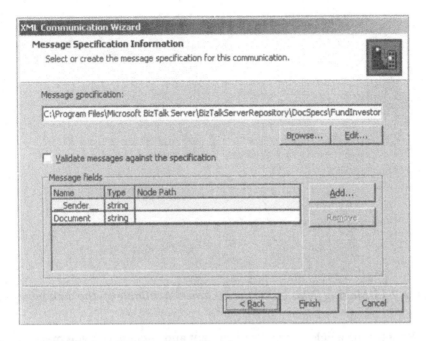

Figure 5-14. Specifying the message specification

This next wizard window is where you enter the message specification (you must provide the full path of the file location, as the WebDAV isn't used here), and the wizard provides you with two options. First, you can validate the document that comes through the port against its document specification. Second, you can pull some fields out of the document and make them available on the data page of the schedule. (I'll discuss the data page in the "Specifying the Data Flow on the Data Page" section, later in this chapter.)

Usually when a document is received from BizTalk Messaging, it has already been validated on the channel, so revalidation may not provide any added value and may slow down the schedule quite a bit. Nevertheless, you do have a chance to validate the document inside the schedule. In this case, leave the Validate messages against the specification checkbox unchecked.

To make fields available on the data page of the schedule, click the Add button in the Message fields section. A Field Selection window will open (see Figure 5-15).

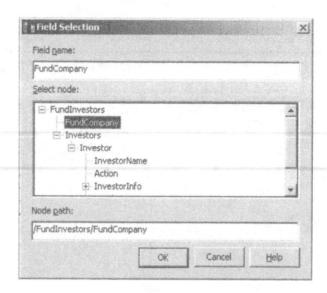

Figure 5-15. Making fields inside the document available on the data page

By selecting a field inside the document and clicking OK, you make this field available on the data page. The message and field on the data page can then be accessed by the implementation shape at runtime. In this example, select FundCompany and click OK. You'll see the data page later and how these fields are linked and accessed by implementation shapes in a schedule.

You have now finished with the XML Communication Wizard, so click Finish. The completed Receive Document action and its implementation are shown in Figure 5-16, with a blue arrow pointing left to the Receive Document action to indicate the direction of the document flow.

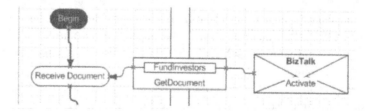

Figure 5-16. A blue arrow points left to the Action shape, indicating the FundInvestors document flow.

Configuring the Implementation for the Customer Management Process and Email Notifications to Investors Actions

The next step on the business process flowchart is the Fork shape, followed by two Action shapes, followed by the Join shape (see Figure 5-17). When it comes to the Fork shape, BizTalk Orchestration will execute the Customer Management Process and Email notifications to investors actions simultaneously.

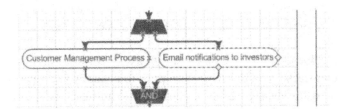

Figure 5-17. Connecting the implementation shapes to the Customer Management Process and Email notification to Investors actions

The "AND" label on the Join shape means that the two Action shapes must both complete before the schedule can continue after the Join shape. You can double-click the Join shape and change the value to OR, in which case the schedule would proceed from the Join shape as soon as one of the two actions completed. However, you must be careful when using the OR operator because all the actions following the Join shape will be executed a second time when the second action completes.

A good place to use the Fork and Join shapes (with the AND operator) is when you have number of actions that take a long time to complete and can be done independently of each other. For instance, if you want to send a number of documents to external clients through the Internet from a schedule, you can set up multiple Action shapes between a Fork shape and a Join shape, and each action would connect to BizTalk Messaging and send a document. In this case, you could send out all the documents in the same time it takes to send one.

In this example, you want to connect a COM component to the Customer Management Process action and a scripting component to the Email notifications to investors action. Assume you have a VB component called FundInvestorCOM that contains a method called Investors, and it looks something like this:

```
Public Function Investors(fundcompany As String, document As String)
'your code here
End Function
```

You can use this COM component via a COM Component implementation shape. Just drag the COM Component shape onto the design space, and the COM Component Binding Wizard will open and ask for the port name. Provide the name for the appropriate orchestration port and click Next.

In the next wizard window you specify how the schedule will instantiate the COM component at runtime. There are three choices: Static, Dynamic, and No instantiation (see Figure 5-18):

- *Static:* The schedule will instantiate the component whenever the message flows to the Action shape that the component is connected to.

- *Dynamic:* The schedule will make calls to a component that has already been instantiated. The interface pointer to that existing component must be provided somewhere in the document so that the schedule can retrieve the pointer and call it.

- *No instantiation:* Used when the component should be instantiated by a process other than the schedule.

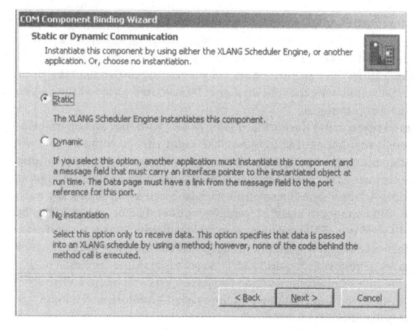

Figure 5-18. Configuring how the COM component is instantiated

In Chapter 11, we'll look at an example in which an external program can interact with a running schedule by instantiating the COM Component shape inside a schedule and passing data into the schedule through the COM component. In such a case, the COM component should be set to No instantiation in this wizard window so that the schedule will wait on the component until it is instantiated by the other program.

In this case, you want to instantiate the component as soon as the data arrives at the Customer Management Process action, so choose Static and click Next to continue to the Advanced Port Properties page of the wizard (see Figure 5-19).

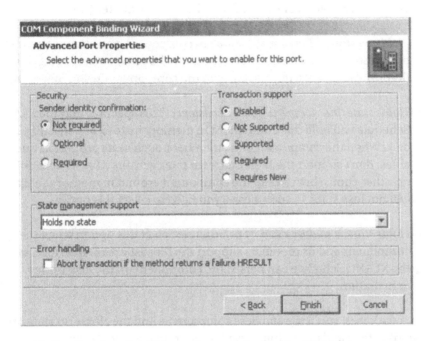

Figure 5-19. Configuring the Advanced properties for the COM component binding

In Figure 5-19, the Security section specifies whether the message will be processed when the sender's identity isn't available:

- *Not Required:* Specifies that the schedule will not check to see whether the sender identity is presented and will process the document regardless

- *Optional:* Specifies that the schedule will put the sender's identity in the _Sender_ field on the data page if available, but will process the message whether the identity is presented or not

- *Required:* Specifies that the schedule will reject the message if the sender identity isn't presented.

The Transaction support section of the window specifies whether this implementation shape will participate in the transaction or not. In order for a COM implementation shape to participate in a transaction, the Action shape it connects to must be bound to a Transaction shape. Since you aren't using any transactions here, the option isn't relevant. We'll look at how you can make a COM component participate in a transaction inside an orchestration in Chapter 10.

The State management support section is where you specify whether the XLANG Schedule should persist the state of the component when dehydrating. (I'll cover the dehydration of the XLANG Schedule in Chapter 10.)

- *Holds no state:* When using a stateless component, you should choose this option so that the schedule will terminate the component during dehydration and create a new instance of the component during rehydration.

- *Holds state, but doesn't support persistence:* This specifies that the XLANG Schedule will hold this component in memory instead of persisting it to disk. When the component or its members, such as its properties and variables, don't support the IPersistStream interface, the XLANG Schedule has no other choice but to keep the component around in memory so that it will not lose state. In such a case, you need to select this option.

- *Holds state, and does support persistence:* Select this option when the component and its members support the IPersistStream interface, so that the XLANG Schedule can persist the component on the disk during dehydration.

In most cases, you'll use stateless components and the Holds no state option. Try avoiding the Holds state, but doesn't support persistence option, which may make your component hold onto system resources for long periods of time. For this example, select Holds no state.

The checkbox in the Error handling section specifies whether the transaction will abort if the component in the transaction returns a bad HRESULT. This checkbox only applies to components that are bound to a transaction shape. In this example, leave it blank, since you don't have any components running in a transaction.

Click Finish to complete the COM component implementation.

The procedure for implementing the Email notifications to investors action with a scripting component is very similar to binding a COM component. You need to specify which scripting component to invoke and which method to call. One particular window you should notice is shown in Figure 5-20. In it, you can specify whether you want the XLANG Schedule to instantiate the scripting component through a moniker or a Prog ID.

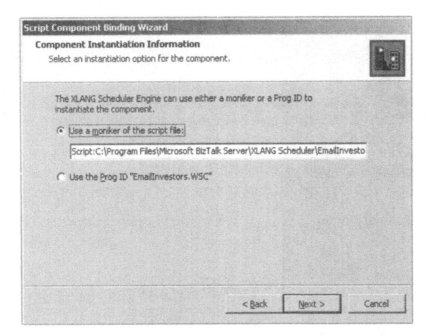

Figure 5-20. Selecting the instantiation option for the component

When you select Use the moniker of the script file as the instantiation method, the XLANG Schedule will load the scripting component from the file location at runtime. This method is location dependent, and the XLANG Schedule must be able to access this script file or an error will be raised.

When you select Use the Prog ID as the instantiation method, the XLANG Schedule will look up this Prod ID in the registry and load the script file based on the value in the registry, as if it were a regular COM component. When you use the Prog ID option, the location of the component is irrelevant, but the scripting component must be registered on the server before it can be instantiated from within a schedule.

Configuring the Ports for the Customer Management Process and Email Notifications to Investors Actions

Now that you have the COM Component and Scripting Component shapes and ports set up, you need to connect the Customer Management Process action to them. When you do so, the wizard shown in Figure 5-21 will appear.

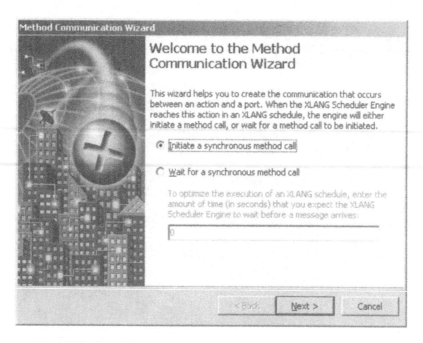

Figure 5-21. Method Communication Wizard

In the first Method Communication Wizard window, select Initiate a synchronous method call. This option enables the schedule to instantiate the method call when a message arrives at the Customer Management Process Action shape. Click Next to move on to the Message Specification Information page of the wizard (see Figure 5-22).

In this wizard window, you can specify in the Methods field which method the action will call. This window also displays the input and output fields for the method the action will call. Notice the __Status__ OUT field—you'll use it later with the Decision shape. Click Finish to complete the link between the Action shape and port.

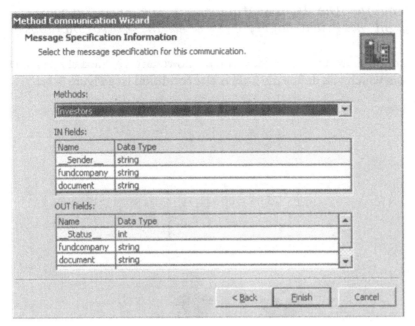

Figure 5-22. Selecting the method the action will call, and viewing the input and output fields

The procedure for linking the Action shape to a scripting component port is identical to that for a COM component. After you complete the bindings for both Action shapes, your workflow should look like the one in Figure 5-23.

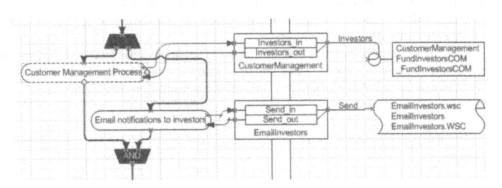

Figure 5-23. Completed bindings for the Customer Management Process and Email notifications to investors actions

Configuring the Implementation for the Send Response Document Back and Notify System Administrator Actions

Let's continue with the next shapes on the flowchart. The next shape is a Decision shape in which you define the if-then-else condition (see Figure 5-24).

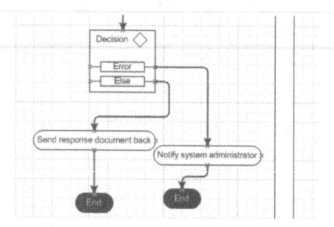

Figure 5-24. Implementing the decision shape on the flowchart

The Decision shape is like a select-case statement in Visual Basic. The process flow will continue on one branch or another based on the conditions being evaluated. In this case, you want to take the Send response document back action if the FundInvestorsCOM component is executed without error, and take the Notify system administrator action if there is something wrong when calling the FundInvestorsCOM component.

To add a condition to a Decision shape, double-click the Decision shape, and a new window will appear. Click Add to add a condition. The Rule Properties window opens, and this is where you can define the condition (see Figure 5-25).

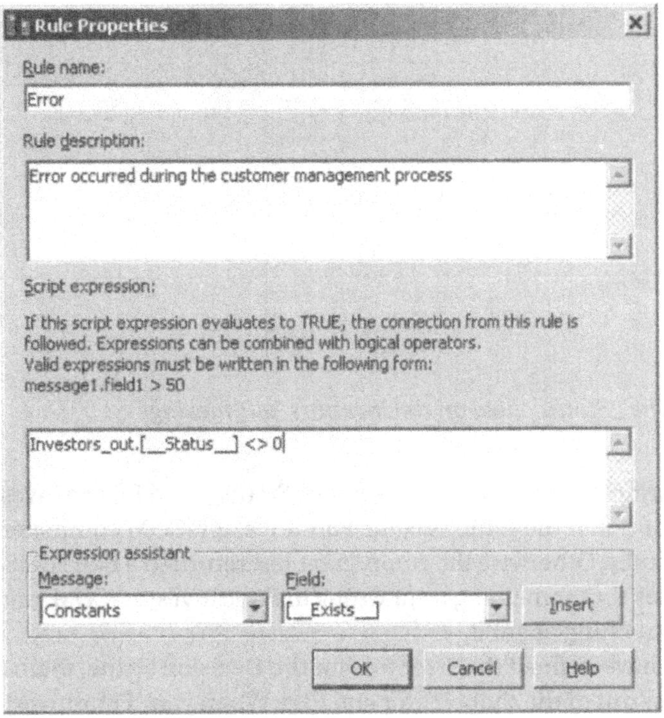

Figure 5-25. Configuring the properties for the Decision shape's rule

To specify a condition to be evaluated, select the message name from the Message list box, and then select a field from the Field list box. Click Insert to add the selections to the text box above the list boxes where the condition is defined. If you know what you're doing, you can also type your condition into the text box by hand.

Whenever you implement a COM component or scripting component, BizTalk Orchestration will create a message on the data page (described later in this chapter) of the orchestration to keep track of all the input and output for the components. Figure 5-26 shows an example. On the data page, which you'll see shortly, there are status fields for every message that is associated with a COM component or scripting component. By checking whether the value in the status field is nonzero after the components are called, you can identify whether the component is processed successfully or not.

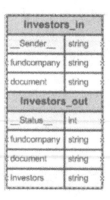

Figure 5-26. The _Status_ field on the Investors_out message

In this example, you want to check if the _Status_ field for the Investors_out message is 0 or not. If the status is 0, the FundInvestorsCOM component executed successfully. Otherwise the component has returned a bad HRESULT, which indicates that something went wrong in FundInvestorsCOM, and you may want to do something about it.

After you have defined the Error rule for the Decision shape, there are two possible routes out of the shape: Error and Else. When your FundInvestorsCOM component fails, you want to store the document in a message queue so that a reporting application can retrieve it later for more tasks. This leads us to the Message Queuing implementation shape.

When you drag and drop the Message Queuing shape on the page, a Message Queuing Binding Wizard opens. Give a name to the port (NotificationQueue), and click Next to proceed.

The next window asks to which type of queue you want to send the document. Choose the static queue because you want to dedicate a message queue for this purpose. Click Next to get to the window shown in Figure 5-27.

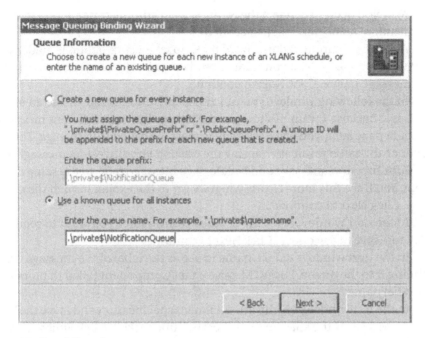

Figure 5-27. Providing the message queue name

You want to consolidate all the messages for which the FundInvestorsCOM component failed in a single queue. Therefore, in the Queue Information window of the wizard, select the Use a known queue for all instances radio button. Specify the format name for the local or remote queue—for the local queue, a shorthand form can be used as shown in Figure 5-27. Click Next to proceed.

On the next window, check the Transaction is required for this queue check-box. If your message queue is a transactional message queue, you must check the Transactions are required with this queue checkbox. Click Finish to complete the wizard.

NOTE   *Transactional message queues allow clients to send and receive messages in a transactional manner. Transactional message queues are discussed in Appendix A.*

Now you need to connect the Notify system administrator action to the NotificationQueue port you just created.

An XML Communication Wizard pops up when connection is made. In the first window, specify that you want to send the FailedMessage document to the message queue. Click Next to continue.

In the following window, you can either create a message or use an existing message. Because I want to show you the linkage between different messages on the data page later, you will create a new message called FailMessage. This will produce the same result as choosing the existing FundInvestors message, since the FundInvestors message and FailMessage message refer to the same document. You'll see this more clearly when we get to the explanation of the data page. Click Next to continue.

In the next window, leave the default settings, since you want to send the XML message to the queue. Click Next to continue.

In the next window, enter a name to use as the label of the message when sending it to the queue. I used "Messages that Component failed to process" as the label name.

In the last window, specify the document specification and leave the Validate messages against the specification checkbox unchecked. Click Finish to complete this binding.

For the Send response document back action, you want to send the response document back to the original sender through BizTalk Messaging, which supports many protocols, such as SMTP, HTTP , HTTPS, etc. You used the BizTalk Messaging shape earlier to get the document into an XLANG Schedule, so now use the same shape to pass the document out of the XLANG Schedule to BizTalk Messaging.

First, drag and drop a BizTalk Messaging shape onto the page—a BizTalk Messaging Binding Wizard will open. Specify a name for the orchestration port (SendResponseDocument), and then click Next to continue.

In the next window, click the Send radio button to indicate that you want to send the message out to BizTalk Messaging. Click Next to continue.

The following window asks about the channel information (see Figure 5-28).

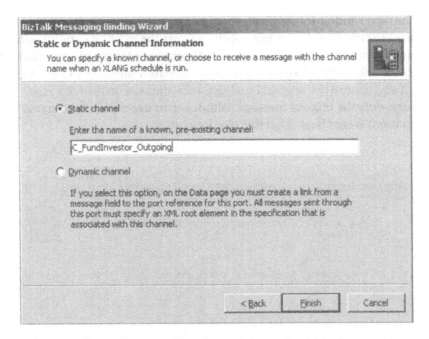

Figure 5-28. Providing the name of the channel through which the response document is sent to the external client

There are two choices in the window shown in Figure 5-28: Static channel and Dynamic channel. If you choose a static channel, the XLANG Schedule will feed the document to this channel at runtime. If you choose a dynamic channel, the XLANG Schedule will retrieve the channel name from a data field in a message on the data page at runtime, and then send the document through that channel. I'll show you a dynamic channel example in Chapter 10. For now, choose the Static channel option and enter the name of the channel: C_FundInvestors_Outgoing. Then click Finish.

Configuring the Ports for the Send Response Document Back and Notify System Administrator Actions

Now you need to link the Action shape to the new BizTalk Messaging implementation shape you just created. When you connect the two shapes, a new XML Communication Wizard opens.

In the first wizard window, leave the default value, and click Next to continue.

The next window is where you enter message information (see Figure 5-29). You want to create a new message—you can't use the existing FundInvestors message because your FundInvestorsCOM component will add error description and status information to the document. It's this new message you want to send back. If you choose the original FundInvestors message instead of a new message, only the original message (without error description and status information) is sent back. That isn't what you want.

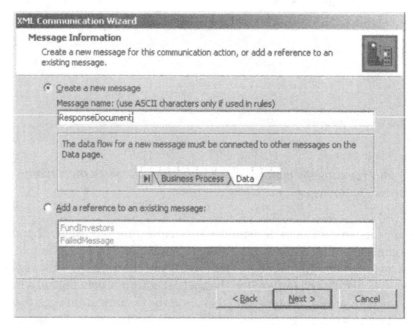

Figure 5-29. Creating a new message for the response document

Select the Create a new message radio button, and name the message ResponseDocument. You'll see later how to provide the data that will be returned from the FundInvestorsCOM component to this message. Click Next to continue.

In the next window, leave the default setting as is and click Next.

The next window asks for the message queue label name. Because you aren't sending this message to a message queue, this label is irrelevant to you, but you must provide a name, so check the Use Instance ID as message label checkbox so that the instance ID will be used as the label name. Click Next to continue.

In the next window, specify the document specification and click Finish. The complete section of the orchestration is shown in Figure 5-30.

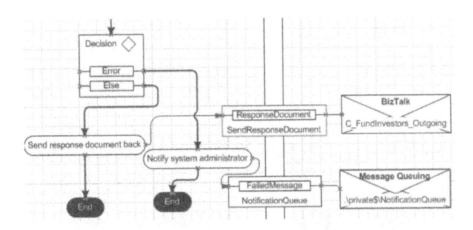

Figure 5-30. Completed bindings for the Send response document back and Notify system administrator actions

If you've followed along to this point, you have completed the flowchart, and it should look more or less like the one in Figure 5-31.

Notice there are many arrows, colored red and blue in BizTalk Orchestration Designer, coming in and out of the "ports." These arrows represent the data flowing back and forth. As the data comes in and out of the ports and implementation shapes, their values may change, so it is critical that you specify how the data is to flow from one shape to the next. This leads us to the topic of BizTalk Orchestration's data page.

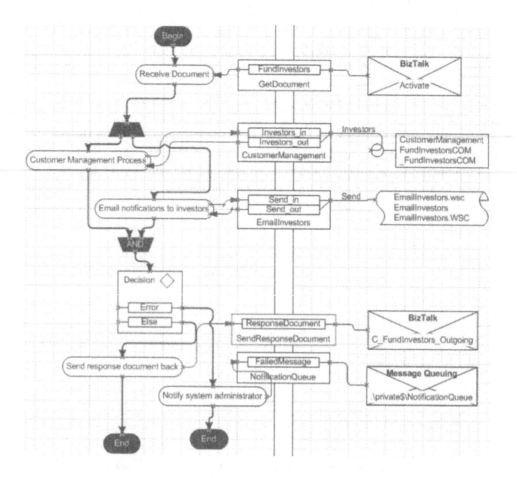

Figure 5-31. The completed flowchart in BizTalk Orchestration Designer

Step 3: Specifying the Data Flow on the Data Page

After you have completed the flowchart, your schedule is still not complete. As you've seen, there are many multicolored arrows coming in and out of the orchestration ports, indicating the data flowing in and out. You must define this data and how each flow of data relates to the others.

During the creation of the flowchart, you created many messages using the binding wizards, but many of these messages are empty shells so far. To get the data into these messages, you must define the relationships among the messages on the data page.

Let's start by seeing what the data page looks like—see Figure 5-32.

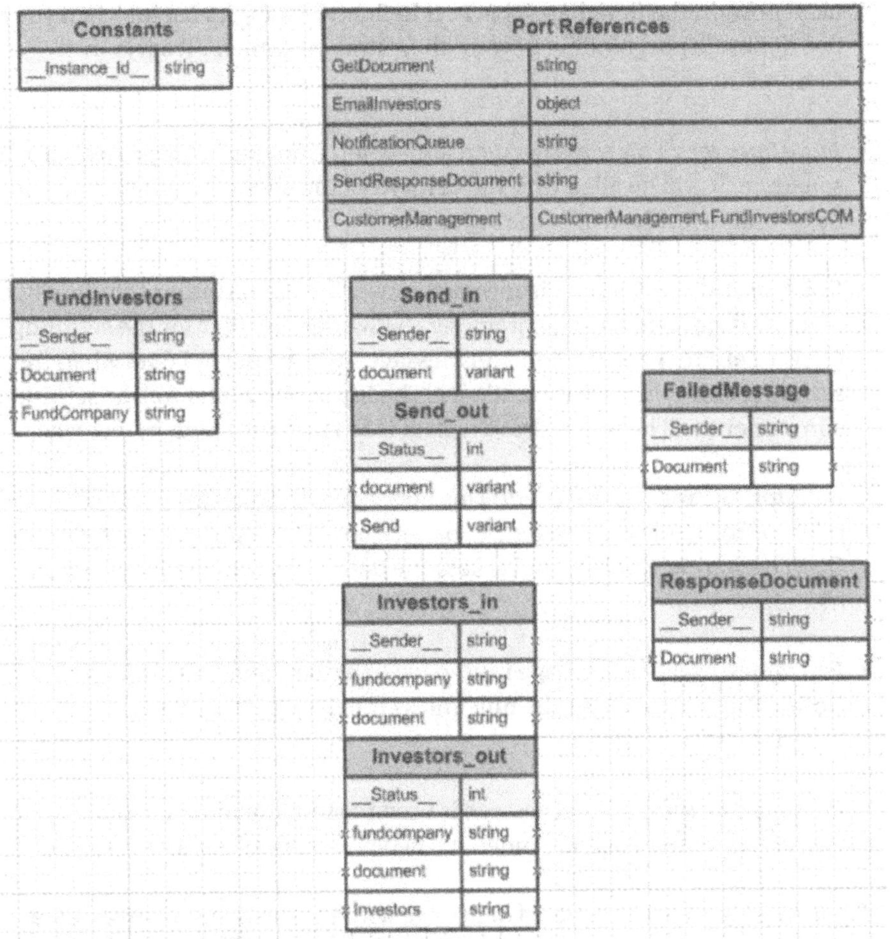

Constants	
__Instance_Id__	string

Port References	
GetDocument	string
EmailInvestors	object
NotificationQueue	string
SendResponseDocument	string
CustomerManagement	CustomerManagement.FundInvestorsCOM

FundInvestors	
__Sender__	string
Document	string
FundCompany	string

Send_in	
__Sender__	string
document	variant

Send_out	
__Status__	int
document	variant
Send	variant

FailedMessage	
__Sender__	string
Document	string

Investors_in	
__Sender__	string
fundcompany	string
document	string

Investors_out	
__Status__	int
fundcompany	string
document	string
Investors	string

ResponseDocument	
__Sender__	string
Document	string

Figure 5-32. The messages on the data page

There are several items on the data page:

- *Constants:* This message contains one or more constant values. The values in this Constants message will not change for the duration of the schedule.

- *Port References:* This message contains a list of values that correspond to each port on the flowchart. This Port References table is useful when you use dynamic port binding in your orchestration, which I'll cover in Chapter 10

- *FundInvestors:* This message is created when a document is passed into the schedule. It will be filled with the content of the client document and will be available for the rest of the schedule.

- *Send_in* and *Send_out:* This message is used by the scripting component to store its input and output parameters. However, in order for the scripting component to work, the Send_in message must be passed data when the scripting component is instantiated. The input parameter for the scripting component will be null unless the data is fed into the Send_in message.

- *Investors_in* and *Investors_out:* This message is used by the COM component to store its input and output parameters. The input parameter for the COM component will be null unless the data is fed into the Investors_in message.

- *FailedMessage:* This message is used when a document is sent to the NotificationQueue. It will be null unless the data is fed into the FailedMessage message.

- *ResponseDocument:* This message is used to store the response document that is sent to the original sender. It will be null unless the data is fed into it.

Figure 5-33 shows a completed data page with the messages appropriated linked. Five linkages appear on the data page for this schedule, and I have numbered each one for reference purposes. Each link indicates the flow of data from one message to another.

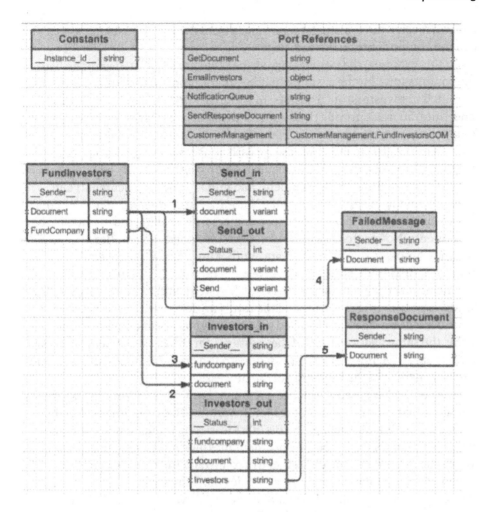

Figure 5-33. Linked messages on the data page

When the FundInvestors document arrives at the P_FundInvestors port, which is a port to your XLANG Schedule, BizTalk Server will activate the FundInvestors schedule. At the same time, BizTalk Messaging will fill the FundInvestors message with the content of the client document as the document comes into the XLANG Schedule. You also pulled the FundCompany field out of the document and made it available on the data page, which is why you see the FundCompany field in the FundInvestors message on the data page.

When the Receive Document action is completed, the two actions between the Fork and Join shapes will be started. The FundInvestorsCOM component, which is connected to the Customer Management Process action, will be instantiated, as will the EmailInvestors scripting component, which is connected to the Email notifications to investors action. When the components are instantiated, they will receive the input parameter values from the message shapes associated with the components on the data page.

In this example, the two message shapes that are associated with the two components (one for the customer management process, and the other for sending e-mail to investors) are Investors_in and Investors_out, and Send_in and Send_out. You must provide the values for these two messages in order for your components to execute properly. In the XLANG Schedule, the way to provide values for a message is to link the message with another message that contains the necessary data. Arrows 1 and 2 in Figure 5-33 do exactly that. By creating links that go from FundInvestors[document] and end at Send_in[document] and Investors_in[document], the content of FundInvestors[document] will be copied to both locations and used as input parameters when calling the method in the components. Notice that FundInvestorsCOM also needs an additional parameter for FundCompany, so you must create another link (arrow 3) between FundInvestors[FundCompany] and Investors_in[FundCompany].

The next action in the schedule is Notify system administrator. In order for the Message Queuing shape to send the resulting document to the message queue, FailedMessage must be filled with the original client document. You can do this the same way as you filled the messages for the COM and scripting components earlier. Arrow 4 fills the message with the original document that came into the schedule at the beginning of the process.

The last action is Send response document back. This action will take the document that is returned from the FundInvestorsCOM component, and then feed it into BizTalk Messaging. The BizTalk Messaging implementation shape for this action uses the ResponseDocument message on the data page. Here, you do the same thing you did earlier to get the data from a message to the ResponseDocument message. Arrow 5 copies the data from Investors_out[Investors], which contains the return value for the COM method call, to ResponseDocument[document].

It is almost time to put an end to this lengthy discussion on BizTalk Orchestration schedules. There is one more step: compiling the workflow.

Step 4: Compiling the Workflow

The next step is to save the work you have done with BizTalk Orchestration Designer into an .skv file, which is a file only BizTalk Orchestration Designer can read. If you want to modify the existing schedule, you must load the .skv file into the designer and then make the changes. However, BizTalk Server can't load an .skv file to execute your schedule at runtime. You must compile the .skv file into an .skx file, which is an XML document that contains all the actions, implementations, and data flows specified in the schedule. BizTalk Server has an engine that can load and parse .skx files and perform your schedule at runtime.

To compile your schedule into an .skx file, Select File ➤ Make [filename].skx from the menu.

NOTE *Be careful about synchronizing the .skx file and .skv files. When you successfully compile the .skx file, don't forget to also save it as an .skv file so that the compiled schedule and "graphic version" of the schedule are in sync.*

Many kinds of errors can occur during the compilation of a schedule, and it can take some time to interpret the special lingo shown in an error message. There are two common errors.

The first error message is shown in Figure 5-34. This error occurs when an Action shape isn't connected to its implementation shape. BizTalk Orchestration requires that every Action shape must be associated with an implementation shape.

Figure 5-34. Compile error: Action shape not attached to an implementation shape

The second common error that occurs during compilation is shown in Figure 5-35. For every message shape that has input message fields, you must provide data for the fields on the data page. If you forget to link the input fields on the data page, this error message will appear. Make sure all the input fields are populated with data on the data page of the schedule.

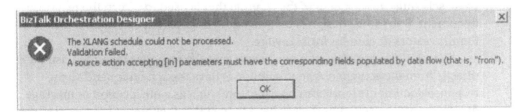

Figure 5-35. Compile error: missing input data

Testing the Workflow

After you have successfully compiled the workflow, you can run it and see how it performs in action. There are several ways to execute a workflow or XLANG Schedule. The most common way is through BizTalk Messaging.

As you learned in Chapter 4, you can set up a Receive Function or Active Server page to submit certain documents to a messaging port, which, in turn, will trigger a particular XLANG Schedule. However, you must first make sure all the necessary channels, ports, and other dependent objects are created.

Creating Additional Channels, Ports, etc.

For the workflow you have just created, you need to create a few more things:

- The message queue that is used by the Notify system administrator action

- A channel, called C_FundInvestors_Outgoing, that is referenced in the schedule by the Send response document back action

- A port that attaches to C_FundInvestors_Outgoing; this messaging port will be responsible for sending the document back to the client through whatever protocols the BizTalk Messaging supports.

However, if you look closely at the channel and port you need to create, you'll see a problem. You learned earlier that a channel can only connect to one port, which represents the destination of the document. Because you hard-coded the channel name inside the schedule, the schedule you just created will only be able to send response documents to one port. If this port is pointing to a client's URL, your schedule could only handle documents from one client. This isn't a good design because it isn't extensible.

Let's imagine Bob just signed up 20 more mutual fund companies that want to use Bob's ASP. Bob now has to get Mike and Joe to create 20 more orchestration schedules, one for each additional client. The only difference among these schedules is the name of the channel that is used to return the response document. Bob's ideal design is to have one schedule that can handle the FundInvestors document from anyone.

To tackle this problem, you must make sure the response document isn't sent directly from the schedule. A good solution is have the schedule send all the response documents to a common data store, such as a file location or message queue, so that the schedule doesn't have to treat the documents from each client differently. You'll then send out the documents with a different method.

Let's create the P_FundInvestors_Outgoing port and
C_FundInvestors_Outgoing channel using BizTalk Messaging Manager with the
specifications in Table 5-3.

Table 5-3. Specifications for P_FundInvestors_Outgoing and
C_FundInvestors_Outgoing

NAME	VALUE
Port name	P_FundInvestors_Outgoing (To an application)
Destination type	Application
Application name	OutgoingMessageQueueApp
Primary address	Direct=OS:.\private$\OutgoingMessageQueue
Channel name	C_FundInvestors_Outgoing (From an application)
Source type	XLANG Schedule
Inbound document	FundInvestors
Outbound document	FundInvestors

By creating the P_FundInvestors_Outgoing port, all the documents that
come out of the XLANG Schedule will be sent to the OutgoingMessageQueue
message queue on the local system. The port has one channel attached to it that
comes from an application called OutgoingMessageQueueApp, which handles
only the FundInvestors document.

Notice that P_FundInvestors_Outgoing is a "to an application" port, and
C_FundInvestors_Outgoing is a "from an application" channel. These properties
are different from the channels and ports created earlier in the chapter—what is
the difference here?

The simple answer is, use a "to an application" port when the destination of
the data is within the organization. Use a "from an application" channel when the
source of the data is within the organization.

These terms are mainly designed to resolve the confusion of data transport
within the Home Organization, where both the source organization and destination organization are the same. By creating different logical applications
within the Home Organization, you can distinguish the channels that route
documents between different internal applications or systems. It is possible
and feasible to make every channel and port organizational ones ("From an
Organization" port), and it is up to the developers to come up with a comprehensive scheme to define the channels and ports.

To create a logical application, open the property page for the organization that you want the application to be associated with. The Organization Properties dialog box is shown in Figure 5-36. Any logical applications defined here will automatically be associated only with that particular organization.

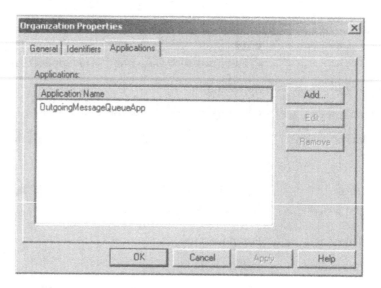

Figure 5-36. Adding an application for an organization

Click the Add button to add an application. The application you define here doesn't have to be related to the physical application in your organization. The applications defined here are merely names used to represent applications and entities instead of using the organizational name inside BizTalk Server.

In the case of P_FundInvestors_Outgoing and C_FundInvestors_Outgoing, the destination is the message queue that exists in the current organization, and the source is the FundInvestors XLANG Schedule, which is also within the current organization. Instead of creating an "organizational" channel that is from Home Organization to Home Organization, you now have a channel that goes from the XLANG Schedule to the OutgoingMessageQueueApp.

Watching the XLANG Schedule with XLANG Monitor Tool

With the channel, port, and message queues completed, it is time to run the schedule from beginning to end. In order to find out exactly what is going on in a schedule running on the system, you can use the XLANG Event Monitor tool.

The tool is excellent for troubleshooting and finding out what processes are executing on a running schedule.

The XLANG Event Monitor executable, XLANGMon.exe, is located under [BizTalk Server installation directory]\SDK\XLANG Tool\. Open the XLANG Event Monitor, and select Recording ➤ New Recording from the menus. XLANG Event Monitor will display all the running schedules in the window.

If you start the recording and use the VB HTTP Post utility to submit a document, you would soon see a schedule appear in the XLANG Event Monitor, as shown in Figure 5-37.

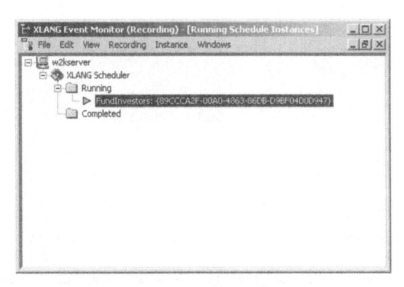

Figure 5-37. A running schedule in XLANG Event Monitor

The green arrow indicates that the schedule is currently in progress. You can also find out exactly which process is being performed inside the running schedule by double-clicking the green arrow. A new window will appear, in which a list of the events is displayed (see Figure 5-38).

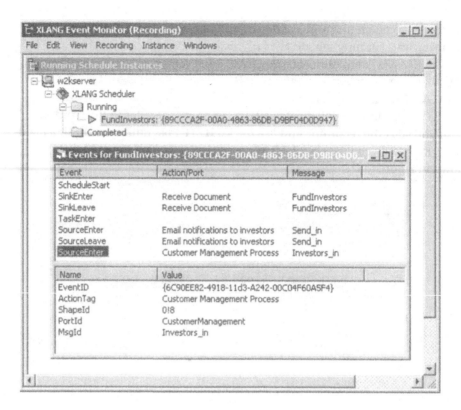

Figure 5-38. Viewing the processes being performed in a running schedule

When the schedule is completed, it will be moved from the Running folder into the Completed folder, and the green arrow will become a black square, which indicates that the processes in the schedule completed correctly and no error occurred. In the first test, FundInvestorsCOM didn't return any error.

The schedule will then take the Send response document back action, as shown in Figure 5-39.

Event	Action/Port	Message
ScheduleStart		
SinkEnter	Receive Document	FundInvestors
SinkLeave	Receive Document	FundInvestors
TaskEnter		
SourceEnter	Email notifications to investors	Send_in
SourceLeave	Email notifications to investors	Send_in
SourceEnter	Customer Management Process	Investors_in
SourceLeave	Customer Management Process	Investors_in
TaskLeave		
SwitchEnter		
CaseExecute		
SourceEnter	Send response document back	ResponseDocu...
SourceLeave	Send response document back	ResponseDocu...
SwitchLeave		
ScheduleDone		

Figure 5-39. A detailed history of the schedule with FundInvestorsCOM completing without error

Notice that the value in the Action/Port column for the SwitchEnter and SwitchLeave events is Send response document back. This indicates that the FundInvestorCOM component has completed successfully, and the Send response document back action is being executed. If you have set up the OutgoingMessageQueue message queue, you should see a new message arrive at that queue.

Now, let's raise an error in the FundInvestorsCOM component and see what happens to your schedule. To raise an error inside your VB component, use Err.Raise. This will generate a bad HRESULT for your component, which, in turn, will generate a nonzero _Status_ field in the message on the data page of the schedule. The VB code could look like the following:

```
Public Function Investors(fundcompany As String, document As String) As String
Err.Raise 10000, "FundInvestors Component", "Error occurred while processing Investors"

'Loop through the document node by node, process the
'content with in each investor node. and plug in the
'status code into the <Status> field for each investor
'    Your code here
'

Investors = document
End Function
```

Now if you run the same test again, you would see that different actions are taken in the XLANG monitor schedule (see Figure 5-40).

Event	Action/Port	Message
ScheduleStart		
SinkEnter	Receive Document	FundInvestors
SinkLeave	Receive Document	FundInvestors
TaskEnter		
SourceEnter	Email notifications to investors	Send_in
SourceEnter	Customer Management Process	Investors_in
SourceLeave	Email notifications to investors	Send_in
SourceLeave	Customer Management Process	Investors_in
TaskLeave		
SwitchEnter		
CaseExecute		
SourceEnter	Notify system administrator	FailedMessage
SourceLeave	Notify system administrator	FailedMessage
SwitchLeave		
ScheduleDone		

Figure 5-40. A detailed history of the schedule with FundInvestorsCOM returning an error

Notice that in this case the action between SwitchEnter and SwitchLeave is Notify system administrator. The Decision shape has chosen the correct action to execute. A message should arrive at the NotificationQueue message queue.

If what you see in the XLANG Event Monitor matches what you expect the workflow to do, you are done with BizTalk Orchestration, at least for now. We'll revisit BizTalk Orchestration in Chapter 10, where you will learn about some advanced features, such as Orchestration transactions, dehydration, schedule correlation, etc.

Summary

In this chapter, you learned how to use flowchart shapes to create a logic design for a workflow, and then to use the implementation shapes to turn a collection of Action shapes into functional code that BizTalk Server can execute at runtime. One of the key points of this chapter is that BizTalk Orchestration can create a workflow that integrates the design and implementation of separate business processes. With BizTalk Orchestration Designer, you have a central place to create, maintain, and modify the workflow of business processes.

CHAPTER 6

Configuring BizTalk Messaging for Outgoing Documents

I'VE ALMOST FINISHED taking you through Bob's first project, and your first end-to-end B2B integration process. As you'll recall, the process starts with the client posting an XML document to Bob's Web site. The process should end with the response document being posted back to the client's URL. So far, the integration process ends with bunch of response documents sitting in a message queue. You must configure BizTalk Messaging so that the messages in the OutgoingMessageQueue will be forwarded to clients instead of remaining in the queue.

Returning Documents to Clients

When messages are sitting in a queue, it's common to use Receive Functions to retrieve them. The question is how to set up the channels and ports so that the messages can be routed to the appropriate client's URL after the message is picked up by a Receive Function. You know that the source organization is embedded in the document. You must identify the destination BizTalk organization that maps to an actual client. It may seem obvious that you can set up the client organization as the destination organization, but how are you going to set up the Receive Function?

If you set up the destination organization as Henry Fonda Inc., all the messages would go back to Henry Fonda Inc., which doesn't make sense.

If you set up the destination port as an application of the Home Organization (BizTalk Server prohibits you from creating a port to the Home Organization), your outgoing document would go through a channel whose source organization is Henry Fonda Inc. and whose destination organization is Home Organization (the destination port for an application is considered to be the destination port of the organization to which the application belongs). However, this still wouldn't work because you've already defined a channel (C_FundInvestors_HenryFonda) that comes from Henry Fonda and goes to an XLANG Schedule (which is also considered to be the Home Organization)—that channel is used to route the document to the port where the schedule starts. If you defined another channel with the same source and destination, a document that came from that client would be passed to two channels at once, which you don't want. In fact, if you created two channels with same source and destination, your processes would get into a loop.

One solution is to define a new organization that can be used as the destination organization for all the outgoing messages. You can define a new organization called Outgoing Messages Gateway, whose only purpose is to create separate channels.

After creating the Outgoing Messages Gateway organization, you need to create the P_Outgoing_HenryFonda port as shown in Table 6-1.

Table 6-1. P_Outgoing_HenryFonda Port Specification

NAME	VALUE
Port name	P_Outgoing_HenryFonda (To an organization)
Destination type	Organization
Organization name	Outgoing Messages Gateway
Primary address	https://www.henryfondamutualfund.com/HTTPSPost.asp

The C_FundInvestors_Outgoing_HenryFonda channel should have the parameters shown in Table 6-2.

Table 6-2. C_FundInvestors_Outgoing_HenryFonda Channel Specification

NAME	VALUE
Channel name	C_FundInvestors_Outgoing_HenryFonda (From an organization)
Source type	Organization
Organization name	Henry Fonda Inc.
Inbound document	FundInvestors
Outbound document	FundInvestors

Next, you also need to create a new message queue Receive Function that watches the OutgoingMessageQueue queue. Table 6-3 shows the configuration information for this new Receive Function.

Table 6-3. Message Queue Receive Function Specification

NAME	VALUE
Receive Function name	OutgoingMSMQ
Pooling location	Direct=OS:.\private$\OutgoingMessageQueue
Source organization qualifier	OrganizationName
Source organization identifier value	<None>
Destination organization qualifier	OrganizationName
Destination organization identifier value	Outgoing Messages Gateway

NOTE *When creating a Receive Function, you should first create the message queue or File folder depending on what type of Receive Function is being created. If you create a Receive Function while its target doesn't exist, BizTalk Server will automatically disable that Receive Function and throw some error messages in the event log. You can correct this problem by creating the Receive Function's target and then unchecking the Disable receive function checkbox on its properties page.*

With the preceding settings, all the outgoing client documents picked up by the OutgoingMSMQ Receive Function are carried to the Outgoing Messages Gateway organization as their destination organization. The source organization information will still be coming from the fields inside the document. For every mutual fund company that should receive the response document, you must set up one channel and one port for its outgoing document, and you need to specify the URL that will be used to send back the documents as the primary address on each of these outgoing ports (see Figure 6-1).

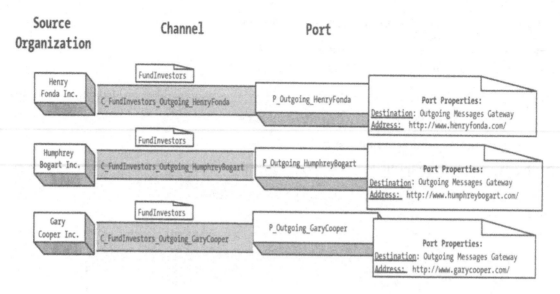

Figure 6-1. Channel and port settings for the outgoing documents

Once you have created the preceding Receive Function, it should start picking the messages from the OutgoingMessageQueue. You should get an error event in the Event View as follows:

```
An error occurred in BizTalk Server.

Details:
_____

[0x80090304] An error occurred during transmission:
A secure connection with the remote server could not be negotiated.
The server's certificate may not be valid.
Request information:

Proxy:
Proxy port:80
URL:https://www.henryfondamutualfund.com/HTTPSPost.asp
Content-Type:text/plain; charset="utf-8"
User name:
Client certificate:
Request body:1136 Bytes
Timeout duration (seconds): 93
Error code:80090304
```

This is an expected error. You haven't set up SSL on www.henryfondamutual-fund.com. In real life, it would be the responsibility of Henry Fonda Inc. to set up SSL on its site to transmit data securely over the Internet. However, since Henry Fonda Inc. hasn't done so, your BizTalk Server raises errors about being unable to establish the secure connection. However, the fact that you saw this BizTalk Server error event means it has started picking the existing messages in the queue and is able to find the correct channel you just created and start sending the response document back.

In order for Bob's application to send response documents back over SSL with mutual authentication, not only do the receiving clients need to set up SSL, you must also configure BizTalk Messaging so that it presents your certificate when establishing a secure connection with the external client's Web site. Doing this is the next topic.

Secure Communication with BizTalk Messaging

To understand secure communications, first consider public key infrastructure (PKI). A *public key infrastructure* is a system of digital certificates, Certification Authorities (CAs), and other registration authorities that verify and authenticate each party involved in an electronic transaction through the use of public key cryptography. The key components of PKI are digital certificates and certification authorities.

Before diving into the details, let's see how you conduct secure communication in the human world and compare that with the concept of PKI in the digital world. The following story is fictional.

I met a Chinese woman named Sherry on campus while I was in school, and planned to call her. I knew she had a couple of roommates, and I wanted to keep our conversation private. I could call her and say, "Hello," hoping that the person on the other end of the line would ask, "Who is this?" I could then verify whether or not the voice was Sherry's before saying anything embarrassing. If the voice was not hers, I could hang up and try later, or ask to talk to Sherry.

After I confirmed that I was talking with Sherry, I could start a private conversation. But what if someone decides to spy on us and picks up another phone on the same line to listen to the conversation? A good way to defend against such intrusions is to talk in an encrypted language. Chinese is just about the most encrypted language you can get in most American situations. I could start talking in Chinese with her. However, if her roommates were also Chinese, there is really nothing I can do about it.

The point of this story is that there are two things you want to ensure secure communication. First, you want to identify the person you are communicating with. Second, you want to make sure that the communication isn't understood by third parties who are eavesdropping on you.

For example, you want to make sure the credit card number you send to Amazon.com can't be stolen by hackers who are network sniffing. You also want to make sure that Amazon.com's Web site is indeed Amazon.com's Web site, and not some hacker's home page that happens to have the same domain name, pretending to be the legitimate site.

In the human world, you can keep communication as secure as possible by recognizing someone's voice and by using code words or an uncommon language. How can you achieve secure communication in the digital world? PKI is the answer.

Symmetric Cryptography

To keep third parties from interpreting messages, you need to encrypt the messages, which normally involves an algorithm and a key. The algorithm specifies how to encrypt and decrypt the message with a given key. The algorithms used to encrypt and decrypt messages today are commonly known, so it's the key that must be kept secret in order to prevent other parties from decrypting the messages and reading them.

The question, however, is how to get the key to the intended recipient so that he or she can use this key for decryption. You must somehow communicate this key securely before you can communicate the message securely—a circular problem. The assumption for this type of secure communication is you have somehow securely given the intended recipient the secret key so that he or she can read your messages. This is called *secret key cryptography* or *symmetric cryptography*.

Asymmetric Cryptography

The issue of how to securely send a secret key is called the *key distribution problem*. This problem was solved by two professors at Stanford University in 1976 when they introduced *public key cryptography*, or *asymmetric cryptography*. The idea is that in order for two parties to engage in a secure communication, each of them must have two keys: one public and one private. A message encrypted by a private key can only be decrypted by a public key, and a message encrypted by a public key can only be decrypted by a private key. The private key is always kept secret by the owner. The public key is made accessible to the public.

If I decide to send a message to a friend of mine, Sherry, inviting her to dinner, I would use my private key to encrypt the message before I send it. After Sherry receives the message, she would have to decrypt it using my public key before she could understand what I was saying (see Figure 6-2). In this scenario, when Sherry successfully uses my public key to decrypt the message, she can be sure the message must have been encrypted with my private key. If it hadn't been, the message could not have been decrypted with my public key. Sherry can be sure the dinner invitation is indeed from me because I should be the only one who has my private key. It's obviously an understatement to say that it's rather important that I keep my private key secure!

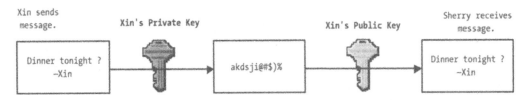

Figure 6-2. Sending an encrypted message using a private key and decrypting it with the public key

When Sherry wants to reply to my invitation, she can apply the same principle so that I can be sure the reply is indeed from her (see Figure 6-3).

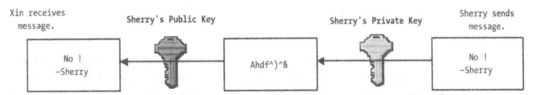

Figure 6-3. Sending an encrypted message using a private key and decrypting it with the public key

Digital Signatures

A *digital signature*, which is based on the preceding example, is a way to guarantee the integrity and origin of data. A digital signature is a combination of two cryptographic technologies: *public key encryption* and *hashing*. To hash something is to produce a very small digest, usually about 128 or 160 bits long, from a large chunk of data. A very small change on the source data will generate a massive change during the hashing of the data, so by comparing the digest of the message before and after the transmission, you can ensure that the message data wasn't tampered with during transmission. In other words, the digest will ensure the integrity of data.

Figure 6-4 outlines how digital signatures with the public key encryption and hashing are used to send a message. If I want to digitally sign my message to Sherry, I would first create a digest for my message using the hash algorithm.

Then I would use my private key to encrypt the digest and attach it to the end of the original message. Both are then sent together to Sherry. It's possible that some hacker could tamper with the message as it's on its way, but the hacker can't make the encrypted digest match the modified message, because the digest needs to be encrypted with my private key.

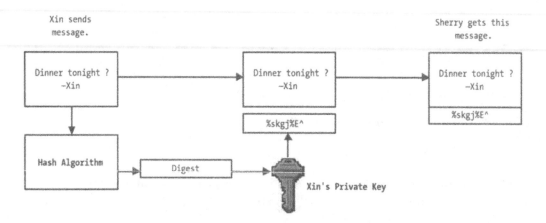

Figure 6-4. Digitally signing a message

Now let's take a look at how Sherry can verify whether the original message has been tampered with. When Sherry receives the message, she'll first use the same hash algorithm to create a digest of the message part of the data. She'll also need to use my public key to decrypt the encrypted digest located at the end of my message. If the digest she generates on her end is same as the one I sent in my message, she can be sure of two things: First, the message came from me, because she used my public key to decrypt the encrypted digest; and second, the message, "Dinner tonight?", has not been tampered with. If the message had been tampered with, the two digests would not match (see Figure 6-5).

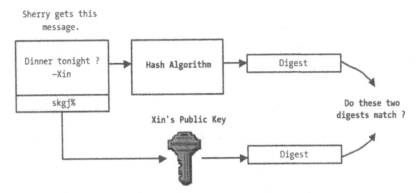

Figure 6-5. Verifying the digest to ensure the message's integrity and origin

Encryption

The preceding examples show how you can use private keys and public keys to authenticate messages and guarantee that they haven't been changed. This use of the keys solves the first problem of secure communication: identifying the person (or entity) you are communicating with. However, it doesn't solve the second problem. There is no way to prevent a third party from getting my public key and intercepting and decrypting the messages I send to Sherry—the public key remains public, after all. We must use our keys differently to prevent other people from understanding the message.

Instead of encrypting the message with my private key, I can encrypt the message with Sherry's public key, and when Sherry receives the message, she can use her private key to decrypt the message. Because only Sherry's private key can decrypt the message, and she is the only one who has that key, anyone who intercepts the message will end up with an unreadable message. This solves the second problem of secure communication: ensuring that the communication isn't understood by third parties. Figure 6-6 illustrates this process.

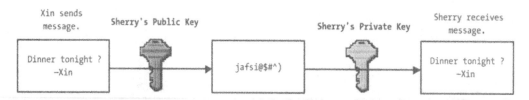

Figure 6-6. Sending a message encrypted using the public key and decrypting it with the private key

In this example, however, Sherry will not be able to ensure it's me who sent her the dinner invitation. Anyone could obtain her public key, encrypt a message, and send it to her.

To summarize: If you have your private key, you can send authenticated messages that others can be sure come from you. If you have someone else's public key, you can send an encrypted message that only that "someone else" can read. To do both these things and achieve truly secure communications, you need to combine the different applications of these two keys and use hash technology.

You should also note that my earlier arguments have been based on an important assumption—that Sherry's public key, which I used to encrypt or decrypt her messages, does indeed come from Sherry. However, unless she physically handed her public key to me, that assumption isn't safe. In today's e-commerce applications, public keys are transmitted over the Internet and are as subject to tampering as the messages they are designed to protect. This brings us to certificates.

Certificates and Certificate Authorities

A *certificate* is a piece of data that is used to identify a person or an entity. It can contain the public key, the private key, and other information that is used to prove its owner's identity. A certificate also identifies its Certificate Authority (CA), which is the organization that issues this certificate. The relationship between the CA and the certificates is like that between the Department of Motor Vehicles (DMV) and a driver license. Before a CA issues a certificate to someone, it does some background checking to make sure the identity information in the certificate is correct. Some well-known CAs, such as VeriSign and Thawte, charge money for performing the background check and issuing the certificate.

In order for Sherry to get a certificate from a CA, she would probably need to use her drive'sr license or birth certificate to prove she is indeed Sherry. After the background check, her name and other identity information would be added to the certificate. In order for me to get her public key, I would request her certificate, which contains her public key. If the name in the certificate is correct, I could then trust that this certificate is indeed from Sherry, and the public key in the certificate also comes from Sherry. The important step here is to verify the information inside the certificate before extracting the public key for use.

However, I still have to make one assumption that will never go away: I have to assume that the CA does do background checks rather than blindly issuing certificates to whoever pays. In the case of well-known CAs, this is valid assumption.

PKI Support in BizTalk Messaging

Now that you know what PKI is, let's take look at how BizTalk Server enables you to transmit data securely.

The first point is that you can specify that you want a document to be encrypted and digitally signed when it's sent out to the client. This is specified when the port properties are configured. If you want to encrypt your document, you need to select S/MIME (short for Secure Multipurpose Internet Mail Extensions) for the Type in the Encryption section of the Messaging Port Properties dialog box (see Figure 6-7).

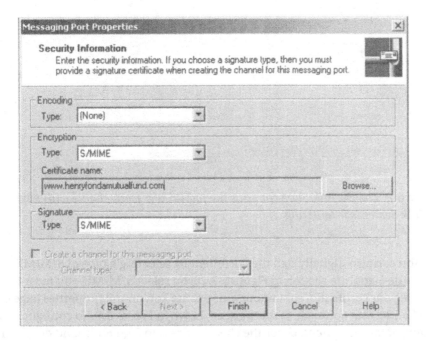

Figure 6-7. Enabling data encryption and signing on the port's properties page

You also need to provide a client certificate so that the client's public key (from the client's certificate) will be used to encrypt the document as it comes out of the port.

To do so, click the Browse button. The window shown in Figure 6-8 will open, asking you to select a certificate from the BizTalk Store. The BizTalk Store is a designated store for client certificates, and this is where you'll put certificates that contain clients' public keys. Whenever you need to encrypt data so that it's readable only by a particular client, you need to select the client's certificate from this BizTalk Store. BizTalk Messaging Manager will not allow you to navigate to other stores for certificates.

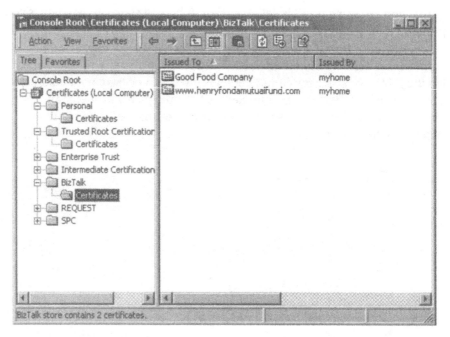

Figure 6-8. The BizTalk Store contains the public keys from clients with whom BizTalk Server is interacting

You can also digitally sign the document by selecting a type of S/MIME under the Signature section in Figure 6-7. If you select S/MIME, you must also provide your certificate, containing your private key, on the properties page of the channel that connects to this port, as shown in Figure 6-9. To configure the signing of the document, check the checkbox next to Sign outbound document on the Outbound Document properties page for the channel. You must also provide a certificate to be used for the signing, and because signing a document involves the use of the private key, you must provide a certificate that contains the private key. Click Browse, and BizTalk Messaging Manager will look in the

Personal Store on the local machine for such a certificate. BizTalk Messaging Manager will not allow you to navigate to other stores for certificates for signing.

 NOTE *The Personal Store stores the certificates associated with the private keys. Such certificates are used to decrypt the data. When BizTalk Server wants to encrypt the outgoing data, it will look in the BizTalk Store for the certificates—the BizTalk Store stores the certificates associated with the public keys of organizations to which the encrypted data is sent.*

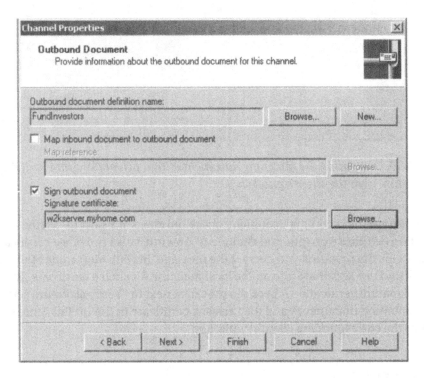

Figure 6-9. Providing a certificate that will be used to sign the outbound document

Besides allowing you to encrypt and sign outgoing documents, BizTalk Messaging also allows you to decrypt incoming documents to verify their integrity and origin by examining their signatures. To configure BizTalk Messaging to do that, open the Inbound Document properties page of the channel (shown in Figure 6-10).

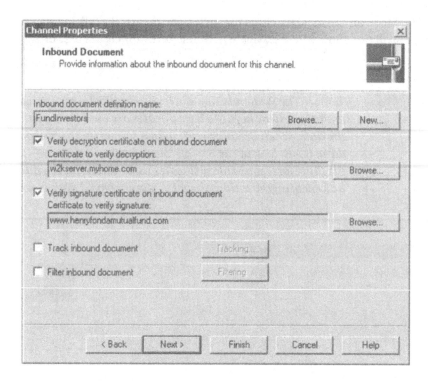

Figure 6-10. Decrypting the incoming document with a private key, and verifying the signature with the client's public key

To decrypt the incoming document, check the checkbox next to "Verify decryption certificate on inbound document". You must also provide a certificate that contains the private key to decrypt the message. BizTalk Messaging Manager will look into the Personal Store on the local machine for such a certificate. To enable signature verification, check the checkbox next to "Verify signature certificate on inbound document", and then select a certificate in the BizTalk Store that contains the corresponding client's public key.

Using SSL

With the PKI support in BizTalk Messaging, you can send encrypted and signed documents to your clients, or transfer the documents from one location to another securely. For most situations, however, you'll want to maximize security when sending data over the HTTP protocol. Instead of configuring the channels and ports for encryption and signing, you can use the native Secure Sockets Layer (SSL) support in BizTalk Messaging to send documents over HTTPS.

SSL is just another application of PKI. Behind the scenes, it will apply the same rules of PKI. SSL has become a bona fide standard for transmitting data over HTTP securely, and it has been adopted by countless businesses as a means of transmitting data securely over HTTP. Because it's so common and is indeed expected, you should use SSL to securely transfer documents over HTTP instead of using the generic method of securing and signing the data you saw in the previous section.

In order to understand how SSL can provide secure communication over HTTP, let's first take a look at the SSL handshaking process illustrated in Figure 6-11.

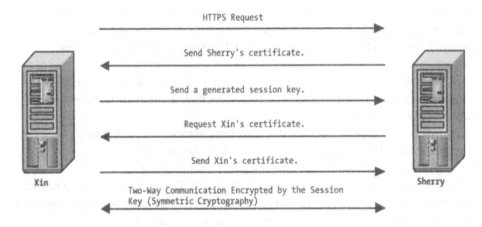

Figure 6-11. SSL handshaking process

When I want to communicate with Sherry using SSL, I would first initiate an HTTPS request to Sherry's Web server, asking for a secure communication. Sherry understands that I'm only interested in a secure conversation, so she sends me her certificate issued by her CA. After I receive the certificate, I'll will examine it to ensure it's indeed from her. The examination includes checking whether the CA who issued her certificate is trusted by me, whether the certificate has expired, etc.

After I'm satisfied with the certificate, I'll generate a session key that I'll use as a secret key for encrypting and decrypting the communication with her in this session. What I need to do now is get this session key to Sherry in a secure manner, because anyone else who gets ahold of this session key will be able to listen to our private conversation. To accomplish this, I'll encrypt the session key with Sherry's public key, which I extract from her certificate. This ensures that only Sherry can decrypt my session key by using her private key.

After I send off this encrypted session key, it will be Sherry's turn to examine who I really am. She does this by requesting my certificate, issued by my CA. I'll send her my certificate, and she'll examine it much the same way I did hers. After she is satisfied with my certificate, we can begin our private conversation, in which every word is encrypted and decrypted by the session key we both hold. The session key acts as a secret key, and it remains a secret between Sherry and me. When we decide to end our conversation, the session key will be destroyed. The next time we have a private conversation, the same handshake process would be done again, and a brand new session key will be generated.

SSL Support in BizTalk Messaging

This may seem to be a very complicated process, but it's actually very simple to implement in BizTalk Messaging. All you need to do is choose a certificate you want to use for the SSL session, and BizTalk Messaging will handle the rest for you.

To enable SSL, open the properties page of a port that points to an HTTPS address. For instance, it could be a Web site to which a client expects secure documents to be sent.

Consider the case of Bob's ASP application. You have a port that sends the return document to Henry Fonda Inc. through the P_Outgoing_HenryFonda port. The destination for this port is HTTPS://www.henryfondamutualfund.com/HTTPSPost.asp. If the protocol for the port is HTTPS, all channels that are connected to this port will have a special properties page when you open the Advanced properties page for the channel, as shown in Figure 6-12. You define the certificate you want to use at the channel level instead of the port level—this gives you the option to use different certificates when communicating with different HTTPS URLs. For example, you could create many channels that connect to one port, and define different certificates for each channel.

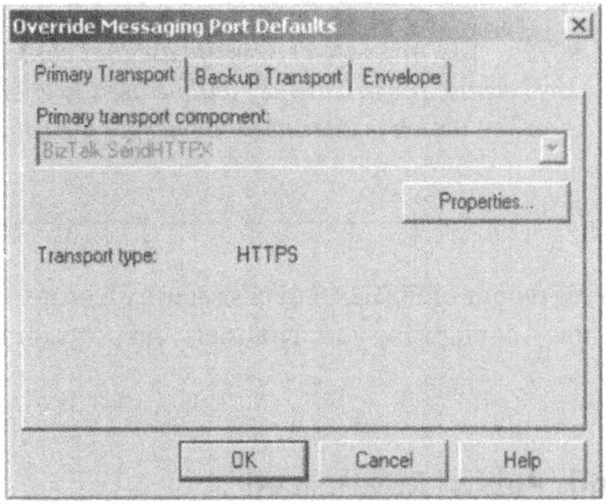

Figure 6-12. Setting certificate information on the advanced properties page of the channel

To specify a certificate, click the Properties button shown in Figure 6-12, and the BizTalk SendHTTPX Properties window will be displayed (see Figure 6-13). The Client certificates list box contains a list of certificates from the Personal Store on the local machine. Choose the correct client certificate, and click OK to save the change.

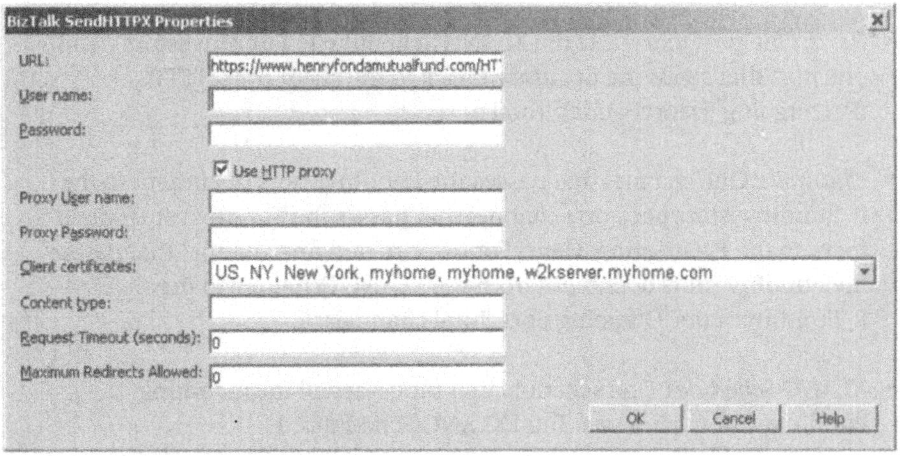

Figure 6-13. Specifying a certificate to use to access an HTTPS site

NOTE *You must select a certificate that contains a private key because the private key will be used to encrypt the session key, which is later used to encrypt the communication.*

Okay, after a big detour of BizTalk Server's security feature, let's get back to the task at hand now—configuring your channels and ports for outgoing messages.

Channels and Ports Revisited

You now have a way of processing a document from end to end. You start with the client sending you a document for processing, and you finish with the processed document being sent back to the original sender, in a secure form, over HTTP(S).

You just have a few things left to create, in order to complete the work for Henry Fonda Inc.:

- *Organizations:* One client organization (Henry Fonda Inc.), and one non-client organization (Outgoing Messages Gateway). Total organizations: 2.

- *Ports:* One port that starts the XLANG Schedule (P_FundInvestors), and one port that sends the document back to the client over HTTPS (P_Outgoing_HenryFonda). Total ports: 2.

- *Channels:* One channel that passes the FundInvestors document to the P_FundInvestors port, one channel that passes the FundInvestors document to the P_Outgoing_HenryFonda port, and one channel that passes the FundInvestors document from the XLANG Schedule to the P_FundInvestors_Outgoing port. Total channels: 3.

- *XLANG Schedules:* One schedule that processes all the incoming FundInvestor documents. Total XLANG Schedules: 1.

These are the BizTalk items you need to create in order to process one document type from one client. How much effort is involved in processing documents for more than one client? How many channels, ports, and organizations would you have to create to facilitate this integration effort? Obviously the number depends on the design. Creating a design that requires huge numbers of channels and ports can decrease the performance, as well as the manageability, of the system when more clients participate in the services. To design a robust and extensible BizTalk application, you need to have a complete understanding of the business requirements for the application, as well as the experience of working with BizTalk Server.

A good way to think about the design of B2B integration using BizTalk Server is to break the end-to-end process into two portions. The first portion gets the document into BizTalk Server and starts the orchestration. The second portion sends the response document from BizTalk Server to the original sender. Let's look at the elements involved in processing the FundInvestors document. The first portion handles the incoming documents and is shown in Figure 6-14.

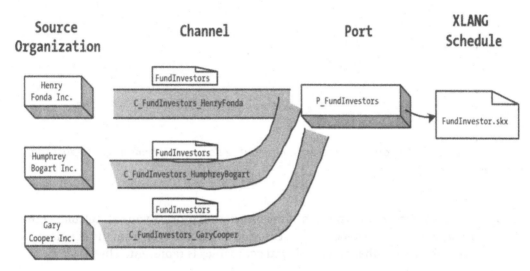

Figure 6-14. The elements involved in processing incoming documents from clients

As you can see in Figure 6-14, you'll need to create an organization to represent every new mutual fund company that sends in documents. You also must create an additional channel to connect the new mutual fund company to the P_FundInvestors port. However, you don't have to create additional ports for the new mutual fund company—all the mutual fund companies will share the same P_FundInvestors port. Similarly, only one XLANG Schedule is required for processing the FundInvestors document. The schedule itself has no knowledge of whose document is coming in—it will process every document of the FundInvestors type.

You also need to forward all the response documents to a central location from where they are sent out to each client later. A combination of one channel and one port can do the job just fine. Figure 6-15 shows the additional channel and port.

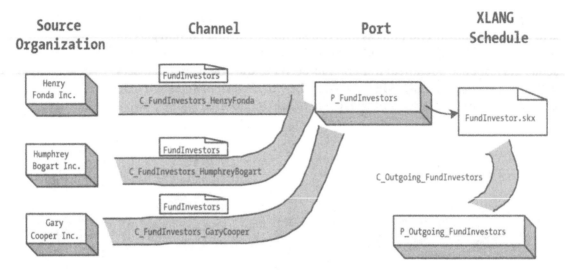

Figure 6-15. The elements involved in processing incoming documents and outgoing document for the clients

Therefore, for this portion of the integration process you can calculate how many elements are needed to process one document type from the clients. Suppose the number of mutual fund companies is represented by n.

- Number of organizations needed: n

- Number of ports needed: $1 + 1$

- Number of channels needed: $n + 1$

- Number of XLANG Schedules needed: 1

Now let's take a look at the second portion of the integration process, which handles the outgoing documents. In Figure 6-16 you can see that for every new mutual fund company, you need an organization to represent it. You don't have to create any new client organizations if those organizations have already been created for the first part of the process. However, you do need to add one additional organization (Outgoing Messages Gateway), which is used to facilitate the routing of the outgoing documents. You also need to create a new channel for each of the mutual fund companies. Finally, you must create a port for each of the new mutual fund companies in order to send the documents back to them.

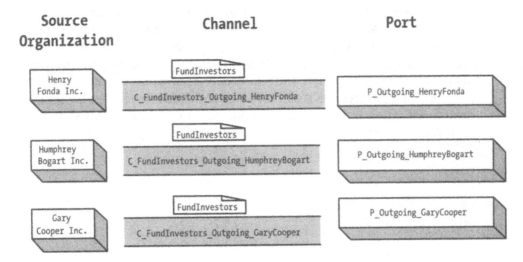

Figure 6-16. The elements involved in processing outgoing documents for the clients

Let's calculate the number of elements involved in the outgoing portion of the process. Again, the number of mutual fund companies is represented by n.

- Number of organizations needed: 1

- Number of ports needed: n

- Number of channels needed: n

If you add the elements from the two parts of the process, you then get the following figures for processing one document type from n mutual fund companies:

- Number of organizations needed: $n + 1$

- Number of ports needed: $n + 2$

- Number of channels needed: $2n + 1$

- Number of XLANG Schedules needed: 1

Summary

In this chapter, you learned more about concept of the secure communications and how BizTalk Messaging achieves secure communication with other parties. You also learned how to process the outgoing document. After reading this and the previous two chapters, you should have a good understanding of how documents are received, processed, and returned to the original sender.

In the next chapter, you'll see how to use XML Editor to create a flat file document specification and use the XML Mapper to convert the flat file document to an XML document.

CHAPTER 7

Flat Files and Mapping

MIKE DUPLICATES some channels and ports so that Bob's ASP application can support three mutual fund companies: Henry Fonda Inc., Humphrey Bogart Inc., Gary Cooper Inc. They then create a demo to show to Bob. Bob is extremely delighted with the work. "Now, I think the system we have can start processing the XML documents from mutual fund companies. But I want to see our system support legacy formats as well as the XML format. Some of our biggest potential customers are still using flat text files when it comes to exchanging documents. Their systems have been in place for many years, and getting them to convert to XML isn't an option right now. We must make our system understand these legacy formats in order to get their business."

Creating Non-XML Document Specifications in XML BizTalk Editor

Mike speaks with me about the non-XML document parse and XML mapping of BizTalk Server, and then he comes to me for more details on how to parse a flat text document and map it to the predefined XML schema you've worked on prior to this chapter.

Creating a Simple Flat File Document

BizTalk Server speaks XML natively. XML is a public standard, and the way tags are used to construct XML documents is standardized and well known. Every system that supports XML can parse an XML document as soon as its format is recognized.

Flat text files are different. Data can be structured in any way in a text file. The flat text can have a positional structure or a delimited structure, in which the data fields are separated by commas, or tabs, or any other character. Since flat text documents can be structured in so many ways, BizTalk Server must know how the flat text document is constructed before parsing it.

In BizTalk Server, document-parsing instructions are included as part of the document specification. For example, suppose the following flat text document is sent from a client:

```
Mike,Fix Income Fund,300
Bob,Growth Fund,100
Joe,Growth Fund,150
```

This is a very simple flat text document that contains three fields in each line or record. (This file is part of the source code available from the Downloads section of the Apress Web site at http://www.apress.com).

Let's look at how a flat file document specification is created in BizTalk Editor. Figure 7-1 shows a flat text file envelope for our flat text document in BizTalk editor. In a flat text document, there is no concept of a root element. The SampleFlatFile name in the figure is merely a logical name that represents the specification.

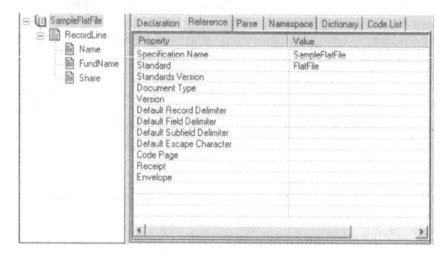

Figure 7-1. A flat text envelope in BizTalk Editor

So what is an envelope, and why do you need one? Just like when you send a letter, you need an envelope that holds information that isn't part of the content of the letter—for example, the destination and reply addresses, and sometimes instructions such as "Picture inside, please don't fold." Such information, although not part of the content of the letter, is necessary for the letter to be delivered and processed properly. Another term used to describe such envelope information is *metadata*—data about data.

When data is sent between BizTalk Servers, you have an option to wrap an envelope around the real content of the document. An envelope in BizTalk Server provides two functions. The first function is to facilitate BizTalk Reliable Messaging, a method that guarantees delivery once and only once between BizTalk Servers. (I'll talk more about BizTalk Reliable Messaging in Chapter 9.) The second function is to provide data-parsing instructions if the document isn't an XML document. In this chapter, you'll see how to use an envelope to provide the parsing instructions for a flat file document, which isn't an XML document since it doesn't contain "<>" tags and doesn't comply with the XML specification.

BizTalk Server natively supports multiple data formats, such as XML, flat files, EDI, and X12. Documents in formats other than XML, including any customized data formats, need to instruct the BizTalk Server document parser how to process them. For example, a flat file can be comma delimited or tab delimited, and BizTalk Server's flat file parser needs to know which character is used to separate the fields before it can successfully parse the document. This information is stored in the BizTalk envelope, and it must come with all non-XML files. BizTalk Server doesn't need envelope information to parse XML documents because XML documents have well-defined rules specifying how they are constructed.

In this example, since the SampleFlatFile specification describes a flat file, an envelope must be created for it. You'll learn how to create an envelope for it in the "Defining a Flat File Envelope" section later in the chapter. For now let's focus on creating the document specification.

In the window shown in Figure 7-1, it is important to change the Standard property to FlatFile. Then click the Parse tab, shown in Figure 7-2. The Parse tab is where you tell BizTalk Server how to parse each record in the flat file document.

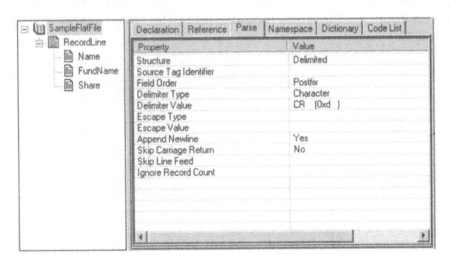

Figure 7-2. Setting the parsing properties for the flat text document

In a nutshell, when you tell BizTalk Server how to parse a flat file document, you tell it how to parse the records and fields within the document. You start by telling BizTalk Server how to parse a record.

To do that, click the root node, SampleFlatFile in the left panel, and then select the Parse tab in the right panel. As you can see in Figure 7-2, the Structure property is set to Delimited, the Delimiter Type property is set to Character, and the Delimiter Value property is set to CR (carriage return). These settings tell BizTalk Server that each record is separated from the next by a carriage return character.

If you want each record in the document to stay on its own line, set the Append Newline property to Yes—this will add a newline character at the end of each record. Many programs on different platforms look for this newline character when parsing a document, and they may not recognize that a record has ended without it.

Since you're using the carriage return as a delimiter in this example, you must set the Skip Carriage Return property to No so that the BizTalk Server parser treats a carriage return character as the end of the record. You should also set the Field Order property to Postfix, which means that the record delimiter is expected at the end of each record rather than at the start of each record (Prefix) or between records (Infix). In other words, in the sample flat text document shown earlier, there will be total of three carriage return characters, one at the end of each line.

After setting the parsing properties at the record level, you must also set the parsing properties at the field level. In order to do that, you need to create a record under the root node—I created a record called RecordLine, but the name isn't important. Let's look at the parsing properties of the RecordLine record shown in Figure 7-3. The parsing properties defined for RecordLine will apply to all the fields within it.

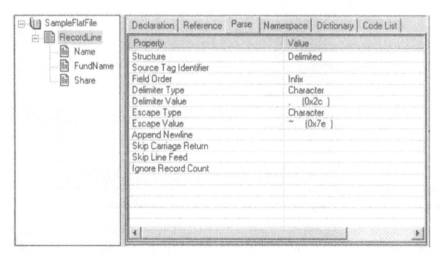

Figure 7-3. Configuring the parsing properties for the fields

Because this document is comma delimited, you need to set the Delimiter Value property to a comma (,) for the RecordLine record. You can also define an escape character to solve the problem of commas that are embedded in fields and that shouldn't be treated as field delimiters, such as when the share of a fund is "2,000,000". If you set the tilde (~) as the escape character, the "2,000,000" share would be written as "2~,000~,000" in the document and it would be parsed correctly.

It is common to set the Field Order property to Infix to avoid the necessity of including a final field delimiter at the end of a record. This means the data will look like "Mike, Fix Income Fund, 300" instead of "Mike, Fix Income Fund, 300,".

Creating a More Complex Flat File Document

It is easy to create a document specification in BizTalk Editor for a simple flat file, as you've seen. But there is one problem that your document specification doesn't address. If an investor is buying ten mutual funds instead of one, how are you going to construct the flat file document? Because the document specification you created is based on a flat structure, you can't define that an investor is buying more than one fund and still make the document valid. This type of document specification wouldn't work with the FundInvestors schema, which contains the hierarchical structure. For instance, under each FundInvestors record there are subrecords, such as Funds, Investor, and so on.

Using what's called a *source tag identifier*, it is possible for a flat file to contain a hierarchical structure. Here is an example:

```
COMPANY:John Wayne
Job:OpenAccount,,|InvestorInfo:Bergman,Ingrid,bingrid@casablanca,
    123-456-7890,1500,1234567892
Job:Trade,,|InvestorInfo:Peck,Gregory,pgregory@spellbound.com,
    123-456-7880,,|MutualFunds:MutualFund:Fonda International Growth,
    Buy,300,45.00+MutualFund:Fonda Fix Income,Sell,300,15
```

Notice the bold text in the preceding example—those parts are source tag identifiers, and they provide the hierarchical structure for the file. The fields are delimited with commas (,) and the subrecords are delimited with pipe characters (|). Subrecords of subrecords are delimited with plus signs (+).

In the preceding document, every line is considered a record (note that the two Job lines, which are too long for the pages of this book, should each be considered a single line). Within each line, you can create subrecords—a record can contain subrecords, such as Job, InvestorInfo, and MutualFunds, which can each contain more subrecords that might contain information on each individual fund.

The challenge now is that one of Bob's top clients, John Wayne Inc., will send the preceding flat text document, and your BizTalk Server must first convert it into an XML document, and then map it into the FundInvestors schema, before it can be passed to the XLANG Schedule for processing. Figure 7-4 shows the flat file specification that represents the previous flat text document.

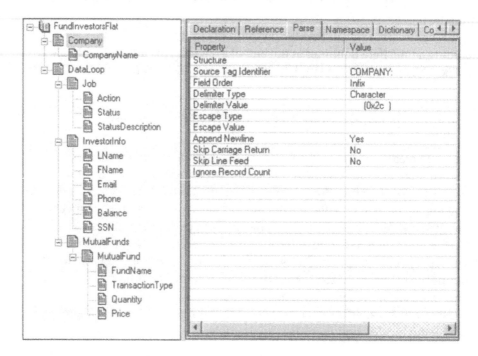

Figure 7-4. Creating a flat file specification for John Wayne Inc.'s document in BizTalk Editor

There are two main records in the specification: Company and DataLoop. The Company record is the very first line of the text file, and it identifies where the document originated. The DataLoop represents the lines of flat text, each line containing information corresponding to the Investor node in the FundInvestors document specification. One DataLoop can be considered one record or one investor.

There are subrecords defined within the DataLoop record, as shown in Figure 7-4. The MutualFunds record also contains another subrecord containing information on each mutual fund.

You can define records as you did in an XML document, but unlike the XML document where the beginning of a new record is indicated with an XML node, flat files don't use such nodes. Instead, each flat file record begins with a source tag identifier—a string located in front of each record that indicates the beginning of a record in a flat file.

To define a source tag qualifier for a record, click the Parse tab and enter a value for the Source Tag Identifier property, as shown in Figure 7-5.

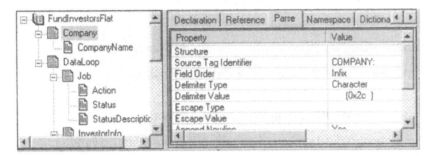

Figure 7-5. Setting the Source Tag Identifier for a record in a flat file document

You want to set the source tag identifier to COMPANY: as shown in Figure 7-5 because the document contains COMPANY:John Wayne at its beginning. You need to set the same properties for your subrecords—Job, InvestorInfo, MutualFunds, and MutualFund. A different delimiter must be used to separate the sub-subrecords, and you can also set that. For example, Figure 7-6 shows that the MutualFund sub-subrecords under MutualFunds are delimited by the plus sign (+), so that they can be differentiated from subrecords, which are separated by the pipe character (|).

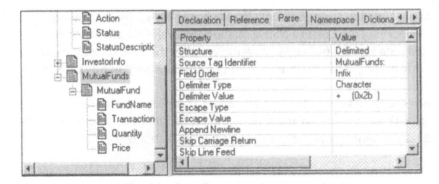

Figure 7-6. Setting a different delimiter for different record levels

Table 7-1 summarizes the relationships between the data in the flat file and the fields defined in the BizTalk Editor as shown in Figure 7-4. This table is based on the second record in the file shown earlier. After you have completed the document specification, save it as "FundInvestorsFlat"—you'll use this document later in this chapter.

Table 7-1. Hierarchical Structure in the Flat File

FIELD IN FLAT FILE	FIELD IN BIZTALK EDITOR
John Wayne	\FundInvestorsFlat\Company\@CompanyName
Peck	\FundInvestorsFlat\DataLoop\InvestorInfo\@LName
Gregory	\FundInvestorsFlat\DataLoop\InvestorInfo\@FName
pgregory@spellbound.com	\FundInvestorsFlat\DataLoop\InvestorInfo\@Email
123-456-7890	\FundInvestorsFlat\DataLoop\InvestorInfo\@Phone
Fonda International Growth	\FundInvestorsFlat\DataLoop\MutualFunds\MutualFund\@FundName
Buy	\FundInvestorsFlat\DataLoop\MutualFunds\MutualFund\@TransactionType
300	\FundInvestorsFlat\DataLoop\MutualFunds\MutualFund\@Quantity
45.00	\FundInvestorsFlat\DataLoop\MutualFunds\MutualFund\@Price
Fonda Fix Income	\FundInvestorsFlat\DataLoop\MutualFunds\MutualFund\@FundName
Sell	\FundInvestorsFlat\DataLoop\MutualFunds\MutualFund\@TransactionType
300	\FundInvestorsFlat\DataLoop\MutualFunds\MutualFund\@Quantity
15	\FundInvestorsFlat\DataLoop\MutualFunds\MutualFund\@Price

You now need to create a sample flat file based on the newly created specification. Select Tools ➢ Create a Native Instance from the menus. Save the generated data in a flat file, and then verify whether the data structure in the file is the same as that of the document coming from the client, in this case, John Wayne Inc.

Once you have verified that the document specification is correct, you can save the work to the WebDAV using the same procedure as in Chapter 4, when the XML document specification was stored in the WebDAV.

Creating an XSLT File Using BizTalk Mapper

Now that you have a completed flat file document specification, you can move to the next task: mapping the flat file document to your FundInvestors document specification. You have already created the FundInvestors XLANG Schedule to handle a FundInvestors document, so it would be ideal if you could process other documents that contain investor information by using that same schedule. In order to do so, you must first convert these variant document specifications into the FundInvestors document specification so your schedule can understand and process them.

I introduced BizTalk Mapper briefly in Chapter 1—it's a powerful graphical tool that can help you create an XSLT file, which allows translation or transformation between two document specifications. The next section describes how you use this BizTalk Server feature.

Using BizTalk Mapper

The first thing you need when creating an XSLT file with BizTalk Mapper is two complete document specifications defined under BizTalk editor. In this case, you want to create a map to convert the FundInvestorsFlat document to FundInvestors document.

To create a map between the FundInvestorsFlat and FundInvestors specifications, open BizTalk Mapper, select File ➤ New from the menus, and the Select Source Specification Type window will open (see Figure 7-7).

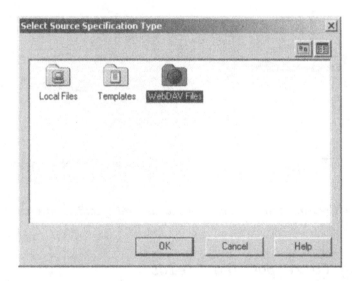

Figure 7-7. Selecting the document specification that is to be converted

Click the WebDAV Files icon, and then click OK.

The Retrieve Source Specification window then opens and asks for the source document specification. Select the flat file document specification you created for John Wayne Inc., FundInvestorsFlat, and click OK. Another window that asks for the destination specification type will open. Select the FundInvestors document specification and click OK.

The BizTalk Mapper window will now look like the one shown in Figure 7-8. Now you're getting to the most fun part of BizTalk Server.

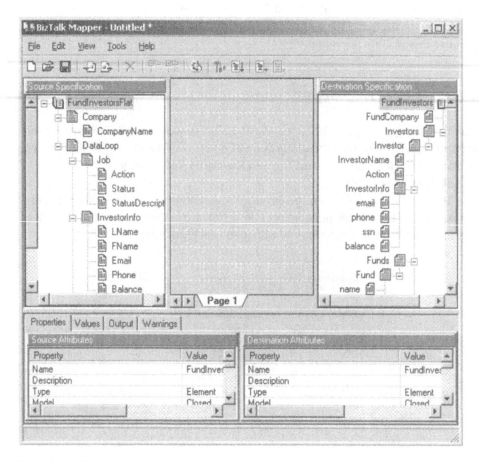

Figure 7-8. *Creating a map between two document specifications using BizTalk Mapper*

Linking Corresponding Fields

The rule of this game is to link the corresponding fields from the two specifications together so that the data from the document on the left is copied to the fields in the document on the right. You can drag and drop links between document specifications the same way you did between messages on the data page in BizTalk Orchestration Designer. Figure 7-9 shows what a completed map looks like.

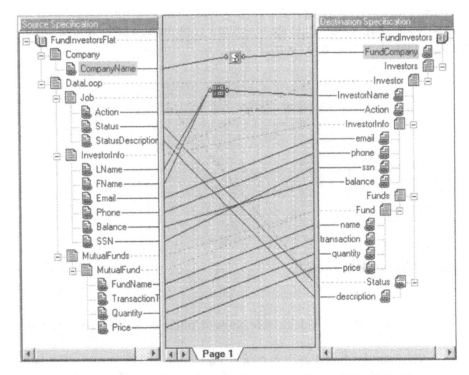

Figure 7-9. A schema map between FundInvestorsFlat and FundInvestors

The solid black lines between fields indicate the data flow from one document structure to the other. The dotted red lines are automatically generated by BizTalk Mapper to show the relationships between data records in the source and destination documents. The colorful square shapes in the middle are functoids, which can be considered mini programs that alter the data as it is being copied from one document to the other. Let's take a look at them in detail.

Modifying Data with Functoids

Functoids are very useful when you want to modify data. The FundInvestorsFlat specification, for example, contains LName and FName fields for the investor, but the FundInvestors document expects the full name of the investor in one field. Using the Concatenation functoid, the LName field can be appended to the FName field before the name is inserted into the InvestorName field. You can also define customized business logic in a functoid by deploying a Script functoid, which allows you to specify a VBScript or JScript program to be executed as the data flows through it.

To use a functoid on a map, click the functoid palette button (the colorful one) on the tool bar. A Functoid Palette window containing a collection of functoids is displayed, as shown in Figure 7-10.

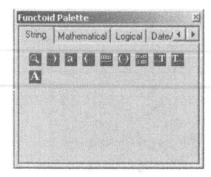

Figure 7-10. The Functoid Palette

The Functoid Palette provides a wide range of functoids in nine tab categories:

- *String:* Contains functions that trim strings, concatenate strings, calculate the length of strings, return portions of strings, etc. (See Table 7-2.)

- *Mathematical:* Contains functions that add, subtract, multiply, and divide numbers, return the maximum or minimum numbers, round numbers to a specific number of decimal positions, etc. (See Table 7-3.)

- *Logical:* Contains functions that compare two items, such as <, >, and =. It also contains functions that check whether a field contains a string or number, etc. (See Table 7-4.)

- *Date/Time:* Contains functions that return the current time and date. (See Table 7-5.)

- *Conversion:* Contains functions that convert between data formats. For example, use these functoids when you want to return a hexadecimal value when given a decimal value, convert a character to its ASCII value, or convert a value to the corresponding ASCII character. (See Table 7-6.)

- *Scientific:* Contains functions that calculate sine, cosine, tangent, x^y, etc. (See Table 7-7.)

- *Cumulative:* Contains functions that calculate the sum of multiple fields in a document, average values for connected fields by iterating over the parent record, etc. (See Table 7-8.)

- *Database:* Contains functions that execute a simple query against a database and extract the values in the columns of the returned recordset. (See Table 7-9.)

- *Advanced:* Contains scripting functoids that allow you to write customized functions to alter the content of the document. It also contains functions that return a count of a particular record inside a document, etc. (See Table 7-10.)

Table 7-2. String Functoids

NAME	PURPOSE
String Find	Returns the position of the beginning of a string inside another string
String Left	Returns the specific number of characters from left side of a string
Lowercase	Returns the lowercase form of a string
String Right	Returns the specific number of characters from right side of a string
String Length	Returns the length of a string
String Extract	Returns a specific part of a string (functions like "mid" in VBScript)
Concatenate	Concatenates multiple strings into one
String Left Trim	Removes leading spaces from a string
String Right Trim	Removes trailing spaces from a string
Uppercase	Returns the uppercase form of a string

Table 7-3. Mathematical Functoids

NAME	PURPOSE
Absolute Value	Returns the absolute value of a number
Integer	Finds the integral portion of a real number
Maximum Value	Returns the maximum value of several numbers
Minimum Value	Returns the minimum value of several numbers
Modulo	Returns the modulus after dividing a number by an integer
Round	Returns a number that is rounded to a specific number of decimal places
Square Root	Returns the square root of a number
Addition	Returns the sum of two or more numbers
Subtraction	Subtracts one number from another
Multiplication	Returns the product of two or more numbers
Division	Divides one number by another

Table 7-4. Logical Functoids

NAME	PURPOSE
Greater Than	Returns "true" if the first parameter is greater than the second parameter
Greater Than or Equal	Returns "true" if the first parameter is greater than or equal to the second parameter
Less Than	Returns "true" if the first parameter is less than the second parameter
Less Than or Equal To	Returns "true" if the first parameter is less than or equal to the second parameter
Equal	Returns "true" if the first parameter is equal to the second parameter
Not Equal	Returns "true" if the first parameter isn't equal to the second parameter
Logical String	Returns "true" if the expression is a string
Logical Date	Returns "true" if the expression is a date
Logical Numeric	Returns "true" if the expression is a number

(continued)

Table 7-4. Logical Functoids (continued)

NAME	PURPOSE
Logical OR	Returns the logical OR of the parameters
Logical AND	Returns the logical AND of the parameters
Logical Existence	Returns "true" if the input record or field exists in the source document

Table 7-5. Date/Time Functoids

NAME	PURPOSE
Add Days	Returns the resulting date in the format YYYY-MM-DD after the additional days have been added to the original date
Date	Returns a string representing the current date in the format YYYY-MM-DD
Time	Returns a string representing the current time in the format hh:mm:ss
Date and Time	Returns a string representing the current date and time in the format YYYY-MM-DDTHH:MM:SS

Table 7-6. Conversion Functoids

NAME	PURPOSE
ASCII from Character	Returns the ASCII value of a given character
Character from ASCII	Returns the character for a given ASCII value
Hexadecimal	Converts a decimal value to a hexadecimal value
Octal	Converts a decimal value to an octal value

Table 7-7. Scientific Functoids

NAME	PURPOSE
Arc Tangent	Returns the arc tangent of a given number
Cosine	Returns the cosine of a given number
Sine	Returns the sine of a given number
Tangent	Returns the tangent of a given number
Natural Exponent Function	Returns the value of e to the given power

(continued)

Table 7-7. Scientific Functoids (continued)

NAME	PURPOSE
Natural Logarithm	Returns the logarithm (base *e*) of a value
10 ^ X	Returns 10 to the X power
Common Logarithm	Returns the logarithm (base 10) of a value
X ^ Y	Returns X to the Y power
Base-Specified Logarithm	Returns the logarithm (base-specified) of a value

Table 7-8. Cumulative Functoids

NAME	PURPOSE
Cumulative Sum	Sums all values for the connected field by iterating over its parent record
Cumulative Average	Calculates the average of all values for the connected field by iterating over its parent record
Cumulative Minimum	Returns the minimum value of the nodes under its parent record
Cumulative Maximum	Returns the maximum value of the nodes under its parent record
Cumulative String	Returns the concatenated string of the string values for the connected field by iterating over its parent record

Table 7-9. Database Functoids

NAME	PURPOSE
Database Lookup	Searches a database for a specific value and retrieves the record that contains the value. This functoid requires four parameters.
Value Extractor	Returns a value from a specific column in an ADO recordset that has been retrieved by the Database Lookup functoid.
Error Return	Returns the error string, if any, returned by Open Database Connectivity (ODBC) when using the Database Lookup functoid.

Table 7-10. Advanced Functoids

NAME	PURPOSE
Scripting	Allows you to create customized VBScript or JScript scripts to be executed at runtime
Record Count	Returns a total count of the records found in the instance
Index	Returns the value of a record or a field at a specified index
Iteration	Returns the iteration number (in a loop) of the source record
Value Mapping	Returns the value of the second parameter if the value of the first parameter is "true"
Value Mapping (Flattening)	Returns the value of the second parameter if the value of the first parameter is "true", and flattens the source document hierarchy
Looping	Creates multiple output records by iterating over each input record

Most of the functoids need parameters, which are normally the data field of the document to which they are connected. For example, to concatenate the LName and FName fields before inserting them into the InvestorName field on the FundInvestors document, connect the LName and FName fields with the concatenation functoid, and connect the functoid to the InvestorName field on the FundInvestors document specification. Double-click the concatenation functoid to configure its properties, as shown in Figure 7-11.

Figure 7-11. Configuring the properties of a functoid

The concatenation functoid shown in Figure 7-11 takes three parameters: "FName", " " (a space), and "LName", and it will concatenate them together. Notice the C icon, which represents a constant value—in this case the constant value is a space that will be inserted between the first name and last name in the result.

In the window shown in Figure 7-11, you can change the order of concatenation by selecting a parameter and clicking the up and down arrows on the upper-left corner of the window. You can also remove an existing parameter from the concatenation by selecting it and clicking the Delete icon.

Click the Script tab to see the code behind the functoid. The script is read-only—in order to define your own program logic, you would have to use the Scripting functoid. For example, to convert the input data to uppercase, write the VBScript or JScript to do the case conversion as shown in Figure 7-12.

Figure 7-12. Creating a customized function with the Scripting functoid

The functoids can also be chained so that the output of one functoid is fed as input to another functoid. By chaining the functoids together, you can perform multiple actions when linking fields. You'll see some examples of this in Chapter 8.

Compiling and Testing the Map

After you complete all the links, you can generate the XSLT file by compiling what you've done so far in BizTalk Mapper. To compile the map, select Tool ➤ Compile Map. An XSLT document will appear under the Output tab at the bottom of the window, as shown in Figure 7-13.

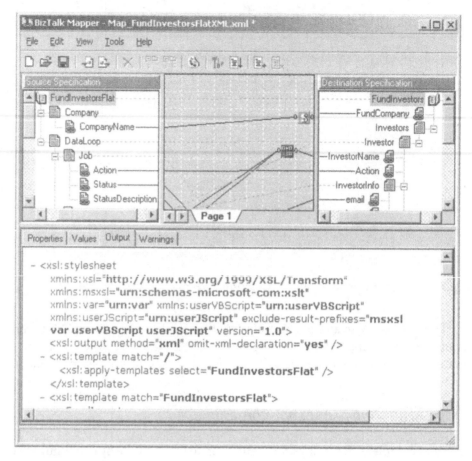

Figure 7-13. Generated XSLT with BizTalk Mapper

To ensure that the generated XSLT will correctly transform your flat text document into a format that fits the FundInvestor document specification, BizTalk Mapper provides a function that can convert one document into another from within the Mapper. Select Tools ➤ Test Map ➤ Native instance to XML. A new file dialog box will open, in which you can select a flat file document that contains some data like the following:

```
COMPANY:John Wayne
Job:OpenAccount,,|InvestorInfo:Bergman,Ingrid,bingrid@casablanca,
123-456-7890,1500,1234567892
Job:Trade,,|InvestorInfo:Peck,Gregory,pgregory@spellbound.com,
123-456-7880,,|MutualFunds:MutualFund:Fonda International Growth,
Buy,300,45.00+MutualFund:Fonda Fix Income,Sell,300,15
```

Click OK, and BizTalk Mapper will try to convert the flat file document into a FundInvestors document based on the linkages and functoids defined in the map. The transformed document will appear in the Output tab at the bottom of the window. The transformed document is now an instance of the FundInvestors specification, as shown in Figure 7-14.

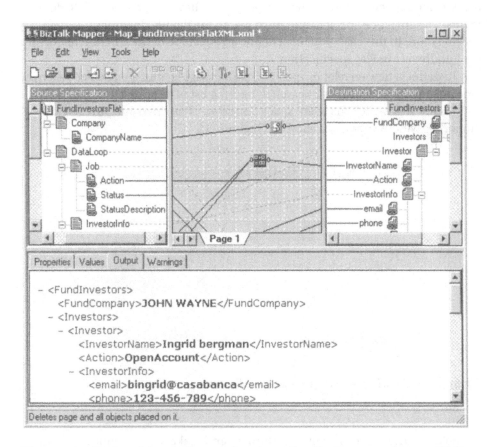

Figure 7-14. Testing the map by transforming a flat file document into an XML document

The generated XML document is what the flat file has become after the transformation. If the XML document looks all right, you can save the map file by storing it in WebDAV. It is always helpful to give it a self-explanatory name, such as Map_FundInvestorsFlatXML.

Defining a Flat File Envelope

With the map done, it is time to create the channels and ports needed to support this new type of document. Before moving on to the channels and ports, though, you must define a flat file envelope definition, because BizTalk Server looks into the envelope specification for the instructions on how to parse non-XML documents. The envelope specification must match the flat file document specification. In this case, you must define an envelope definition that refers to the FundInvestorsFlat specification.

To define a new envelope, open BizTalk Messaging Manager. Select the envelope link on the left, and click Search to return a list of existing envelope definitions. Right-click the white space and select New Envelope. An Envelope Properties window opens, as shown in Figure 7-15.

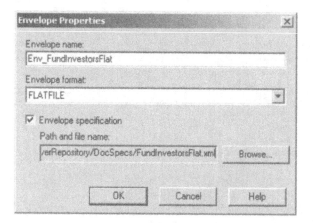

Figure 7-15. Creating a new envelope specification

Select FLATFILE as the envelope format, and make the envelope specification the same as the document specification that it is associated with—in this case, FundInvestorsFlat.

Next, you need to attach the C_FundInvestorsFlat_JohnWayne channel to the P_FundInvestors port so that you can transform the incoming flat files. Use the settings shown in Table 7-11.

Table 7-11. Settings for Attaching the C_FundInvestorsFlat_JohnWayne Channel to the P_FundInvestors Port

NAME	VALUE
Channel name	C_FundInvestorsFlat_JohnWayne
Source type	Organization
Inbound document	FundInvestorsFlat
Outbound document	FundInvestors
Map file	Map_FundInvestorsFlatXML

You must also create a new Receive Function for the flat file document, because you must specify the envelope information on the Receive Function. You also must create a new message queue to store the flat file documents that the Receive Function watches for—call the message queue IncomingFlatMSMQ. Create a Receive Function based on the specifications in Table 7-12.

Table 7-12. Specifications for the Receive Function of the Flat File Document

NAME	VALUE
Receive Function name	IncomingFlatMSMQ
Polling location	Direct=OS:.\private$\IncomingDataStoreFlat
Envelope name	Env_FundInvestorsFlat
Source organization qualifier	OrganizationName
Source organization identifier value	<None>
Destination organization qualifier	Organization Name
Destination organization identifier value	Home Organization

Notice that the envelope name (specified on the advanced property page of the Receive Function) refers to the envelope definition you just created. If you didn't include the envelope information on the Receive Function, BizTalk Messaging would not be able to parse the flat file document that is picked up by that Receive Function.

You also need to consider the outgoing route as well as the incoming route. You have to create one channel and one port for sending the response document back to John Wayne Inc., so you must find out what type of document John Wayne Inc. is expecting to be returned. If you create a channel and port similar to the ones for Henry Fonda Inc., the response document sent back to John Wayne Inc. would be a FundInvestors document. However, if John Wayne Inc. is expecting the response document to be of the same type as the document it sends to us (a flat file document), you'll have to make sure the XML document that comes out of your schedule is mapped back to the flat file format before sending it back.

As it turns out, John Wayne Inc. does want a flat file document returned, so you need to do two things: First, create a new map file that will convert the FundInvestors document to a FundInvestorsFlat document. Second, tell BizTalk Messaging to stream the document into a flat file document before it is sent back to John Wayne Inc.

The procedure for creating a map file to map the FundInvestors document back to a FundInvestorsFlat document is similar to what you did earlier to create Map_FundInvestorsFlatXML. In this case, though, you must specify the FundInvestors document specification as the source, and FundInvestorsFlat as the destination specification. You'll also have to re-create all the links and functoids (reversing their functionalities). When you are finished, save the map to the WebDAV with a self-explanatory name, such as Map_FundInvestorsXMLFlat.

When you use this reverse map, the document that comes out of the channel is a FundInvestorsFlat document in XML form, and it needs to be streamed into a flat file document. To tell BizTalk Sever to output the document as a flat file document, you need to specify the envelope that is used to serialize the XML document into a non-XML document. The envelope information is specified in the configuration of the P_Outgoing_FundInvestorsFlat_JohnWayne port, as shown in Figure 7-16.

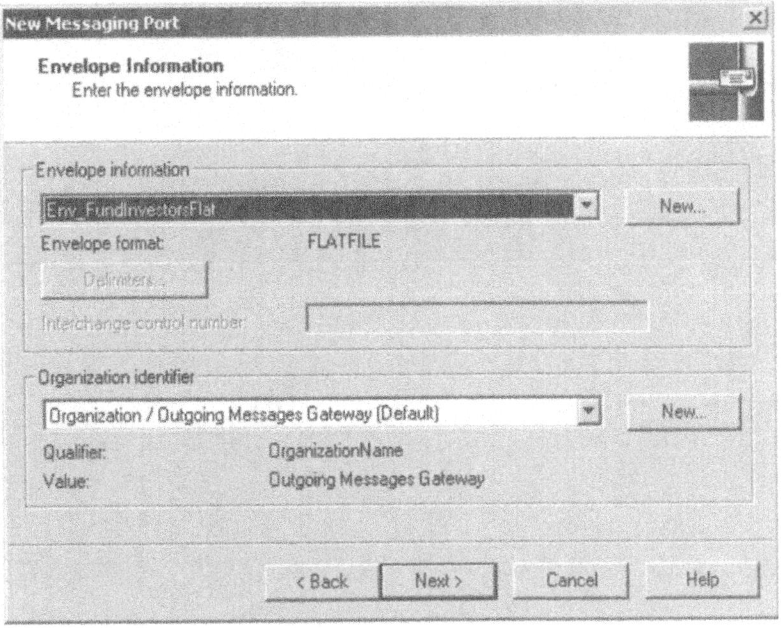

Figure 7-16. Specifying the envelope information on the port

On the port, select the Env_FundInvestorsFlat envelope from the list. The envelope provides BizTalk Messaging with enough information for it to output the document as a flat file document before sending it back. If you run a quick test, you would find that the document that is posted back to https://www.johnwayne.com/HTTPPost.asp is actually a flat file document that contains all the comma (,) and pipe (|) delimiter characters.

Summary

In this chapter, you learned how to define a flat file document specification in BizTalk Editor. BizTalk Editor can define both simple flat file documents and ones that contain complex hierarchical structures.

You also learned how to use BizTalk Mapper to transform documents from one schema to another. The chapter also introduced several functoids, which can be used in the maps to provide greater flexibility during the data transformation.

There are many interesting features in BizTalk Mapper, and you'll learn more about them in Chapter 9.

Other BizTalk Server Features

IN THIS CHAPTER I'll show you the features of BizTalk Server that you didn't use in Bob's ASP project. You'll see some of the protocols BizTalk Messaging supports, some more functoid examples, some handy features of the BizTalk Editor, and the While shape in BizTalk Orchestration Designer.

Destination Protocols

You've seen ports point to XLANG Schedules and to HTTPS URLs in Bob's ASP project. BizTalk Server supports many other types of protocols besides those two, such as files, message queues, SMTP, HTTP, and application integration components.

Files

To send a document to a file location through a port, you need to set the transport type on the port to File, as shown in Figure 8-1. You can access the Primary Transport dialog box shown in Figure 8-1 by opening the properties page of the port and clicking the Browse button next to the port address field.

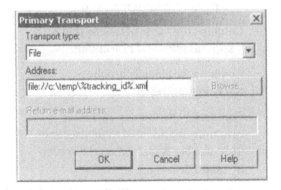

Figure 8-1. Setting an address for the file location

In this dialog box, you need to specify the file location in the Address field in this format: file://[drive]:\[directory]\[filename]. An example would look like this: file://c:\temp\sample.xml.

 NOTE *BizTalk Server doesn't automatically create the destination file folder if it doesn't already exist. For the example shown in Figure 8-1, BizTalk Server will raise a runtime error when sending data to the c:\temp folder if that folder doesn't exist.*

Notice the %tracking_id% part of the address in Figure 8-1. It is a variable that holds the tracking ID for the document that is coming through this port, and it is being used as the filename. For this document, BizTalk Messaging will create a file with tracking_id as its filename. Because the tracking ID is always a unique number, you can add %tracking_id% as part of the filename to create a unique filename, preventing the file from being overwritten. There are many other variable values that can be used in the File Transport property, as listed in Table 8-1.

Table 8-1. Variables for the File Transport Property

VARIABLE	DESCRIPTION	UNIQUE FILENAME
%datetime%	Contains the date and time, in milliseconds,of file creation. The time is based on Greenwich mean time (GMT) rather than local time.	No
%document_name%	Contains the name of the document definition used to process the source file.	No
%server%	Contains the host name of the server that processed the document.	No
%src_filename%	Contains the name of the file that is being submitted for processing.	No
%tracking_id%	Contains the globally unique tracking number.	Yes
%uid%	Contains a counter that increases over time, represented in milliseconds. This number is reset when the server is restarted.	No

You can also combine several variables to generate a filename; for example, file://c:\temp\%server%_%datatime%_%tracking_id%.xml would result in a filename like this: file://c:\temp\server1_631650895164926224_{bd70c020-2d24-11d0-9110-00004c752752}.xml.

On the channel that is connected to the port using the File transport type, you can set additional properties. In the Advanced properties page on the channel, shown in Figure 8-2, you can specify a user name and password pair that you want BizTalk Messaging to use to access the target file. You can also choose how the document is written to the file: Overwrite file, Append to file (the default setting), and Create a new file.

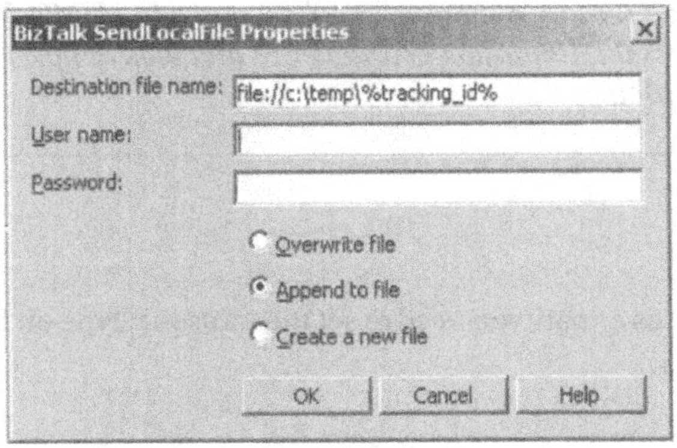

Figure 8-2. Advanced properties for the File transport type

Message Queues

To send documents to a local or remote message queue through a port, you can set the transport type on the port to Message Queuing (see Figure 8-3).

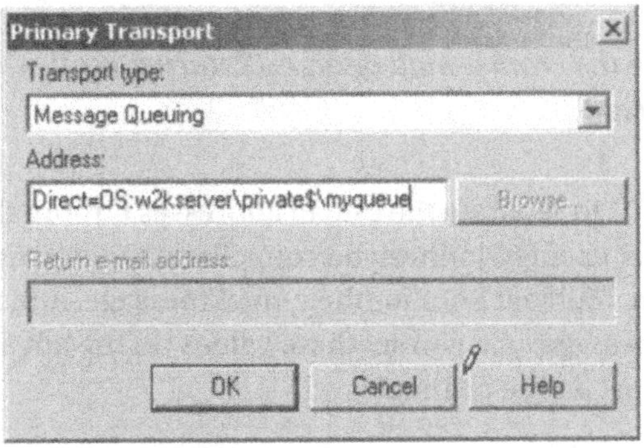

Figure 8-3. Setting the address for a message queue

In the Address text box, enter the format name of the message queue. The format name may look like any of the following: DIRECT=OS:<ServerName>\<QueueName>, PUBLIC=<QueueName GUID>, and DIRECT=TCP:<IPAddress\QueueName>.

You can configure many other settings on the advanced properties page for channels that are connected to such ports, including the message label, the priority of the message, the transaction level, and the delivery type (express or recoverable). These settings are used when sending the document to the target message queue.

 NOTE   *The message size limit in MSMQ is 4MB. Messages that are larger than 4MB can't be stored in MSMQ. I'll discuss this limitation in Chapter 13 and look at how to deal with it.*

SMTP

To send a document as e-mail, you need to set the transport type on the port to SMTP (see Figure 8-4).

Figure 8-4. Specifying the From e-mail address (Return e-mail address) and the To e-mail address (Address)

Use semicolons (;) to separate the e-mail addresses if more than one is specified, like this—mailto: client1@johnwayne.com;client2@johnwayne.com. If you want to set the CC and Subject lines for the e-mail message, and the authentication type for the message, you can set these values on the advanced properties page for the SMTP port on the channel level.

You'll also need to specify the SMTP host used to send e-mail. This is done on the BizTalk Server group's properties page, shown in Figure 8-5.

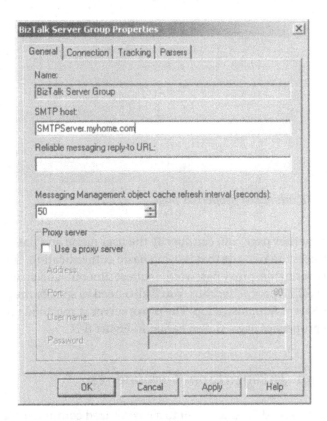

Figure 8-5. Configuring the SMTP host for the BizTalk Server group

HTTP

The advanced properties page for the HTTP Transport Type is the same as the one for HTTPS, which you saw in Chapter 6 (see Figure 8-6).

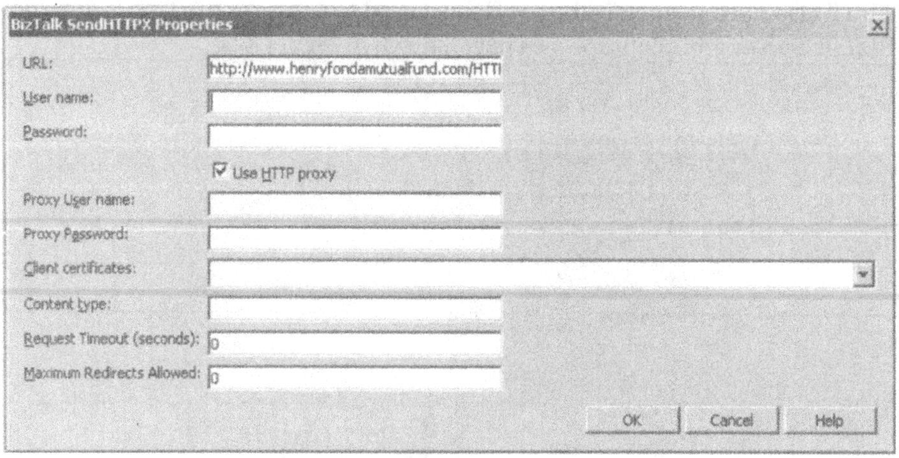

Figure 8-6. HTTP advanced properties page

In this properties page, you can specify the user name and password required to access the Web site that is using basic authentication. You can also set the proxy user name, proxy password, request timeout, and so on. If you check the Use HTTP proxy checkbox, you'll also need to specify the proxy server using BizTalk Server Administration. The proxy server is specified on the BizTalk Server group properties page, shown earlier in Figure 8-5.

Application Integration Components

When you want to send the document to a customized component for further processing, you need to set the transport type to Application Integration Component. In order to qualify as an application integration component that can be instantiated by a BizTalk Messaging port, the component has to implement either the IBTSAppIntegration or the IPipelineComponent interface. I'll cover the use of application integration components in detail in Chapter 11.

Now that we've looked at the variety of destination port protocols available in BizTalk Server, let's go on and take a look at some of the features available in the BizTalk Editor.

BizTalk Editor Features

You learned how to create a schema from scratch using BizTalk Editor in Chapter 7. However, creating a schema from scratch normally involves significant time and effort. Fortunately, BizTalk Editor includes features that allow you to import into BizTalk Editor document schemas that use different standards. These can then be modified and saved as BizTalk schemas.

On the tool menu of BizTalk Editor, select Tools ➤ Import to open the Select Import Module dialog box shown in Figure 8-7. You can import a schema from three sources: Well-Formed XML Instance, Document Type Definition, or XDR Schema.

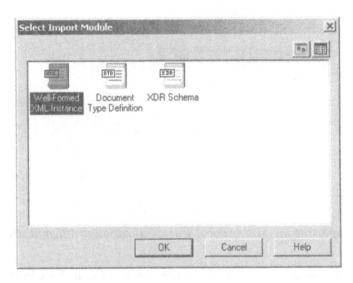

Figure 8-7. Selecting the source of import

The Well-Formed XML Instance option allows you to generate a BizTalk schema from an XML document instance. For example, if you have crafted a sample document, you can select this option and have BizTalk Editor automatically generate a BizTalk schema based on the structure of your sample document. You can then verify, modify, and save the schema as a BizTalk schema. You can also import a DTD schema or XDR schema into BizTalk Editor in similar fashion and then modify and save it as a BizTalk schema.

Another cool feature about BizTalk Editor is its ability to export an existing document specification to different schemas, such as XSD and XDR. To export a specification, you first need to load an existing document specification in BizTalk Editor. Then open the Tools menu and choose one of the two export options on the menu, as shown in Figure 8-8. Unfortunately, although BizTalk Editor allows you to export document specifications to XSD schemas, it doesn't yet have the ability to import from an XSD schema.

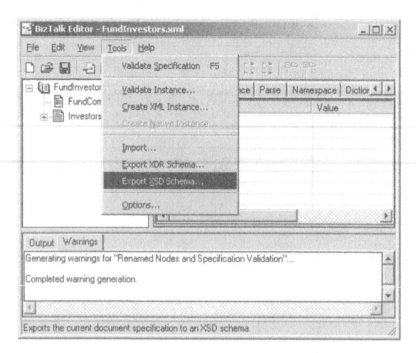

Figure 8-8. Exporting an existing document specification to different schemas

Other tools are available in BizTalk Editor, such as Create XML instance, which generates a sample XML document for the document specification. The Create Native instance option generates a sample document of a non-XML format (flat file, EDI, etc.), if the document specification is of a non-XML standard type.

The While Shape in Orchestration

In Chapter 7 you saw all the flowchart shapes in action except the Transaction shape and the While shape. I'll cover the Transaction shape in Chapter 10. Here, I'll show you the While shape works.

Sometimes you'll want to have some kind of looping logic in your schedule. For example, you may want to perform a certain process several times, or to process certain work until something occurs. In these cases, you can use the While shape in an orchestration.

Loop statements in programming languages need a counter of some sort to keep track of how many times the loop has been executed, and the counter also needs to be incremented in the loop accordingly. Such programming is fairly easy in any language. Unfortunately, BizTalk Orchestration isn't a common programming language, and there are many simple things that aren't supported in BizTalk Orchestration. For instance, you can't define a variable in an orchestration, which means you can't define a counter variable for the loop in the orchestration.

To get around this problem, you have to implement some kind of counter inside your component, and then communicate the value of the counter variable to the orchestration. The other important thing you have to keep in mind is that this counter variable in the component must remember its previous value as the while loop continues—this requires the state of the component to be maintained for the duration of the while loop.

The While shape is best understood through looking at an example. Figure 8-9 shows a schedule that contains a while loop. In this schedule, you have a LoopXLANG component that contains two methods: Increment and DoWork. The DoWork method does the real work, and the Increment method maintains the loop counter.

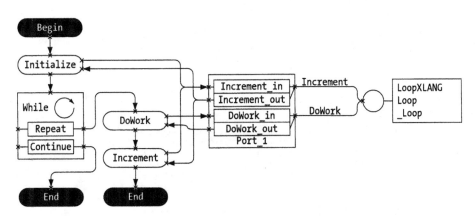

Figure 8-9. A schedule with While shape

Here is the code for the LoopXLANG component:

```
Private counter
Public Function Increment()
    'increment the counter variable by 1
    counter = counter + 1
    Increment = counter
End Function

Public Function DoWork()
    'Add your code here.
```

```
      MsgBox ("loop #" & counter)
End Function

Private Sub Class_Initialize()
      'initialize the variable
      counter = 0
End Sub
```

When the schedule is started, the first Action shape is Initialize, which will call the Increment method. The counter variable will be set to 1.

The next shape is a While shape, and you need to create a Repeat rule to define how many times the While shape repeats its actions. The properties for Repeat are set in the Rule Properties dialog box, shown in Figure 8-10.

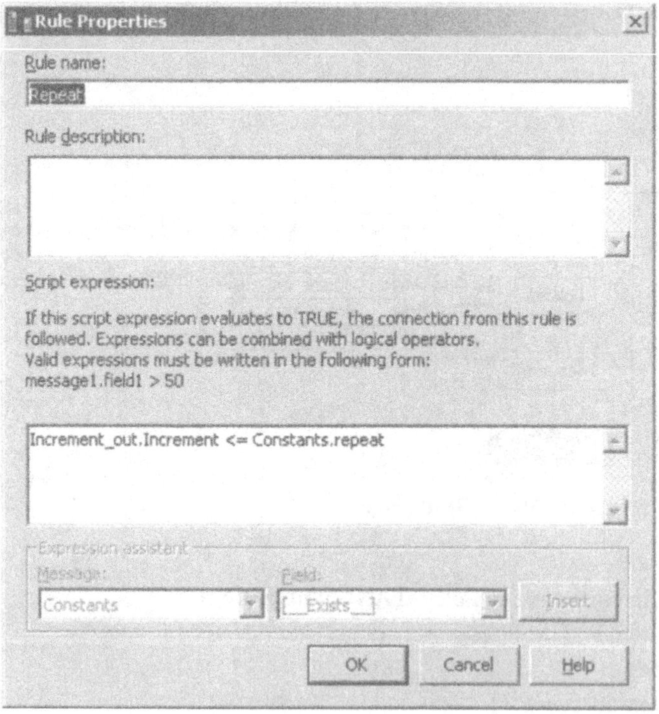

Figure 8-10. The rule property of a While shape

The Script expression area of the Rule Properties dialog box contains the condition that will be evaluated in every pass through the While loop. In this example, you want the Increment method to run the number of times that is set in the repeat constant, so the condition being tested is whether the counter is less than or equal to the repeat constant—if it is, the loop will continue. The

Constants.repeat constant is defined on the data page of the orchestration. If the condition is true, then the DoWork and Increment methods will be executed.

As the Increment method is executed, the Increment_out.Increment data field will be increased by one, because Increment_out.Increment is actually the return value of the Increment method. When Increment_out.Increment is greater than the constant value defined on the data page, the while loop ends and execution continues with the Action shapes below the While shape.

It is important that you call the Increment method at least once before the While shape is reached (in this case, the Initialize Action shape calls the Increment method); otherwise, the Increment_out message in the condition of the While shape will be null, and a runtime error will be generated, complaining that Increment_out.Increment doesn't exist. Another important point is that in order for this While shape to work, the private variable counter must maintain its state for as long as the While loop runs. Therefore, you must configure the component's State Management Support property as either "Holds state, but doesn't support persistence" or "Holds state, and does support persistence" in the COM Component Binding Wizard. The former option will keep the component in memory because it can't persist its state to disk. The latter option allows the component to be persisted to disk and brought back to memory when it is accessed again. In order to select this option, the component must support either the IPersistStream or IPersistStreamInit interface.

There are a number of ways you can test the schedule. Because this schedule doesn't expect any data from BizTalk Messaging, the easiest way to test it is through XLANG Monitor. Open XLANG Monitor and select Instance ➤ Run from the menu. Enter the file location of the .skx file you want to run, and click OK. Each time the loop runs, a message box will display the counter value, so you will see as many message boxes as the constant value you set on the data page.

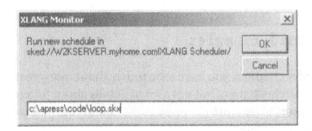

Figure 8-11. Starting an XLANG Schedule from the XLANG Monitor

Another good application of the While shape is to create an infinite loop (by setting the condition to something like "1 = 1"). Within this infinite loop, you can continually poll the messages from some data source, such as a message queue or BizTalk Messaging (see Figure 8-12).

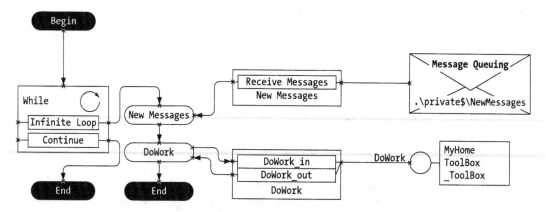

Figure 8-12. Creating an infinite loop using the While shape

In the schedule in Figure 8-12, the Infinite Loop rule inside the While shape will always return true. Within each occurrence of the loop, the New Messages action will receive a message from the message queue. If there is no message in the message queue, the schedule will wait at the New Messages action, and the process flow will continue as soon as a new message arrives at the message queue. The good thing about this schedule is that it never ends. It will simply stay in memory and wait for the next message to arrive.

You can also set the State Management Support property of the COM component to "Holds state, and does support persistence" so that the running schedule can be persisted (dehydrated) to the disk to free the memory as it waits for messages, and it can be rehydrated when the message arrives. With this technique, you can make one running schedule route all the incoming messages to a message queue or BizTalk Messaging.

More Functoid Examples

In this and earlier chapters, you have seen much about many features of BizTalk Messaging and Orchestration, but not a lot of details about functoids. I'll use the rest of this chapter to demonstrate some of the cool things you can do with functoids in the BizTalk Mapper.

We looked at some simple functoid examples in Chapter 7. In the following sections, I'll describe some common functoids you can deploy to customize conversions.

Cumulative Sum

The Cumulative Sum functoid is commonly used to get a summary of data from a source document and put the result into the destination document. For instance, the example in Figure 8-13 uses the Cumulative Sum functoid to calculate the total sales of all transactions.

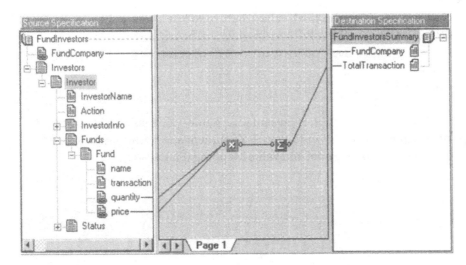

Figure 8-13. Calculating the cumulative sum for all transactions

The map in Figure 8-13 involves two functoids: Multiplication and Cumulative Sum. First you find out the transaction amount for each fund by using the Multiplication functoid, and then you sum up the transaction amounts for all the funds in the document by using the Cumulative Sum functoid. You make the result of the Multiplication functoid be the input parameter for the Cumulative Sum functoid, and the total amount returned by Cumulative Sum will be inserted into the TotalTransaction field on the destination document.

Value Mapping (Flattening)

Documents generated by applications may contain name/value pairs, such as the data stored in a dictionary object. You'll sometimes want to convert data in such a structure to a document specification that is more user friendly. The Value Mapping functoid can help make that conversion easier.

For example, suppose you have the following XML document that you want to convert into a FundInvestors document.

```
<FundInvestorsApp>
<Record1 Name="FundCompany" Value="Henry Fonda Inc."></Record1>
<Record2>
    <Record3 Name="InvestorName" Value="Fernando Rey"></Record3>
    <Record3 Name="Email" Value="frey@frenchconnection.com"></Record3>
    <Record3 Name="Action" Value="OpenAccount"></Record3>
</Record2>
<Record2>
    <Record3 Name="InvestorName" Value="Toshiro Mifune"></Record3>
    <Record3 Name="Email" Value="tmifune@highandlow.com"></Record3>
    <Record3 Name="Action" Value="OpenAccount"></Record3>
</Record2>
</FundInvestorsApp>
```

The investor information is presented as name-value pairs. To convert this type of document to your FundInvestors document specification, you need to combine two functoids: Equal and Value Mapping (Flattening).

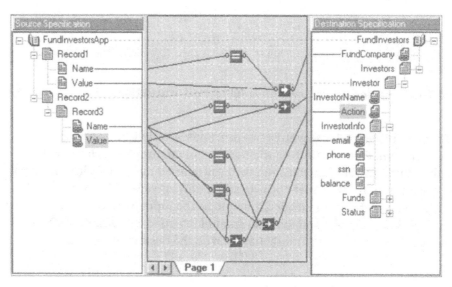

Figure 8-14. Using the Value Mapping (Flattening) functoid to map the data between two schemas

In this example, under Record3 in Figure 8-14, the Name field is connected to three Equal functoids. The properties of one of the Equal functoids is shown in Figure 8-15.

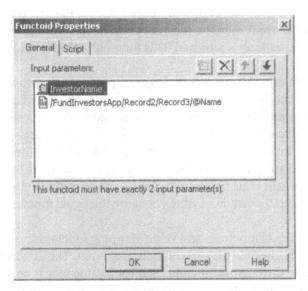

Figure 8-15. The properties for one of the Equal functoids

The purpose of this functoid is to verify whether the data in the Name field is equal to InvestorName. If it is, then the value "true" is returned to the Value Mapping functoid, which it connects to as its first parameter. If it isn't, then the value "false" is returned to the Value Mapping functoid as its first parameter. Now, let's take a look at what's in the Value Mapping functoid (see Figure 8-16).

Figure 8-16. The properties for Value Mapping functoid

The Value Mapping functoid takes two parameters. If the first parameter contains the value of "true", then the second parameter is returned from the functoid; otherwise, nothing is returned. This functoid acts as a kind of if-then statement.

The data for the Value Mapping functoid's two parameters comes from the Equal functoid and the Value field in the source document as shown in Figure 8-16. Then, the Value Mapping functoid's output is connected to the InvestorName field in the destination document. It works like this: When the Name field under Record3 is equal to InvestorName, the functoid takes the value of the Value field from under Record3 and plugs it into the InvestorName field of the FundInvestors document. If Name field value isn't InvestorName, but something else, then the Value Mapping functoid won't do anything because the Equal functoid will return "false".

The rest of the Equal functoids and Value Mapping functoids on the map will check whether the Name field fits each of their properties. This is why each Name field is connected to three Equal functoids and each Value field is connected to three Value Mapping functoids. This arrangement is similar to the statement "if . . . then, if . . . then, if . . . then".

Database Lookup and Value Extractor

Database access is almost certain to exist in any enterprise application. The need to access the database store is so prevalent that the BizTalk Server development team at Microsoft even added this ability to its mapping features. BizTalk Server offers three database-related functoids: Database Lookup, Value Extractor, and Error Return.

In the following example, the source document provides an investor ID instead of detailed information about the investors. All the detail information is stored in the database. In order to extract the detailed information and then insert it into the destination document, you need to deploy some database functoids. Here is a sample of the source document:

```
<FundInvestorsDatabase>
<FundCompany>Henry Fonda Inc.</FundCompany>
    <InvestorID>100</InvestorID>
    <InvestorID>101</InvestorID>
</FundInvestorsDatabase>
```

You have a data table on your system that stores the detailed information about each investor, such as the InvestorID, Investor Name, Phone number, etc. This data table will be accessed by the functoids on the map. The map between the two documents is shown in Figure 8-17.

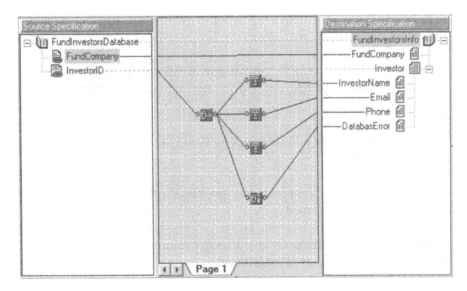

Figure 8-17. Database functoids extracting the detailed information from the database for the destination document

The mapping area contains five functoids: one Database Lookup functoid, three Value Extractor functoids, and one Error Return functoid. Let's take a look at the Database Lookup functoid first, which is connected to the InvestorID record on the source document. Its properties are shown in Figure 8-18.

Figure 8-18. Database Lookup functoid properties

The Database Lookup functoid has four input parameters, and they must be in the following order:

- *Value:* In the current example, this parameter will contain the investor ID from the document, which you'll use to find its matching record in the data table.

- *Connection string:* This is the connection string the functoid will use to access the database.

- *Database table name:* This parameter specifies the data table against which the search query is executed.

- *Column name:* This parameter identifies the column in the table that the Value parameter is expected to be found.

The Database Lookup functoid is connected with the three Value Extractor functoids, each of which represents one of the three fields in the destination document. The Value Extractor takes exactly two parameters (see Figure 8-19). The first is the ADO record returned by the Database Lookup functoid. The second is the name of the column in the returned record that contains the value for the destination document.

Figure 8-19. Value Extractor functoid properties

The Value Extractor functoid shown in Figure 8-19 will return the value in the InvestorName column of the ADO record that is returned from Database Lookup. The Value Extractor functoid sends this value to the InvestorName field in the destination document.

The Error Return functoid is used to output any database error information. It takes only one parameter, Database Lookup, which is automatically added when the two functoids are connected. If a database error occurs, the Error Return functoid will return the error information, which can be inserted in the destination document.

To test this map, select Tools ➤ Test Map ➤ Instance XML to XML. The output document should now contain the detailed investor information from the database:

```
<FundInvestorsInfo>
<FundCompany>Henry Fonda Inc.</FundCompany>
<Investor>
  <InvestorName>Fernando Rey</InvestorName>
  <Email>frey@frenchconnection.com</Email>
  <Phone>212-555-1515</Phone>
  <DatabaseError />
</Investor>
<Investor>
  <InvestorName>Toshiro Mifune</InvestorName>
  <Email>tmifune@highandlow.com</Email>
  <Phone>212-555-1516</Phone>
  <DatabaseError />
</Investor>
</FundInvestorsInfo>
```

Summary

In this chapter, you learned about additional data transport protocols supported by BizTalk Server, and about schema importing and exporting in BizTalk Editor. You also learned about the While shape in BizTalk Orchestration and several functoids that you can use in BizTalk Mapper to customize document conversions.

Although I've covered a huge amount about BizTalk Server so far in the book, there are still many advanced BizTalk Server features I haven't yet touched. In the next several chapters, I'll discuss these advanced features and their application by implementing a modified version of Bob's ASP application.

CHAPTER 9

Advanced BizTalk Messaging Features

IN PREVIOUS CHAPTERS, I've shown you how to build a robust B2B application, but BizTalk Server offers many features you haven't seen yet. In this chapter, I'll cover the advanced features of BizTalk Messaging. You'll learn about HTTP Receive Functions, open destination ports, open source channels, distribution lists, tracking features, reliable messaging, and BizTalk SEED packages.

Many of the features covered in this chapter require the basic knowledge of BizTalk Server that I covered in previous chapters. These topics will once again be presented in the context of Bob's ASP application and his continuous need to add new requirements and features to his application.

Using HTTP Receive Functions

Some time after Bob's ASP application has been set up, he arranges a meeting with Mike. Bob says "I've looked at our B2B application architecture, and I found that we have Active Server Pages installed on the same server as BizTalk Server, and it is open to the Internet. This makes our application too vulnerable. I've heard too many horror stories about hackers damaging banks and some well-known Web sites. I haven't been able to sleep well for the past week. Can we change our application so that our BizTalk Server isn't exposed to the Internet as it is now?"

Mike replies, "How about only exposing the Web server to the Internet, and deploying Active Server Pages on the Web server to make BizTalk Interchange submit DCOM calls to the remote BizTalk Server? We can also put a firewall between the Web server and BizTalk Server."

Mike continues, "We still need to open a bunch of firewall ports to allow the DCOM calls to pass through. It isn't a good security practice to have too many ports open on the firewall. After all, the firewall is supposed to eliminate open ports on a system. What can we do to solve this problem?"

One way to solve this problem is to use HTTP Receive Functions, which are new to BizTalk Server 2002. To understand how HTTP Receive Functions can help, let's look at how one would fit into Bob's ASP application (see Figure 9-1).

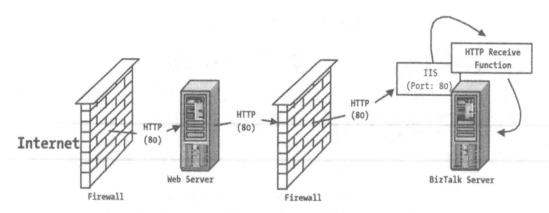

Figure 9-1. HTTP Receive Functions in Bob's ASP application

In Bob's application's new architecture, a firewall resides between the Internet and the Web server. Another firewall resides between the Web server and the BizTalk Server. Only port 80 is open on both firewalls. When a mutual fund company submits a document to Bob's Web server through port 80, the Web server will need to forward the HTTP post to BizTalk Server. Instead of making a DCOM call to BizTalk Server using the BizTalk interchange component, which requires many ports to be opened on the firewall, the Web server will simply make an HTTP redirect and post the client document to the BizTalk Server's IIS through port 80. BizTalk Server's HTTP Receive Function will detect the incoming document posted to IIS, and can pull it into BizTalk Server's work queue as it arrives.

In this kind of arrangement, you can configure the firewall between the Web server and BizTalk Server so that it only allows communications between the Web server and BizTalk Server. This will prevent hackers from establishing a direct link with your BizTalk Server and will significantly increase the resistance of your application to malicious attacks from the Internet.

Setting Up HTTP Receive Functions

Following along with this example, now that you'll be putting BizTalk Server behind the second firewall and using your Web server to redirect client documents to BizTalk Server, let's look at what you need to set up BizTalk Server to accept these HTTP posts and pull them into the BizTalk Server work queue for processing.

In Chapter 4, you saw some Active Server Pages (ASP) code. You can create a similar ASP page and deploy it on BizTalk Server's IIS. From within this ASP page, you can make local Interchange submit calls to bring the posted document into BizTalk Server.

It is certainly possible for you to create such ASP pages yourself, but BizTalk Server's HTTP Receive Functions provide a high performance ISAPI component that does the same thing. Also, the HTTP Receive Function is integrated in the BizTalk Server Administration Console, and it can be configured using a Receive Function properties page.

Three major steps are involved in setting up an HTTP Receive Function:

1. Set up the virtual directory that hosts the ISAPI DLL.

2. Configure the IIS COM+ package.

3. Create the HTTP Receive Function using the BizTalk Server Administration Console.

Step 1: Setting Up the Virtual Directory

When your Web server redirects the client's document to BizTalk Server, it will need to post the document to a specific file under a virtual directory on BizTalk Server. Therefore, you must first set up a virtual directory on the BizTalk Server.

To create a new virtual directory, open the Internet Information Service console on the BizTalk Server. Right-click the Default Web Site and select New ➤ Virtual Directory. Follow the steps on the Virtual Directory Creation Wizard to create a virtual directory.

When you are finished, right-click the newly created virtual directory and select Properties. The Properties page for the virtual directory will open (see Figure 9-2).

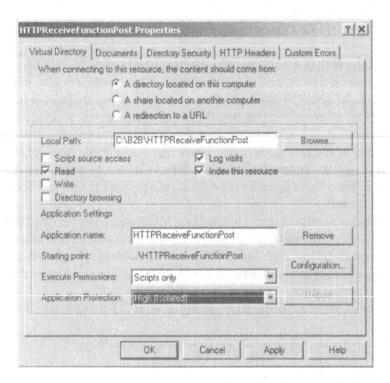

Figure 9-2. The Properties page for the virtual directory HTTPReceiveFunctionPost

Select the Virtual Directory tab of the Properties page, and under the Application Settings section change the Execute Permissions setting to Scripts and Executables. This setting enables the virtual directory to execute the ISAPI application hosted under it. You'll also need to change the Application Protection setting within the same section. Change it to High (Isolated). In the next section, I'll explain the difference between the three values: Low (IIS Process), Medium (Pooled), and High (Isolated). Click Apply to accept the changes.

In my case, I have my virtual directory pointing to C:\B2B\HTTPReceiveFunctionPost on the BizTalk Server, as you can see in Figure 9-2. However, there is no file under this directory. Since you want to host an ISAPI DLL in your virtual directory, you need to copy the DLL that is used by the HTTP Receive Function to this directory. BizTalkHTTPReceive.dll is the ISAPI DLL that the HTTP Receive Function uses, and it is located under the [BizTalk installation directory]\HTTP Receive\ folder. Copy it to the physical file folder that the virtual directory is pointing to.

Step 2: Configuring the IIS COM+ Package

Now let's move on to the configuration of the IIS COM+ package. Open Component Services under Administrative Tools (see Figure 9-3).

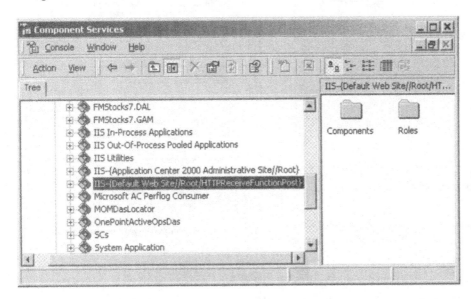

Figure 9-3. IIS COM+ package for your virtual directory

There are three types of COM+ applications associated with IIS, and they correspond to the three application protection levels that can be defined for the virtual directory you just created. To better understand what this Application Protection setting means, let's first look at the role the application protection levels play in IIS.

When a Web application is created with Low (IIS Process) as its application protection level, requests for the Web application are performed under the InetInfo.exe process. All Web applications that are configured as Low (IIS Process) will be running under the same InetInfo.exe process (indicated as IIS In-Process Application shown in Figure 9-4), so if one Web application under this process crashes, it will crash the whole process, and IIS will be unable to process any request to any Web application. Web applications running under this protection level are faster than they can be in other protection levels, but they can also inflict the most damage to IIS.

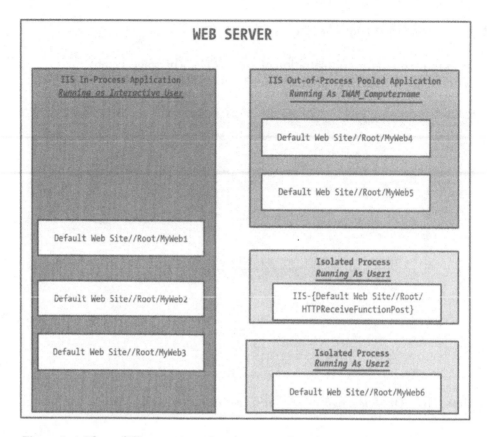

Figure 9-4. Three different types of processes under which a Web application can run

When a Web application is created with Medium (Pooled) as its application protection level, requests for the Web application are performed outside the InetInfo.exe process. All Web applications that are configured as Medium (Pooled) will be running under the same Dllhost process (indicated as IIS Out-Of-Process Pooled Application in Figure 9-4), hence the use of the term "pooled." When one Web application under this process crashes, it will crash the whole process and make all Web applications under this process unusable. However, Web applications under IIS In-Process will not be affected, since it is a totally separate process (indicated as IIS Out-of-Process Pooled application in Figure 9-4).

This protection level is slower than the Low (IIS Process) protection level, since there will be data marshaling between InetInfo.exe and Dllhost.exe. (Data marshaling occurs when method calls pass across process boundaries—in the case of a Web server, data marshaling occurs when page requests are passed between InetInfo.exe and the hosted application in Dllhost.exe.) This Dllhost runs under the IWAM_Computername account by default and is subject to change through the Component Services window. This Dllhost is located under Component Server under the name of IIS Out-Of-Process Pooled Applications.

The third protection level is High (Isolated). When a Web application is configured with this protection level, requests for this Web application will run under a separate Dllhost process, and no other Web application will be running under this process. In other words, a Web application with a high protection level will run in its own dedicated process—one process per application. When such an application crashes, it only crashes its own Dllhost, and no other Web application is affected. This protection level is the slowest, but it offers the most protection to other Web applications on the server. This Dllhost process runs under the IWAM_Computername account by default, and it can be changed through the Component Services window. For each Web application with a high protection level, there is a COM+ application hosting its Dllhost. The COM+ application is located under Component Services and has a name beginning with "IIS-{Default Web Site//Root/ . . . }" and ending with the name of the virtual directory created for the purpose—in this case, the name is IIS-{Default Web Site//Root/HTTPReceiveFunctionPost} (see Figure 9-3 earlier).

Step 3: Creating the HTTP Receive Function

Once you've created the virtual directory, in this case, HTTPReceiveFunctionPost, it's time to create an HTTP Receive Function that watches this virtual directory for any posted documents.

To create an HTTP Receive Function, open the BizTalk Server Administration Console, right-click the Receive Function node, and then select New ➤ HTTP Receive Function. An Add an HTTP Receive Function window will open (see Figure 9-5).

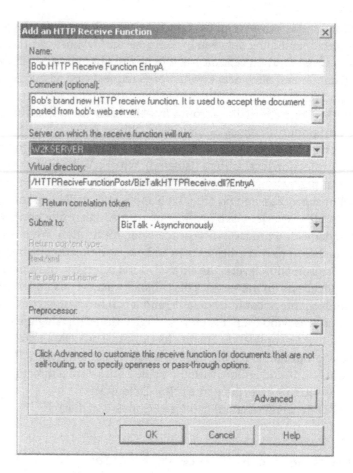

Figure 9-5. The Add an HTTP Receive Function window

There are couple of properties in this window that deserve some explanation. First is the Virtual directory property. You need to specify the location of the BizTalkHTTPReceive.dll file in the following format:

```
/[virtual directory]/BizTalkHTTPReceive.dll?[querystring]
```

In the example in Figure 9-5, the location is as follows:

```
/HTTPReceiveFunctionPost/BizTalkHTTPReceive.dll?EntryA
```

The "/" (slash) at the beginning of the URL (the preceding file path) indicates the default Web server root. The query string (EntryA, in this example) at the end of the URL allows you to create multiple HTTP Receive Functions that reference one BizTalkHTTPReceive.dll. For example, you can create two separate HTTP Receive Functions named Bob HTTP Receive Function EntryA and Bob HTTP Receive Function EntryB. Their virtual directory properties would be /HTTPReceiveFunctionPost/BizTalkHTTPReceive.dll?EntryA and /HTTPReceiveFunctionPost/BizTalkHTTPReceive.dll?EntryB, respectively. If a client posts the document to the URL that ends with "?EntryA", the first Receive Function will be triggered. If the same client posts the document to the URL that ends with "?EntryB", the second Receive Function is triggered, even though both URLs refer to the same ISAPI DLL. In other words, it is possible to invoke different Receive Functions by varying the query string of the URL.

The second property that is specific to the HTTP Receive Function is the Submit to property. It instructs the Receive Function what to do with the posted document. Three options appear in the drop-down list for this property:

- *BizTalk Server - Asynchronously:* The HTTP Receive Function will send the posted document to the BizTalk Server work queue with the Interchange.submit() call.

- *BizTalk Server - Synchronously:* The HTTP Receive Function will use the Interchange.submitsync() call to send the posted document to the BizTalk Server work queue. (I'll discuss the difference between the submit() and submitsync() method calls in Chapter 11.)

- *File:* The HTTP Receive Function will save the posted document to a file location. When you select this option, you must provide additional information in the "File path and name" property.

For Bob's application, you need to set the submit method to BizTalk Server - Asynchronously.

Once you have done this, click the Advanced button to open a window in which you can provide routing information for this HTTP Receive Function. The advanced properties page for Receive Functions are all identical. You'll set up the properties for this Receive Function the same way you did for the IncomingMSMQ Receive Function you created in Chapter 4 (see Table 9-1).

Table 9-1. HTTP Receive Function Settings

NAME	VALUE
Receive Function name	Bob HTTP Receive Function EntryA
Pooling location	/HTTPReceiveFunctionPost/BizTalkHTTPReceive.dll?EntryA
Submit method	BizTalk Server - Asynchronously
Source organization qualifier	OrganizationName
Source organization identifier value	<None>
Destination organization qualifier	OrganizationName
Destination organization identifier value	Home Organization

With the HTTP Receive Function completed, you can test it to see if it yields the results you expect. Open the HTTP post utility, specify http://localhost/HTTPReceiveFunctionPost/BizTalkHTTPReceive.dll?EntryA in the URL field, and click Post. You will probably get a "500 internal error" message because the HTTPReceiveFunctionPost Web application is running under an account that doesn't have permission to access the BizTalk Messaging database.

NOTE   *The HTTP post utility is my VB program that contains methods allowing you to easily open an HTTP connection and post data to a URL. This utility was discussed in Chapter 4, and the source code is located in the Downloads section on the Apress Web site (*http://www.apress.com*).*

To make our Web application run as a different account, open the Component Services window, and then open the Properties page for IIS-{Default Web Site//Root/HTTPReceiveFunctionPost} (see Figure 9-6).

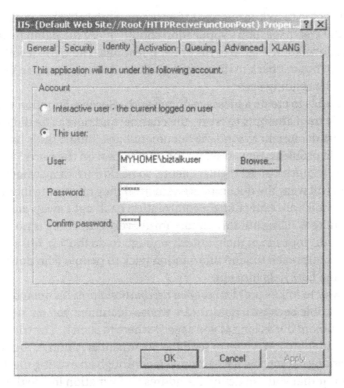

Figure 9-6. Changing the identity for the COM+ application used by the example Web application

The default user is IWAM_Computername, and you need to change this specification to a user who has full access to the BizTalk Messaging database. Make this change and click OK.

After saving this change, you should get a "200 OK" response when you resubmit the document again. If you have your XLANG Event Monitor turned on, you should see an XLANG Schedule start in a short while.

Assume this HTTP Receive Function has worked as expected, and Mike is happy with the result. He sets up a meeting with Bob to report what has been done, and he gets a new assignment.

Using Open Destination Ports

Bob wants to set up a new client inquiry page on his Web site. This page will allow potential customers to specify what information about Bob's ASP application they would like to receive. The questions can be business questions, such as these: What type of business is this ASP? How does it work? How much does it cost? Or they may be technical questions involving technical documents or document specification information. After the potential client completes the inquiry on the Web page, Bob's application should query the database and retrieve all information related to his or her questions. Then, the resulting document needs to be sent back to the potential client. Bob wants to use BizTalk Server to do the sending part.

Mike decides to create a message queue and a Receive Function to watch the queue. He then attempts to create the channel and port as he did for the FundInvestors document to send the document back. But he finds himself running into a big problem: How to set up the destination on the port? The people who send the inquiries aren't regular clients, so he doesn't know what reply address they will want the document sent to until they fill out the inquiry form online. These folks are expecting the information back right away, and there could be hundreds filling out this inquiry form every day. There is no way Mike can create a port for each of them quickly enough to do the job. Mike has to come up with a new approach to send information back to people who don't have an account set up. Let's help him out.

The answer to Mike's problem is *open destination ports*. An open destination port is very flexible because it doesn't care whose document you are sending; it will send the document out as long as you specify where to send it. The trick is telling the open destination port where to send the document at runtime. You still have to provide an address somehow if it isn't provided through an existing message port.

It turns out that you can define the address information inside the document. The open destination port can extract this address information and send the document accordingly at runtime. As you saw in Chapter 4, in order to provide BizTalk Server with the destination information for a document, you must specify which field in the document holds this information. This is done with the document's dictionary property. When the document arrives at an open destination port, this port will look at the destination value information in the document. The open destination port will accept the destination value as the address information and send the document out.

To summarize, you must do three things to get the open destination port to work:

1. Create an open destination port.

2. Define a field as the destination value in the document's dictionary properties.

3. Tell BizTalk Server that this document is intended for an open destination port rather than a traditional port when the document is brought into the work queue by the interchange component or a Receive Function. If you don't explicitly tell BizTalk Server what type of port the document is heading for, the destination value will be considered to be the organization name instead of the actual address.

First, create a messaging port using BizTalk Messaging Manager. Select Open destination as shown in Figure 9-7. When you click the Open destination radio button, you will not be able to select a destination organization. The open destination port isn't associated with any organization. Click Next until you finish with the wizard.

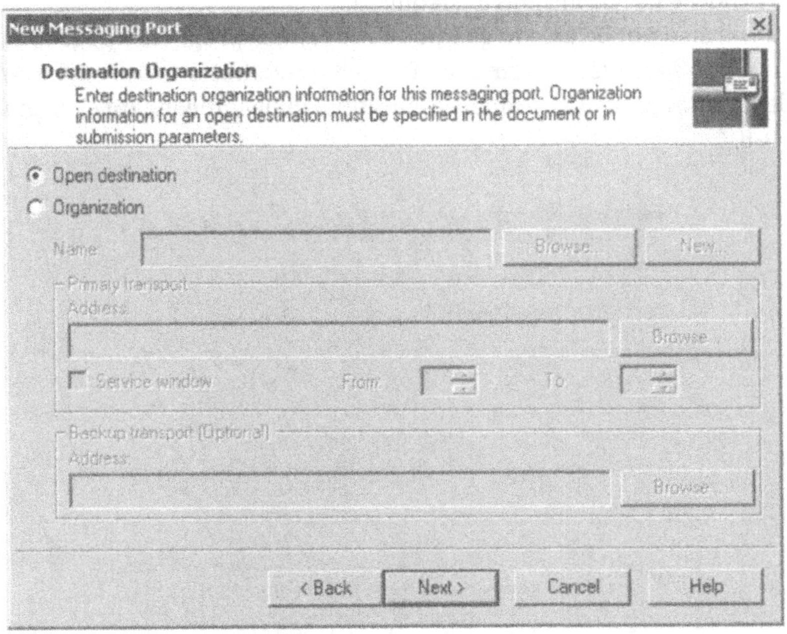

Figure 9-7. Creating an open destination port

Next, you need to make sure your document contains a destination field that holds the destination address, such as "http://www.client2.com/post.asp" or "mailto:client1@client1.com". You need to set this field as the destination value in the document's dictionary properties.

Last, when you set up a Receive Function to pull such a document into BizTalk Server, you need to tell BizTalk Server that this document is headed to an open destination port. To do that, set the Openness property at the top of the Receive Function's properties page to Open destination. This will tell BizTalk Server that every document pulled from this location goes to an open destination port. If you use the Interchange submit method, you will need to set the first parameter, which indicates the value of Openness, to BIZTALK_OPENNESS_TYPE_DESTINATION, or 4. If you use the Receive Function to submit the document, you will need to set the Openness option on the advanced properties page of that Receive Function.

An important thing to remember about open destination ports is that they will not allow you to encrypt the document, because each document is sent to a different organization and address, and BizTalk Messaging has no knowledge of the destination organization or what certificate to use at runtime to encrypt any given document. For the same reason, open destination ports can't send a document to an HTTPS site that requires mutual authentication, since BizTalk Server wouldn't know what certificates are required.

You will also not be able to go into the advanced properties page to set additional configuration information for a channel that is connected to an open destination port. The Properties button will become inactive, as shown in Figure 9-8.

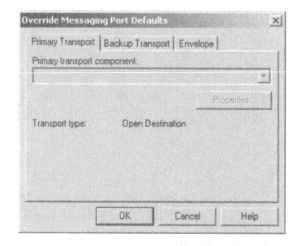

Figure 9-8. The advanced properties page will not be available if an open destination port is used.

BizTalk Server locates channels for self-routing documents differently than for other documents. Because the destination embedded in the document is actually the physical destination address (as opposed to the organization's name), BizTalk Server can't locate the channel based on information in the document alone. (There is no destination organization, and this is one of the three pieces of information needed to locate a channel). Instead, you must notify BizTalk Server that the document is intended for an open destination port so that BizTalk Server can search on all the channels that connect to "Open destination" as their destination organization. To do so, you must set the Openness setting to Open destination or 4 on the Receive Function or Interchange submit parameter, respectively. That way, when the self-routing document is picked up, BizTalk Server will have enough information about the destination of the document to locate the correct channel.

NOTE *Only a "To an Organization" port can be set as an open destination port. If you create a "To an Application" port, you must provide the destination information on the port.*

Using Open Source Channels

The concept of an open source channel is similar to that of an open destination port. The open source allows you to route documents from multiple sources to one destination. In some situations you'll care where the document is going but not where the document is from.

Bob changes his mind about how a client inquiry should be processed. Automatically generating information that potential clients request, and sending it back, and expecting them to come back for business is really poor salesmanship. Bob wants to give each potential client some personal attention when it comes to providing information. Bob wants to have all the information sent to him by e-mail, so he can then analyze the data from the potential client to come up with a good sales pitch targeting him or her. He'll then personally call the potential client to sell his product. Bob has asked Mike to fix it so that all the inquiries will be sent to him by e-mail.

This is a good place to implement an open source channel, because Mike really doesn't care what organization each inquiry is from. All Mike wants to do is send each message to Bob's mailbox.

To do this for Mike, create an SMTP port that points to Bob's e-mail box. Then create a channel to the port, and set the channel type to Open source, as shown in Figure 9-9.

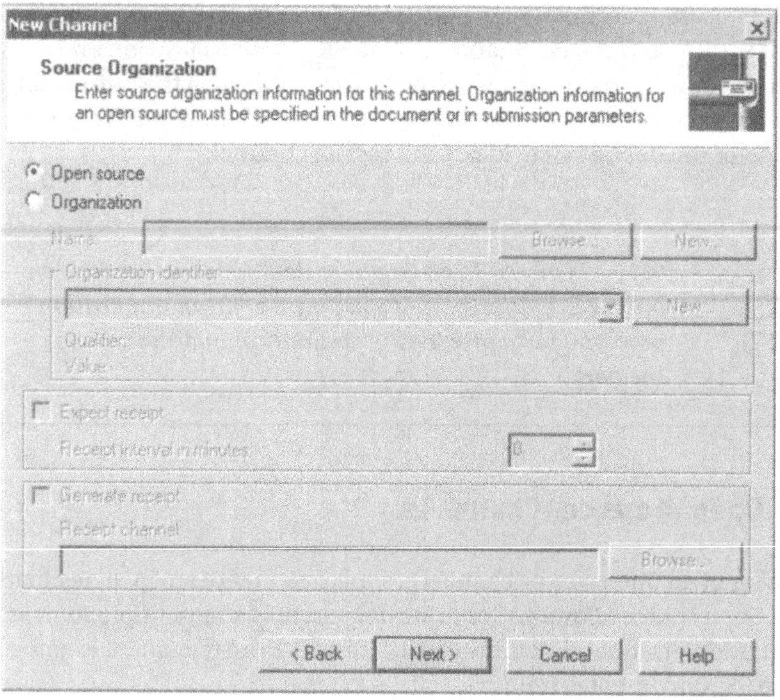

Figure 9-9. Creating an open source channel

When you set the channel to Open source, you will not get to set the source organization. You still, however, need to provide a document type for the channel, and you'll have an opportunity to apply the map file. As in the case of the open destination port, you also have to set the openness type to Open source on the Receive Function that is used to pull the document into BizTalk Server.

When using the Interchange submit method, set the first parameter to BIZTALK_OPENNESS_TYPE_SOURCE, or 2, to indicate that the document is submitted through an open source channel. BizTalk Messaging will apply the same rule described previously to locate the channel for the open source document, except the source organization is considered to be "Open source". If a Receive Function is used, make sure the Openness setting on its advanced properties page is Open source.

If Bob later decides that other types of documents should be sent to him regardless of where they come from, all you need to do is attach a new open source channel to the same SMTP port that is pointing to Bob's e-mail box and specify the inbound document type for the channel. BizTalk Server will automatically locate the right open source channel based on the type of incoming document. You could use the same code and Receive Function created for the first open source example.

Using Distribution Lists

As much as Bob would prefer giving personal attention to his clients on business matters, he has decided to send most of the less important information to his clients electronically. Providing information such as the server maintenance schedule, company news, and upcoming events over the phone can be tedious and time consuming. Bob wants to send such generic information to all of his clients electronically so that he can get more sleep. Unfortunately, Bob has stolen the sleep from Mike. Now Mike has to come up with an application that allows this generic information to be sent to each of Bob's clients.

By this time, Bob's BizTalk Server is servicing a total of 25 clients. Things are looking up. Mike has created a program to pull information from the database and generate a document type called BobNewsLetter. Normally, if Mike needs to send a document to a client, he would create a channel and attach it to the outgoing messaging port for this client—for example, Mike would create a channel called C_BobNewsLetter_Outgoing_HenryFonda and attach it to P_Outgoing_HenryFonda so that the document could be sent to Henry Fonda Inc. However, this time Mike feels a little overwhelmed. As more and more customers join the service, Mike feels the workload of having to create so many channels and ports. He wants to find an easier way to do this.

There is, in fact, a better way to send generic documents to all of Bob's clients—a distribution list. With a distribution list, Mike needs to only create one channel instead of 25 to send the document to all of Bob's clients. Let's come to Mike's rescue once more by investigating how distribution lists can save so much work.

When you define a distribution list, you need to provide the names of the ports that are on this list, such as P_Outgoing_HenryFonda. In order for a document to arrive at a port on the distribution list, you must also define a channel for the distribution list in the same way you do for a regular port. When a document comes out of this channel, it will be forwarded to every port on the distribution list. As you can see in Figure 9-10, you only need to include one port on the distribution list and one channel to achieve what Bob has asked.

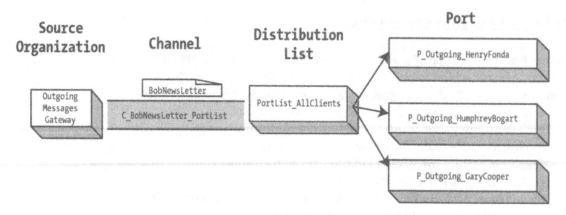

Figure 9-10. The distribution list forwards the document to multiple ports.

To create a distribution list, open BizTalk Messaging Manager, click Distribution lists in the left panel, and then click Search. Right-click the empty space in the right panel and select New Distribution. The New Distribution List window will open, as shown in Figure 9-11.

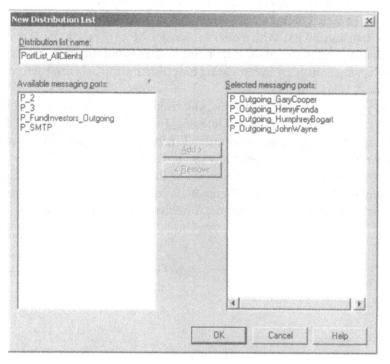

Figure 9-11. Creating a distribution list for the ports

Select the outgoing ports that are responsible for actually sending the document from the Available Messaging Ports list and click the Add button in the middle to add them to the Selected Messaging Ports list. Click OK to save the changes.

Next, you must create a channel for the distribution list. Right-click the PortList_AllClients distribution list in BizTalk Messaging Manager and select New Channel ➤ From an Organization. Create a channel with the settings shown in Table 9-2.

Table 9-2. Distribution List Channel Settings

NAME	VALUE
Channel name	C_PortList_BobNewsLetter_AllClients
Source organization	Outgoing Messages Gateway
Inbound document	BobNewsLetter
Outbound document	BobNewsLetter

If you open the advanced properties page for the newly created channel (see Figure 9-12), you can overwrite the settings for each port on the list. The settings you make through this override window will only affect the documents that arrive at these ports through the distribution list.

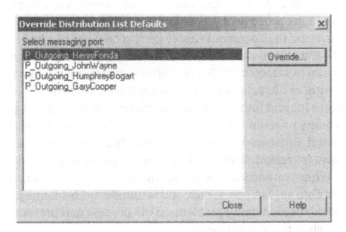

Figure 9-12. Overriding the settings on each individual port on the distribution list

When you select a port in the Override Distribution List Defaults window and click the Override button, the Advanced properties page for that port will open. You can then configure the way the document is sent after arriving at this port through the distribution list.

To route the document to this distribution list, you must specify the channel the distribution list is associated with. In this case, you can either specify the channel parameter on the Interchange submit method, or specify the name of the channel on the Receive Function.

With the newly created distribution list, Mike can easily send a copy of Bob's newsletter to every client on the list. Through the distribution list, Mike can also specify who will receive the document simply by adding or removing ports to and from the distribution list.

NOTE *Open destination ports can't be added to a distribution list because open destination ports don't contain a destination as part of their configuration. The distribution list depends on the destination information from each port's configuration settings.*

Tracking Documents

So far, you've seen a lot of things BizTalk Server does, but what happens when something goes wrong? What happens when a client sends a document, but the document doesn't get processed? Whose fault is it? Did the client really send the document, or did the document simply get lost because of a bug in your application? Or if the document did get processed, whose fault is it if the data inside the document is incorrect? Did the original document contain incorrect data to begin with, or did your application simply get it wrong?

The ability to log and track every document that passes through an application and to query on them is very important. People are less forgiving when money is involved. Businesses such as banks and financial firms have the most strict procedures for recording every piece of information that is involved in a transaction. When transactions are made online, as in a B2B scenario, a system that can record data as it arrives, leaves, and is transferred from one process to the next is critical for identifying problems in the process and preventing legal complications when problems do arise.

BizTalk Server's document tracking ability provides you with an out-of-the-box solution for recording data at various stages of processing. It also provides a Web interface that allows you to query and examine a particular document as it flows through BizTalk Server.

Bob wants his ASP application to be able to track documents. He brings this challenge to Mike: "I want to add some tracking functionality to our application.

I want to be able to track every single document. I also want to be able to search for documents we have logged. And I want to do some business analysis on these documents. For instance, I want to find out who is making the most transactions, dollarwise. Can we do that?"

We certainly can. There are different levels of tracking in BizTalk Server:

- *Interchange-level tracking:* An *interchange* in BizTalk Server is a submission that contains one or more document instances. This means you can put multiple documents into one interchange and submit it to BizTalk Server, and every document inside the interchange is tracked.

- *Channel-level tracking:* This type of tracking allows you to track a document that is sent through a specific channel. It also gives you the freedom to track only specific types of data. There are situations in which you'll want to track a document as it arrives from a client, and you can track that kind of data by turning on the tracking feature on the specific channel that brings that data into BizTalk Server. In some situations data is simply transferred from one location to another location internally, and you don't need a copy of such data, so you can turn off the tracking on those channels.

- *Document field-level tracking:* With the interchange-level and channel-level tracking, the document content is stored in BizTalk Server's Tracking database, but there is no way to associate a document with the data values inside the document. If you want to find out which document has a total transaction amount (which is one field in a document) greater than a million dollars, you would have to examine the content of each document, one by one, to find out which has a greater total transaction amount. This is very counterproductive. With document field-level tracking, you can specify certain fields inside the document to be pulled out and tracked, in conjunction with the document. When you want to retrieve a document with a specific field value, BizTalk Server will query on the tracked document fields for the matching values and then retrieve the documents that are associated with those data fields. You can specify data fields inside the document on a global basis as well as on a channel-by-channel basis.

When a document is tracked, there are two types of information saved to the BizTalk Tracking database. The first type is routing data about this document, such as the source and destination organizations, when the document was processed, etc. The second type of data is the document's content. You can access both types of information using a Web-based tool called BizTalk Document Tracking, which I'll discuss in more detail later.

Bob doesn't really know what kind of data he wants to track, so he tells Mike to track every document just to be safe. Mike decides to go with interchange-level tracking.

Configuring Interchange-Level Tracking

Before you implement any tracking features, you must first turn on tracking for the BizTalk Server group. Open the BizTalk Server Administration Console, and open the properties page for the BizTalk Server Group. Select the Tracking tab (see Figure 9-13).

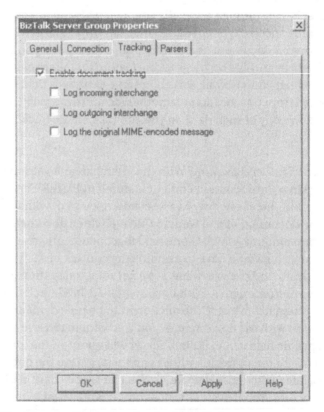

Figure 9-13. Tracking configuration for the BizTalk Server group

The Tracking tab contains four checkboxes. The Enable document tracking checkbox turns on tracking for this BizTalk Server group. You need to check this checkbox. If this checkbox isn't checked, no documents will be tracked in this BizTalk Server group regardless of the settings for channel-level tracking and document field-level tracking.

The next three checkboxes specify the type of data you want to track. Checking the Log incoming interchange checkbox will track all the interchange submissions before they go through the channel. Checking the Log outgoing interchange checkbox will track all the interchange submissions coming out of the channel. And when a client's interchange is encrypted and digitally signed, you can check the Log the original MIME-encoded message checkbox to track the original document before it is decrypted and its signature information is removed. By storing this original copy, which contains the digital signature, you'll have real proof that the data was sent by the client, since no one can change digitally signed data except its owner.

In this case, you only need to log the incoming and outgoing interchanges. You don't want to log the original MIME-encoded message because the content inside the documents isn't encrypted or signed when it reaches the BizTalk Server (you're using SSL to handle the decryption and signature verification).

With these settings, all the interchange information will be tracked, along with the document routing information, which is always available as long as you check the Enable document tracking option. Because you'll also log the incoming and outgoing interchanges, BizTalk Server will store a copy of every interchange that goes through the system.

Accessing Tracked Information

For now, assume channel-level tracking and document field-level tracking isn't turned on, and let's see what BizTalk Server's tracking system stores when a client document arrives and is processed. Open the HTTP post utility and submit a FundInvestors document. When the whole process is complete, you can look at what BizTalk Document Tracking has recorded.

Open the BizTalk Document Tracking tool by selecting Start ➢ Programs ➢ BizTalk Server 2002 from the menus (see Figure 9-14). BizTalk Document Tracking is a Web-based tool you can use to search the tracking data in the BizTalk Tracking database.

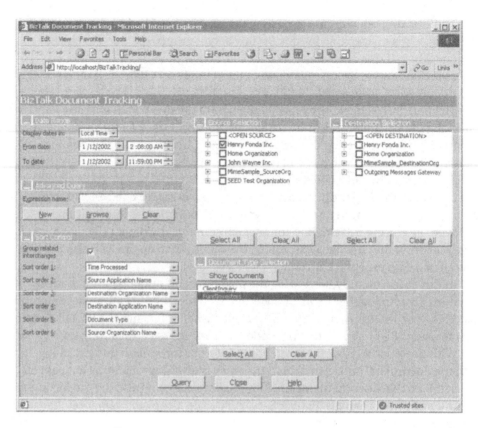

Figure 9-14. BizTalk Document Tracking application

 NOTE   *If you are getting the message "This page accesses data on another domain. Do you allow this?" always click the Yes button. To permanently get rid of this message, you must add your http://localhost to the trusted site list. Select Tools ➤ Internet Options from the Internet Explorer menus, select the Security tab, and then select the Trusted Sites icon. Click the Sites button to add your http://localhost to the list.*

With BizTalk Document Tracking, you can search for a logged document based on the source organization, destination organization, and document type, as shown in Figure 9-14. You can also filter the results by time and change the sort order of the results.

When you have set the search criteria, click the Query button to start the search. A Query Results window will be displayed, containing the search results (see Figure 9-15).

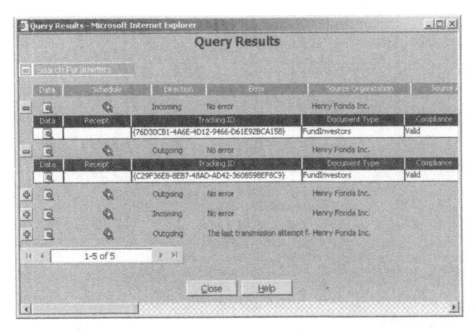

Figure 9-15. Query results for a tracking search

The Query Results page provides both routing data and document content for the matching interchanges. Each interchange is represented by a record with a + (plus sign) icon beside it. Routing information, such as the source organization, destination organization, etc., is associated with each interchange.

To look at the interchange data, click one of the notepad icons (the icon shows a notepad with a magnifying glass) in the first column next to the + icons. A View Interchange Data window containing the content of the interchange will be displayed. In this example, it contains the sample FundInvestors document submitted through the HTTP post utility (see Figure 9-16).

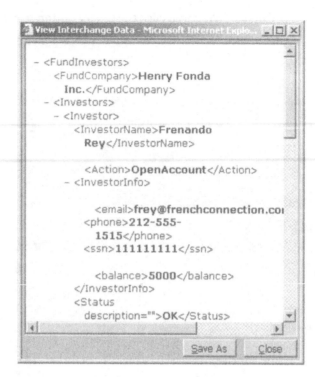

Figure 9-16. The content of an interchange submission can be viewed by clicking the notepad icon.

When you click one of the + icons and expand the entry, the tracking information for the documents in the interchange is returned. In this example, there is only one document in our interchange submission. The tracking information for the document includes the document type, tracking ID, validation error, etc.

A similar notepad icon appears at the beginning of the tracking information. If you click it, a new window will open, but no data is shown in the window. This is because you only specified tracking for the interchange when you set the configuration in the BizTalk Server Administration Console. In order to track the document instances inside a interchange, you would have to configure tracking on the channel that the document flows through.

Using Channel-Level Tracking

To configure the tracking of each document on the channel level, open the properties page of a channel, as shown in Figure 9-17.

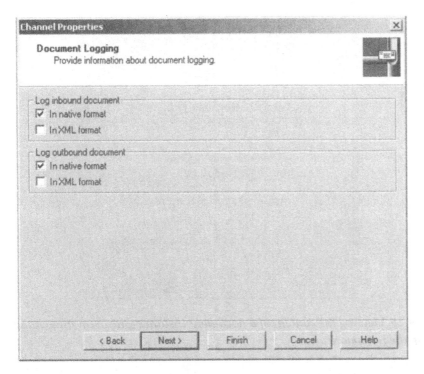

Figure 9-17. Document logging properties on the channel level

For every messaging channel, there are four formats of document you can track: The content of both inbound and outbound documents can be stored in either native format or XML format. In Figure 9-17, I have set tracking to log the inbound and outbound documents in native format.

Apply these settings to the C_FundInvestors_Outgoing_HenryFonda channel and resubmit the document with the HTTP post utility. Once you've done that, run the BizTalk Document Tracking program again and query the tracking information for the document you just submitted. On the Query Results page, expand the + icon for the tracked interchange, and then click the notepad icon that represents the document instance within the interchange. The View Document Instance Data window will be displayed again, but this time it will contain the content of the document that passed through the C_FundInvestors_Outgoing_HenryFonda channel (see Figure 9-18).

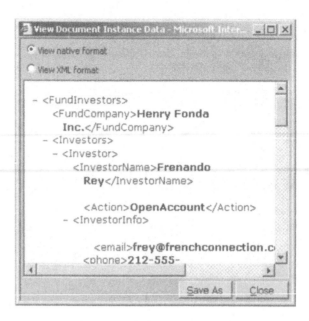

Figure 9-18. Viewing the content of a document instance within an interchange by clicking the notepad icon

As you can see in Figure 9-18, two radio buttons are located at the top of the window. Because you have only chosen to track the document in native format on the channel's properties page, you'll get a message saying "data not available" when you choose to view the XML format.

NOTE *Figure 9-18 shows XML format because the data is an XML document; native format for an XML document is still XML format.*

BizTalk Server tracking enables you to track documents on both the interchange level and channel level. When you enable interchange tracking through the appropriate properties page setting on the BizTalk Server group, every single interchange that goes through the system will be tracked. You only need to check two checkboxes to configure this type of tracking, and it is very easy to maintain. However, the negative side of interchange-level tracking is that there is no way for you to selectively turn off tracking for certain interchanges if it isn't necessary. Logging every interchange indiscriminately will adversely affect system performance, especially when the documents are quite large, due to excessive database writing. You can reduce the tracking overhead by turning off logging for both incoming and outgoing interchanges and instead enabling document logging on the channels where the tracking is indeed necessary for business purposes. For instance, you could track only two documents: the incoming documents on the channel that brings in the data to BizTalk Server, and the outgoing document on the channel that sends out the data to clients. You could disable the logging of documents that come through other channels. That way, you can selectively track the documents that have the most business value and keep the performance overhead to a minimum.

NOTE *The maximum supported size limit for a document submitted to BizTalk Server is 20MB in Unicode. When the document is in ASCII code, then it should not exceed 10MB, since BizTalk Server will convert it to Unicode first, which will double the original size. Documents that are larger than the supported limit may not be processed properly if the document is unable to be saved to the database within the database timeout limit. Document logging involves significant database writing, so it is recommended that you turn off document logging for very large documents to reduce its effect on system performance.*

Using Document Field-Level Tracking

When you log a document in the BizTalk Tracking database, BizTalk Server stores a copy of the document. So far, though, I haven't shown you a convenient way to search on the content of the logged document. Let's take a look at field-level tracking, which provides a way to extract certain data fields inside the document and make them available during the document search.

There are two places where you can specify the fields in a document you want to track. The first one is document global tracking, and it is defined during the configuration of the document specification. Open BizTalk Messaging Manager, open the properties page of an existing document definition, and click the Global Tracking tab (see Figure 9-19).

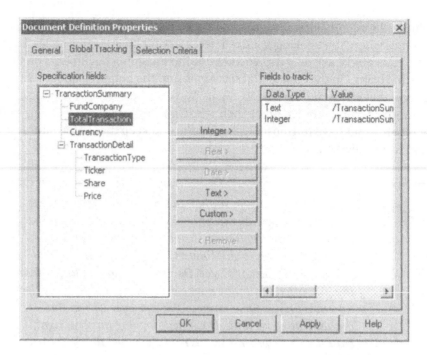

Figure 9-19. Global Tracking properties for the document definition

In the Global Tracking tab, select an existing data field in the Specification fields list, and click the button in the middle that matches its data type. This will move the data field to the Fields to track list. Unfortunately, you can't select more than two data fields with the same data type. If you want to track more data fields, you'll need to use the Custom type, which can be used for any data type and doesn't have a limit on how many data fields can be tracked.

When you set the global tracking property for a document type, BizTalk Server will extract the value in the document's global tracking fields and associate these values with the document instance. When you want to search on the document in the Tracking database later, you can define a query on these global tracking fields, and any document instance associated with matching field values will be returned.

To see this in action, configure the TransactionSummary document's global tracking properties as shown in Figure 9-19. You want to track the FundCompany data field and the TotalTransaction data field. Once you have done that, submit three TransactionSummary documents to BizTalk Server as follows:

Submission 1:

```
<TransactionSummary>
  <FundCompany>Henry Fonda Inc.</FundCompany>
  <TotalTransaction>2500</TotalTransaction>
  <TransactionDetail>
  <Currency>US Dollar</Currency>
    . . . . . . . . .
  </TransactionDetail>
</TransactionSummary>
```

Submission 2:

```
<TransactionSummary>
  <FundCompany>Henry Fonda Inc.</FundCompany>
  <TotalTransaction>1500</TotalTransaction>
  <TransactionDetail>
  <Currency>UK Pound</Currency>
    . . . . . . . . .
  </TransactionDetail>
</TransactionSummary>
```

Submission 3:

```
<TransactionSummary>
  <FundCompany>Gary Cooper Inc. </FundCompany>
  <TotalTransaction>3000</TotalTransaction>
  <TransactionDetail>
  <Currency>US Dollar</Currency>
    . . . . . . . . .
  </TransactionDetail>
</TransactionSummary>
```

After you've submitted these three documents, open BizTalk Document Tracking. Under the Advanced Query section, click the New button. This will open the Advanced Query Builder window shown in Figure 9-20.

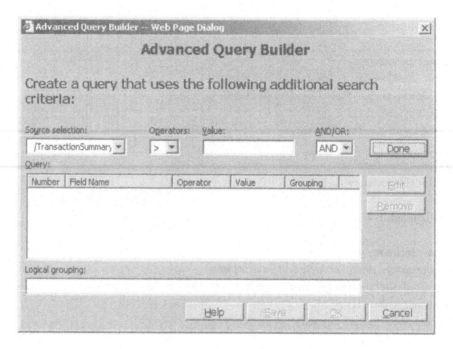

Figure 9-20. Advanced Query Builder allows you to create queries against the tracked fields inside a document.

The Source selection field contains a list of tracked fields defined in the document specification on the system. Select /TransactionSummary/TotalTransaction (Integer) from the list box, and then select the greater than operator (>) in the Operators list box. Enter 2000 in the Value text box, and then click the Done button to add these settings to the Query list box.

Now you have a query that will return document instances from the Tracking database that meet the condition of /TransactionSummary/TotalTransaction > 2000. You can also use the AND/OR list box to assemble a condition that consists of many source/field selections, as you would do in a SQL statement, such as " . . . where A=B and C=D or E=F".

Click the Save button at the bottom of the window, and enter an expression name for the query in the dialog box that opens. For this example, name the query "Transaction amount over 2000", and click OK to finish.

To run the advanced query you just created, click the Browse button in the Advanced Query section. A window that lists all the existing advanced queries on the system will open (see Figure 9-21).

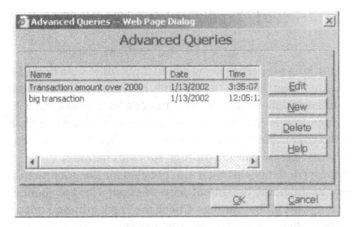

Figure 9-21. A list of existing advanced queries on the system

Select the Transaction amount over 2000 expression name and click the OK button to return to the main window (shown earlier in Figure 9-14). Then click the Query button at the bottom of the main window to view the result of this query.

In this case, you should receive a result containing four records. Two of them are incoming and outgoing TransactionSummary documents from Henry Fonda Inc., and the other two are from Gary Cooper Inc. You also entered another submission from Henry Fonda Inc, but it isn't returned by the query because the TotalTransaction field in that document is 1500.

To see that the returned document is indeed the one you're looking for, you can check the values stored in the tracked fields. When you examine the tracking information, you'll see columns with name of data types, as shown in Figure 9-22. These are the tracked fields that BizTalk Server has extracted for that document instance. In this case, String 1 is Gary Cooper Inc. and Integer 1 is 3000. These values correspond to the FundCompany field and TotalTransaction fields specified on the document's global tracking properties page.

Integer 1	Integer 2	Date 1	Date 2	String 1
3000				Gary Cooper Inc.

Figure 9-22. The tracked fields show on the Query Results page

Overriding Field-Level Tracking for Specific Channels

A document's global tracking properties allow you to track some data fields for certain documents as they pass through the channel. However, you may sometimes want to track different data fields than the ones defined in the Global Tracking properties page. In this case, you can override the document's global tracking settings on the channel level so that BizTalk Server will track different data fields for documents that are passing through specific channels.

To track a different set of data fields than are specified for the document's global tracking, open the Incoming document properties page for the channel where you want to change the global settings. Check the Track inbound document checkbox, and then click the Tracking button next to it. A Tracking for Inbound Document window will open (see Figure 9-23).

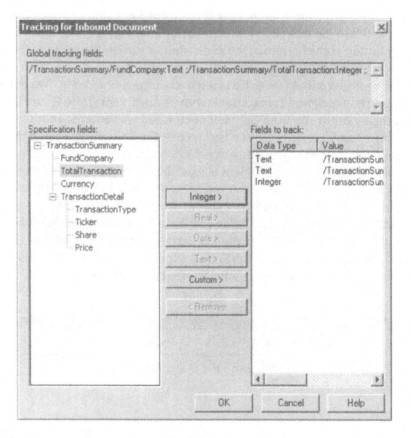

Figure 9-23. Overriding the global tracking fields on the channel by configuring the tracking properties for the inbound document

The Tracking for Inbound Document window is similar to the document's Global Tracking tab. The difference is that this window contains a text box that shows the existing global tracking fields defined for this type of document. To override these global tracking settings, simply add data fields to or remove them from the Fields to track list on the right. Whatever appears in the Fields to track section will be the data fields BizTalk Server tracks in the document that passes through this channel. In other words, this tracking list (on the channel level) overrides the tracking list defined in the document's global tracking properties.

For this example, you'll track the FundCompany, TotalTransaction, and Currency fields of the incoming document. Click OK. After you save the configuration on the channel, you need to define a new advanced query to return the documents whose Currency field is US Dollar, like this: \TransactionSummary\Currency = US Dollar.

When you run this new query, you'll get only two documents on the Query Results page: one incoming and one outgoing document from Henry Fonda Inc. Of the three documents you submitted, two have a Currency value of US Dollar. However, because you configured the incoming document field tracking on the channel that is associated with Henry Fonda Inc., you won't see the document from Gary Cooper Inc. on the Query Results page, even through the document from Gary Cooper also has US Dollar as the Currency field value. Without the tracking setting on the channel, BizTalk Server will not be able to extract the Currency field values from the document and associate them with documents that fit the condition \TransactionSummary\Currency = US Dollar.

 NOTE *BizTalk Server only tracks the first occurrence of a value for document fields that are specified for tracking. If a record inside a document appears more than once, only the field values from the first record are tracked.*

Using Reliable Messaging

Bob receives a number of calls from his clients complaining they've been receiving several duplicate documents, and the duplicate data has caused major trouble on their databases. Some investors complain that their purchase order of 500 shares of Enron had somehow turned into purchases of 1000 shares, which hurt them badly. Bob asks Mike to resolve this duplicate document problem, and to achieve once-and-only-once delivery for documents.

In Chapter 7, you learned about the BizTalk Messaging envelope. You can store the document-parsing information inside the envelope when the document being transmitted isn't an XML document. The other use for the BizTalk Messaging envelope is to support *reliable messaging*.

The goal of BizTalk Server's reliable messaging is once-and-once-only delivery of the document in a heterogeneous environment across the Internet. To fully appreciate the concept of reliable messaging, let's reexamine the part of Bob's ASP where the documents are sent out to clients through HTTP(S). This is achieved by configuring a messaging port that uses HTTP(S) and points to the client's URL, where the document will be posted.

BizTalk Messaging transmits the document by performing an HTTP post to the client's URL and waiting for the return of response code 200 or 202. If BizTalk Server receives either of these response codes, it will consider the document delivered successfully. If BizTalk Server receives an error response such as "500 Internal Error", or "401 page not found", it will attempt to resend the document according to the retry configuration on the messaging port. BizTalk Server will put the document on the suspended queue if all the retries are exhausted and it is still unable to get a either a 200 or 202 response code.

Things are pretty straightforward, right? However, this is the ideal scenario for sending a document through the Internet. In some situations BizTalk Server doesn't receive any response code at all after posting the document to the client's URL. HTTP isn't a reliable protocol. There is no guarantee that a message will reach its destination in a timely manner.

Other reasons may prevent BizTalk Server from receiving a response code. For example, perhaps the client's system or network is shut down right after it received the document but before a response code was sent out. How can you be sure whether the document reached the destination successfully? The chance of this type of situation occurring is small, but you must consider it, especially when a network is slow or many documents are sent at once. Such scenarios can cause application latency on both the sending and receiving end and can increase the probability of lost response codes.

BizTalk Server approaches this problem by treating the documents that don't have response codes returned from clients in the same way as documents that result in a bad response code. In other words, if there is a bad response code or a missing response code, BizTalk Server will move the document to the retry queue after the timeout limit is reached. BizTalk Server will resend the message until the retry limit is reached. By increasing the number of retries, the chance of a missing response code decreases significantly. Keep in mind that BizTalk Server knows how to handle documents that result in either success or failure response codes. The purpose of retrying a document that results in a missing response code is to make it result in a received response code.

BizTalk Server can eliminate the missing response code document by retrying the same document multiple times. However, using multiple retries when there are missing response codes (when you don't know whether the document was accepted by the client or not) means that clients may accept the same document more than once.

This is where BizTalk reliable messaging envelopes come in. As you saw in Chapter 7, envelopes contain a lot of metadata, such as document-parsing instructions. However, unlike the envelopes used to carry document-parsing information, BizTalk reliable messaging envelopes contain information that uniquely identifies a particular instance of a document.

When a document is sent using the reliable messaging envelope, BizTalk Server will generate a SOAP envelope and store some metadata in it. The most important information in the SOAP header is a field called "identity", which contains a unique ID in this format: "uuid:xxxxxxxx-xxxx-xxxx-xxxx-xxxxxxxxxxxx". BizTalk Server will make sure that this unique ID is the same for each retry.

When BizTalk Server sends a document with the reliable messaging envelope to a client, the client must watch for this field and add this ID to a log when the document is successfully received. For every document that carries the reliable messaging envelope, the client must check whether the identity field contains a number that already exists in its log. If it does, the client simply discards the message, and no harm is done. Figure 9-24 illustrates this process.

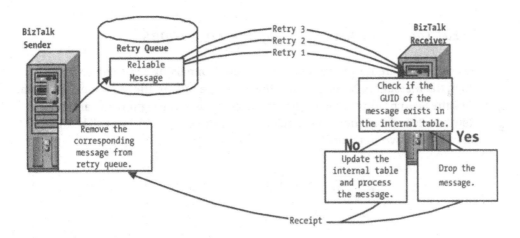

Figure 9-24. The BizTalk Server reliable messaging concept

The actual implementation of reliable messaging is a bit different, but its principle is as I just described. In reality, BizTalk Server first puts every message marked for using a reliable messaging envelope in the retry queue. When the message is sent to the client, the sender's reply-to URL is embedded inside the envelope header. The client will send the receipt to the sender's reply-to URL after it successfully receives the document—the receipt is another message that looks like the original reliable message, except it doesn't contain the original document in its SOAP body. The value in the original document's identity field is also copied to the identity field in the receipt, and when BizTalk Server (the document sender) receives this receipt from the client, it will remove the document from the retry queue that contains the identical identity field. There is no reason to retry the message if the client has already got it. If a receipt that contains a document's ID has not arrived after the last retry, BizTalk Server will move that document to the suspended queue.

Don't worry if you don't get the whole idea just yet. It'll make more sense after I show you how to implement reliable messaging in BizTalk Server.

There are three things you need to do to implement reliable messaging:

- Create a reliable messaging envelope.

- Configure BizTalk Server (document sender) to attach the envelope with each outgoing document.

- Configure BizTalk Server (document receiver) to accept the document with the reliable messaging envelope.

Creating Reliable Messaging Envelopes

You can easily create a reliable messaging envelope using Messaging Manager. Open the Messaging Manager, click the Envelope link on the left panel, and then click the Search button. Right-click the white area of the right panel and select New Envelope from the pop-up menu. A New Envelope window will be displayed, as shown in Figure 9-25.

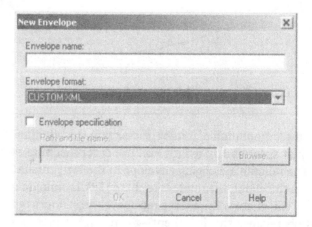

Figure 9-25. Creating a new envelope with Messaging Manager

Change the Envelope format from CUSTOM XML to RELIABLE, and then enter a name for this envelope, such as MyReliableEnv. That's it. You have just created a reliable envelope. Impressive, isn't it?

Configuring the BizTalk Server (Document Sender) to Support Reliable Messaging

The next step is to configure the BizTalk Server (document sender) to use this reliable messaging envelope when it sends out the messages to external parties. There are two steps involved in this task:

1. You must configure where BizTalk Server (document sender) expects to receive the receipt from the document receiver.

2. You must bind the reliable envelope to the messaging port that you want to use to send out the reliable messages.

For the first step, open the BizTalk Server Administration Console, and open the BizTalk Server Group Properties page. Set the "Reliable messaging reply-to URL" option to a Web location that contains a script that can process the receipt. Figure 9-26 shows an example of such a configuration, where Server.myhome.com is the BizTalk Server (document sender), and ReliableMsgReceipt.asp is the script file that processes the receipts. This script file is provided by Microsoft and can be found under [BizTalk Installation folder]\SDK\Messaging Samples\ReliableMessaging\.

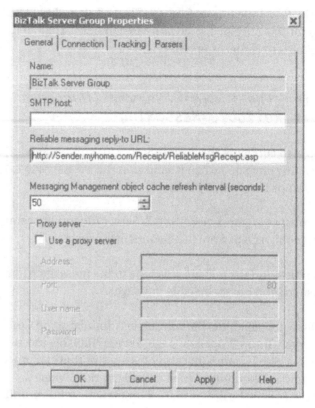

Figure 9-26. Setting the reply-to URL

NOTE   *This reply-to URL must be accessible from the document receiver because the document receiver will send the receipt to this address. Therefore, you shouldn't use "localhost" as the host name for this URL.*

BizTalk Server can receive receipts over multiple protocols, such as File, SMTP, MSMQ, and HTTPS. The formats of the reply-to URL start with "file://", "mailto:", "queue://Direct=OS:<servername>\<queuename>", and "https://", respectively.

For the second step, you need to configure the message port to use the envelope as documents come out of it. Open a messaging port's properties page under the Messaging Manager, and click Next until you reach the Envelope Information window shown in Figure 9-27.

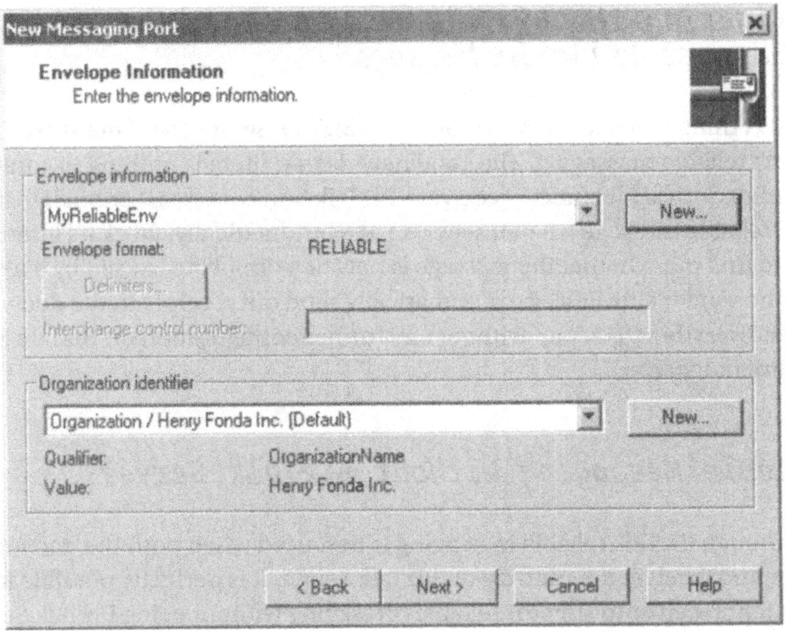

Figure 9-27. Configuring the envelope information on the messaging port

Select MyReliableEnv from the drop-down list to enable reliable messaging for this messaging port. You also need to configure the retry count on the channel that connects to this messaging port to a value greater than zero. The retry count determines how many document retries BizTalk Server will wait for before moving the document to the suspended queue if no receipt is received by that time. This retry count must be set to a number greater than zero for reliable messaging to work properly.

NOTE   *If a reliable messaging envelope isn't used on the messaging port, the retry count can be set to any number.*

Configuring the BizTalk Server (Document Receiver) to Support Reliable Messaging

The next thing you need to do is configure BizTalk Server (document receiver) to support reliable messaging. The good news is that there is nothing to configure on BizTalk Server (document receiver). BizTalk Server is smart enough to recognize a reliable message when it sees one. It'll automatically check its internal table to find out whether the message is new or a duplicate caused by a retry from the sender side. It'll also automatically send out receipts to the document sender. Everything is set up without any further configuration on BizTalk Server (document receiver).

Reliable Messaging Without BizTalk Server

Even though BizTalk reliable messaging is best used when both the document sender and receiver are running on BizTalk Server, it is perfectly possible for the document receiver to support reliable messaging without using BizTalk Server. You may want to use reliable messaging to enforce the once-and-once-only delivery, but you don't want to force your business partners to use BizTalk Server for the sake of reliable messaging. In such a case, each business partner must have an application that understands BizTalk reliable messaging on their end.

Creating such an application requires developers to basically replicate the processes that occur on BizTalk Server for dealing with reliable messages, such as determining whether a message is a duplicate, sending the receipt back to the document sender, and so on. In order to implement this functionality yourself, you need to refer to the BizTalk Framework (BTF) 2.0 specification. This specification describes how the SOAP envelope is constructed by BizTalk Server, and the use of each element inside the envelope. You can find out more about this specification on Microsoft's Web site: `http://microsoft.com/biztalk/techinfo/framwork20.asp`.

Reliable Messaging Example

Before I end the discussion of reliable messaging, let's take a look at a reliable message. Figure 9-28 shows a sample reliable message (displayed in Internet Explorer for easy viewing).

```
<?xml version="1.0" ?>
- <SOAP-ENV:Envelope xmlns:SOAP-ENV="http://schemas.xmlsoap.org/soap/envelope/"
    xmlns:xsi="http://www.w3.org/1999/XMLSchema-instance">
  - <SOAP-ENV:Header>
    - <eps:endpoints SOAP-ENV:mustUnderstand="1" xmlns:eps="http://schemas.biztalk.org/btf-2-
        0/endpoints" xmlns:biz="http://schemas.biztalk.org/btf-2-0/address/types">
      - <eps:to>
          <eps:address xsi:type="biz:OrganizationName">Henry Fonda Inc.</eps:address>
        </eps:to>
      - <eps:from>
          <eps:address xsi:type="biz:OrganizationName">Outgoing Messages
            Gateway</eps:address>
        </eps:from>
      </eps:endpoints>
    - <prop:properties SOAP-ENV:mustUnderstand="1" xmlns:prop="http://schemas.biztalk.org/btf-2-
        0/properties">
        <prop:identity>uuid:A004D514-E729-491E-A03A-26E3608F41F9</prop:identity>
        <prop:sentAt>2002-09-10T18:51:41+00:00</prop:sentAt>
        <prop:expiresAt>2002-09-10T18:55:41+00:00</prop:expiresAt>
        <prop:topic>root:FundInvestors</prop:topic>
      </prop:properties>
    - <services xmlns="http://schemas.biztalk.org/btf-2-0/services">
      - <deliveryReceiptRequest>
        - <sendTo>
            <address
              xsi:type="biz:httpURL">http://Sender.myhome.com/Receipt/ReliableMsgReceipt.asp</address
          </sendTo>
          <sendBy>2002-09-10T18:55:41+00:00</sendBy>
        </deliveryReceiptRequest>
      </services>
    </SOAP-ENV:Header>
  + <SOAP-ENV:Body>
  </SOAP-ENV:Envelope>
```

Figure 9-28. A sample reliable message

The SOAP-ENV:Header section contains all the necessary information for a BizTalk Server (document receiver) to process the reliable message. For instance, <prop:identity>uuid:A004D514-E729-491E-A03A-26E3608F41F9</prop:identity> uniquely identifies this message, and <sendTo><address xsi:type="biz:httpURL">http://Sender.myhome.com/Receipt/ReliableMsgReceipt.asp</address></sendTo> specifies where the document receiver will send back the receipt. The actual content of the document (the FundInvestors document) is stored in the <SOAP-ENV:Body> elements (collapsed for ease of viewing).

NOTE   *If a document with a reliable messaging envelope is moved to the suspended queue due to a transmission error (if, for example, the receiver didn't return a receipt in time or the receiver is down for a while), you can't simply resubmit such a document in the BizTalk Server Administration Console as you would for a document without a reliable messaging envelope. This is because the reliable messaging envelope contains an <expiresAt> element that will be examined at the time of the resubmission. If the value of <expiresAt> exceeds the current time, which is almost always the case, BizTalk Server will omit the resubmission and leave the message in the suspended queue. To resubmit the document for reliable messaging, you must extract the SOAP body from the message, and send it through the channel to resubmit it again. This means that you must either perform some extra manual steps or create a program to extract and submit it to the channel automatically.*

Using the BizTalk SEED Package

"We have a working prototype for the FundInvestors document, so I would like to get our mutual fund clients to start sending and receiving the document," Bob says to Mike. "Several of our clients are also using BizTalk Server to process documents—is there any feature in BizTalk Server 2002 that can help them get their system ready to exchange documents with us easily?" Turns out I've got the answer to Bob's question: SEED.

SEED is a new addition to BizTalk Server 2002. B2B applications are about exchanging documents, so all the participants in a B2B system must make sure their systems are ready to exchange documents. SEED provides a convenient way to help business partners set up their systems to exchange documents with minimum effort. The business partners must use BizTalk Server for exchanging documents to be able to take advantage of what SEED offers.

Requirements for Sending and Receiving Documents

In order to help Bob's business partners make their system ready, you need to make their systems capable of sending a document to you and receiving a document from you.

First let's take a look at what it takes to make their systems ready to send you a document (see Figure 9-29).

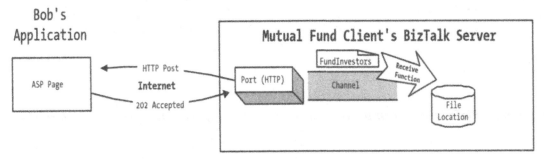

Figure 9-29. *BizTalk Server components involved in setting up a client to send documents*

When a client wants to send a FundInvestors document to you, they will need the following items set up:

- Organization that represents Bob's organization

- Messaging port that points to your Web entry point

- Messaging channel that connects to the port

- Document specification and definition for FundInvestors

- Receive Function to pull the data that is to be sent

Next, let's take a look at what items are involved for setting up a client's system for receiving a document (see Figure 9-30).

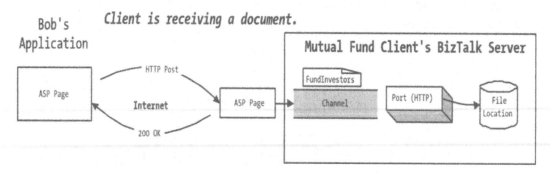

Figure 9-30. BizTalk Server components involved in setting up a client for receiving a document

When a client wants to receive the response document from you, that client will need the following items set up:

- ASP page to accept the posted document from you

- Organization that represents Bob's organization

- Messaging port that saves the response document to a file location

- Messaging channel that connects to the port

- Document specification and definition for the response document

Creating a SEED Package

Now let's look at how a BizTalk SEED package can help clients set up the necessary items for sending and receiving documents. Open the BizTalk SEED Wizard by selecting Start ➢ Programs ➢ BizTalk Server 2002. Figure 9-31 shows this wizard's Welcome page.

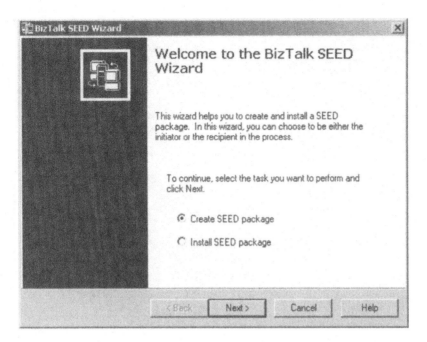

Figure 9-31. BizTalk SEED Wizard

You can use the BizTalk SEED Wizard to either create a SEED package or install a SEED package. Because you want to create a package for the client to install on his or her system, select Create SEED package and click Next. You will now see the wizard page shown in Figure 9-32.

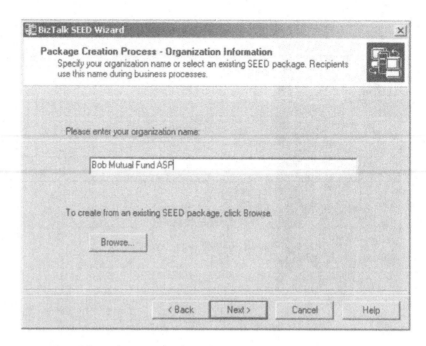

Figure 9-32. Providing the organization name

On this window, you specify the organization's name. This name will be used to create an organization on the client's BizTalk Server. The Browse button is used for selecting an existing SEED package for modification. Click Next to proceed, since you are creating a brand new package.

The next window contains a text box that lists the documents that currently exist in the SEED package. There is nothing in the text box, so click the Add button to add the document you want to exchange with the client. A Configure Document window opens, allowing you to configure the document (see Figure 9-33).

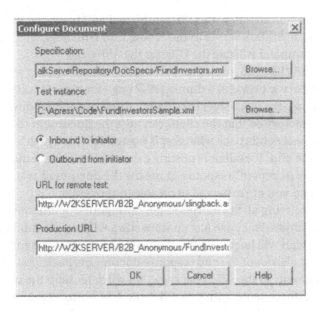

Figure 9-33. Configuring the inbound to initiator document and the URLs

There is quite bit of information in this Configure Document window, so let's look at the steps one by one. You first need to identify the document specification. Click the Browse button next to the Specification field and select FundInvestors from WebDAV. Next, you need to specify a test instance of the document that the clients can use to send back to you during the document exchange.

The two radio buttons indicate whether you'll receive this document from the client or whether you'll send it to the client. The term *initiator* refers to the system that is creating this package (in this case, the initiator is Bob's ASP application), so inbound to initiator means "inbound to Bob's ASP application." In other words, you are now configuring a document that will be sent to you from the client system. The Outbound from Initiator option refers to the response document Bob's ASP application will send to the client, and you'll configure it later.

The two URLs at the bottom of the window represent the Web addresses the client will post the document to. These two addresses will both be part of the package. During the testing phase, a client may choose to send the document to the URL for remote test. Later, if he or she deploys this SEED package to production, the production URL will be used to send the real document to you.

Therefore, you should enter the URL for the real ASP page that will bring the document into your BizTalk Server in the Production URL field.

In this example, I will use the URL for the ASP page http://W2KSERVER/B2B_Anonymous/FundInvestorsPost.asp as the production URL. BizTalk Server provides a dummy ASP page for remote testing called slingback.asp (under [BizTalk Server installation directory]\SEED directory). Copy it to a virtual directory so that the client can post the document to it. This ASP page is very simple—it sends back whatever is posted to it along with a "202 Accepted" response at the end. If a client is posting a document to the remote testing URL and gets a "202 Accepted" response, it means the document reached Bob's ASP application and you are expected to be able to process it.

After completing all the entries in the Configure Document window, click OK to save the changes. You have just completed specifying the inbound to initiator document, which will later help the client set up a system to send documents to you. Since you also want to send response documents back, you must add another document to the SEED package that will later help the client set up a system to accept documents from you. Click the Add button again to add another document to the SEED package. The same Configure Document window will appear (see Figure 9-34).

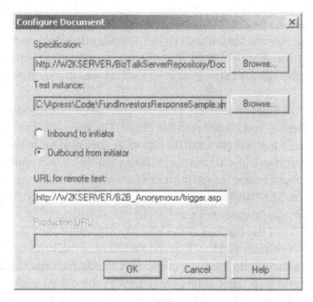

Figure 9-34. Configuring the outbound from initiator document and the URLs

As you did previously, you need to provide the document specification for the response document and a test document. Next, select the Outbound from initiator radio button, which indicates that the document is outbound from you; in other words, you are doing the sending this time.

Notice that the URL for the remote test is
http://W2KSERVER/B2B_Anonymous/trigger.asp. The file trigger.asp is another
file for testing a SEED package, and it can be found at [BizTalk Server installation
directory]\SEED directory. You need to copy it to the virtual directory where it
can be reached by clients.

You may be wondering why you need to specify an ASP page on your server.
Shouldn't it be an ASP page on the client's server? After all, you are the one who is
sending the document. To answer this question, you need to first understand
how testing is done using the SEED package. When a client tests the sending of
a document, all he or she needs is the URL to post the document to. The client
can post the document anytime. On the other hand, when the client is testing the
system for receiving a document, he or she can't initiate such a test. The client
depends on Bob's ASP application to send him or her the document. Normally, in
order for a client to test that part of the system, the client would call someone at
Bob's company and ask that person to send a document. However, it's better not
to have to depend on another for testing your application. The SEED package
comes with a solution that allows the client to initiate the sending of a document
from the other party.

It works like this: Let's say Henry Fonda Inc. wants to test whether their system is able to receive a response document from Bob's application. The SEED
Wizard first wraps the expected response document with a document envelope
containing a URL to an ASP page on Henry Fonda Inc.'s Web server, where it
expects the response document to be posted. Next, it sends this document to the
trigger.asp location on Bob's Web server. This trigger.asp file contains the code
that extracts the URL from the envelope and makes an Interchange submit call to
submit the response document to Bob's BizTalk Server through a channel named
BTMSeedTestChannel. This channel connects to an open destination port, and
the URL address that trigger.asp has extracted will be used as the destination.
Therefore, whenever Henry Fonda Inc. posts a document to trigger.asp, it will get
the same document (without the envelope) posted right back to the URL (on
Henry Fonda's Web server) that it specified in the document. This way Henry
Fonda Inc. can initiate a response document from Bob's ASP application.

NOTE *BTMSeedTestChannel and BTMSeedTestPort are the
channel and port installed during the BizTalk Server installation. These two items are hidden, so they aren't shown in
the BizTalk Messaging Manager. However, you will find that
they do indeed exist by looking into the bts_port table in the
InterchangeBTM database. The sole purpose of this channel
and port is to facilitate testing with the SEED package.*

Now, come back to the SEED Wizard. After you have completed the configuration for the outbound from initiator document, click OK to save the changes. You now have two documents in the package: one that is inbound and one that is outbound. Click Next to proceed.

In the next window, the SEED Wizard saves what you have configured into a package. Let's name this package FundInvestorsPackage.xml and click Finish. If there are no errors, you will receive a message saying the package has been successfully created.

Installing a SEED Package

You have just created a SEED package. The next step is for the client to install this package on his or her BizTalk Server. After the client receives this SEED package, he or she will need to open the BizTalk SEED Wizard on his or her BizTalk Server to install it.

Imagine you are on the BizTalk Server of Henry Fonda Inc. Open the BizTalk SEED Wizard, and select Install SEED package in the first page. Click Next to proceed. In the next page, you need to specify which package you want to install by clicking the Browse button and selecting the predefined SEED package (see Figure 9-35).

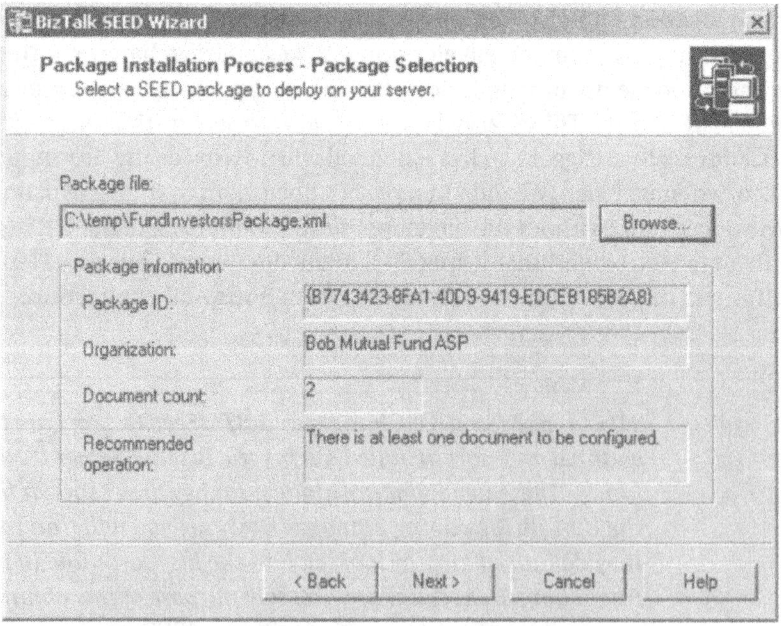

Figure 9-35. Installing the SEED package

The SEED Wizard extracts the value in the package and displays it in the window. It indicates that the package is from the organization Bob Mutual Fund ASP, and it contains two documents. Click Next.

The next window asks about the timeout value and interval value. If a large document is involved, you may want to increase the timeout to accommodate the longer time required to post a large document over the Internet. Click Next to proceed.

In the next window, you can configure the package and create all the necessary BizTalk Server items used for testing. After all the channels, ports, and Receive Functions are set up, you can also start testing both locally and remotely in this window (see Figure 9-36).

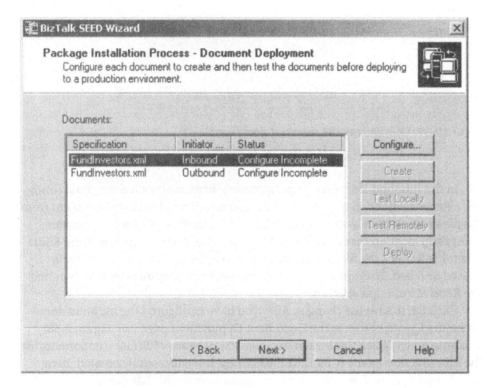

Figure 9-36. Document deployment process

Notice in Figure 9-31 that the status for the two documents in the package is Configure Incomplete. You must first configure these two documents before the SEED package can create the necessary BizTalk Server components for testing. To configure these two documents, select the inbound document, and click configure.

Select the inbound document in the Document Deployment page, and click the Configure button (see Figure 9-36). The Inbound Document (to Initiator) Configuration window will open (see Figure 9-37).

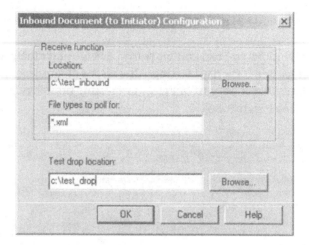

Figure 9-37. Configuring the inbound document

In the Inbound Document (to Initiator) Configuration window, you'll configure a Receive Function that will be used later to pull the inbound document from the file location to be sent to Bob's ASP application. You also need to provide a test drop location that will be used when you perform the local test. The SEED Wizard will check the file in this test drop location to determine if the test is passed or failed. This test drop location must be different from the location that the Receive Function watches.

Click OK to save the changes. After you have configured the inbound document, the Create button in the Document Deployment page (see Figure 9-36) becomes active. Click this button to create the necessary BizTalk components for the inbound document. After the SEED Wizard has successfully created them, you should find the following new components on the BizTalk Server:

- A messaging port called FundInvestorsPackage_FundInvestors pointing to file://c:\test_drop\FundInvestorsSample.xml.

- A messaging channel that connects to the preceding port.

- A Receive Function called FundInvestorsPackage_FundInvestors, with a polling location of c:\test_inbound*.xml. The channel name associated with this Receive Function is FundInvestorsPackage_FundInvestors.

After these BizTalk components have been installed, the status for the inbound document changes to Create Passed, and the Test Locally button becomes activated. Click the Test Locally button to start the local test.

The local test does the following: The SEED Wizard copies the sample inbound document in the package to the c:\test_inbound folder, and the Receive Function it has just created pulls the document and passes it to the FundInvestorsPackage_FundInvestors channel. When the sample document arrives at the FundInvestorsPackage_FundInvestors port, it is written to the c:\test_drop folder. The SEED Wizard then checks whether the sample document is successfully delivered to the c:\test_drop folder. If it is, the SEED Wizard concludes that the sample document it dropped to the file location has been picked up and delivered to the proper messaging port, and that the messaging port successfully delivered the document to its destination target. Therefore, the local test is considered successful. The status for the inbound document will become Local Test Passed.

After a successful local test, the Test Remotely button will become activated. Click this button to start a remote test. BizTalk Server first changes the destination for port FundInvestorsPackage_FundInvestors from file://c:\test_drop\FundInvestorsSample.xml to http://W2KSERVER/B2B_Anonymous/slingback.asp, which is what you specified during the creation of the SEED package earlier. Now, the SEED Wizard copies a sample document to c:\test_inbound folder, and a Receive Function picks it up and eventually posts the document to http://W2KSERVER/B2B_Anonymous/slingback.asp. The slingback.asp file (on Bob's Web server) returns the document and a "202 Accepted" response code. When the SEED Wizard receives this "202 Accepted" response code, it knows the document has reached the remote server and come back successfully. Therefore, it considers the remote test also successful. The status for the inbound document becomes Remote Test Passed, and the Deploy button becomes activated.

When you click the Deploy button, the SEED Wizard changes the destination of the port from http://W2KSERVER/B2B_Anonymous/slingback.asp to http://W2KSERVER/B2B_Anonymous/FundInvestorsPost.asp, which is the real production URL where posted documents will be processed by Bob's BizTalk Server.

After finishing the configuration, testing, and deployment for the inbound to initiator document, you do the same for the outbound from initiator document, which is the document that clients will receive from Bob's ASP. The steps are similar, but there is no deployment step as there is for the inbound document.

Select the outbound document in the Document Deployment page, and click the Configure button (see Figure 9-36). The Outbound Document (to Initiator) Configuration window, which contains two fields, will open (see Figure 9-38).

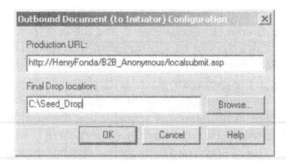

Figure 9-38. Configuring the outbound document

In the Production URL field, you need to specify the ASP page on your Web server that will accept documents posted by someone else. You then must specify a file location for the Final drop location setting. This drop location serves the same purpose as the Test drop location setting for the inbound document. Click OK to save the changes.

After you configure the outbound document, click the Create button to create the necessary BizTalk components. When this process is completed, the following BizTalk components will have been created:

- A messaging port called FundInvestorsPackage_FundInvestors_response 1, which points to file://c:\Seed_Drop\FundInvestorsResponseSample.xml

- A messaging channel called FundInvestorsPackage_FundInvestors_response 1, which connects to the port.

Once you have done this, click the Test Locally button. The SEED Wizard sends the sample document in the package to the FundInvestorsPackage_FundInvestors_response 1 channel. This sample document eventually ends up as a file under c:\Seed_Drop called FundInvestorsResponseSample.xml. The SEED Wizard then checks whether the document is indeed there, and if it is, it means that documents that arrive at the new channel will reach their target successfully. Therefore, the SEED Wizard considers the local test successful, and it deletes the file in the c:\Seed_Drop folder for the next test.

Click the Test Remotely button to start the remote test. The remote test is quite different from the local one. First, the SEED Wizard wraps the sample response document with an envelope and posts it to http://W2KSERVER/B2B_Anonymous/trigger.asp on Bob's Web server, which you configured for the outbound from initiator document when you created the

SEED package (refer to Figure 9-34). Inside the envelope is a field called RemoteURL that contains the value http://HenryFonda/B2B_Anonymous/localsubmit.asp (localsubmit.asp is located under [BizTalk Server installation directory]\SEED directory). Another field called Channel contains the value FundInvestorsPackage_FundInvestors_response 1. When trigger.asp accepts the post, it then submits it to a hidden open destination port (BTMSeedTestPort) on Bob's BizTalk Server. The RemoteURL field will be used as the destination of the open port.

BizTalk Messaging will then make a post to the URL http://HenryFonda/B2B_Anonymous/localsubmit.asp; localsubmit.asp contains codes that extract the value in the Channel field and then submit the document to that channel. The port connected to this channel writes the response documents to a file called FundInvestorsResponseSample.xml under the c:\Seed_Drop folder. The SEED Wizard then checks whether the file exists there. If it does, the SEED Wizard considers the remote test successful and deletes the file in the c:\Seed_Drop folder.

With the remote tests completed for both inbound and outbound documents, you just need to save the configuration of the SEED package by clicking Finish (see Figure 9-39).

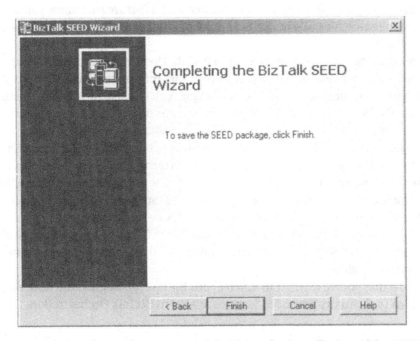

Figure 9-39. Saving the configuration and finishing the installation of the SEED package

You have just successfully installed the SEED package on Henry Fonda Inc.'s BizTalk Server. Whenever Henry Fonda Inc. wants to test the sending and receiving of documents with Bob's ASP, they can simply open the SEED Wizard, select Install SEED package, load the same package, and then start testing the inbound and outbound documents remotely or locally with a click of a button. They can also modify the configuration for the documents and test those documents with the SEED Wizard.

There is one more thing you have to remember to change. Henry Fonda Inc. should modify the localsubmit.asp for the production environment. Because Bob won't send response documents containing the channel name information, the code that extracts the channel name from the posted document should be replaced with the predefined channel that is used to bring the outbound from initiator document into Henry Fonda Inc.'s BizTalk Server.

Summary

You've seen many advanced BizTalk Messaging concepts in this chapter. You now know more about the HTTP Receive Function, and its configuration and applications. You also learned about the features of open destination ports and open source channels, which allow you greater flexibility when routing documents in BizTalk Server. Distribution lists are another useful feature that allow you to distribute the same message to multiple predefined destinations with minimal configuration.

You also got an in-depth look at the BizTalk Document Tracking Web application, which provides a powerful searching tool for tracking BizTalk Server data. Combined with document field-level tracking, you can use the BizTalk Document Tracking Web application to generate various reports based on the content of the documents, such as reports on documents that contain specific zip codes, or purchasing amounts that are greater than some predefined threshold number.

Reliable messaging is another BizTalk Messaging feature you learned about in this chapter, and it provides a great alternative to best-effort message delivery over the Internet. Reliable messaging's once-and-only-once delivery feature makes transmitting critical data over the unreliable Internet reliable.

Last, but not least, the BizTalk SEED package offers an easy way to quickly configure BizTalk Server and test data transmission on both the data sending and data receiving sides.

Now that you've learned so much about BizTalk Messaging, the next chapter will turn to the many advanced features related to BizTalk Orchestration.

CHAPTER 10

Advanced BizTalk Orchestration Features

In Chapter 9, you learned about some advanced features of BizTalk Messaging. In this chapter, I'll show you the many advanced features of BizTalk Orchestration: orchestration transactions, XLANG Schedule throttling, orchestration correlation, Web services in BizTalk Orchestration, orchestration dehydration, and so on. You'll continue to update Bob's ASP as you explore these features, because Bob always wants to add to his application.

Using Orchestration Transactions (Short, Long, and Timed)

In Chapter 5, you created an orchestration that processes the FundInvestors document. You used a Decision shape to determine whether your COM+ component completed successfully, but because the orchestration didn't have any transactional support, the actions that were performed couldn't be rolled back in the event of failure. Bob wants Mike to build a trading workflow that can process the buy and sell orders for the mutual fund companies, but he wants the trading XLANG Schedule to support transactions so that when an error occurs, any changes that have been made will automatically be rolled back to maintain the integrity of the data in the system. Let's take a quick look at transactions before tackling this assignment.

A *transaction* is a group of operations that are processed as a single unit. In the computer world, transactions follow these four rules, collectively known as the ACID rules:

- *Atomicity:* A transaction represents an atomic unit of work. Either all modifications within a transaction are performed, or none of the modifications are performed. In other words, if one job in the transaction fails, the work performed by the previous jobs in that transaction should be reversed as if nothing happened.

- *Consistency:* When a transaction is finished, whether committed or aborted, all the data must be in the proper state, with all the internal rules and relationships between data being correct.

- *Isolation:* Modifications made by one transaction must be isolated from the modifications made by other concurrent transactions. Isolated transactions that run concurrently will perform modifications that preserve internal database consistency exactly as they would if the transactions were run serially. In other words, all the data related to an ongoing transaction should be locked to prevent other transactions from interfering with this transaction.

- *Durability:* After a transaction has been committed, all modifications are permanently in place in the system. The modifications persist even if a system failure occurs. In other words, after the data in the transaction has been committed, any system failure shouldn't change the committed data in any way.

Types of Transactions

In BizTalk Orchestration, you can make your Action-shape implementations participate in a transaction in one of two ways: Run your XLANG Schedule as a traditional transactional COM+ component or as an XLANG Schedule transaction that is specific to BizTalk Orchestration.

When making an XLANG Schedule run as a COM+ component, external COM+ components can start such a XLANG Schedule as if it were a COM+ component. The transactional behavior of this type of XLANG Schedule is the same as a COM+ component.

To configure an XLANG Schedule to run as a COM+ component, open the properties page of the Start shape at the top of the workflow, and for the Transaction model field, select "Treat the XLANG Schedule as a COM+ Component" (see Figure 10-1).

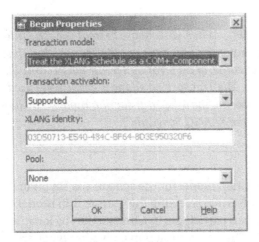

Figure 10-1. Configuring the transaction model for the orchestration

There are four transaction activation options available for this type of XLANG Schedule (which are the same as for COM+ components):

- *Not supported:* The schedule won't participate in the transaction. When the creator of the schedule aborts the transaction, the change made by the schedule won't be rolled back.

- *Supported:* The schedule will participate in the transaction of its creator, but it won't create one if its creator doesn't participate in a transaction. If its creator participates in a transaction, an abort in its creator will roll back all the actions performed inside the schedule.

- *Required:* The schedule will participate in its creator's transaction. If its creator doesn't participate in a transaction, the schedule will create a new transaction and make all the actions within the schedule participate in this transaction. An abort in its creator will roll back all the actions performed inside the schedule.

- *Required new:* The schedule will create a new transaction regardless of whether its creator already has a transaction. All the actions inside the schedule will participate in this new transaction created by the schedule. An abort in its creator won't roll back all the actions performed inside the schedule.

NOTE *When you choose to treat the schedule as a COM+ component, you can't use the Transaction shape on the schedule, or an error will occur when compiling the schedule. The Transaction shape is exclusively used when choosing the other transaction model ("Include transaction in the XLANG Schedule").*

The other transaction model for the schedule is "Include transaction within the XLANG Schedule". When selecting this transaction model, the actions within the schedule can participate in a transaction by locating them inside a Transaction shape. The four transaction activation types are also available for this transaction model.

When it comes time to choose which transaction model to use for your schedule, there are a number of factors to consider. In terms of performance, running the schedule as a COM+ component is much faster than using the other model. However, when running as an XLANG-style transaction, your schedule will be able to support Distributed Transaction Coordinator (DTC) style transactions, long-term transactions, timed transactions, and nested transactions. I'll discuss these transaction types later in this chapter. The COM+ transaction model only supports DTC-style transactions.

In fact, the Transaction shapes aren't even allowed in an orchestration unless the orchestration's transaction model setting is "Include Transaction within the XLANG Schedule" on the Begin shape. If the orchestration isn't configured this way and contains transactions, it will cause a compile error when you try to compile it into an .skx file.

NOTE *DTC provides services to manage transactions that span different transactional sources. COM+ replies on DTC for its transactional support. For example, by using DTC, a COM+ component can write to a database and MSMQ, two separate transactional resources, in a single transaction.*

With XLANG-style transactions, your schedule can also define actions to be taken in event of a transaction failure. This feature isn't available in COM+-style transactions. A schedule with XLANG-style transactions is shown in Figure 10-2.

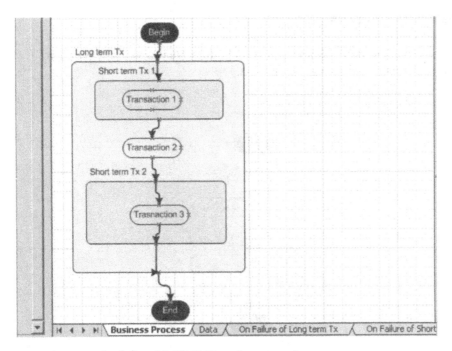

Figure 10-2. A schedule with XLANG-style transaction

To create a transaction inside another transaction, you need to first drag and drop a Transaction shape from the flowchart panel onto the Business Process page (which creates a new transaction), and then drag another transaction into the boundary of the first Transaction shape. You must make sure that all four sides of the second (inner) Transaction shape fit inside the four sides of the first (outer) Transaction shape, or the inner transaction won't be considered nested inside the outer one. To verify whether the transaction is nested properly, you can drag the outer Transaction shape around a bit—if the inner Transaction shape moves with the outer one, the inner transaction is properly nested. You can resize the Transaction shapes so that one can fit inside another.

NOTE *If you delete the outer Transaction shape, the inner transaction, along with the shapes inside it, is deleted as well. If you want to keep the inner Transaction shape, make sure you move the inner transaction outside of the boundary of the outer one, unnesting the inner one, before deleting the outer transaction.*

Short-Lived Transactions

Let's come back to Bob's trading XLANG Schedule. He wants the schedule to perform the actions shown in Figure 10-3.

Figure 10-3. Actions involved in Bob's trading schedule

Five actions are involved in this trade schedule:

- *Receive Doc:* This action receives the document from the client.

- *Pre-Trade Database Update:* This action will update the database to indicate that the buy and sell transactions inside the client document are being processed. The information in this database will be exposed to the Internet so that each client can check the status of his or her trade orders.

- *Execute Trade:* This action will start Bob's existing trading component, which will execute the trade order and return a document that contains information on the transaction, such as fulfillment of the trade, final price per share, etc.

- *Post-Trade Database Update:* This action will take the document returned from the trading component and update the status information on the client's trade order in the database.

- *Sending Trade Status Back:* This action will send the document returned from the trading component back to the client.

Bob already has a document specification for this schedule, named Trade, defined in XML editor (see Figure 10-4).

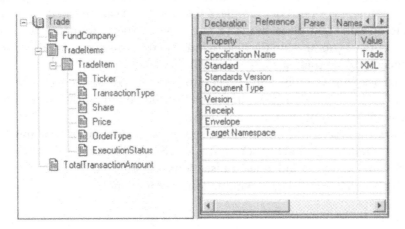

Figure 10-4. Trade document specification

A sample trade from a client would look like this:

```
<Trade>
  <FundCompany>Henry Fonda Inc.</FundCompany>
  <TradeItems>
    <TradeItem>
      <Ticker>IBM</Ticker>
      <TransactionType>Buy</TransactionType>
      <Share>10000</Share>
      <Price/>
      <OrderType>Market Order</OrderType>
      <ExecutionStatus/>
    </TradeItem>
    <TradeItem>
      <Ticker>MSFT</Ticker>
      <TransactionType>Buy</TransactionType>
      <Share>15000</Share>
      <Price>65.50</Price>
      <OrderType>Limit Order</OrderType>
      <ExecutionStatus/>
    </TradeItem>
  </TradeItems>
  <TotalTransactionAmount/>
</Trade>
```

The <ExecutionStatus> field will contain the execution information for each individual stock transaction in the document. Its content will be filled by Bob's trading component, and it will contain information on whether a specific transaction completed or not. For example, if the limit price isn't reached, the transaction won't take place; in such a case, the trading component will insert "Limited price is not met" in the field to indicate that this particular order was not processed. The trading component will also fill the <TotalTransactionAmount> and <ExecutionStatus> fields under each TradeItem record. The TotalTransactionAmount is the total dollar amount for each individual trade that is completed in the document.

In this trade schedule, you want to use XLANG-style transactions. You'll use short-term transactions in this schedule. Later in this chapter, I'll show you how to work with long-term and timed transactions, but for now, let's find out what advantages can be gained by making actions transactional.

The Trade Schedule

The Business Process page for Bob's trade schedule using transactions is shown in Figure 10-5. There are still five Action shapes in this schedule, but four of them are inside two short-term transactions. The Pre-Trade Database Update and Execute Trade actions are in the Trade Proc transaction. The Post-Trade Database Update and Sending Trade Status Back actions are in the Post-Trade Proc transaction.

Short-term transactions are also known as *DTC-style transactions*. These follow the same rules as DTC transactions in COM+. For instance, if the Execute Trade process aborts the transaction, any changes made by the Pre-Trade Database Update action will be automatically rolled back. After the transaction is committed, the changes made by both actions will be committed.

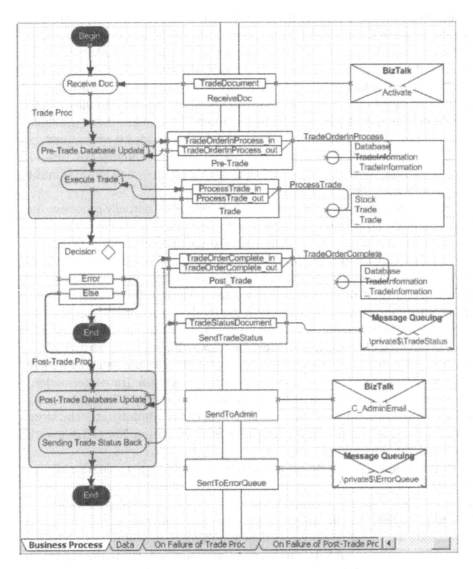

Figure 10-5. Business Process page of an orchestration with short-term transactions

Before you set up the properties for the Transaction shapes and specify what they should do in the event of failure, you must first define what you want the schedule to do. When a trade document enters the Trade Proc transaction and arrives at the Pre-Trade Database Update action, the TradeInformation COM+ component will be kicked off, and will update Bob's database with the order information in the document. The component will set the status in the database to In Process for each trade listed in the document. This means that if the client goes to the Web site, he or she will see the updated status for his or her outstanding buy and sell orders. If the TradeInformation COM+ component fails for whatever reason, the first thing you want to do is send an e-mail to the administrator to inform that person of this failure.

The next action is Execute Trade. This is the step that actually processes the document using Bob's trading component. The trading component is a COM+ component that will examine each individual trade in the document to verify whether the transaction is compliant with SEC rules and whether there are sufficient funds to make the transactions happen. If all the information in the document is correct, the component processes the orders, fills the status fields for the individual transactions along with the TotalTransactionAmount field, and returns the trade document. If a problem exists with the information in the document, the trading component will abort the transaction and end the current schedule, since there is no reason to continue. In this case, the database update will be rolled back, and you need to make another call to the TradeInformation component to mark the client's submission with the message "Contains errors, unable to process", and you must send an e-mail to the administrator and store the client document in the error queue for later examination. After all this work is completed, the schedule will end.

Unfortunately, there is no automatic way to terminate a whole schedule when a transaction aborts. When this happens, the schedule simply starts the process on its On Failure page and returns to the main business process after the actions on the On Failure page are performed. In some situations you'll want to terminate the schedule altogether if an important transaction fails, such as if the trading component fails—in that case, you want to perform the actions on the On Failure page and then terminate the schedule.

To achieve this goal, you can use a Decision shape to check whether or not the transaction has aborted by evaluating the value of ProcessTrade_out.[__Exists__]. ProcessTrade_out is the message that contains the output of the trading component. If the transaction succeeds, ProcessTrade_out.[__Exists__] will return true. If the transaction aborts, ProcessTrade_out.[__Exists__] will return false. Based on this test in the Decision shape, you can either continue the process flow or end it.

If the process flow enters the Post-Trade Proc transaction, the Trade Proc transaction has been successful and committed. It's now time to update the database with the new trade status information of each individual trade—the In Process status will be changed to whatever is in the status field of the document. If a client goes to Bob's Web site, they will find the status information for each individual trade he or she has sent. If this Post-Trade Database Update fails for whatever reason, you want to first send an e-mail to the administrator and then terminate the schedule. However, all the transactions have been committed at this point, so the administrator will need to inform the client that his or her transactions have been committed.

If the Post-Trade Database Update transaction is processed successfully, you want to send the document that is returned by the trading component to the client so that he or she will have a digital copy of this document. You can do this by sending the response document to a message queue to be picked up and forwarded later by BizTalk Messaging. If the schedule is unable to write the document to the message queue, it will roll back the database update that the Post-Trade Database Update transaction made, and it will send out an e-mail to the administrator to inform him or her of the situation.

Implementing the Transactions

To implement the transactions described in the previous section, you must set the transaction model of this schedule to "Include Transaction with XLANG Schedule" on the Start shape's properties page (refer back to Figure 10-1).

Next, double-click the Trade Proc transaction to open its Transaction Properties page (see Figure 10-6).

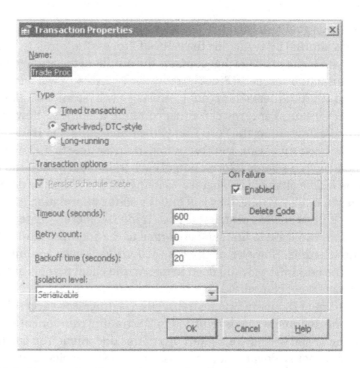

Figure 10-6. Transaction Properties page for the Trade Proc transaction

In the Type section of the Transaction Properties page, select Short-lived, DTC-style. Under the Transaction options section are three properties:

- *Timeout (seconds):* This specifies how long the transaction may run before it's aborted or retried. This option is available for timed and short-lived, DTC-style transactions.

- *Retry count:* This specifies how many times the transaction can be retried if it can't be completed before the timeout.

- *Backoff time (seconds):* This specifies how long the schedule will wait before continuing with the next retry. The actual wait time depends on the backoff time and the retry number: The formula is wait time = B^R (B to the Rth power, where B equals the backoff time in seconds and R equals the number of retries). This option is available only for short-lived, DTC-style transactions.

The time it takes the trading component to complete depends on many factors, such as the size of the transaction and the activity on the stock market. You'll set the timeout time to 10 minutes (600 seconds) for this transaction. Set the retry count to zero, since you don't want to execute the transaction again if it times out. The backoff time is irrelevant when you set the retry count to zero.

The Isolation level setting allows you to configure how this transaction will lock the resources it uses when it's running. There are four isolation levels:

- *Uncommitted read:* A transaction set with this isolation level will be able to read data regardless of whether the data is committed. For example, if a first transaction is updating a record but hasn't yet committed the change, a second transaction (with a setting of Uncommitted read) won't care about whether the first transaction will commit the change or abort. It simply reads what it sees in that record at that moment. This type of transaction is very fast, since it always gets the data it wants right away, but the data it reads may not be consistent, since it could read data that is rolled back later.

- *Committed read:* A transaction set with this isolation level will only read data that has been committed by other transactions. If data has been changed by another transaction but not yet committed, this transaction will wait until the data it wants to read has been committed. This type of transaction won't lock the data it reads, so other transactions could change the data before this transaction ends. This may cause inconsistencies if the transaction updates the data and assumes that the data is the same, because another transaction may have changed it. This type of transaction is slower than the uncommitted read, since it has to wait for all the uncommitted data to clear.

- *Repeatable read:* A transaction set with this isolation level locks all the data reads so that it can't be changed by other transactions until the repeatable read transaction is finished. This solves the problem with committed reads, but it's slower than a committed read because it has to lock all the data it reads, not just the data it updates. Repeatable reads are also slow in the sense that other transactions won't able to update the data locked by the repeatable read transaction until the repeatable read transaction finishes.

- *Serializable:* A transaction set with this isolation level will lock the table to prevent inserts, updates, and deletes. This means that everything this transaction sees and doesn't see at the beginning of the transaction will remain exactly the same at the end of the transaction, except for changes made by the transaction itself. One problem with repeatable reads is that they don't prevent another transaction from inserting new data, which may cause some inconsistency in calculations that rely on information such as the total number of records—the Serializable isolation level solves this problem. Because this isolation level forces each transaction to be carried out and committed one at a time, it's the most restrictive of the four isolation levels, and it's the only isolation level that meets the ACID criteria.

For this example, choose the Serializable isolation level, which is the default setting, for the Trade Proc transaction. In the On failure section, check the Enabled checkbox, and then click the Add Code button to add a Business Process page that will be triggered when the transaction fails.

When you click the Add Code button, Orchestration Designer will add a new tab at the bottom of the window called On Failure of Trade Proc, to indicate that a new Business Process page exists for the transaction Trade Proc (see Figure 10-7).

Figure 10-7. A new On Failure page for the Trade Proc transaction

This On Failure page is similar to the regular Business Process page—here you can define Action shapes and implementation shapes. The process on the On Failure page starts right after the transaction it's associated with aborts. You have some idea of what you want to do in the case of the transaction aborting, so let's define those actions on the On Failure of Trade Proc page (see Figure 10-8).

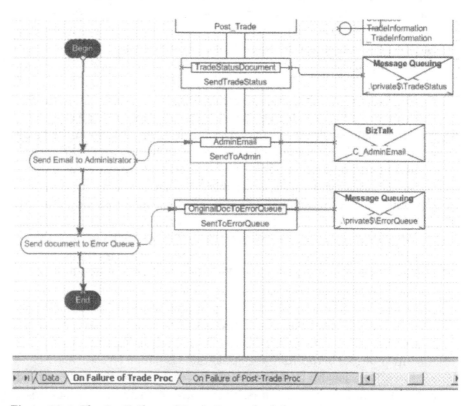

Figure 10-8. The On Failure of Trade Proc schedule

On the On Failure page, all the implementations on the Business Process page will still be available and can be linked with the Action shapes defined on this page. It's perfectly all right to create new transactions by dropping Transaction shapes on the On Failure page, and creating another On Failure page for this On Failure page. As far as the orchestration is concerned, the On Failure page is just another Business Process page.

In this case, you first want to send an e-mail to the administrator, so you need to implement a BizTalk Messaging shape on the page and link it with the Send Email to Administrator implementation. Next, you want to send the original document to a message queue so that the administrator can examine it later. (All the messages created on the Business Process page are still available in the BizTalk Messaging Binding Wizard.)

You've now completed the On Failure of Trade Proc page. The actions on this page will be processed when the transaction aborts. But what makes a transaction abort?

Many conditions can make a transaction abort, such as the following:

- The Abort shape is encountered within the process flow.

- A COM+ component or Scripting component returns a failure HRESULT (these components need to be configured to abort a transaction if a failure HRESULT is returned during the port binding).

- An abort transaction is called inside a COM+ or scripting component.

- A failure is introduced by a binding technology at a system level (for example, Message Queuing might fail to put a message on a queue).

- The XLANG Scheduler Engine (the COM+ application that executes instances of schedules) encounters an error (such as a DTC error) that causes it to abort a transaction within a given instance.

- A schedule is paused (this might require all transactions within that schedule to abort).

- A transaction time-out within the transaction properties.

To configure a component to abort the transaction when it causes a failure HRESULT, open the component's Binding Wizard (see Figure 10-9). Under the Error handling section, select the sole checkbox option so that the transaction this component is in will automatically abort when a bad HRESULT is returned from this component. Under the Transaction support section, you must select Supported to make this component participate in the existing transaction.

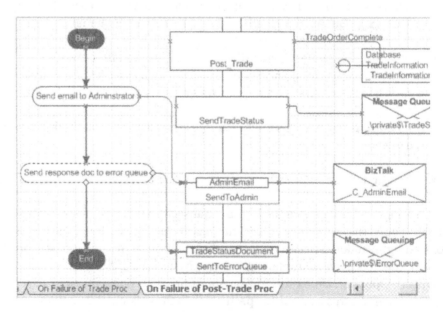

Figure 10-9. COM Component Binding Wizard

You also need to configure these properties for the TradeInformation and Trade components inside the Trade Proc transaction.

Next, you need to create an On Failure page for the Post-Trade Proc transaction (see Figure 10-10).

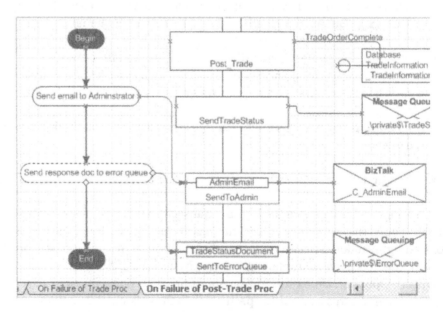

Figure 10-10. On Failure page for the Post-Trade Proc transaction

To test whether the On Failure page really works, let's raise an error in the trading component. Because the trading component is configured to abort the transaction when it encounters a bad HRESULT, you can watch what action will be taken in such a case in the XLANG Event Monitor (see Figure 10-11).

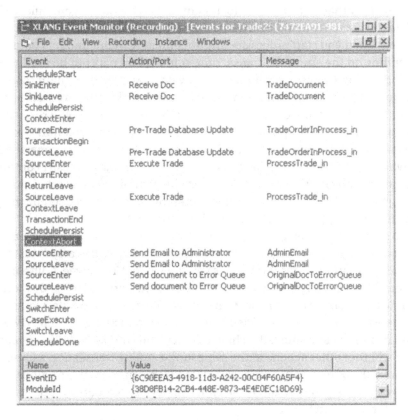

Figure 10-11. Actions taken for the trade schedule with an aborted transaction

Because you've raised an error in the trading component (for example, with the Err.Raise method in VB), and the trading component is configured to abort the transaction when encountering a bad HRESULT, the first transaction, Trade Proc, is aborted at the ContextAbort event. The process flow then continues with the On Failure of Trade Proc page where an e-mail is sent to the administrator and the document is sent to the message queue.

After the schedule finishes the process on the On Failure page, it enters the Decision shape, where it identifies that an error has occurred in the previous transaction, and it terminates the current schedule.

Long-Lived Transactions

It sounds like short-lived transactions do exactly what you ask them to do, so you may be wondering why you need long-lived transactions. Let's reexamine the previous schedule.

You know that when a client document first arrives at the schedule, you'll update the database to indicate that the transactions in the document are in progress. Then you start processing the document with the trading component. Depending on the size of the transaction, some orders may not be fulfilled for a long time. For example, if a fund company decides to buy a million shares of IBM, you really have no idea when the order can be fulfilled. It may take 3 minutes or 3 hours. If it indeed takes 3 hours to fulfill the order, do you really want to lock up the data you've updated (or read, depending on the isolation level) in the database so that no one else can read or update it? The answer is generally no. But what else can you do? As long as the trading component doesn't commit or abort, the database changes you made can't be committed or aborted either. Having too much data locked up for too long will dramatically degrade the performance of an application that depends on such data.

To solve this problem, BizTalk Orchestration introduced a new type of transaction called a *long-running transaction*. (Timed transactions are almost the same as long-running transactions, as you'll see later.) The biggest difference between long-running transactions and short-lived transactions is that long-running transactions aren't really transactions. Every action inside a long-running transaction will be committed or aborted as soon as it completes. When an action has been committed, the change is final and can't be rolled back regardless of whether other actions in the same long-running transaction succeed or fail. The only difference between processes in long-running transactions and those without any transaction is that you can perform certain actions in the event of transaction failure.

Here's the benefit of long-running transactions over short-lived transactions: Because everything is committed or aborted right away, the length of time locks are held on the data source is significantly reduced. For example, all the data that is updated by the Pre-Trade Database Update will become available for other applications immediately after the action completes. This means, though, that automatic rollback won't be available when the transaction aborts, since committed data can't be rolled back.

To better understand the properties of a long-running transaction, let's modify the schedule you created earlier to include a long-running transaction (see Figure 10-12). Here you have a long-running transaction, and as with a short-lived transaction, you can define an On Failure page for it. Only the actions wrapped in the long-running transaction won't be rolled back automatically—for those actions you'll need to reverse the changes yourself on the On Failure of Long Tx page.

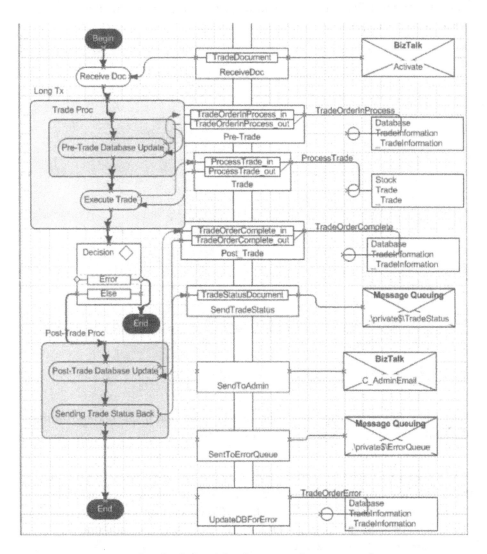

Figure 10-12. The trade schedule with a long-running transaction

Things are getting a little complicated with the short-lived transaction nested inside the long-running transaction in Figure 10-12. With nested transactions, you can delegate tasks that can be completed in relatively short time to short-lived transactions to take advantage of automatic rollback, and leave the tasks that take more time to run in the long-running transaction to take advantage of the faster release of resources.

In a nested transaction, there are two Business Process pages that are used to handle the "on failure" situation. The first one is the regular On Failure page, and the second one is called the *Compensation page,* and both are specified in the Transaction Properties window (see Figure 10-13).

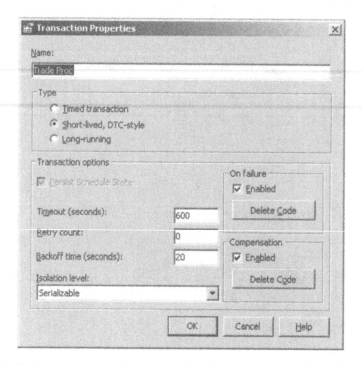

Figure 10-13. Properties page for a short-lived transaction inside a long-running transaction

When a short-lived transaction resides inside a long-running transaction, you can define a Compensation page on top of an On Failure page. In this case, you'll have a total of three "transaction failure" pages for the Long Tx transaction. There will be two On Failure pages for Long Tx and Trade Proc and one Compensation page for Trade Proc.

The Compensation page is only called when the Trade Proc transaction has been committed but the Long Tx transaction is calling for an abort. The processes on the Compensation page are defined in exactly the same way as those of the On Failure page. Keep in mind that the actions in the corresponding transaction have been committed by the time the Compensation page is called, so actions that are taken on this page must reverse the changes that were committed.

To test the new schedule, raise an error in the trading component, and watch it run in the XLANG Event Monitor. You should see the actions from the Compensation of Trade Proc page and from the On Failure of Long Tx page being called.

Timed Transactions

With long-running transactions, your trading component can run for hours without locking other data sources. However, at some point, you want to terminate the schedule. In such cases, you want to use timed transactions. The features and behavior of timed transactions are exactly the same as those of long-running transactions, except that you can define how long a transaction will run before it times out or aborts. With a timeout property, you can put a lid on how long a long-running transaction can run in the system.

A Review of Transactions

As you saw, there are two transaction models for XLANG Schedules: COM+ component–style transactions and XLANG-style transactions. Only with XLANG-style transactions can you define short-lived, long-running, and timed transaction types.

Short-lived transactions are DTC-style transactions, and they give you the benefit of automatic rollback when the transactions abort, but they also have the shortcomings associated with DTC transactions, such as locking up data for extended periods, which could hurt the performance of other applications accessing the same data.

Long-running transactions solve the data-locking problem by committing the changes as soon as each action in the transaction completes, but you have to provide your own rollback logic for when the transaction aborts.

When a short-lived transaction is nested inside a long-running transaction, two pages are called when the process aborts: The On Failure page defines actions that will be called when the short-lived transaction fails, and the Compensation page defines the actions that will be called when the short-lived transaction is committed and the surrounding long-running transaction is aborted.

Timed transactions are simply long-running transactions with a timeout limit.

Using XLANG Schedule Throttling

Schedule throttling is a new feature in BizTalk Server 2002. It makes your BizTalk application scalable and also solves a very real problem. Let's use the trade schedule as an example.

When clients send a document to Bob's BizTalk Server for processing, the XLANG engine will start an instance of the schedule and will start loading the components to process the document. What happens when Bob's client tries to send several documents at once? For example, the news of a federal interest-rate hike was just released, and every client reacts to the news and starts buying or selling stocks. Bob's ASP will receive over 50 trade orders at once. How will BizTalk Server react to these sudden demands?

If you don't control how many trade schedules can run at once, BizTalk Server will attempt to start 50 trade schedules, and each of the schedules will attempt to instantiate all the components it needs to process the document. Having so many schedules running at once will significantly degrade the performance of every schedule running on the machine. The situation will become worse if the components used in the schedule are also making database reads or modifications. You can run into problems when the maximum number of database connections is reached. The performance of the database will also significantly degrade because the database server is overwhelmed with managing so many data locks at once.

The result is that all the schedules are running on the system, but none of them are getting any work done. What you need is a way to manage how many instances of a particular schedule can run at one time so that BizTalk Server won't be overwhelmed by a huge number of running schedules. The solution to this problem is XLANG Schedule throttling or pooling, which allows you to specify the maximum number of instances of a specific schedule that can run at one time.

To enable and configure this feature, open the schedule in Orchestration Designer, and open the Properties page of the Begin shape (see Figure 10-14).

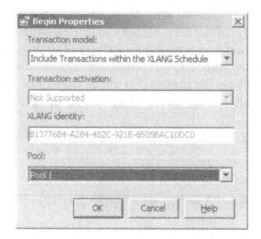

Figure 10-14. Configuring an instance pool for an XLANG Schedule

By default, the value selected in the Pool list box is None, which means schedule pooling isn't enabled for this XLANG Schedule. Change this value to a pool number—for the purposes of this example, select Pool 1. Click OK to save the changes. This is the only thing you need to do in the schedule.

Next, open Component Services. Under COM+ applications, locate the XLANG Schedule Pool application, and then expand its Components folder (see Figure 10-15). Under the XLANG Schedule Pool are 25 components. Each component will control the instance pooling for an XLANG Schedule. The default maximum number of instances for each of these components is 25, and you can modify these through the activation property of the components. Note that there are only 25 components under the XLANG Schedule Pool application. This number can't be changed.

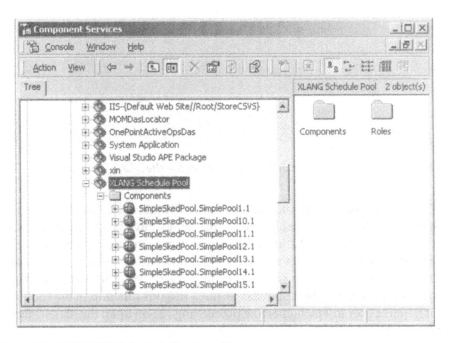

Figure 10-15. XLANG Schedule Pool application

To configure the XLANG Schedule pooling application, open the properties page for SimpleSkedPool.SimplePool1.1, which corresponds to the Pool 1 setting you selected on the Begin shape of the schedule (see Figure 10-16).

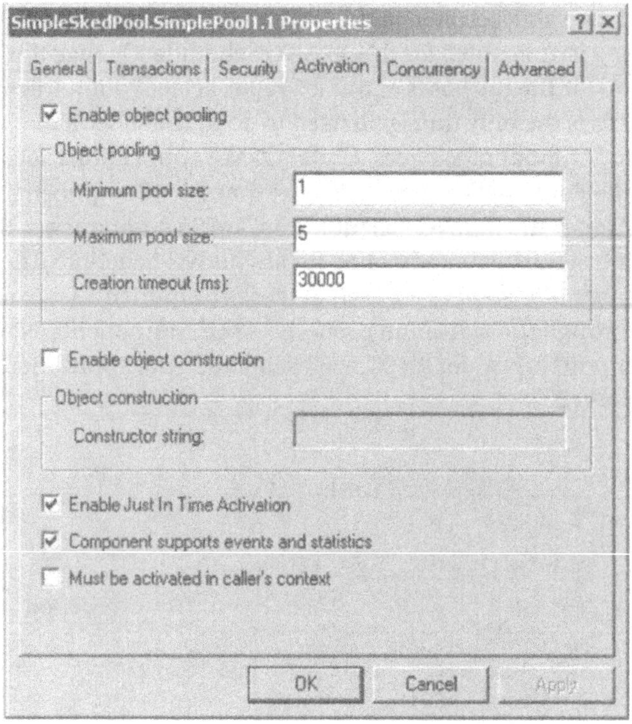

Figure 10-16. Configuring the pooling properties for the XLANG Schedule

On the properties page, select the Activation tab. Check the Enable object pooling checkbox and the Enable Just In Time Activation checkbox. Set the maximum pool size to 5 to specify that a maximum of five running instances of the trade schedule can exist on the system at one time. Click OK to save the changes.

To test the configuration, add some code to the trading component so that it will take longer to complete (for instance, put a msgbox function in the code so that it requires user interaction before proceeding). Then open the XLANG Event Monitor (see Figure 10-17).

Now start ten trade schedules by dropping ten copies of the document in the folder that is watched by the Receive Function that starts the trade schedule. Only five instances will run on the system at once.

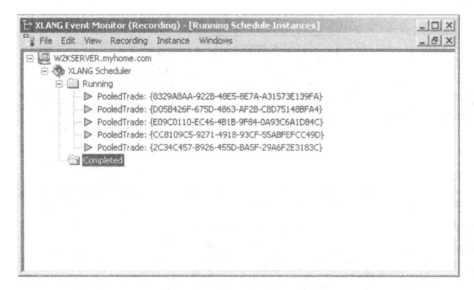

Figure 10-17. With pooled XLANG Schedules, you can limit the number of schedule instances running at one time.

If you look into the Queues folder in the BizTalk Server Administration Console, there will be five trade documents waiting in the Work Queue folder to be picked up as soon as a free spot becomes available in the schedule pool. As soon as a schedule instance is completed, a spot in the pool will become free for the next schedule instance.

In Bob's case, when 100 trade documents arrive, the BizTalk XLANG engine will process the documents 5 at a time, and the system resources won't be over-loaded by the excessive outstanding schedule instances.

Dehydrating and Rehydrating XLANG Schedules

So far, you've seen many features of XLANG Schedules. You've looked at the Action shapes and implementation shapes and what they can do for schedules, but there is another less obvious, yet very important feature of XLANG Schedules. In this section, you'll learn about the *dehydration* and *rehydration* of XLANG Schedules.

When an XLANG Schedule is dehydrated, all the schedule's instance-related state information is persisted to the database, and that schedule's instance is erased from memory, freeing system resources. The rehydration of an XLANG Schedule reverses the dehydration process; it restores the dehydrated instance back to memory so that it can continue its processes. Figure 10-18 outlines the dehydration and rehydration processes.

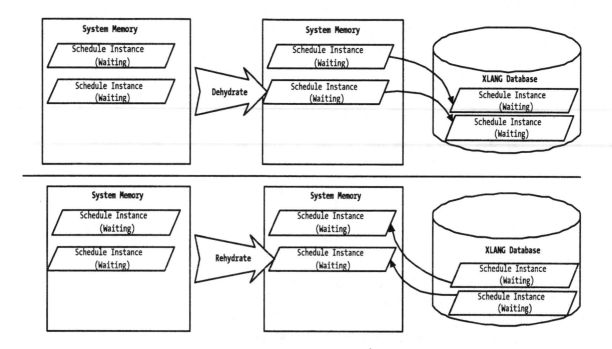

Figure 10-18. The dehydration and rehydration processes

In many B2B scenarios, a process in a workflow can be blocked for long periods of time before the workflow can continue. If a worker sent an order to the manager for approval and didn't expect to have the order approved for a couple of days, it would certainly be unacceptable for the worker not to do any other work while waiting for the approval. The same issue exists in XLANG Schedules—when a schedule instance is stopped and is waiting for a message to arrive before it can continue its process, BizTalk Server will consider dehydrating this particular instance so that the freed system resources can be used by other applications.

When a schedule is waiting on a port, for instance, one of the actions in the schedule will receive the document from a Message Queuing shape. If there is no message in the queue, the schedule will be blocked at that port until a message arrives at the message queue. In addition to the blockage, the following conditions must also be met before BizTalk Server will actually dehydrate this schedule instance to the database:

- The schedule instance must be in a quiescent state. All the actions in the schedule must remain inactive when a port is being blocked. If some components connected to the ports haven't yet completed, BizTalk Server won't dehydrate that schedule instance.

- The schedule instance must not contain any running DTC-style transactions. The XLANG engine won't dehydrate a schedule instance if it's
  running a short-lived transaction that hasn't yet aborted or committed.

- The implementation for the port must support persistence if it holds the
  state. For example, if the COM component connecting to the port holds
  the state but doesn't support the IPersist interface, then the XLANG engine
  can't dehydrate the schedule instance, because it will be unable to persist
  the state held by the component to the XLANG database.

- The latency setting for the port must be greater than 180. The latency setting assigned in the XML Communication Wizard should be greater than
  180 seconds (see Figure 10-19). BizTalk Server will never dehydrate
  a schedule instance if the latency value for the blocked port is less than or
  equal to 180 seconds.

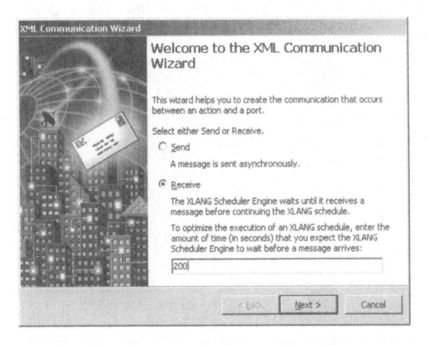

*Figure 10-19. Configuring the latency value for the port in the XML
Communication Wizard*

The rehydration process is much simpler. When a message arrives at the port
that has been blocked, the XLANG engine will instantiate the schedule and
return the state information and persisted components of that dehydrated

schedule instance back to system memory, where the schedule can continue from where it left off.

Using Orchestration Correlation

In Chapter 5, you saw that BizTalk Orchestration can send data to BizTalk Messaging and to message queues by using BizTalk Messaging implementation shapes and setting the data flow on the port to Send. Similarly, BizTalk Orchestration can receive data from BizTalk Messaging and message queues by setting the data flow on the port to Receive. However, there is a problem that I haven't directed your attention to.

Consider the scenario in Figure 10-20. The schedule is simple. It receives a document from BizTalk Messaging and sends the document to a NewOrder message queue, where the document is picked up by another application for processing. The schedule then waits for a confirmation message. When the order is fulfilled, a confirmation message is sent to the Confirmation message queue, and the schedule will retrieve it from the queue and process the rest of the actions.

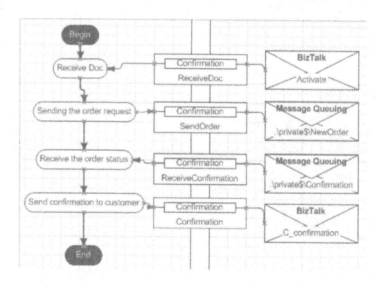

Figure 10-20. A schedule that sends and receives documents using message queues

If you have one schedule instance running on the system, you won't have any problem retrieving the document from the Confirmation queue, because the confirmation document in the queue must have originated from the order document the schedule was processing. However, when multiple instances of this schedule are running on the system, and each instance is processing an order document from a different client, you'll have a problem. How do you determine which schedule instance will pick up the document that just arrived at the Confirmation queue? How do you know which schedule instance was processing the order document that this confirmation matches?

To this point, you've been thinking about XLANG Schedules in a single-instance scenario, but in the real B2B world, it's common to have multiple instances of the same schedule running on a system at once. You must find a way to ensure that the messages a schedule instance receives are indeed intended for that particular instance. This means that whenever a schedule instance receives a document, either from BizTalk Messaging or a message queue, it won't simply assume that the arriving document is associated with the document it has been processing. Instead, BizTalk Server has a technique called *orchestration correlation* to handle this problem.

Orchestration Correlation Through Message Queues

Mike has discovered some performance problems in the trade schedule. The problem lies with the trading component. Currently, the trade schedule makes a synchronous call to the trading component, which sometimes can take a long time to process the order, and many smaller orders have to wait on the queue even though they could be processed very quickly. Mike wants to change the current schedule to remove the direct synchronous calls to the trading component.

Mike decides to make the schedule send the trade order to a remote message queue instead of calling the trading component. The trading components will be moved to the server that hosts the remote message queue and will process the documents as soon as they arrive from the trade schedule. Multiple instances of the trading component will be activated to process the trade orders as quickly as possible. After an order is executed, the response document (which contains the execution status information) is sent to another message queue that is watched by the running trade schedule instances. As soon as a response document arrives, the correct schedule instance will pick up the response document and will process the Post-Trade Database Update transaction and forward the response documents back to the original clients.

To ensure that the running schedules will pick up the correct response documents from the message queue, the orchestration correlation technique will be used in this new trade schedule. The new trade schedule replaces the Execute Trade action with two new Action shapes that are connecting to message queuing shapes (see Figure 10-21).

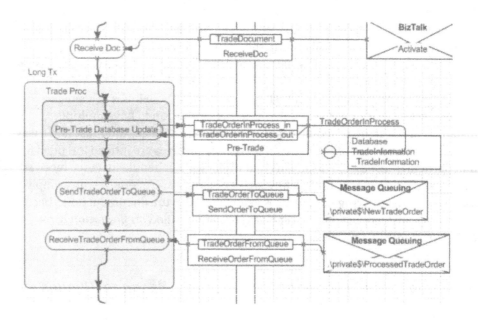

Figure 10-21. Revised trade schedule

The SendTradeOrderToQueue action will send the trade order to the message queue called NewTradeOrder, where it will be picked up to be processed by the trading component. After the trading component completes the trade order, it will generate a response document that contains the transaction status information, and will send the response document to a separate message queue called ProcessedTradeOrder. The ReceiveTradeOrderFromQueue action will then receive the correct response document from the queue and go on to the subsequent actions.

Now, let's add two Message Queuing implementation shapes to support orchestration correlation. Drag and drop the first Message Queuing shape onto the Business Process page. In the Message Queuing Binding Wizard, specify the port name as SendOrderToQueue and the static message queue path as .\private$\NewTradeOrder.

Next, connect the SendTradeOrderToQueue action with the appropriate port, and an XML Communication Wizard will open. You need to create a new message to represent the document that will be sent to the queue.

The next window will ask for the message label information (see Figure 10-22). Check the "Use Instance Id as Message Label" checkbox. The Message type field will then contain an uneditable value, __Instance_Id__. The instance ID is a GUID that uniquely identifies a schedule instance. This ID is critical in identifying which document is associated with a specific schedule instance. Click Next until you finish the wizard.

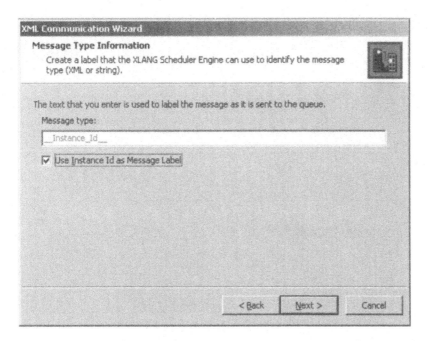

Figure 10-22. Using the instance ID as the message label

Now you can drag and drop the second Message Queuing shape onto the Business Process page, and specify ReceiveOrderFromQueue as the port name and .\private$\ProcessedTradeOrder as the message queue path. Connect the ReceiveTradeOrderFromQueue Action shape with this Message Queuing shape.

In the XML Communication Wizard that opens, specify that this port is to receive messages. If you expect that the trade order will take a long time to process, you may want to set the wait time to a number greater than 180 seconds, which will allow the XLANG engine to dehydrate the schedule instance while it waits for messages to arrive. For this example, set it to 200 seconds.

In the next window, create a new message called TradeOrderFromQueue to represent the response document that arrives at the message queue.

Click Next to proceed to the window shown in Figure 10-23. Check the Use Instance ID as Message Label checkbox. This setting is important because a schedule instance will only accept a message from a queue whose message label is equal to its instance ID. You also must provide a Message type name, but this value is irrelevant if you are using the instance ID as the message label, so just type in anything and click Next until you finish the wizard.

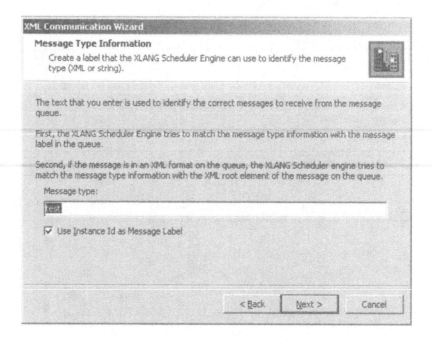

Figure 10-23. *Specifying the message type information for the port*

The central idea of using the instance ID as the message label for orchestration correlation is that all the running schedules will check the message label of the messages as they arrive at the queue. If the message label of a message in the queue has the same value as the instance ID of one of the running schedules, that particular running schedule will pick up the message and process it. Other running schedules won't pick up that document since none of them has the matching instance ID.

To make the whole correlation process work, the trade component must make sure the message label (which contains the instance ID) of the message it picked up from the queue has the same message label when the message is sent out after processing. Throughout the whole process, the message label must remain the same, or the correlation won't work. BizTalk Server wouldn't be able to match the messages with the correct running schedules otherwise.

NOTE *You can read and assign message labels for messages in the queue programmatically though the use of the MSMQ object model. In this example, the trade component will need to call these MSMQ methods to read and assign the message labels to ensure they stay the same. For more information about the MSMQ object model, refer to Appendix A.*

You also need to modify the data page to make sure all the messages are linked correctly.

After you compile the schedule, you are ready to test it. However, you must set up some Receive Functions, channels and ports for this schedule before you can test it. Figure 10-24 shows the CorrelationTrade schedule in the XLANG Event Monitor. Notice the snowflake icon beside CorrelationTrade—it indicates that the schedule instance has been dehydrated. Open the detailed events for the schedule instance (shown in the Events for CorrelationTrade window in Figure 10-24) to reveal that schedule is indeed dehydrated and is waiting on the ReceiveTradeOrderFromQueue action.

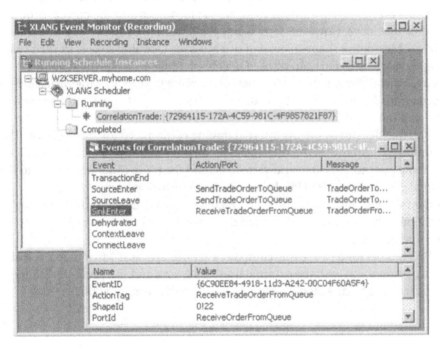

Figure 10-24. Dehydrated schedule instance is waiting for a message to arrive.

The next step is to send a message to the .\private$\ProcessedTradeOrder queue so that the schedule instance can continue. To test it, handcraft multiple response documents and give one of them the same label name as the GUID shown in the XLANG Event Monitor, in this case {72964115-172A-4C59-981C-4F9857821F87}. Shortly after you send these messages to the ProcessedTradeOrder queue, that dehydrated CorrelationTrade instance will be rehydrated and will start processing the message. When it's completed, you should find that there are still some messages in the queue, and only the matching message is removed.

With orchestration correlation, you can convert the many synchronous tasks into asynchronous ones by implementing this "send-receive" pair in the schedule. This asynchronous approach removes the binding between the schedule and the business components, and when combined with the XLANG Schedule's ability to be dehydrated, will greatly improve the resource management and scalability of the XLANG Schedules under a heavy load.

Orchestration Correlation Through BizTalk Messaging

In the example you just saw, the message label is a critical piece of information that helps BizTalk Orchestration correlate the messages and the correct running schedule instances. However, sometimes you'll want to send the document to a BizTalk Messaging shape instead of to a Message Queuing shape. In such cases, using message labels to keep track of which schedule instance the document belongs to won't be feasible, since there is no place to store this message label information. You must come up with a different solution to correlate the messages and the schedule instances.

Bob decides not to use his internal trading component for some reason. He has found a company on the Internet that can offer the trade execution service to his clients instead. All clients need to do is send the trade order document to the external provider over HTTPS. As soon as the trades have been executed, a response document containing the execution status information is sent back to the clients, who can then update their database or perform any further post-trade operations.

Bob has decided to use this company's service and asks Mike to replace his trading component with the external trading system, and integrate this trading service into the trade schedule. Figure 10-25 shows the general plan.

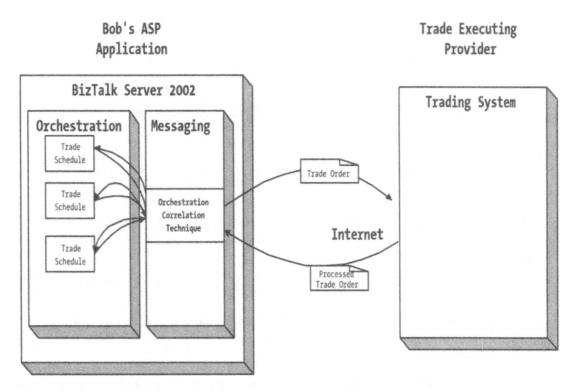

Figure 10-25. A revised system to process trades for clients

To help Mike make this change, you need to revise your trade schedule
to replace your trading component and integrate with an external provider. You'll
replace the two Message Queuing shapes with two BizTalk Messaging shapes,
which are responsible for sending the trade order to the external provider
through the Internet, and receiving the response document and correlating it
with the correct trade schedule instance. Because you have to remove the message queuing part of the picture, and your external provider is outside the
organization, you need to provide two pieces of information to the external
provider. You need to tell them where you expect to receive the response document and what the instance ID should be for this response document.

One way to provide this information is to embed it inside the document
when it's sent out. Let's modify the trade document specification to add a field
called ReplyTo right below the FundCompany field. Figure 10-26 shows the trade
schedule revised for this new change.

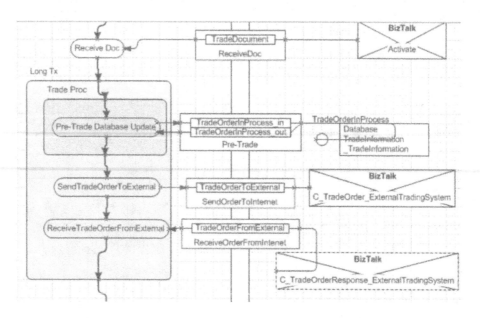

Figure 10-26. BizTalk Messaging shapes are used instead of Message Queuing shapes for sending and receiving documents.

As you can see in Figure 10-26, the two message queuing shapes are replaced by the two BizTalk Messaging shapes. The SendTradeOrderToExternal action will send the mutual fund company's trade order document to a C_TradeOrder_ExternalTradingSystem channel, which is connected to a port with the URL of the external trade execution provider as the destination.

When configuring this shape with the XML Communication Wizard, you need to pull out the ReplyTo message field to make it available for access on the data page, which you'll see shortly. Give any name for the message label for the XML message—the name doesn't matter here since you aren't writing it to the message queue.

Next, you need to add the BizTalk Messaging shape used for receiving the response document. Drag and drop the BizTalk Messaging shape onto the page. The BizTalk Messaging Binding Wizard will open, as shown in Figure 10-27.

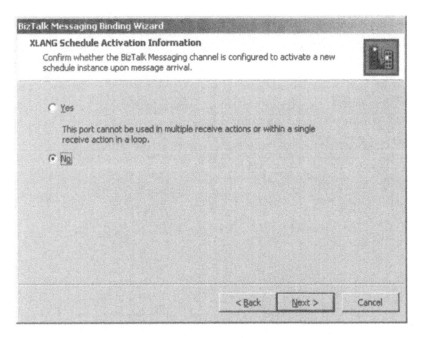

Figure 10-27. XLANG Schedule activation information

You've seen this window many times before in earlier chapters, and in it you've usually selected Yes. This time, though, you need to select No. When Yes is selected, BizTalk attempts to create a brand new schedule instance to process the document. When No is selected, BizTalk Server won't attempt to create a new instance of the schedule. In this case, you already have a running schedule instance—all you want to ask BizTalk Server to do is feed the data into this port.

Click Next to proceed to the window shown in Figure 10-28, which you haven't seen before.

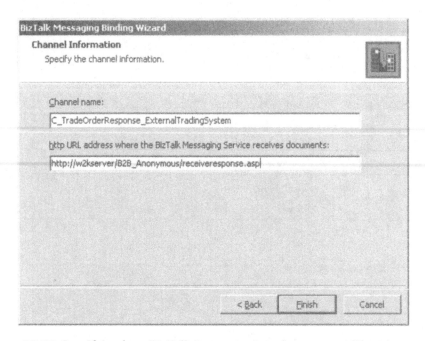

Figure 10-28. Specifying how BizTalk Server receives the response document

In this Channel Information page, you need to provide two important pieces of information to configure how BizTalk Messaging will receive the document before it can pass the document to the running schedule instance. In Figure 10-28, you are instructing the external trade execution provider to send the response document to http://w2kserver/B2B_Anonymous/receiveresponse.asp, and you can add the channel name C_TradeOrderResponse_ExternalTradingSystem as one of its query strings. In other words, you are specifying that your URL for accepting the response document is http://w2kserver/B2B_Anonymous/receiveresponse.asp?channel= C_TradeOrderResponse_ExternalTradingSystem.

You might ask why you specify this information in BizTalk Server. Shouldn't you tell your provider this information instead? Bear with me for a second, I'm getting to that. Click Finish to save the change.

Next, you must connect the ReceiveTradeOrderFromExternal action with the port. During the XML Configuration Wizard, specify the Message type as Trade, which is the root name for the response document. This value is important, because when documents arrive at BizTalk Server, this Action shape will only retrieve the documents with Trade as their root name. Leave the instance ID alone, since you aren't dealing with the message queue now.

After you finish the configuration of the BizTalk Messaging shapes on the business page, there is still something you must do to get the whole thing to work. You've provided the channel and URL that are used to receive the response document on the port, as is shown in Figure 10-28. Next you must send them along with the document to the external system provider. To do so, you need to link the port reference and the ReplyTo field in the document, as shown in Figure 10-29. The value of the ReplyTo field is dynamically created when an instance of this schedule is started. You'll see what value it takes later.

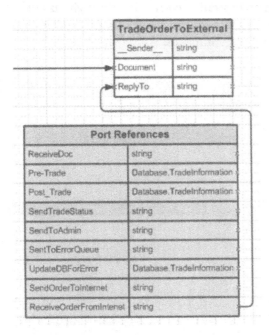

Figure 10-29. Connecting the port reference to the ReplyTo field in the document

If you caught the document posted to the external service provider, you would see that the ReplyTo field contains the following value:

```
<ReplyTo>http://w2kserver/B2B_Anonymous/receiveresponse.asp?Channel=
C_TradeOrderResponse_ExternalTradingSystem&
QPath=W2KSERVER.myhome.com\private$\c_tradeorderresponse_externaltradingsystem
{8c2786fd-7e6f-4d07-a96b-92852f4151ec}</ReplyTo>
```

This ReplyTo field contains a URL to an ASP page with two query string items: Channel (Channel=C_TradeOrderResponse_ExternalTradingSystem) and Qpath (QPath=W2KSERVER.myhome.com\private$\c_tradeorderresponse_external-tradingsystem{8c2786fd-7e6f-4d07-a96b-92852f4151ec}). In order for the schedule to correlate the response document with the right running schedule instance, the sender (external system provider) must post the response document to the URL that is embedded in the document.

If you have a question about where the QPath value in the query string is coming from, just check the local message queue. You'll find that the QPath is actually the path to a local queue that is created by the schedule at runtime (see Figure 10-30). The name of this queue is formed by combining the channel name and the instance ID of the schedule. This name is unique, since the instance ID is always unique. With orchestration correlation through BizTalk Messaging, BizTalk Server actually creates one message queue for each running instance of the schedule for correlation purposes.

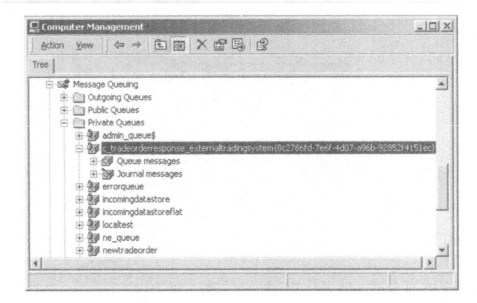

Figure 10-30. A local queue is created by BizTalk Server for storing the incoming message.

After the trade schedule sends out the trade order, the schedule will be dehydrated while it waits for the response document to arrive. In order for the dehydrated schedule instance to continue, the response document must arrive at the BizTalk Server. To be exact, a response document must arrive at this message queue, which is dynamically created to handle the document returned to this port for this particular schedule instance. As soon as a message arrives at this c_tradeorderresponse_externaltradingsystem{8c2786fd-7e6f-4d07-a96b-92852f4151ec} queue, the schedule will be rehydrated and will pull the message out of this queue, bring it into the rehydrated schedule, and continue with the rest of the orchestration. After the schedule is complete, this local queue will be automatically removed.

The external trading service provider doesn't have to know how to get the message to the dehydrated schedule instance. All they need to do is post the response document using the URL stored in the ReplyTo field. Your job is to create an ASP page that will transfer the posted documents to those dynamically created local queues.

BizTalk Server provides an ASP page for this task. The file is located under [BizTalk Server installation directory]\SDK\ReceiveScripts\ReceiveResponse.asp. In this ASP page, there are a number of key lines of code that will do the trick:

```
'retrieve the parameter in the query string
queuepath = Request.QueryString("qpath")
queuepath = "queue://Direct=OS:" & queuepath
channelname = Request.QueryString("channel")
'add you code to extract the posted document
'submit to the BizTalk Server
call interchange.submit (4,PostedDocument,,,,,queuepath,channelname)
```

The submit call uses 4 as its first parameter to specify that the document is sent to an open destination. The destination value for this document is queuepath, which will be used as the destination target for the open port. The channelname is the channel that connects to the open destination port.

NOTE *The channel information is optional, but it's helpful to provide it in the submit call if it's available. In order for BizTalk Server to find a channel on its own, you have to make sure the source and destination information provided is sufficient for BizTalk Server to find a distinct channel. In many cases, it's easier to provide a channel name in the submit call than to decide whether less information is sufficient. If you do provide a channel name, BizTalk Server will recognize it and will bypass the search for the channel and use the one you provide. This also applies to the Receive Function. When channel information is provided on the advanced properties page of the Receive Function, BizTalk Server will use it to pass the document to the port.*

To complete the process, you also must create a channel and an open destination port to be used for correlating the posted document back to the schedule-instance message queue, where the schedule instance will pick up the document and continue on its processes.

Using Dynamic Port Binding

I discussed open destination ports in BizTalk Messaging in Chapter 10. This is where the destination of the port is unknown until it's provided by a data field in the document or in submit call parameters. This concept decouples the destination from the port, and it's very useful when you don't know the destination beforehand. In BizTalk Orchestration, you need to provide either a channel name and message queue path during the configuration of the implementation shapes in order to send a document to BizTalk Messaging or to a message queue. You may be wondering whether there is a way to decouple the destination address from the implementation shape so that your schedule can have the flexibility of an open destination port.

The answer is yes. Dynamic port binding allows you to provide the address information to the implementation shapes at runtime. First, let's take a look at a dynamic port binding connected to a Message Queuing shape (see Figure 10-31).

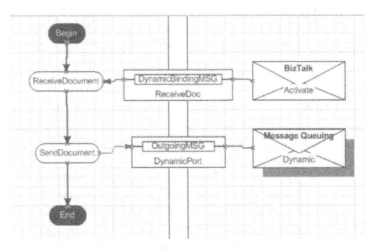

Figure 10-31. A schedule with dynamic port binding to a message queue

When you are using the Message Queuing Binding Wizard, specify a dynamic queue instead of a static queue. A Message Queuing shape with a shadow will appear on the page. To provide the address, you need to link a data field containing the address information to the port the dynamic messaging queue connects to on the data page (see Figure 10-32).

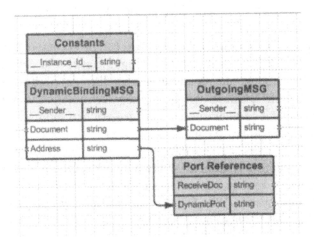

Figure 10-32. Providing the address information by linking the address data field to the dynamic port reference

Inside the document, you must have a data field that contains the address information for the message queue or this dynamic port binding won't work. Here is a sample document that can be used in this schedule:

```
<message>
  <Address>.\private$\DynamicBindingQueue</Address>
  <Data>this is a test message</Data>
</message>
```

When you run this schedule, the message is written to the message queue specified in the message queue information in the document.

You can create dynamic binding ports for BizTalk Messaging shapes the same way you did for the Message Queuing shape. When the BizTalk Messaging Binding Wizard asks for the channel information, specify a dynamic channel. You'll also need to link a data field that contains the name of the messaging channel to the port reference on the data page, and the address field in the document must be protocol specific. In other words, if you use dynamic binding on a message queue, the address field must be a queue path. If you use dynamic binding on BizTalk Messaging, then the address field must be a channel name. Here's an example, with C_Message_ExternalClient being the channel name:

```
<message>
  <Address>C_Message_ExternalClient</Address>
  <Data>this is a test message</Data>
</message>
```

Using Web Services in BizTalk Orchestration

A *Web service* is an application or program that can be accessed through the Internet using the HTTP(S) protocol. The intriguing aspect of Web services is their ability to integrate applications running on different platforms in different locations. This benefit has been sought by many technologies in the past, such as DCOM, but they all faced a common challenge—each of them used a proprietary protocol to communicate with clients and servers.

Simple Object Access Protocol (SOAP) provides a standard way to access applications on a remote system. SOAP is a network protocol, and it has no programming model. It's merely a specification for how to invoke and receive the services of a remote system. With SOAP as the communication protocol between client and server, Web services have become easier than ever to use and implement.

Web services can be also be integrated with BizTalk Orchestration. There are two ways of integrating the Web services and BizTalk Orchestration:

- Accessing Web services within an XLANG Schedule

- Exposing XLANG Schedules as Web services

I'll discuss each in turn.

Accessing Web Services Within XLANG Schedules

BizTalk Orchestration doesn't provide a way to invoke Web services directly. However, because it can call COM components, you can make BizTalk Orchestration access the Web service through a COM implementation shape (see Figure 10-33).

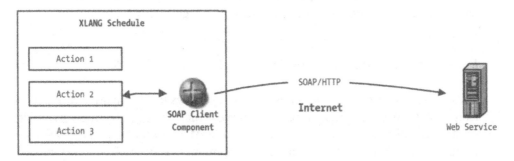

Figure 10-33. *Accessing a Web service from within an XLANG Schedule through a COM component binding*

Bob wants to retrieve a list of quotes from the stock exchange so that he can use it to calculate the current market values for the portfolios of his mutual fund clients. He heard that the major stock exchanges have implemented something called a Web service, which allows clients to request quotes through the Internet. He wants Mike to make their schedule capable of accessing this quote information through the Internet.

To enable the schedule to access the Web service, you need to develop a COM component that can access the Web service. The following code will create a SOAP client in Visual Basic:

```
Function QuoteServiceClient(doc As String) As String
Dim SoapClient As New MSSOAPLib.SoapClient
SoapClient.mssoapinit "http://w2kserver/QuoteService/QuoteService.wsdl",
"QuoteService", "QuoteServiceSoapPort"
QuoteServiceClient = SoapClient.ReceiveQuotes(doc)
End Function
```

You need to add "Microsoft SOAP Type library" to the VB project reference in order to access its functionality. First, you must instantiate a SoapClient object, since you are requesting the Web service as n client. Next, you need to initialize the SoapClient object with the Web Services Description Language (WSDL) file for the quote service. The WSDL file tells clients what methods and properties are available for service, and it also contains the data type for the parameter, and the result for the method calls. In other words, it's effectively a type library for the Web service.

To make a request for the Web service, you simply make a method call on the SoapClient object. All the work of generating a SOAP message and sending the message over to the other side are handled by the SoapClient object behind the scenes. With all the complex tasks being handled for you, you can simply call a method of the Web service as you do with a regular COM component.

Exposing XLANG Schedules As Web Services

XLANG Schedules can also be exposed as Web services to the outside, with help from a COM component. An XLANG Schedule is BizTalk Server technology, and it can't be directly exposed as a Web service as a COM component can be. However, there is a BizTalk API that allows a COM component to start an XLANG Schedule. You can use such a COM component as a wrapper for the XLANG Schedule, which will provide the real service.

Suppose the Stock Exchange is using BizTalk Orchestration to provide the quote service, and it has decided to expose this quote service as a Web service so that clients can request the stock quotes through the Internet (see Figure 10-34).

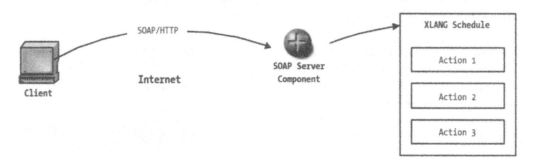

Figure 10-34. Exposing an XLANG Schedule as a Web service through a COM component

Three steps are involved in exposing an XLANG Schedule as a service:

1. Create an orchestration that has entry points for programmatic access from external applications.

2. Create a COM component that can interface with the XLANG Schedule.

3. Create the WSDL and WSML files for this COM component, and expose these files to the Internet for clients to access.

Step 1: Create an Orchestration with Entry Points

Figure 10-35 shows the Quote Service schedule running on a stock exchange's BizTalk Server to provide the quote service.

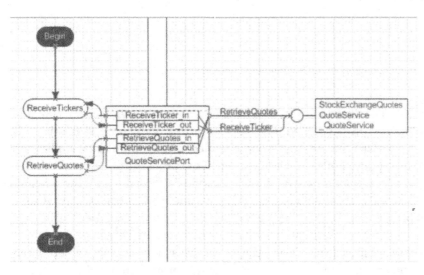

Figure 10-35. An orchestration that provides a quote service for clients

An important aspect of this schedule is that it contains entry points for external applications to start and control its flow. There are two actions on the schedule: ReceiveTickers, which receives documents that contain stock tickers from clients, and RetrieveQuotes, which returns the quotes for each ticker in the document.

When you configure the Method Communication Wizard for both actions, you'll see the window in Figure 10-36.

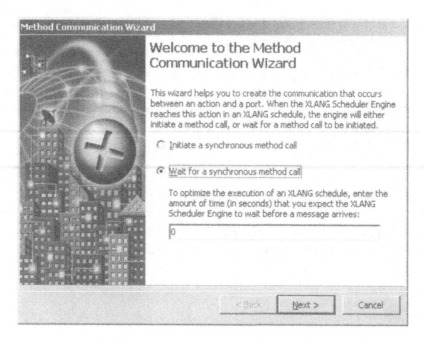

Figure 10-36. Method Communication Wizard

In the earlier situations, you've selected the "Initiate a synchronous method call" option, because the schedule is really in control of the process flow in earlier examples. This isn't the case in the quote service, where the external application (the COM wrapper in this case) is in control of the process flow of the schedule. When you select "Wait for a synchronous method call" on the port, the schedule process flow will stop when it reaches this port, and it won't continue until an external program makes a call to the method that the port is connecting to.

If you still feel unclear about this option, don't worry. Things will be clearer when you take a look at the COM wrapper for this schedule. That's where you'll see how you can control the flow of this schedule programmatically.

Step 2: Create a COM Component to Interface with the Schedule

The following code creates the COM wrapper that you'll expose as a Web service shortly:

```
Public Function QuoteServiceController(Tickers As String) As String
   Dim ssked_URL As String
   Dim sked As Object
```

```
'set the URL for quote service schedule.
ssked_URL = "sked:///C:\Program Files\Microsoft BizTalk Server\
XLANG Scheduler\quoteservice.skx/QuoteServicePort"
'Load and start the schedule
Set sked = GetObject(ssked_URL)

'Provide Ticker document by calling the method on the port
sked.ReceiveTicker (Tickers)

'Retrieve the quote result by calling the method on the port
QuoteServiceController = sked.RetrieveQuotes()
End Function
```

There are four key points you should know about the preceding code:

- *ssked_URL:* This is the path for the schedule. Port reference (QuoteServicePort) is part of the path.

- *set sked = GetObject(ssked_URL):* The GetObject method takes one parameter—the path of the skx file for the schedule you want to load. After you call this method, you have a running schedule that can be referenced by the object sked.

- *sked.ReceiveTicker (Tickers):* Before this method is called, the schedule you've just started is waiting on the QuoteServicePort port. This is because you've configured the port to wait until someone else initiates the ReceiveTicker method. By calling the ReceiveTicker method and passing in the ticker document, the process flow of the schedule can now continue to the next action: RetrieveQuotes.

- *sked.RetrieveQuotes:* Before this method is called, the schedule waits at the QuoteServicePort port. The schedule can't continue until something calls the RetrieveQuotes method. The RetrieveQuotes method returns the quotes for the tickers, and the return value is then assigned to the return value of the QuoteServiceController function. The schedule is then finished after the method call is completed.

As you can see, if you didn't set the schedule to wait for the initiation of the method, the schedule wouldn't wait for the external application to provide input data, and it wouldn't extract the output data at the right moment.

Step 3: Create the WSDL and WSML Files and Expose Them to the Internet

Once you've compiled this VB code into a DLL, you have a COM component that contains a method called QuoteServiceController. This method takes a ticker document as its input parameter and returns the quotes document. The next step is to enable the Web service on this COM component, and expose the QuoteServiceController method.

To enable the Web service on the COM component, you must create a WSDL file to describe the service provided in this component, and a WSML file to map the service in WSDL to the component. Creating these two documents can be an extremely tedious task. However, it only takes few clicks to create them if you use the WSDL generator that comes with SOAP Toolkit 2.0. SOAP Toolkit is a separate product, and you can download it free from the Microsoft Web site.

After you've installed SOAP Toolkit 2.0, open the WSDL generator by selecting Start ➤ Programs ➤ Microsoft SoapToolkit (see Figure 10-37). In the first SOAP Toolkit window, specify the name of the Web service and .dll file for which you'll be generating the WSDL file, and click Next to proceed.

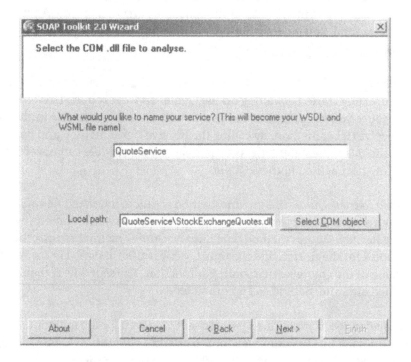

Figure 10-37. Defining the name and COM component for the Web service

When you click the Next button, the wizard will examine and gather information about the interface and methods of the COM component. In the window shown in Figure 10-38, the SOAP Toolkit displays the possible interfaces and methods you can expose for clients to access. Click the QuoteServiceController method, and click Next to proceed.

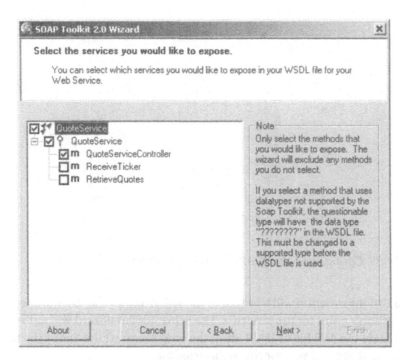

Figure 10-38. Selecting the method to expose through SOAP Toolkit

In the next window, shown in Figure 10-39, you need to provide the Uniform Resource Identifier (URI) of the listener file and the type of the listener. The listener can be either an ASP file or ISAPI .dll, as these are the files responsible for accepting the HTTP requests from clients and returning the results of their requests back to clients.

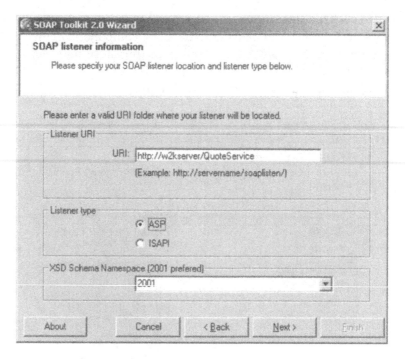

Figure 10-39. Configuring the SOAP listener for the service

The URI information will be saved to the WSDL file so that clients know where the entry point for the service is. The SOAP Toolkit Wizard will automatically generate the ASP file or ISAPI .dll at the end. You must then copy the files to the location of the URI you specify in this window.

Click Next to proceed. In the next window, specify the location where you want the SOAP Toolkit Wizard to save the generated file. Click Next until you finish.

The SOAP Toolkit Wizard has just created three files: QuoteService.wsdl, QuoteService.wsml, and QuoteService.asp. The last thing you need to do before you can start testing is to copy these three files to the file directory that http://w2kserver/QuoteService references.

Test the Web Service

To test the integration between the Web service and BizTalk Orchestration, you can start the QuoteServiceClient.skx file (included as part of the source code, available on the Downloads section of the Apress Web site, at http://www.apress.com). The QuoteServiceClient schedule will call the QuoteServiceClient component, which will make a SOAP call to the QuoteServiceController method hosted as a Web service under the http://w2kserver/QuoteService directory. QuoteServiceController will then start the QuoteService.skx file (included in the source code) to process the document and return the quotes back to the QuoteServiceController method, which in turn will pass the quotes back to the QuoteServiceClient component hosted inside the QuoteServiceClient XLANG Schedule.

In my case, both the QuoteServiceClient schedule and the QuoteService schedule are on the same machine. However, the communication between them is through a Web service. When I start the QuoteServiceClient schedule, my XLANG Event Monitor shows what you can see in Figure 10-40.

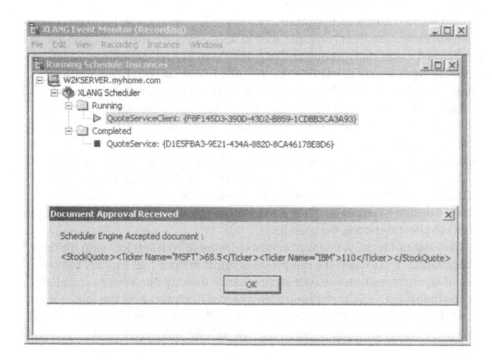

Figure 10-40. QuoteServiceClient schedule is calling the QuoteService schedule through a Web service.

In this test, you learned that you can make an XLANG Schedule access a Web service through a SOAP client component, and you can also turn an XLANG Schedule into a Web service by exposing it through a COM component that controls it.

Summary

You've learned several important features about BizTalk Orchestration in this chapter. You started with an exploration of orchestration transactions, and the three transaction styles—short-lived, long-running, and timed—and you saw their application in different business scenarios.

You also learned about XLANG Schedule throttling, a useful feature that allows you to control how many active XLANG Schedule instances are running at a time, hence controlling how much resources can be used for each type of orchestration on the system. This feature significantly boosts the scalability of XLANG Schedules on BizTalk Server.

You learned about orchestration correlation features, which allow you to correlate documents to their corresponding XLANG Schedule instances, and you also learned about dehydration and rehydration of XLANG Schedules, which are BizTalk Server's way of persisting running schedules to disk to free up system memory used by the schedules, boosting the system resources on that server.

Combining the dehydration/rehydration feature, orchestration correlation, and long-running transaction support in BizTalk Orchestration, you have an excellent solution for handling large amounts of workflow that can take hours or even days to complete, while still using minimum amounts of system resources.

Dynamic ports is another feature covered in this chapter that adds value to BizTalk Orchestration. With dynamic ports, your orchestrations now have the ability to decide where to send the document at runtime, as opposed to having to specify the destination at design time.

Last, but not least, you looked at how to leverage Web services with BizTalk Orchestration. You looked at a sample stock quote service that exposes the services of an orchestration as a Web service, hence making the services of BizTalk Orchestration available to multiple clients across the Internet at the same time.

In the next chapter, I'll show you what BizTalk Server offers from a programming perspective, and what you can achieve with BizTalk Server APIs.

CHAPTER 11

BizTalk Server Programming

IN THIS CHAPTER, you'll learn about the programming aspects of BizTalk Server. Up to this point, I've walked you through the process of creating a BizTalk Server application without writing much code, which was one of goals for developing a fast-to-market B2B and EAI solution. However, at times you'll want to have more control over how processes are done, and you'll want to customize the existing BizTalk features to fit your needs. In such cases, you need to write your own code to make things happen the way you want.

BizTalk Server offers a set of APIs that will help you create more flexible BizTalk Server solutions. I'll show you how to add custom business logic to BizTalk Messaging through the use of AICs (short for application integration components) and pipeline AICs, how to configure BizTalk Messaging programmatically though the BizTalk Configuration API, how to access the data store in the tracking database programmatically using the Tracking API and Interchange API, and how to interact with running XLANG Schedules through moniker activation. You'll continue working on Bob's ASP application as I discuss BizTalk Server programming.

Interchange Interface

Bob starts noticing that quite a few documents are accumulating in the BizTalk Server suspended queue. He wants Mike to create a simple Web application that will allow him to view all the details on the documents in the suspended queue and analyze them to find out why the documents failed to be processed. He also wants to be able to delete documents from the suspended queue. Mike is planning to write a Visual Basic program to handle this job. He just needs to find a way to get the information out of the suspended queue.

You've used the Interchange submit method in earlier chapters to get a document into BizTalk Server. It turns out that there are many methods available on this Interchange interface that you haven't seen yet. Some of the lesser known methods will help Mike get the information out of the suspended queue:

- *Submit():* By now you've used this method many times to submit a document into BizTalk Server's work queue.

- *SubmitSync():* This method functions much like the Submit method, except it is a synchronize call. The interchange is complete when this method returns.

- *CheckSuspendedQueue():* This method returns a list of handles for the document in the suspended queue. It can also filter documents based on its parameter values.

- *GetSuspendedQueueItemDetails():* This method obtains the interchange details for a document handle.

- *DeleteFromSuspendedQueue():* This method deletes one or more documents from the suspended queue.

The last three methods seem to fit Mike's needs perfectly. The finished SuspendDocTool program is shown in Figure 11-1.

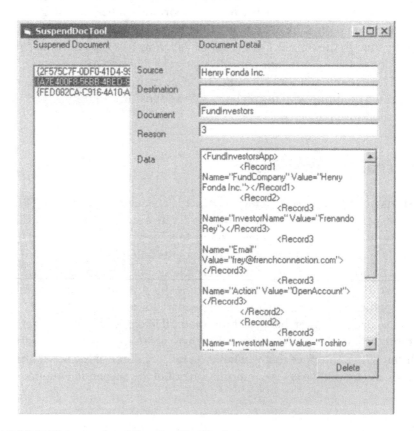

Figure 11-1. The completed SuspendDocTool program

This program has three major functions. On the left side of the window, it has a list box that shows the GUID for the documents in the BizTalk Server suspended queue. When one of the items on the list is clicked, the details about the selected suspended document will appear in the text boxes on the right side of the window. This information includes the source organization, destination organization, content of the document, etc. At the bottom of the window is a Delete button, which removes a specific document from the suspended queue. Let's look at the code.

The following code displays all the document handles in the suspended queue:

```
Private Sub Form_Load()

    Dim Doclist As Variant
    Dim interchange As BTSInterchangeLib.interchange

    Set interchange = New BTSInterchangeLib.interchange
    Doclist = interchange.CheckSuspendedQueue()

    For i = 0 To UBound(Doclist)
        List1.AddItem (Doclist(i))
    Next

End Sub
```

Before you start coding using the Interchange object, you need to add a reference to the BizTalk Interchange type library to the project. On the Visual Studio tool bar, select project ➤ Reference, then select Microsoft BizTalk Server Interchange 1.0 Type Library in the References window. The type library file for this reference is called cisapi.tlb and is located under the BizTalk Server Installation folder (for example, C:\Program Files\Microsoft BizTalk Server).

Following is the method signature of CheckSuspendedQueue:

```
Function CheckSuspendedQueue( _
    DocName As String, _
    SourceName As String, _
    DestName As String_
)
```

As you can see in the preceding code, the CheckSuspendedQueue method takes three optional parameters. If no parameter is provided, the method will return a list containing all the documents in the suspended queue. When one or more parameters are provided, the method will return a list of matching documents. For example, CheckSuspendedQueue("FundInvestors") will return all the FundInvestors documents in the suspended queue. To extract the document handle for the list box, you can loop through the document list that is returned from the method call.

The document handle has very little meaning for you, but the GetSuspendedQueueItemDetails method will need it to retrieve the detailed information about a specified document. This is the signature of the method:

```
Sub GetSuspendedQueueItemDetails( _
    ItemHandle As String, _
    SourceName As Variant, _
    DestName As Variant, _
    DocName As Variant, _
    ReasonCode As Variant, _
    ItemData As Variant
)
```

When one of the items is selected in the list box, the following code will fire and retrieve the detail information for the selected document:

```
Private Sub List1_Click()
On Error Resume Next
    Dim src, dst, doc, reas, data
    handle = List1.Text
    interchange.GetSuspendedQueueItemDetails handle, src, dst, doc, reas, data

    sourcevalue.Text = src
    destinationvalue.Text = dst
    documentvalue.Text = doc
    reasonvalue.Text = reas
    datavalue.Text = data

End Sub
```

You'll need to call the GetSuspendedQueueItemDetails method with the first parameter, which is the handle of the document. GetSuspendedQueueItemDetails doesn't have a return value. Instead, it will fill the second parameter with document's source organization name, the third parameter with the destination organization name, the fourth parameter with the document type name, the fifth parameter with the error code (the reason for failure), and the sixth parameter with the contents of the document.

The fifth parameter contains the numeric value that indicates different types of errors. Use the following list, taken from BizTalk Server online help, to find out what each one means:

- *noReason [0]:* Not supported for this release.

- *rtdlqParserFailure [1]:* Specifies that the instance of the document was placed in the queue because of failure of the parser.

- *rtdlqParserDocFailure [2]:* Specifies that the instance of the document was placed in the queue because the business document was invalid.

- *rtdlqDocValidation [3]:* Specifies that the document was placed in the queue because document validation failed.

- *rtdlqChannelSelectFailure [4]:* Specifies that the instance of the document was placed in the queue because of failure in selecting the correct IBizTalkChannel object.

- *rtdlqInvalidMap [5]:* Specifies that the instance of the document was placed in the queue because the map referred to by the IBizTalkChannel object was formatted incorrectly.

- *rtdlqFieldTrackingFailure [6]:* Specifies that the instance of the document was placed in the queue because the server was unable to track the requested fields within the document.

- *rtdlqMappingFailure [7]:* Specifies that the instance of the document was placed in the queue because of failure of transformation.

- *rtdlqSerializerFailure [8]:* Specifies that the instance of the document was placed in the queue because the server could not convert this document to its native format.

- *rtdlqEncodingFailure [9]:* Specifies that the instance of the document was placed in the queue because the server was unable to encode this interchange.

- *rtdlqSigningFailure [10]:* Specifies that the instance of the document was placed in the queue because the server was unable to sign this interchange.

- *rtdlqEncryptionFailure [11]:* Specifies that the instance of the document was placed in the queue because the server was unable to encrypt this interchange.

- *rtdlqTransmissionFailure [12]:* Specifies that the instance of the document was placed in the queue because the server was unable to deliver this document.

- *rtdlqUserMove [13]:* Specifies that the administrator moved this instance of the document to the queue.

- *rtdlqTimeout [14]:* Specifies that the instance of the document was placed in the queue because a time-out occurred.

- *rtdlqCustomCompFailure [15]:* Specifies that the instance of the document was placed in the queue because of failure of a custom component.

- *unkReason [16]:* Specifies that this item was marked as "In Process" by an inactive server. On restart of this server, this item was automatically moved to the suspended queue. There was probably a catastrophic failure on the original server. Contact the system administrator for more information.

- *rtdlqNoChannel [17]:* Specifies that the instance of the document was placed in the queue because the BizTalkChannel object was deleted.

- *rtdlqMissingChannel [18]:* Specifies that the instance of the document was placed in the queue because the BizTalkChannel object specified by the Submit method of the Interchange interface was not found.

- *rtdlqInvalidChannel [19]:* Specifies that the instance of the document was placed in the queue because the BizTalkChannel object specified by the Submit method of the Interchange interface specifies an open IBizTalkPort object. This isn't permitted.

- *rtdlqOutOfMemory [20]:* Specifies that your computer has run out of memory. Rebooting is recommended.

- *rtdlqBTFRecReqExpired [21]:* Specifies that the document was placed in the queue because the BTF timestamp receiptRequiredBy expired.

- *rtdlqBTFExpiresAtExpired [22]:* Specifies that the document was placed in the queue because the BTF timestamp expiresAt expired.

- *rtdlqCorrelationFailure [23]:* Specifies that the document receipt failed.

Last, let's look at the code behind the Delete button.

```
Private Sub Delete_Click()
On Error Resume Next
    interchange.DeleteFromSuspendedQueue (handle)
    List1.RemoveItem (List1.ListIndex)
    sourcevalue.Text = ""
    destinationvalue.Text = ""
    documentvalue.Text = ""
    reasonvalue.Text = ""
    datavalue.Text = ""
End Sub
```

In this code, the DeleteFromSuspendedQueue(handle) method removes the document from the suspended queue permanently.

You've just seen three methods of the Interchange interface that are related to the suspended queue. There is another method in the interface I haven't discussed yet: the SubmitSync method.

SubmitSync is similar to the Submit method, but the SubmitSync method forces the document to be processed in a synchronous manner. When you submit a document using the Submit method, the document is first put into the work queue where a member server in a BizTalk Server group will retrieve it later for additional processing. However, when you submit a document using the SubmitSync method, the document will bypass all the queues and execute all the components required by the messaging port on the calling thread. In other words, the document is processed in a synchronous manner, and the method call will not return until the document has completed processing.

One thing to note is that when multiple channels are matched for a document submission, only the Submit method can be used. SubmitSync will fail if the document needs to pass through more than one channel at once. If the destination of the document is an HTTP site or an AIC, then the document handle and response document can be returned to the SubmitSync call if they are available.

The signature of SubmitSync is as follows:

```
Sub SubmitSync( _
    Openness As BIZTALK_OPENNESS_TYPE, _
    Document As String, _
    DocName As String, _
    SourceQualifier As String, _
    SourceID As String, _
    DestQualifier As String, _
    DestID As String, _
    ChannelName As String, _
```

```
    FilePath As String, _
    EnvelopeName As String, _
    PassThrough As Long, _
    SubmissionHandle As Variant, _
    ResponseDocument As Variant
)
```

As you can see in this signature, the SubmitSync method takes two more optional parameters than the Submit method. When the last two parameters are provided, they will be filled with the value of the submission handle and the response document if available when the method returns. You can then access the values stored in the last two parameters.

In some situations you may want to use the SubmitSync method, such as when you have an AIC that processes a document and returns a response document indicating the status of the processing. You would then have to use the SubmitSync method to receive this returned document, since the Submit method isn't able to receive the response document.

Later in the chapter, I'll show you an example of this when developing the AIC component.

NOTE   *The SubmitSync method forces BizTalk Server to process the document in a synchronous manner. It eliminates the benefit of load balancing that BizTalk Server groups offer.*

AIC

In earlier examples, to invoke some customized business logic to process a document, you first created an orchestration and implemented the COM component or script component inside the orchestration. In this section, I'll demonstrate another way to invoke customized business logic. Application integration components (AICs) allow you to process a document without ever starting BizTalk Orchestration, as shown in Figure 11-2.

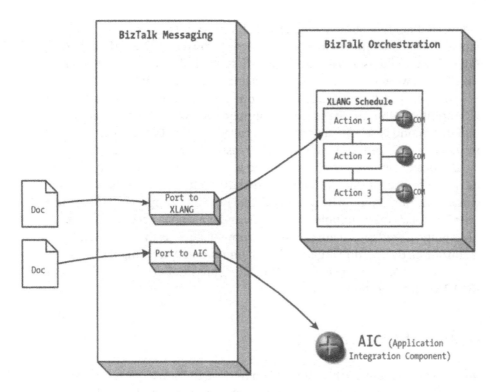

Figure 11-2. Processing a document with either an XLANG Schedule or an AIC

So how do you choose which method to use when both XLANG Schedules and AICs can eventually do the same thing? The answer lies in the type of business processes that need to be applied to the document. If a number of tasks are performed in a sequential manner on the document, and this workflow is formed by many plug and play components, using an orchestration will be a better choice. However, at times the tasks to be performed on the document can be treated as more or less a single action, and in this case an AIC is a good choice.

Let's use the SOAP client schedule as an example. As you learned in Chapter 10, Mike has created an orchestration to retrieve the stock quotes from a stock exchange's Web service. The orchestration then saves the document in the database to complete the process. This task can be done with orchestration, as you saw, but it would probably be much simpler to create an AIC component that requests the stock quote from the Web service and updates the database at once.

Another example is the FTP AIC component. Let's say you want to send a document to an external FTP site, because BizTalk Server doesn't support FTP natively. You'll need to write a COM component that will send the document through FTP. Do you really want to create an orchestration with only one task in it, which is to invoke the FTP component? Probably not. What is the point of adding all that orchestration overhead if all you want to do is call a COM component and pass a document to it? In such a case, you'd be better off developing an FTP AIC whose job is to pass the document to the FTP site. You could then call this FTP AIC whenever you are sending a document via FTP.

There are two types of AIC. The first one is the lightweight AIC, also known as BTSAppIntegration AIC. Its strength is simplicity, and it's much easier to create than the second type. The second type is called PipelineComponent AIC, or simply pipeline AIC, and as you've probably guessed it's relatively hard to create.

Besides the amount of effort involved in developing these two types of AIC, the real difference is that the BTSAppIntegration AIC only takes one parameter, which is the document to be processed. The PipelineComponent AIC, on the other hand, can take multiple parameters, and it also has access to all the messaging-related information of the document, such as the document's source organization, destination organization, submission ID, tracking ID, etc.

A number of steps are involved in creating an AIC. Let's start with the easier AIC: BTSAppIntegration.

BTSAppIntegration AIC

Mike wants to create a lightweight AIC to retrieve the stock quotes from the external Web service using SOAP, and then save it in the database. The QuoteServiceClient schedule created in Chapter 10 currently serves this purpose, but Mike feels this kind of operation is straightforward and doesn't need to be performed by an orchestration. He wants to create this AIC using Visual Basic.

AIC As a COM Component

Three major steps are involved in creating and deploying an AIC component:

1. Create the AIC component.

2. Register the AIC component.

3. Choose the AIC component as the destination for the BizTalk Messaging port.

The key difference between an AIC component and a regular COM component is that at runtime BizTalk Messaging will pass the document to the component through a common interface called IBTSAppIntegration, as shown in Figure 11-3. In other words, AIC is a COM component that implements the IBTSAppIntegration interface. To make an AIC, you must implement this interface on the component.

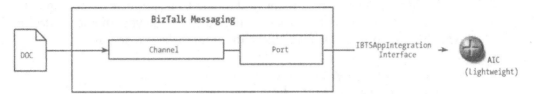

Figure 11-3. The document is passed from the port to the lightweight AIC through the IBTSAppIntegration interface.

Creating the AIC

To create the AIC, open Visual Basic and start a new project. You need to add a reference to the project, so on the Visual Basic menu, select project ➤ references, and then check the Microsoft BizTalk Server Application Interface Component 1.0 Type Library checkbox. You also need to add the Microsoft Soap Library so you can make SOAP calls in your program. MSSOPA1.dll, the library file for this reference, is located under the C:\Program Files\Common Files\MSSoap\Binaries folder.

There is only one method you have to implement for this IBTSAppIntegration interface: IBTSAppIntegration_ProcessMessage. Here is the code that does this:

```
Implements IBTSAppIntegration
Private Function IBTSAppIntegration_ProcessMessage(ByVal document As String)
 As String
On Error GoTo ErrorHandler
    Dim ResponseDoc As String
    ResponseDoc = QuoteServiceSoapClient(document)
    UpdateDB (ResponseDoc)
    IBTSAppIntegration_ProcessMessage = "Stock quotes update completed"
    Exit Function
ErrorHandler:
    On Error GoTo 0
    Err.Raise Err.Number, Err.Source,Err.Description
End Function
```

Notice the "Implements IBTSAppIntegration" on the very first line. You must include this line of code to make this component an AIC. The IBTSAppIntegration_ProcessMessage method takes the document that comes out of the message queue as the input parameter. If the method is completed successfully, the return value of this method would be "Stock quotes update completed".

Within the QuoteServiceSoapClient method, you perform two actions. First you call the Web service for the stock quote, and second you update the database with the latest quotes. Here are the methods for these two actions:

```
Private Function QuoteServiceSoapClient(document As String)
    Dim SoapClient As New MSSOAPLib.SoapClient
    SoapClient.mssoapinit "http://w2kserver/QuoteService/QuoteService.wsdl",
  "QuoteService", "QuoteServiceSoapPort"
    QuoteServiceClient = SoapClient.QuoteServiceController(document)
End Function


Private Sub UpdateDB(ResponseDoc)
'you code here to update the database
End Sub
```

The next step is to compile this program into a DLL file, and then to register this component in a way that is BizTalk Messaging friendly.

There are two ways to register this AIC component. You can register it using regedit or register it in COM+ to make it a configured component. First, let's see how to register with regsvr32.

Registering the AIC with regsvr32

After you compile the component in Visual Basic, the DLL is automatically registered on the system. However, to make this component show up on the list of available AIC components when specifying the destination of the message port, you must also add the following registry keys:

```
[HKEY_CLASSES_ROOT\CLSID\AIC_CLSID\Implemented Categories\
{5C6C30E7-C66D-40e3-889D-08C5C3099E52}]


[HKEY_CLASSES_ROOT\CLSID\AIC_CLSID\Implemented Categories\
{BD193E1D-D7DC-4b7c-B9D2-92AE0344C836}]
```

The instances of AIC_CLSID in the preceding lines should be replaced with the component's class ID before adding those lines to the system registry. To determine the class ID of a registered component, you can search the registry with the regedit.exe tool for the ProgID of the AIC component, which is in the form of ProjectName.ClassName. When the registry entry is found, look for the CLSID key under the returned registry entry.

The first of the two preceding registry keys tells BizTalk Server that the component is a valid BizTalk Server component and that the component can be used as a preprocessor. (Preprocessors are discussed in the "Preprocessors" section in this chapter.) The second registry key tells BizTalk Server that the component is an AIC component.

Choosing the AIC As the Destination for the Messaging Port

After you add the preceding registry keys, the next step is to select the new AIC component as the destination of a messaging port, as shown in Figure 11-4.

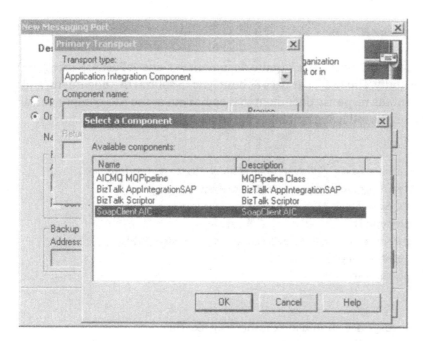

Figure 11-4. Selecting the component from the AIC list as the destination for the message port

If you hadn't added the two registry keys, the SoapClient.AIC wouldn't show up in this list even though the component has implemented the necessary interface.

Registering the AIC in COM+

There is a second way to register the AIC that is much easier. Instead of editing the system registry, you can simply drag and drop the DLL to an application under the COM+ component service. No additional steps are necessary to register the component. By registering AIC as a COM+ application, you can take advantage of the features COM+ offers, such as transaction support, pooling, security authentication, etc.

One thing to note is that if the AIC component is configured to perform a security check, you'll need to allow the account used by BizTalk Messaging to access the AIC, since the Messaging service will be the one to instantiate the AIC component. If you are using AIC as an unconfigured component, then the AIC will be running in the same process as BizTalk Messaging. When the AIC crashes, it may bring down the BizTalk Messaging service. Therefore, I recommended that you make the AIC a configured component to provide better protection for BizTalk Messaging.

Testing the AIC

To test the AIC, post a stock quote document to GenericPost.asp using the VB HTTP utility. The ASP page uses SubmitSync to submit the document, and to write out the response document that comes out of the AIC component, as shown in the following section of the code:

```
<%
    set oInterchange = Server.CreateObject("Biztalk.Interchange")
    oInterchange.submitsync 1,PostedDocument,,,,,, _
        "C_SoapClient_AIC",,,,handle,responsedoc
    Response.write " Handle is: " & handle
    Response.write " Response Document is  " & responsedoc
    set oInterchange=nothing
    Response.Status="200 OK"
%>
```

The response should look something like this:

```
200 - OK    Handle is: {974BB032-1C3B-470A-AA38-940481FD152E}
Response document is:  Stock Quotes have been updated successfully
```

If the result was not what you expected, you could always debug the AIC component just as you would any other component.

AIC As a .NET Component

The preceding sections showed how to create an AIC component as a COM component. But what do you need to do if you plan to create an AIC using C# or VB .NET? Does this still work well with BizTalk Messaging, which isn't built on the .NET Framework? The answer is yes, of course.

Before you start to build your AIC component in .NET, you need to understand two important concepts: shared assemblies and the Runtime Callable Wrapper (RCW).

In .NET, there are two types of assemblies: private and shared. When you compile an assembly in Visual Studio .NET, a private assembly is automatically created and saved in the project folder or subfolder of the project folder. These folders are isolated from the rest of the system. The private assembly is intended for access by one application only. If you want to create an assembly that can be shared by multiple applications, the way the DLLs are shared among different applications, you then need to compile the assembly as a shared assembly and place it into the Global Assembly Cache (GAC). The GAC, which is located under C:\WINNT\Assembly, contains all the shared assemblies that exist on the system.

In this case, because you want BizTalk Messaging to access your .NET AIC component, you'll need to make this .NET component a shared assembly.

One way .NET is backward compatible with COM is through a proxy that sits between the .NET component and the COM component called a *callable wrapper*. There are two types of callable wrappers: RCW and CCW.

RCW, or Runtime Callable Wrapper, enables a .NET object to access a COM object. For example, if you're creating a .NET AIC that will need to access the COM interface IBTSAppIntegration, you'll need to access it through the RCW, which acts as a proxy and marshals the call between the .NET object and the COM object, as shown in Figure 11-5.

Accessing COM Object Through
Runtime Callable Wrapper

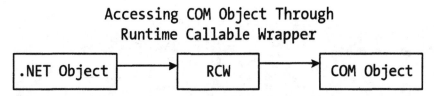

Figure 11-5. Accessing a COM object through RCW

CCW, or COM Callable Wrapper, on the other hand, enables a COM object to access a .NET object. In this case, after you've created your .NET AIC, you must create a CCW in order for BizTalk Messaging service to access it, as shown in Figure 11-6.

Accessing .NET Object Through
Component Callable Wrapper

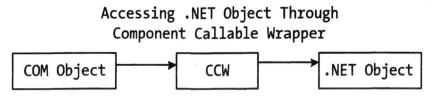

Figure 11-6. Accessing a .NET component through CCW

With that said, here's what's involved in re-creating your AIC in C# and making it available to BizTalk Messaging Service:

1. Import the BizTalk Server Application Interface type library into GAC.

2. Create the C# AIC component.

3. Expose the .NET AIC component as a COM component through regasm.exe (a utility to register and expose the .NET component COM client). or make it a configured COM+ component.

4. Select the .NET AIC as the destination of the message port.

Importing the BizTalk Server Application Interface Type Library

The first thing you need to do is import the BizTalk Server Application Interface type library to GAC so that your C# program can access its interface. Every assembly in the GAC has a strong name that is used to sign the wrapper assembly for the BizTalk Server Application Interface type library.

Open the command prompt, and type in following command (see Figure 11-7):

```
c:\>sn -k c:\BTSAppIntegration.snk
```

Figure 11-7. Creating a strong name file for the wrapper assembly

A key pair will be created at the location you specified. The Strong Name tool (sn), which comes with the .NET Framework, allows you to create a key pair to be used to provide a globally unique name for the assembly and also to digitally sign the assembly to ensure it has not been tampered with.

The next step is to create the RCW assembly for the BizTalk Server Application Interface type library. You also want to sign this new RCW assembly with the key you've just created. Type in the following command (see Figure 11-8):

```
tlbimp "c:\Program Files\Microsoft BizTalk
Server\btscomplib.tlb" /out: c:\temp\BTSAppIntegration.dll /namespace:
BTSAppIntegration /asmversion:1.0 /keyfile:
c:\BTSAppIntegration.snk /primary
```

Figure 11-8. Using tlbimp to create an RCW assembly for the btscomplib type library

You use tlbimp to create an RCW assembly for a given COM type library. As you can see in Figure 11-8, the new RCW assembly is being copied to c:\temp\BTSAppIntegration.dll.

The next step is to register this assembly into the GAC. You can either drag and drop the BTSAppIntegration.dll file to the c:\Winnt\Assembly folder, or use the following command:

```
gacutil /i BTSAppIntegrationLib.dll
```

If successful, the new assembly should appear under the GAC folder (c:\Winnt\Assembly), as shown in Figure 11-9.

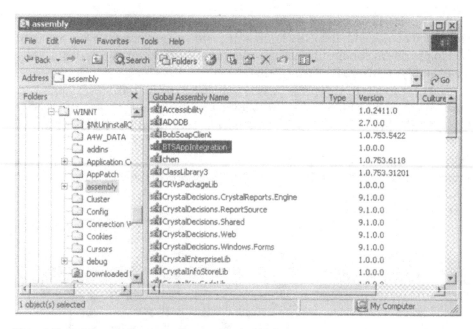

Figure 11-9. The newly created assembly in GAC

Creating the C# AIC Component

The next step is to create your AIC component in C#. Open Visual Studio .NET, and create a new project called SoapClientDotNet. Then add a new class file called AIC.cs.

Before you start coding, you should add the references you'll need to use in the project. Open the menu bar of Visual Studio .NET, select Project, and then select Reference. You want to add two references, as shown in Figure 11-10.

The first reference shown in Figure 11-10 is the System.EnterpriseServices component, which you'll need for making your .NET AIC component a configured component. The second reference is the wrapper assembly you just created. You'll need to access the BizTalk Server Application Interface type library through it. Click OK to add them to the project.

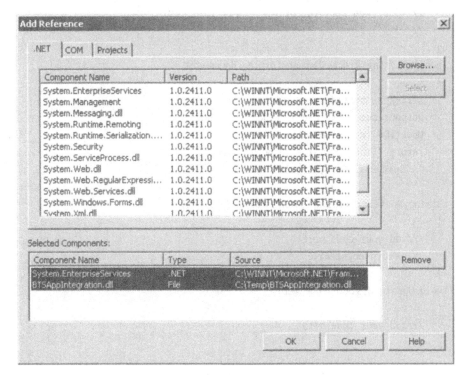

Figure 11-10. Adding references to the project

Next, add the following code to the AIC.cs file:

```
using System;
using BTSAppIntegration;
using System.EnterpriseServices;
using System.Runtime.InteropServices;

namespace SoapClientDotNet
{
    /// <summary>
    /// Summary description for AIC.
    /// </summary>

        [Guid("2BC73916-FB97-4049-B1AF-DF6BBB43CDB2")]
    public class AIC : ServicedComponent, IBTSAppIntegration
    {
        public AIC()
        {
            //
```

```
        // TODO: Add constructor logic here
        //
    }
    public string ProcessMessage(string document)
    {
        string responsedoc;
        responsedoc = QuoteServiceSoapClient(document);
        UpdateDB (responsedoc);
        return "Stock Quotes have been updated _
            successfully by .NET AIC";
                        }
    string QuoteServiceSoapClient(string document)
    {
        ///add your code here
            return document;
    }
    void UpdateDB(string document)
    {
        ///add your code here
    }
  }
}
```

In the preceding code, there are three additional classes you'll be using in the code: BTSAppIntegration, System.EnterpriseServices, and System.Runtime.InteropServices. The public class AIC extends the ServicedComponent class and IBTSAppIntegration interface. The class also has to implement the ProcessMessage method required by IBTSAppIntegration.

Because you'll export this class as a configured COM+ component, you need to add the [GUID] attribute for your class. The [GUID] attribute is used to specify a globally unique identifier (GUID) for a class or an interface. In Visual Basic 6, the IDE will generate a GUID for you when you compile the component. In C#, you need to provide this attribute manually. The easiest way to obtain a GUID is to find an existing GUID in your system registry and modify several of its bits to produce a new globally unique identifier.

You also need to modify the Assembly.cs to set the attribute for the COM+ package that hosts your AIC class. Here's the code of the Assembly.cs file under the SoapClientDotNet project.

```
using System.Reflection;
using System.Runtime.CompilerServices;
using System.EnterpriseServices;
```

```
// some default assembly directive.
// Add reference to the strong name
[assembly: AssemblyKeyFile(@"c:\BTSAIC.snk")]
// Add the COM+ Application configuration
[assembly: ApplicationName("SoapClientDotNet")]
[assembly: ApplicationID("7F8DB6A1-9CFC-433c-B907-AA892687D539")]
[assembly: Description("BTS AIC As Dot Net Component")]
[assembly: ApplicationActivation(ActivationOption.Server)]
```

To host this class under COM+, you need to first add a reference to
System.EnterpriseServices, as shown in the preceding code. You also must create
a strong name file to be used as AssemblyKeyFile when the class is hosted under
COM+. You can create this with "sn -k" as you did earlier for the RCW assembly.

The attribute settings in the preceding code specify that you're creating a
COM+ Server application called SoapClientDotNet. Its application ID is
7F8DB6A1-9CFC-433c-B907-AA892687D539. (This GUID is only for this example;
you should generate your own GUID to be the application ID for your AIC component.)

Finally, you need to compile this project by clicking Rebuild All on the
menu bar.

Exposing the .NET AIC Component As a COM Component

If the compile succeeds, your next step is to register your newly created .NET
assembly to COM+ using the following command (see Figure 11-11):

```
C:\C#\BTSAICDotNet\bin\Debug>regsvcs SoapClientDotNet.dll
```

*Figure 11-11. Registering the .NET component into COM+ with the regsvcs
command*

If the .NET assembly is registered successfully, you should find
a COM+ application called SoapClientDotNet and a component called
SoapClientDotNet.AIC under it, as shown in Figure 11-12.

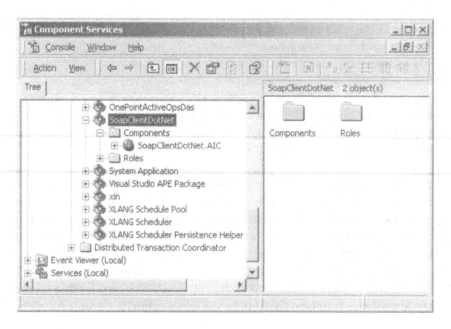

Figure 11-12. The .NET component SoapClientDotNet.AIC, hosted under the COM+ application

Because you've just registered the AIC as the COM+ application, you don't have to manually add the registry keys you used earlier with the unconfigured AIC component.

Selecting the .NET AIC As the Destination for the Messaging Port

The last step is to make this .NET AIC the destination of the message port, as shown in Figure 11-13.

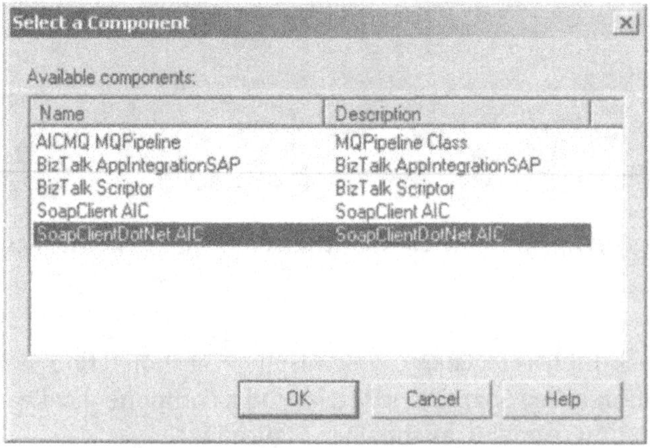

Figure 11-13. Selecting the SoapClientDotNet.AIC as the destination for the message port

If you post a document to GenericPost.asp, which uses the SubmitSync method to submit the document to BizTalk Server, you will get the following response back, which indicates that the request has been passed to and processed by your new .NET AIC.

```
200 - OK    Handle is: {BB666DBE-0948-4860-8B7E-A85E9F88AB7B}
Response document is:  Stock Quotes have been updated successfully by .NET AIC
```

IPipelineComponent AIC

In the previous section, you learned about the lightweight BTSAppIntegration AIC, and how to create AICs as COM and .NET components. I'll now show you what the Pipeline AIC can offer that is worth the additional effort.

The lightweight AIC is simple and easy to develop, but it lacks flexibility because it doesn't take parameters other than the document itself. Every document is processed the same way, as long as the same AIC is involved. If you want to customize the way the document is processed inside a lightweight AIC, you would have to create another AIC with different business logic.

BizTalk Server provides another type of AIC for this situation, called a pipeline AIC. The biggest difference between a lightweight AIC and a pipeline AIC is that the pipeline AIC can have multiple parameters or properties, which can be set during the configuration of the messaging port that uses it. Once these properties are configured, their values are persisted and are available to the BizTalk Messaging service at runtime.

Even though you haven't created a pipeline AIC yet, you've certainly seen one in action. The file transport type, which you select during the advanced properties configuration of a channel, is a perfect example of the use of pipeline AICs (see Figure 11-14).

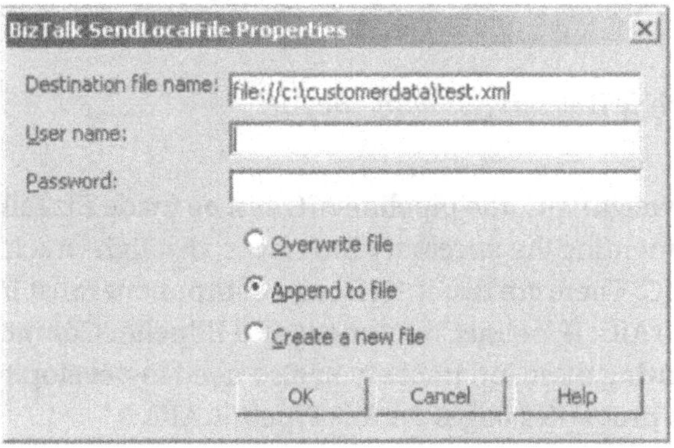

Figure 11-14. A file transport's Properties page

When you select a transport type for the port, you are actually selecting the pipeline AIC that comes with BizTalk Server—you specify the parameters for the pipeline AIC on the Properties page during the advanced configuration of the channel. As you can see, a lightweight AIC would not be able to do the job, since it would take the documents coming out of every channel and deal with them the same way. You wouldn't have the flexibility to change the behaviors and attributes of the AIC by simply modifying its property values.

Bob wants to extend the global reach of his business. He wants to provide his clients with the ability to trade in the overseas market. So he asks Mike to modify the existing SoapClient AIC, which currently can request the quotes from only one stock exchange, to enable the quote service for all the major stock exchanges in the world. Each of these exchanges have their own Web service address and request user ID and password to access the service.

Because this operation requires inputting many parameters, Mike decides to build a pipeline AIC to handle the job. Figure 11-15 shows how this pipeline AIC fits into what Bob wants to accomplish.

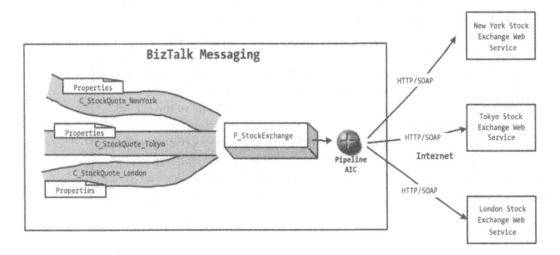

Figure 11-15. Connecting multiple Web services with one AIC

Like the lightweight AIC, the pipeline AIC can be made BizTalk Messaging friendly by implementing the necessary interfaces, through which the document is passed to the AIC. There are two interfaces a component must implement to become a pipeline AIC: IPipelineComponent and IPipelineComponentAdmin. Besides implementing these interfaces, you also need to develop two ASP pages, which are used as properties pages for this Pipeline AIC.

There are three steps involved in deploying a pipeline AIC component:

1. Create the pipeline AIC component.

2. Register the component and select it as the destination for the port.

3. Create the properties page used by this pipeline component.

Creating the Pipeline AIC Component

First, I'll walk you through creating a pipeline AIC in Visual Basic. Open Visual Basic and start a new project called SoapClient2. Then add a class named PipelineAIC.

Before you go into the code, you first need to add a couple of references to the project. From the menu bar of Visual Basic, select Project ➤ References, and then check the Microsoft Commerce 2000 Default Pipeline Component Type Library and Microsoft Commerce 2000 Core Component Type Library check-boxes.

The pipeline AIC is based on the pipeline component technology that was first introduced in Microsoft Site Server, the predecessor of Commerce Server. Because of this, you have to implement these two interfaces: IPipelineComponent and IPipelineComponentAdmin.

IPipelineComponent contains following two methods:

```
Function Execute(DispOrder As Object, DispContext As Object, Flags As Long _
) As Long
Sub EnableDesign(Enable As Boolean)
```

IPipelineComponentAdmin contains following two methods:

```
Function GetConfigData() As Object
Sub SetConfigData(ConfigDictionary As Object)
```

First, let's take a look the Execute method. The Execute method is similar to IBTSAppIntegration_ProcessMessage(document as String), except Execute takes three parameters: DispOrder, DispContext, and Flags. When the BizTalk Messaging port calls the Execute method of IPipelineComponent, it will provide values for these three parameters.

DispContext is a null object, because it isn't used by BizTalk Server. Flags is a reserved parameter and isn't used either. The only meaningful object that is passed to the Execute function by the message port is the first parameter, DispOrder. DispOrder is a transport dictionary object (a type of CDictionary object, which is a generic object, originally from Commerce Server, for storing name/value pairs). It contains the document itself and values for many other messaging-related fields.

Table 11-1 lists some commonly used fields inside this transport dictionary object. To retrieve the values stored in these fields, use the DispOrder(field_name) method.

Table 11-1. Commonly Used Fields in the Transport Dictionary Object

DICTIONARY FIELD NAME	DESCRIPTION
working_data	Contents of the submitted document
doc_type	Root node of the inbound document
out_doc_doc_type	Root node of the outbound document
Src_ID_Type	Source identifier type
Src_ID_Value	Source identifier value
Tracking_ID	Document tracking ID
Document_name	Outbound document's definition name
Dest_ID_Type	Destination identifier type
Dest_ID_Value	Destination identifier value
Responsefield	Response document

The second method is EnableDesign, which takes one Boolean parameter. This method is called when the dictionary properties are being set at design time, which is when you change the values through the advanced properties page, during channel configuration.

Now let's take a look at the methods in the IPipelineComponentAdmin interface: GetConfigData() and SetConfigData(ConfigDictionary as object).

GetConfigData() retrieves the current property data from the component properties page and displays it on the advanced properties page during channel configuration.

SetConfigData(ConfigDictionary as object) is called to save the property settings to the properties page of the component when the changes have been made on the advanced properties page during channel configuration. This method is also called immediately before BizTalk Messaging sends the document to the pipeline component. It passes in the dictionary object containing the AIC's property settings configured for the channel so that the properties can be accessed at runtime.

Figure 11-16 summarizes how these methods are called at both design time and runtime.

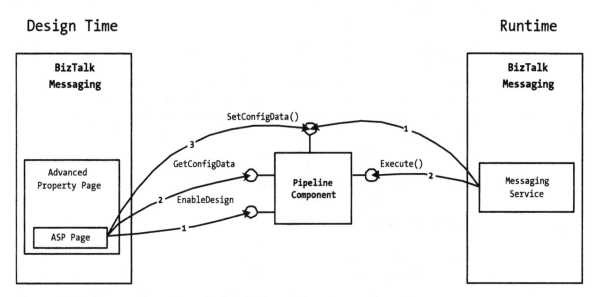

Figure 11-16. Comparison of methods called at design time and runtime

Design time is when you configure the properties on the component. Whenever you open the advanced properties page for the pipeline component, a couple of Active Server Pages will be called. These ASP pages will configure the component for design mode by calling the EnableDesign method, and they will then call the GetConfigData method to retrieve and display the current property values. If users make changes to the properties, the SetConfigData method is called to save the changes.

At run time, when the BizTalk Messaging service is about to send a document to a pipeline component, it will first call the SetConfigData method and pass in the dictionary object containing the properties configured on the channel's advanced properties page. It will then call the Execute method and pass it another dictionary object containing the document and other message-related fields. After the Execute method has completed, the Responsefield of the dictionary object will be returned to the caller.

Now that you've seen an overview of the interfaces and methods involved in the pipeline AIC component , let's return to the Visual Basic program. Here is the sample code in the Pipeline AIC class:

```
Implements IPipelineComponentAdmin
Implements IPipelineComponent
Const success = 0
```

```vb
Const failure = 2
'declare variables to store property values
Private url As String
Private method As String
Private userid As String
Private password As String

Private Sub IPipelineComponent_EnableDesign(ByVal fEnable As Long)
'Do Nothing (the code in this subroutine will not be executed, the
'existence of this subroutine is only to comply with the requirements of
'fully implementing the interface.)
End Sub 'IPipelineComponent_EnableDesign

Private Function IPipelineComponent_Execute(ByVal dictTransport As Object, _
    ByVal pdispContext As Object, _
    ByVal lFlags As Long) As Long

 On Error GoTo ExecuteError
 Dim ResponseDoc As String

 'Overwrite configuration defaults with any values passed in
 IPipelineComponentAdmin_SetConfigData dictTransport

 If Not pdispContext Is Nothing Then
    IPipelineComponentAdmin_SetConfigData pdispContext
 End If

 'call the web service
 ResponseDoc = QuoteServiceSoapClient(url, method,
 dictTransport("working_data"), _
    userid, password)
 UpdateDB (ResponseDoc)
 'set the response document
dictTransport("Responsefield") = "Stock Quotes from " & _
     url & " have been updated successfully by Pipeline AIC"
 'return success
 IPipelineComponent_Execute = success
 Exit Function

ExecuteError:
    IPipelineComponent_Execute = failure   'Serious Error Occurred
End Function 'IPipelineComponent_Execute
```

```
Private Function IPipelineComponentAdmin_GetConfigData() As Object
    Dim objectConfig As New CDictionary

    objectConfig.Value("url") = url
    objectConfig.Value("method") = method
    objectConfig.Value("userid") = userid
    objectConfig.Value("password") = password

    Set IPipelineComponentAdmin_GetConfigData = objectConfig
End Function 'IPipelineComponentAdmin_GetConfigData

Private Sub IPipelineComponentAdmin_SetConfigData(ByVal pDict As Object)
    'set value for url
    If Not IsNull(pDict("url")) Then
        url = CStr(pDict("url"))
    End If
    'set value for method
    If Not IsNull(pDict("method")) Then
        method = CStr(pDict("method"))
    End If
    'set value for userid
    If Not IsNull(pDict("userid")) Then
        userid = CStr(pDict("userid"))
    End If
    'set value for method
    If Not IsNull(pDict("password")) Then
        password = CStr(pDict("password"))
    End If
End Sub 'IPipelineComponentAdmin_SetConfigData

Private Function QuoteServiceSoapClient(ByVal url As String, _
 ByVal method As String, _
        ByVal working_dat, ByVal userid As String, _
 ByVal password As String) As String
    Dim ResponseDoc
    'Add your code to call the web service,
    'and save the return data to ResponseDoc
    QuoteServiceSoapClient = ResponseDoc
End Function

Private Sub UpdateDB(document As String)
    'add your code to update stock quotes in database
End Sub
```

In the general declarations section of the class, you need to implement the two interfaces required for pipeline AIC components and declare the four private variables that store the values of the AIC's properties.

In the IPipelineComponent_Execute method, you can perform whatever business logic is necessary, and then create a response document to be returned to the caller by setting dictTransport("Responsefield").

In the IPipelineComponentAdmin_SetConfigData method, you'll assign the private variables declared at the top of the code to the property values stored in the dictionary object parameter.

Registering the Component and Selecting It As the Destination for the Port

After you have completed the Visual Basic program, you can either register it and manually add the two category IDs to the registry keys for this component, or you can simply install it in a COM+ application.

If the pipeline AIC component is registered successfully, the SoapClient2.PipelineAIC component should appear as one of the items on the AIC list for the destination of the messaging port, as shown in Figure 11-17.

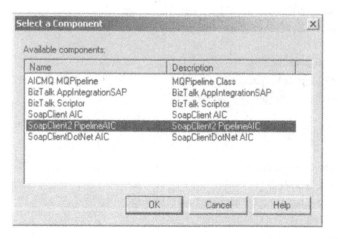

Figure 11-17. Selecting SoapClient2.PipelineAIC as the destination of the messaging port

Creating the Properties Page

The next step is to create the properties page for this pipeline AIC component so that you can set the values for the property fields needed by this component. There are two ASP files that set and retrieve property values, and they must meet two special requirements for the properties pages to be loaded properly.

First, these two ASP pages must be named [projectname]_[classname].asp and [projectname]_[classname]_post.asp. For example, the progid for this pipeline component is SoapClient2.PipelineAIC, so the ASP filenames are SoapClient2_PipelineAIC.asp and SoapClient2_PipelineAIC_post.asp, respectively.

Second, these two files must be copied to the directory under [BizTalk installation directory]\MessagingManager\pipeline. With these restrictions on the filenames and locations, BizTalk Messaging is able to load the correct ASP file based on the progid of the AIC component.

The Projectname_classname.asp file contains the user interface for the properties of the AIC component. This is the code for SoapClient2_PipelineAIC.asp:

```
<%@ LANGUAGE = VBScript %>
<!--#INCLUDE FILE="pe_edit_header.asp" -->
<%
call InputText("url")
call InputText("method")
call InputText("userid")
call InputPassword("password")
%>
<!--#INCLUDE FILE="pe_edit_footer.asp" -->
```

As you can see, this ASP page is very simple. There are four InputText method calls between the header include file and the footer include file. The InputText method is one of many methods provided by the header file and files included in the header file.

Table 11-2 lists several useful methods that are available when designing the user interface of the component's properties page. If you are interested in how each of these methods is defined, check out the pe_global_edit.asp file located under [BizTalk Server Installation Folder]\MessagingManager\pipeline (for example, C:\Program Files\Microsoft BizTalk Server\MessagingManager\pipeline).

Table 11-2. Methods Available When Designing the User Interface of a Component's Properties Page

METHOD NAME	DESCRIPTION
InputTextArea(field)	Displays a text area box for the AIC's property field
InputText(field)	Displays a textbox for the AIC's property field
InputTextAccel(field,accel)	Displays a textbox for the AIC's property field and creates an accelerator key to access it
InputPassword(field)	Displays a textbox with password mask for the AIC's property field
InputPasswordAccel(field,accel)	Displays a textbox with password mask for the AIC's property field and creates an accelerator key to access it
DisplayReadonlyText(field)	Displays a read-only textbox for the AIC's property field
InputSelection(field, list, accel)	Displays a drop-down list that contains the possible values this AIC's property field can take and creates an accelerator key to access it
InputArray(field)	Equivalent to InputSelection, except you can't specify an accelerator key
InputArrayAccel(field,arr,accel)	Equivalent to InputSelection
InputSimpleList(field,listname)	Displays a drop-down combo box with field as the label, from a dictionary object called listname
InputSimpleListAccel(field,listname,accel)	Displays a drop-down combo box with field as the label, from a dictionary object called listname, and creates an accelerator key
InputOption (name,value)	Displays an option with a specific name and value to a drop-down combo box
InputRadio (name,value,custom_title,table_entry)	Displays a radio button with a different display name, customer_title, and optional descriptive text represented by table_entry
InputRadioAccel (name,value,custom_title,table_entry,accel)	Displays a radio button with a different display name, customer_title, and optional descriptive text represented by table_entry, and creates an accelerator key to access it
InputCheckbox(name)	Displays a checkbox for the AIC property field
InputCheckboxAccel(name,accel)	Displays a checkbox for the AIC property field, and creates an accelerator key to access it
InputNumber(field)	Displays a text box for a number field of AIC properties

(continued)

Table 11-2. Methods Available When Designing the User Interface of a Component's Properties Page (continued)

METHOD NAME	DESCRIPTION
InputNumberAccel(field,accel)	Displays a text box for a number field of AIC properties, and creates an accelerator key to access it
InputFloat(field)	Displays a text box for a floating-point field of AIC properties
InputFloatAccel(field,accel)	Displays a text box for a floating-point field of AIC properties and creates an accelerator key to access it

The projectname_classname_post.asp page is called when you click OK to save the changes made on the properties page. The projectname_classname_post.asp doesn't contain any UI code as the other one does. Its sole purpose is to save the property settings for the pipeline AIC component. As with the other page, there is a set of predefined methods that you can call to save the property settings.

The following code is from SoapClient2_PipelineAIC_post.asp:

```
<%@ LANGUAGE = VBScript %>
<!--#INCLUDE FILE="pe_global_edit.asp" -->
<%
call GetInputText("url", 0, bufsize_medium)
call GetInputText("method", 0, bufsize_medium)
call GetInputText("userid", 0, bufsize_medium)
call GetInputPassword("password", 0, bufsize_medium)
%>
<!--#INCLUDE FILE="pe_post_footer.asp" -->
```

The code contains four method calls that correspond to the four method calls in the SoapClient2_PipelineAIC.asp. GetInputText, along with the other "Get" methods, will retrieve the property values specified in data fields on the SoapClient2_PipelineAIC.asp page and save them to a dictionary object. This dictionary object is then stored in the pipeline AIC component.

The "Get" method must be comparable with the UI object from which it retrieves the data. For example, the GetInputPassword method can only retrieve values in UI objects created by the InputPassword method. Table 11-3 lists available methods that retrieve the data from the UI object in the projectname_class.asp page.

Table 11-3. Methods Available When Retrieving the Configuration Information from the Component's Properties Page

METHOD NAME	DESCRIPTION
GetInputText(field, min, max)	Processes the data from a corresponding text box field with specified minimum and maximum lengths. Comparable UI objects: InputText, InputTextAccel, InputTextArea, DisplayReadonlyText
GetInputPassword(field, min, max)	Processes the data from a corresponding password field with specified minimum and maximum lengths. Comparable UI object: InputPassword
GetSelection(field, min, max)	Processes the data from a corresponding Select field with specified minimum and maximum lengths. Comparable UI objects: InputSelection, InputArray, InputArrayAccel, InputSimpleListAccel, InputSimpleList
GetInputNumber(field, min, max)	Processes the data from a corresponding number text box field with specified minimum and maximum lengths. Comparable UI objects: InputNumber, InputNumberAccel
GetInputFloat(field, min, max)	Processes the data from a corresponding floating-point text box field with specified minimum and maximum lengths. Comparable UI objects: InputFloat, InputFloatAccel
GetCheckBox(field)	Processes the data from a corresponding checkbox field with specified minimum and maximum lengths. Comparable UI objects: InputCheckbox, InputCheckboxAccel

After you save these two ASP files to the [BizTalk installation directory]\ Managing Manager\pipeline folder, you're ready to see them in action. Open the advanced properties page of the channel that connects the Pipeline AIC port, and click the Property button in the Primary Transport tab. A Properties window, which is an ASP page, pops up (see Figure 11-18).

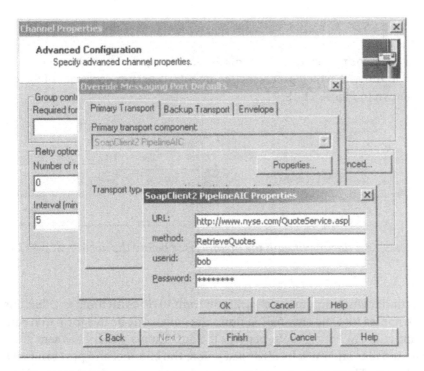

Figure 11-18. Specifying the property settings for the pipeline AIC component during the channel configuration

The Properties window shows the four property fields you defined in the ASP page. Click OK to save the changes.

To test this component, post the quote document using the VB HTTP utility. The response should look like this:

```
200 - OK    Handle is: {F0980FD2-5499-4645-AD11-3CDBE03C7619}
Response document is:   Stock Quotes from http://www.nyse.com/QuoteService.asp
have been updated successfully by Pipeline AIC
```

Pipeline AIC As a .NET Component

To create a .NET pipeline component, you need to follow the same procedure as for creating the lightweight .NET AIC. The principle of creating and deploying a pipeline .NET AIC is same as that for a lightweight .NET AIC. In the case of the pipeline .NET AIC, you need to create two RCWs for the two interfaces that are implemented in the component: IPipelineComponentAdmin and IPipelineComponent.

Preprocessors

The preprocessor processes documents before they go into the channel, as opposed to the AIC, which processes documents after they come out of the channel, as shown in Figure 11-19.

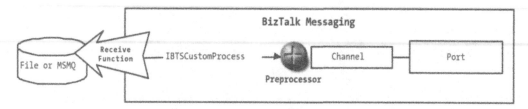

Figure 11-19. Processing a document with the preprocessor before the document goes into the channel

But under what circumstances will you want to do something to a document before it comes into the channel? At times the data won't be in a form that can be used immediately. For example, perhaps the documents a client has sent are compressed files and must be unzipped before the channel and port can make sense of them. The process of unzipping the documents can be performed inside a preprocessor component just before the document goes into the channel. The preprocessor also allows you to treat certain documents differently before they are passed into the channel for further processing.

The preprocessor can only be used with Receive Functions, because you don't really have an opportunity to add any customized code. If you have sent the document to BizTalk Server with an Interchange submit call, you would have to add customized code or call additional components to process the document before calling the Interchange submit method.

As with the AICs, a component has to implement a special interface to become a preprocessor component. Every preprocessor must implement the IBTSCustomProcess interface. The IBTSCustomProcess contains two methods: Execute and SetContext.

Here is the Execute method:

```
Sub Execute( _
DataIn As Variant, _
CodePageIn As Long, _
IsFilePath As Boolean, _
CodePageOut As Variant, _
DataOut As Variant _
)
```

This method takes five parameters:

- *DataIn:* This input parameter represents the data being read by the Message Queue Receive Function. If File Receive Function is used to pick up the document, this parameter then contains the file path, and the IsFilePath parameter also contains the value true.

- *CodePageIn:* This input parameter contains the code page of the input data. The code page indicates the character set and keyboard layout used on a computer.

- *IsFilePath:* This input parameter indicates whether the DataIn parameter contains the data or file path to the data. Its value is true when the DataIn is a file path and the data is read from a File Receive Function; otherwise its value is false and the DataIn parameter contains the data that is read from the Message Queue Receive Function.

- *CodePageOut:* This input parameter contains the code page of the output data. The code page indicates the character set and keyboard layout used on a computer.

- *DataOut:* This is an output parameter, and it contains the data sent to the BizTalk Server channel for further processing.

The other method of the interface, SetContext, contains only one input parameter, the BTSCustomProcessContext object. This object is read-only and contains the configuration information of the Receive Function to which the pre-processor is attached. The configuration information is stored as a property member of the BTSCustomProcessContext object.

To create a preprocessor in Visual Basic, open a new Active DLL project called BOBPreProcessor and add a class called Unzip. Add the Microsoft BizTalk Server Application Interface Component 1.0 Type Library to the project reference.

Next, add implementation code for the two methods as shown in the following example:

```
Implements IBTSCustomProcess
Dim src_id as string
Dim dest_id as string
Sub IBTSCustomProcess_SetContext(ByVal pCtx As IBTSCustomProcessContext)
    ' Note: This sample only demonstrates how to obtain context information...
```

```
        src_id = pCtx.SourceID
        dest_id = pCtx.DestID


End Sub

Sub IBTSCustomProcess_Execute(ByVal vDataIn, ByVal nCodePageIn As Long,
  ByVal bIsFilePath As Boolean, ByRef nCodePageOut, ByRef vDataOut)
On Error GoTo ErrorHandler
    vDataOut = Unzip(vDataIn)
Exit Sub

ErrorHandler:
    On Error GoTo 0
    Err.Raise Err.Number, Err.Source, Err.Description
End Sub
Private Function Unzip(ByRef ZippedData as String) As String
'add your code to unzip the data
End Function
```

If the Execute method returns an error, the document picked up by the Receive Function will then be sent to the suspended queue.

To register this component, compile the program in Visual Basic, and then manually add the following registration key to the system registry. This will make BizTalk Server recognize the component as a preprocessor.

```
[HKEY_CLASSES_ROOT\CLSID\AIC_CLSID\Implemented Categories\
{20E8080F-F624-4401-A203-9D99CF18A6D9}]
```

In the preceding key, AIC_CLSID represents the class ID of the preprocessor component.

After adding the key to the system registry, you are ready to use the preprocessor. To specify the preprocessor for the Receive Function, open the properties page of the Receive Function, as shown in Figure 11-20, and then select BOBPreProcessor. Unzip from the drop-down list of existing preprocessors.

NOTE *Unlike the AIC components, you must add the additional registry key for the preprocessor to the system registry, even when you have registered the component in COM+. Otherwise the component isn't shown in the list on the Receive Function's properties page.*

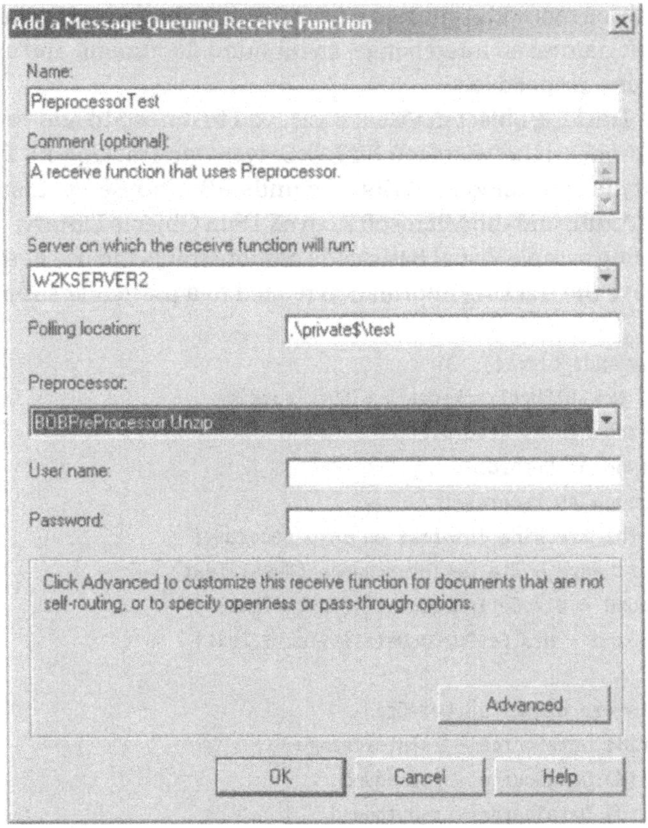

Figure 11-20. Specifying which preprocessor to use on the Receive Function's properties page

BizTalk Tracking Object Model

In Chapter 9, you looked at the Document Tracking feature in BizTalk Server. Document Tracking is a Web interface that allows you to see the detail information of specific submitted documents, such as the source organization, destination organization, and inbound and outbound documents of the submission. The BizTalk Tracking object provides you with the ability to retrieve this information about a specific submission programmatically, so that you can incorporate the tracking information in your application.

The Tracking object contains three methods: GetInterchanges, GetInDocDetails, and GetOutDocDetails. They all take one parameter, the submission ID that is returned by the Interchange submit call. For example:

```
SubmissionId = oInterchange.submit( 1,PostedDocument)
```

Each of these three methods returns an ADO Recordset containing the details implied by their names: an interchange, an inbound document, and an outbound document, respectively.

To use the Tracking object in Visual Basic, you first need to add two things to the project references: the Microsoft BizTalk Server Doc Tracking 1.0 Type Library (the type library for this reference is located under [BizTalk Server Installation folder]\ CISDTA.dll), and the Microsoft ActiveX Data Objects Library.

The following sample Visual Basic code demonstrates the use of this object model to retrieve the tracking information related to a particular submission:

```
Private Sub Command1_Click()
    Dim dta As New BTSDocTrackingLib.BTSDocTracking
    Dim rsInterchange As Recordset
    Dim rsInbound As Recordset
    Dim rsOutbound As Recordset
    'retrieve the tracking information into recordset
    Set rsInterchange = dta.GetInterchanges(Text1.Text)
    Set rsInbound = dta.GetInDocDetails(Text1.Text)
    Set rsOutbound = dta.GetOutDocDetails(Text1.Text)

    'display the recordset in DataGrid
    Set DataGrid1.DataSource = rsInterchange
    Set DataGrid2.DataSource = rsInbound
    Set DataGrid3.DataSource = rsOutbound
End Sub
```

Figure 11-21 shows the program in action. It takes the submission ID from the top text box and generates its tracking information. The window contains three data-grid controls. The Interchange data grid lists all the interchanges that are associated with the submission ID. The Inbound Document data grid and Outbound Document data grid list the inbound and outbound documents associated with the submission ID.

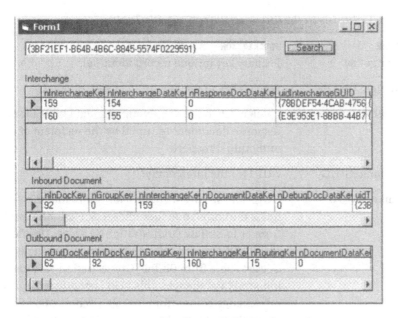

Figure 11-21. Sample program using the BizTalk Tracking object

The result sets returned by the Tracking object contain many columns that represent the data stored in the following three data tables in the BizTalk Tracking database: dta_interchange_details, dta_indoc_details, and dta_outdoc_details. Each of these three tables contains a great deal of information about the interchange and the document associated with each data submission.

- *dta_interchange_details table:* Contains the information for each interchange submitted to BizTalk Server. (See Table 11-4.)

- *dta_indoc_details table:* Contains the tracking information for all the inbound documents processed by BizTalk Server. It contains the details of the document instances for inbound interchange records in the dta_interchange_details table. (See Table 11-5.)

- *dta_outdoc_details table:* Contains the tracking information for all the outbound documents processed by the BizTalk Server. It contains the details on the document instances for the outbound interchange records in the dta_interchange_details table. (See Table 11-6.)

Table 11-4. Columns in the dta_interchange_details Table

COLUMN NAME	DESCRIPTION
nInterchangeKey	Primary key unique record identifier.
nInterchangeDataKey	Foreign key to the dta_interchange_data table.
nResponseDocDataKey	Foreign key to the dta_document_data table for the response document returned by the recipient of an outbound transport.
uidInterchangeGUID	GUID for the interchange.
uidSubmissionGUID	GUID for the parent submission. Note that this GUID holds the correlation identifier (correlationID) provided from or to BizTalk Orchestration Services. This field is empty if the record is for an inbound interchange that doesn't come from BizTalk Orchestration Services. For inbound interchanges, this field is populated only if the interchange comes from BizTalk Orchestration Services. For outbound interchanges, this field is always populated.
dtProcessedTimeStamp	Time the record was created.
nvcSyntax	Code for document syntax (XML, X12, EDIFACT, HL7, and so on). In the case of unrecognized syntax due to parsing failure or pass-through submission, this field has a value of UNKNOWN.
nvcVersion	Version of the syntax.
nvcControlID	Unique control number for electronic data interchange (EDI) interchanges or an identifier for BizTalk reliable messages.
nDirection	Flag indicating whether the interchange is incoming or outgoing. Possible values are 0 (outbound) or 1 (inbound). This is a foreign key to dta_direction_values, the table that contains the direction values.
etTimeSent	Timestamp for a successful transmission.
nError	Code that indicates the occurrence of an error. This is a foreign key to dta_error_message, the table that contains the error message descriptions.
nTestMode	Test or production indicator. This field is reserved and isn't used.

(continued)

Table 11-4. Columns in the dta_interchange_details Table (continued)

COLUMN NAME	DESCRIPTION
nvcSrcAliasQualifer	Sender qualifier value extracted from the submitted or transmitted interchange.
nvcSrcAliasId	Sender identifier value extracted from the submitted or transmitted interchange.
nvcSrcAppName	Interchange level identifier for the source application extracted from the submitted or transmitted interchange.
nvcDestAliasQualifier	Recipient qualifier extracted from the submitted or transmitted interchange.
nvcDestAliasID	Recipient identifier value extracted from the submitted or transmitted interchange.
nvcDestAppName	Interchange level identifier for the destination application extracted from the submitted or transmitted interchange.
nAckStatus	Code for the status of the receipt. This is a foreign key to dta_ack_status_values, the table that contains the receipt status descriptions.
nvcSMTPMessageID	SMTP transport message identifier (for EDIINT). This field is reserved and isn't used.
nDocumentsAccepted	Number of documents accepted in the interchange.
nDocumentsRejected	Number of documents rejected in the interchange.
nTransportType	Transmission protocol indicator code. This is a foreign key to the dta_transport_type_values table.
nvcTransportAddress	Address of the transport target.
nvcServerName	Server that processed the interchange.
nNumberOfBytes	Size of the interchange, in bytes. This field represents what is tracked in the related dta_interchange_data record and can be different from what is actually transmitted. The size can be increased by additional envelope processing and data format conversion during transmission.
nNumOfTransmitAttempts	Transmission attempt counter.

Table 11-5. Columns in the dta_indoc_details Table

COLUMN NAME	DESCRIPTION
nInDocKey	Primary key unique record identifier.
nDocumentDataKey	Foreign key to the dta_document_data table.
nDebugDocDataKey	Foreign key to the dta_debugdoc_data table for the XML form of the received document, even if the received document itself is in XML.
nGroupKey	Foreign key to the dta_group_details table.
nInterchangeKey	Foreign key to the dta_interchange_details table.
uidTrackingGUID	Master tracking key value based on a GUID.
dtProcessedTimeStamp	Time the record was created.
nvcSyntax	Code for document syntax (XML, X12, EDIFACT, HL7, and so on). In the case of unrecognized syntax due to parsing failure or pass-through submission, this field has a value of UNKNOWN.
nvcVersion	Version of the syntax.
nvcRelease	Release of the version.
nvcDocType	Document type or transaction set identifier.
nvcControlID	Unique control number for electronic data interchange (EDI) documents and functional groups.
nlsValid	Code that indicates validation results. Possible values are 0 0 (invalid), 1 (valid), or 2 (pass-through).
nError	Code that indicates the occurrence of an error. This is the foreign key to dta_error_message, the table that contains the descriptions of the error messages.

Table 11-6. Columns in the dta_outdoc_details Table

COLUMN NAME	DESCRIPTION
nDocumentDataKey	Primary key unique record identifier.
nDebugDocDataKey	Foreign key to the dta_indoc_details parent record.
NGroupKey	Foreign key to the dta_document_data table.
NInterchangeKey	Foreign key to the dta_debugdoc_data table for the XML form of the outgoing document, even if the outgoing document is XML. When an outbound document is sent to a port group, only one copy of the dta_debugdoc_data record is stored, and all resulting dta_outdoc_details records point to it.
UidTrackingGUID	Master tracking key value based on a GUID.
DtProcessedTimeStamp	The time the record was created.
NvcSyntax	Code for document syntax (XML, X12, EDIFACT, HL7, and so on). In the case of unrecognized syntax due to parsing failure or pass-through submission, this field has a value of UNKNOWN.
NvcVersion	Version of the syntax.
NvcRelease	Release of the version.
NvcDocType	Document type or transaction set identifier.
NvcControlID	Unique control number for EDI documents and functional groups.
NlsValid	Code that indicates validation results. Possible values are 0 (invalid), 1 (valid), or 2 (pass-through).
NError	Code that indicates the occurrence of an error. This is a foreign key to dta_error_message, the table that contains the error message descriptions.
NAckStatus	Code for the status of the receipt. This is a foreign key to dta_ack_status_values, the table that contains the receipt status descriptions.
NRoutingKey	Foreign key to the dta_routing_details table.
NReceiptFlag	Flag that indicates to which table a receipt is associated. Possible values are 1 (interchange), 2 (group), 4 (indoc), or 8 (outdoc).

(continued)

Table 11-6. Columns in the dta_outdoc_details Table (continued)

COLUMN NAME	DESCRIPTION
NReceiptKey	Unique number that identifies the receipt.
DtReceiptDueBy	Receipt deadline timestamp, computed as the processing timestamp.
nRealName1	Foreign key to the dta_custom_field_names table.
rlRealValue1	Real capture field 1. This field must be an 8-byte real value.
nRealName2	Foreign key to the dta_custom_field_names table.
rlRealValue2	Real capture field 2. This field must be an 8-byte real value.
nIntName1	Foreign key to the dta_custom_field_names table.
nIntValue1	Integer capture field 1.
nIntName2	Foreign key to the dta_custom_field_names table.
nIntValue2	Integer capture field 2.
nDateName1	Foreign key to the dta_custom_field_names table.
dtDateValue1	Date capture field 1.
nDateName2	Foreign key to the dta_custom_field_names table.
dtDateValue2	Date capture field 2.
nStrName1	Foreign key to the dta_custom_field_names table.
nvcStrValue1	String capture field 1.
nStrName2	Foreign key to the dta_custom_field_names table.
nvcStrValue2	String capture field 2.
nvcCustomSearch	Binary large object for concatenated string capture as XML.

To obtain more tracking information, such as the content of the document, you can first retrieve the document key or interchange key by calling the GetInterchangeDetails, GetInDocDetails, or GetOutDocDetails methods, and then execute the SQL query against the dta_interchange_data or dta_document_data table by providing the value "key" field. The dta_interchange_data and dta_document_data tables store the actual content data in binary format in the imgInterchangeData and imgDocumentData data columns respectively. You can then call the Write method of the ADO.Stream object to read the binary stream, change the Type property to adTypeText, and then call the ReadText method to return the text representation of the image data.

The following is sample code that outputs the content of the interchange as text:

```
'Declare variables
set adostream = CreateObject("ADODB.Stream")
adostream.Type = 1 'adTypeBinary
'Add your ADO code to retrieve the image data from tracking database
adostream.Write rs.Fields("ImgInterchangeData")
adostream.Type = 2 'adTypeText
adostream.Read strInterchange
'strInterchange is string containing the content of a interchange.
```

NOTE *You should try to use BizTalk APIs to access the data in the Tracking database instead of directly accessing the data through ADO. This will guard you against potential database table schema changes in future BizTalk Server releases.*

As you can see, with the help of BizTalk Server Tracking object and an understanding of the relationship between tracking tables, you should be able to create customized applications similar to the BizTalk Document Tracking application.

BizTalk Messaging Configuration Object Model

The BizTalk Messaging configuration object model provides you a means to add, update, remove, and retrieve the BizTalk Messaging configuration programmatically.

In earlier chapters, you saw how to configure channels, ports, etc., with BizTalk Messaging Manager, so you may be wondering why you need to use the Messaging configuration object when the same type of work can be done with BizTalk Messaging Manager.

The answer to the question is twofold. One obvious answer is scripted deployment. When you have to deploy the Messaging configuration from a development environment to staging, QA, and production environments, the worst deployment strategy is to rely on people to duplicate the Messaging configuration in each environment using BizTalk Messaging Manager. Manual deployment isn't only error prone, but is also labor intensive. Depending on the BizTalk solution, tech support personnel might need to spend hours duplicating hundreds of items in Messaging Manager during a manual deployment. By using Messaging configuration objects, you can deploy the BizTalk configuration settings in a matter of a few seconds. Some time must be invested upfront to create such a deployment script, but having a deployment strategy that is fast, simple, and error free is almost always worthy of such investment.

There is another reason that Messaging configuration objects can provide significant benefits to your applications. With these objects, you can modify the configuration settings at runtime without human intervention. For example, suppose in Bob's case one of his clients decided to change the URL that will receive the response document and the password used to access that URL. Without using configuration objects, Bob would have to go into the production environment and change the settings with BizTalk Messaging Manager. It may not seem to be a big deal to change the configuration for one client, but it would be an enormous task when hundreds of clients are requesting similar changes.

In such a situation, it would be more efficient to delegate the task of maintaining the client-specific Messaging configuration to the clients themselves. Clients can interact with BizTalk Messaging and modify its settings through a customized program that uses Messaging configuration objects to make the configuration changes on the BizTalk Server.

Messaging configuration objects can also be used to create a customized application for the product support staff to view and maintain BizTalk Messaging. Additional tools and security features that don't exist in Messaging Manager can also be added to provide more specialized functions for end users.

To access the BizTalk Messaging configuration object model programmatically, you need to add a reference to BizTalk Server Configuration Objects 1.0 Type Library in your program. BizTalkObjectModel.dll, the dll file for this reference, is located under [BizTalk Server Installation Folder].

Messaging Configuration Interfaces

The BizTalk Messaging configuration object model contains the following interfaces:

- *IBizTalkConfig:* Defines the methods and properties that are used to create other Messaging configuration objects

- *IBizTalkBase:* Defines the methods and properties that are inherited by several configuration objects

- *IBizTalkChannel:* Defines the methods and properties for configuring the BizTalk Messaging channel

- *IBizTalkDocument:* Defines the methods and properties for configuring the BizTalk document definition

- *IBizTalkEnvelope:* Defines the methods and properties for configuring the BizTalk envelope definition

- *IBizTalkOrganization:* Defines the methods and properties for configuring the BizTalk Organization

- *IBizTalkPort:* Defines the methods and properties for configuring the messaging port.

- *IBizTalkPortGroup:* Defines the methods and properties for configuring the messaging port list.

The relationship between these interfaces is illustrated in Figure 11-22.

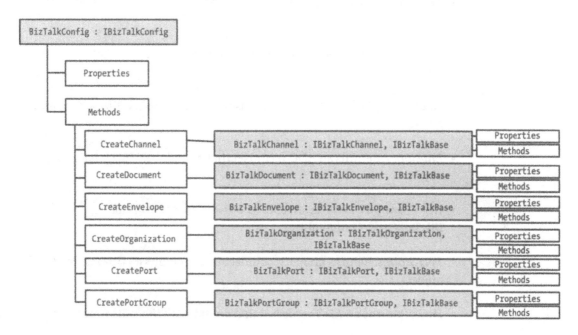

Figure 11-22. BizTalk Messaging configuration object model

To change any Messaging configuration, you first need to create a BizTalkConfig object that implements the IBizTalkConfig interface. The BizTalkConfig object has six methods that return the six different types of Messaging configuration objects, each of which implements IBizTalkBase and one of six Messaging configuration interfaces. For example, calling the CreateDocument method on BizTalkConfig will return a BizTalkDocument object that implements the IBizTalkDocument and IBizTalkBase interfaces.

After obtaining the Messaging configuration object, you can then call its methods and properties to retrieve, add, remove, or update the Messaging configuration of the BizTalk Server. Let's take a look at each of these objects and see how they can be used to change the Messaging configuration settings.

Objects

To obtain the six types of Messaging configuration objects, you first need to create a BizTalkConfig object. BizTalkConfig implements IBizTalkConfig, which contains the properties and methods described next.

There are seven properties in IBizTalkConfig:

- *Certificates:* Returns an ADO recordset that contains all specified certificates

- *Channels:* Returns an ADO recordset that contains all IBizTalkChannel objects

- *Documents:* Returns an ADO recordset that contains all IBizTalkDocument objects

- *Envelopes:* Returns an ADO recordset that contains all IBizTalkEnvelope objects

- *Organizations:* Returns an ADO recordset that contains all IBizTalkOrganization objects

- *PortGroups:* Returns an ADO recordset that contains all IBizTalkPortGroup objects

- *Ports:* Returns an ADO recordset that contains all IBizTalkPort objects

There are six methods in IBizTalkConfig:

- *CreateChannel:* Returns a new IBizTalkChannel object

- *CreateDocument:* Returns a new IBizTalkDocument object

- *CreateEnvelope:* Returns a new IBizTalkEnvelope object

- *CreateOrganization:* Returns a new IBizTalkOrganization object

- *CreatePort:* Returns a new IBizTalkPort object

- *CreatePortGroup:* Returns a new IBizTalkPortGroup object

The following sample code creates the BizTalkConfig object and six Messaging configuration objects:

```
Dim BTConf
Dim doc
Dim env
Dim org
Dim port
Dim portGroup
Dim channel

Set BTConf = CreateObject("BizTalk.BizTalkConfig")

Set doc = BTConf.CreateDocument
Set env = BTConf.CreateEnvelope
Set org = BTConf.CreateOrganization
Set port = BTConf.CreatePort
Set portGroup = BTConf.CreatePortGroup
Set channel = BTConf.CreateChannel
```

Before you look at the six types of Messaging configuration objects in detail, you should understand the dependency among these objects. When you created channels and ports using BizTalk Messaging manager in earlier chapters, you learned some dependency rules, such as you can't create a channel without first creating a port, and you can't create an port without first creating a organization. Such rules also apply when you add and remove configuration settings programmatically.

The dependency rules are illustrated in Figure 11-23. The arrows indicate the direction of dependency.

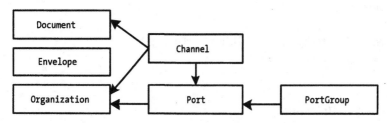

Figure 11-23. BizTalk Messaging configuration dependency

Let's first look at the three Messaging configuration objects that don't depend on others: Document, Envelope, and Organization. Then I'll show you the configuration objects for Port, PortGroup, and Channel.

BizTalkDocument

The BizTalkDocument object contains many properties and methods. Here is a list of the commonly used properties:

- *Name:* Name of the document definition

- *Handle:* Handle for the document definition

- *Reference:* WebDAV URL for the document specification

Following are the commonly used methods for this object (inherited from IBizTalkBase):

- *Create:* Creates a new object

- *Remove:* Removes an existing object from BizTalk Messaging Database

- *Load:* Loads a specified object in the memory given its handle

- *LoadByName:* Loads a specified object in the memory given its name

- *Save:* Saves the object into the BizTalk Messaging database after modifying its setting

- *Clear:* Clears the object from the memory

You can add a new document definition with code like this:

```
Dim BTConf
Dim doc
Set BTConf = CreateObject("BizTalk.BizTalkConfig")
Set doc = BTConf.CreateDocument

doc.clear
doc.name = "FundInvestors"
doc.reference = "http://w2kserver/BizTalkServerRepository/DocSpecs/
FundInvestors.xml"
doc.Create
```

You can also modify the existing document definition with code like the following:

```
Dim BTConf
Dim doc
Set BTConf = CreateObject("BizTalk.BizTalkConfig")
Set doc = BTConf.CreateDocument

doc.clear
doc.LoadByName("FundInvestors")
doc.name="New_FundInvestors"
doc.reference = "http://w2kserver/BizTalkServerRepository/DocSpecs/
New_FundInvestors.xml"
doc.save
```

To delete a document specification, you can use the following code sample:

```
Dim BTConf
Dim doc
Set BTConf = CreateObject("BizTalk.BizTalkConfig")
Set doc = BTConf.CreateDocument

doc.clear
doc.LoadByName("FundInvestors")
doc.Remove
```

Before you remove a document definition, you must first remove all the objects that depend on this document definition; otherwise, the Remove call will fail. For example, if two channels depend on this document definition, those two channels must be removed before the document definition can be successfully removed.

BizTalkEnvelope

The BizTalkEnvelope object has properties and methods similar to BizTalkDocument. Here is an example of adding an envelope to BizTalk Messaging:

```
Dim BTConf
Dim env
Set BTConf = CreateObject("BizTalk.BizTalkConfig")
Set org = BTConf.CreateEnvelope
```

```
env.clear
env.name = "FundInvestorsFlat"
env.reference = "http://w2kserver/BizTalkServerRepository/DocSpecs/
FundInvestorsFlat.xml
env.format = "FLATFILE"
env.Create
```

BizTalkOrganization

The BizTalkOrganization object is used to create the organization and its alias and applications. It has quite few more properties and methods than BizTalk Document or BizTalkEnvelope, because organization aliases and applications are also created with this object. These are the properties that are commonly used:

- *Alias:* Contains an ADO recordset of aliases that refer to the object

- *Applications:* Contains an ADO recordset of applications that refer to the object

- *Name:* Name of the organization

- *Handle:* Handle of the organization

And here are some of the more common methods of this object:

- *IBizTalkBase methods:* Basic methods inherited from IBizTalkBase, such as Load, Create, Save, Remove, etc.

- *CreateAlias:* Creates an alias for the organization

- *CreateApplication:* Creates an application for the organization

- *LoadAlias:* Loads the existing alias into memory

- *LoadApplication:* Loads the existing application into memory

- *RemoveAlias:* Removes the existing alias

- *RemoveApplication:* Removes the existing application

- *SaveAlias:* Saves the changes made to the existing alias

- *SaveApplication:* Saves the change made to the existing application

- *GetDefaultAlias:* Retrieves the default alias of an organization

The following three examples show how to add and modify an organization and its aliases and applications using the BizTalkOrganization object. First, let's see how to add a new organization:

```
Dim BTConf
Dim org
Set BTConf = CreateObject("BizTalk.BizTalkConfig")
Set org= BTConf.CreateOrganization

org.Clear
org.Name = "Henry Fonda Inc."
org.Comments ="Bob's best client"
org.Create

org.CreateAlias "TaxID",false,"TaxID","123456789"
org.Save
```

The Create method in the preceding code must be called before you can add the organization alias. The CreateAlias method takes four parameters, and the second one determines whether this alias is the default alias or not. By default, the Organization name is the default alias, but by setting the second parameter of CreateAlias to true, the newly created alias will become the default alias.

The following example will modify the existing organization:

```
Dim BTConf
Dim org
Dim AppHandle
Set BTConf = CreateObject("BizTalk.BizTalkConfig")
Set org= BTConf.CreateOrganization

org.Clear
org.LoadByName("Home Organization")
org.Name = "Bob's organization"

'Create new organization application and alias
org.CreateApplication "BobApp"
org.CreateAlias "TaxID",false,"TaxID","987654321"
org.Save
```

```
'Modify the existing settings
org.SaveApplication GetAppID("BobApp",org), "New_BobApp"
org.SaveAlias GetAliasID("TaxID","TaxID","987654321",org),"TaxID",false,"TaxID",
"999999999"
org.save

'Following function returns the alias handle
Function GetAliasID(sName, sQual, sValue, org)
    Set aliasrs = org.Aliases
    Do While Not aliasrs.EOF
        If (aliasrs("name") = sName) And (aliasrs("qualifier") = sQual) _
                    And (aliasrs("value") = sValue) Then
            GetAliasID = aliasrs("id")
            Exit Do
        End If
        aliasrs.MoveNext
    Loop
End Function

'Following function returns the application handle
Function GetAppID(sName, org)
    Set Apprs = org.Applications
    Do While Not Apprs.EOF
        If Apprs("name") = sName Then
            GetAppID = Apprs("id")
            Exit Do
        End If
        Apprs.MoveNext
    Loop
End Function
```

There are two utility functions in the preceding example: GetAliasID(sName, sQual, sValue, org) and GetAppID(sName, org). They return the object handle for either an existing organization alias or organization application. Each function loops through all the existing aliases and applications and returns the ID field of the record that matches the input parameters. The handle is used to reference the object in the Messaging configuration object model, so that the reference to the object can still be valid even when the object name has changed.

The program first loads the Home Organization by calling LoadByName("Home Organization"), and it then sets the name property to "Bob's Organization". Next, the program creates a new organization alias called TaxID and an organization application called BobApp. It then calls the SaveAlias and SaveApplication methods to reset the values of the TaxID alias and BobApp application. After the method calls, the value of the TaxID alias becomes 999999999 and the application name changes from BobApp to New_BobApp. Last, it calls the Save method to save the changes made by the program.

 NOTE *You can only define applications for Home Organizations in BizTalk Messaging Manager.*

BizTalkPort

The BizTalkPort object allows you to retrieve, add, modify, and remove messaging ports programmatically. Here are the commonly used properties in the BizTalkPort object:

- *DestinationEndpoint:* Contains the destination information for the port

- *PrimaryTransport:* Contains the detail information on the transport used by the destination end point

- *Name:* Name of the messaging port

- *Handle:* Handle of the messaging port

- *Channels:* Contains an ADO recordset that includes information about all channels that connect to this messaging port

Following are the methods for this object:

- *IBizTalkBase methods:* Basic methods inherited from IBizTalkBase, such as Load, Create, Save, Remove, etc.

When you are creating a messaging port using BizTalkPort, the organization that the port is associated with must exist on the system. The DestinationEndpoint point needs to know the handle of the associated organization. To obtain the organization handle, you can use the return value of the LoadByName(organization name) method. Here is a sample showing how you can add a new message port:

```
Const BIZTALK_OPENNESS_TYPE_EX_TOWORKFLOW = 16
Const BIZTALK_TRANSPORT_TYPE_ORCHESTRATIONACTIVATION = 8192

Dim BTConf
Dim port
Dim org
Set BTConf = CreateObject("BizTalk.BizTalkConfig")
Set port= BTConf.CreatePort
set org = BTConf.CreateOrganization

'retrieve the handles for organization and alias
org.LoadByName("Bob's Organization")
orghandle = org.handle
aliashandle = org.GetDefaultAlias

port.Clear
port.Name = "P_FundInvestors"
'set the endpoint object - port.DestinationEndPoint
port.DestinationEndPoint.Organization = orghandle
port.DestinationEndPoint.Alias = aliashandle
port.DestinationEndPoint.Openness = BIZTALK_OPENNESS_TYPE_EX_TOWORKFLOW
' set transport info for port.PrimaryTransport
port.PrimaryTransport.Address = "C:\Program Files\Microsoft BizTalk Server\XLANG
Scheduler\FundInvestors.skx"
port.PrimaryTransport.Parameter = "GetDocument"
port.PrimaryTransport.Type = IZTALK_TRANSPORT_TYPE_ORCHESTRATIONACTIVATION
port.Create
```

Because the messaging port needs to reference the organization, you need in the preceding code to first obtain the handle for the destination organization and its alias. Org.Handle and org.GetDefaultAlias can be used to retrieve these handles.

Next, you need to set the values for the DestinationEndpoint and PrimaryTransport objects for the message port. Besides these two objects, you can also set values for the ServiceWindowInfo object, the EncryptionCertificateInfo object, etc., if necessary.

The procedure for modifying an existing messaging port is very similar to that of modifying an organization. You need to first load the port, then set its values, and save it. For example, the following code changes the PrimaryTransport address of the port to a different schedule file:

```
Dim BTConf
Dim port
Set BTConf = CreateObject("BizTalk.BizTalkConfig")
Set port= BTConf.CreatePort

port.Clear
Port.LoadByName("P_FundInvestors")
port.PrimaryTransport.Address = "C:\Program Files\Microsoft BizTalk Server\
XLANG Scheduler\New_FundInvestors.skx"
port.Save
```

To remove a messaging port, you must first remove all its dependency objects, such as channels and port groups. Then you can use the LoadByName and Remove methods to delete the messaging port. Here's an example:

```
Dim BTConf
Dim port
Set BTConf = CreateObject("BizTalk.BizTalkConfig")
Set port= BTConf.CreatePort

port.Clear
Port.LoadByName("P_FundInvestors")
port.Remove
```

BizTalkPortGroup

The BizTalkPortGroup object allows you to create and modify the port distribution list programmatically. It contains the following commonly used properties:

- *Ports:* Contains an ADO recordset that includes information about all ports referenced by this port group

- *Name:* Port distribution list name

- *Handle:* Port distribution list handle

The methods for this object are as follows:

- *IBizTalkBase methods:* Basic methods inherited from IBizTalkBase, such as Load, Create, Save, Remove, etc.

- *AddPort:* Adds the port to the distribution list

- *RemovePort:* Removes the port from the distribution list

To create a new distribution list, you first need to create a new distribution list and then add the port to the list. You must retrieve the handle for the port in the distribution list first for same reason you retrieved the handle for the organization in the messaging port example. The following code sample creates a distribution list that contains two messaging ports:

```
Dim BTConf
Dim port
Dim portgroup
Dim p_handle1
Dim p_handle2
Set BTConf = CreateObject("BizTalk.BizTalkConfig")
Set portgroup= BTConf.CreatePortGroup
set port = BTConf.CreatePort

port.LoadByName("P_Outgoing_HenryFonda")
p_handle1=port.handle
port.LoadByName("P_Outgoing_GaryCooper")
p_handle2=port.handle

portgroup.Clear
portgroup.Name="PortList_AllClients"
portgroup.AddPort(p_handle1)
portgroup.AddPort(p_handle2)
portgroup.Create
```

To modify the distribution list, load PortGroup with the LoadByName method first, and then call either AddPort or RemovePort. Here's an example:

```
Dim BTConf
Dim port
Dim portgroup
Dim p_handle1
```

```
Set BTConf = CreateObject("BizTalk.BizTalkConfig")
Set portgroup= BTConf.CreatePortGroup
set port = BTConf.CreatePort

port.LoadByName("P_Outgoing_HenryFonda")
p_handle1=port.handle

portgroup.Clear
portgroup.LoadByName("PortList_AllClients")
portgroup.RemovePort(p_handle1)
portgroup.Save
```

The following example removes the distribution list:

```
Dim BTConf
Dim portgroup

Set BTConf = CreateObject("BizTalk.BizTalkConfig")
Set portgroup= BTConf.CreatePortGroup

portgroup.LoadByName("PortList_AllClients")
portgroup.Remove
```

BizTalkChannel

The BizTalkChannel object allows you to add, update, and delete a messaging channel in BizTalk Server Messaging. The channel depends on the messaging port and document definitions, so you must first retrieve the handles for these dependency objects before you can create a message channel. The following are some of the commonly used properties of the BizTalkChannel object:

- *Expression:* Contains a complete set of equations that filter the selection of the object

- *InputDocument:* Contains the handle to the input IBizTalkDocument object that describes the input document specification

- *OutputDocument:* Contains the handle to the output IBizTalkDocument object that describes the output document specification

- *LoggingInfo:* Contains information about logging the document

- *MapReference:* Contains the full Web Distributed Authoring and Versioning (WebDAV) URL of the map that provides instructions on how the input document in the format used by the source organization is to be rendered in the format used by the destination organization, if different

- *Port:* Contains the handle to the associated IBizTalkPort object

- *PortGroup:* Contains the handle to the associated IBizTalkPortGroup object

- *SourceEndpoint:* Contains information about the source

Here are the commonly used methods for this object:

- *IBizTalkBase methods:* Basic methods inherited from IBizTalkBase, such as Load, Create, Save, Remove, etc.

- *GetConfigComponent:* Returns the CLSID of the component associated with the IBizTalkPort object.

- *GetConfigData:* Returns an IDictionary object that contains the primary transport configuration information.

- *SetConfigComponent:* Sets the CLSID of the component associated with the IBizTalkPort object.

- *SetConfigData:* Sets the IDictionary object that contains the configuration data for the transport object. The fields in the dictionary object depend on the protocols being used. Refer to Tables 11-7 (for HTTP and HTTPS), 11-8 (for local files), and 11-9 (for message queuing) for the fields in the dictionary object. This dictionary represents the advanced properties during the configuration of the channel.

Table 11-7. HTTP and HTTPS Fields in the IDictionary Object

DICTIONARY FIELD	DESCRIPTION
URL	URL of the document destination. (Required)
ContentType	Value for the Content-Type HTTP/HTTPS property that appears in HTTP headers during transmission. The default value is an empty string ("").
ClientCert	Reference to the certificate used with SSL connections using HTTPS. The default value is an empty string ("").
ProxyName	URL of the proxy server used when sending documents outside a firewall.
ProxyPort	Port number used by the proxy server.
UseProxy	Value that indicates whether the proxy server is used. The default value is true.

Table 11-8. Local File Fields in the IDictionary Object

DICTIONARY FIELD	DESCRIPTION
Filename	Name and path of the file to be created (required).
CopyMode	Value that indicates how the file should be written. Use a value of 0 for overwrite mode, a value of 1 for append mode, and a value of 2 to create a new file. The default value is append mode (1).
UserName	Windows user name needed to access a file share
Password	Windows password needed to access a file share

Table 11-9. Message Queuing fields in the IDictionary Object

DICTIONARY FIELD	DESCRIPTION
QueueName	Name of the Messaging Queue to which the document is sent (required).
MessageLabel	Value specified in the message label field on the queue.
Priority	Priority of the message placed in the queue. This must be a value between 0 and 7, where a higher value indicates a higher priority. The default value is 3.
AuthLevel	Value indicating whether the message needs to be authenticated using a digital signature. Use a value of 0 to bypass authentication. A value of 1 indicates that authentication will be used. The default value is 0.
Delivery	Value indicating how a message is delivered to a queue. Use a value of 1 to indicate that the message should be backed up until it is delivered to the queue. A value of 0 indicates that the message is only resident in memory. The default value is 0.

The following code sample creates a new channel that connects to an HTTPS messaging port. The LoadByName method is used to retrieve the handle for the organization and port that are referenced by the channel.

```
Const BIZTALK_CONFIGDATA_TYPE_PRIMARYTRANSPORT = 0
Dim BTConf
Dim port
Dim org
Dim channel
Dim doc
Dim port_handle
Dim org_handle
Dim alias_handle
Dim indoc_handle
Dim outdoc_handle
Set BTConf = CreateObject("BizTalk.BizTalkConfig")
Set port= BTConf.CreatePort
set org = BTConf.CreateOrganization
set channel = BTConf.CreateChannel
set doc = BTConf.CreateDocument
```

```
'get all the handles used by the channel
port.LoadByName("P_Outgoing_JohnWayne")
port_handle = port.handle
org.LoadByName("John Wayne Inc.")
org_handle = org.handle
alias_handle = org.GetDefaultAlias
doc.LoadByName("FundInvestorsFlat")
indoc_handle=doc.handle
doc.LoadByName("FundInvestors")
outdoc_handle=doc.handle

channel.Clear  'Set the channel properties to their default values first.
channel.Name = "C_FundInvestorsFlat_JohnWayne"

' set the endpoint object - channel.SourceEndPoint
channel.SourceEndPoint.Organization = org_handle
channel.SourceEndPoint.Alias = alias_handle
channel.InputDocument = indoc_handle
channel.OutputDocument = outdoc_handle
channel.MapReference = "http://w2kserver/BizTalkServerRepository/Maps/
Map_FundInvestorsFlatXML.xml"
channel.port = port_handle

' Logging info
channel.LoggingInfo.LogNativeInputDocument = 0
channel.LoggingInfo.LogNativeOutputDocument = -1
channel.LoggingInfo.LogXMLInputDocument = 0
channel.LoggingInfo.LogXMLOutputDocument = 0
channel.RetryCount = 0
channel.RetryInterval = 5

channel.Create

' set port configuration for P_Outgoing_JohnWayne
Set dict = CreateObject("Commerce.Dictionary")
dict.ProxyName = ""
dict.URL = "https://www.JohnWayne.com/post.asp"
dict.RequestTimeout = "0"
dict.Password = ""
dict.ProxyPort = "80"
dict.UseProxy = "1"
```

```
dict.ContentType = ""
dict.ClientCert = "BobCert"
dict.UserName = ""
channel.SetConfigData BIZTALK_CONFIGDATA_TYPE_PRIMARYTRANSPORT, port_handle, dict
Set dict = Nothing
channel.save
```

The program first retrieves five handles that are referenced by the channel—they are handles for the source organization, organization alias, port, inbound document, and outbound document. It then sets many channel properties and calls the Create method to create the channel.

Next, the program creates a dictionary object and sets the name-value pairs that are used as the advanced property settings for the channel. You only need to set the fields that will take different values from the values already set on the port.

The program then calls SetConfigData and passes it the dictionary object that was created. Finally, the Save method is called to save the configuration data as the advanced properties of the channel.

Programs that modify an existing channel can be significantly shorter. The following code is an example that modifies MapReference and the channel's dictionary object:

```
Const BIZTALK_CONFIGDATA_TYPE_PRIMARYTRANSPORT = 0
Const BIZTALK_TRANSPORT_TYPE_HTTPS = 1024
Dim BTConf
Dim port
Dim port_handle
Dim dict
Dim channel

Set BTConf = CreateObject("BizTalk.BizTalkConfig")
Set port= BTConf.CreatePort
set channel = BTConf.CreateChannel

'get all the handles used by the channel
port.LoadByName("P_Outgoing_JohnWayne")
port_handle = port.handle


channel.Clear
channel.LoadByName( "C_FundInvestorsFlat_JohnWayne")
channel.MapReference =
"http://w2kserver/BizTalkServerRepository/Maps/New_Map_FundInvestorsFlatXML.xml"
```

```
'Retrieve and modify the dictionary object
dict = channel.GetConfigData
(BIZTALK_TRANSPORT_TYPE_HTTPS,port_handle,BIZTALK_CONFIGDATA_TYPE_PRIMARYTRANSPORT)
dict.RequestTimeout = "30"
'Attach the dictionary object to the channel and save the change
channel.SetConfigData BIZTALK_CONFIGDATA_TYPE_PRIMARYTRANSPORT, port_handle, dict
Set dict = Nothing
channel.save
```

To load the dictionary object, the preceding program calls the GetConfigData method, which returns a dictionary object representing the current configuration. The program then resets the value for the field and calls the SetConfigData method to attach the dictionary with the new value back to the channel. Then the program calls the Save method to save the changes.

A program that deletes a channel is even easier. The following example deletes an existing channel:

```
Dim BTConf
Dim channel
Set BTConf = CreateObject("BizTalk.BizTalkConfig")
set channel = BTConf.CreateChannel

channel.Clear
channel.LoadByName( "C_FundInvestorsFlat_JohnWayne")
channel.Remove
```

IWFWorkflowInstance and IWFProxy

The IWFWorkflowInstance interface offers you a way to interact with a new or running XLANG Schedule programmatically. IWFProxy, on the other hand, provides a way to interact with a particular port inside a schedule programmatically.

Most of the time, a schedule is started by BizTalk Messaging when a messaging port is configured to start a new XLANG Schedule. Occasionally, however, you may want to invoke a schedule with your own program, or interact with a running schedule. In such cases, you can take advantage of these two interfaces to control the schedule in a more customized way.

IWFWorkflowInstance contains the following method:

- *WaitForCompletion:* Blocks and doesn't return until the schedule instance that is referenced has completed

The properties for IWFWorkflowInstance are as follows:

- *CompletionStatus:* Contains a value that indicates the success or failure of the XLANG Schedule instance.

- *FullPortName:* Contains the full name of a port in a form usable by the associated technology, such as a COM moniker, message queue pathname, or channel name.

- *FullyQualifiedName:* Contains the fully qualified name of this XLANG Schedule instance.

- *InstanceId:* Contains the GUID assigned to the current XLANG Schedule instance.

- *IsCompleted:* Contains a value that indicates whether the XLANG Schedule instance has finished executing.

- *ModuleId:* Contains the GUID of the XML module associated with the current XLANG Schedule instance.

- *ModuleName:* Contains the name of the XML module associated with the current XLANG Schedule instance.

- *ParentInstanceID:* Contains the GUID assigned to the parent XLANG Schedule instance of the current schedule instance.

- *Port:* Contains an IWFProxy reference to the named port. This is applicable only to COM-based port bindings.

The Port property of IWFWorkflowInstance returns an IWFProxy reference, which allows you to reference a specified port in an XLANG Schedule. Through the reference to the port, you can call the COM method that is bound to that particular port from an external application.

IWFProxy contains only two properties:

- *FullyQualifiedName:* Contains the fully qualified name of a COM-bound port

- *WorkflowInstance:* Contains a reference to the current XLANG Schedule instance

To start a new instance programmatically, you call the VB GetObject method and pass in the moniker of the XLANG Schedule. GetObject returns a reference to an object indicated by the moniker at runtime. A *moniker* is a string name that uniquely identifies a COM+ object on a system. To start a schedule, you must pass the moniker of the intended schedule to GetObject as its parameter.

The format of a moniker of an XLANG Schedule is as follows:

```
sked://[host_name]![XLANG_host_application_name]/path_of_skx
```

By default, the host_name is the local host name, and the XLANG_host_application_name is "XLANG Schedule", which is a COM+ application installed as part of BizTalk Server. So, if you want to start a new schedule locally, you can write the moniker as follows:

```
sked:///c:\temp\myschedule.skx
```

You can also reference a running XLANG Schedule by including the instance ID of the schedule as part of moniker, like

```
sked:///{999A9650-9A47-431D-AC18-F364AA99E3D8}
```

or

```
sked://localhost!XLANG Schedule/{999A9650-9A47-431D-AC18-F364AA99E3D8}
```

Using the instance ID is important, since there could be multiple instances of the same XLANG Schedule running on a system. You must be able to uniquely identify the instance you are referring to.

When you add the port name as part of the moniker, you get a reference to a specific port of a specific running schedule, such as the following:

```
sked://localhost!XLANG Schedule/{999A9650-9A47-431D-AC18-F364AA99E3D8}/WaitForReply
```

By being able to reference a specific port on a schedule, you can then pass data to the schedule, as well as get data out of the schedule. This feature greatly enhances interoperability between the XLANG Schedules and other Windows applications.

 NOTE *When a moniker contains the port name, the port must be connected to a COM component or a scripting component.*

To access a COM component that binds to a port from an external application, you also must make sure the port will wait for the external application's call when the schedule's process flow reaches the port. To ensure the process flow will stop at the port instead of continue on, you need to configure the method binding, as shown in Figure 11-24.

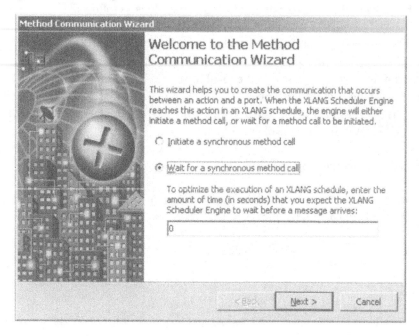

Figure 11-24. Configuring the method to wait for the method call from an external source

By making the schedule wait for a synchronous method call, it gives control of the schedule to the external application that will make the method call bound to the port.

Now, let's see how you can interact with a schedule programmatically through the IWFWorkflowInstance and IWFProxy interfaces. To create such a program in Visual Basic, you need to add the XLANG Scheduler Runtime Type Library to the project references. SkedCore.dll, the DLL for this reference, is located under the [BizTalk Server Installation Folder]\XLANG Schedule folder.

The following sample code starts a new schedule and then calls the MyMethod method that is bound to the PortToExternal port. The string "this is external data" is passed to the MyMethod method as an input parameter.

```
Dim schedule As IWFWorkflowInstance
Dim port As IWFProxy
```

```
'load the schedule
Set schedule = GetObject("sked:///c:\temp\myschedule.skx")
Set port = schedule.port("PortToExternal")
'call the method bound to the "PortToExternal" port
port.MyMethod ("this is external data")
```

The same program could also be written as follows:

```
Set port = GetObject("sked:///c:\temp\myschedule.skx/PortToExternal")
port.MyMethod ("this is external data")
```

To work with a running schedule, you need to use the instance ID in the moniker when calling the GetObject method. The following sample code loads the dehydrated schedule and passes the data to the ReceiveData method, which has been waiting to be called.

```
Set port = GetObject("sked:///{1ACD8407-8BCA-4BE7-8FCA- 515AE34E2980}\WaitForData")
port.ReceiveData ("here is the data you are waiting for")
```

Summary

In this chapter, you learned about the programming aspects of BizTalk Server. You learned how to create AIC components in both VB and C#, which extends the reach of BizTalk Server.

You also learned about working with BizTalk Server's Tracking object model programmatically. The Tracking object model allows you to search against the BizTalk Tracking database without relying on the BizTalk Tracking Web application. You can use these object models to create applications that allow users to create customized searches and generate reports from the BizTalk Tracking database.

The BizTalk Messaging Configuration object model enables you to do everything you can do in Messaging Manager programmatically. With the ability to add, edit, and remove the Messaging configuration settings, you can create scripts to deploy predefined Messaging configurations to BizTalk Server without manually configuring it.

Finally, through the use of IWFProxy, you can now send and receive data to and from a running XLANG Schedule and increase integration between XLANG Schedules and third-party applications.

Securing BizTalk Server

In previous chapters, you've seen how to develop quite a few full-blown BizTalk Server applications. You've tested the applications and are satisfied with the results. Now it's time to put some armor on your applications. In this chapter, I'll talk about the security issues that surround BizTalk Server and the applications that are built on top of it.

This chapter will be divided into two main topics. The first topic is the security issues of BizTalk Server COM+ applications, BizTalk Server services and security accounts, and BizTalk Server–related databases. The second topic is how to secure an application that is running on top of BizTalk Server, and how to identify who the documents that pass through BizTalk Server are from. This is important, because you may have multiple business partners who are sending documents to you, and you need to make sure the documents are processed under their owner's identity.

BizTalk Server COM+ Application Security

In earlier chapters, I talked about some security features in BizTalk Server related to document encryption/decryption, document signing, and authentication. In this section, I'll show you BizTalk Server security from a different perspective. You'll see how you can manage BizTalk Server's applications and its services in a secure environment.

Interactive Account vs. Application Identity

After you install BizTalk Server, there are number of newly installed applications running as interactive user accounts. The interactive account is the user account of the person who is currently logged on to the system, and when I say "currently," I mean the person whose face is in front of the computer monitor. In other words, if a domain administrator logs on, the applications on the machine that are running as interactive user are actually running as the domain administrator. If Mr. John Public logs on to the server, those same applications are now running as JPublic. If you restart the computer, and no one has yet logged on to the machine with a user ID and password, those same applications will be running as nobody, which means those applications can't be started. An error will be generated on the Event Viewer, indicating a security violation if some program tries to execute the application.

When you have your application running on a COM+ server application, you can't assume or guarantee the system is always logged on with the user account you want your application to run under. Therefore, you must provide a specific user account for your application so that no matter who is logged on to the server or if no one is logged on to the server, your application will always run under that user account you specified.

BizTalk Server comes with three server applications and two library applications. Library applications run under their caller's security context, and you can't make them run as a predefined user account. For the three server applications, however, you must define the user account under which the application should run. These are the three server applications that come with the BizTalk Server installation:

- *BizTalk Server Interchange Application:* Contains the Interchange class, which is responsible for submitting documents into BizTalk Server's work queue

- *XLANG Schedule:* Contains the XLANG engine, which processes the BizTalk orchestrations

- *XLANG Schedule Pool:* Similar to the XLANG Schedule, except you can specify how you want each XLANG Schedule processed, such as setting the maximum pool size allowed for certain XLANG Schedules

Setting a Server Application's Identity

To specify the user account under which each server application should run, open Component Manager from Administrative Tools. Right-click the server application name and select Properties, as shown in Figure 12-1.

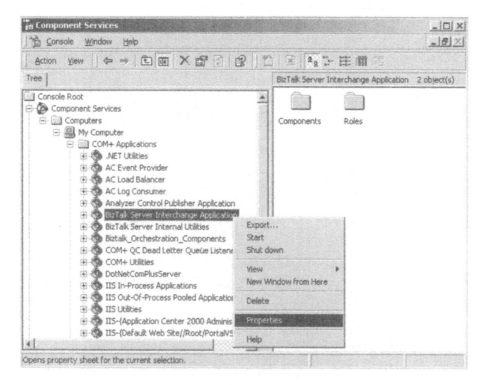

Figure 12-1. Configuring the application's user account under Component Services

> **NOTE** *The Component Services console is an application that allows you to view and configure the properties of COM+ components, such as transactional support, role-based security, component pooling, etc. It's located under Administrative Tools.*

When the Properties page appears, the fields are all grayed out and not editable. You need to make this application's properties editable first. To do so, select the Advanced tab on the Properties page, and uncheck the Disable deletion and Disable changes checkboxes in the Permission section, as shown in Figure 12-2.

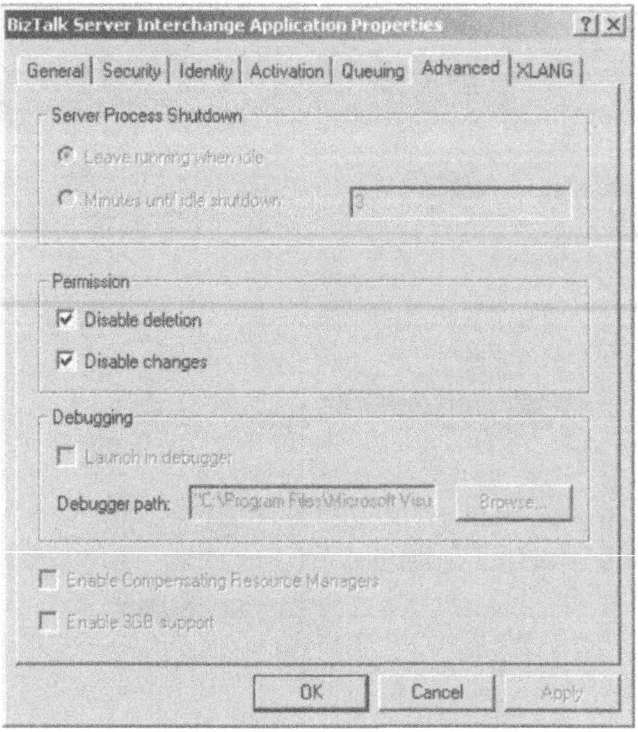

Figure 12-2. Unchecking the checkboxes in the Permission section to make the properties editable

Click OK, and you will see a confirmation dialog box. Click Yes. Now, open up the Properties page of this application again, and all the fields will be editable.

On the Properties page of the BizTalk Server Interchange Application, select the Identity tab. Under the Account section, select the This user radio button, and type in or browse to an existing user account. Type in the password and click OK.

In my case, I want this BizTalk Server Interchange Application to run under the biztalkuser account in the myhome domain (see Figure 12-3). You can use either a domain account or a local account for this application. You'll have to consider which account you really want to use to run this application shortly. Not every user account will be able to successfully run this application.

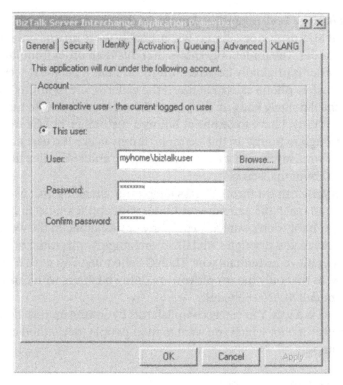

Figure 12-3. Setting the identity for the BizTalk Server Interchange Application

Now you can duplicate this process for other BizTalk Server applications so that they won't be running under interactive user.

> **NOTE** *There is nothing wrong with using the interactive user account on your own development computer. Since you'll almost always log on to your own computer to do any work, these applications will always be running under your user account, which is preferable during the development stage.*

Role-Based Security

COM+ applications support simple but powerful role-based security. In the previous section, I showed you how to define your server application's identity. That application identity specifies who you want this application to run as, but not who can call and execute the application—there's a big difference between the two.

For example, if I call my broker, Jimmy, on the phone, and ask him to buy 100 shares of Microsoft stock, Jimmy will probably write up one order ticket and hand it to a trader. The trader only knows that this is an order from Jimmy, even though the order is originally from me. Jimmy also has a personal secretary, Lisa, who only transfers phone calls to Jimmy if the caller is one of Jimmy's customers. Otherwise she'll politely hang up the phone. In order for Jimmy to buy 100 shares of Microsoft for me, I have to be one of Jimmy's customers, or Lisa won't let my order get through to Jimmy. In this example, Jimmy is like the user account (or identity) that your server application is running as, and Lisa is like the role-based security I am about to discuss.

Not everyone can get through Lisa's telephone screening, just as not every method call can reach the components under your applications. In BizTalk Server, you probably don't want any company or individual in the world to submit documents to you through a BizTalk Interchange Application, nor do you want those people to instantiate your XLANG Schedules. You need a way to filter those people so that only the people you are doing business with can submit documents or call XLANG Schedules.

Well, there is a way. You can accomplish this by setting up role-based security for each application for which you want to filter people (or method calls). This takes a few steps.

- Enable security checking.

- Set up security roles.

- Assign users to the roles.

- Grant access permissions to the roles.

Enabling Security Checking

To enable security checking on any server application, open the Properties page of the application under the Component Services console and select the Security tab (see Figure 12-4). Under the Authorization section, check the "Enforce access checks for this application" checkbox. Also, under the Security level section, select the second option, which specifies access checks at the process and component levels. Then click OK.

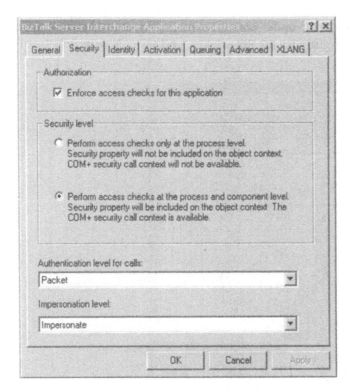

Figure 12-4. Enabling security checking on the application

If the checkbox in the Authorization section is left unchecked, anyone could call the Interchange Application to submit a document to your BizTalk Server's work queue.

The difference between the two radio button options in the Security level section is that when you select the first radio button, the security context would not be available to your program, and your program couldn't programmatically check who is accessing the components. You also couldn't define a fine-grained role-level security under the application. This may not seem like a problem for an application that has only one component in it, but it would prevent you from setting different role-level securities on different components if there were more than one component under the application.

Setting Up Security Roles

Now that security checking is set up, let's define some roles that can access your BizTalk Server Interchange Application. The first thing you need to do is create new roles under this application. Each application under Component Services has its own set of roles, and they are completely independent of each other.

To create a role under BizTalk Server Interchange Application, expand the application, right-click the Roles folder, and select New ➤ Role (see Figure 12-5).

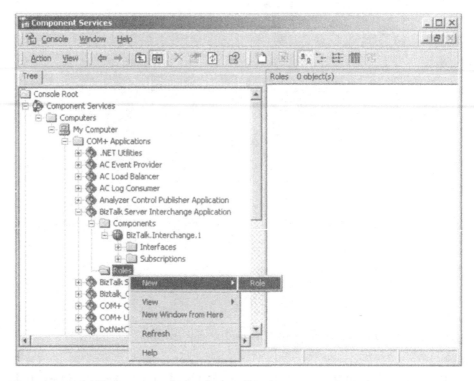

Figure 12-5. Adding a new role for the application

A new dialog box appears, in which you can specify the name of the new role. This name allows you to easily identify the purpose of this role. It doesn't need to be the same name as that of the user or group assigned under this role. In my case, I wanted to set up the system so that my customers from North America, Asia, and Europe can submit their documents to my BizTalk Servers, so I added the following roles: North American Customers, Asian Customers, and European Customers.

After I created these roles, my BizTalk Server Interchange Application looks like what you see in Figure 12-6.

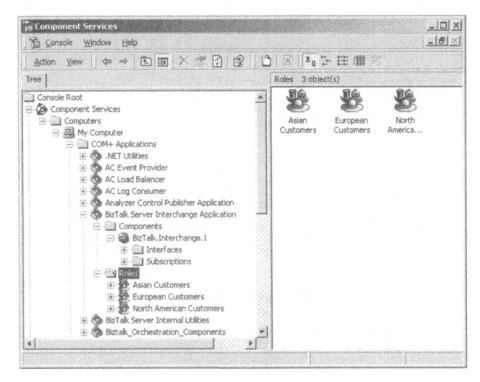

Figure 12-6. New roles added under the BizTalk Server Interchange Application

Assigning Users to Roles

Now that you've seen how to add roles, you need to learn how to assign the
Windows 2000 users or groups to each role. The reason for doing this is that you
want to convert the Windows user-based security to role-based security when
someone calls your Interchange Application. In COM+, role membership is the
only thing that an application recognizes.

To assign a Windows user or group to a role, expand a role under the Roles
folder, and you will see a Users folder under it. Right-click the user folder and
select New ➢ User, as shown in Figure 12-7.

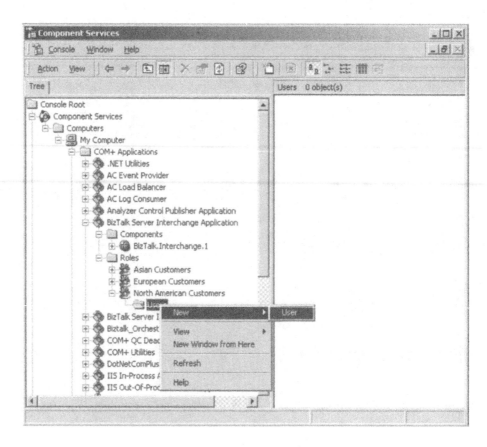

Figure 12-7. Assigning a Windows user or group to a role

When you select User, a new dialog box opens and shows all the users and groups in the domain. Select the desired users or groups, and click OK.

After adding users or groups to each role, your screen should resemble Figure 12-8, with users and groups showing under the various roles.

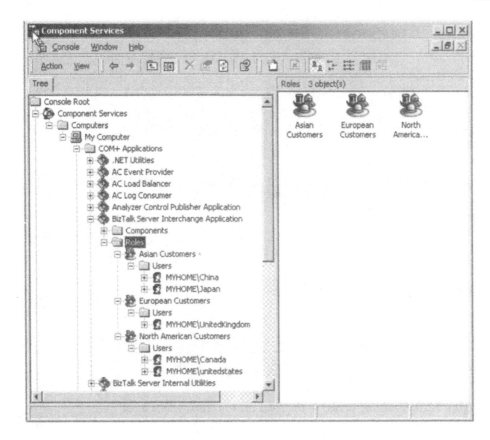

Figure 12-8. Users and groups assigned to roles

Granting Access to Roles

The next step is to enable access for the roles under each component so that users will be able to access the components. To allow a role to access a component, right-click the component and select Properties. For this example, select the BizTalk.Interchange.1 component from the Components folder. The Properties page will open.

On the Properties page, select the Security tab, and you should see the roles you just added to the application listed there. To allow access for all these roles, check the checkbox next to each role, and then click OK to save the changes (see Figure 12-9).

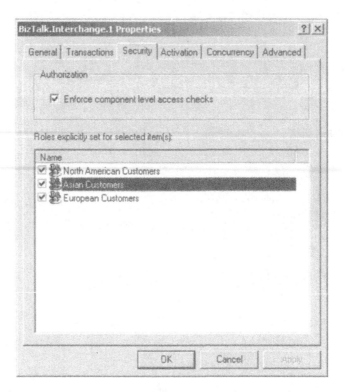

Figure 12-9. Enabling access to the roles on the component level

After you've configured the BizTalk Interchange component, only users who belong to one of the roles you created can submit documents to you. For instance, in my case, if a user called Korea tries to submit a document to me, then he or she would get a COM error complaining of a security failure, since there is no user called Korea under any of the three roles I've created.

By now you may have realized the amount of configuration that can go into these applications. Would it be better if you could do this without so much mouse clicking and keyboard knocking? You bet. In Chapter 14, I'll talk about deploying BizTalk Server applications, and the configuration of COM+ applications is part of the deployment. I'll show you a way to configure all these settings with scripts using ComAdminCatalog APIs. ComAdminCatalog is a set of objects for viewing, creating, and modifying COM+ applications programmatically.

Securing BizTalk Server Tools and Services

Let's now look at the security of the BizTalk Messaging service. By default, this service runs as the local system account, which has administrative privileges only on the local server. The local system is fine as long as all the resources the BizTalk Messaging service is accessing are local resources. This may not always be true, though.

The Messaging service sometimes needs to access remote resources, which will cause problems when using the local system account. For example, BizTalk Receive Functions are controlled by the Messaging service, and when the destination of a Receive Function is a file location on a remote server or a message queue on another computer, the Receive Function will try to read and delete the file or message using its local system account. It will get an access denied error if the remote resources don't recognize this local system account from another machine. Although there is a way to configure an account other than the local system account for the Receive Function, this may add a lot of managing overhead for those account-password pairs, especially if you have many Receive Functions. The Messaging service also needs to access the BizTalk Server databases, but if these databases are located on a remote SQL server, the Messaging service will fail because the local system account doesn't have access to the remote SQL server database by default.

In order to allow a Messaging service that is running as the local system account to work with remote SQL servers, you must explicitly grant the BizTalk Server database access to that local system account. This adds a lot of administrative work that can be avoided.

To eliminate the excess management overhead associated with the use of the local system account, you can set up BizTalk Server to run under a domain user that is recognizable on the remote resources within the same domain. Let's call the user MYHOME\BizTalkuser and add this user under the local groups on BizTalk Server. This user will be the one that handles all the BizTalk Server–related operations. You now can run all your BizTalk Server COM+ applications and Messaging services as this domain user.

You now have all the basic information for setting up a secure BizTalk environment, so you will now put them together to get a complete strategy. You'll learn what you need to configure on BizTalk Server to achieve your goal. You'll first see how to secure BizTalk Server from a human user's perspective, and consider users' access privileges for the BizTalk tools. After that, you'll look at this from an application's perspective and consider the security requirements of BizTalk Server services, to see how you need to set things up to make your BizTalk Server services work in a secure environment.

Securing BizTalk Server Tools

There are several BizTalk Server tools to consider: BizTalk Messaging Manager, BizTalk Server Administrator, BizTalk Document Tracking, XLANG Monitor, BizTalk Orchestration Designer, BizTalk Editor, and BizTalk Mapper.

BizTalk Messaging Manager is used by users only, so your application may interact with the BizTalk Messaging service, but not directly with the GUI. For a user to interact with BizTalk Messaging Manager, his or her user account must meet two criteria:

- The user must be a member of the BizTalk Server Administrators group. This is a local group on BizTalk Server.

- The user must be a member of the db_owner database role and have full control of the BizTalk Share Queue database and the BizTalk Messaging database.

 NOTE *Being a member of the local administration group isn't enough to use Messaging Manager. The user must be a member of the BizTalk Server Administrator group to use BizTalk Messaging Manager.*

The BizTalk Server Administrator program has the same criteria as BizTalk Messaging Manager, just described.

BizTalk Document Tracking is also only directly used by users. It requires the users to meet the following criteria:

- The user must be a member of the BizTalk Server Report Users group. This is a local group on BizTalk Server.

- The user must be a member of the db_owner database role and have full control of the BizTalk Tracking database and the BizTalk Messaging database.

XLANG Monitor is a utility that developers can use to watch the progress of running XLANG instances. In order to run this application, the user must meet the following criterion:

- The user must be a member of the XLANG Schedule Creator role of XLANG Scheduler application under Component Services. By default, the user under this role is Everyone, so every user logged on to the server can run XLANG Monitor.

BizTalk Orchestration designer, BizTalk Editor, and BizTalk Mapper require no special privileges from the user to run these programs.

Securing BizTalk Server Services

To secure BizTalk Server from the application perspective, you need to focus on the BizTalk Server services and BizTalk COM+ applications.

BizTalk Messaging

The BizTalk Messaging service touches almost every aspect of BizTalk Server. For the BizTalk Messaging service to work properly, the following criteria must be met:

- The BizTalk Messaging service account must have the "Log on as a service" right assigned. You configure this setting through Local Security Settings under Administrative Tools (see Figure 12-10). Double-click the policy called "Log on as a service" to open it. The Messaging service account must be added to the list. In this example, I added the domain user MYHOME\biztalkuser. The strategy here is to run BizTalk Server services and applications under a common domain user account, and add whatever security privileges are necessary for BizTalk Server to operate properly to this user account.

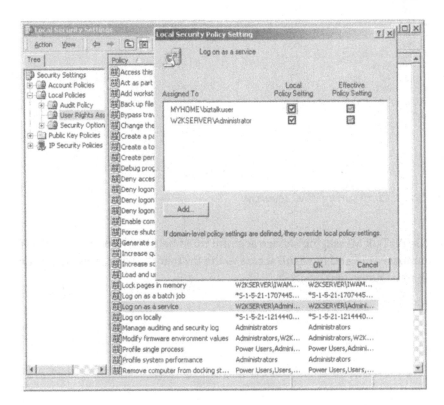

Figure 12-10. Configuring the local security policy

- The BizTalk Server Messaging service account must also have full control over the Root\MicrosoftBizTalkServer namespace under Windows Management Instrumentation (WMI). To configure the security on specific WMI namespaces, you need to open the WMI control from the Computer Management console, as shown in Figure 12-11. Right-click WMI Control, and select Properties. Select the Security tab (as shown in Figure 12-12), expand the Root folder, select MicrosoftBizTalkServer, and click the Security button at the right. Then add the BizTalk Messaging service account.

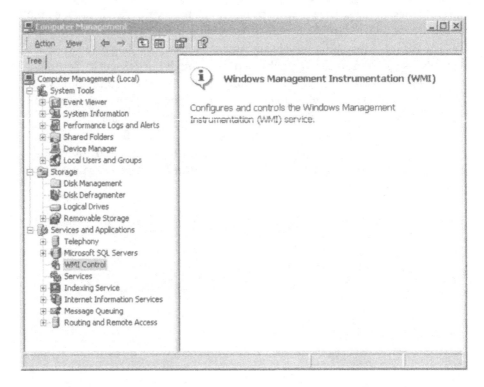

Figure 12-11. Configuring WMI security

- The BizTalk Messaging service account must be a member of the db_owner database role and have full access to the BizTalk Tracking, Messaging , and Shared Queue databases.

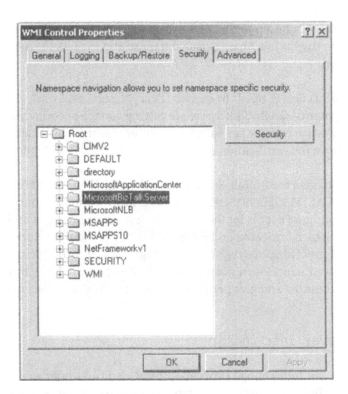

Figure 12-12. Configuring security on the MicrosoftBizTalkServer namespace

- If there is a Receive Function defined on the BizTalk Server that will access the resource using a separate user name and password, the BizTalk Messaging service will also be responsible for impersonating that new user when accessing that resource. The impersonation operation requires the BizTalk Messaging service to run under an account that has the "Log on locally" and "Act as part of operating system" rights assigned to it. These can be configured using the same procedure as for configuring the "Log on as a service" right described earlier.

BizTalk Messaging configuration objects are a set of objects that can be used to add, modify, and delete the BizTalk Messaging configuration programmatically. BizTalk Messaging Manager uses this set of objects to do the work behind the scenes. To make sure BizTalk Messaging configuration objects function properly, the following criteria must be met:

- The user who is making the calls to the Messaging configuration object must be a member of the BizTalk Server Administrators group. If the user isn't in the group, an error will be thrown.

- The user must be a member of the db_owner database role and have full access to the BizTalk Share Queue database and BizTalk Messaging database.

When BizTalk Server needs to encrypt, decrypt ,sign, and verify digital signatures on documents, the BizTalk Server Messaging service account has to have access to the system registry key called SystemCertificates. This enables BizTalk Server to retrieve the certification and perform encryption, decryption, digital signing, etc.

You need to give the BizTalk Server Messaging service account full control of the HKEY_LOCAL_MACHINE\SOFTWARE\Microsoft\SystemCertificates registry key. To configure access for the registry key, you need to use a tool called Regedt32.exe, which is located under the C:\WINNT\System32 folder. When you locate the SystemCertificates registry key in Regedt32, click the Security tab on the menu bar and select Permission. A dialog box will open in which you can add users to the access list and give permissions to users for the registry key.

BizTalk Server Interchange

The BizTalk Server Interchange application must also run under an account with some special privileges in order to operate properly. As you've seen earlier in this chapter, you can change the account (identity) under which this application runs. The account must meet these criteria:

- The BizTalk Server Interchange Application's identity must have full control over the Root\MicrosoftBizTalkServer namespace under WMI.

- The BizTalk Server Interchange Application's identity must be a member of the db_owner database role and have full access to the BizTalk Tracking, Messaging , and Shared Queue databases.

XLANG Scheduler

The XLANG Scheduler application is responsible for processing XLANG orchestrations, and saving and retrieving the transaction state to and from the database during orchestration process. In order for the XLANG Scheduler application to perform this work, it must have full access to the XLANG database (Orchestration Persistence database).

XLANG Scheduler accesses the XLANG database through a file DSN. This file DSN will access the XLANG database through either Windows integrated security or SQL login. To verify the settings inside the DSN file, open Data Sources (ODBC) from Administrative Tools. Select the File DSN tab, and click the Configure button on the right (see Figure 12-13).

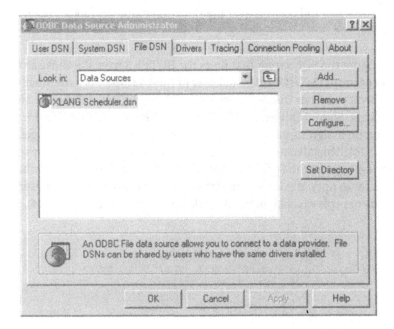

Figure 12-13. Checking the DSN settings used by the XLANG Scheduler application

If the DSN accesses the database using Windows integrated security, this application's identity must be a member of the db_owner role of the XLANG database and have full control of the database. If the DSN accesses the database using SQL security, then this SQL login must be a member of the db_owner role of the XLANG database and have full control of the database.

Checklist for Setting Up User Accounts for BizTalk Server Services and Applications

The following check list summarizes all the topics I've just discussed, providing a quick to-do list you can refer to when configuring user accounts for BizTalk Server services and applications.

- Create a new domain user such as MYHOME\biztalkuser (you can name it anything you want).

- Add this user account (biztalkuser) to the BizTalk Administrators local group.

- Modify the local security policy to give this user the rights to "Log on locally", "Log on as a service", and "Act as part of operating system".

- Give this user full control over the Root\MicrosoftBizTalkServer WMI namespace.

- Configure the SQL server that hosts the BizTalk Server database so that the user account (MYHOME\biztalkuser in this example) is a member of db_owner and has full access to each of these BizTalk databases: Messaging, Tracking, Shared Queue, and XLANG. Consult your SQL Server documentation on assigning access rights to a user. To find out the privileges of MYHOME\biztalkuser on the database server, open SQL Enterprise Manager, select the Security folder, and locate the user. Then double-click the user to open the logon Properties page, and verify that this user has a db_owner role on each of the BizTalk databases (see Figure 12-14).

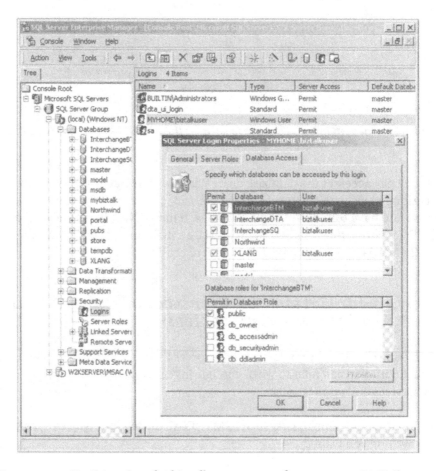

Figure 12-14. Verifying that the biztalkuser account has access to BizTalk databases through SQL Server Enterprise Manager

- Change the BizTalk Messaging Server account to this new user account (MYHOME\biztalkuser in this example). This is done through the Service console under Administrative Tools.

- Give this user account full control over the registry key HKEY_LOCAL_MACHINE\SOFTWARE\Microsoft\SystemCertificates if encryption/decryption or digital signing/verifying are used when processing documents on BizTalk Server.

- Make all the BizTalk Server COM+ server applications' identities be this new user account (MYHOME\biztalkuser).

The next important step is to test the application vigorously. Your applications may perform some operations that require more security rights, and you can find that out by testing your applications well after the security lockdown of the server. Locate and fix whatever problems occurred in this locked-down environment.

Document Identification

Now that you've seen security from the perspective of BizTalk Server's services and applications, let's take a look at security from the document identity point of view.

With Windows applications, either GUI or COM applications, there is always a user security context attached to the thread that is executing the program. When your application makes COM calls to a configured component, COM+ checks for the security context of the caller to make sure the caller has access to the component through the role-based security mentioned earlier.

In a B2B environment, data is transmitted in XML or some other standard data format, and there is no such security context that attaches to the document itself. Especially with asynchronous processes, such as those going on inside BizTalk Server, security contexts on the processing threads are lost after the data is persisted to MSMQ or a database. How are you going to secure the application if you don't have the security context that you use in a COM environment?

In this half of the chapter, I'll discuss several ways to get around this problem, but first let's take a look at a simple B2B solution.

Concept Overview

When Mike submits an XML document to his business partner's Web site using Basic authentication over the Internet (see Figure 12-15), he has a Windows account on his business partner's system. When he posts a document to the IIS server, IIS recognizes the Basic authentication and checks if the logon is successful. If it is, IIS's impersonation process will impersonate Mike and make the calls to the Post.asp, which contains the COM method calls to some business objects.

The Post.asp then runs with Mike's identity, and the COM calls made within the ASP page carry Mike's identity. If the business object is a library application that accesses a SQL database using Windows integrated security, then all the database access calls will also carry Mike's identity (as in the case of Business Object B in Figure 12-15).

It's important that each process is aware of who is making the request. You may want to have code inside business components to validate the user and perform different tasks based on the identity of that user. Obviously, you don't need to write any extra code to make every process along the way run under the original sender's identity, because Windows can keep the caller's user security context accessible when the caller is making calls to other objects inside a program.

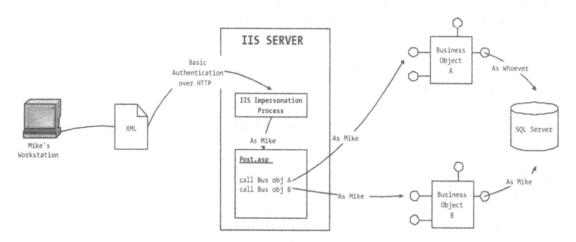

Figure 12-15. A simple B2B situation

The situation I just described covers the basics, but it's oversimplified, and more importantly, it's a synchronous process.

A lot could be said about the pros and cons of synchronous and asynchronous processes, but more and more applications, especially B2B and EAI applications, are being deployed these days using asynchronous processes because of their scalability. With asynchronous processes, all the work is put into a pool, and the work can be picked up from the pool and processed at a later time. Unfortunately, when you put the work in the pool, it loses its identity information.

A good analogy for asynchronous and synchronous processing is the difference between waiting in line at the bank or at the supermarket. When I line up for a bank teller to deposit a check or ask some questions, I wait in one long line.

There may be four or five bank tellers serving at once, and whichever teller is done with their current customer will take the next one from the line. Even through the process is sometimes ridiculously slow, it's an efficient use of the resources (tellers). How could you speed it up if every bank teller is already busy serving the customers?

In a supermarket, people wait in one of several lines for a particular cashier. If you are in line behind someone pushing two carts of food and carrying a handful of newspaper coupons, you know it's not your day. In this case, one person could block five customers even when the other cashiers have finished serving their customers and have nothing to do. Of course, people are smart enough to move to another line to speed up the process. Computing processes waiting in queues, however, don't have their own discretion to act upon.

If you build your B2B application using BizTalk Server, chances are that 99 percent of the time you will be using an asynchronous model, because BizTalk Server will save all the documents into its shared queue first, which is a data table. This effectively erases any identity information that attaches to the thread and the user security token that may have come from the original sender of the document. So how can you know the identity of the sender? What happens if the business component that processes the data needs to make a decision based on the identity of the user who sent the data?

You need to find a way to identify who the data is from at every step of the process. There are many solutions to choose from, but I'll talk about one I think is easy to understand and implement.

Extracting and Persisting Document Identity

There are four ways a document can get into your BizTalk Server system: by file, MSMQ, HTTP(S), and COM (Interchange submit) calls. The first two are persistent stores, such databases after things are stored there. You really can't figure out where they are from—all the documents in those stores look alike, even though they may come from 20 different senders.

When a document comes in through one of the latter two ways, it does carry an identity, and you must do something to persist this piece of information. The best way to persist it is to save it as part of the document. In a more complex B2B scenario, a piece of data can be persisted many times to many data stores, and having the identity information as part of the data guarantees that the identity won't get lost during the transmission of the data.

This identity information should be located at some node of the document schema. When a customer sends in a document, an additional empty element in the document acts as a placeholder for the identity information. It's extremely important to not delegate this task of entering the identity information to the customer. Because you need to use this identity information at every step of the process, you must be absolutely sure that the person who sends the document matches the identity information inside the document. If customer A intentionally or unintentionally put customer B as the value in the identity field inside the document, and you simply accepted that value, there would be no difference between it and a document from customer B.

In this section, I'll show you a couple of examples, and you'll see how to extract the identity information and save it inside the document when someone sends a document over the Internet. The implementation for HTTP(S) and COM (Interchange submit) calls are very similar.

In these examples, assume you have a customer who is sending a document to you through HTTP Basic authentication. You can set up an ASP page to first accept the document, verify the identity of the sender, plug this identity information into the document, and then make a COM call using the Interchange submit method to move the document into the BizTalk work queue for further attention.

Before you start coding, though, there is one thing that you should decide. If you're going to add this new identity element to the document, you can either tell customers that the documents they submit must include the empty identity element at the right position, or don't mention the identity element, since the identity element is related to how your application works and isn't related to the content of the document.

If you decide to choose the first option, and make the customer supply an empty identity element in the document, all you need to do is confirm who this customer really is and put this customer's identity value in the element.

However, if you choose the second option, whereby the customer has no knowledge of the element, you must define your schema so that it won't reject the document as invalid after your program adds this extra undefined element to it. This can be done by changing the element's model property from closed to open in BizTalk Editor. The other thing to watch out for with this choice is that if you decide to send the response document (containing the original document and some indication of the status of the processing) back to the customer, you may need to remove this identity element, because the customer won't be expecting the extra element. This is not a problem if the customer's system that receives the response document doesn't mind some extra undefined elements.

The first example I'll present will obtain the document identity when a document is sent through Basic authentication over HTTP. The second example will use Secure Socket Layer (SSL) authentication.

> **NOTE** *Basic authentication isn't considered secure when used by itself because the data, including the password, is transmitted in an unencrypted form and can be intercepted by people monitoring the network traffic. However, if it's combined with SSL (without the requirement of client certification), it can be a much more secure way of transmitting data, since all the data will be encrypted at all times through SSL.*

Basic Authentication Example

Here is some simple ASP code to do the work. This code uses ASP's Request object to extract the user account of the caller and add it to the document before submitting it to BizTalk Messaging. This code isn't for production implementation—to keep it fairly short, I've left out error-handling code that would be needed in production code. It can be found in the BasicAuthenticationPost.asp file, available from the Downloads section of the Apress Web site (http://www.apress.com).

```
<%
    Const TYPE_BINARY = 1
    Const TYPE_TEXT = 2
    Dim account
    Dim stream
    Dim PostedDocument
    Dim EntityBody
    Dim position
    Dim oInterchange
    'extract the account information from ASP Request object
    account=Request.ServerVariables("AUTH_USER")

'code to extract the data from HTTP Post.
    EntityBody=Request.BinaryRead(Request.TotalBytes)
    Set Stream = Server.CreateObject("AdoDB.Stream")
    Stream.Type = TYPE_BINARY
    stream.Open
    Stream.Write EntityBody
    Stream.Position = 0
    Stream.Type =  TYPE_TEXT
    Stream.Charset = "us-ascii"
    PostedDocument = PostedDocument & Stream.ReadText
```

```
'Identify the type of the document and add the account information
'inside a predefined position.(In our sample, we will add it right after
'the Root element, if you choose a different the location for the element, you
'must implement different code below.

'find out the position of the end of the first element(Root)
position = instr(1,PostedDocument,">")
PostedDocument=mid(PostedDocument,1,position) & _
            "<identity>" & account & "</identity>" & _
            mid(PostedDocument,position + 1)

set oInterchange = Server.CreateObject("BizTalk.Interchange")
'Depending on your situation, you may need to provide more optional parameters
oInterchange.submit 1,PostedDocument

set oInterchange=nothing
set stream=nothing

Response.Status="200 OK"
%>
```

To demonstrate that it really works, I have set up a testing BizTalk Server
channel and port that point to the following page on my IIS server:
http://w2kserver.myhome.com/B2B_Basic/BasicAuthenticationPost.asp. On the
advanced properties page of the channel, I provided myhome\Mike as the user
ID, and "password" as the password. B2B_Basic is the virtual directory, and this
virtual directory is configured to use Basic authentication as its authentication
access method. This virtual directory will recognize the account from the
myhome domain (see Figure 12-16).

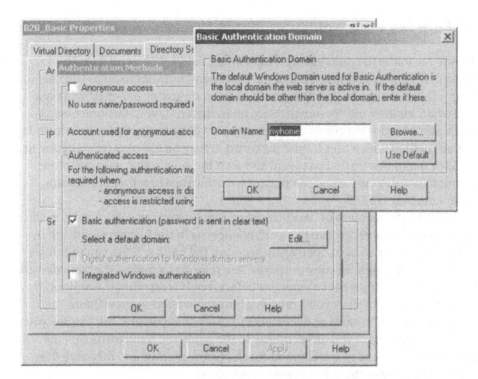

Figure 12-16. To configure the authentication method on a virtual directory, open the properties page for the virtual directory and set the domain name.

When I run my test, the data that is saved to the BizTalk Server queue looks like·this, with the identity element embedded in it:

```
<Order>
  <identity>myhome\mike</identity>
  <id>12345</id>
  <items>
    <item>
      <name>Windows XP Home</name>
      <price>199</price>
      <quantity>15</quantity>
    </item>
    <item>
      <name>Windows XP Professional</name>
      <price>299</price>
      <quantity>15</quantity>
    </item></items>
</Order>
```

SSL Example

The ASP file in the previous example can extract the user account from the sender's HTTP post and insert it into the document, but that requires the user to set up a user account on your Windows system and provide a user ID and password when sending the document. More often than not, your customer won't have a user account in your system, or won't be willing to trust the whole authentication method with a user ID and password. It may be too easy for someone to get his or her hands on that password and start impersonating your customer. Fortunately, today customers can present a certificate when they are sending documents over HTTPS.

A certificate is a piece of data that sits on your system and uniquely identifies you. A certificate is very much like a driver's license in the human world. When someone goes to a bank to open up an account, the bank will ask you to bring a driver license for identification purposes. The reason is simple—the bank doesn't trust you, because they haven't met you before, but it trusts the government. If the government is to issue you a driver's license, you need to show them several identification cards or documents to prove that you are who you say you are. When you present you driver license to the bank, the bank trusts that the government has done its background check on you already, and therefore they assume you are who the driver license says you are.

There are a few companies, called Certificate Authorities (CAs), whose business is based on providing identification for people and businesses—VeriSign being one of these CAs. Most companies trust VeriSign to do a background check on people or businesses. By holding a VeriSign certificate, you are basically saying that VeriSign has done their checking, and all the information they found out about you is on the certificate.

To use SSL, you'll need to send your document with the certificate attached so that the receiver can look at the certificate and be sure whom this document is from.

Web Site SSL Configuration

To set up a Web site that accepts customers' data over HTTPS and verifies the sender's certificate, a few steps need to be taken. The following steps are standard configuration steps for Web sites that use certificates and SSL:

- Obtain a server certificate for your Web server, so that your customers are sure to whom they are sending sensitive information.

- Each customer must obtain a certificate from a CA whose certificates you both agree to accept.

- Configure the Web server so that it only processes requests when the client certificate is presented.

- Map a client certificate with a predefined Windows account for accessing resources on your system.

- Write the code to extract the identity information from the client certificate and insert it into the document at a predefined position so that the sender's identity information is included with the document every step of the way.

I'll discuss each of these steps in turn.

To obtain a server certification, you need to contact the CA agreed on by you and your customers. After obtaining the certificate, you can install it on your Web server through the Web site's Properties page. Open the Properties page of the Default Web Site, and select the Directory Security tab, as shown in Figure 12-17.

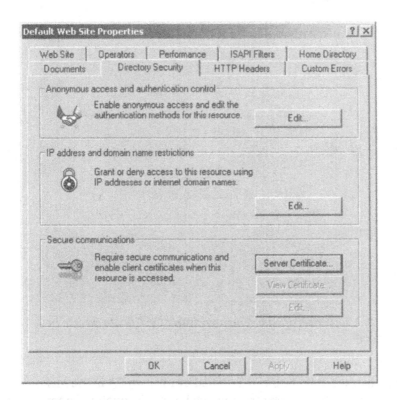

Figure 12-17. Adding a server certificate to a Web site

Click the Server Certificate button, and a Web Server Certificate Wizard will start up. Follow the instructions for installing a server certificate.

If you're only at the development phase of the project and don't want to get a real certificate, or don't know which server will get the certificate, you can generate your own certificate using the Certificate service that comes with Windows 2000 Server and later versions. By installing the Certificate service, you become your own CA and are capable of issuing certificates. Although no one will trust you as a CA, it's great for testing your application without using a real certificate.

For demonstration purposes, I created a server certificate using my own CA service. Figure 12-18 shows what a server certification looks like.

Figure 12-18. A server certificate generated using Certificate service in Windows 2000

As you can see, this certificate is issued by my own CA in the myhome domain. It's issued to my Web server, which has a fully qualified domain name (FQDN) of w2kserver.myhome.com.

The second step is for your customers to get their own certificates from the CA to identify themselves. No additional work needs to be done on your part (the receiving end).

The third step is to configure the virtual directory on the Web server so that the only communication between the virtual directory and customers is through SSL. Also, the virtual directory must be expecting a client certificate when data is sent to it. If no client certificate from the agreed-on CA is presented, an HTTPS error will be returned to the client.

To configure this, open the Properties page of the virtual directory that you will expose to the outside world for document posting, and select the Directory Security tab, as shown in Figure 12-19.

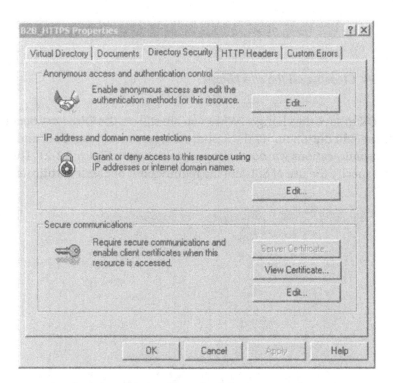

Figure 12-19. Configuring SSL for the virtual directory

Click the Edit button in the Anonymous access and authentication control section. You are going to uncheck all the checkboxes, as shown in Figure 12-20.

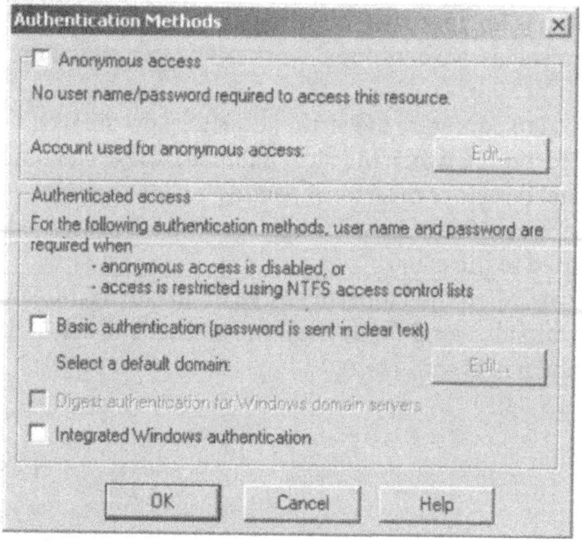

Figure 12-20. Clearing all the checkboxes

Click OK to save the changes. While you are still on the Directory Security tab, click the Edit button under the Secure communications section, and a new Secure Communications window will open, as shown in Figure 12-21. This is where you specify the use of SSL and the requirement of client certificates.

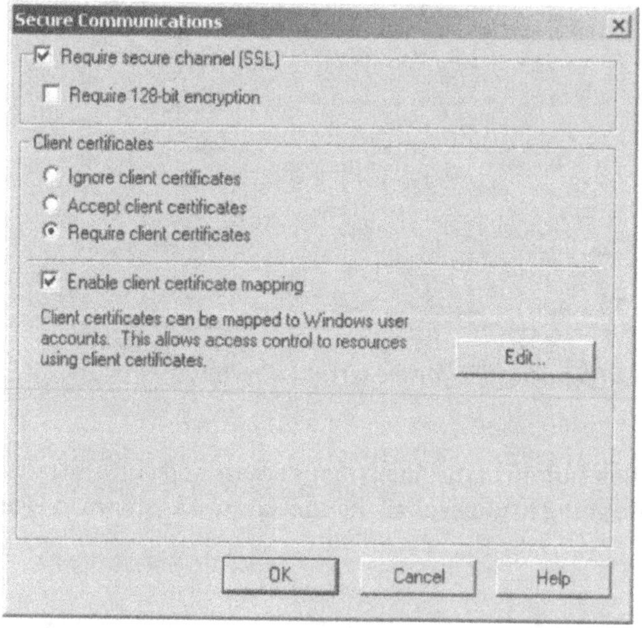

Figure 12-21. Enabling SSL and requirement for client certificates for the virtual directory

By checking the Require secure channel (SSL) checkbox, customers must now use "https://" in their URL when posting the document. Selecting the Require client certificates radio button enforces the presence of a client certificate from the CA when a document is posted to your site.

One thing to keep in mind is that the CA that issues these certificates must exist in the list of trusted root Certification Authorities on both the client machine and server machine. You can add that CA to this list through the MMC Certificates console if it isn't already there.

The Enable client certificate mapping checkbox needs to be checked also.

What you've done so far is allow the client with a certificate to submit a document to your system through the Web site. However, the customer can't do anything just yet, including posting a document to an ASP page. To allow these outsiders to access your resources, you need to take extra steps to map them to a Windows account for that purpose. To map them, click the Edit button in the Enable client certificate mapping section to bring up the Account Mappings dialog box (see Figure 12-22).

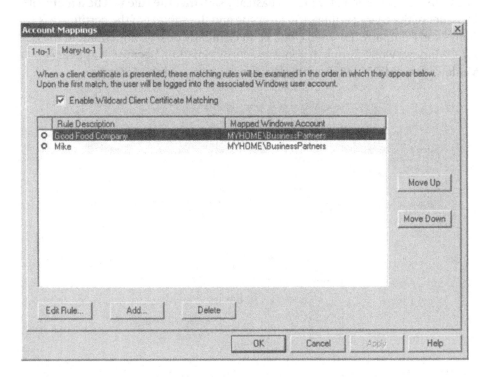

Figure 12-22. Mapping the certificates to a Windows account

You have a choice to map a client certificate to an account one by one (1-to-1), or you can map a bunch of certificates together to an account (Many-to-1). It makes more sense here to use the latter choice. You may have many people and companies who are submitting documents to you. By choosing Many-to-1, you need only map all the people and companies to a generic Windows account so that they can access your ASP pages. This doesn't mean you forget about your customers' original identities. You'll deal with their identities using an ASP in the next step. For now, let's see how to map a bunch of certificates to a Windows account.

As you can see in Figure 12-22, I've added a couple of rules: one is for Good Food Company, and one is for Mike. Let's take a look at what they define. Double-clicking a rule brings up its properties. If you were to double-click the Good Food Company rule, you'd get the window shown in Figure 12-23.

Every time a request comes to this site, IIS will check whether the client certificate satisfies any of these rules. Upon the first match, IIS will impersonate this client as the MYHOME\BusinessPartners account, in this example. The rule's properties window shown in Figure 12-23 basically says that the rule will be a match if the issuer of the client certificate is myhome and the subject of the certificate is Good Food Company. So, when Good Food Company posts a document to the ASP page, Windows won't complain about a security violation, because it appears that a Windows user (MYHOME\BusinessPartners) is accessing the ASP page.

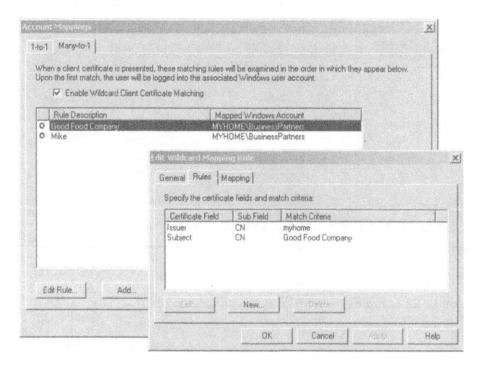

Figure 12-23. Creating mapping rules when mapping many certificates to one Windows account

The SSL Code

Now your customers can successfully post documents over HTTPS with their client certificates. They aren't your internal Windows users, and they don't need to provide a user ID and password as in the Basic authentication example you looked at earlier. But how do you find out the identity of the client at runtime so that you can plug that information into the document before submitting it to your BizTalk Server? Fortunately, there aren't too many code changes needed.

Here is the modified code based on the earlier code. The name of the file is HTTPSPOST.asp.

```
<%
    Const TYPE_BINARY = 1
    Const TYPE_TEXT = 2
    Dim subject
    Dim stream
    Dim PostedDocument
    Dim EntityBody
    Dim position
    Dim oInterchange

    'extract the subject information from ClientCertificate object.
    'SubjectCN means the Common Name field in the Subject of the certificate
    subject=Request.ClientCertificate("SubjectCN")

    'code to extract the data from HTTP Post.
    EntityBody=Request.BinaryRead(Request.TotalBytes)
    Set Stream = Server.CreateObject("AdoDB.Stream")
    Stream.Type =  TYPE_BINARY
    stream.Open
    Stream.Write EntityBody
    Stream.Position = 0
    Stream.Type = TYPE_TEXT     Stream.Charset = "us-ascii"
    PostedDocument = PostedDocument & Stream.ReadText

    'Identify the type of the document and add the account information
    'inside a predefined position.(In our sample, we will add it right after
    'the Root element, if you choose a different location for the element, you
    'must implement different code below.
```

```
'find out the position of the end of the first element(Root)
position = instr(1,PostedDocument,">")
PostedDocument=mid(PostedDocument,1,position) & _
            "<identity>" & Subject & "</identity>" & _
            mid(PostedDocument,position + 1)

set oInterchange = Server.CreateObject("BizTalk.Interchange")
'Depending on your situation, you may need to provide more optional parameters
oInterchange.submit 1,PostedDocument

set oInterchange=nothing
set stream=nothing

Response.Status="200 OK"
%>
```

When I post the document using the Good Food Company's client certificate over HTTPS to https://w2kserver.myhome.com/B2B_HTTPS/HTTPSPost.asp, the document being submitted to BizTalk Server looks like this:

```
<Order>
  <identity>Good Food Company</identity>
  <id>12345</id>
  <items>
    <item>
      <name>Windows XP Home</name>
      <price>199</price>
      <quantity>15</quantity>
    </item>
    <item>
      <name>Windows XP Professional</name>
      <price>299</price>
      <quantity>15</quantity>
    </item></items>
</Order>
```

As you can see, the subject information from the client certificate is plugged into the identity element.

In both previous samples, the ASP page acts as a proxy between the customers who are submitting the document through the Internet and the BizTalk Server Interchange Application. What happens if the customers aren't submitting documents through the Internet, but rather by calling the BizTalk Interchange component through DCOM? In many cases, it doesn't have to be an external customer making a direct DCOM call—it could be one of the internal applications that is making the DCOM method calls. How do you get the caller's identity information and insert it into the document before submitting the document to BizTalk Server through the Interchange Application?

The ASP page solution you've seen in the HTTP(S) scenarios won't work here. To solve this problem, you need to deploy a proxy, not with an ASP page, but rather through a customized configured COM component. You need to ask the clients, both internal and external, who want to submit documents through DCOM, to call this customized component of ours. This customized component contains a wrapper function for the BizTalk Interchange submit method. By deploying such a component, you have a chance to extract the caller's identity and save it inside the document before passing the document to the BizTalk Interchange submit method. The idea is similar to the ASP page, but you need to use other technology to get the identity information from the caller.

Here is the sample code in Visual Basic:

```
Public Function Submit( _
    Openness As BIZTALK_OPENNESS_TYPE, _
    Document As String, _
    DocName As String, _
    SourceQualifier As String, _
    SourceID As String, _
    DestQualifier As String, _
    DestID As String, _
    ChannelName As String, _
    FilePath As String, _
    EnvelopeName As String, _
    PassThrough As Long
    ) As String


Dim OInterchange as new Interchange
Dim tracknum as string
Dim objcontext As ObjectContext
Dim directcaller as string
Dim newDocument as string        'document with identity element

'obtain object context
Set objcontext = GetObjectContext

'Extract the caller's identity through security property object
directcaller = objcontext.security.GetDirectCallerName
```

```
'Add the directcaller into the identity element inside the document

'//
'//   add you code here to save the identity into the document.
'//

tracknum = oInterchange.submit (Openness,newDocument,,SourceQualifier,SourceID, _
            DestQualifier, DestID, ChannelName,,_
            EnvelopeName, PassThrough)
submit = tracknum
End Function
```

NOTE *objcontext.security.GetDirectCallerName is only accessible when the component being called has the "Enforce access checks for this application" and "Perform access checks at the process and component level" options enabled. Figure 12-4, earlier in the chapter, shows these settings in the Component Services console.*

You now need to compile this class to a DLL and make it part of a new server application under Component Services. You also need to make sure this application has access to the BizTalk Interchange component, and you need to apply appropriate role-based security to it. You then can instruct your clients to call this method instead of the one in the BizTalk Server Interchange Application.

Summary

In summary, you need to set up a domain user that handles all the BizTalk-related operations, and grant this user the access and privileges that are required for BizTalk applications and the Messaging service to run properly. You also need to configure the rule-based security for your COM+ server applications so that they are only accessible to people or companies you approve.

In terms of document security, you want the identity of the original sender to be carried around with the document at all times so that you know the identity of the document at every step of the processes in the system.

To obtain the identity information of the sender, you can set up a site using Basic authentication or SSL that requires a client certificate. You need to do some level of IIS configuration to get this to work the way you intend, and you also need to implement ASP pages to extract the identity information.

Request.ServerVariable("AUTH_USER") returns the user ID in the Basic authentication scenario. Request.ClientCertificate("SubjectCN") returns the common name of the subject of the client certificate in the SSL scenario.

The ASP page also inserts this identity information in the customer document at a predefined position and then sends it to your BizTalk Server with the submit method of the BizTalk Interchange component.

When customers are submitting documents through DCOM, you can extract the customer's identity by redirecting the calls to a wrapper function, where you extract the caller's identity through the Security Property object of ObjectContext, and then you can call the BizTalk Interchange component to submit the document. In the next chapter, you'll learn techniques for building an effective BizTalk Server solution.

CHAPTER 13

Building an Effective BizTalk Application

You've learned a great deal about the features of BizTalk Server in previous chapters and how to put these features together to build an application. In this chapter, I'll take a different approach, and show you how to design a better and more effective BizTalk Server application.

What exactly does it take to build an effective BizTalk application? Foremost, an effective BizTalk Server application should be up and running 24/7, so you need to include fault tolerance in a BizTalk Server application. An effective BizTalk Server application also needs to provide acceptable performance under heavy load, so you must also consider the scalability of the application. Performance optimization is another consideration—you need to make the application serve the client as well as possible on the client's existing computer hardware. Besides those considerations, you also need to understand some of the loopholes in BizTalk Server, and design your application accordingly to avoid running into such problems. Even the best thought-out BizTalk applications will produce errors of one kind or another. The ability to react to and resolve these errors in a timely fashion is another important factor when building an effective BizTalk application.

In this chapter, I'll discuss BizTalk Server groups and examine BizTalk Server database clustering. I'll then analyze a number of BizTalk Server application designs and their pros and cons. I'll also demonstrate how to work on the problem of document size limit, and look at other loopholes you should think about when building a BizTalk application. At the end of the chapter, I'll show you how you can proactively react to errors that occur in the BizTalk Server application.

BizTalk Server Groups

Bob has set up another meeting with Mike about clustering. "I am glad we have got most of the work out of the way," says Bob. "But I have just got another Dell server, and I want to set up our system so that we can tell our clients that our system is capable of providing uninterrupted service 24/7. I also want to make a claim that our service is scalable too, so they won't have to worry about the performance of the service being affected adversely when our business is expanding." Mike has preparing for this day, and he has been reading about BizTalk Server groups lately.

 NOTE *BizTalk Server groups are supported in the BizTalk Server 2002 Enterprise Edition. BizTalk Server Standard Edition, Partner Edition, and Developer Edition don't support BizTalk Server groups. Keep this in mind when you choose which edition to use.*

The Basics of BizTalk Server Groups

The basic idea behind the BizTalk Server group is to achieve horizontal scaling with a shared BizTalk Server database. A shared BizTalk Server database results in a pool of work from which each member server can pick up documents and process them independently of other member servers. Therefore, if one BizTalk Server goes down, the other servers in the group can continue their work.

 NOTE Horizontal scaling *is a practice of implementing multiple systems that serve the same set functionalities to boost the overall performance and achieve fault tolerance. An example of this type of scaling is a Web farm, in which multiple Web servers with the same Web content serve user requests.* Vertical scaling, *on the other hand, is a practice of adding additional system resources at certain points of application flow to boost its performance. An example of this would be allocating business objects and data access objects on separate servers to increase performance.*

If a BizTalk Server is to participate in an existing BizTalk Server group, this BizTalk Server must use the existing Messaging database, Shared Queue database, and Tracking database, instead of creating a new set of databases. The member servers in a BizTalk Server group aren't required to share the XLANG database, though. Each member can reference a different XLANG database, either local or remote.

To make a new BizTalk Server join an existing BizTalk Server group during installation, you must choose the Select an existing database option when configuring its BizTalk Messaging database, as shown in Figure 13-1.

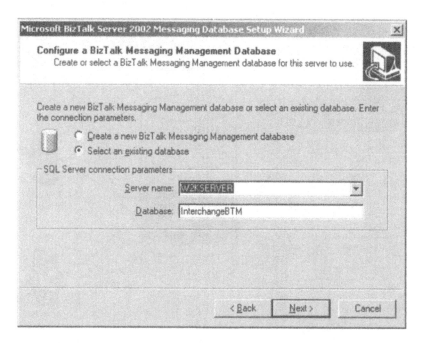

Figure 13-1. Selecting an existing database for the BizTalk Messaging database in order to join an existing server group

You can also make a stand-alone BizTalk Server join a BizTalk Server group by changing its Messaging database configuration through the BizTalk Server Administration Console. Open the BizTalk Server Administration Console, select Microsoft BizTalk Server 2002 on the left panel, right-click it, and select Properties. A dialog box will open. You can change the values of the BizTalk Messaging database name and the SQL Server name for this BizTalk Server so that the Messaging database and SQL Server name point to the centralized databases of the existing BizTalk Server group.

You'll also need to change the configuration for the Shared Queue database and Tracking database to make each truly a "team member." To change the configuration for the Shared Queue and Tracking databases, right-click the BizTalk Server group on the left panel of the BizTalk Server Administration Console, select Properties, and then select the Connection tab on the properties window. You can change the database information for both the Messaging database and the Tracking database.

BizTalk Server groups provide you with two benefits: load balancing and fault tolerance. Let's take a look at how BizTalk Server achieves these. Figure 13-2 shows a BizTalk Server group that involves three BizTalk Servers.

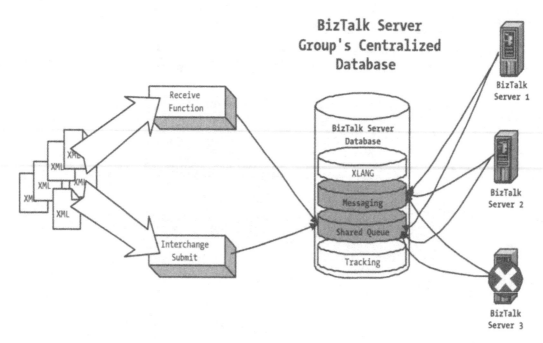

Figure 13-2. A BizTalk Server group

Load balancing in this context doesn't refer to component load balancing or network load balancing as in a Windows system. Instead, it refers to the BizTalk Server group's ability to allow member servers to receive the workload from the central work queue and process that work independently. The work queue in a BizTalk Server group is a database table called cs_WorkQ under the InterchangeSQ database.

It works like this: Whenever a document arrives at BizTalk Server through a Receive Function or Interchange submit call, its content and other routing information is inserted into this cs_WorkQ table as a data record. Some of the data columns in this table will sound very familiar to you, such as nvcSrcOrgName, nvcDestOrgName, and nvcDocName. After the document is persisted into this table as a record, it will stay in the table until one of the BizTalk Servers in the group retrieves it from the table, processes it according to the configuration, and at last deletes it from the table after the document is successfully processed. If some error occurs during the processing, the BizTalk Server will move the record from the cs_WorkQ table to a central retry queue or suspended queue. If the process still generates an error during the retries, the document will go to the suspended queue and stay there until someone explicitly deletes it using the BizTalk Server Administration Tool. An appropriate locking mechanism is used when a record is being processed, which ensures that documents being processed by one of the BizTalk Servers will not be retrieved and processed again by another BizTalk Server in the group.

Load Balancing and Fault Tolerance

With this centralized work queue, many BizTalk Servers can participate in retrieving and processing documents saved in a work queue, which achieves the goal of load balancing. Each BizTalk Server is only responsible for a fraction of the total workload in the system.

The other benefit of BizTalk Server groups is fault tolerance, which comes from having the centralized BizTalk Messaging database. Every time an XML document arrives, BizTalk Server must find out how to process this particular document—what schema it will be validated against, what channel it will be passed to, what XLANG Schedule to start, etc. This information is defined using BizTalk Messaging Manager, and it is stored in a centralized BizTalk Messaging database in tables such as bts_channel, bts_document, bts_port, etc. By accessing the data stored inside these tables, any BizTalk Server in the BizTalk Server group will have enough information to process whichever document it retrieves. When one of the member servers goes down, the remaining BizTalk Servers will still be able to access the processing information for the documents they retrieve. From the point of view of the external client, the service continues without interruption.

So what happens if the server that is hosting the Receive Function and Interchange component fails? What good is the BizTalk Server group if the data can never reach its Share Queue database?

First, let's look at how you can solve this problem in the case of Receive Functions. When a BizTalk Server in the group fails, its Receive Function fails as well. If its Receive Functions are watching a file location or message queue, the documents stored there will not be retrieved by this BizTalk Server. You must do two things to solve this problem.

First, you need to set up a centralized data store for the Receive Functions to target. In Chapter 4, I set up a message queue (IncomingMSMQ) on the same machine as BizTalk Server. This isn't a very good design, because all the documents inside this queue will become unreachable if the server goes down. The idea is to not have any important data persisted on the machine that runs BizTalk Server. Because BizTalk Server Receive Functions are able to watch a remote location, such as files on a network drive and messages in a remote message queue, you can set up a remote server to store all the documents in either a file directory or a message queue. (Even with a remote server, there are questions about how to keep this remote server up all the time, and some there are some transaction issues related to the message queue. You can find out more in Appendix A.)

The second thing you need to do is make more than one BizTalk Server watch your data target. In other words, for every data target (either a file location or message queue) that you want to watch for incoming documents, you need to set up two Receive Functions for it on separate BizTalk Servers. This design ensures that if one BizTalk Server goes down, along with its Receive Functions, there is at least one other BizTalk Server that is still watching the same data target, so the data will be continuously pulled from that data target. This is shown in Figure 13-3.

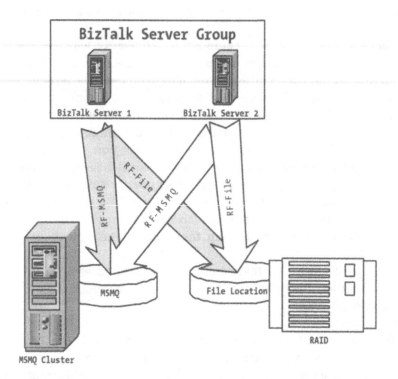

Figure 13-3. Creating multiple Receive Functions for each data target

As you can see in this figure, if BizTalk Server 1 goes down, the data stored in the remote MSMQ and remote File Location will continue to be pulled by BizTalk Server 2 into the work queue of the BizTalk Server group. Clustering technology should be applied on the server that is hosting the MSMQ, and RAID (short for Redundant Array of Independent Disks) should be applied to the file location to prevent any data from becoming inaccessible.

That takes care of the Receive Functions. Now let's take a look at the Interchange submit calls, which is another way to get the data into the Shared Queue database. In many situations, you may decide to use the Interchange submit method to get the data into the BizTalk Server group. Because the Interchange component is a configured component installed on every BizTalk Server, you'll need to create a proxy for the Interchange component and deploy it to clients wanting to submit documents to BizTalk Server through DCOM calls. You also must make the "remote server" setting for a client's proxy component point to one of the BizTalk Servers in the group. However, hard-coding the remote server name on the proxy will tie this client to a specific BizTalk Server in the group. The client will receive a COM error when the target BizTalk Server goes down. The service would be interrupted from the client's perspective, even though the BizTalk Server group is still functional.

To resolve this problem, the DCOM calls between the client and the BizTalk Server need to be load balanced in such a way that the load balancing service will not route the DCOM calls to a BizTalk Server that has gone down or that isn't responding to COM requests. One of the software applications that can offer this type of load balancing is Application Center, shown in Figure 13-4.

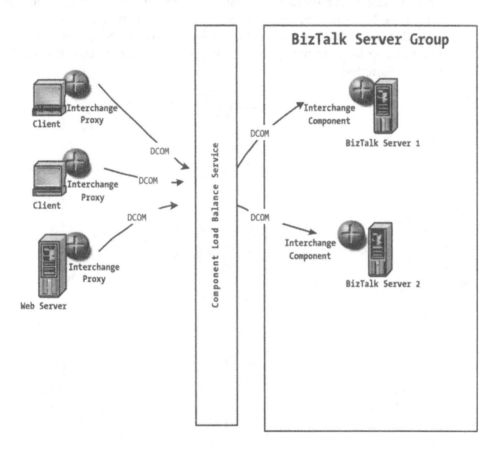

Figure 13-4. Load balancing the Interchange submit DCOM calls with the Component Load Balancing service in Application Center

The Component Load Balancing (CLB) service in Microsoft Application Center constantly communicates with each of the BizTalk Servers in the group. If BizTalk Server 1 goes down, CLB will mark it as unavailable on its internal routing table so that all the DCOM calls will be routed to the remaining servers. In this case, BizTalk Server 2 would take on all the DCOM calls from the clients. When BizTalk Server 1 is rebooted or comes online again, the CLB service will mark it as available again on its routing table so that future DCOM calls can be forwarded to BizTalk Server 1. To make the component load balancing service work, you must install the Application Center software on the clients that make the DCOM calls to BizTalk Server and on BizTalk Server itself. This kind of load balancing service is very useful, but keep in mind that the cost of this application will increase when introducing additional software into the picture.

An alternative to load balancing the incoming document is to use the HTTP Receive Function I introduced in Chapter 9. Like File and Message Queue Receive Functions, HTTP Receive Functions provide a way for an external source to submit a document to BizTalk Server for processing. Figure 13-5 shows a solution that achieves load balancing similar to the previous solution by using HTTP Receive Functions.

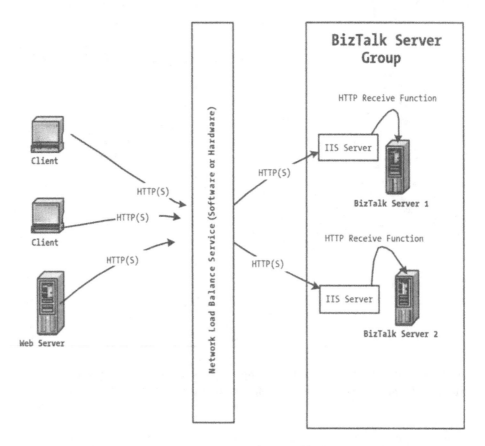

Figure 13-5. Using HTTP Receive Functions to load balance the document submissions

One of the biggest advantages of using HTTP Receive Functions for load balancing is its simplicity of configuration. No additional software is needed to support this type of load balancing, except the Network Load Balancing service that comes with Windows 2000 Server. You can install the Network Load Balancing service through Add/Remove Programs under the Control panel. You can also replace the software solution with a hardware-based network routing solution.

When a client is ready to submit a document to BizTalk Server, the client will post the document as an HTTP(S) request to the URL on a virtual cluster that has been created by the network load balancing server, such as http://VirtualBizTalkServer.myhome.com/HTTPReceiveFunctionPost/BizTalkHTTPReceive.dll?EntryA. In this example, VirtualBizTalkServer is the virtual server name that is used by the BizTalk Server member servers in the group.

As the document is passed through the Network Load Balancing service (or any other HTTP load balancing software or hardware), the load balancing service will find out which of the "real" BizTalk Servers under VirtualBizTalkServer.myhome.com (this virtual server is nothing more than a name that identifies a collection of "real" servers) is best able to process the HTTP request (or the document). The load balancing service then forwards the document to the appropriate "real" BizTalk Server. There would be an HTTP Receive Function set up on the "real" BizTalk Server to watch for any incoming documents that arrive at the URL of /HTTPReceiveFunctionPost/BizTalkHTTPReceive.dll?EntryA, and it would save the documents to the BizTalk Server's work queue as they arrive. If one of the BizTalk Servers in the group goes down, the Network Load Balancing service will drop that server from its routing list so that no further documents are routed to the unavailable server. The remaining BizTalk Servers will simply pick up the extra load. To the clients, the service appears to be uninterrupted, even though one of the BizTalk Servers is offline.

To summarize this discussion of BizTalk Server groups, there are two things you must consider as you make your BizTalk Servers fault tolerant. First, you must ensure that the document can arrive at the BizTalk Server. You can accomplish this by using the HTTP Receive Function and setting up Receive Functions on multiple BizTalk Servers to watch the same file location or message queue. Second, you must ensure that the documents will get processed after they arrive. You can make sure of this by adding additional BizTalk Servers to the same group so that multiple BizTalk Servers will share the same work queue for the document.

Resource Clustering

It seems that once you have taken fault tolerance and load balancing into account, you should be able to build a BizTalk Server application that is 100 percent fault tolerant, but unfortunately, that isn't the case. What happens if the SQL server that hosts the BizTalk Server database goes down, or the very server the MSMQ and File Receive Functions are set up to watch for incoming documents goes down? In those situations, the BizTalk Server or BizTalk Server group will not be able to process any messages. Even though this type of system downtime isn't directly related to BizTalk Server per se, you have to take these issues into account. After all, the customers don't really care which of your servers cause the problems if you fail to process their documents.

To keep your customers happy, you must think about how to handle situations when the BizTalk Server application's supporting servers go offline. In this section I'll talk about Windows 2000's clustering service and its usefulness in your BizTalk application.

The Basics of Clustering

Clustering is something you should always keep in mind when designing applications that can't afford to go down. Clustering offers two benefits to your application: load balancing and fault tolerance. Depending on how you implement clustering, you can take advantage of one or both of these benefits.

There are two types of clustering. The first type is *active/active mode*. In this mode, the servers within the cluster will participate in providing the services. If one node of the cluster goes offline, the other nodes will pick up the additional load and continue providing the services. As far as clients are concerned, the services are uninterrupted. Figure 13-6 illustrates this active/active mode.

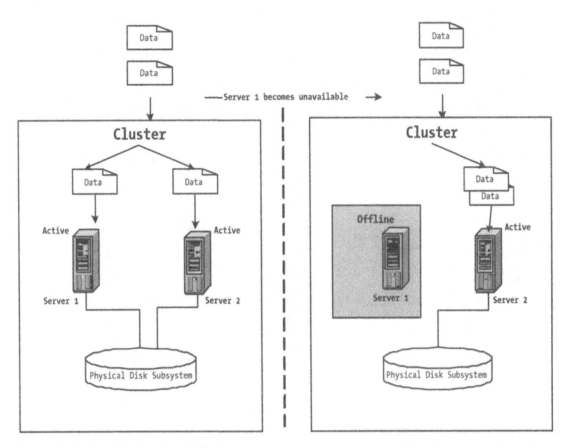

Figure 13-6. An active/active mode cluster

The second clustering mode is *active/passive mode*, as shown in Figure 13-7. This clustering mode designates one server node to provide the services to the client, and the other server node to stay idle and not provide any services to the client. The passive node is only brought to life when the active node fails. In such a case, the passive node will become the active node and will start providing services to clients.

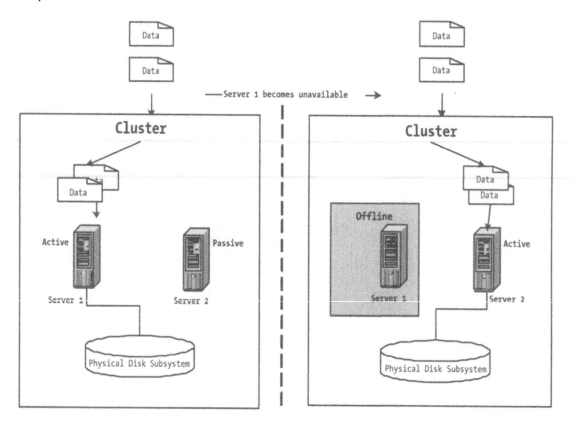

Figure 13-7. An active/passive mode cluster

When you comparing these two modes, it's easy to notice that while both provide fault tolerance, only the active/active mode provides load balancing and scales better than the active/passive mode, since more than one server is providing the service in the ideal situation where no system failure has occurred.

It seems to be a no-brainer to choose active/active mode over active/passive mode for your application and servers. However, not every application and resource can support active/active clustering mode. For example, SQL Server only supports active/passive mode. BizTalk Server also only supports active/passive mode. I'll show you how you can cluster your BizTalk Server and achieve load balancing even with the active/passive mode in the next section.

Clustering BizTalk Server and Related Resources

As you have learned earlier in this chapter, BizTalk Server groups already offer an easy model for load balancing requests and providing fault tolerance, assuming the SQL Server that hosts its database is always up and running. To remove the uncertainty about the availability of the SQL Server, you can cluster the SQL Server using Windows 2000's Cluster service.

BizTalk Server Groups with Active/Passive SQL Server Clusters

Figure 13-8 shows a BizTalk Server group using a clustered SQL Server to host its database. The SQL Server is configured as active/passive mode.

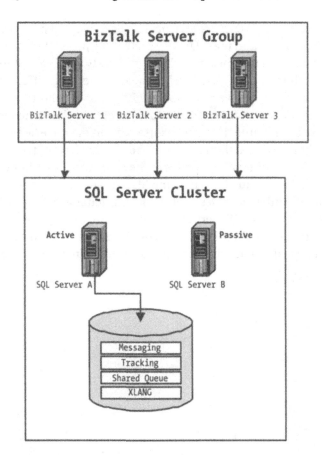

Figure 13-8. A BizTalk Server group with a SQL Server cluster

In Figure 13-8, each BizTalk Server in the group will reference the database on the clustered SQL Server. The clustered SQL server consists of two nodes of SQL Server, one being in active mode and the other in passive mode. The actual BizTalk Server database files are hosted on a RAID in a remote location, where both nodes in the cluster can access them independently. With this design, you can ensure that BizTalk Server can serve its clients continually if the client's documents arrive at the BizTalk Server successfully.

Although this type of design meets your requirements for fault tolerance, the request isn't load balanced on the database level. All the database requests will have to be processed by SQL Server A or SQL Server B (when Server A fails), but never by both.

BizTalk Server Groups with Active/Active SQL Server Clusters

If you read certain marketing material on SQL Server, you'd probably be surprised by Microsoft's claim that SQL Server 2000 supports the active/active mode. That may seem to contradict what I've already said. Well, it turns out that Microsoft uses the term "active/active" to mean something different.

The original active/active mode for database servers allows each database server in the cluster to read data from and write data to the same table of the same database at the same time. Microsoft's version of active/active mode for SQL Server allows each database server in the cluster to read data from and write data to the tables in different databases at the same time. In other words, you can configure a SQL Server cluster so that one SQL Server node accesses one of your databases and the other accesses another of your databases. Figure 13-9 shows this type of active/active SQL Server cluster. Because the SQL Servers in the cluster are accessing the databases (although different ones), it provides some level of load balancing, and that is the reason Microsoft claims it is active/active mode.

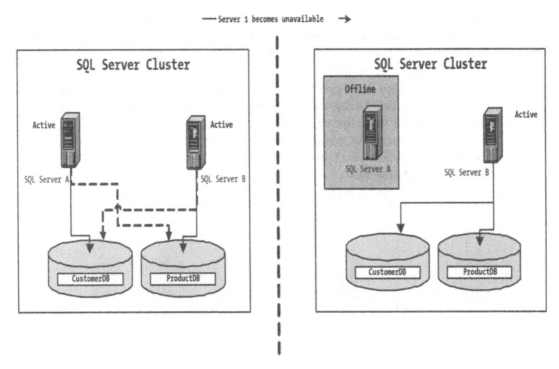

Figure 13-9. An active/active SQL Server cluster

As you can see in Figure 13-9, SQL Server A is configured as the active node in the cluster and owns the control for CustomerDB, and it's the passive node for ProductDB. SQL Server B is configured as the passive node (or standby server) for CustomerDB, and it is the active node for ProductDB. This means that SQL Server B can take over both databases when SQL Server A fails. The same is true for SQL Server A.

To enable this active/active mode, you need to create a new SQL Server instance to host ProductDB on SQL Server B and make it the active node for the new SQL Server instance. At the same time, you also need to configure SQL Server A as the passive node for the new SQL Server instance. With this design, you have each node in the cluster act as the active node on a separate SQL Server instance, and each uses the other node as the passive node for the database it owns. When a failure occurs on one of the nodes in the cluster, the other node will simply take ownership of the database controlled by the failed server.

By using active/active SQL Server mode, you can achieve a certain level of load balancing, since each of the servers in the cluster is active and is serving the requests for its clients. However, to fully take advantage of the active/active mode, you must have two databases running on two separate SQL Server instances, and the processing that occurs on each database must be somewhat significant. If you have only a single database where heavy processing occurs, the active/active mode will not provide the level of load balancing you expect, since the majority of the processing will still occur on one node.

BizTalk Server databases can benefit from the active/active SQL Server cluster. There are four databases used by BizTalk Server, and among them, the Shared Queue and Tracking databases are the most frequently accessed. By processing the requests for these two databases on different SQL Servers, you can effectively load balance the client requests and significantly boost the performance. Figure 13-10 shows a BizTalk Server group used with an active/active SQL Server cluster as its back end.

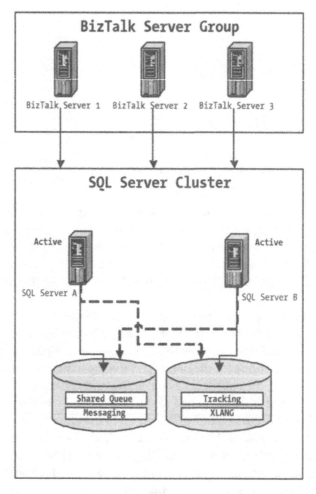

Figure 13-10. A BizTalk Server group with an active/active SQL Server cluster

If you compare the architecture in Figure 13-10 with Figure 13-8, you can see that using active/active mode provides you with the same level of protection against system failure, and furthermore it allows the requests on the Shared Queue and Tracking databases to be handled on two separate servers, therefore providing a more efficient solution than using an active/passive SQL Server cluster for the BizTalk Server group's back end.

The BizTalk Server group combined with a clustered SQL Server is usually sufficient to be considered truly fault tolerant. However, if you think harder, you can find that even this design, under certain circumstances, may not guarantee that it will always process client requests continually.

Clustering BizTalk Server

Let's take a look at a couple of examples where this strategy doesn't provide complete fault tolerance. Figure 13-11 shows one of these situations.

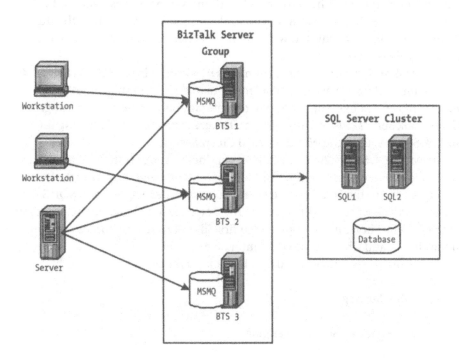

Figure 13-11. BizTalk Server group with clustered BizTalk Server database

Figure 13-11 shows a number of systems sending documents to the local queue of the BizTalk Server group members. Each of servers in the BizTalk Server group will have a Receive Function set up to pick up documents from the queue and process them. However, what happens if a BizTalk Server goes down after a document arrives at its message queue, but before the document is picked up and saved to the shared work queue on the SQL Server cluster? In such a case, the document will stay at the local queue until the BizTalk Server that went down is brought back online again. The document wouldn't get lost, but the client wouldn't see his or her document being processed right away.

This kind of problem happens when BizTalk Server persists some data locally. I'll show you some architecture designs that provide a solution for this problem, but for now, you can see why a BizTalk Server group can't provide fault tolerance if a BizTalk Server goes down before it sends all the client documents stored locally to the shared work queue.

The second situation where the BizTalk Server group may fail to provide fault tolerance is when you use the long-term XLANG Schedule in your application. A dehydrated XLANG Schedule can only be rehydrated and processed by the same BizTalk Server that dehydrates it in the first place. As you can see, if a BizTalk Server goes down, all the dehydrated XLANG Schedules created by this BizTalk Server can't be rehydrated until the server comes back online, even if there are other BizTalk members up and running in the group. If the dehydrated schedule is rehydrated while its BizTalk Server creator is not available, the schedule will fail.

You can resolve both of these problems by introducing a *BizTalk Server cluster*. The term "BizTalk Server cluster" may mean different things in different documents and books (some documents refer to this as a BizTalk Server group). The BizTalk Server cluster I am referring to here is created by clustering the BizTalk Servers using the Windows 2000 Cluster service.

As with SQL Server 2000, BizTalk Server doesn't support the real active/active mode. However, you can achieve BizTalk Server load balancing though the same principle used in the SQL Server cluster you saw earlier, where each SQL Server node is "active" for separate resources. To effectively load balance the processing on the BizTalk Server node, you need to first identify what resources are available in the cluster and which are process intensive.

These are the resources used by a BizTalk Server cluster:

- BizTalk Messaging

- BizTalk XLANG Schedule engine

- File folder (for File Receive Functions)

- Message queue (used for Message Queue Receive Functions, BizTalk Messaging, and the XLANG Schedule engine)

- MSDTC (required by BizTalk Messaging)

- WebDAV (used by BizTalk Messaging for retrieving the XML schema and map file)

- BizTalk XLANG Schedule Restart service (for restarting the XLANG application after the reboot)

- SQL Server (for storing the BizTalk Server databases)

You could host all these resources on one node of the cluster and make the other node serve as the failover node in an active/passive cluster, or you could host these resources on different nodes and make each node use the other as the failover node, as you saw in the active/active SQL Server cluster. Figure 13-12 shows one of the active/active options for allocating these resources within a BizTalk Server cluster.

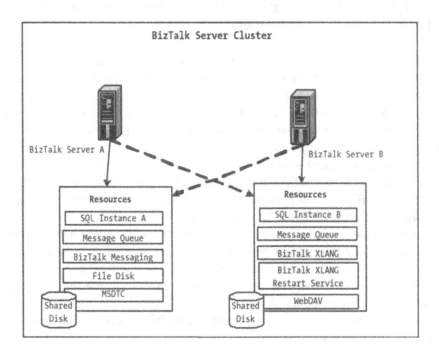

Figure 13-12. An active/active BizTalk Server cluster

In the BizTalk Server cluster shown in Figure 13-12, each node of the cluster hosts a number of resources and treats the other node as the failover for these resources. When one of the nodes fails, the remaining node will take over the resource and continue to serve the client. In this cluster scenario, all the local data stores, such as the message queue and file folder that are referenced by the Receive Function, are clustered resources, so the active node will still be able to access them when one BizTalk Server in the cluster fails. The BizTalk Server cluster also resolves the problem related to the dehydrated schedules. Since the dehydrated schedule is associated with the virtual server name or network name, instead of the real machine name in the BizTalk Server cluster, the dehydrated schedule can now be processed by the BizTalk Server node that isn't its original creator.

There are detailed step-by-step instructions on how to set up Windows 2000 clusters and BizTalk Server clusters, and these must be followed rigidly to make a cluster work. Refer to the Microsoft white papers "Microsoft BizTalk Server 2000: High-Availability Solutions Using Microsoft Windows 2000 Cluster Service" and "Step-by-Step Guide to Installing Cluster Service" for more details on clusters and their setup.

MSMQ Message Size Limit and Its Implications for BizTalk Server Development

Another very important issue that can greatly affect how you design your BizTalk application is the fact that message queue messages can't exceed 4MB in size. This limitation implies that you can only store documents that are less than 4MB. If you want to convert and store a document in Unicode (the encoding standard that uses 2 bytes to represent each character), you can only store documents that have less than 2MB of characters.

This problem isn't new—it has been around since the release of MSMQ 1.0, though you may not have noticed this problem if you have been using MSMQ for sending very small messages between applications. For the most part, messages aren't larger than a few kilobytes. However, the problem emerges when MSMQ is used in conjunction with BizTalk Server, which is expected to handle documents that may potentially grow very large, such as purchase orders from a large retail store, or product catalogs. Also, all the metadata in XML (element names and attribute names) used in many of these documents takes so much space that it results in a much larger document size.

Let's take a look at how this size limit affects BizTalk Server and how you can design your applications to take this into account.

MSMQ in BizTalk Server

BizTalk Server uses MSMQ in two main areas. The first is the Message Queue Receive Function, which is one of the data channels that clients use to move data into BizTalk Server. The second area is in XLANG Schedules, which can interact with MSMQ to retrieve data or send data when you use the Messaging Queue implementation shape inside your BizTalk Orchestration.

However, there is another place inside an XLANG Schedule where MSMQ is used. It turns out that BizTalk Orchestration uses MSMQ as the data buffer when data is transferred in and out of BizTalk Orchestration. Figure 13-13 shows a simplified orchestration that uses the BizTalk Messaging shape to retrieve and send messages to and from the BizTalk Messaging service.

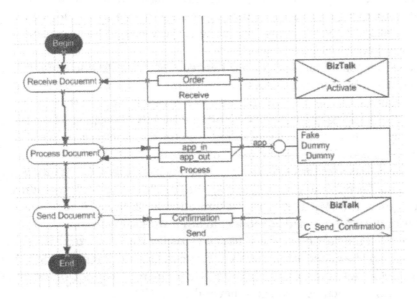

Figure 13-13. A BizTalk Messaging implementation used in BizTalk Orchestration

The Size-Limit Problem

BizTalk Server will create a message queue behind the scenes at runtime for each BizTalk Messaging shape in an orchestration. In the orchestration in Figure 13-13, when an order document arrives from a client, BizTalk Server will first create a temporary message queue, and save the client document to this queue. BizTalk Server will then start an orchestration and pass in the name of the newly created message queue for this instance of the schedule. The XLANG Schedule will retrieve the client document from this queue before it starts processing it.

NOTE   *The very early beta version of BizTalk Server 2000 didn't even have the BizTalk (Activate) Messaging shape. The only way you could get the document into an orchestration was to implement a Message Queue shape at beginning of the orchestration yourself. The released version of BizTalk Server makes it easier for you to pass the data to the orchestration by creating the BizTalk (Activate) Messaging shape.*

At the bottom of Figure 13-13, the confirmation document is sent from the orchestration to BizTalk Messaging through a BizTalk Messaging shape. BizTalk Server again uses a message queue to transfer the document from within the orchestration to the BizTalk Server work queue. When the orchestration is completed, the temporary message queue will be deleted. If the orchestration takes a long time to complete, such as when there is a long-term transaction in the orchestration, you can see the temporary message queue created for a particular instance of an XLANG Schedule by looking at the Message Queue console under the Computer Management console.

Now that you understand the link between the orchestration and message queues, it isn't hard to realize the set of problems you'll face if the size of the document you want to process with BizTalk Orchestration is bigger than the size limit of the message queue. Keep in mind that BizTalk Messaging will convert the ASCII data to Unicode before processing it, so the document can't exceed 2MB if it is in ASCII code. There are also many other factors that can affect the document size as it passes through BizTalk Server. For example, if the client document is in flat file format, and you want to map the flat file to XML before sending it the orchestration, the 4MB document size limitation (or 2MB ASCII code limit) applies to the post-mapped document. In other words, the maximum size limit for a flat file document would be even smaller, since the extra metadata (or XML tags) will be added when BizTalk Server converts the flat file to XML. Also, when your business processes add extra data to the response document, the size of the response document can grow beyond the 4MB limit.

Unfortunately, the error message raised by BizTalk Server that is associated with this 4MB document limit is rather vague. The error message will read like the following when the document is too large to be processed by the XLANG Schedule:

```
[0x0159] The server encountered a transport error while processing
the messaging port "P_FundInvestors", which uses a transport component
with a ProgID of "BizTalk.BPOActivation.1".
```

BizTalk.BPOActivation is the component that BizTalk Server uses to process the XLANG Schedule. Because the document is too big to fit in the temporary message queue, BizTalk Server will generate this type of error message to indicate that the XLANG Schedule has failed to process the document.

NOTE   *The 4MB document size limit only applies to orchestrations that send and receive large documents to and from the BizTalk Messaging service. When the document is processed by methods other than orchestrations, such as AIC, the 4MB document size limit doesn't apply. The only document size limit that applies in such a scenario is about 20MB. This 20MB number isn't an absolute limit, but rather the recommended (or supported) size limit that produces adequate performance on BizTalk Server. You can extend this size limit by using a faster server and disabling the Tracking feature for large documents.*

Two Solutions to the Size-Limit Problem

Now that you understand the problem, you need to come up with a solution for handling documents that are larger than 4MB in BizTalk Orchestration. There are two ways to solve the problem. The first one is easy to implement. The second one is endorsed by Microsoft, but it takes some extra coding to get it right.

Both methods solve the problem by avoiding the use of the BizTalk Messaging implementation shape inside an orchestration. Let's take a look at the easy method first.

The Easy Solution

In Chapter 11, you learned about the BizTalk AIC IWFWorkflowInstance and IWFProxy interfaces, which allow you to interact with an XLANG Schedule and pass data in and out of a schedule instance. You can use a combination of these two technologies to get around the 4MB problem.

Figure 13-14 illustrates the high-level design for this easier solution.

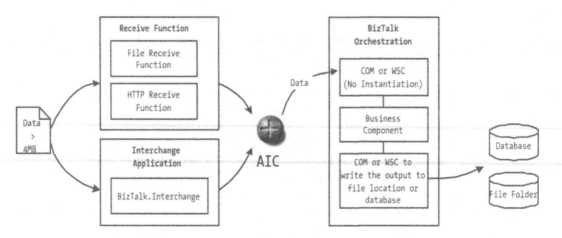

Figure 13-14. The easy solution

In this solution, when a large client document arrives, BizTalk Server can pick it up using one of the following: a File Receive Function, an HTTP Receive Function, or a BizTalk Interchange component. The Message Queue Receive Function can't be used, since the message queue can't hold messages that are more than 4MB.

After BizTalk Server picks up the document, it will send the document off to a messaging port that is connected to an AIC instead of an orchestration. The AIC will be responsible for instantiating the XLANG Schedule and passing the document to a specific entry point in the schedule. The XLANG Schedule that is used in this solution will employ a noninstantiation COM or WSC component as the entry point for the document to enter the schedule. The XLANG Schedule can then instantiate the number of components needed to process the documents. When the processes are complete, the XLANG Schedule can call a COM or WSC component to save the optional response document to a database or a file location, from which it can be picked up and sent in a separate operation. This allows you to avoid the use of the BizTalk Messaging shape in the orchestration.

The key take-away of this solution is to use the AIC to pass large documents to an orchestration. The orchestration also must provide a special entry point for the AIC. Figure 13-15 shows the prototype for such an orchestration.

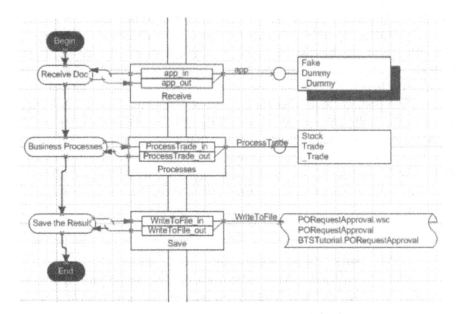

Figure 13-15. BizTalk Orchestration used in the easy solution

The orchestration shown in Figure 13-15 includes three actions: Receive Doc, Business Processes, and Save the Result. The only implementation shapes in the orchestration are either COM or WSC components.

To create an entry point for an AIC to pass in the data to the orchestration, you must do two things. First, you must bind the Receive Doc action to a COM (or WSC) implementation shape that is configured with the setting No Instantiation. The dark shadow beneath the implementation shape indicates that when this XLANG Schedule is started, the XLANG Schedule will not attempt to instantiate the component.

NOTE   *The method in the COM or WSC component used as the entry point in the orchestration shouldn't contain any implementation code. The BizTalk XLANG engine will not execute the code inside the method. The method is used purely as a means to pass the data into the orchestration.*

Second, you must specify the "wait for synchronous method call" setting in the Method Communication Wizard when you connect an Action shape to the appropriate port. (In the case of Figure 13-15, you set "wait for synchronous method call" when you connect the Receive Doc action to the Receive port.)

After the Receive Doc action, you can set numerous actions that call the business components to process the document. If the business processes produce a response document that you want to send to an external source, you will persist the response document to a location that doesn't reply on MSMQ, such as a database or file location. The documents stored in the database or file location will have to be dealt with later by a separate operation through the BizTalk Messaging service or another customized operation to deliver the document to the client.

NOTE   *If the response document is small and doesn't exceed the 4MB size limit, it would be perfectly all right to use the BizTalk Messaging implementation shape to send the document.*

After you create an orchestration file, you also must create the AIC to instantiate the XLANG Schedule and pass in the document to it. The following code is a sample AIC program to start the XLANG Schedule:

```
Dim schedule As IWFWorkflowInstance
Dim port As IWFProxy

'load the schedule
Set schedule = GetObject("sked:///c:\temp\LargeDocument.skx")
Set port = schedule.port("Receive")
'call the method bound to the "Receive" port
port.app ("this is a very large document")
```

There are three major steps in the preceding code that pass the document to BizTalk Orchestration. First, GetObject is called to start an XLANG Schedule, and it returns a reference to the running schedule. Second, you get a port reference to the entry point of the schedule by calling schedule.port([port name]). Last, you call the method of the COM or WSC component that connects to that port. For example, port.app("this is very large document") calls a method named "app" (which resides in the Fake.Dummy component on the Receive port) and passes in the content of a very large document (which can be bigger than 4MB) as its string parameter.

After the data has been passed into the running XLANG Schedule, the XLANG Schedule can continue with the additional processes defined in the orchestration. If the orchestration produces a response document that should be sent to an external source, you can implement a COM or WSC component that saves the document to database or file location. You can then set up an additional process to send the response document out. For example, you can create a schedule task to retrieve the response document from the data table and send it out to clients. You can also create a File Receive Function to retrieve the response documents that are stored in the file location and send them to the clients through BizTalk Messaging. You could also use the BizTalk Messaging shape to send the document directly, if the response document is smaller than 4MB.

As you can see, using the AIC to start and pass documents to the XLANG Schedule eliminates the need to use the BizTalk Messaging shape, and so it removes the size limitation on the documents an XLANG Schedule can process.

Microsoft's Solution

As in the previous solution, Microsoft's recommended solution also uses the AIC to avoid the direct instantiation of an XLANG Schedule by BizTalk Messaging. This solution, however, doesn't directly pass the document to the XLANG Schedule either—it uses a SQL database as the temporary data repository for the incoming document. Figure 13-16 shows the high-level design for this solution.

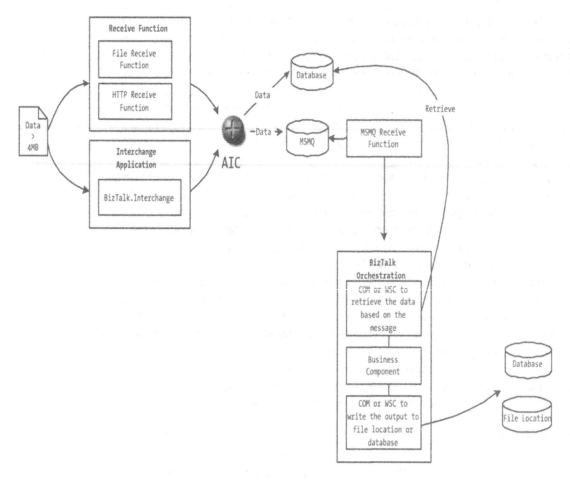

Figure 13-16. Microsoft's recommended solution

The solution in Figure 13-16 may look intimidating, but it is actually very simple. It works as follows. When a client sends a large document to BizTalk Server, the document is picked up by either a Receive Function (but not the Message Queue Receive Function) or an Interchange component. BizTalk Server will pass the document to an AIC, and the AIC does two things. It first saves the document to a predefined database table, and then it generates a very small trigger document that simply identifies what type of document has just arrived. For example, if the client document is a FundInvestor document, the trigger document may look like this:

```
<FundInvestorTrigger Company = "Henry Fonda Inc."/>
```

or like this:

```
"<TradeTrigger/>"
```

You can also add some additional attributes to identify specific instances of the client, if necessary. After the AIC generates the trigger document, it will send it to the message queue. The Message Queue Receive Function will be configured to retrieve the trigger documents as they arrive at the queue, and bring them to the appropriate message port where an XLANG Schedule is started. Because BizTalk Messaging can't pass in the client document, except for a trigger document that notifies that a new client document has arrived; the XLANG Schedule is responsible for retrieving the document from the data table.

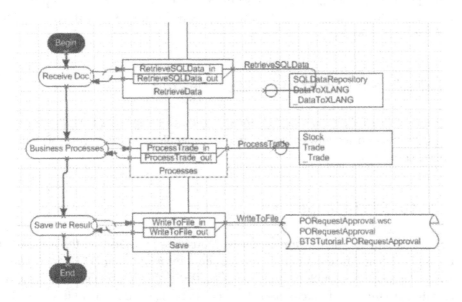

Figure 13-17. A BizTalk orchestration used in Microsoft's recommended solution

Figure 13-17 shows the orchestration used in this solution. In this orchestration, the very first action after the schedule starts is to call the RetrieveSQLData method of the DataToXLANG component. Depending on the nature of the orchestration, you can set some constant values on the data page that are used as the RetrieveSQLData's input parameters to determine what kind of data the component will retrieve at runtime.

After the component retrieves the document from the database, it passes the document to the business processes. At the end, you can save the optional response documents to a database or file location where they can be retrieved later to be sent to the client.

You've now seen two solutions for handling large documents in BizTalk Orchestration. The easier solution uses a dummy component inside an orchestration to receive the document from the external source, which uses the BizTalk API (IWFProxy) to communicate with the running schedule. The second solution, which is Microsoft's recommended solution, creates a data access component that is used from within the orchestration to retrieve and update the data coming from the external source.

BizTalk Server Application Design

In this section, I'll review a number of architecture designs for BizTalk Server applications and see how each design offers specific benefits to your BizTalk Server solutions.

IIS to BizTalk Server

In most situations, you'll be interacting with business partners over the Web. IIS will be used to accept the documents from the client through either HTTP or HTTPS. You've seen examples in Bob's project that use ASP pages to accept the document and that use the local Interchange submit call to bring the document into BizTalk Server's work queue. However, when you move the application from development to the production environment, you need to consider security requirements that may require BizTalk Server to be located behind a firewall. In that case, you must rearrange IIS and BizTalk Server. Figure 13-18 shows one of the designs that you can use to move BizTalk Server behind the demilitarized zone (DMZ).

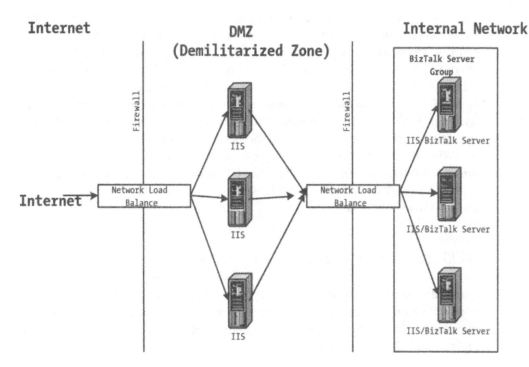

Figure 13-18. BizTalk Server design: IIS to BizTalk Server

NOTE   Demilitarized zone *is a military term referring to an area where military forces, operations, and installations are prohibited. This term has made its way into the IT context to identify a computer host or small network inserted as a "neutral zone" between a company's private network and the outside public network. It prevents outside users from getting direct access to a server that has company data.*

In the design shown in Figure 13-18, the client documents first arrive at the IIS servers in the DMZ, and network load balancing helps to balance the HTTP requests to each of the IIS servers. The ASP page is deployed on each of the IIS servers in the DMZ to accept the documents from the clients, and it uses the Response.Redirect method to redirect the documents to the IIS running on the BizTalk Servers in the internal network. A Network Load Balancing service is used between the DMZ and the Internal Network to ensure that all the redirected documents are loaded evenly among the BizTalk Server members in the group.

With this design, you achieve the goal of moving the BizTalk Server group behind the internal firewall so that it is better protected against malicious attacks. You can also provide better protection for your internal network by locking down the firewall so that only traffic through port 80 is allowed.

MSMQ to BizTalk Server

In the MSMQ to BizTalk Server design, you use a clustered MSMQ as the intermediary data storage between the IIS server in the DMZ that accepts the client documents. The BizTalk Server group is again behind an internal firewall. Figure 13-19 illustrates this design.

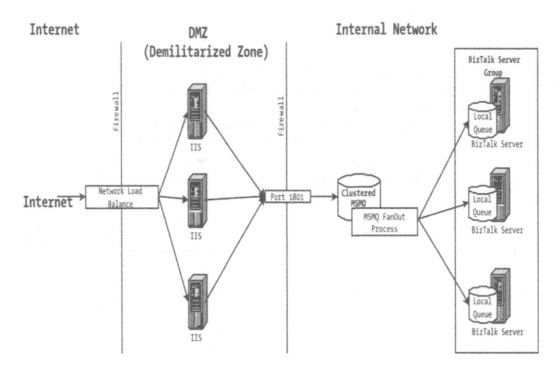

Figure 13-19. BizTalk Server design: MSMQ to BizTalk Server

As the documents arrive at the DMZ, the ASP page on the IIS server will transfer the client's document to the system behind the internal firewall. However, instead of transferring them to another IIS server as you saw in the first design, the ASP page will send the client document to a clustered MSMQ located behind the internal firewall by using a transactional write. It is important that the message queue is clustered to provide uninterrupted message queuing service for the IIS server in the DMZ.

The MSMQ fan-out process runs on the clustered MSMQ. This fan-out process retrieves the messages from the local queue and distributes them to the remote message queues. In this case, the messages are distributed to message queues on each of the BizTalk Server members located on the internal network through remote transactional writes. The reason for implementing the fan out is to work around the fact that MSMQ doesn't support remote transactional reads, which means the BizTalk Server members aren't able to retrieve the messages from the clustered queue in a transactional manner. Refer to Appendix A for more detail on MSMQ and its transaction-related issues.

After the messages are fanned out to message queues on each of the BizTalk Server members, the BizTalk Servers can use the Message Queue Receive Function to retrieve them and process them accordingly. With this design, port 1801 instead of port 80 is opened for the message to cluster MSMQ through the firewall so that IIS server can send the documents to the MSMQ server, which is located behind the firewall. To distribute the queued messages from the clustered MSMQ to the remote BizTalk Servers, you need to create a program that constantly watches for the arrival of new messages and distributes them as they arrive. Besides that, this design is pretty straightforward. Keep in mind that documents can't exceed 4MB in size, because MSMQ is used.

It is important to be aware that it may take a few minutes for the standby node to take over the MSMQ cluster when the active node fails, and during this time, the MSMQ service will not be available to clients. However, if an independent MSMQ is installed on each of the IIS servers in the DMZ, clients can continue to submit documents to the IIS server without noticing the problem. This is because the independent MSMQ has the ability to store the outgoing messages if the destination queue isn't available. The independent MSMQ will try to connect to the destination queue periodically and will resend messages that are in its outgoing queue when the destination queue comes back online.

Figure 13-20 shows what the outgoing queue looks like on IIS if the destination queue isn't available. When the MSMQ cluster is temporarily not available, clients can continue to submit their documents without the fear of losing them.

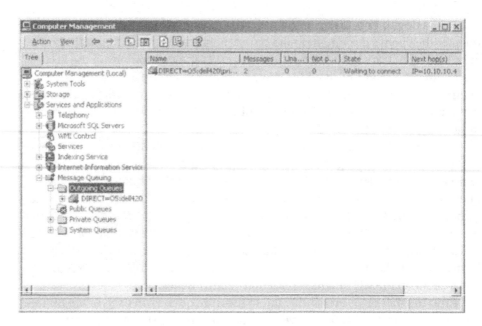

Figure 13-20. The outgoing queues of an independent MSMQ can store messages when the destination queues aren't available.

BizTalk Server (Receive Only) to BizTalk Server

In some situations, there may be many XLANG Schedules running on the BizTalk Server, consuming significant system resources. The server may not be able to allocate enough processing power for Receive Functions to provide adequate service to clients who are submitting their documents. In such a case, you may want to dedicate a number of BizTalk Servers in the group to perform only the Receive Functions, and the rest of the BizTalk Server members can process the documents.

With BizTalk Servers dedicated to receiving documents from clients, you can receive the client documents quickly, even when document processing consumes large amounts of system resources. By separating the functionality of receiving the documents and processing the documents, you can scale out the BizTalk Server group to fit the specific demands of the application. You can add more receive-only BizTalk Servers when the amount of document submissions increases, or you can add more processing servers when more XLANG Schedules are processed.

To configure a BizTalk Server to become a receive-only server, open the BizTalk Administration Console. Right-click one of the BizTalk Server nodes under the BizTalk Server group, and select Properties to open its Properties window, as shown in Figure 13-21.

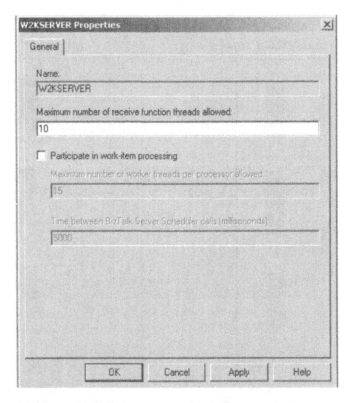

Figure 13-21. Making a BizTalk Server a receive-only server

Notice the option "Participate in work-item processing" on the Properties page of each BizTalk Server. By unchecking this option, the BizTalk Server's ability to retrieve and process documents from the work queue is turned off. However, it can still use its Receive Functions to accept documents and send them to the work queue.

 NOTE *By disabling the "Participate in work-item processing" checkbox, BizTalk Server will not be able to peek into the work queue. Therefore, it won't be able to do any processing work except storing the incoming documents that are picked up by the Receive Functions to the work queue.*

You can create logical groups within the BizTalk Server group, with each having specific tasks, namely the receiving group and processing group, as shown in Figure 13-22.

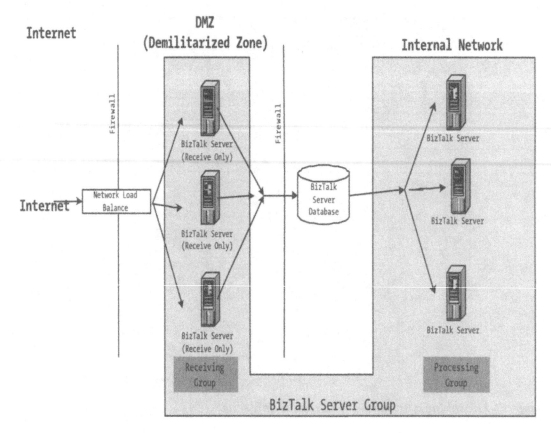

Figure 13-22. BizTalk Server design: BizTalk Server (Receive Only) to BizTalk Server

The design in Figure 13-22 partitions the receiving part of a task from the processing part within a BizTalk Server group. You can set up the first "logical group" of BizTalk Server members in the DMZ to only receive documents from external clients. As they accept documents, they will send them to the work queue on the BizTalk Server database server located behind the internal firewall. Because all the receive-only BizTalk Servers have the setting "Participate in the work-item processing" turned off, they will not be able to retrieve the documents from the work queue.

The second logical group of BizTalk Server members is located behind the firewall. Their job is to retrieve the documents from the work queue and process them. With this design you can easily scale out the BizTalk Server members in each logical group independently to meet increasing demands on either the receiving or processing parts of the task.

NOTE *You can set up Receive Functions on the processing servers to transfer data internally, but you should avoid setting up Receive Functions to directly receive documents from external sources. Such tasks should be delegated to the receive-only servers in the DMZ.*

Optimizing BizTalk Server

In this section, you'll learn how to tune and optimize BizTalk Server to provide the best performance on given hardware. You'll see how optimization works for BizTalk Messaging and for BizTalk Orchestration.

Optimizing BizTalk Messaging

You can optimize the performance of BizTalk Messaging in a number of ways. Let's take a look at the following areas:

- Server settings

- Registry settings

- AICs

- Document definitions and maps

Server Settings

When you install BizTalk Server, a set of default settings are configured as part of the installation. You can optimize BizTalk Server by modifying these settings to achieve faster performance under certain scenarios. These server settings can be accessed through the BizTalk Server Administration Console.

Let's first take a look at the BizTalk Server group settings. Open the BizTalk Server Administration Console, right-click the BizTalk Server group name, and select Properties. Figure 13-23 shows the Properties window that appears.

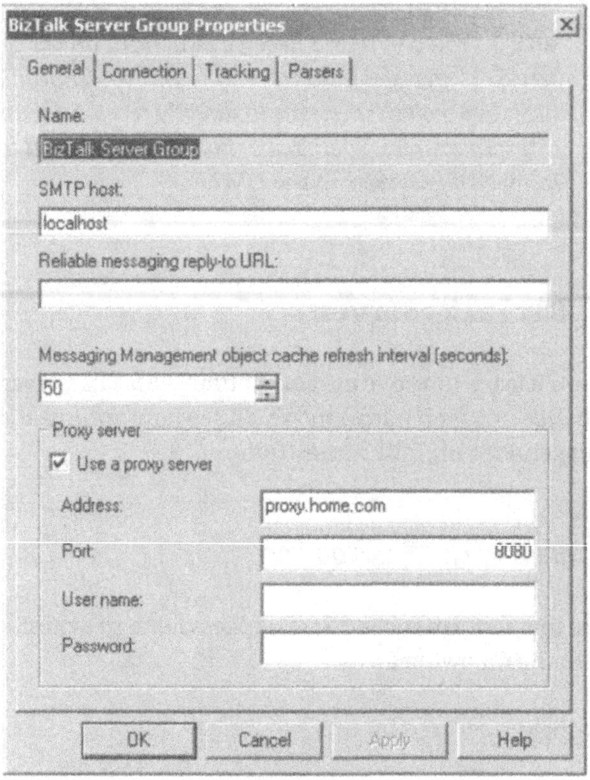

Figure 13-23. Configuring the BizTalk Server group settings

On the General tab of the Properties window, you can change the value for the "Messaging Management object cache refresh interval (seconds)" property. This property determines how often BizTalk Server will refresh the cache that stores messaging information on channels, ports, etc. Normally, this messaging information stays the same after you've completed the BizTalk Messaging configuration. By increasing this value, you can reduce the frequency with which BizTalk Server queries the Messaging database, hence reducing the burden on the database server as well as the BizTalk Servers.

On the Tracking tab, you can enable or disable logging for incoming and outgoing interchanges. When interchanges are logged, every client submission will be saved to the Tracking database. This can potentially become a bottleneck for BizTalk Server when many large documents are coming through the BizTalk Server. Depending on the network connection between the BizTalk Server and the database server that hosts the Tracking database, and on the performance of the database server, the overall performance may or may not be adequate. If it isn't adequate, you can turn off the interchange tracking on this tab. You can always log documents that come through specific channels by explicitly enabling Document Tracking on the channel level.

On the Parsers tab, you can add, remove, and rearrange the document parsers installed on the system. You should use the up and down buttons to move the most frequently used document parsers to the top of list so that BizTalk Server can find the appropriate document parser quickly at runtime. The XML document parser (BizTalk.ParserXML.1) is at the top of the list by default.

Besides the settings for the BizTalk Server group, you can also optimize BizTalk Server's performance by tuning the settings associated with each individual BizTalk Server. These settings can be accessed through the BizTalk Server Administration Console.

Open the BizTalk Server Administration Console, right-click one of the BizTalk Server nodes under the BizTalk Server group, and select Properties. A Properties window will open, as shown in Figure 13-24.

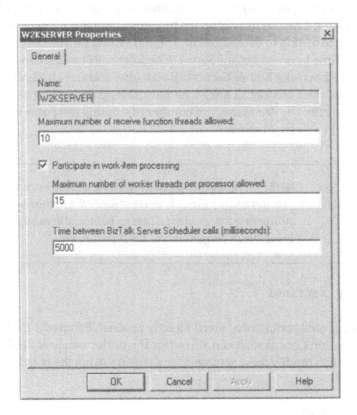

Figure 13-24. Configuring BizTalk Server settings

The "Maximum number of receive function threads allowed" property determines how many worker threads are allocated for Receive Function. Allocating more threads for Receive Function can speed up retrieving documents into the

BizTalk work queue, but allocating too many worker threads may add overhead to the operating system. The recommended value for this setting is 4 threads.

The "Participate in work-item processing" checkbox determines whether this BizTalk Server will retrieve documents from the work queue and process them. Unchecking this checkbox will make the server a receive-only BizTalk Server. When this option is checked, the two settings below it become editable.

The "Maximum number of worker threads per processor allowed" option determines the maximum number of worker threads that can be allocated for processing documents. The recommended value for this setting is from 10 to 15. Setting this figure too low can cause BizTalk Server to wait for available work threads to free up before processing additional documents, causing a performance bottleneck. Setting this figure too high can add operating system overhead as the system manages the additional threads. The appropriate value for this setting depends heavily on the individual situation. You can do some performance testing to determine the optimal setting for your application.

The "Time between BizTalk Server Scheduler calls (milliseconds)" setting determines how long BizTalk Server will wait after starting an XLANG Schedule before it will start another XLANG Schedule. Raising this setting can produce a throttling effect by decreasing the number of running instances of XLANG Schedules in a single moment.

 NOTE *The worker threads referred to in the preceding discussion are the threads that perform the actual work of processing a document, such as validation, mapping, delivering the document to the destination, etc.*

Registry Settings

There are several settings that aren't directly accessible from the BizTalk Server Administration Console that can also affect the performance of BizTalk Messaging. You can modify these settings in the registry using the regedit.exe program.

NoValidation Key

BizTalk Messaging spends significant resources to validate the document against its schema as the document arrives at BizTalk Server. The schema validation provided by BizTalk Messaging removes the need for you to include validation code inside your programs to ensure the document is compliant with the specification.

However, sometimes you may want to skip the schema validation. For example, if your internal applications generate some XML documents and send them through BizTalk Server, you may not want to validate them. It is more efficient to make sure the processes the internal applications use to generate the XML are bug free and will always generate valid documents. That way you know the documents are valid, and you don't need to validate documents inside BizTalk Server.

To turn off document validation in BizTalk Server, you can add the NoValidation registry key under the \HKEY_LOCAL_MACHINE\SYSTEM\CurrentControlSet\Services\BTSSVC node, and set its value to a nonzero number.

ParserRefreshInterval Key

By default, BizTalk Server will check its Messaging database every 60 seconds for new document parsers that are added to the server. Although performing this action may not use many resources, you should turn it off if you are using a fixed set of document parsers on BizTalk Server. To turn off the checking, add the ParserRefreshInterval key under the \HKEY_LOCAL_MACHINE\SYSTEM\CurrentControlSet\Services\BTSSVC node, and set its value to 0.

BatchSize Key

The BatchSize key is specific to Message Queue Receive Functions. By default, BizTalk Message Queue Receive Functions grab 20 messages from the message queue at once and send them to the work queue as one transaction. By increasing this number, you can significantly improve the performance of Message Queue Receive Functions, since they can pull in more messages at once. However, because the whole batch is sent as one transaction, if one of the messages causes an error, the whole batch will be rolled back and resubmitted.

To change the default value, add the BatchSize key under \HKEY_LOCAL_MACHINE\SYSTEM\CurrentControlSet\Services\BTSSVC node, and set its value to the number of messages to be pulled in in a single batch.

WorkerThreads Key

When HTTP Receive Functions are used, there are two registry keys you may want to consider when tuning the performance. The first key is WorkerThreads. This key determines the maximum number of threads used to accept the HTTP posts to the HTTP Receive Function. If clients are posting large numbers of documents to an HTTP Receive Function, you can increase this key value to allow more threads to process the HTTP documents posted.

The default value for the maximum worker threads for HTTP Receive Functions is 6. To change its value, add the WorkerThreads key under the \HKEY_LOCAL_MACHINE\SYSTEM\CurrentControlSet\Services\BTSSVC\HTTP Listener node, and modify its value.

QueueFactor Key

Even with an increased number of worker threads for HTTP Receive Functions, the number of HTTP posts at certain moment can potentially be much larger than the maximum number of worker threads allocated for HTTP Receive Functions. In such a case, the HTTP posts that aren't immediately processed by the worker threads will be put on the queue. The items in the queue will be pulled in and processed as soon as a worker thread is freed up. However, there is a limit on the number of HTTP posts that can be in the queue. This concept is similar to the queue in a Web server. When the HTTP requests exceed the queue size, the Web server will reply to clients with a "Server too busy" error message.

The default queue size for the HTTP Receive Function is 3. To increase the value, add the QueueFactor key under the \HKEY_LOCAL_MACHINE\SYSTEM\CurrentControlSet\Services\BTSSVC\HTTP Listener node, and increase its value.

AICs

In Chapter 11, you learned about the use of AICs, and how to create them in Visual Basic by implementing AIC interfaces. Although Visual Basic allows you to quickly develop AICs, due to the nature of the Visual Basic language, you may encounter performance issues when a large number of documents that are processed by AICs arrive at the BizTalk Server at the same time.

When you create a component using Visual Basic, the component is created as a Single Threaded Apartment (STA) in VB, by default. When the BizTalk Messaging Service, which runs in a Multithreaded Apartment (MTA), calls the Visual Basic AIC, COM+ will create an STA to host the AICs activated by the BizTalk Server. Because all the instances of the AICs are hosted by this STA, only one single thread is used to process all the method calls among the instance of component. This results in all the calls to Visual Basic AIC being serialized, which causes the performance problem. In addition, parameters of calls between BizTalk Messaging (MTA) and Visual Basic AIC (STA) have to be marshalled, further degrading the performance.

As you can see, if many AICs are instantiated at the same time, the performance will be significantly affected. However, if the AIC is created as a free-thread component, then every available worker thread can process the method calls. Unlike the STA component, free-thread components are hosted in an MTA, and any worker thread in the MTA can directly call the components.

This allows all the available BizTalk Server's worker threads to process the AIC instances hosted in its MTA.

To create free-threaded AICs, you need to code them using Visual C++ and mark them as "Free threaded" components, or you can use .NET languages, such as C# and VB .NET. Therefore, to improve the performance of BizTalk Server applications that use AICs, you should write your AICs in Visual C++ or a .NET language.

Document Definitions and Maps

When a document arrives from a client, BizTalk Server will take a number of steps before it hands the document off to the destination, such as the XLANG Schedule, AIC, or remote location. BizTalk Server will load the document into its memory and validate it against the schedule, then pass the document through a channel where a document mapping may be applied.

When you define the document schema, you should keep in mind that every field and condition you define in the document schema will be validated against every document of that type by BizTalk Server. You should keep only the necessary fields and field conditions that you absolutely need. Having excessive data fields or validation conditions will increase the time and memory BizTalk Server uses to complete the document validation.

Under certain situations, you may want to turn off the validation altogether. This is done through registry changes, as you saw in the "NoValidation Key" section earlier in this chapter.

The size of the documents that are processed by BizTalk Server is also worth considering. When the document size grows too large, you can turn off tracking for this type of document to eliminate the time and resources needed to save such documents to the Tracking database. Microsoft recommends that the documents don't exceed 20MB in Unicode. Turning off tracking was discussed in the "Server Settings" section earlier in the chapter.

Optimizing BizTalk Orchestration

When your BizTalk Server applications use XLANG Schedules to process documents, there are a few areas where you can improve performance.

Setting the ADO Threading Mode

The XLANG engine uses ActiveX Data Objects (ADO) to persist state and transactional information to the XLANG database. ADO's threading mode is set to Apartment by default, and this threading model can cause performance problems when multiple XLANG Schedule instances are running at the same. You can change ADO's threading mode to Both, which will greatly improve the performance of XLANG Schedule engine.

To change the threading mode of ADO, you can use a registry file called adofre15.reg, which is located under the Program Files\Common Files\System\ado folder. To modify the registry, simply double-click this registry file in Windows Explorer. To switch the threading mode back to Apartment mode, you can run adoapt15.reg under the same directory.

Choosing a Transaction Model

As you learned in earlier chapters, BizTalk Orchestration supports two transactional models: "Include Transaction within the XLANG Schedule" (the native XLANG transactional model) and "Treat the XLANG Schedule as COM+ Component" (the COM+ transactional model). The COM+ transactional model is much faster than the XLANG native transactional model. The tradeoff is that the XLANG native transactional model has many great features that don't exist in the COM+ model, such as timed and long-term transactions, the On Failure transaction page, etc.

If you decide the speed of the schedule is more important than the benefits the XLANG native transactional model offers, you should create the orchestration using the COM+ transaction model.

Using Transaction Shapes

When a BizTalk orchestration involves the use of transactions, you should keep in mind that the XLANG engine will write the transactional state to the XLANG database when the process flow passes in and out of the Transaction shape boundary. To improve performance, you should try to use as few Transaction shapes as possible.

Using Short-Lived Transactions

When you are using short lived (DTC-style) transactions in an orchestration, the transaction will not commit until the end of process flow exits out of the short-lived transaction. During that time, the resources that are modified are locked and become inaccessible to other applications. You should keep the transactions as short as possible, and only use short-lived transactions when it is absolutely necessary.

Using In-Process COM Components

COM components that are configured as in-process components operate much faster than out-of-process components because in-process components don't carry the overhead caused by the data marshaling that occurs between different processes. Using in-process COM components inside an orchestration will significantly boost the performance of XLANG Schedules. However, using an in-process component carries special risks of bringing down the entire XLANG application. You should make sure the components used in the orchestration are well tested before you turn them into in-process components.

Installing the XLANG Database Locally

If the COM component used in an orchestration is located on the BizTalk Server, you should install the XLANG database locally. With the XLANG database located on the local BizTalk Server, you can eliminate the network traffic associated with persisting the component state to the XLANG database.

Using Asynchronous Processes

When certain components inside an orchestration are processing intensive and take a long time to complete, they may cause performance issues when many XLANG Schedules are created and are waiting on this component to complete. You should consider turning this synchronized process (direct COM binding inside the orchestration) into an asynchronous process by deploying "Send" and "Receive" ports. You can then use the correlation technique described in Chapter 10 to bring back the results to the correct running XLANG Schedule when a specific instance's component completes its work. Figure 13-25 shows one example of this technique.

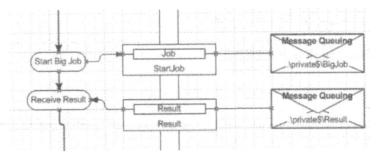

Figure 13-25. Converting the processes to asynchronous processes

Dehydrate Waiting Schedules

If you don't want your system to hold onto precious memory space while waiting for a result to come back, you can configure the latency setting for the "Receive" port to more than 180 in the XML Communication Wizard. This configuration will make the XLANG Schedule dehydrate, which saves its state to the XLANG database and removes it from memory. When the result finally arrives at the result port, the XLANG engine will rehydrate the schedule and continue with further process flow.

Performance Monitoring

When your clients are experiencing slow response and service, the first thing you need to do is find out where the performance bottleneck is. There are a few tools that can assist you in troubleshooting the performance problem:

- *Windows Performance Monitor:* This contains many commonly used performance counters that allow you to find out how well your system is operating. I'll talk about Performance Monitor in this section.

- *Microsoft Operations Manager (MOM):* This tool allows you to create more customized performance queries and performance threshold for alerts. I'll talk about MOM in Chapter 15.

- *Health Monitor:* This comes with Microsoft Application Center.

These tools all work around the concept of recording data for a specific performance counter to determine how well the system is operating.

Following is a list of the useful counters tracked in the Windows Performance Monitor. You can check them to find out about the performance of BizTalk Server.

- *Disk I/O—Disk Read % and Disk Write %:* These counters help you determine whether excessive disk operations are occurring on the system. Certain operations, such as XML parsing and mapping, require great amounts of memory to do the job, and if there isn't enough physical memory available on the system, you will see these two counters increase significantly, which indicates performance will be hurt.

- *CPU—% Processor Time:* This counter helps you determine whether the processing power on the system is adequate to handle the job. It isn't uncommon for the counter to reach 100 percent for very brief times. However, if the CPU stays fully utilized for long periods of time, you may need to add more processors to the system, or upgrade the system with faster CPUs.

- *BizTalk Server—Document Received/Sec, Document Processed/Sec:* The first counter tells you how quickly BizTalk Server takes the documents received from the client and saves them to the work queue. The second counter indicates how quickly BizTalk Server takes the documents from the work queue and processes them. By comparing these two counters, you may identify the need to add hardware resources to the system that has low results on this counter.

- *Active Server Pages—Request Queued, Request Wait Time:* These two counters can help you determine the performance of the HTTP Receive Function and the ASP page that receives the post from the client. If this number becomes too large, it means the Receive Function or ASP page isn't bringing the data to the work queue quickly enough, and more client requests are waiting in the queue to be served. In this situation, you may consider adding more BizTalk Servers to the group to help load balance the document posts.

Handling Errors Effectively

Although you've learned a lot about building an effective BizTalk Server application, you can't absolutely prevent errors from happening on your system. Being able to handle these errors is critical to building effective BizTalk Server applications. In this section, you'll learn ways to proactively treat these errors and unexpected events.

Before you can handle the errors in your system, though, you must first know where potential errors may occur. The errors on BizTalk Server can be categorized as three types: BizTalk Messaging errors, BizTalk Orchestration errors, and general BizTalk Server errors.

Errors in BizTalk Messaging

Errors related to BizTalk Messaging take the form of documents that end up in the suspended queue. For example, invalid documents or document transmission errors are considered to be BizTalk Messaging errors.

One way to handle these errors is to constantly check the new arrivals in the suspended queue and process them accordingly. The last thing you want to do is let these failed documents sit in the suspended queue and collect electronic dust. After all, these documents are from clients who expect these document to be processed successfully.

One way to handle documents in the suspended queue is to run some type of scheduled task that will retrieve all the suspended queue items and do something about them. You can send them off to the system administrator by e-mail, so that he or she can investigate the problem, or send an e-mail to the project manager to notify him or her that the failure has occurred. The project manager can then involve the development team in troubleshooting and fixing the problem.

These are situations where you are certain the fault isn't on your side. For example, if the document failed because of an invalid schema, you know this is the document sender's problem, so you can send the invalid document back to the sender in a special schema to notify the sender that the error has occurred in his or her document. Here is an example of such a special schema:

```
<Error>
<Description><![CDATA[Invalid document, expecting "FundCompany" field...]]>
</Description>
<OriginalDocument><![CDATA[<FundInvestors><Investors>.... ]]></OriginalDocument>
</Error>
```

With this technique, you can react to some well-known errors quickly, and eliminate the need for human intervention on your side.

To run this suspended queue cleanup job periodically, you can rely on the Scheduled Tasks or a SQL Server job to run a certain script or executable at a certain time of the day. Scheduled Tasks, shown in Figure 13-26, is located under the Control Panel.

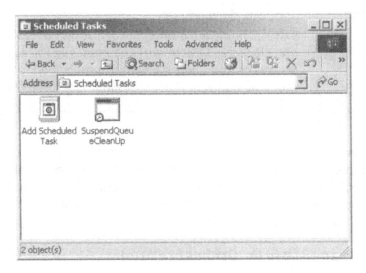

Figure 13-26. The Scheduled Tasks tool

To create a scheduled task, just double-click the Add Scheduled Task icon and follow the instructions of the wizard that appears to create a new scheduled task.

SQL Server jobs are created through SQL Server Enterprise Manager. Figure 13-27 shows where you will find the SQL Server jobs under the Enterprise Manager. When creating SQL Server jobs to execute the suspended queue cleanup, the SQL Server Agent service must be running.

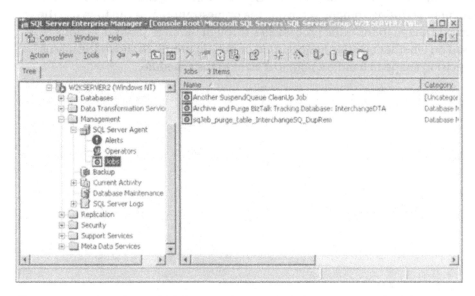

Figure 13-27. Creating a SQL Server job using SQL Server Enterprise Manager

NOTE *The default installation of SQL Server doesn't config-ure SQL Server Agent to start automatically. You can use the Services console under the Administrative Tools to make it start automatically. The service name is SQLSERVERAGENT.*

In Chapter 11, you learned about the Interchange component and its ability to query and retrieve documents from the BizTalk Server suspended queue. You can use this feature of the Interchange component inside the script program you scheduled to execute the Schedule Task and SQL Server jobs.

Errors in BizTalk Orchestration

When a document is processed by an XLANG Schedule, you need to guard against potential errors occurring inside the XLANG Schedule. It is important that you pay more attention to the error handling in BizTalk Orchestration than other type of errors, since the document may get lost if the errors aren't handled properly. (You can keep a copy of every document that passes through BizTalk Server by turning on Document Tracking, but you shouldn't use that feature to guard against potential document loss due to unhandled errors in Orches-tration.)

There are basically two ways to handle errors inside an orchestration. The first method is to check the __status__ field after making calls to the COM com-ponent or scripting component inside the orchestration. You can then use the Decision shape to route the process flow through different paths of actions based on whether an error has occurred or not. Figure 13-28 shows the use of a Decision shape to handle a potential error in the schedule.

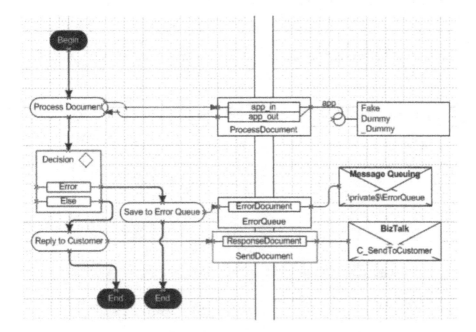

Figure 13-28. Using a Decision shape in a schedule to handle an error

The decision shown in Figure 13-28 results in two process flows. The Save to Error Queue action will save the document to the message queue and terminate the orchestration if the Fake.Dummy component returns a bad HRESULT. Otherwise, the process flow will reach the Reply to Customer action.

The other way you can provide error handling for your orchestration is through the transaction's On Failure page. However, to take advantage of the On Failure page, you must enclose the actions within the Transaction (XLANG-style) shape. Figure 13-29 shows an orchestration saving a document to the message queue on the transaction's On Failure page.

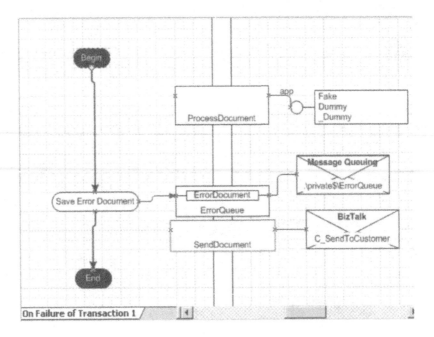

Figure 13-29. Error handling on a transaction On Failure page

General Errors in BizTalk Server

Some types of errors that occur in BizTalk Server don't belong to either category mentioned previously. I categorize these as general BizTalk Server errors. You may have seen this type of error after working with BizTalk Server for a while. For example, you may get errors about the connectivity between BizTalk Server and its database, errors about the Messaging service being unable to start, errors about the Receive Function being unable to locate its targets, etc. There may not be an automatic way to handle these types of errors eloquently, since the problems normally are so fundamental and unpredictable. For example, there is really not much you can do if the database or network is down. Under such circumstances, the best thing you can do is send out a notification about those errors to the system administrator or BizTalk Server developers so that they can take appropriate steps to resolve the problem.

There are two ways you can make sure you are notified about such errors on BizTalk Server: the hard way and the easy way. The hard way is to write a lot of WMI code to query the application events, and write a lot of other code to notify the appropriate people. However, I would not recommend this method unless there is a compelling reason for it.

The easy way is to rely on monitoring software to take care of event notification. Some monitoring tools are also equipped with the ability to run customized code on the target system when certain events occur. MOM is one of these tools (MOM will be discussed in Chapter 15). Although many of these errors, especially those that are infrastructure related, can't be fixed by simply running some code on the target system, the ability to run customized code in the event that something happens does help you automate error handling in some specialized cases.

For example, suppose you have a file or Message Queue Receive Function that is configured to watch specific resources using a given set of user IDs and passwords. You'll normally get a BizTalk Server error about the Receive Function when the network or active directory (or domain control) becomes unavailable for a short period of time, because the file folder and message queue need to contact the active directory or domain control to determine whether the requests from the BizTalk Server Receive Function are permitted. In such a case, BizTalk Server will disable the Receive Functions that are unable to reach their targets, and you must explicitly enable those Receive Functions to make them functional again. You could write some WMI code to enable those Receive Functions and instruct the monitoring software to run it on the BizTalk Server in the event that the Receive Functions are disabled, so that documents don't accumulate in the file folder or message queue for too long. I will talk about MOM in more depth in Chapter 15.

Summary

In this chapter, you learned some techniques for building an effective BizTalk Server application. You learned how to build a fault-tolerant and scalable BizTalk application through the use of BizTalk Server groups, HTTP Receive Functions, MSMQ, network load balancing, and database clustering.

By understanding the limitations of MSMQ, you also learned how to build BizTalk applications that can handle very large documents. And you learned some things you can do to enhance BizTalk Server's performance by tweaking the BizTalk Server configuration, the system registry, AICs, document definitions and transformations, and BizTalk Orchestration.

Last, you looked at a number of ways to handle different types of errors that can occur on a BizTalk Server. In the next chapter, you'll get a chance to explore yet another very important aspect of BizTalk Server application: deployment.

CHAPTER 14

Deployment Strategies and Solutions

Now THAT YOU KNOW HOW to create a B2B application using BizTalk Server, you'll learn how you can deploy it. Developing an effective deployment strategy is critical to product rollout. The last thing you want is to see the application working in the development environment but not in the production environment. As your BizTalk application moves from development, to staging, to QA, and finally to the production environment, it's your responsibility to ensure that those environments, or more specifically, the files and configurations, are synchronized with the development environment, which you know has the latest and greatest version of your application.

If you've been following along with the examples thus far, you've been doing most of your system configuration in the development environment manually. In most cases, however, manually duplicating such settings in each environment is both labor intensive and error prone. In this chapter, I'll show you a number of strategies and techniques that make deploying your BizTalk Server application both accurate and fast.

Deployment Overview

Before you can develop a strategy for deploying a BizTalk Server application, you need to know what components are involved in your BizTalk application. Generally, you can group the components of a BizTalk Server application into three categories:

- *Infrastructure:* This includes the operating system setup, database setup, installation of BizTalk Server, etc.

- *Files:* These are files such as the XML schema and schedule files.

- *Configuration settings:* These are the configuration settings for BizTalk Server and BizTalk Messaging.

Infrastructure Deployment Considerations

Besides ensuring that the installation of the operating system, database, and BizTalk Server is correct, you also need to pay attention to the security and firewall port configuration between the servers that support the application.

When you develop your code in the development environment, the accounts the BizTalk Server service and applications use may be the local administrator's account or an interactive account. As you move your application from one environment to the next, you need to replace those accounts with a domain account. A set of specific privileges must be granted to this account in order for the BizTalk Server application to work properly. Such security settings should be configured before you start to deploy components that are specific to your BizTalk application.

To configure the security on the new environment, you can refer to Chapter 12 for detailed information on how to set up the security configuration to make the BizTalk application work properly.

The firewall configuration is another area that may cause a headache when it comes to getting the infrastructure ready for deployment. Firewalls are used to restrict communications between the networks on each side. Figure 14-1 shows a typical network protected by firewalls.

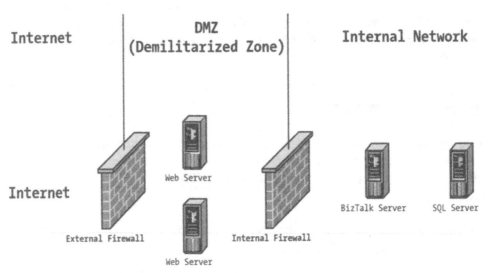

Figure 14-1. A simple BizTalk Server network protected by firewalls

In the simplified network diagram in Figure 14-1, the network has three segments: the Internet, the DMZ, and the internal network. These three network segments are separated by firewalls.

The external firewall separates the Internet and the DMZ. By deploying a firewall between these two networks, you can reduce the amount of access the public has to the Web server in the DMZ. Firewalls restrict access by controlling which ports are open for communications and what type of network packets can pass through the open ports. For example, if you implement an ASP page on the Web server to accept documents from clients on the Internet, you can open port 80 while leaving the other ports closed. With only port 80 open, any attempt to access services on the other ports will fail, such as DCOM calls, which use port numbers between 1024 to 65535. With a firewall between the Internet and DMZ, you can open only those ports that are intended for the services that your server will provide.

The servers in the DMZ normally have to be directly exposed to the Internet to provide their services. For example, the Web server will supply the HTML requested by the user on the Internet, the DNS server will provide the IP addresses, and the SMTP server will need to receive and send e-mail through the Internet. Therefore, even if you try to lock down as many ports as possible, there will still be a number of ports that must be open on the firewall so that users on the Internet can access the intended servers.

This exposes a security problem. What happens if the user decides to access another server on the network through the open port? For example, the user can modify the URL to access the virtual directory on the BizTalk Server, one of the virtual directories pointing to the Document Tracking Web application.

You certainly don't want users to access just any server that has IIS running on port 80. To solve these problems, you can deploy another firewall between the DMZ and the internal network. In that firewall, you can open only the port that is required for the Web server to communicate with the servers in the internal network. For example, the only interaction between the Web server and the BizTalk Server is through MSMQ, so you can configure the internal firewall so that only port 1801 is open, which will be used to send messages through the firewall. A hacker on the Internet can access the Web server through port 80, but not the message queue behind the internal firewall, since port 1801 isn't open on the external firewall. You can also configure the internal firewall so that only network packets originating from your server in the DMZ are allowed to pass through.

With the DMZ behind the external firewall and in front of the internal firewall, you expose the servers in the DMZ to the Internet while keeping the internal network from the direct reach of users on the Internet. The firewall configuration directly depends on the application architecture that is in place. You must be able to configure the firewall so that it will block requests to servers and services that aren't intended for the users on the Internet.

After you have locked down all the ports, you must find a way for the server behind the firewall to send data to the Internet. For example, BizTalk Messaging may send documents to clients over the Internet through HTTP(S) or SMTP. To enable BizTalk Server to send outbound data, you can deploy a gateway server whose job is to forward the requests to the Internet, as shown in Figure 14-2.

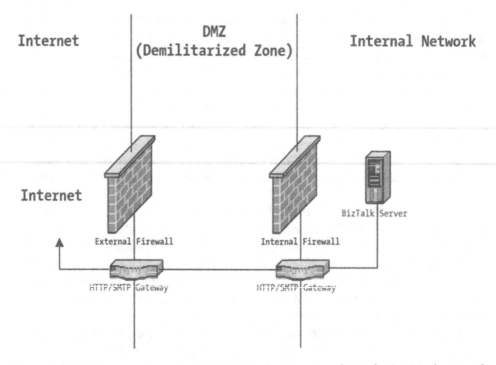

Figure 14-2. Using a gateway/router to route the messages from the internal network to the Internet

When it comes to firewall configuration for BizTalk Servers, what you really need to do is allow BizTalk Server to communicate with other resources across the firewall. Let's take a look at the resources BizTalk Server will potentially need to access:

- MSMQ

- Databases

- DCOM

- Other BizTalk Server members in the group

If the BizTalk Server will communicate with MSMQ across a firewall, the following ports should be open for BizTalk Server to send and receive messages:

- *TCP:* 1801

- *Remote procedure call (RPC):* 135, 2101, 2103, 2105

- *User Datagram Protocol (UDP):* 3527, 1801

TCP (port 1801) is used for general message sending and session management. Because MSMQ operations are build on RPC, ports 135, 2101, 2103, and 2105 should be open for the remote message reads. MSMQ also uses ports 3527 and 1801 for internal PING mechanisms and broadcasts.

BizTalk Server needs to talk to its database. If you move the SQL Server database used by BizTalk Server to a remote host, you need to make sure communication between BizTalk Server and that remote database is possible. By default, SQL Server talks on port 1433. However, just opening this port isn't enough for BizTalk Server to communicate with it. BizTalk Server uses Distributed Transaction Coordinator (DTC) to make transactional calls to its database. This means you need to open the RPC ports for DTC, since DTC is based on RPC. RPC requires port 135 for the handshake, and then it chooses dynamic ports that are above 1024 and below 65535 for the RPC calls. You can tie up security by only leaving a range of ports open for RPC to work.

On top of that, depending on the database setup, port 1434 may also need to be opened for the names instance of the database. If BizTalk Server isn't talking to the default database, it must be talking to a named instance, and the format of such a name looks like server\instance1. This is supported in SQL Server 2000 only.

When BizTalk Server invokes remote COM components, such as an orchestration calling a component on a remote box through DCOM, the firewall configuration must accommodate such communication to allow DCOM calls to flow from BizTalk Server to the remote server. On the other hand, some remote servers may be calling the Interchange component on BizTalk Server to pass data into the BizTalk Server database. In such a case, the firewall also needs to allow the DCOM calls to flow from the other server to BizTalk Server.

To configure the DCOM port on BizTalk Server and other servers, open the command prompt, enter **dcomcnfg**, and the Distributed COM Configuration Properties window will open, as shown in Figure 14-3.

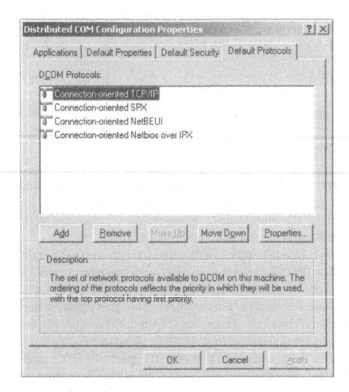

Figure 14-3. Configuring the DCOM port with dcomcnfg.exe

Select the Default Protocols tab, select the Connection-oriented TCP/IP item in the DCOM Protocols list, and click the Properties button. The Properties for COM Internet Services window will pop up, in which you can specify the range of ports this system will use to communicate the DCOM calls from the remote clients. You can then configure the firewall to open this range of ports to allow the DCOM calls to pass through. Click the Add button in this window to add a range of ports used by DCOM, as shown in Figure 14-4.

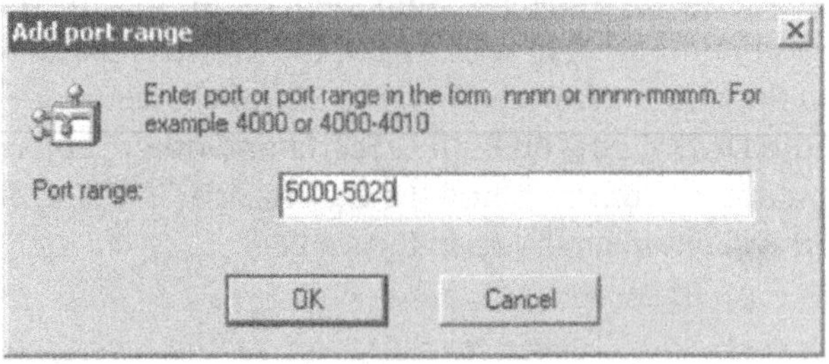

Figure 14-4. Configuring a range for DCOM calls

In Figure 14-4, you see I've allocated ports from 5000 to 5020 to be used for DCOM calls. When a remote client initiates a component on the system, the client will first make a request about which port will be employed for later DCOM calls, by using port 135. The server that hosts the component will then randomly pick a port from the port range and send that port number back to the client, who would then open this port to make the DCOM requests on the server. By narrowing the port range used by DCOM, you only need to open a limited port on the firewall to allow a DCOM request to pass through.

When you have multiple BizTalk Servers within a server group, NetBIOS has to be enabled in order for the BizTalk Server members to communicate with each other. This should not be a concern if the BizTalk Server members aren't separated by firewalls. However, if you do separate them with a firewall, such as when you have a BizTalk Server member receiving documents in front of the firewall, and the other BizTalk Server members behind the firewall processing the documents, you need to make sure the appropriate firewall ports that are required by NetBIOS are open, namely ports 137, 138, and 139.

File Deployment Considerations

After ensuring that the infrastructure is stable and ready for application deployment, the next step is to figure out what type of files are part of the application to be deployed. Depending on the application, there could be various types of files involved. In this book, I'll only focus on the deployment of files that are related to BizTalk Server.

File deployment is mostly a matter of copying the files related to the BizTalk Server application from one environment to another. In general, there are six types of files you should consider:

- BizTalk schema files (*.xml)

- BizTalk map files (*.xml)

- BizTalk Orchestration files (*.skx)

- AIC, preprocessor component files (*.dll)

- ASP pages for pipeline AICs (*.asp)

- ASP pages for receiving the documents posted (*.asp)

BizTalk schema files are normally located in the [BizTalk Installation Directory]\BizTalkServerRepository\DocSpecs directory. It's recommended that you copy the schema files to the same BizTalkServerRepository\DocSpecs folder under the BizTalk installation directory on the target BizTalk Server, since BizTalkServerRepository is referenced by a virtual directory that is created during the BizTalk Server installation.

BizTalk Map files that will be referenced by channels should also be copied to the target server. Map files, by default, are located under the [BizTalk Installation Directory]\BizTalkServerRepository\Maps directory.

The compiled version of BizTalk Orchestration files, .skx files, should also be copied as part of the BizTalk Server application. It isn't important where these files are located on the target server, as long as the location for these files matches the path information specified on the message port that needs to load the orchestration file. As far as BizTalk Orchestration is concerned, BizTalk Server only needs the .skx file to start a schedule, but you may want to deploy the .skv file (the Orchestration Designer file) anyway, so that you can to open the orchestration file in Orchestration Designer, in case you need to investigate or troubleshoot a problem.

If the BizTalk application uses the AIC (either the lightweight AIC or pipeline AIC) or preprocessors, you need to also register the components on the target server, but first you need to copy the DLL files to the target server. I'll talk about the registry later in the chapter.

There are two sets of ASP pages you also need to deploy. The first set is used by the pipeline AIC to allow the user to configure its properties in BizTalk Messaging Manager. These files are located under the [BizTalk Installation Directory]\MessagingManager\pipeline directory. For each AIC you want to deploy, you need to copy two ASP files, Projectname_classname.asp and Projectname_classname_post.asp, to the [BizTalk Installation Directory]\MessagingManager\pipeline directory on the target location. BizTalk Messaging Manager will look to this location for the ASP files to load during the configuration of the channel.

The second set of ASP pages are the document-receiving ASP pages that accept the data posted to the BizTalk Server. The location of these files on the target server depends on the virtual directory configuration.

Configuration Considerations

The bulk of the deployment work is related to the transfer of all the configurations that are part of the BizTalk Server application to the target server. These configurations can be categorized into four types:

- *BizTalk Messaging configuration:* This includes the configuration for channels, ports, organizations, etc. It comprises all the settings you are able to configure through BizTalk Messaging Manager.

- *BizTalk Server configuration:* This includes the BizTalk Server properties settings, such as Receive Functions, tracking information, and SMTP host and proxy servers that are used by the Messaging service to send documents out to the Internet. Anything that can be configured with BizTalk Administration Console falls into this type of configuration.

- *Component registration:* This includes the registration of components and configuration of COM+ applications and components, such as security and transaction support.

- *MSMQ and file folder configuration:* This includes the creation of message queues and file folders that will be used by either Message Queue Receive Functions or File Receive Functions.

Now that you know what kind of configurations are involved in the deployment of the BizTalk Server application, let's take a look at exactly how you can deploy these things. In the remainder of this chapter, I'll focus on the actual deployment of files and configurations, and assume the infrastructure is ready and stable.

Application Center Deployment

There are two strategies you should consider when it comes to actual deployment. You can either use the new BizTalk Server 2002 deployment feature through Application Center (which is a separate product from Microsoft, and not part of BizTalk Server), or you can develop an in-house deployment script with popular scripting languages, such as VBScript.

The advantage of using Application Center to deploy a BizTalk Server application is that it involves the least amount of development work. Unfortunately, it has the noticeable disadvantage of inflexibility when it comes to some specific business requirements. For instance, you can use Application Center to deploy the BizTalk Messaging configuration as a new addition, but Application Center doesn't automatically allow you to deploy an updated configuration. To deploy an updated configuration, you must first delete the existing configuration on the target BizTalk Server and then redeploy the whole configuration again with the latest update. While the Messaging configuration is being deleted from the BizTalk Server and reinstalled, clients will not be able to access the functionality related to BizTalk Messaging.

Application Center is best used to deploy BizTalk Messaging when you don't expect a lot of updates to the existing messaging configuration. If there are likely to be many updates, such as adding new clients to the system, you should look into a different deployment strategy, such as script deployment, which I'll discuss later in the chapter. You can use Application Center to deploy files, such as orchestration files, as well as the BizTalk Messaging configuration.

 NOTE *To use Application Center to deploy BizTalk Server resources, Application Center SP1 must be installed. For detailed information, refer to the Application Center SP1 installation document.*

Three steps are involved in deploying a BizTalk Server application using Application Center:

1. Create a cluster, if one doesn't exist.

2. Define the application, or collection of resources.

3. Deploy the application to the target server or cluster.

Creating a Cluster

Clusters in Application Center represent the environments of various applications. In order to deploy an application from one environment to another using Application Center, you need to first establish clusters, and then move the application from one cluster to the next.

To create a cluster, open the Application Center console from Administrative Tools, right-click the Application Center icon, and select Connect. A Connect to Server window opens, as shown in Figure 14-5.

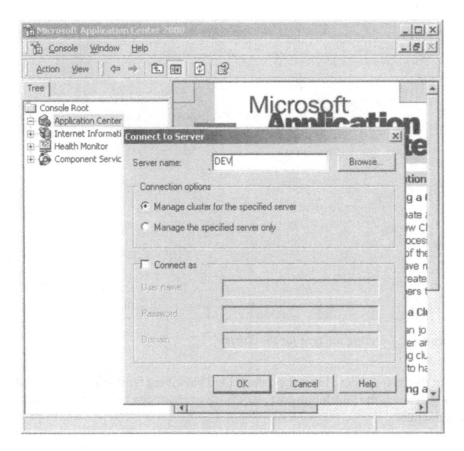

Figure 14-5. Creating a new cluster

Type the name of the server you want to connect to, leave the connection option as "Manager cluster for the specified server", and click OK to continue.

If this server isn't part of a cluster, you will be asked to either create a new cluster or join an existing cluster. Select "Create a new cluster" and continue.

In the next window, you need to give a name to the new cluster (I named it DEVCluster for this example), and then click OK to continue.

In the following New Cluster Wizard window, shown in Figure 14-6, you need to select the type of new cluster. Because this cluster will be used for deploying your application, select General/Web cluster, and click OK to continue.

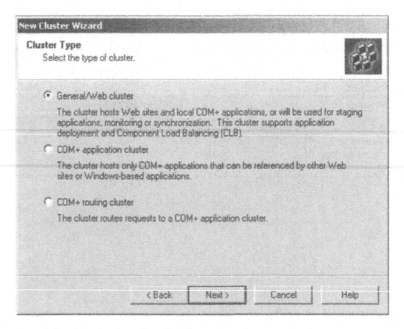

Figure 14-6. Selecting the type for the cluster

In the next window, leave the default load balancing type, and then click OK until you reach the Finish button. Click Finish to create the cluster, which may take a while.

Defining the Application

After the cluster is created, select the Applications icon under DEVCluster in the left panel, and the right panel will display the existing applications that are defined on the system, as shown in Figure 14-7.

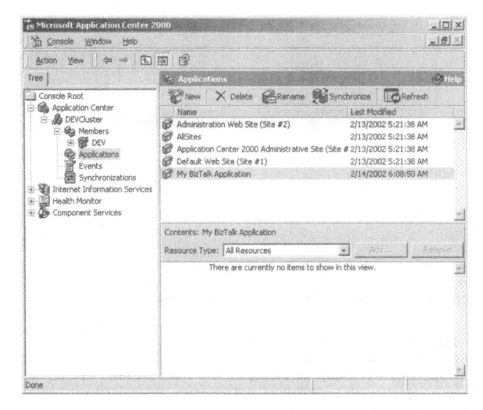

Figure 14-7. Defining a new application

What you need to do here is define a BizTalk application. Click the New icon at the top of the right panel, and a dialog box will ask for the name of the application. Type **My BizTalk Application** and click OK. A new application will appear on the application list (see Figure 14-7).

Now you can add resources to this application so that when you deploy this application later, the specified resources will be deployed too. Select My BizTalk Application, and open the Resource Type list by clicking the Add button next to the Resource Type list box. An item called BizTalk should appear on the list—select that item and click the Add button next to it to add the BizTalk resource to the application.

An Add Resource window will open, as shown in Figure 14-8, in which you can add the specific BizTalk Server resources.

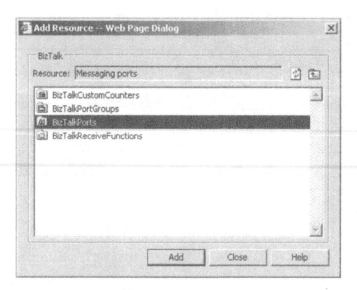

Figure 14-8. Adding the specific BizTalk Server resources to the application

This is the window where you specify what ports and Receive Functions are to be included as part of the deployment. Double-click BizTalkPorts to select the individual ports to be included in the deployment. When you select a port, the associated channels, organizations, and document definitions are also automatically selected for deployment.

After adding the BizTalk Server resource, you can also add the file resource for the XLANG files and the configured AICs. To add more resources to the system, select File System Path and COM+ application on the resource type list, and add them to My BizTalk Application.

Deploying the Application

After you've created an application and added resources to it, you can deploy the application to another cluster or server. To deploy an application, right-click the Application icon on the left panel under the cluster, and select New Deployment. A New Deployment Wizard will start up.

Click Next to go to the Deployment Target Options window, shown in Figure 14-9. Select the "Deploy content outside the current cluster" option to deploy the BizTalk Server application to another cluster. Click Next to continue.

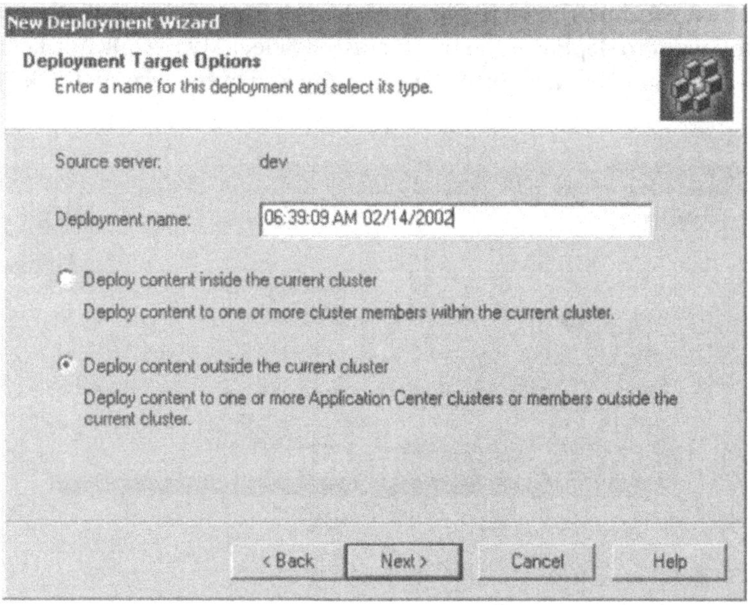

Figure 14-9. Deploying the application to another cluster

In the next window, shown in Figure 14-10, you specify what cluster you will deploy the application to. On the Deployment Targets window, you need to specify the controller server for the cluster to which the application is being deployed. Click the Add button to add multiple cluster controllers if the application is to be deployed to more than one cluster. Click Next to continue.

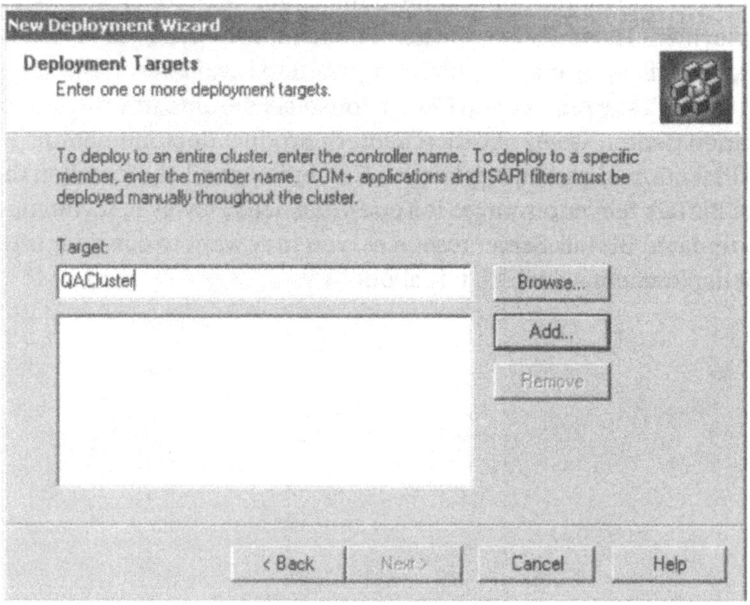

Figure 14-10. Specifying the target cluster of the application

The next window, shown in Figure 14-11, is where you choose what application you want to deploy to the target cluster. Select My BizTalk Application from the list, and click Next until you get to the end of the wizard. Click Finish.

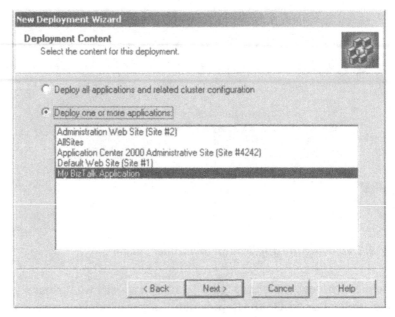

Figure 14-11. Selecting the application for deployment

When you click the Finish button, Application Center starts deploying the resources defined for the application to the target server or cluster. When the deployment is completed, the new application, in this case My BizTalk Application, will appear as one of the applications available on the system when viewed through the Application Center console. For more information on using Application Center, see Application Center's product documentation.

As I mentioned earlier, Application Center is a good choice when the deployment of BizTalk Server resources is a one-time deal. However, if you must deploy updated BizTalk Server resources, you may want to consider using a script deployment, which I'll talk about next.

Script Deployment

In this section, you'll see how to deploy the configuration with scripts. You'll be creating scripts to deploy the four types of configuration I discussed earlier:

- BizTalk Messaging configuration

- BizTalk Server configuration

- Component registration

- MSMQ and file folder configuration

Deployment of BizTalk Messaging Configuration

Let's look first at the most important part of the deployment—the BizTalk Messaging configuration. In Chapter 11, you saw that the BizTalk Messaging configuration can be added, updated, and deleted programmatically with the BizTalk Configuration object model. In essence, the automatic deployment of the BizTalk Messaging configuration involves using a customized program that calls these Messaging configuration objects to add necessary BizTalk channels, ports, etc.

BizTalk Server Configuration Assistant Tool

Before you get too discouraged by the thought of all the effort involved in creating all these channels and ports, let's first take a look at what tools are available that can help you get the coding done faster. BizTalk Server comes with a very useful tool called BizTalk Server Configuration Assistant, shown in Figure 14-12. It can be found at [BizTalk Server Installation directory]\SDK\Messaging Samples\BTConfigAssistant\EXE\BTConfAssistant.exe. The BTConfAssistant.exe is supplied as a VB sample, and it isn't a supported Microsoft product. However, it comes with the VB source code, so feel free to modify it if you know what you are doing.

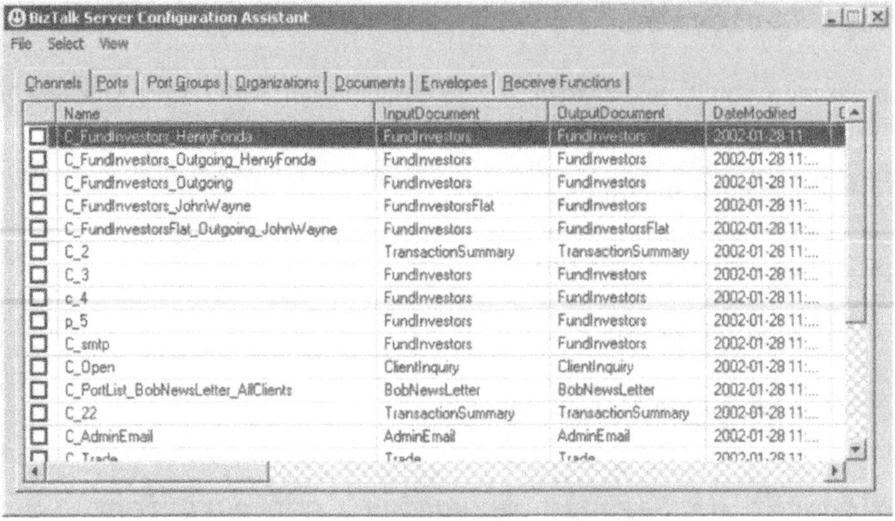

Figure 14-12. The BizTalk Server Configuration Assistant tool

Configuration Assistant helps you create an installation script for the configuration items you want to deploy. The program has seven tabs across the top, each representing a type of Messaging configuration in BizTalk Server, except for the last one, which represents the Receive Functions that currently exist on the local server. You can select the items you want to deploy to another server by clicking the checkbox next to the desired configuration items. The related items are also selected automatically, so when C_FundInvestors_HenryFonda is selected, the P_FundInvestors on the Ports tab, FundInvestors on the Documents tab, and Henry Fonda Inc. on the Organizations tab are also selected. The tool automatically figures out that a channel can't be installed until those related items are installed first.

After you select the items you want to deploy, the tool will generate the code for you. To make that happen, select View ➤ Selected Items from the menus. An XML Representation window opens, as shown in Figure 14-13.

This window contains two tabs: XML and VBScript. The XML tab contains the XML representation of the configuration items you have selected. The second window contains the generated VBScript that you can use to install the items you have selected, as shown in Figure 14-13.

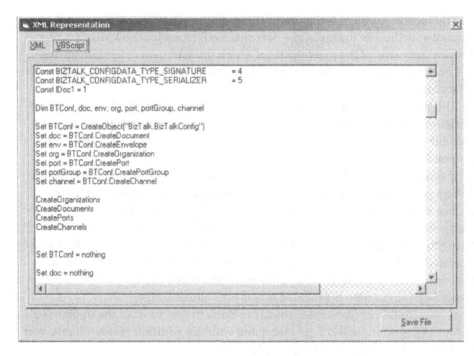

*Figure 14-13. VBScript generated by the BizTalk Server Configuration
Assistant tool*

You can save this VBScript by clicking the Save File button at the lower-right corner. To install all the items you've selected, simply run the VBScript on the target BizTalk Server.

Using Configuration Assistant allows you to deploy the BizTalk Messaging configuration quickly, with little development effort, but using only this tool for your BizTalk application deployment has its own set of problems.

Like the Application Center deployment you saw earlier, the script that Configuration Assistant generates can only be run on a brand new BizTalk Server with no existing channels or ports. To update any configuration that has already been installed on the target server, you must first uninstall the whole configuration, generate code that reflects the update, and then run the script again on the target server. This may present a problem when you want to keep your application up and running 24/7. The assumption you have to make when executing this generated script is that the target server doesn't have any BizTalk Messaging configuration for channels, ports, etc. If this assumption isn't correct, you can't use this generated script for your deployment.

The second problem is that many things in the script are machine and environment specific. For example, the document reference for the XML schema contains the name of the machine from which the script was originally generated. Some of the destination URLs for the ports may also point to testing server URLs instead of production URLs.

Although the generated script alone is unable to update the Messaging configuration and contain environment- and server-specific information, it can be a feasible deployment solution if the problems associated with this design are acceptable and can be dealt with.

If you take Bob's ASP as an example, using the generated code alone would not be a good deployment solution. Bob's client base will increase, and this requires Bob to add the configurations for new clients to BizTalk Messaging constantly, since channels and ports need to be added for each additional client. Having to delete the configuration on the production server and reload the newly generated configuration could interrupt the service for too long. Also, when problems occur, it would be difficult to locate the source of the problems, since the whole configuration is included in this monolithic script.

If your BizTalk application is similar to Bob's in that most of the updates to the Messaging configuration are associated with the addition of new clients, you should consider using a two-script deployment.

The Two-Script Deployment

The scripts in a two-script deployment are the base script and the add-on script.

The *base script* adds the infrastructure configuration for the BizTalk Server application. The configuration this script adds will be same whether your BizTalk Server needs to support one client or one hundred clients. For example, in Bob's case, the FundInvestors document definition can be considered part of the base script since you have to add such an item no matter how many clients you have to support—each of the clients will have to use the same FundInvestors document definition. Another example is the P_FundInvestors port, which starts the FundInvestors schedule when a new document arrives. This port isn't associated with any specific client. As you learned in earlier chapters, channels and ports are associated with an organization, so if the organizations they are associated with aren't the client organizations, you can configure them as part of the base script.

The *add-on script*, on the other hand, installs the configurations that are associated with specific clients. In Bob's case, C_FundInvestors_HenryFonda and P_Outgoing_HenryFonda are considered part of the configuration for the add-on script, since both are associated with the Henry Fonda Inc. client organization.

With this two-script deployment strategy, you can add new clients to your BizTalk Server without deleting any existing configuration. After the initial base script installation, any future expansion of the client base will only involve deploying a client-specific configuration through the use of the add-on script. Figure 14-14 illustrates the concept of two-script deployment.

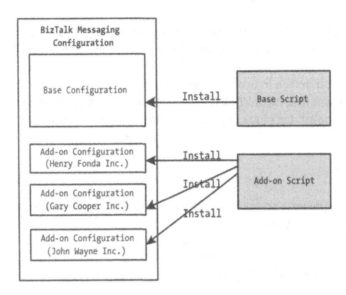

Figure 14-14. Deploying BizTalk messaging configuration with a base script and an add-on script

With two-script deployment, you eliminate the need to uninstall and reinstall the whole configuration when adding a new client to BizTalk Messaging. If your BizTalk Server has many new configurations that need to be added, but very few changes need to be made to existing configurations, this two-script strategy is a good fit for your deployment.

Another problem you may encounter is that a lot of information in the script is server specific. You must replace such hard-coded values with variables that get their values from either the input parameters of the script or function calls that return the correct values for the environment. For example, to assign a variable with input parameters, you could use WScript.Arguments, as shown in the following code (in BaseScript.vbs):

```
dim vArgs
dim Installation_Environment

Set vArgs = WScript.Arguments
Installation_Environment = vArgs(0)
```

WScript.Arguments returns an array that represents the parameters of the script. For example, running

```
C:\BaseScript.vbs "Production"
```

will make the variable Installation_Environment equal to "Production". You can then add logic in your script to perform the configuration using the input parameters.

Even if you decide to use the base script and add-on script for your deployment, the script that the BizTalk Configuration Assistant generated can be used as a starting point. Let's look at some sample code for both the base script and add-on script.

Base Script

Here is a sample base script that shows the installation of configuration for the FundInvestor document:

```
Const BIZTALK_OPENNESS_TYPE_EX_TOWORKFLOW      = 16
Const BIZTALK_TRANSPORT_TYPE_ORCHESTRATIONACTIVATION = 8192
dim vArgs
dim BizTalk_Installation_Location
dim ServerName
'retrieve the parameter
Set vArgs = WScript.Arguments
BizTalk_Installation_Location= vArgs(0)
'obtain the local machine name
Set WshNetwork = WScript.CreateObject("WScript.Network")
ServerName=WshNetwork.ComputerName
'-----------------------------------------------
'declare other constant value
'declare variable
Dim BTConf, doc, env, org, port, portGroup, channel
Set BTConf = CreateObject("BizTalk.BizTalkConfig")
Set doc = BTConf.CreateDocument
Set env = BTConf.CreateEnvelope
Set org = BTConf.CreateOrganization
Set port = BTConf.CreatePort

'Call the functions to add the base configurations
CreateOrganizations
CreateDocuments
CreatePorts
```

```
'clear the object at the end
Set BTConf = nothing


Set portGroup = nothing
Set channel = nothing
'----------------------------------------------
Function CreateOrganizations
    Create_lOrg110001
    Set org = nothing
End Function 'CreateOrganizations
Function CreateDocuments
    Create_lDoc140002
    Set doc = nothing
End Function 'CreateDocuments
Function CreatePorts
    Create_lPort160002
    Set port = nothing
End Function 'CreatePorts
'----------------------------------------------
Dim lOrg110001
'declare alias(es)
Dim lAlias120001
Dim lAlias120002
'declare application(s)
Dim lApp130002
Dim lApp130001
Function Create_lOrg110001
    org.clear
    Call LoadDefaultOrg (BTConf, org)
    lOrg110001 = org.Handle
    org.CreateApplication "AdminEmailApp"
    org.CreateApplication "OutgoingMessageQueueApp"
    org.Save
    Call ErrCheck(lOrg110001)
    lAlias120001 = GetOrgNameAliasID ( org )
    lAlias120002 = GetAliasID ("Reliable Messaging Acknowledgement SMTP From
 Address", "SMTP", "<acknowledgement email address>", org)
    lApp130002 = GetAppID ("AdminEmailApp", org)
    lApp130001 = GetAppID ("OutgoingMessageQueueApp", org)
End Function 'Create_lOrg110001
```

```
'declare doc handle
Dim lDoc140002
Function Create_lDoc140002
    doc.clear
    doc.name = "FundInvestors"
    doc.reference = "http://" & Servername &
"/BizTalkServerRepository/DocSpecs/FundInvestors.xml"
    ' set track fields
    doc.TrackFields.s_value1 = "/FundInvestors/Investors/Investor/InvestorName"
    doc.TrackFields.s_value2 = "/FundInvestors/FundCompany"
    lDoc140002 = doc.Create
    Call ErrCheck(lDoc140002)
End Function 'Create_lDoc140002

'declare the port handle
Dim lPort160002
Function Create_lPort160002
    port.clear
    port.name = "P_FundInvestors"
    port.Comments = "The port receives FundInvestors Document"
    ' set the endpoint object - port.DestinationEndPoint
    port.DestinationEndPoint.Organization = lOrg110001
    port.DestinationEndPoint.Alias = lAlias120001
    port.DestinationEndPoint.Openness = BIZTALK_OPENNESS_TYPE_EX_TOWORKFLOW
    ' set transport info for port.PrimaryTransport
    port.PrimaryTransport.Address = BizTalk_Installation_Location &
 "\XLANG Scheduler\FundInvestors.skx"
    port.PrimaryTransport.Parameter = "GetDocument"
    port.PrimaryTransport.Type = BIZTALK_TRANSPORT_TYPE_ORCHESTRATIONACTIVATION
    ' create object and check errors
    lPort160002 = port.Create
    Call ErrCheck(lPort160002)
End Function 'Create_lPort160002
'Utility functions here
```

Notice that the doc.reference in the function Create_lDoc140002 is equal to

```
"http://" & Servername & "/BizTalkServerRepository/DocSpecs/FundInvestors.xml"
```

The Servername variable is the local machine name, which is obtained using WScript.Network at the beginning of the code. The port.PrimaryTransport.Address in the function Create_lPort160002 is equal to

```
BizTalk_Installation_Location & "\XLANG Scheduler\FundInvestors.skx"
```

where BizTalk_Installation_Location is the input parameter for the script file. By replacing the hard-coded values in the script with these variables, you don't need to make any code modifications as you install the script from one environment to another.

The key steps in developing a base script are as follows:

1. Run BizTalk Server Configuration Assistant to generate the VBScript, which you can use as a start point.

2. Remove any Messaging configuration that is associated with the clients.

3. Replace the hard-coded values, such as URLs or file paths, that are server or environment specific with variables that will be assigned appropriate values dynamically via parameters passed in as command line arguments or derived in the script.

After you've created the base script, you can start creating the add-on script, which only contains the client-specific Messaging configuration.

Add-On Script

Add-on scripts are a bit tricky. When you install an add-on script, the base script should have already been installed on the server, and many client-specific Messaging configurations will be associated with the configurations that are part of the base script. Therefore, you must obtain references to existing configurations before the add-on configuration can be installed successfully. For example, suppose you want to install the C_FundInvestors_HenryFonda channel. Because this channel is attached to the P_FundInvestors port, which is part of the base script, you have to first get the handle of the port using the handle property on the BizTalkPort object before you can create the messaging channel.

To get a better understanding of the add-on script, let's take a look at the add-on scrip for the base script you saw in the previous section.

```
Const BIZTALK_CONFIGDATA_TYPE_PRIMARYTRANSPORT     = 0
dim vArgs
dim BizTalk_Installation_Location
dim ServerName
'retrieve the parameter
Set vArgs = WScript.Arguments
BizTalk_Installation_Location = vArgs(0)
Org_Name = vArgs(1)
Tax_number = vArgs(2)
Org_Short_Name = vArgs(3)
```

```
'obtain the local machine name
Set WshNetwork = WScript.CreateObject("WScript.Network")
ServerName = WshNetwork.ComputerName
'------------------------------------------------
Dim BTConf, doc, env, org, port, portGroup, channel
Set BTConf = CreateObject("BizTalk.BizTalkConfig")
Set doc = BTConf.CreateDocument
Set org = BTConf.CreateOrganization
Set port = BTConf.CreatePort
Set channel = BTConf.CreateChannel

CreateOrganizations
CreateDocuments
CreatePorts
CreateChannels

Set BTConf = nothing

Set portGroup = nothing

'------------------------------------------------
Function CreateOrganizations
    Create_lOrg110002
    Set org = nothing
End Function 'CreateOrganizations
Function CreateDocuments
    Retrieve_lDoc140002
    Set doc = nothing
End Function 'CreateDocuments
Function CreatePorts
    Retrieve_lPort160002
    Set port = nothing
End Function 'CreatePorts

Function CreateChannels
    Create_lChannel180002
    Set channel = nothing
End Function 'CreateChannels
'------------------------------------------------
Dim lOrg110002
'declare alias(es)
Dim lAlias120003
Dim lAlias120004
```

```
Function Create_lOrg110002
    org.clear
    org.name = Org_Name
    org.Comments = "The mutual fund firm is using bob's ASP application"
    org.CreateAlias "TAX_ID", False,  "TAX_ID", Tax_number
    lOrg110002 = org.Create
    Call ErrCheck(lOrg110002)
    lAlias120003 = GetOrgNameAliasID ( org )
    lAlias120004 = GetAliasID ("TAX_ID", "TAX_ID", Tax_number, org)
End Function 'Create_lOrg110002


Dim lDoc140002
Function Retrieve_lDoc140002
    doc.clear
    doc.LoadByName("FundInvestors")
    lDoc140002 = doc.handle()
End Function 'Create_lDoc140002


Dim lPort160002
Function Retrieve_lPort160002
    port.clear
    port.LoadByName("P_FundInvestors")
    lPort160002 = port.handle()
End Function 'Create_lPort160002


Dim lChannel180002
Function Create_lChannel180002
    channel.clear
    channel.name = "C_FundInvestors_" & Org_short_name
    ' set the endpoint object - channel.SourceEndPoint
    channel.SourceEndPoint.Organization = lOrg110002
    channel.SourceEndPoint.Alias = lAlias120003
    channel.InputDocument = lDoc140002
    channel.OutputDocument = lDoc140002
    channel.Port = lPort160002
    ' Logging info
    channel.LoggingInfo.LogNativeInputDocument = 0
    channel.LoggingInfo.LogNativeOutputDocument = 0
    channel.LoggingInfo.LogXMLInputDocument = 0
    channel.LoggingInfo.LogXMLOutputDocument = 0
    channel.RetryCount = 0
    channel.RetryInterval = 5
    ' set port component configuration for lPort160002
```

```
' create object and check errors
lChannel180002 = channel.Create
Call ErrCheck(lChannel180002)
' set port configuration for lPort160002
Set dict = CreateObject("Commerce.Dictionary")
dict.SkedFile = BizTalk_Installation_Location &
"\XLANG Scheduler\FundInvestors.skx"
dict.Port = "GetDocument"
channel.SetConfigData BIZTALK_CONFIGDATA_TYPE_PRIMARYTRANSPORT,
lPort160002, dict
Set dict = nothing
channel.Save
End Function 'Create_lChannel180002
'Utility functions
```

To make this add-on script generic, you should also replace all client-specific information with variables, so that you can use the same add-on script to add multiple clients. I added the following code segment to dynamically determine the name of the client and the name of the channel:

```
Set vArgs = WScript.Arguments
BizTalk_Installation_Location = vArgs(0)
Org_Name = vArgs(1)
Tax_number = vArgs(2)
Org_Short_Name = vArgs(3)

'Function that creates organization
org.name = Org_Name
org.CreateAlias "TAX_ID", False,  "TAX_ID", Tax_number

'Function that creates the channel
channel.name = "C_FundInvestors_" & Org_short_name
```

When executing the script, you need to pass in four parameters as follows:

```
C:\add-on.vbs "E:\Program Files\Microsoft BizTalk Server" "Henry Fonda Inc."
 123456789 "HenryFonda"
```

To add additional clients and associated configurations, you can simply call the same script and pass in different parameters for a different client.

The preceding script will create two BizTalk Server configuration items: the organization of Henry Fonda Inc., and C_FundInvestors_HenryFonda. Because this channel references the P_FundInvestors port and the FundInvestors document definition, you must retrieve their handles first.

The Retrieve_lDoc140002 function assigns the handle of the FundInvestors document to the lDoc140002 variable. It does this by first calling doc.LoadByName("FundInvestors") and then calling doc.handle() to return the document handle. Similar methods are called in the Retrieve_lPort160002 function to return the port handle to lPort160002. These object handles will be referenced when creating the C_FundInvestor_HenryFonda channel with the following code:

```
channel.InputDocument = lDoc140002
channel.OutputDocument = lDoc140002
channel.Port = lPort160002
```

 NOTE *Ignore the number that appears as part of the variable name and function name. The variable names are generated by combining the handle type and the ID that represents the object in the BizTalk Messaging database. The number in the variable name need not match the variable's value.*

With LoadByName() method, you can now create the script that updates the existing messaging configuration. In Chapter 11, you were introduced to BizTalk Messaging Configuration APIs, which allow you to programmatically add, modify, and delete the messaging configuration. The following is an example for updating a port's primary transport address to a different XLANG Schedule. For detailed information on this API, refer to Chapter 11.

```
Dim BTConf
Dim port
Set BTConf = CreateObject("BizTalk.BizTalkConfig")
Set port= BTConf.CreatePort

port.Clear
Port.LoadByName("P_FundInvestors")
port.PrimaryTransport.Address = "C:\Program Files\Microsoft BizTalk Server\
XLANG Scheduler\New_FundInvestors.skx"
port.Save
```

Now that you have looked at using scripts to deploy the BizTalk Messaging configuration, let's see how to deploy the general BizTalk Server configuration using scripts.

Deployment of BizTalk Server Configuration

Configuration for BizTalk Server refers to the three types of properties you are able to set using the BizTalk Messaging Administration Console:

- Receive Function properties

- BizTalk Server properties

- BizTalk Server Group properties

Windows Management Instrumentation (WMI), which you briefly saw in Chapter 12, is the tool for the job. You'll be creating a WMI script to set the properties of BizTalk Server.

To find out what BizTalk Server properties are available and can be configured with your WMI script, open the WMI CIM studio and connect to the root\MicrosoftBizTalkServer namespace to view the available classes, as shown in Figure 14-15.

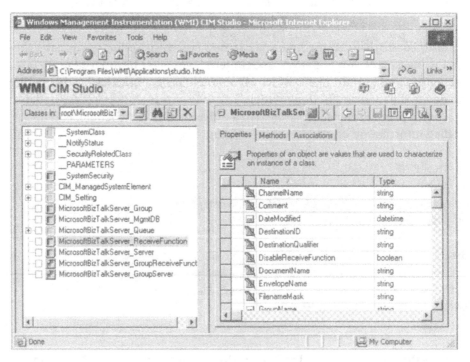

Figure 14-15. Viewing the available properties that can be set under the BizTalk Server namespace

Let's take a look at the each of the three type of configurations that you can modify with WMI.

Configuring Receive Function Properties

The BizTalk Server Configuration Assistant tool generates the VBScript for installing the Receive Functions on the target server. You can modify this code to create a helper function to add Receive Functions, as shown here:

```
dim WshNetwork
Set WshNetwork = WScript.CreateObject("WScript.Network")
servername=WshNetwork.ComputerName


CreateFileRcvFunc("file_pooling_" & servername, "BizTalk Server Group",
 servername, "C:\file_pooling",null,1,"File",null,"","","","",true,"*.xml ")


'A helper function for creating a receive function
Function CreateFileRcvFunc(strName, strGroupName, ProcessingServer,
 PollingLocation, strChannelName, nOpennessFlag, strRcvFuncType, strEnvelopeName,
 strSourceQualifier,strSourceID,strDestQualifier,strDestID,bdisable, strMask)

    On Error Resume Next
    Set WBEMLocator = CreateObject("WbemScripting.SWbemLocator")
    Set WBEMService = WBEMLocator.ConnectServer(, "root/MicrosoftBizTalkServer")
    Set objBTSRecvFunc= WBEMService.Get("MicrosoftBizTalkServer_ReceiveFunction")
    'create new instance of MicrosoftBizTalkServer_ReceiveFunction class
    Set objBTSRecvFuncInstance = objBTSRecvFunc.SpawnInstance_(0)

    strServername = servername
    objBTSRecvFuncInstance.groupname = strGroupName
    objBTSRecvFuncInstance.Name = strName
    strServername = servername
    If strRcvFuncType = "File" Then
        objBTSRecvFuncInstance.FilenameMask = strMask
        objBTSRecvFuncInstance.ProtocolType = 1 'ADMIN_PROTOCOL_TYPE_FILE
    ElseIf strRcvFuncType = "MSMQ" Then
        objBTSRecvFuncInstance.ProtocolType = 2 'ADMIN_PROTOCOL_TYPE_MSMQ
    End If
    objBTSRecvFuncInstance.ChannelName = strChannelName
    objBTSRecvFuncInstance.PollingLocation = PollingLocation
    objBTSRecvFuncInstance.ProcessingServer = ProcessingServer
    objBTSRecvFuncInstance.EnvelopeName = strEnvelopeName
```

```
            objBTSRecvFuncInstance.OpennessFlag = nOpennessFlag
            objBTSRecvFuncInstance.SourceQualifier = strSourceQualifier
            objBTSRecvFuncInstance.SourceID = strSourceID
            objBTSRecvFuncInstance.DestinationQualifier = strDestQualifier
            objBTSRecvFuncInstance.DestinationID = strDestID
            objBTSRecvFuncInstance.DisableReceiveFunction = bdisable
            'Create a new receive function.
            objBTSRecvFuncInstance.Put_ (2) ' Create
         'set objects to nothing after finish
End Function
```

To create a Receive Function, you first need to create an instance of the ReceiveFunction class with the following code:

```
Set WBEMLocator = CreateObject("WbemScripting.SWbemLocator")
Set WBEMService = WBEMLocator.ConnectServer(, "root/MicrosoftBizTalkServer")
Set objBTSRecvFunc= WBEMService.Get("MicrosoftBizTalkServer_ReceiveFunction")
Set objBTSRecvFuncInstance = objBTSRecvFunc.SpawnInstance_(0)
```

The first two lines connect to the namespace MicrosoftBizTalkServer, and the last two lines create an instance of the MicrosoftBizTalkServer_ReceiveFunction class, and you can set its properties values. After you set all the necessary properties, you can use the Put_ method on the instance to create or update the Receive Function.

Configuring BizTalk Server Properties

You can use WMI code similar to that for the Receive Function to create an instance of the MicrosoftBizTalkServer_Server class and modify its properties. The following code modifies several BizTalk Server properties:

```
Dim servername,WshNetWork
Set WshNetwork = WScript.CreateObject("WScript.Network")
servername=WshNetwork.ComputerName

Set WBEMLocator = CreateObject("WbemScripting.SWbemLocator")
Set WBEMService = WBEMLocator.ConnectServer(, "root/MicrosoftBizTalkServer")
Set objBTSsserver= WBEMService.Get("MicrosoftBizTalkServer_Server")
Set objBTSsserverInstance = objBTSsserver.SpawnInstance_()

objBTSsserverInstance.name="W2KSERVER"
objBTSsserverInstance.SchedulerWaitTime =5000
```

```
objBTSserverInstance.MaxRecvSvcThreadsPerProcessor = 10
objBTSserverInstance.MaxWorkerThreadsPerProcessor = 15
'must shut down the server first to save the changes.
objBTSserverInstance.StopServer()
objBTSserverInstance.put_(1)
objBTSserverInstance.startserver()
'set objects to nothing after finish
```

After running this script, you can verify the changes are saved by right-clicking the BizTalk Server icon, which in this example is W2KSERVER, and selecting Properties. The Properties window associated with the MicrosoftBizTalkServer_Server object comes up, as shown in Figure 14-16.

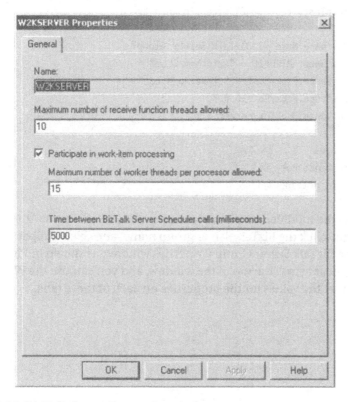

Figure 14-16. BizTalk Server Properties window

Configuring BizTalk Server Group Properties

There are great number of properties related to the BizTalk Server group. The following sample code will modify some of these properties through WMI:

```
Dim servername,WshNetWork
on error resume next
Set WshNetwork = WScript.CreateObject("WScript.Network")
servername=WshNetwork.ComputerName

Set WBEMLocator = CreateObject("WbemScripting.SWbemLocator")
Set WBEMService = WBEMLocator.ConnectServer(, "root/MicrosoftBizTalkServer")
Set objBTSgroup= WBEMService.Get("MicrosoftBizTalkServer_Group")
Set objBTSgroupInstance = objBTSgroup.SpawnInstance_

objBTSgroupInstance.Name = "BizTalk Server Group"
objBTSgroupInstance.SMTPHost = "smtp.home.com"
objBTSgroupInstance.ProxyHost = "proxy.home.com"
objBTSgroupInstance.ProxyPort = 8080
objBTSgroupInstance.UseProxyServer = 1

'Save the changes
objBTSgroupInstance.Put_ (1)
'set objects to nothing
```

To verify the modified configuration, open the BizTalk Server Administration Console, right-click the BizTalk Server group name, and select Properties. This will open the BizTalk Server Group Properties window, as shown in Figure 14-17. Four tabs appear across the top of the window, and you can use the WMI script to retrieve and set the values for the properties on each of these tabs.

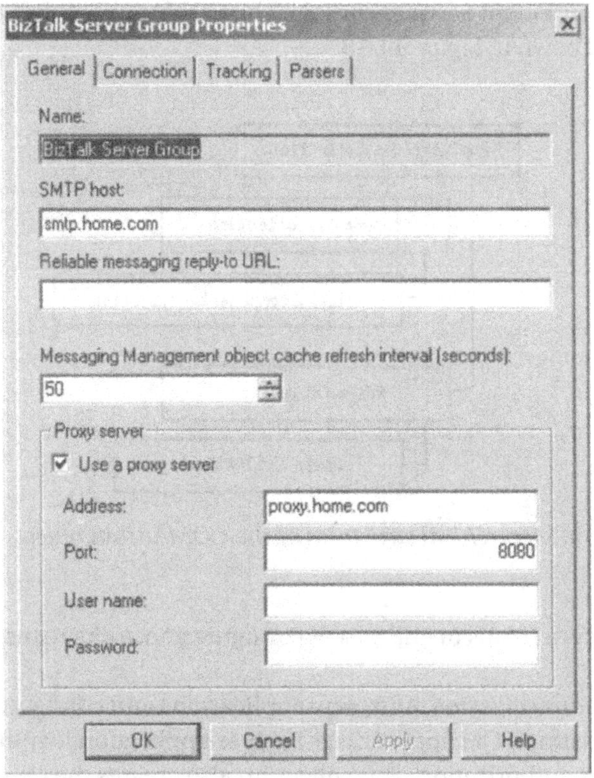

Figure 14-17. BizTalk Server Group Properties window

With the BizTalk Server configuration settled, the next topic I'll discuss is the deployment of the COM components.

Deployment of COM Components

A couple of sets of COM components are involved in a BizTalk Server application. First there is the BizTalk Server Interchange Application. In Chapter 12, I talked about how to enable role-based security on this component to allow only the intended clients to submit documents to BizTalk Server. You need a way to deploy the configuration of these role-based security properties on the component. The other set of components are the AICs used in a BizTalk application. If you make these AICs configured components, you also need a way to register them on the target BizTalk Server as such.

COMAdmin objects enable you to read and write information that is stored in the COM+ catalog. This allows you to script anything you are able to configure through the Component Services console. The COMAdmin object contains five collections, as shown in Figure 14-18.

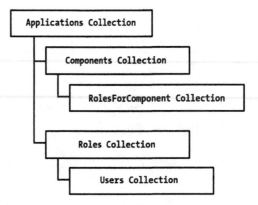

Figure 14-18. The hierarchical structures of the COMAdmin object

Each collection maps to one area of configuration, as its name implies:

- *Applications collection:* Adds new applications and configures the properties of existing COM applications, such as application identities and securities authorization. This collection also creates the Components collection and Roles collection.

- *Components collection:* Adds and configures the components under the application. This collection also creates the RolesForComponent collection.

- *Roles collection:* Creates and modifies roles under an application. This collection also creates the Users collection.

- *RolesForComponent collection:* Assigns the roles to components under the application.

- *Users collection:* Adds or removes Windows users from the roles of an application.

I'll discuss the deployment of COM components in two parts. The first part describes how to configure an existing component. The second part examines how to register a brand new component in COM+.

Configuring an Existing Application

Let's use the BizTalk Server Interchange Application as an example. The security setting on the component is turned off by default when you install BizTalk Server. You need to develop a script that will enable security, create roles, and assign those roles to the components of the application. The following sample code uses the COMAdmin to achieve this goal:

```
'define constant for the appid and class id used by
'BizTalk Server Interchange Application.
Const AppID = "{0C9B9BBE-E0F2-4485-9BE8-C40BAC8D0677}"
Const CLSID = "{7D2A8C8B-645C-11D2-B605-00C04FC30E1A}"
'Declare variables
'actual declaration omitted here

Set cat = CreateObject("COMAdmin.COMAdminCatalog")
'modify the properties of COM application
Set apps = cat.GetCollection("Applications")
apps.Populate
For Each app In apps
    If app.Name = "BizTalk Server Interchange Application" Then
        'must enable the modification on the application first.
        app.Value("Changeable") = 1
        app.Value("Deleteable") = 1
        apps.SaveChanges
        app.ApplicationAccessChecksEnabled = true
        app.AccessChecksLevel = 1 'access checks at process and component level
        apps.SaveChanges
        Exit For
    End If
Next

'Add a new role to the application
Set roles = apps.GetCollection("Roles", AppID)
Set role = roles.Add
role.Value("Name") = "MutualFundClients"
roles.SaveChanges

'Add two users under the "MutualFundClients" role
Set users = roles.GetCollection("UsersInRole", role.Key)
Set user = users.Add
user.Value("User") = "Home\HenryFonda"
Set user = users.Add
```

```
user.Value("User") = "Home\GaryCooper"
users.SaveChanges

'Specify the role-level access on the Interchange component
Set comps = apps.GetCollection("Components", AppID)
comps.Populate
'enable the access for "MutualFundClients" role to
'the Interchange component.
For Each comp In comps
    If comp.Key = CLSID Then
        Set RolesForComp = comps.GetCollection("RolesForComponent", CLSID)
        Set RoleForComp = RolesForComp.Add
        RoleForComp.Value("Name") = role.Name
        RolesForComp.SaveChanges
        Exit For
    End If
Next

'set objects to nothing
```

The preceding script performs four major actions:

- It makes the properties of the BizTalk Server Interchange Application editable.

- It creates a new role under the BizTalk Server Interchange Application called MutualFundClients.

- It creates two Windows users and adds them under the new role.

- It binds the new role to the Interchange component so that the MutualFundClients role can access it.

To change the application properties, the script first gets a reference to the COMAdminCatalog class, and then calls GetCollection("Applications") to get a list of the COM+ applications installed on the system. The script then loops through the applications to find one called BizTalk Server Interchange Application. After it finds this application, the properties Changeable and Deleteable are set to true so that further properties are allowed to be set. Because you need to make sure this application performs the access check, you need to set ApplicationAccessChecksEnabled to true and AccessChecksLevel to 1 so that access checks are performed on both the process level and component level.

After the script finishes the settings on the application level, it creates a role for the application. It first gets a reference to the roles collection of the application, which represents all the existing roles under this application. It then adds a new role called MutualFundClients.

The script then adds two Windows users to this new role. It calls GetCollection("UsersInRole", role.Key) to get a collection of all the users under the new role. The role.Key still refers to MutualFundClients at this point. The script then adds Home\HenryFonda and Home\GaryCooper to the user collection, and saves the change.

The last step in the script is to bind the new role, after filling it with real users, to the Interchange component. It first gets a collection of all the components under BizTalk Server Interchange Application and loops through them to find one that matches the Interchange component's CLSID. After you get the reference to the Interchange component, you call comps.GetCollection("RolesForComponent", CLSID) to get a collection of roles assigned to the Interchange component. You then add MutualFundClients to this collection and save the change.

Creating New Applications and Adding New Components

You can also use COMAdmin for creating new applications and adding new components to them.

If you have created and used AICs in your BizTalk application, you can choose to make them either unconfigured components or configured components. To make them unconfigured components, follow the instructions for registering AICs in Chapter 11.

Such procedures can also be scripted for automatic deployment. However, if you want to make the AICs take advantage of COM+, such as for security and transaction support, you should register them as configured COM+ components. I'll be focusing on deploying AICs as configured components in the following section.

To register the AIC as a configured component, you need to do two things. First, you need a COM+ application. (Creating this application is optional, though, since you can always add the AIC to an existing COM+ application.) Second, you need to add the AIC to the application.

The following code sample creates a COM+ application called "AIC Application" and installs the component SoapClient.dll under it:

```
Const AppID = "{B0895DB1-59B2-4888-88A8-B3CFA587EBF9}"
Const ComponentPath = "C:\Apress\Code\SOAPClientAIC\SoapClient.dll"

Dim AICApp
Set cat = CreateObject("COMAdmin.COMAdminCatalog")
```

```
Set apps = cat.GetCollection("Applications")
'Create a new COM+ application
Set AICApp= apps.Add
AICApp.Value("Name") = "AIC Application"
AICApp.Value("ID") = AppID
AICApp.Value("Description") = "Application that host AICs"
apps.SaveChanges.

'install the component under the application
cat.InstallComponent AppID, ComponentPath,"",""
'set objects to nothing
```

At the beginning of the script, you define two constants: one for the application ID, and the other for the file path of the DLL, which will be added to the application. The application ID is a GUID, and it's required when creating a COM+ application. This ID can be any GUID as long as it's unique.

To add the DLL to the application, you call the InstallComponent method on the COMAdminCatalog object and pass in the application ID and the file path for the DLL.

After the application is created and the component is added, you can also add code similar to that in an earlier code sample to modify the properties as needed.

To check the result of the script, open the Component Services console, locate AIC Application, and expand the node. There should be a component called SoapClient.AIC under it, as shown in Figure 14-19.

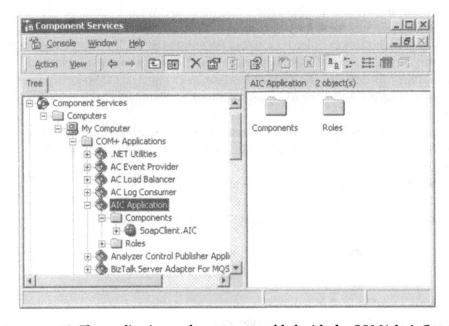

Figure 14-19. The application and component added with the COMAdminCatalog object

As you saw through the scripts using COMAdminCatalog, you're able to create deployment scripts for configured COM+ components that configure them as desired, with quite a bit of flexibility.

Deployment of MSMQ and File Folders

When you deploy Receive Functions that watch for MSMQ and file locations, it's your responsibility to deploy the message queues and file folders to meet the requirements of the Receive Functions. To create message queues and file folders through scripts, you can use the MSMQ object model and FileSystemObject.

The following code creates a message queue and file folder on the local machine:

```
CreateQueue (".\private$\IncomingMSMQ")
CreateFolder ("C:\temp\data")

Function CreateQueue(strpath)
on error resume next
    Dim msmqinfo
    set msmqinfo=Createobject("MSMQ.MSMQQueueInfo")
    msmqinfo.PathName = strpath
    msmqinfo.Create True, True 'a transactional and world readable queue
End Function

Function CreateFolder(strfolderpath)
on error resume next
    dim fileobj
    set fileobj=createobject("Scripting.FileSystemObject")
    If not fileobj.FolderExists(strfolderpath) Then
     fileobj.CreateFolder (strfolderpath)
    end if
end Function
```

For further details on the MSMQ object model, refer to Appendix A.

Summary of Script Deployment

As you've seen, four types of scripts are available to you.

The first type is the script that installs the BizTalk Messaging configurations. You can either create a single script that installs any message configuration, or create two separate scripts as a base script and an add-on script. The base script installs the configuration that isn't client specific, and the add-on script installs the configuration that is associated with specific clients. By developing a two-script deployment strategy, you can install the configuration for new clients without deleting the existing Messaging configuration on BizTalk Server.

The second type is the script that installs the BizTalk Server Receive Functions and configures the properties for both BizTalk Server groups and BizTalk Server through the use of the WMI's MicrosoftBizTalkServer namespace.

The third type of script installs and configures the COM+ application and the components that are involved in the BizTalk application by using the COMAdminCatalog object.

The last type of script creates the necessary message queues and file folders to be used by the BizTalk Server Receive Functions.

Summary

This chapter focuses on the deployment of BizTalk Server applications. You examined several elements related to deployment: infrastructure, files, and configuration.

In terms of the actual deployment implementation, you saw deployment through Application Center. You then learned how to create a more flexible deployment through using a two-script deployment strategy: base script and add-on script.

With the BizTalk Server API, WMI, and COMAdmin object model, you're now equipped with all the tools needed for scripting BizTalk Messaging configuration, BizTalk Server configuration, and COM+ configuration.

This lengthy discussion of BizTalk Server 2002 is almost over. In the last chapter, I'll show you what you can do to keep your BizTalk Server application in good shape after it starts running in production.

CHAPTER 15

BizTalk Server with Microsoft Operations Manager

THE EARLIER CHAPTERS OF THIS BOOK dealt with designing, developing, and deploying BizTalk applications. In this last chapter of the book, I'll focus on the management side of BizTalk Server operations. This chapter deals with what happens after the BizTalk Server application is deployed to the production environment.

What exactly happens after the application is deployed? You need to monitor the performance of the application as it runs on BizTalk Server. You also want to be notified when a problem or error event occurs on the server, so that you can react accordingly to resolve whatever the problem may be.

BizTalk Server doesn't come with tools that perform such management and maintenance tasks. To handle these tasks after the BizTalk Server application is deployed, you need some type of software management tool to help you monitor and maintain the application. There are quite a few such tools on the market. One that stands out is a separate Microsoft product called Microsoft Operations Manager, a.k.a. MOM. BizTalk Server comes with a MOM package, which allows you to implement and deploy management services for BizTalk Server very easily.

Introducing MOM

MOM is a monitoring and management tool that can help you know exactly what problems occur on the server and also give you the ability to automate reactions for some such problems. This feature enables you to react to these problems proactively.

Use MOM's performance monitoring capabilities to find out how well your application runs on the server, and set up actions to be performed when certain performance counters fall below critical levels.

MOM can handle events in computer groups as well as in individual computers. This consolidates the information about computers that perform similar tasks and simplifies the monitoring of services provided by a group of computers.

MOM also comes with a comprehensive reporting tool and a Web Administrator Console that allows you great flexibility in monitoring and managing the application from remote locations.

MOM contains six major components:

- *Agent:* This service runs on the machine you want to monitor, and it will communicate with the Consolidator to get the latest processing rules. The agent is also responsible for processing the rules and collecting the events and performance data, and sending them to the Consolidator.

- *Agent Manager:* This service will install, uninstall, and configure the agents installed on the computers.

- *Consolidator:* This service is responsible for sending the updated processing rules down to the agents' computers, and sending the information collected from the agents' computers to the Data Access Server (DAS). The Consolidator can also function as an agent.

- *Data Access Server:* This service acts as an interface between the MOM central database and the other components that need to update and retrieve data from this central database, such as the Consolidator, MOM Administrator Console, and MOM Web console.

- *MOM Web console:* This is a Web application installed as part of MOM. It provides a way for people to manage MOM through the Internet or an intranet.

- *MOM central database:* This database contains all the configuration information, and information collected from the monitored computers.

The relationship among these six MOM components is illustrated in Figure 15-1.

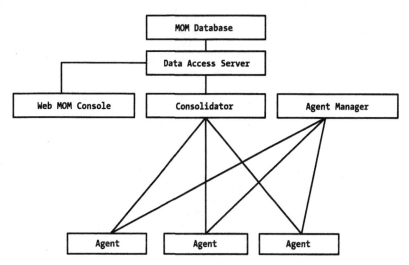

Figure 15-1. Relationship among the different MOM components

Before MOM can monitor your application for you, you must set up MOM to start watching for the server you want to monitor and manage. I'll walk you through a series of procedures to set MOM up to monitor a couple of BizTalk Servers running Bob's ASP application.

Setting Up MOM

Mike has successfully deployed Bob's application to the production environment, which is a server-hosting facility at a remote location. Mike wants to use MOM to notify him of error events that occur on his BizTalk Servers. He also wants to set it up to perform specific actions for certain known error events. Bob has also requested a weekly report on the performance of and problems with his newly deployed ASP application.

Figure 15-2 outlines what Mike has in mind to get the job done using MOM.

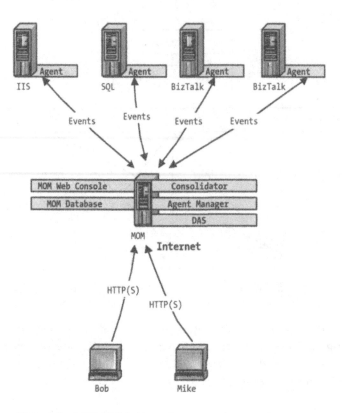

Figure 15-2. Using the MOM Web Console to monitor and manage servers at a remote location

There are five steps for setting up MOM to monitor and manage the servers:

1. Install MOM

2. Install Agents on the machines you want to monitor

3. Create computer groups

4. Create event processing rules, alert processing rules, performance processing rules, and the responses for the rules

5. Assign the rules to the computer groups

After you complete these five steps, MOM will finally be ready to do its work.

Installing MOM

With exception of Agent Manager and Consolidator, which have to be installed on the same server, you can distribute these MOM components to multiple systems to boost the performance.

During the installation of MOM, you'll be asked to choose the type of installation. If you want to install only some of the components on the server, you'll choose a Custom installation, which will prompt you with the window shown in Figure 15-3, where you can select the components you want to install. For the purposes of this chapter, you'll install everything on the same server. Click Next to continue.

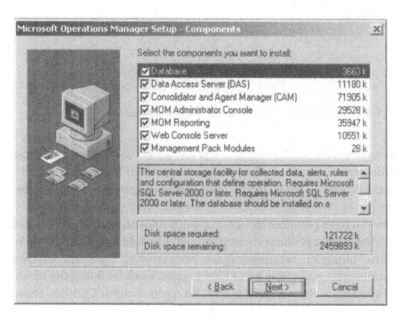

Figure 15-3. Choosing one or more components to be installed on the system

In the following window, you are asked to provide the user account for the Data Access Server, Consolidator, and Agent Manager, as shown in Figure 15-4.

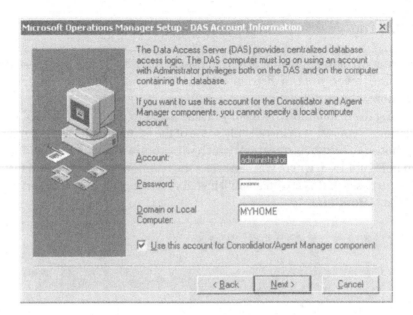

Figure 15-4. Specifying the user account for the services

You must specify a user account that has access to the DAS and database server. You can also make the Consolidator and Agent Manager run under the same user account by checking the checkbox at the bottom of the window. Then click Next.

Once you have provided the user account information, MOM Setup starts installing the software. When it completes, you should find that the Microsoft Operations Manager program group has been created. There are two items in it: MOM Administrator Console and MOM Report. You'll be doing the rest of the configuration and setup through this MOM Administrator Console, shown in Figure 15-5.

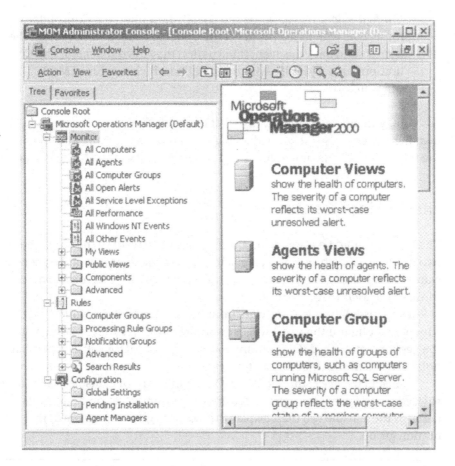

Figure 15-5. MOM Administrator Console

The MOM Administrator Console window is divided into two panels. The left panel has three major categories: Monitor, Rules, and Configuration. These categories function as follows:

- *Monitor:* This contains different views of the data concerning events, alerts, and performance counters that have been collected from the machines on MOM's watch list. You can also define customized views. For example, you could create a view on the events generated by all the BizTalk Servers you have, and ignore the events from other servers.

- *Rules:* This contains all the defined rules that are available in MOM. These rules are categorized into different groups, and MOM will assign the rules to the agent computers according to their computer type. For example, MOM can apply the BizTalk Server rules to the all the BizTalk Servers on the network, and the IIS rules to all the IIS servers on the network.

- *Configuration:* This is where you specify how often the Consolidator communicates with its agents to get the updated rules, and how often the agents send back the event information they have collected. The Configuration category is also where you define which machines MOM will watch.

After you have successfully installed MOM on the server, the next step is to install the agents. As you learned earlier, the agents are responsible for collecting the information on their machines and sending it back to the MOM Consolidator.

Installing the Agents

The agents should be installed on the machines you want to monitor. There are two ways to install the agent on a machine. You can either install the agent software through the MOM CD-ROM, or you can install the agent on the machine through the MOM Administrator Console.

If you install the agent software from the MOM CD-ROM, you need to specify which Consolidator the agent will communicate with. However, when you install the agent through the MOM Administrator Console, MOM will automatically notify the agent which Consolidator to use.

To install the agent through the MOM Administrator Console, open the console, click the Agent Managers folder under the Configuration node, and the right panel of the console will then display the existing Agent Managers in this configuration group.

NOTE *The configuration group is used to uniquely identify the MOM server on the network. Each configuration group must have a MOM central database, one or more Agent Managers and Consolidators, one or more DAS, and one or more agents. In other words, the MOM components within a given configuration group will write and read from the same MOM central database.*

Right-click the Agent Manager and select Properties to open the Agent Manager Properties window, shown in Figure 15-6.

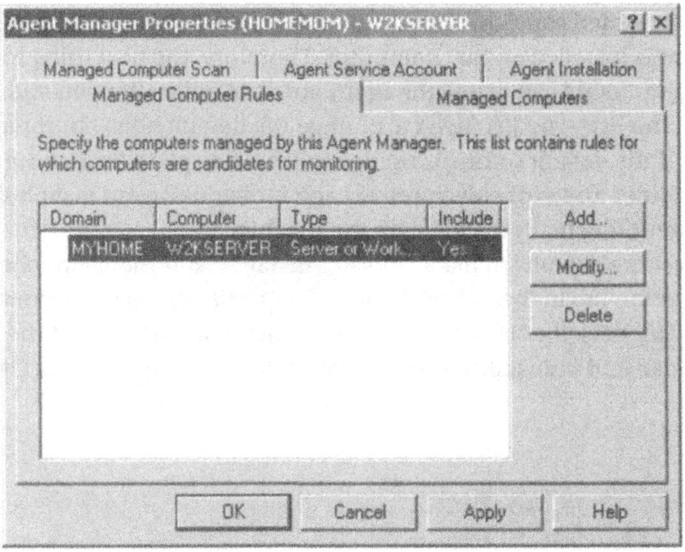

Figure 15-6. Specifying computers to be managed by the Agent Manager

You must configure a number of important properties for the Agent Manager. First, you need to add the computers that can be managed by this Agent Manager. In Figure 15-6, there is only one machine, W2KSERVER, on the list. To add another machine to MOM's watch list, click the Add button on the right. A Computers window opens, asking for the details about the computer to be added, as shown in Figure 15-7.

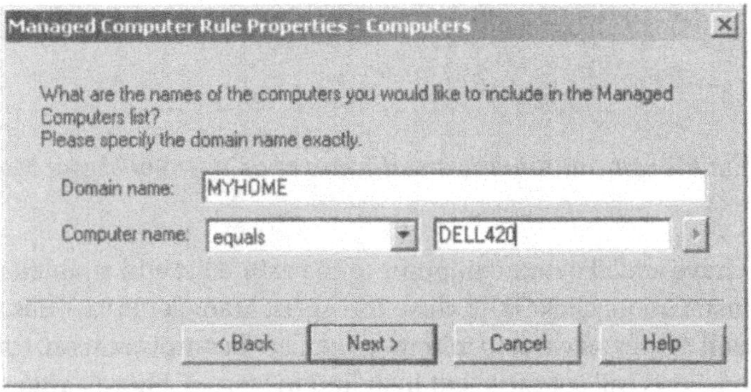

Figure 15-7. Adding a new computer to the watch list

You can either provide an exact computer name or an expression. For example, if you specify "Computer name matches wildcard BizTalk*", this will include all the computers whose names start with "BizTalk". The rest of the steps are straightforward.

The newly added computer is still not able to participate in MOM's activity until an agent is installed on that computer. Therefore, the next thing to do is install an agent. MOM can install the agent automatically after you add the computer to the list—you just need to change the default behavior for agent installation. If the default setting is used, you'll have to go to the Pending Installation folder and explicitly approve each individual agent installation before the agent is actually installed on the machine.

To change the default so that agents are installed automatically, click the Agent Installation tab in the Agent Manager Properties window, as shown in Figure 15-8. Uncheck the "Use global settings" checkbox, and select the "Automatically install and uninstall agents as required" radio button. Click OK to save the changes.

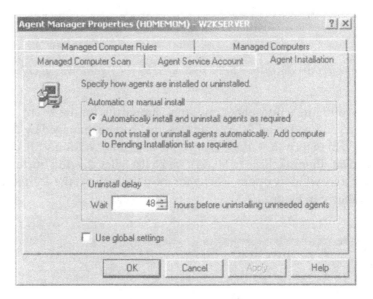

Figure 15-8. Enabling the automatic installation of an agent on Agent Manager

After you have added a new computer to the watch list and enabled automatic agent installation, click OK to close the Agent Manager Properties window. A dialog box will ask if you want to initiate a managed computer scan. Click Yes to perform a scan—this will get the agent installation started. Shortly after the computer scan, you should see the new computer appear on the Managed Computers tab, as shown in Figure 15-9.

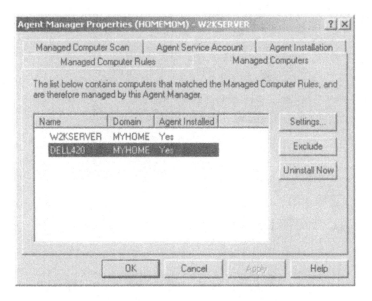

Figure 15-9. The list of computers with agents installed

Notice that in Figure 15-9, the value in the Agent Installed column for Dell420 is Yes. This means the agent has been successfully installed on the machine, and Dell420 can start participating in whatever MOM activities are defined in its rules. If you log on to Dell420 and check its Service console, you would find that a service called OnePoint has been installed and started. This OnePoint service is actually the MOM agent service.

NOTE *Microsoft bought a software management tool from NetIQ and rebranded it for MOM. OnePoint is the name of the service used in the NetIQ product, and that name is still referenced in many places within MOM.*

Setting the Agent Properties

Now that the agent is installed, you can customize the agent's properties. Such properties include how often the agent will send event and performance data, how often the agent checks its system's service availability, etc.

To customize an agent on a specific computer, bring up the Agent Manager Properties on that computer and click the Managed Computers tab (shown in Figure 15-9). Then, click the Settings button on the right to open its Properties window, as shown in Figure 15-10.

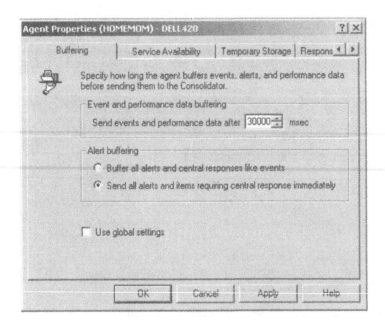

Figure 15-10. Customizing the settings for the agent

The properties shown in this window are grayed out by default. To make them editable, you must first uncheck the Use global settings checkbox at the bottom of the window. If you want to change settings for all the agents installed on all the computers watched by MOM, you can modify the global settings of the agent. To do so, right-click the Global setting folder and select Edit agent setting.

You can also configure the global settings of the MOM server. Such configurations include information on where the MOM Web Console is located, what e-mail server is used to send out the alert, and what network port is used for communication between agent computers and their Consolidators. To configure these settings, open the MOM Administrator Console and right-click the Global Settings folder under the Configuration category, and select Edit general settings to open the Configuration Group Global Settings window shown in Figure 15-11.

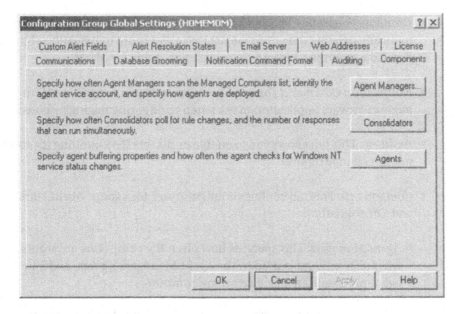

Figure 15-11. Configuring the global settings of MOM

Here is a quick description of what you can do on the tabs in this window:

- *Custom Alert Fields:* This tab allows you to define fields that are displayed in alerts. Any alerts generated in the configuration group will contain these fields.

- *Alert Resolution States:* This tab allows you to add and modify the alert resolution states for the generated alerts. Resolution states— New, Acknowledged, Resolved, etc.—indicate whether you have begun to resolve the alert.

- *Email Server:* This tab allows you to specify the e-mail settings used by the Consolidator to send e-mail responses.

- *Web Addresses:* This tab allows you to specify the location of the Web Console and any reports saved to the Web.

- *License:* This tab displays the license information and applies a new license file or product key.

- *Communications:* This tab allows you to specify the TCP/IP ports, both encrypted and unencrypted, that agents will use when communicating with the Consolidators.

- *Database Grooming:* This tab allows you to specify parameters for automatically deleting data from the database. For more information about database grooming, refer to the installation guide for MOM.

- *Notification Command Format:* This tab allows you to specify a third-party paging software application to use when configuring paging responses.

- *Auditing:* This tab allows you to enable or disable DAS auditing for configuration change reports.

- *Components:* This tab contains configurations for agents, Agent Managers, and Consolidators:

  - *Agent Managers:* This specifies how often the computers are scanned, what user account is used by the Agent Manager's agents, and how the agent programs are installed on the computers.

  - *Consolidators:* This specifies how often Consolidators poll for rule changes, the number of responses that can run simultaneously, and how the Consolidator buffers data.

  - *Agents:* This specifies the agent's buffering properties, heartbeat parameters, and other communication properties.

 NOTE Heartbeat *is a term used figuratively in MOM to represent a signal that agents broadcast to other systems as an indication that they are up and running.*

You have just installed an agent on a computer. This computer now has all the equipment for processing the rules you define for it. But before you start creating the rules, you need to consolidate the computers that provide the same service into one group, so that it is easy to manage.

Creating Computer Groups

Creating a computer group requires you to first identify the computers of similar types. For instance, in Bob's case, two BizTalk Servers are providing services to clients as a whole. Instead of dealing with each BizTalk Server, you can put all the BizTalk Servers into group, and monitor the events and performance of this group. When you want certain rules to be executed on each BizTalk Server, you only need to create and deploy the rules for the group (this is a computer group in the context of MOM, not a BizTalk Server group) rather than deploy them for individual BizTalk Servers on the network. You'll next create a computer group called Bob's BizTalk Servers and place the two BizTalk Servers into that group.

Creating the Group

Open the MOM Administrator Console, select the Computer Groups folder under the Rules category, and the console will list all the existing computer groups set up by MOM, as shown in Figure 15-12.

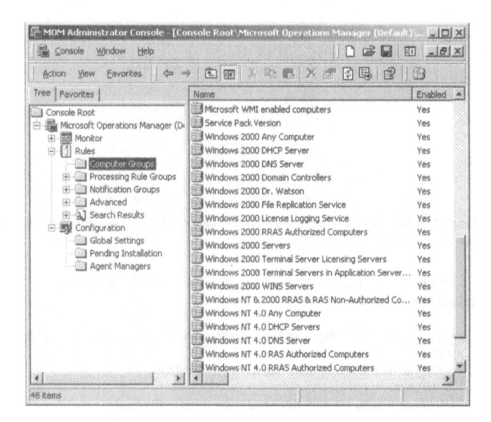

Figure 15-12. MOM's Computer Groups list

Right-click the Computer Groups folder and select Create Computer Groups. A new window opens, asking for the type of computers that are to be included in this group. Check the checkbox next to Windows NT Server, and click Next.

In the next window, select the radio button next to All Computers and click Next to continue.

In the next window, you'll specify the kind of computers that will be included in your new computer group. This window is shown in Figure 15-13. Here is where you define the formula that MOM will use to get a collection of computers that fit the definitions. By deciding what formula to use here, you can choose the target computers for your computer rules.

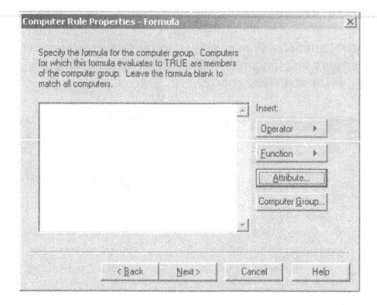

Figure 15-13. Specifying which computers will be included as the members of the new computer group

MOM allows you to specify what computers are part of this new group through three methods:

- You can include computers from other groups in this new computer group.

- You can include computers that have certain attributes.

- You can specifically add individual computers to the group.

You can also use a combination of the three methods to define which computers are included in the group.

Adding Computers from an Existing Group

To add all the computers from an existing computer group, click the Computer Group button and select the groups to add from a list of computer groups. For example, if you add the Internet Information Server 5 group and Windows 2000 Domain controller group to the new group, then the new group would automatically include machines that have IIS 5 installed, and the machines that are domain controllers. Because there is no such group that contains only BizTalk Servers, this method of adding existing groups won't help you include only the BizTalk Server machines in your group.

Adding Computers by Attribute

MOM provides you with a way to define computer attributes, After you do so, MOM will then search all the computers on its watch list to find the ones that match the attributes, and put them into the group. An attribute, in MOM, is nothing more than some characteristic registry key of a machine.

To create an attribute or select an existing attribute for the group, click the Attribute button. A new window will open, listing existing attributes on the system. Click the New button on the right to create a new attribute that uniquely identifies the BizTalk Servers only. The window shown in Figure 15-14 will be displayed.

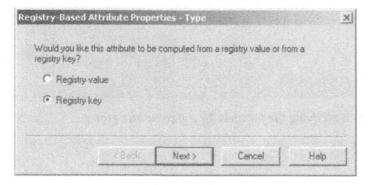

Figure 15-14. Configuring a registry-based attribute

You can create an attribute to check either for the existence of a registry key or for the value of a registry key. Because all computers that have BizTalk Server 2002 Enterprise Edition installed will contain the registry key HKEY_LOCAL_MACHINE\SOFTWARE\Microsoft\BizTalk Server\1.0, you can identify whether a computer is a BizTalk Server by checking for the existence of this key. Therefore, you can select the Registry key radio button and click Next. You'll then need to provide information on the registry location, and give a name for the new attribute. For the purposes of this example, call it Bob's BizTalk Servers.

After you have created the new attribute, you need to select it as the qualification for the computers to be included in this new group. Figure 15-15 shows the format for inputting the attribute condition. RegistryChecker is the name of the attribute. If you want to use multiple attributes and conditions to define the computer group, you can use the Operator and Function buttons to assemble a more complex formula. The Operator button provides operators such as And, Or, Not, etc. The Function button provides the MatchWildcard and MatchRegEx functions.

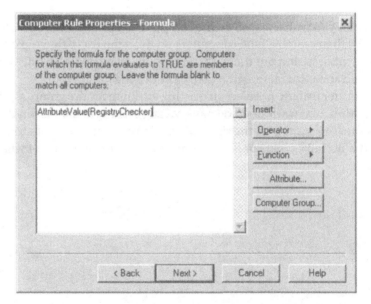

Figure 15-15. Specifying the formula for the computer group

Adding Individual Computers

You also can add additional computers to the group that may not match the specified attributes. When creating a computer group, you'll see an Included Computers window, as shown in Figure 15-16. This is the window you use to add any computer you want to the computer group. Just click the Add button, and specify the name of the computer to be included in the group. This gives you more flexibility in terms of what computers are included in the group.

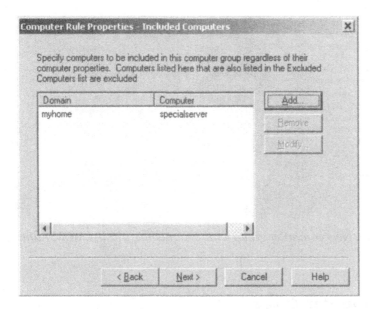

Figure 15-16. Including additional computers in the computer group

Naming the Computer Group

At the end, after specifying the computers in the group, you need to provide a name for your group. For this example, call it Bob's BizTalk Computer Group. You can then make the Agent Manager scan all the computers to determine which computers qualify as members of the new computer group. Figure 15-17 shows that MOM has indicated two computers as members of Bob's BizTalk Computer Group.

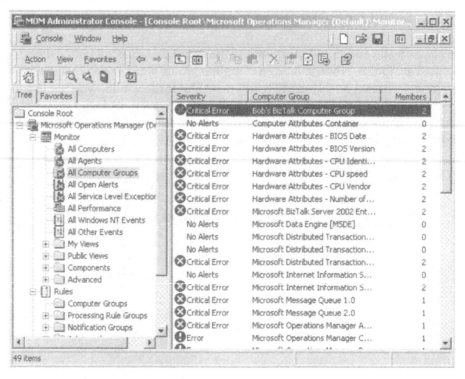

Figure 15-17. New computer group with two members in the MOM Administrator Console

Viewing Computer Groups

To view the existing computer groups, their member counters, and overall error status, click the All Computer Groups folder under the Monitor category, in the MOM Administrator Console. In Figure 15-17, you can see that Bob's BizTalk Computer Group contains two members, and that errors have occurred in the group. To get the details of the events, double-click the computer group to open the detail window, where the status for each member server is displayed,as shown in Figure 15-18. You can also double-click each individual computer shown in Figure 15-18 to view the detailed event logs for the computer.

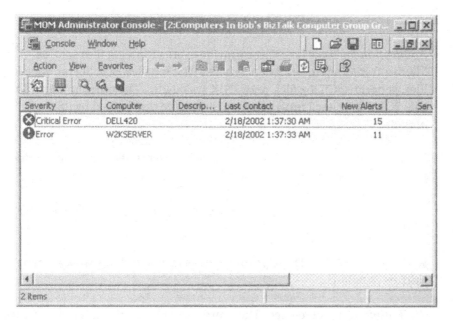

Figure 15-18. Member servers of the computer group and their status information

Creating Processing Rules

After you have added computers to the group, the next step is creating the processing rules for the new group. A *processing rule* specifies what actions the computer will take when certain events occur. There are three types of processing rules:

- Event processing rules

- Alert processing rules

- Performance processing rules

To understand processing rules, though, you must first understand MOM providers.

MOM Providers

MOM collects information about computers from a number of providers. MOM providers provide runtime information to the processing rules so that these rules can decide whether or not to perform certain actions.

There are seven types of MOM providers:

- *Application log providers:* These provide events from log files such as Microsoft Internet Information Services (IIS) log files, SQL Server trace log files, generic ASCII log files, and UNIX syslog files. The other application (IIS, SQL Server, etc.) must generate the log file that is used by this provider.

- *Windows Event Log providers:* These provide events generated by Windows, such as the events that are displayed in the Event Viewer console.

- *Timed event providers:* These provide events generated by MOM at scheduled times.

- *WMI event providers:* These provide events from Windows Management Instrumentation.

- *WMI numeric data providers:* These provide sampled WMI numeric values.

- *Performance counter providers:* These provide the performance statistics for a number of applications.

- *Generic providers:* These provide events that MOM generates internally, such as when an agent heartbeat doesn't occur on time.

It is important to understand where the event data is coming from when you define the processing rules, because the rules will expect a specific type of data to come from the providers.

For example, if you want to take some action when the database connection between BizTalk Server and the database server is dropped, you need to know that this event will be raised in the Windows Event Log so you can define the processing rules to capture this information from the Windows Event Log provider. Or, if you want to be notified when the BizTalk Server suspended queue contains more than 10 items, you need to create a processing rule that receives information from the WMI numeric events. Even through the Windows Event Log records that a document is sent to the suspended queue, there is no way to make the Windows Event Log raise an event when the suspended document count reaches 10.

Types of Processing Rules

You can create three types of processing rules in MOM:

- *Event processing rules:* These allow you to react to events from numerous MOM providers. The possible reactions to such events include executing a script, notifying user groups, etc. The majority of processing rules are event processing rules.

- *Alert processing rules:* These allow you to consolidate the alerts that are raised by event processing rules and treat them in a collective manner.

  For example, there may be many alerts raised by event processing rules, and some of them will be more important than others. You can set up a few alert processing rules to process all the outstanding alerts. For example, management teams could be notified when alerts from BizTalk Server with a severity of critical error occurs, and developer teams could be notified when alerts that are less severe occur. You can also set up notifications for each processing rule; however, this would be very difficult to manage, since you would have to configure each event processing rule to send alerts to the notification group individually. With alert processing rules, you only need to set up a couple of rules (depending on the situation) to process all the notifications you need.

- *Performance processing rules:* These include two types of rules. The first type is the measuring type, these will generate statistics on the performance of agent computers, which can be used to create performance charts and reports. The second type is the threshold type, which will allow you to define certain actions to be taken when certain performance statistics fall below or rise above specific levels.

Let's look at how you can create these processing rules in MOM.

Creating Event Processing Rules

From time to time, Bob gets complaints from his clients who claim they didn't get a response document. It turns out that the reason some response documents are never returned is that the original documents didn't comply with the document specification.

Normally it takes hours, if not days, to get back to clients about what happened to their document. Bob wants to handle this type of problem so that the invalid documents are automatically sent back to the original client with a reason for the failure. By processing the invalid documents automatically, clients can get an instant reply about what is wrong with their document, and they can correct it and resubmit it quickly. Bob wants Mike to use MOM to handle this job.

Mike wants to develop an event processing rule that triggers when an error event associated with document validation failure occurs, and he also wants to run a script on the BizTalk Server to retrieve the invalid document and send a copy of the document content, along with the error description, back to the original sender. The event processing rule will also raise an alert to inform the management team about the situation. You'll see how all this is done through MOM.

Creating the Processing Rule Group

The first thing I'll show you how to do is create a processing rule group, which will be used for all the future rules that come from Bob. Open the MOM console, right-click the Processing Rules folder under the Rules category, and select Create Processing Rule group. A new window will open—enter **Bob's Rule** as the name, and click OK to save it.

Creating the Event Processing Rule

Under the Bob's Rule folder, right-click the Event Processing Rules folder and select New ➤ Event Processing Rule. A Select Event Processing Rule Type window opens, as shown in Figure 15-19.

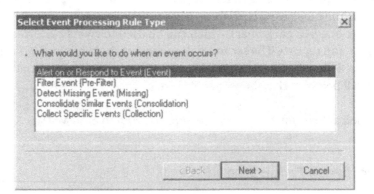

Figure 15-19. Selecting the type for the new event processing rule

There are five types of event processing rules to choose from:

- *Alert on or respond to event:* This allows MOM to raise an alert or run a response when specific events occur. This is the most common type of event processing rule.

- *Filter event:* This allows MOM to block certain kinds of events that aren't considered important by the MOM user.

- *Detect missing event:* This allows MOM to raise an alert and run a response when certain events don't occur at a specific time.

- *Consolidate similar events:* This allows MOM to group multiple similar events on an agent computer into a single summary event. MOM stores summary events in the database.

- *Collect specific events:* This allows MOM to identify events with specific criteria to be collected from specific sources.

Because you want to raise an alert and run a response when a document invalidation error occurs, you need to create an event processing rule of the Alert or Respond to Event type. Click that type and click Next.

Specifying the Event

The next window, shown in Figure 15-20, asks for the MOM provider that provides the information for this event processing rule. When a document invalidation error occurs on BizTalk Server, BizTalk Server always raises an error event under the Application event of Windows Event Log. Therefore, you need to select Application as the Provider name ("Application" represents the Application log under Windows NT Event Log) for this event processing rule. Click Next.

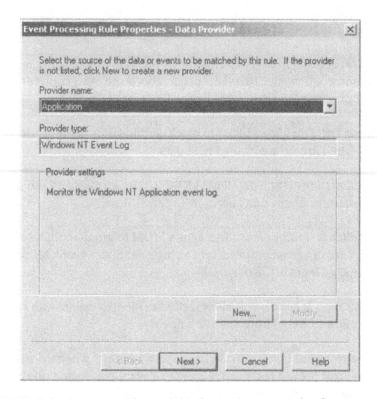

Figure 15-20. Selecting a provider as the information source for the new event processing rule

The next window, shown in Figure 15-21, asks for information about this error event. This is where you tell MOM how to identify a BizTalk Server document invalidation error. When the information you provide here matches an event MOM receives from its agents, this event processing rule will be triggered.

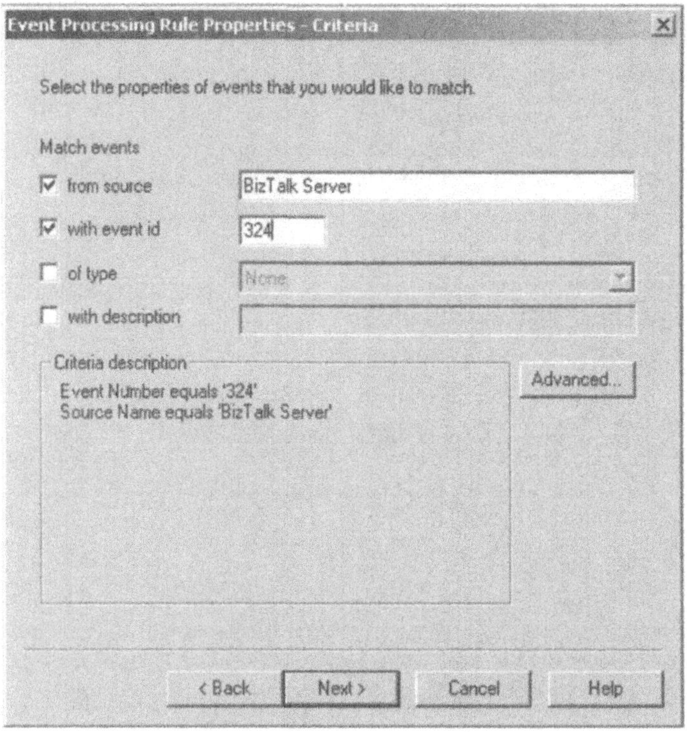

Figure 15-21. Providing the detail information on the event for the event processing rule

To be able to provide this detail information, you need to know the error event better. If you go through the Event Viewer on BizTalk Server, you should be able to find an earlier error that related to document invalidation. Figure 15-22 shows an example of a document invalidation error that occurred on the BizTalk Server. You can study this error and get some of its characteristic information, such as Event ID, Event Source, etc.

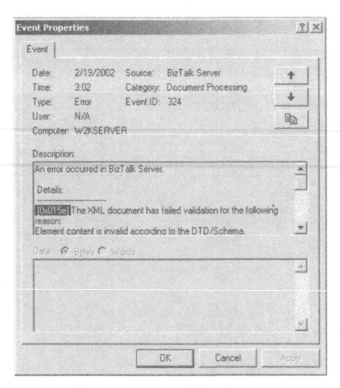

Figure 15-22. A document invalidation error on BizTalk Server

Comparing Figure 15-21 and Figure 15-22, you can see that much of the information required by MOM to create an event processing rule is shown in a typical Windows event. However, only providing the event source, event type, and event ID isn't enough for MOM to uniquely identify a document validation–related event, since there are many BizTalk Server events with the same properties. However, notice the highlighted code in the event description in Figure 15-22. This code is the ID that identifies it as a document validation–related error. You must make this code a part of the matching criteria for this event processing rule.

The description field in Figure 15-21 must match the event exactly, in order to be considered a match. You won't use this field to identify the event; instead click the Advanced button to add more matching criteria for this event processing rule. Figure 15-23 shows this Advanced Criteria window.

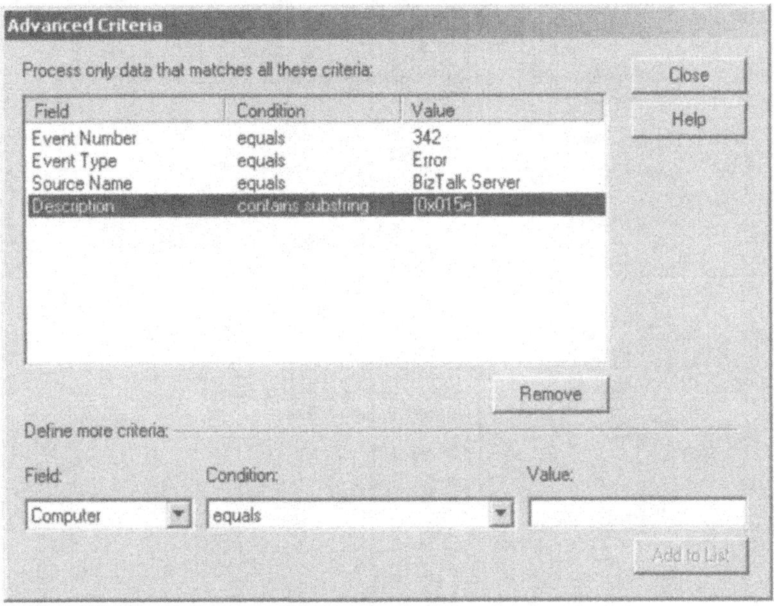

Figure 15-23. Providing additional information to help MOM identify the event

In the Define more criteria section at the bottom of the window, you can define additional matching criteria. As you can see in Figure 15-23, I have added Description contains substring [0x015e] to the list of criteria. This ensures that this event processing rule will trigger only when all four conditions shown in Figure 15-23 are met. Click Close to save the changes.

Defining an Alert

After you have modified the matching criteria, you have a chance to specify whether an alert will be raised when the event processing rule is triggered, as shown in Figure 15-24.

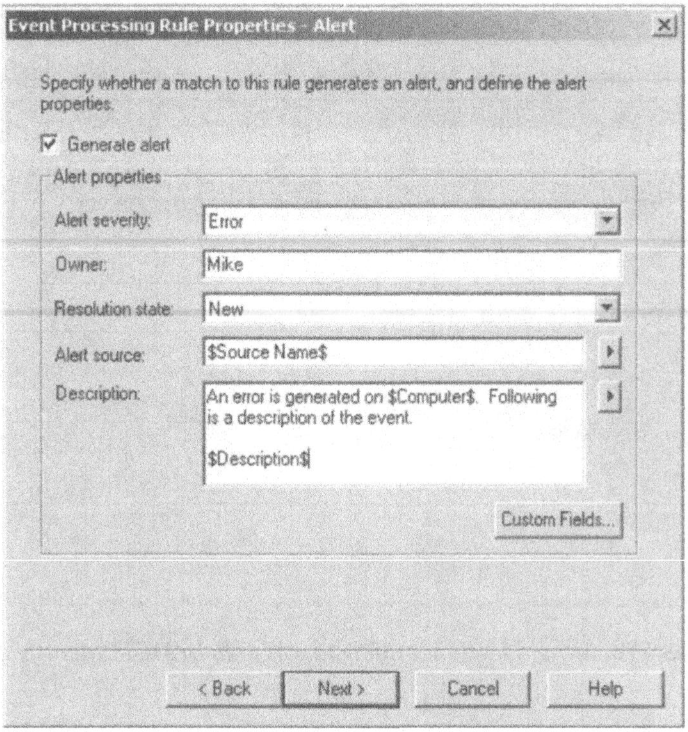

Figure 15-24. Generating an alert for the event processing rule

In this Alert window, the variables are surrounded with dollar signs ($). These variables hold the information MOM obtains at runtime about the particular event. For example, $Description$ represents the description text of the error event you saw in Figure 15-22. You can also customize the values for the fields that appear in the Alert Properties section of the window by clicking the arrow buttons next to the Alert source and Description fields. This allows you to choose different variables from the pop-up menu. Click Next to go to the Alert Suppression window, shown in Figure 15-25.

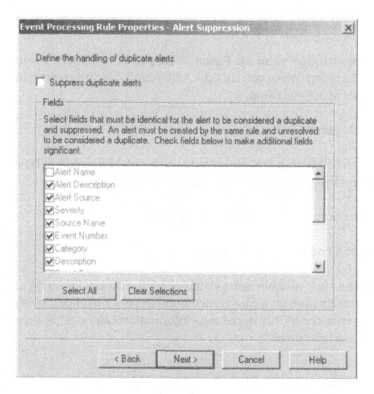

Figure 15-25. Defining the handling of duplicated alerts

In the Alert Suppression window, shown in Figure 15-25, you can suppress duplicate alerts. When you check the Suppress duplicate alerts checkbox, MOM will drop alerts if they match an outstanding or unresolved alert. For example, if there are 10 invalid document error events being generated by BizTalk Server, the event processing rule you are defining will generate 10 alerts. In some situations, one alert is enough to direct people's attention to the problem, and many duplicated alerts indicating the same problem may cause unnecessary management concern. In such situations, you can suppress the duplicate alerts of an event processing rule so that only unique alerts are raised.

The alerts generated by an event processing rule are considered unique when the selected fields of the alert are identical to those of an existing unresolved alert. You can modify this selection of fields to change the rules that determine the uniqueness of the alert by checking or unchecking the checkboxes in the Fields section in Figure 15-25. You want to be alerted about every invalid document in this case, so you won't suppress duplicated alerts for this event processing rule. Click Next to continue.

Specifying the Response Actions

The Responses window, shown in Figure 15-26, provides you with the means to respond to the event. When you click the Add button, a pop-up menu appears, with five types of actions listed:

- Launch a script.

- Send an SNMP trap (SNMP, or Simple Network Management Protocol, is a network protocol used to manage TCP/IP networks).

- Send a notification to a notification group.

- Execute a command and batch file.

- Update a state variable (state variables are the means for MOM to store state information on either agent computers or Consolidators when certain events occur. This stored state information can be retrieved and acted upon at a later time).

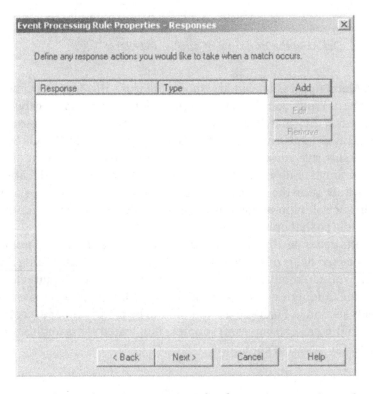

Figure 15-26. Defining the response actions for the event processing rule

Since Mike wants to be notified, and he wants to run a script to send back the invalid document to the client, he needs to define two response actions. On the pop-up menu, you need to select the "Send a notification to a notification group" option. The window shown in Figure 15-27 will open.

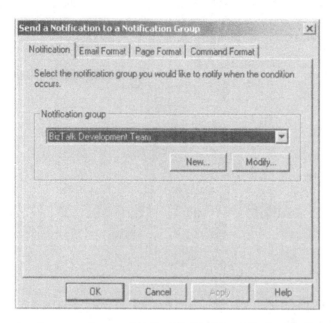

Figure 15-27. Configuring the notification for the event processing rule

In the window shown in Figure 15-27, you can specify which group you want to notify, and the format of the notification. The notification can be sent through either e-mail, pager, or in a third-party format. There are several predefined notification groups in MOM. (These are logical groups for MOM, used for grouping many operators into a single unit; the groups aren't the same as NT groups). Select the notification group you want to use; in this case, it would be BizTalk Development Team, and click OK.

You can also create your own customized notification group. To create a notification group, click the New button in the window shown in Figure 15-27, and a Notification Group Properties window will open, as shown in Figure 15-28. You can add existing operators, shown in the Available Operators list, to the new notification group's Group Operators list, by clicking the left arrow button between the lists. Click the New Operator button to create a new operator.

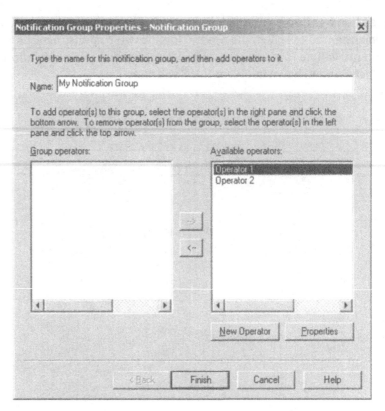

Figure 15-28. Creating a new notification group

Each operator is associated with an e-mail address and a page address. When a notification group receives an alert, the alert will be sent out to each of its operators through their e-mail address, or page address, or both.

You have so far added the one response action of notifying the BizTalk development team group. You'll now add another response action to launch a script. Click the Add button in the Responses window (shown in Figure 15-26) again, and then select Launch a script. A Launch a Script window will open, as shown in Figure 15-29.

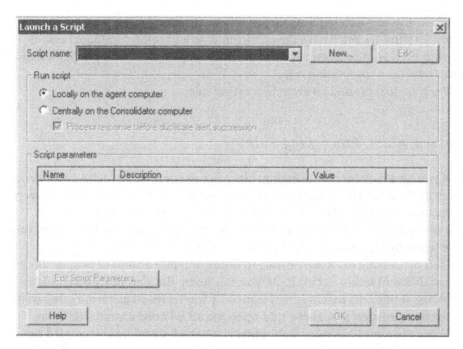

Figure 15-29. Specifying a script to launch as the response action to the event processing rule

When you use a script as the response action for an event processing rule, you need to provide three pieces of information: the script name, the location where the script is executed, and any optional script parameters. The Script Name drop-down list in Figure 15-29 contains many commonly used scripts that are installed as part of the MOM installation. In this case, you need to create a customized script to handle the documents in the BizTalk Server suspended queue.

To create a new script, click the New button, and a new window will open, where you can enter the code for the script you want to run when the event processing rule triggers.

Besides specifying which script to launch, you also need to specify where the script is to be executed. You can run the script on either the agent computer or the Consolidator computer. For example, you may want to write a script using WMI and Interchange components to resubmit certain suspended queue items. Because a script that interacts with the BizTalk Server suspended queue needs to run on the BizTalk Server, you can configure the script to run locally on the agent computer, which in this case would be the BizTalk Server.

When you are done defining the response actions, click Next in the Responses window. You'll have the opportunity to add some comments associated with this event processing rule to the knowledge base and to provide a name for this new event processing rule.

You have just created an event processing rule.

Creating Alert Processing Rules

When you create an event processing rule, you can specify that MOM generate an alert to indicate that a problem has occurred. However, generating alerts this way will become hard to manage, and it will be difficult to react to the alerts when event processing rules generate a lot of alerts. By using alert processing rules, you can ease the management of the alerts that are generated.

Alert processing rules can be used to notify different groups of people about alerts of different levels. For example, you can set up the alert processing rule so that MOM notifies the management team only when critical alerts are generated.

To create an alert processing rule, open the MOM Administrator Console, right-click the Alert Processing Rule under the Bob's Rule folder you created earlier, and select New ➤ Alert Processing Rule. An Alert Criteria window will open, as shown in Figure 15-30.

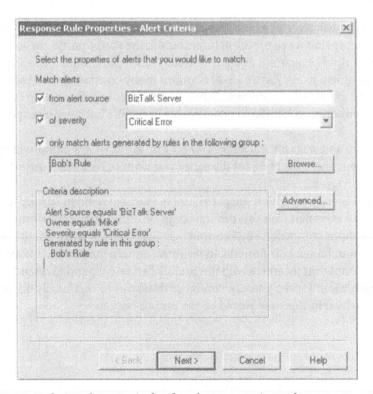

Figure 15-30. Defining the criteria for the alert processing rule

In this Alert Criteria window, you can define the matching criteria for this alert processing rule. If an event processing rule raises an alert that matches an alert processing rule, the alert processing rule triggers, and the alert's response actions will be executed. You can filter the generated events to raise appropriate alerts by providing specific matching criteria. For example, the settings in Figure 15-30 indicate that this rule will only trigger when the alert's owner is Mike, the alert is critical, and it is from BizTalk Server. The alert must also be generated by the rules in the Bob's Rule group.

To get more details on the matching properties of the alert, you can refer to the information in the Alert window (see Figure 15-24) where the alert was first defined. As you can see, with alert processing rules, you can focus on very specific alerts.

After you have provided MOM with the matching criteria, you can define what response action should be taken. The procedures for defining the response actions for an alert processing rule is identical to that for the event processing rules. You want this particular alert processing rule to notify the management team. Refer to the "Specifying the Response Actions" section earlier for details on how to set up the response actions.

Creating Performance Processing Rules

As discussed earlier, performance processing rules consist of two types of rules: the measuring rule and threshold rule.

- *Measuring rules:* These retrieve the performance data from the agent machine in order to create the performance chart and report. This type of performance processing rule allows you to define the response action to be taken when performance falls below some predefined level.

- *Threshold rules:* These watch certain performance counters on the agent machine and trigger when the performance numbers fall below a predefined level. You can define response actions that fire when this type of performance processing rule triggers.

Creating Measuring Performance Processing Rules

Let's take a look at how to create a measuring performance processing rule. Open the MOM Administrator Console, right-click the Performance Processing Rule folder under Bob's Rule, and select New ➤ Performance Processing Rule. The Performance Processing Rule Type dialog box will open, as shown in Figure 15-31. Select the Sample Performance Data (Measuring) option, and click Next to continue.

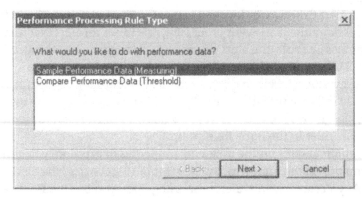

Figure 15-31. Choosing the type of performance processing rule to create

In the following window, you can either select an existing performance processing rule that was installed as part of MOM or create a new rule. Click the New button, since you want to create a rule to measure BizTalk Server performance.

The next window is shown in Figure 15-32. It asks the provider type for the performance information.

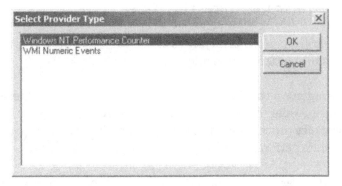

Figure 15-32. Selecting the provider type for the performance processing rule

As with event processing rules, you'll need to provide information on where your rule will receive the performance data from. The Windows NT Performance Counter option provides information such as average CPU utilization and average memory consumption. In the case of BizTalk Server performance counts, it will provide information such as how many documents are received per second on average, how many XLANG Schedules are completed per second on average, etc. The WMI Numeric Events option provides performance information such as the number of documents in the BizTalk Server suspended queue. In this example, you'll select Windows NT Performance Counter, and click OK.

The next window, shown in Figure 15-33, is where you select the specific performance counters to monitor. You specify what performance counters MOM will query at certain time intervals, and the data collected by MOM will be stored in the database to be retrieved later for reports or graphs.

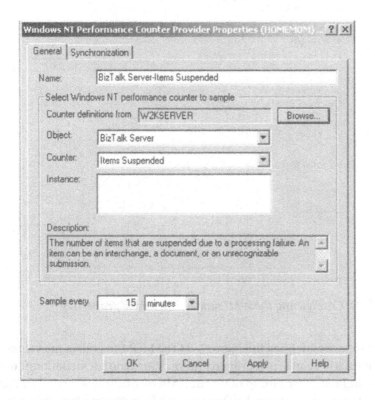

Figure 15-33. Choosing the performance counter for the measurement performance processing rule

The configuration shown in Figure 15-33 indicates MOM will collect the number of suspended documents on the BizTalk Server every 15 minutes. Click OK to save this new performance processing rule.

Creating Threshold Performance Processing Rules

The second rule you'll create is a threshold performance processing rule. You want to notify the management team when the suspended queue contains more than 10 documents.

You'll create another performance processing rule as you did for the previous measuring rule, except that you select the Compare Performance Data (Threshold) option as the processing rule type in the window shown in

Figure 15-31,. and select WMI Numeric Event as the provider type in the window shown in Figure 15-32. A General Properties window opens, as shown in Figure 15-34.

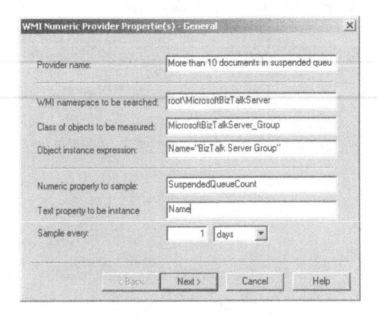

Figure 15-34. Configuring the WMI numeric provider properties

The properties defined in Figure 15-34 tell MOM to collect the values (these must be numeric values) of a property named SuspendedQueueCount of class MicrosoftBizTalkServer_Group of the root\MicrosoftBizTalkServer WMI namespace once every day. SuspendedQueueCount is a property that indicates how many items are in the BizTalk Server suspended queue.

Click Next to save the settings and return to the threshold performance processing rule window. Click Next until you reach the window shown in Figure 15-35.

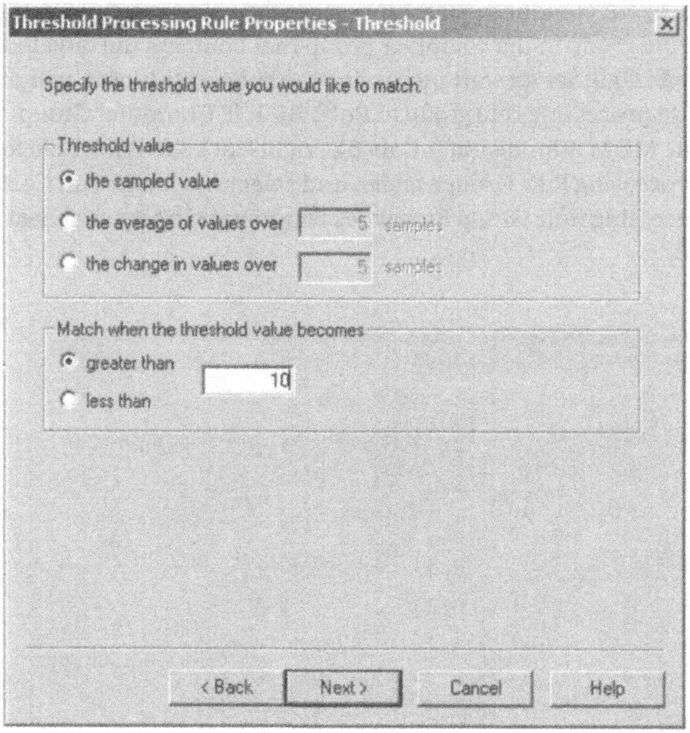

Figure 15-35. Configuring the threshold for the performance processing rule

In this window, you want to set the threshold for this performance processing rule to be equal to 10 so that MOM will trigger this performance processing rule if more than 10 documents are in the suspended queue. Click Next.

After you specify the threshold, you'll go through a series of windows to define whether to generate an alert, and which response actions to fire when the rule is triggered. The configuration procedures are the same as for the event processing rule you saw earlier. Refer to the "Defining an Alert" and "Specifying the Response Actions" sections earlier in the chapter.

Attaching Processing Rules to Computer Groups

You have just learned how to create event processing rules, alert processing rules, and performance processing rules. However, these processing rules aren't activated until you attach these rules to a specific computer group. Until then, no agent computer can start processing the rules.

To make agent computers start processing the rules, you must assign the processing rule group to the computer group that contains the targeted computers. To make BizTalk Server start processing the rules in this case, you must bind the Bob's Rule processing rule group to Bob's BizTalk Computer Group.

Open the MOM Administrator Console, right-click the Bob's Rule folder under the Processing Rule Groups folder, and select Associate with Computer group. A Processing Rule Group Properties window will open, as shown in Figure 15-36.

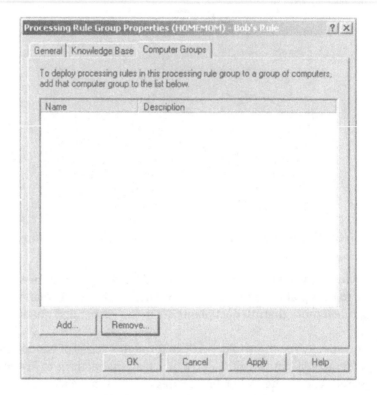

Figure 15-36. Associating the processing rule group with computer groups

Click the Add button and select Bob's BizTalk Computer Group from the list of computer groups defined on MOM. Then click OK.

After you have associated Bob's BizTalk Computer Group with this processing rule group, the MOM Consolidator will put out the processing rules defined in Bob's Rule to each of the agent computers that are part of Bob's BizTalk Computer Group at their next heartbeat, and these agent computers will start processing the rules as soon as they receive them.

Monitoring MOM

You have just learned how to configure the processing rules. These rules allow the agent computer to automatically react to certain events and performance data, but they don't provide an interface for people to examine the events and alerts that occur on the agent machines. To view what is happening on the agent computers, you need to rely on the monitoring tools that come with MOM.

The monitoring tools are located under the Monitor category of the MOM Administrator Console, as shown in Figure 15-37. There are many types of views that can provide you with pictures which give different perspectives on what is happening on the agent computers.

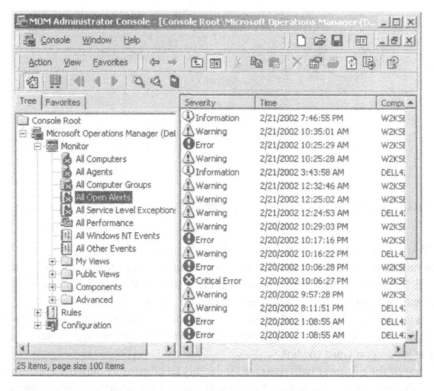

Figure 15-37. Monitoring agent computers with predefined views

The MOM console comes with a number of default views that allow you to see what has happened on each agent computer, and on the computer group as a whole. For example, clicking the All Open Alerts view will display all the unresolved alerts raised by all the computers watched by MOM.

You can also create a customized view that only lists the information that meets certain criteria. For example, suppose you want to create a view that will list all the error events that occurred on the BizTalk Servers. You can create such a view by right-clicking the My Views folder and selecting New ➤ Event View. An Event View Properties window for the view opens, as shown in Figure 15-38.

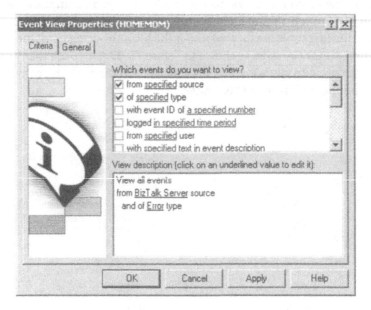

Figure 15-38. Configuring a customized event view

You can narrow the events that are listed by this view by providing some information about what type of event you are expecting. In this case, you specify BizTalk Server to be the event source, and Error to be the event type. This new view will only list the events that meet these two conditions.

In addition to customized event views, you can also create customized alert views, performance views, computer group views, etc., by specifying the criteria for the items you want to view.

One of the biggest challenges we face today in computer networks is monitoring computers from a remote location. Because of security concerns, many monitoring tools can't monitor the remote computers due to the restrictions on the firewall. MOM provides a solution for this problem through a MOM Web console that mimics the functionality of the MOM Administrator Console. MOM's Web Console can let you monitor computers from a remote location across the Internet or an intranet. With its Web Console, you can monitor computers and computer groups, and view events, alerts, and reports on each agent computer and computer group. You can also create new customized views from Internet Explorer.

To access MOM's Web Console, open
`http://MOMWebConsole/OnePointOperations/default.htm` in Internet Explorer. In
this URL, "MOMWebConsole" should be replaced with the name of the computer
that has the MOM Web Console installed.

The home page of the MOM Web Console is called OpsPortal, and it displays
a summary report on MOM and the agent computers it watches. Click the Go to
views hyperlink in the upper-left corner of the home page to be redirected to the
page shown in Figure 15-39, which resembles the interface of the MOM
Administrator Console.

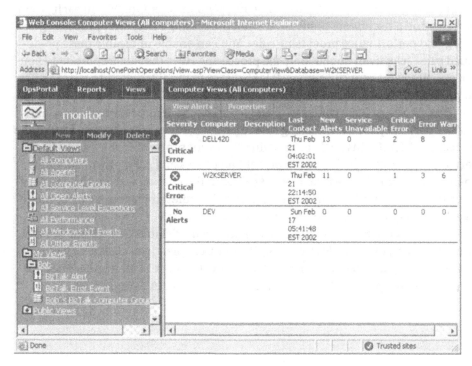

*Figure 15-39. Using MOM's Web Console to monitor computers on the network
remotely*

MOM Management Package

MOM has provided a set of excellent tools for monitoring and managing the
computer system. However, to fully take advantage of MOM, you must know how
to create the processing rules that will raise alerts and react to problems automatically. This requires you to become familiar with the potential events that
may occur on the system you want to monitor.

The more complete and selective you can make the processing rules on the agent computers, the more efficiently you can manage the computers and applications running on them. However, creating the processing rules from scratch requires a great deal of effort and in-depth knowledge about the events that may be generated by the agent computer. To reduce the burden of creating the processing rules, Microsoft introduced the MOM management package.

A MOM management package contains a set of predefined processing rules that are normally targeted to a specific service or application. When you open the Processing Rule Groups folder in the MOM Administrator Console, you'll find a list of rule groups. In fact, these rule groups are there because of the management packages that were added during the MOM installation. Within each group, you can find a number of predefined event processing rules, alert processing rules, and performance processing rules. You can enable or disable these predefined rules selectively so that only the processing rules that are important to you get executed on agent computers. It is also easy to modify these processing rules to produce the customized results you are looking for.

BizTalk Server 2002 comes with a MOM management package that contains BizTalk Server–specific processing rules that are ready to run after you import the package to MOM. This package contains 900 event processing rules and 36 performance processing rules. These predefined processing rules are no different than the homemade ones you created earlier in the chapter, except that you don't have to create them. You can add new processing rules or customize these predefined processing rules to produce the results you want.

To import the BizTalk management package model to MOM so that you can use these rules, open the MOM Administrator Console, right-click Processing Rule Groups under the Rules category, and select Import Management Pack. An Import Management Pack window will open, as shown in Figure 15-40.

Figure 15-40. Import Management Pack window

Click the Browse button and select the BizTalk2002.ask file, which is located under the MOM folder on the BizTalk Server installation CD-ROM. Click Import to import the management pack.

When the process is complete, there will be a folder called Microsoft BizTalk Server created under Processing Rule Groups. The Microsoft BizTalk Server folder contains another folder called Microsoft BizTalk Server 2002 Enterprise Edition, which contains many predefined processing rules.

One last thing you have to do before these predefined processing rules start working is to associate the computer groups to these processing rule groups. That was explained earlier in the "Attaching Processing Rules to Computer Groups" section.

If you need more information on MOM, you can take a look at MOM's user group on Microsoft's Web site (http://communities.microsoft.com/newsgroups/default.asp?icp=mom&lcid=US). Microsoft has also published several articles on MOM, such as "Microsoft Operations Manager Deployment Guide" and "Microsoft Operations Manager 2000 Operations Guide," which can be found at http://www.microsoft.com/mom.

Summary

In this last chapter of the book, you learned about using MOM in the context of BizTalk Server. You first saw how MOM works and discussed some important components and concepts, such as MOM providers, MOM agents, the Agent Manager, Consolidators, etc. You then learned how MOM manages the computers and their events through the use of computer groups and different types of processing rules. You saw how to set up processing rules to trigger customized scripts and notify people when certain events occur.

In terms of the monitoring aspect of MOM, you learned how to monitor the system using the MOM Administrator Console and MOM's Web Console. You also looked at the BizTalk Server 2002 MOM package, which comes with a huge number of predefined processing rules for BizTalk Server. With these predefined processing rules, you can more effectively monitor and react to different types of events that occur on the BizTalk Server and its applications in the production environment.

APPENDIX A

Microsoft Message Queue

MICROSOFT MESSAGE QUEUE (MSMQ) is one of the most important and overlooked components for building scalable enterprise applications. In earlier chapters of the book, I've demonstrated how important MSMQ is in the internal workings of BizTalk Server.

In BizTalk Messaging, MSMQ Receive Functions are able to bring the documents that are stored in the MSMQ into BizTalk's work queue. Messaging ports support MSMQ as one of the protocols for transporting documents to different locations. BizTalk Server also uses MSMQ as the data buffer when sending and receiving data between BizTalk Orchestration and Messaging. And with the support of MSMQ inside BizTalk Orchestration, you can create XLANG Schedules that interact with MSMQ. XLANG Schedule also depends on MSMQ for its ability to correlate related messages. The list goes on and on.

MSMQ is asynchronous by nature, and it has been somewhat overlooked because synchronous applications are in style. Many applications, however, don't require real time responses from the server, and there are more of them than you might expect. Human society provides a very good insight on how the digital world can improve itself. Tax filing, driver license registrations, and checkout counters at supermarkets are all asynchronous processes. Although people often complain about them, they rarely come up with a better system to serve a great number of customers economically. As more people realize the benefits of asynchronous processes in their applications, MSMQ will become more popular with developers who want to build applications that service a great number of clients. In this appendix, you'll see specifically how to use MSMQ to provide the asynchronous services in your applications.

MSMQ Overview

In this appendix, I'll focus on MSMQ 2.0, which comes with all editions of Windows 2000 and is installed as a Windows service. MSMQ consists of two parts: the data store and APIs. The data store is used to store messages so they can be retrieved later. The APIs are used to send and retrieve messages inside the message queue data store. When you put these two parts together, you have a new way to share data between different systems or applications, as shown in Figure A-1.

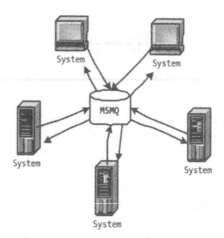

Figure A-1. Sharing data between multiple systems using MSMQ

As the data is sent to MSMQ, it's saved as a message in a message queue. A message is simply some string or binary data. The message queue is a storage unit where these messages are stored. The retrieval of messages follows the rule of first in, first out.

During the installation of the message queue service, you can specify what type of role the system will play. The system can be installed as one of five types of MSMQ:

- *MSMQ primary controller:* A MSMQ primary controller has to be on a Windows 2000 domain controller. It's responsible for storing all the information about each of the MSMQ servers or clients in the domain. This information is used to decide where to route messages in the network. The MSMQ primary controller will modify this routing information as new MSMQs participate in the domain.

- *MSMQ server (with routing):* A MSMQ server with routing (a routing server) is the server that actually routes the messages between different machines—it obtains a read-only copy of the routing information from the MSMQ primary controller. The MSMQ routing server can send and receive messages, and it can also store messages while the destination of the message is offline and forward it again whenever the destination is back online. A routing server makes decisions about how a message is delivered by looking at the cost of various site links and determining the quickest and most efficient way to deliver the message across multiple sites. The MSMQ routing server must be installed on a Windows 2000 Server or greater.

- *MSMQ server (without routing):* An MSMQ server without routing can do everything an MSMQ server (with routing) can do except route messages for other clients. It must be installed on a Windows 2000 Server or greater.

- *Independent client:* A MSMQ independent client consists of the message queue data store and a set of MSMQ objects that can be called to send and retrieve messages to and from the message queue, either locally or remotely. It can also send and receive messages and store the message while the destination is offline and forward it again when the destination comes back online. The only difference between an MSMQ routing server and MSMQ independent client is that the independent client doesn't route the messages for other clients. It's the same as a MSMQ server (without routing), except the MSMQ independent client can be installed on Windows 2000 Professional.

- *MSMQ dependent client:* A MSMQ dependent client doesn't have its own message queue store. It only consists of a set of MSMQ objects. Because dependent clients don't have their own message queue stores, they can only send and retrieve messages from the remote queue, and certain features won't be available for dependent queues, such as the store-and-forward feature, because its functionality depends on the local queue.

The relationships between these servers and clients are illustrated in Figure A-2.

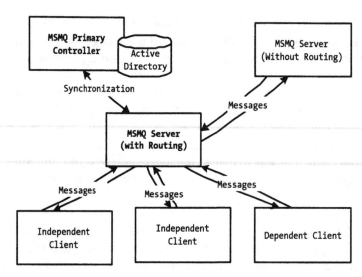

Figure A-2. Different MSMQ types in a domain

By implementing a MSMQ routing server, the dedicated connection between each system is significantly reduced. It also reduces the bandwidth usage in the network by consolidating the connections among systems. When MSMQ servers and clients are located in many different sites, the MSMQ routing server can act as a gateway to route messages between the sites for its clients, as shown in Figure A-3.

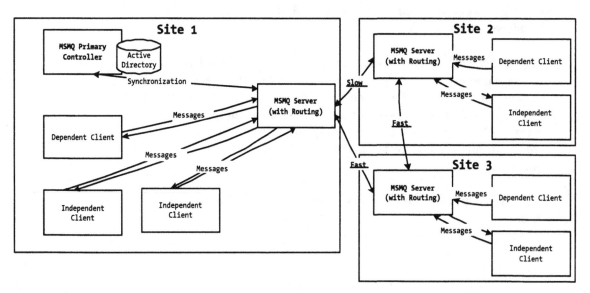

Figure A-3. Message routing between sites through the MSMQ routing server as the gateway to external systems

You can also configure the cost of links between each site in Active Directory, and the MSMQ routing server will use this information to find a route to deliver the messages in the most efficient way. In Figure A-3, the link between Site 1 and Site 2 is slow, but the link between Site 1 and Site 3 is fast, as is the link between Site 2 and Site 3. To optimize the performance, you can configure the cost of the link in Active Directory as shown in Figure A-4, so that the messages from Site 1 first will be routed to the MSMQ routing server in Site 3; then from Site 3, they will be further routed to Site 2, and eventually to the message queue in Site 2. The link cost can range from 1 to 4,294,967,295. Higher numbers indicate higher costs. A cost of zero means the two sites aren't connected.

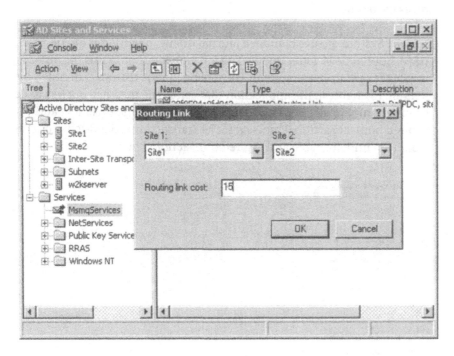

Figure A-4. Setting up the routing link cost between sites in Active Directory

There are four types of message queues, as shown in Figure A-5:

- *Outgoing:* Outgoing queues on a computer are used to store messages temporarily before they are sent to their destinations. If the network is down, MSMQ will defer sending out messages in the outgoing queues until a later time when the network is up again.

- *Public:* Public queues can be accessed without the explicit knowledge of the physical location of the message queue. Every public queue is registered in Active Directory, and applications can query on a public queue using the MSMQQuery object to retrieve information, such as the physical location of the message queue.

- *Private:* Private queues can only be accessed if other applications know the physical location of the queue since it isn't published in Active Directory. To access a private queue on the system, you must first know the name of the machine where the message queue is located, and the name of the message queue.

- *System:* System queues contain a journal queue, dead-letter queue, and transactional dead-letter queue. The journal queue contains the outgoing messages sent from the system. The journal queue feature is disabled by default; to enable it, the application that sends the message out has to do so programmatically. The dead-letter queue stores undeliverable and expired nontransactional messages. The transactional dead-letter queue stores the undeliverable and expired transactional messages.

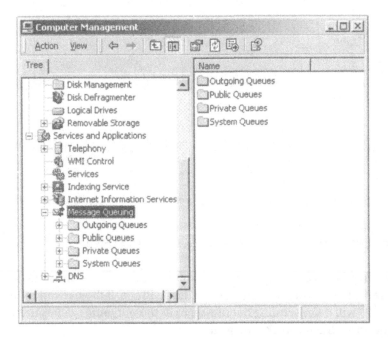

Figure A-5. The four types of message queues on an MSMQ system

Message Queuing

Message queuing turns synchronous processing into asynchronous processing by decoupling the sending of the request and the receiving of the response in the application, as shown in Figure A-6.

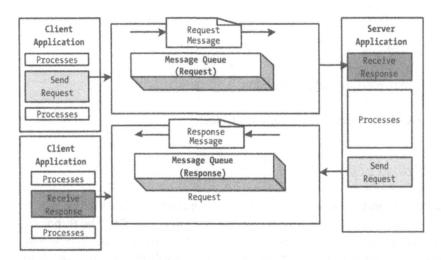

Figure A-6. The use of message queues makes the interaction between client and server an asynchronous process.

When a client wants to use the service provided by the server application, the client will send a request in the form of a message to the message queue, instead of making a direct link to the server application through a synchronous protocol such as COM. After the message is delivered to the message queue, the client application continues on with other processes.

To process the client's request in the message queue, the server application needs to watch for any incoming messages in the queue. When a new message arrives at the queue, the server application will perform whatever processing needs to be done for the message. If the client is expecting a response or return message from the server application, the server application will send the response as a message to another message queue, which is watched by the client application.

Because the client doesn't establish a direct link with the server application, the server doesn't need to pay immediate attention to the request. It will process the response whenever it sees fit. The same is true for sending the response message back. Because the server doesn't establish a direct link with the client application, the client doesn't need to pay immediate attention to the response from the server. It will process the response when it has time.

Why are you going through all this trouble to implement message queues between the client and server when a simple COM or DCOM call seems to achieve the same result? To truly understand why you should use the message queue, let's take a look at the benefits the message queue can bring to applications:

- Continuous availability

- Scalability

- Cross-platform interoperability

- COM+ and MSMQ transaction support

Availability

In a synchronous process, the server must be online and ready to process requests when a client requests its service. The client must also be responsive when the server responds. However, making sure all the systems involved in a process are up and running at all times isn't a simple task. Systems go down because of hardware failure, software failure, or scheduled maintenance. If a process is synchronous between the client and server, the service can potentially be interrupted whenever one of the systems involved in the process goes down.

By replacing the direct link with a message queue between the client and server, the client can continuously send requests even when the server goes down, and the server can continuously send responses even when the client is down. When one of the two is down, the messages simply stay at the message queue and wait to be picked up. These messages eventually get processed when the systems come back online and start pulling the messages from the message queue.

With the message queue, you are able to remove the machine dependency from your application, but what happens if the system that hosts the message queue goes down, or the network goes down? In this case, the message wouldn't even be able to reach the message queue.

MSMQ has a useful feature called the *outgoing queue*. This feature allows the system sending a message to store the message on a local queue if it's unable to send the message out due to network disturbances or the remote location being offline. The MSMQ service will try to resend these messages at a later time.

MSMQ servers can be clustered in both active/active and active/passive modes to provide better reliability to the application. For more information about active/active and active/passive modes, refer to Chapter 13.

Scalability

One of the most interesting features in MSMQ is its ability to increase the scalability of an application. With a centralized MSMQ, it becomes very easy to add servers to process a client's requests with little or no change to the application itself. Because of the asynchronous nature of message queues, you can add servers to pull and process request messages from a centralized queue, as shown in Figure A-7.

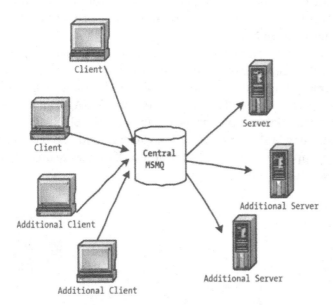

Figure A-7. Scaling out the application by adding additional servers to process requests in a centralized MSMQ

As you see in Figure A-7, MSMQ provides a excellent means for load balancing requests from the client. By adding two servers to process the request messages in the centralized message queue, each server only takes about one-third of the workload as opposed to one server processing all of the workload. The great benefit of using MSMQ for load balancing requests is that it's simple to deploy. To balance client requests, you can simply add identical call processing servers, and make them watch for the same MSMQ.

Interoperability

MSMQ can also prove an excellent cross-platform integration solution for applications in a heterogeneous environment. In a heterogeneous environment, the client and the server may be located on different platforms, and more often than not, the applications on the client cannot make direct calls to the application on the server because of incompatible application interfaces. To solve this problem, you can use MSMQ to change the communication to an asynchronous process. As long as both the client and server applications know how to send and retrieve messages from MSMQ, you can enable communications between such heterogeneous applications through MSMQ.

MSMQ is a Microsoft technology, so systems must be able to support COM to interact with MSMQ. A number of products allow applications on non-Microsoft platforms to interact with MSMQ. The MSMQ-MQSeries bridge, which is part of SNA 4 or Host Integration Server (HIS), a later version of SNA, from Microsoft allows applications in Microsoft platforms to interact with IBM's MQSeries on the mainframe. Combining MSMQ and MQSeries, you can send and retrieve messages to and from applications on the mainframe as if they were on a Microsoft platform, as shown in Figure A-8.

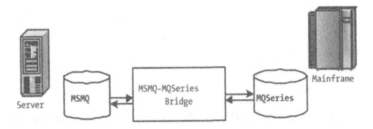

Figure A-8. Integration of applications on different platforms through an MSMQ-MQSeries bridge

Transaction Support

MSMQ supports two types of transactions: COM+ transactions and native MSMQ transactions.

With COM+ style transactions, you can read and write messages as you read and write data to an SQL database. You can commit or roll back the sending and retrieving of messages to and from the queue by committing or aborting the transaction context. You can enlist the MSMQ calls as well as other transactional resources within a single transaction.

Compared with COM+-style transaction, the native version is much faster. However, with native MSMQ transactions, you cannot enlist other transactional resources in a single transaction. In other words, if you want to make a database update and read from a message queue in a single transaction, you would have to use COM+-style transaction, because MSMQ native transaction doesn't support other transactional resources. To create an application that takes advantage of MSMQ, rely on the MSMQ object model to interact with MSMQ. In the next section I'll show you a number of these MSMQ objects to better understand how to use them in your application to interact with MSMQ.

MSMQ Programming Model

The MSMQ programming model comes with ten objects, and each performs a specific task:

- *MSMQQuery:* Used to query for existing public queues in Active Directory.

- *MSMQQueueInfos:* A collection of MSMQQueueInfo objects.

- *MSMQQueueInfo:* A single queue object, which can be used to create, update, and delete a single queue.

- *MSMQQueue:* Used to open a queue and receive messages in the queue.

- *MSMQMessage:* Used to create a message and send the message to the queue.

- *MSMQApplication:* Used to obtain information about the Message Queuing service on the local computer, including the name of the local computer.

- *MSMQEvent:* Used to provide event handling. This object creates applications that process the events asynchronously.

- *MSMQTransactionDispenser:* Used to create an MSMQTransaction object that represents a new internal transaction object. The new MSMQTransaction object can then be used in calls to send or retrieve messages.

- *MSMQCoordinatedTransactionDispenser:* Used to obtain an MS DTC transaction object. When the transaction is obtained, an MSMQTransaction object is returned that can be used to send or retrieve messages.

- *MSMQTransaction:* Represents a transaction object obtained externally using the MSMQCoordinatedTransactionDispenser object, or created internally using the MSMQTransactionDispenser object.

Five of these objects are commonly used in most message queue operations. The relationships among these five objects are represented in Figure A-9.

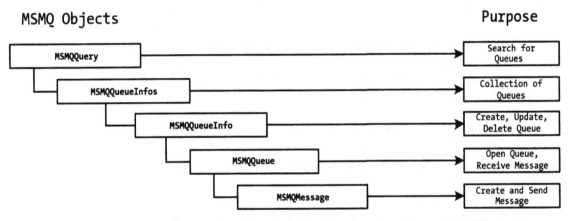

Figure A-9. MSMQ objects and their purposes

MSMQQueueInfo (Creating, Refreshing, and Deleting the Queue)

The MSMQQueueInfo object provides methods and properties for creating new message queues and managing existing message queues, such as changing the properties for a queue.

The methods and properties for the MSMQQueueInfo object are listed in Tables A-1 and A-2.

Table A-1. Methods of the MSMQQueueInfo Object

METHOD NAME	DESCRIPTION
Create	Creates a queue based on the queue properties of the MSMQQueueInfo object
Delete	Deletes an existing queue
Open	Opens a queue, returning an MSMQQueue object
Refresh	Refreshes the property values of the MSMQQueueInfo object with the values stored in the directory service (for public queues) or the local computer (for private queues)
Update	Updates the directory service or the local computer with the current property values of the MSMQQueueInfo object

Table A-2. Properties of the MSMQQueueInfo Object

PROPERTY NAME	ACCESS/DATA TYPE	DESCRIPTION
Authenticate	Access: Read/write Data type: Long	Specifies whether the queue accepts only authenticated messages
BasePriority	Access: Read/write Data type: Long	Specifies a base priority for all messages sent to a public queue
CreateTime	Access: Read-only Data type: Date Variant	Provides the time and date when the public or private queue was created
FormatName	Access: Read/write Data type: String	Specifies the format name of the queue
IsTransactional	Access: Read-only Data type: Short	Indicates whether the queue supports transactions
IsWorldReadable	Access: Read-only Data type: Short	Indicates whether everyone can read the messages in the queue
Journal	Access: Read/write Data type: Long	Specifies whether or not messages retrieved from the queue are stored in a queue journal
JournalQuota	Access: Read/write Data type: Long	Specifies the maximum size of the queue journal
Label	Access: Read/write Data type: String	Specifies a description of the queue or message
ModifyTime	Access: Read-only Data type: Date Variant	Provides the time and date when the stored properties of the queue were last updated

(continued)

Table A-2. Properties of the MSMQQueueInfo Object (continued)

PROPERTY NAME	ACCESS/DATA TYPE	DESCRIPTION
PathName	Access: Read/write Data type: String	Specifies the Message Queuing pathname of the queue
PathNameDNS	Access: Read-only Data type: String	Provides the DNS pathname of the queue
PrivLevel	Access: Read/write Data type: Long	Specifies the privacy level of a queue or message
QueueGuid	Access: Read-only Data type: GUID	Provides the identifier of the public queue associated with the MSMQQueueInfo object
Quota	Access: Read/write Data type: Long	Specifies the maximum size of the queue
ServiceTypeGuid	Access: Read/write Data type: GUID	Specifies the type of service provided by the queue

The MSMQQueueInfo object is used to perform functions such as creating a queue, retrieving the name or GUID of a queue, etc. The following code demonstrates how you can create a queue and retrieve its properties using MSMQQueueInfo object:

```
Dim queueInfo As MSMQ.MSMQQueueInfo
Dim queuename As String

Set queueInfo = New MSMQ.MSMQQueueInfo
'create a public queue
queuename = "FirstQueue"
queueInfo.PathName = ".\" & queuename
queueInfo.Create

'create another public queue on remote server
'with the same queue name

queueInfo.PathName = "Dell420\" & queuename
queueInfo.Create

'create a private queue
queuename = "SecondQueue"
queueInfo.PathName = ".\private$\" & queuename
queueInfo.Create
```

The PathName property determines where the queue is created. In the preceding code example, the program creates three message queues. The first two queues are public queues: .\FirstQueue and Dell420\FirstQueue. The period (.) in the first queue name indicates that it's a public queue that will be created locally. If a public queue is to be created on a remote machine, then you need to replace the period (.) with the machine name in the queue's pathname. The second queue is a public queue on the Dell420 computer. Because the local machine name is W2KSERVER, the two public queues created are W2KSERVER\FirstQueue and DELL420\FirstQueue.

After these two queues are created, they are registered in Active Directory. Each public queue in the domain must have a unique name, and an error will be raised if you try to add a public queue with the same pathname of an existing public queue.

The third queue is a local queue, and it's registered in Active Directory. The private queue is identified with "private$" as part of the pathname. To create the message, simply call the Create method on the MSMQQueueInfo object after providing the pathname property.

MSMQQuery and MSMQQueueInfos (Searching for the Queues)

The MSMQQueueInfo object manages only one message queue. By combining the MSMQQuery and MSMQQueueInfos objects, you can query all the existing public and private message queues and get MSMQQueueInfo references to the queues.

The MSMQQueueInfos object provides methods for enumerating through the collection of public queues returned by the MSMQQuery.LookupQueue method. It contains the two methods listed in Table A-3 and no properties.

Table A-3. Methods of the MSMQQueueInfos Object

METHOD NAME	DESCRIPTION
Next	Returns the next queue in the collection
Reset	Returns the cursor to the start of the results of a query

The MSMQQuery object allows you to query the Active Directory for all the existing public queues. Its LookupQueue method returns a single MSMQQueueInfos object that represents a set of MSMQQueueInfo objects, each of which contains information about a public queue. MSMQQuery contains only one method, which is listed in Table A-4, and no properties.

Table A-4. Method of the MSMQQuery Object

METHOD NAME	DESCRIPTION
LookupQueue	Returns a collection of public queues

The LookupQueue method can search for public queues by specifying any of the following properties:

- Queue identifier

- Service type

- Queue label

- Create time

- Modify time

- Multicast address

The signature for the LookupQueue method is as follows:

```
queryObject.LookupQueue( _
  [QueueGuid] _
  [, ServiceTypeGuid] _
  [, Label] _
  [, CreateTime] _
  [, ModifyTime] _
  [, RelServiceType] _
  [, RelLabel] _
  [, RelCreateTime] _
  [, RelModifyTime] _
  [, MulticastAddress] _
  [, RelMulticastAddress] _
)
```

The following code shows how you can use the MSMQQuery and MSMQQueueInfos objects to retrieve information about the public queues in Active Directory.

```
Dim queueInfo As MSMQ.MSMQQueueInfo
Dim queuequery As MSMQ.MSMQQuery
Dim queueinfos As MSMQ.MSMQQueueInfos
Dim queuename As String
```

```
Set queuequery = New MSMQ.MSMQQuery
'Lookup queue with the search parameter
'Important - queue names are case-sensitive
Set queueInfos = queuequery.LookupQueue(, , "FirstQueue")
'Move to first record in queue set
set queueInfo = queueInfos.Reset
Set queueInfo = queueInfos.Next

Do While Not IsNull(queueInfo)
    MsgBox (queueInfo.PathName)
    Set queueInfo = queueInfos.Next
Loop
```

The queueInfos object is a collection of queueInfo objects for message queues that have FirstQueue as their label. The first use of the Next method after the Reset method moves the cursor to the first record in the queue set. You can then loop through the queue set to retrieve the properties for each matching public queue.

To retrieve a list representing all the existing public queues in Active Directory, you can call the LookupQueue() method with no parameters.

MSMQQueue, MSMQMessage, and MSMQQueueInfo (Receiving and Sending Messages)

MSMQQueueInfo, MSMQQueueInfos, and MSMQQuery are objects used to manage the message queues. To send and retrieve messages from the queues, you need to use another set of objects, namely, MSMQQueue and MSMQMessage.

The MSMQQueue Object

First, let's take a look at the MSMQQueue object. Its primary purpose is to open an existing message queue for reading. It contains methods that allow you to loop through messages in the queue and retrieve the content of the messages. The methods and properties for the MSMQQueue object are listed in Tables A-5 and A-6.

Table A-5. Methods of the MSMQQueue Object

METHOD NAME	DESCRIPTION
Close	Closes this instance of the queue.
EnableNotification	Starts event notification for asynchronously reading messages in the queue.
Peek	Returns the first message in the queue, or waits for a message to arrive if the queue is empty. The Peek method doesn't remove any messages from the queue.
PeekCurrent	Returns the current message, but doesn't remove the current message from the queue.
PeekNext	Returns the next message in the queue, but doesn't remove it from the queue.
Receive	Retrieves the first message in the queue, removing the message from the queue.
ReceiveCurrent	Reads the message at the current cursor location.
Reset	Returns the cursor to the start of the queue.

Table A-6. Properties of the MSMQQueue Object

PROPERTY NAME	ACCESS/DATA TYPE	DESCRIPTION
Access	Access: Read-only Data type: Long	Provides the access rights of the open queue
Handle	Access: Read-only Data type: Long	Provides the handle of the opened queue
IsOpen	Access: Read-only Data type: Short	Provides an indication of whether or not the queue is open
QueueInfo	Access: Read-only Data type: MSMQQueueInfo	Provides an MSMQQueueInfo object that contains the initial settings used to open the queue
ShareMode	Access: Read-only Data type: Long	Provides the share mode of the open queue

The MSMQMessage Object

The MSMQQueue's Receive (and ReceiveCurrent) and Peek (and PeekCurrent, PeekNext) methods return an MSMQMessage object. MSMQMessage objects contain methods and properties that allow you to retrieve detail information about a particular message that has been peeked at or retrieved. The methods and properties for the MSMQMessage object are listed in Tables A-7 and A-8.

Table A-7. Methods of the MSMQMessage Object

METHOD NAME	DESCRIPTION
AttachCurrentSecurityContext	Used when sending authenticated messages. This method retrieves security context information from a specific certificate.
Send	Sends the message to the specified queue.

Table A-8. Properties of the MSMQMessage Object

PROPERTY NAME	ACCESS/DATA TYPE	DESCRIPTION
Ack	Access: Read/write Data type: Long	Specifies the type of acknowledgment messages that MSMQ returns to the administration queue
AdminQueueInfo	Access: Read/write Data type: MSMQQueueInfo	Specifies the queue used for acknowledgment messages
AppSpecific	Access: Read/write Data type: Long	Specifies application-generated information for filtering messages
ArrivedTime	Access: Read-only Data type: Date Variant	Provides the time when the message arrived at the queue
Authentication ProviderName	Access: Read/write Data type: String	Specifies the name of the provider used to authenticate the message
Authentication ProviderType	Access: Read/write Data type: Long	Specifies the type of provider used to authenticate the message
AuthLevel	Access: Read/write Data type: Long	Specifies whether the message should be authenticated when received by the queue
Body	Access: Read/write Data type: Variant	Specifies the body of the message
BodyLength	Access: Read-only Data type: Long	Provides the size of the message body

(continued)

Table A-8. Properties of the MSMQMessage Object (continued)

PROPERTY NAME	ACCESS/DATA TYPE	DESCRIPTION
Class	Access: Read-only Data type: Long	Provides the type of message
Connector TypeGuid	Access: Read/write Data type: String	Indicates that some properties typically set by Message Queuing were set by the sending application
CorrelationId	Access: Read/write Data type: Variant (array of bytes)	Specifies the correlation identifier of the message
Delivery	Access: Read/write Data type: Long	Specifies how the message is delivered (optimize throughput or recoverability)
Destination QueueInfo	Access: Read-only Data type: MSMQQueueInfo	Provides the queue where the message resides (the queue to which the message is sent)
Destination SymmetricKey	Access: Read/write Data type: Variant (array of bytes)	Specifies the symmetric key used to encrypt the message
EncryptAlgorithm	Access: Read/write Data type: Long	Specifies the algorithm used to encrypt the message body
Extension	Access: Read/write Data type: Variant (array of bytes)	Specifies additional application-defined information
HashAlgorithm	Access: Read/write Data type: Long	Specifies the hash algorithm used when authenticating messages
Id	Access: Read-only Data type: Variant (array of bytes)	Provides the MSMQ-generated identifier for the message
IsAuthenticated	Access: Read-only Data type: Short	Indicates whether the message was authenticated by MSMQ
IsFirstIn Transaction	Access: Read-only Data type: Short	Indicates whether the message was the first message in a transaction
Journal	Access: Read/write Data type: Long	Specifies whether a copy of the message is stored in the computer journal
Label	Access: Read/write Data type: String	Specifies an application-defined label for the message
MaxTimeTo ReachQueue	Access: Read/write Data type: Long	Specifies how long the message has to reach the queue

(continued)

Table A-8. Properties of the MSMQMessage Object (continued)

PROPERTY NAME	ACCESS/DATA TYPE	DESCRIPTION
MaxTime ToReceive	Access: Read/write Data type: Long	Specifies how long the receiving application has to remove the message from the queue
MsgClass	Access: Read/write Data type: Long	Specifies the type of message
Priority	Access: Read/write Data type: Long	Specifies the priority of the message (where it's placed in the queue)
PrivLevel	Access: Read/write Data type: Long	Specifies whether the message is private (encrypted)
Received Authentication Level	Access: Read-only Data type: Short	Provides the authentication level specified by the sending application
Response QueueInfo	Access: Read/write Data type: MSMQQueueInfo	Specifies the queue for sending responses to the message
SenderCertificate	Access: Read/write Data type: Variant (array of bytes)	Specifies the sender certificate
SenderId	Access: Read/write Data type: Variant (array of bytes)	Identifies the user who sent the message
SentTime	Access: Read-only Data type: Date Variant	Provides the date and time that the message was sent
Signature	Access: Read/write Data type: Variant (array of bytes)	Specifies the digital signature used to sign the message
SourceMachine Guid	Access: Read-only Data type: String (GUID format)	Provides the identifier of the computer where the message originated
Trace	Access: Read/write Data type: Long	Specifies whether the route of the message is traced
TransactionId	Access: Read-only Data type: Variant (array of bytes)	Provides the transaction identifier for the message
TransactionStatus QueueInfo	Access: Read-only Data type: MSMQQueueInfo	Provides the transaction status queue

Sending a Message

To send a message to a queue, you need to create a new MSMQMessage object to represent the message you want to send to the queue. You can then set the properties of the message, such as label, body, delivery priority, etc. After you set the properties on the MSMQMessage object, you call its Send method, and pass in the MSMQQueue object for the queue you are sending the message to.

Here is a code example:

```
Const MQMSG_DELIVERY_RECOVERABLE = 1
Const MQ_SINGLE_MESSAGE = 3

Dim queuemsg As MSMQ.MSMQMessage
Dim queue As MSMQ.MSMQQueue
Dim queueinfo As MSMQ.MSMQQueueInfo

'create a new message
Set queuemsg = New MSMQ.MSMQMessage
queuemsg.Label = "test message"
queuemsg.Body = "This is a testing message"
queuemsg.Delivery = MQMSG_DELIVERY_RECOVERABLE
queuemsg.Priority = 7

'specify the target queue
Set queueinfo = New MSMQ.MSMQQueueInfo
queueinfo.PathName = ".\TargetQueue"
Set queue = queueinfo.Open

'specify the response queue
Set queueinfo = New MSMQ.MSMQQueueInfo
queueinfo.PathName = ".\ResponseQueue"
queuemsg.ResponseQueueInfo = queueinfo

'send the message
If queue.IsOpen Then
    queuemsg.Send queue, MQ_SINGLE_MESSAGE
End If
queue.Close
```

There are quite a few properties for the MSMQMessage object. Let's take a look at the ones in the sample.

The Delivery property determines how MSMQ handles and delivers the message. It has two possible values:

- *MQMSG_DELIVERY_RECOVERABLE (1):* In every hop along its route, the message is forwarded to the next hop or stored locally in a backup file until delivered. This guarantees delivery even in the case of a computer crash.

- *MQMSG_DELIVERY_EXPRESS (0):* The message stays in memory until it can be delivered. (This is also referred to as in-memory message store and forward.) This is the default value.

When sending a recoverable message, MSMQ will always keep a local copy of that message so that in case of system failure, MSMQ won't lose the message. Use this delivery type when you want to make sure that no message is lost. The express type of message doesn't persist the message to the disk, so it runs the risk of losing the message if the system goes down before the message is sent out. However, by limiting disk access, the express delivery type is much faster than the other type.

The Priority property ranges from 0 to 7, where 7 is the highest priority. Messages with higher priority will be put at the front of the queue's message list so that they can be picked up earlier by applications. When a message is sent as a transactional message, the priority property will be set to 0.

The ResponseQueueInfo property specifies the queue where the sender is expecting to receive the response message. This response queue can be any message queue. By specifying the ResponseQueueInfo property for the MSMQMessage object, the receiving application is able to dynamically determine which message queue it will use to receive the response message for a particular message. By using this property, the sender can decide where the response message will be sent for a particular message.

To actually send the message, you need to call the Send method on the MSMQMessage object. The Send message takes two parameters: The first represents the target queue for the message, and the second is an optional parameter that defines the kind of transaction used to send the message. There are four types of transaction that can be used:

- *MQ_NO_TRANSACTION (0):* Specifies that the call isn't part of a transaction.

- *MQ_MTS_TRANSACTION (1):* Specifies that the call is part of the current Microsoft Transaction Server (MTS) transaction. This is the default.

- *MQ_SINGLE_MESSAGE (3):* Sends a single message as a transaction.

- *MQ_XA_TRANSACTION (2):* Specifies that the call is part of an externally coordinated, XA-compliant transaction (or global transaction).

When a transaction parameter isn't provided, MQ_MTS_TRANSACTION is assumed. MQ_SINGLE_MESSAGE allows you to send only one message to the queue in a transactional manner. To send more than one message, or to join an existing COM+ transaction, you have to set the transaction to MQ_MTS_TRANSACTION.

Receiving a Message

To retrieve a message from a queue, you need to obtain an MSMQQueueInfo object that references the message queue. It must call the Open method of MSMQQueueInfo to create an MSMQQueue object that you can use to manage the messages in the queue.

Here is a code sample for opening and retrieving messages from a message queue:

```
Const MQ_PEEK_ACCESS = 32
Const MQ_SEND_ACCESS = 2
Const MQ_RECEIVE_ACCESS = 1
Const MQ_DENY_NONE = 0
Const MQ_DENY_RECEIVE_SHARE = 1
Const MQ_TRANSACTIONAL = 1
Const MQ_TRANSACTIONAL_NONE = 0


Dim queueinfo As MSMQ.MSMQQueueInfo
Dim queue As MSMQ.MSMQQueue
Dim responsequeue As MSMQ.MSMQQueue
Dim responsequeueinfo As MSMQ.MSMQQueueInfo
Dim responsemsg As MSMQ.MSMQMessage

Dim queuemsg As MSMQ.MSMQMessage

Set queueinfo = New MSMQ.MSMQQueueInfo
queueinfo.PathName = "Dell420\TargetQueue"
Set queue = queueinfo.Open(MQ_RECEIVE_ACCESS, MQ_DENY_NONE)

queue.Reset
Set queuemsg = queue.PeekCurrent
Queue.reset
Set responsemsg = New MSMQ.MSMQMessage
```

```
Do While Not IsNull(queuemsg)
    Set queuemsq = queue.ReceiveCurrent(MQ_TRANSACTIONAL, , , 1000)
    'return a response message to the response queue
    Set responsequeueinfo = queuemsg.responsequeueinfo
    Set responsequeue = responsequeueinfo.Open(MQ_SEND_ACCESS, MQ_DENY_NONE)
    responsemsg.Label = "Receipt for : " & queuemsg.Label
    responsemsg.Body = "Message received"
    responsemsg.CorrelationId = queuemsg.Id
    responsemsg.Send responsequeue
Loop
queue.Close
```

The first thing you need to do to read the message from the queue is get a reference to the MSMQQueueInfo object for the message queue from which you want to read the messages. You then call the MSMQQueueInfo Open method to get the queue ready to retrieve messages.

The Open Method

The Open method takes two parameters: AccessMode and ShareMode. These parameters determine whether the queue allows the read or write operation, and whether the queue can be accessed by more than one process.

The AccessMode parameter can have the following values:

- *MQ_PEEK_ACCESS (32):* Messages can only be looked at. They cannot be removed from the queue.

- *MQ_SEND_ACCESS (2):* Messages can only be sent to the queue.

- *MQ_RECEIVE_ACCESS (1):* Messages can be retrieved from the queue or peeked at. See the description of the ShareMode parameter for information on limiting who can retrieve messages from the queue.

The ShareMode parameter can have these values:

- *MQ_DENY_NONE (0):* The queue is available to everyone—this is the default. This setting must be used if the AccessMode parameter is set to MQ_PEEK_ACCESS or MQ_SEND_ACCESS.

- *MQ_DENY_RECEIVE_SHARE (1):* Limits who can retrieve messages from the message queue. If the queue is already opened for retrieving messages by another process, this call fails and returns MQ_ERROR_SHARING_VIOLATION. MQ_DENY_RECEIVE_SHARE is applicable only when access is set to MQ_RECEIVE_ACCESS.

The Receive and ReceiveCurrent Methods

The Open method returns an MSMQQueue object. To receive the message, you can call either ReceiveCurrent or Receive. The Receive method reads the first message in the queue, and the ReceiveCurrent method reads the message pointed to by the current cursor. The messages will be deleted after they have been read.

The ReceiveCurrent method takes five optional parameters. This is the method signature:

```
set messageObject = queueObject.ReceiveCurrent( _
  [ Transaction] _
  [, WantDestinationQueue] _
  [, WantBody] _
  [, ReceiveTimeout] _
  [, WantConnectorType] _
)
```

The Transaction parameter can be either an MSMQTransaction object or one of the following constants:

- *MQ_NO_TRANSACTION (0):* Specifies that the call isn't part of a transaction.

- *MQ_MTS_TRANSACTION (1):* Specifies that the call is part of the current MTS transaction. This is the default.

- *MQ_XA_TRANSACTION (2):* Specifies that the call is part of an externally coordinated, XA-compliant transaction.

The WantDestinationQueue parameter defines whether MSMQMessage.DestinationQueueInfo will be updated to indicate that the message has been removed from the queue. This can significantly slow down the system; the default is false.

The WantBody parameter is optional, and it specifies whether the body of the message is needed. Set this property to false to optimize the speed of the application if the body of the message isn't needed. The other properties of the message will still be available when WantBody is set to false, which is false.

The ReceiveTimeout parameter indicates the number of milliseconds that will pass before the receive action times out. The default is -1 (infinite). If the message queue is empty, and ReceiveTimeout is -1, the queue object will be blocked at the receive method until a message arrives.

The WantConnectorType parameter indicates whether the receiving application wants to retrieve the ConnectorTypeGuid property of the message.

The MSMQQueueInfo Peek Method

To check whether messages exist in the queue without removing them, and to read them, you can call PeekCurrent or Peek. Here is an example of peeking at the messages in the queue:

```
'set the cursor to the first message in the queue
Set queuemsg = queue.PeekCurrent

Do While Not IsNull(queuemsg)
    msgbox(queuemsg.Label)
    Set queuemsg = queue.PeekNext
End Sub
```

The PeekCurrent or Reset method must be called to initialize the cursor before you can call PeekNext.

Responding to a Message

After receiving a message, you can send a response message. The response queue information can be retrieved through the ResponseQueueInfo property of the MSMQMessage. Then, you can create a new MSMQMessage object and set its CorrelationId equal to the original message's Id property. This gives the sending application the ability to match up the response message with its originally sent counterpart when it arrives at the response queue.

After the message is sent, the Close method is called to close the message's response queue.

So far, you've seen how to use the MSMQQueue object to retrieve and process messages after they arrive at the queue, but how do you know when to run this program to receive messages? One way to solve this problem is to run the program in an infinite loop, but that is far from a good solution. To find a better solution for this problem, let's look at the MSMQEvent object.

MSMQEvent

The MSMQEvent object turns message receiving from a synchronous operation to an asynchronous one through the event notification capability of MSMQ. The MSMQEvent object contains only two events: Arrived and ArrivedError.

To enable event notification for MSMQ, you'll do three things in your code:

1. Create an MSMQEvent.

2. Enable the notification on the queue you want to watch.

3. Implement the event handler method to fire when a message arrives at the queue.

The following example receives the message using MSMQ's event notification feature:

```
Private WithEvents QueueEvent As MSMQEvent

Public Function Start()
    Dim QueueInfo As MSMQ.MSMQQueueInfo
    Dim RequestQueue As MSMQ.MSMQQueue

    Set QueueInfo = New MSMQ.MSMQQueueInfo
    QueueInfo.PathName = "Dell420\TargetQueue"
    Set RequestQueue = QueueInfo.Open(MQ_RECEIVE_ACCESS, MQ_DENY_NONE)
    'start the event notification
    RequestQueue.EnableNotification QueueEvent
End Function

Sub QueueEvent_Arrived(ByVal queue As Object, ByVal cursor As Long)
    Dim RequestQueue As MSMQ.MSMQQueue
    Dim RequestMsg As MSMQ.MSMQMessage

    Set RequestQueue = queue
    Set RequestMsg = RequestQueue.Receive()
    If Not IsNull(RequestMsg) Then
        'Process the message
    End If
    'restart the event notification after each event fire
    RequestQueue.EnableNotification QueueEvent
End Sub
Sub QueueEvent_ArrivedError(ByVal queue As Object, ByVal cursor As Long)
    'Process the event
End Sub
```

In order to work with the event in the preceding code, you need to first create an event sink object, QueueEvent, using the WithEvents keyword. Next, you need to enable event notification by calling the EnableNotification method of the MSMQQueue object, and pass in the new event object you've just created.

Once you've enabled event notification, whenever a new message arrives at the queue, MSMQ will trigger the program's event handlers. There are two event handles implemented in the program: QueueEvent_Arrived and QueueEvent_ArrivedError.

It's important that you call the EnableNotification method again after each Arrived event is fired, because the method only sets up the notification for single event firing. The program remains idle until a message arrives. After the program processes the new message, it will return to idle state again to wait for the next message to arrive.

Internal and External MSMQ Transactions

MSMQ supports both nontransactional messaging and transactional messaging. It's much faster to send and receive messages in a nontransactional manner, but there are four problems associated with nontransactional messaging:

- Messages may be dropped or duplicated.

- There is no guarantee about the order in which messages are sent and received.

- There is no way to send and receive multiple messages as a single unit so that they either all succeed or are all rolled back.

- The caller application isn't guaranteed to be informed when an error occurs, so it cannot react to a failure.

To battle these problems, you can send and receive messages in either MSMQ internal transactions or MSMQ external transactions.

Internal MSMQ Transactions

MSMQ internal transactions are fast, but they don't allow the participation of other transactional resources, such as SQL Server. In other words, the MSMQ internal transactions can be used on MSMQ only.

Because you can send and receive messages in transactions, you must make sure the message queue is transactional. You need to specify that the queue supports transactions by checking the Transactional checkbox when you create the message queue, as shown in Figure A-10. After a message queue is marked as a transactional queue, it can no longer accept nontransactional messages.

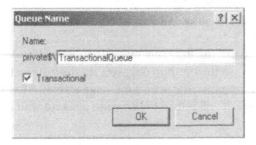

Figure A-10. Creating a message queue as a transactional queue

After you have a transactional queue, you can start sending single messages in a transaction in one of two ways. The following example shows messages sent using the MSMQTransaction object:

```
'declare and set the queuemsg and queue
Dim td As MSMQ.MSMQTransactionDispenser
Dim tx As MSMQ.MSMQTransaction
Set td = New MSMQ.MSMQTransactionDispenser
'start a transaction
'code for setting up queue object is omitted for easy viewing
Set tx = td.BeginTransaction()
queuemsg.Send queue, tx
'end the transaction
If Err <> 0 Then
    tx.Abort
Else
    tx.Commit
End If
```

This program first creates a new MSMQTransactionDispenser object. It then calls the MSMQTransactionDispenser object's BeginTransaction method to start a transaction. The method also returns a MSMQTransaction object, which will be passed to the Send method as a parameter. This makes the message-sending process a part of this transaction. When message has been sent, you can call either the Commit or Abort method of the MSMQTransaction object to end the transaction.

The same program can also be written without using the MSMQTransaction object, as shown here:

```
'declare and set the queuemsg and queue
queuemsg.Send queue, MQ_SINGLE_MESSAGE
```

Obviously, this second method of sending transactional messages is much easier when you are sending a single transactional message. However, you'll have to use the MSMQTransaction object when you want to send and receive multiple messages in one transaction. Here's an example:

```
On Error Resume Next
Dim td As MSMQ.MSMQTransactionDispenser
Dim tx As MSMQ.MSMQTransaction
Set td = New MSMQ.MSMQTransactionDispenser

'start a transaction
Set tx = td.BeginTransaction()
Set queuemsg1 = queue1.Receive(tx)
queuemsg1.Send queue2, tx
queuemsg1.Send queue3, tx
'end the transaction
If Err <> 0 Then
    tx.Abort
Else
    tx.Commit
End If
```

In this example, the message received from queue1 is sent to queue2 and queue3 in one transaction. Therefore, if the program were unable to send to queue3, the transaction would abort, causing the message sent to queue2 to be deleted and the original message received from the queue1 to be returned to queue1.

External MSMQ Transactions

Internal MSMQ transactions are fast and easy to create, especially when sending or receiving a single message from a queue. However, there is one major shortcoming—MSMQTransactionDispenser is unable to include other transactional resources in its transaction. Although MSMQ comes with MSMQCoordinatedTransactionDispenser to make MSMQ internal transactions work with other transaction resources, this approach requires you to add many low-level calls to your program to handle the coordination between different types of transactional resources. To avoid writing code to coordinate the resources yourself, you can rely on the COM+ runtime to handle the transaction for you. The COM+ runtime supports many transactional resource managers, such as those in MSMQ and SQL Server.

Here is an example of performing an MSMQ operation and SQL operation within one transaction:

```
On Error Resume Next
'declare queue and message
Dim ctx As ObjectContext
Set ctx = GetObjectContext()
'add code to modify the database...
'database code goes here.
'send and receive message with MQ_MTS_TRANSACTION
Set queuemsg1 = queue1.Receive(MQ_MTS_TRANSACTION)
queuemsg1.Send queue2, MQ_MTS_TRANSACTION
queuemsg1.Send queue3, MQ_MTS_TRANSACTION
If Err <> 0 Then
    ctx.SetAbort
Else
    ctx.SetComplete
End If
```

To access the ObjectContext object, you need to first include the COM+ Service Type Library in the project references. In the preceding example, the database modification and MSMQ operations will run in the same existing transaction context of the COM+ component. To provide this COM component with a transaction, you can configure the COM component to require a transaction in the Component Services console. The Require a transaction setting ensures the component will be running under either a newly created transaction or a transaction inherited from other COM components.

There is one problem in terms of receiving transactional messages from the message queue. In MSMQ 2.0, a message can only be received in a transactional manner from a local queue. If the message queue is located on a remote server, MSMQ can't guarantee that messages will be received in a transactional manner. This problem can potentially prohibit you from using a centralized message queue to route data to different applications. This leads to the next topic, the Message Queue Dispatcher, which takes care of this problem.

Message Queue Dispatcher

The key to solving the transactional remote receiving problem is to convert a transactional remote receive operation to a transactional local receive operation. When you implement a centralized MSMQ server to host all the messages, you can use the method shown in Figure A-11 to ensure that all the message transfers are done transactionally.

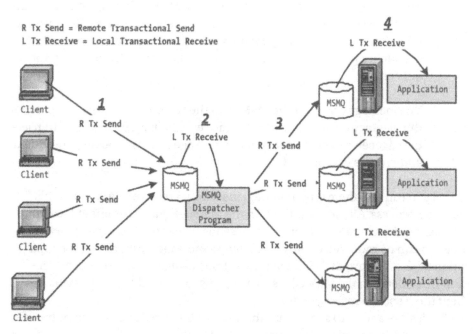

Figure A-11. Converting a remote transactional receive operation to a local transactional receive operation

Normally, when you implement a centralized MSMQ, the client will send the message to a queue, and the server will receive the message remotely. Since remote transactional receive operations aren't supported in MSMQ 2.0, you must do things a little differently. Basically, the solution can be broken down into four steps as shown in Figure A-11.

1. The client sends the message to a queue on the remote MSMQ server. Because MSMQ supports the remote transactional send operation, you can guarantee that the message is delivered once, and only once.

2. An MSMQ dispatcher program on the centralized MSMQ server watches for new messages to arrive at local queues. When a new message arrives, the dispatcher will pull the message out and forward it to the remote server that will eventually process the message for the client. Because this MSMQ dispatcher program is running on the MSMQ server, it performs a local transactional receive operation, which is supported in MSMQ 2.0.

3. The message is sent from the MSMQ server to the message queue on the remote server that actually processes the client's messages. Because this operation is another remote transactional send operation, the MSMQ dispatcher program can guarantee the message is delivered once and only once.

4. The message arrives at the MSMQ on the remote server that will process the messages. The application on the server will perform a local transactional receive operation to pull the message into its local message queue and process it as needed.

As you can see, there is no remote transactional receive operation in this four-step process. All the operations on the message queue are either local transactional receives or remote transactional sends. The same MSMQ dispatcher program can be modified to forward response messages from the server application back to the original client in transactions using the same concept. The ResponseQueue on the MSMQMessage object can be used to identify which client the response message is for.

Tables A-9 and A-10 summarize the support for transactional and nontransactional send and receive operations in MSMQ 2.0.

Table A-9. Send Operations in MSMQ 2.0

| | LOCAL QUEUE | | REMOTE QUEUE | |
	Transactional queue	Nontransactional queue	Transactional queue	Nontransactional queue
Transactional send operation	Yes	No	Yes	No
Nontransactional send operation	No	Yes	No	Yes

Table A-10. Receive Operations in MSMQ 2.0

	LOCAL QUEUE		REMOTE QUEUE	
	Transactional queue	Nontransactional queue	Transactional queue	Nontransactional queue
Transactional receive operation	Yes	No	No	No
Nontransactional receive operation	Yes	Yes	Yes	Yes

New Features in MSMQ 3.0

With the release of Windows XP, Microsoft introduced MSMQ 3.0. MSMQ 3.0 is only available for Windows XP and .NET servers currently. I have compiled a list of new key features in this latest version of MSMQ, and hopefully they'll spur your imagination on how they can be used in your future applications.

The first new feature I'll discuss is *Internet-ready message queuing*. Until MSMQ 3.0, all messages were sent and received behind the firewall. It was possible to send and receive messages to and from a message queue over the Internet, but this had almost never been done because many ports would have to be open to make communication between queues possible, and this has network security implications. MSMQ 3.0 resolves this problem by creating a hybrid of Web services and MSMQ, which allows messages to travel between different message queues across the Internet. You can use this feature out of the box to transmit messages across the Internet with a minimum of configuration.

MSMQ 3.0's object model handles the creation of SOAP messages when sending messages. On the receiving side, the close integration between IIS 6 and MSMQ 3.0 will take care of the processing of SOAP messages and of saving to the destination queue.

MSMQ 3.0 also implements SOAP extensions to handle reliable messaging so that queued messages are delivered once and only once. The concept behind the reliable messaging of MSMQ 3.0 is the same as that behind reliable messaging in BizTalk Server.

The next new feature to consider is the *one-to-many messaging model*. MSMQ 3.0 allows clients to send a message to multiple queues through messaging multicast and queue distribution lists. Messaging multicast is similar to a broadcast in which you "ping" a server. Messaging multicast supports only an "at-most-once" quality of service, and doesn't support transactional reads or writes. The benefit of this feature is that it allows you to send out messages to a huge number of recipients very effectively.

Queue distribution lists are similar to port distribution lists in BizTalk Server, in the sense that they take one message and send it out to a number of destinations. MSMQ 3.0 allows clients to send a message to each of the message queues on the list, and the list can be either generated at runtime or retrieved from Active Directory, where a predefined list can be stored. With queue distribution lists, multiple copies of the message are sent out from the client. Such operations will use many more network resources than messaging multicast, where only one copy of a message is sent to the network. However, the benefit of queue distribution lists is that they support transactional send operations.

MSMQ 3.0 also includes *additional management features*. The MSMQ 3.0 object model includes a set of APIs for managing and monitoring message queues. With these new APIs, you can write programs to retrieve message queue statistics, control and monitor the Message Queue service, track an individual queued message, etc.

Finally, let's look at *MSMQ trigger*. Actually, this isn't a new feature. MSMQ trigger has been around for some time and can still be downloaded as a separate program (that is, separate from Windows 2000) from Microsoft's Web site. MSMQ 3.0 includes this feature as part of its offering.

The idea of MSMQ trigger is simple. You tell it what COM component or executable file MSMQ trigger will run when a message arrives at a particular queue. It's similar to the MSMQ Receive Function, except MSMQ trigger sends the message to COM components and executables instead of to BizTalk Server's shared queue.

There are other new features besides those just mentioned. MSMQ 3.0 boosts performance significantly over previous versions. It also increases the queue storage limit to 1 terabyte from 2 gigabytes in MSMQ 2.0. The queue storage limit refers to the maximum amount of disk space that can be used to store the messages.

NOTE *MSMQ 3.0 still has a 4-megabyte size limit on a single message. It's also still unable to perform transactional reads from a remote queue.*

MSMQ 3.0 also sees a change in several features existing in previous versions. For example, IPX is no longer supported in MSMQ 3.0, which means you can't use MSMQ 3.0 in an IPX network such as a NetWare network. An MSMQ 3.0 dependent client only supports MSMQ 2.0-level functionalities.

For more information on MSMQ 3.0, visit `http://www.microsoft.com/msmq`.

Additional Resources on MSMQ

Several interesting whitepapers, available from Microsoft, can help you learn more about MSMQ and its application. You can find them at `http://www.microsoft.com/msmq/whitepapers.htm`.

Here is a list of some of these white papers:

- "Programming Best Practices with Microsoft Message Queuing Services (MSMQ)" discusses the best practices for building, troubleshooting, and testing distributed applications with Microsoft Message Queuing Services.

- "Optimizing Message Queuing Performance" discusses the MSMQ application designs that affect performance the most. It also includes a number of benchmarks done by Microsoft to show the performance impact of several designs and configurations.

- "Microsoft Message Queuing Services (MSMQ) Tips" discusses a number of tips and strategies for building MSMQ applications. It's a good source of sample code, too.

- "MSMQ 3.0 White Paper" tells all about the new features of MSMQ 3.0 in XP if you're interested in learning more about this version of MSMQ.

Summary

MSMQ has become a very important building block in the development of asynchronous applications today. Here you learned about the concepts of messaging queues, and the different types of message queues, such as MSMQ independent queue, MSMQ dependent queue, MSMQ server, etc. You also learned about scalability, interoperability, and transaction support in MSMQ.

You also saw MSMQ's programming models, illustrated by several code examples that used these object models to do some real work with MSMQ. Finally, you learned more about how to send and retrieve messages in a transactional manner, and how to create an MSMQ dispatcher to handle the problems associated with the transactional remote write operation.

BizTalk Server API Reference

THIS APPENDIX PROVIDES a convenient reference for the BizTalk Server APIs, culled from Microsoft's BizTalk online help. (Copyright 2002 Microsoft Corporation. All rights reserved.)

IInterchange Methods

NAME	DESCRIPTION
CheckSuspendedQueue	Returns a list of documents from the suspended queue that match the request criteria.
DeleteFromSuspendedQueue	Deletes all specified documents from the suspended queue.
GetSuspendedQueueItemDetails	Retrieves information about a single entry in the suspended queue.
Submit	Sends an interchange or document to BizTalk Server 2002 for asynchronous processing. BizTalk Server 2002 places the document in a queue until the next available server can process it.
SubmitSync	Sends an interchange or document to BizTalk Server 2002 for synchronous processing. An optional response document is returned to the caller.

IBTSAppIntegration Method

NAME	DESCRIPTION
ProcessMessage	Processes a document and returns a response document, if available. This method is called at run time when the server is sending a document to the component.

IPipelineComponent Methods

NAME	DESCRIPTION
EnableDesign	Configures the component for execution in one of two modes: design mode or execution mode
Execute	Executes the operation expected of the component, given the transport IDictionary object and other configuration settings

IPipelineComponentAdmin Methods

NAME	DESCRIPTION
GetConfigData	Returns an IDictionary object that contains the configuration data for the component to be used to display these values
SetConfigData	Sets the configuration for a component, using the contents of an IDictionary object

IBTSCustomProcess Methods

NAME	DESCRIPTION
Execute	Performs the custom processing on data obtained from a Receive Function
SetContext	Retrieves context information associated with the data being processed

IBizTalkTrackData Methods

NAME	DESCRIPTION
GetInDocDetails	Returns an ADO recordset that contains a list of the documents that were submitted to BizTalk Server by using the Interchange submit method
GetInterchanges	Returns an ADO recordset that contains a list of interchanges that were submitted to BizTalk Server by using the Interchange submit method, including all the data from the Tracking database
GetOutDocDetails	Returns an ADO recordset that contains a list of the documents that were generated as a result of the Interchange submit method

IBizTalkConfig Methods

NAME	DESCRIPTION
CreateChannel	Returns a new IBizTalkChannel object
CreateDocument	Returns a new IBizTalkDocument object
CreateEnvelope	Returns a new IBizTalkEnvelope object
CreateOrganization	Returns a new IBizTalkOrganization object
CreatePort	Returns a new IBizTalkPort object
CreatePortGroup	Returns a new IBizTalkPortGroup object

IBizTalkChannel Properties

NAME	DESCRIPTION
Comments	Contains user comments for the object
ControlNumberValue	Contains the value of the group control number
DateModified	Contains the date and time at which the information in the object was created or last modified
DecryptionCertificateInfo	Contains information about the certificate that decrypts the input document
ExpectReceiptTimeout	Contains the time, in minutes, in which to expect the receipt for the current document before treating the document as expired
Expression	Contains a complete set of equations that filter the selection of the object
Handle	Contains the identifier of the object
InputDocument	Contains the handle to the input IBizTalkDocument object that describes the input document specification
IsReceiptChannel	Contains the flag that indicates whether the object is a receipt channel
LoggingInfo	Contains information about logging the document
MapContent	Contains the contents of the map that provide instructions on how the input document in the format used by the source organization is to be rendered in the format used by the destination organization, if different
MapReference	Contains the full Web Distributed Authoring and Versioning (WebDAV) URL of the map that provides instructions on how the input document in the format used by the source organization is to be rendered in the format used by the destination organization, if different
Name	Contains the name of the object
OutputDocument	Contains the handle to the output IBizTalkDocument object that describes the output document specification
Port	Contains the handle to the associated IBizTalkPort object
PortGroup	Contains the handle to the associated IBizTalkPortGroup object
ReceiptChannel	Contains the handle to the receipt channel for this object
RetryCount	Contains the number of times to retry submitting a document when a destination connection failure occurs

(continued)

IBizTalkChannel Properties *(continued)*

NAME	DESCRIPTION
RetryInterval	Contains the amount of time, in minutes, between retry attempts when a destination connection failure occurs during document submission
SignatureCertificateInfo	Contains information about the certificate that signs the output document
SourceEndpoint	Contains information about the source
TrackFields	Contains the IDictionary object that points to the specification that contains fields to track interchange data on input documents for this IBizTalkChannel object
VerifySignatureCertificateInfo	Contains information about the certificate that verifies the signature of the input document

IBizTalkChannel Methods

NAME	DESCRIPTION
Clear	Clears the object from memory
Create	Creates a new object in the database
GetConfigComponent	Retrieves the CLSID of the component associated with the IBizTalkPort object
GetConfigData	Retrieves the configuration associated with the specified IBizTalkPort object
Load	Loads an object in memory
LoadByName	Loads an object by name in memory
Remove	Removes the object from the database
Save	Saves the object in the database
SetConfigComponent	Sets the CLSID of the component associated with the IBizTalkPort object
SetConfigData	Sets the configuration information for the associated IBizTalkPort object

IBizTalkDocument Properties

NAME	DESCRIPTION
Content	Contains the content of the document specification described by the object
DateModified	Contains the content of the document specification described by the object
Handle	Contains the handle to the object
Name	Contains the name of the object
NameSpace	Contains the string that resolves naming conflicts between elements in a document
PropertySet	Contains an IDictionary object that contains the electronic data interchange (EDI) selection criteria (name/value pairs) by which the server extracts information from the functional group header of the EDI document to identify the object when the document is input
Reference	Contains the full Web Distributed Authoring and Versioning (WebDAV) URL for the document specification referred to by this IBizTalkDocument object
TrackFields	Contains the full Web Distributed Authoring and Versioning (WebDAV) URL for the document specification referred to by this IBizTalkDocument object
Type	Contains the type of document specification
Version	Contains the version of the document standard

IBizTalkDocument Methods

NAME	DESCRIPTION
Clear	Clears the object from memory
Create	Creates a new object in the database
Load	Loads a specified object in memory
LoadByName	Loads a specified object by name in memory
LoadByPropertySet	Loads the document object by its PropertySet object
Remove	Removes the object from the database
Save	Saves the object in the database

IBizTalkOrganization Properties

NAME	DESCRIPTION
Aliases	Contains an ADO recordset of aliases that refer to the object
Applications	Contains an ADO recordset of applications that refer to the object
Comments	Contains user comments for the object
DateModified	Contains the date and time at which the information in the object was created or last modified
Handle	Contains the handle to the object
IsDefault	Contains a value that indicates whether the object is the default organization
Name	Contains the name of the object

IBizTalkOrganization Methods

NAME	DESCRIPTION
Clear	Clears the object from memory
Create	Creates a new object in the database
CreateAlias	Creates an alias for the object
CreateApplication	Creates a new application
GetDefaultAlias	Retrieves the default alias for the object
Load	Loads a specified object in memory
LoadAlias	Loads an existing alias for the object in memory
LoadApplication	Loads an application in memory
LoadByName	Loads a specified object by name in memory
Remove	Removes the object from the database
RemoveAlias	Removes an alias
RemoveApplication	Removes an application
Save	Saves the object in the database
SaveAlias	Saves the alias
SaveApplication	Saves the application

IBizTalkPort Properties

NAME	DESCRIPTION
Channels	Contains an ADO recordset that includes information about all IBizTalkChannel objects that refer to the object
Comments	Contains the user comments for the IBizTalkPort object
ControlNumberValue	Contains the value of the interchange control number
DateModified	Contains the date and time at which the information in the object was created or last modified
Delimiters	Contains an IDictionary object that includes all delimiters used in the document specification
DestinationEndpoint	Contains information about the destination
EncodingType	Contains an enumeration value that indicates the type of document encoding
EncryptionCertificateInfo	Contains information about the certificate that encrypts the document
EncryptionType	Contains an enumeration value that indicates the type of document encryption
Envelope	Contains a handle to the IBizTalkEnvelope object associated with this IBizTalkPort object
Handle	Contains the handle to the object
Name	Contains the name of the object
PrimaryTransport	Contains the primary transport component information
SecondaryTransport	Contains the secondary transport component information
ServiceWindowInfo	Contains the service window information
SignatureType	Contains an enumeration value that indicates the type of digital signing and verification

IBizTalkPort Methods

NAME	DESCRIPTION
Clear	Clears the object from memory
Create	Creates a new object in the database
Load	Loads a specified object in memory
LoadByName	Loads a specified object by name in memory
Remove	Removes the object from the database
Save	Saves the object in the database

IBizTalkEnvelope Properties

NAME	DESCRIPTION
Content	Contains the contents of the selected envelope format specification
DateModified	Contains the date and time at which the information in the object was created or last modified
Format	Contains a string that identifies the type of envelope
Handle	Contains the handle to the object
Name	Contains the name of the object
NameSpace	Contains a string that resolves naming conflicts between elements in an envelope specification
Reference	Contains a full Web Distributed Authoring and Versioning (WebDAV) URL name of the envelope format specification file
Version	Contains the version of the envelope format specification

IBizTalkEnvelope Methods

NAME	DESCRIPTION
Clear	Clears the object from memory
Create	Creates a new object in the database
Load	Loads a specified object in memory
LoadByName	Loads a specified object by name in memory
Remove	Removes the object from the database
Save	Saves the object in the database

IBizTalkPortGroup Properties

NAME	DESCRIPTION
Channels	Contains an ADO recordset that holds information about all IBizTalkChannel objects that refer to this object
DateModified	Contains the date and time at which the information in the object was created or last modified
Handle	Contains the handle to the object
Name	Contains the name of the object
Ports	Contains an ADO recordset that contains information about all IBizTalkPort objects that refer to this object

IBizTalkPortGroup Methods

NAME	DESCRIPTION
AddPort	Adds an IBizTalkPort object to this port group. There must be at least one IBizTalkPort object in the port group.
Clear	Clears the object from memory.
Create	Creates a new object in the database.
Load	Loads a specified object in memory.
LoadByName	Loads a specified object by name in memory.
Remove	Removes the object from the database.
RemovePort	Removes an IBizTalkPort object from the port group. There must be at least one IBizTalkPort object in the port group.
Save	Saves the object in the database.

IWFWorkflowInstance Properties

NAME	DESCRIPTION
CompletionStatus	Contains a value that indicates the success or failure of the XLANG schedule instance
FullPortName	Contains the full name of a port in a form usable by the associated technology, such as a COM moniker or message queue pathname or a channel name
FullyQualifiedName	Contains the fully qualified name of this XLANG schedule instance
InstanceId	Contains the globally unique identifier (GUID) assigned to the current XLANG schedule instance
IsCompleted	Contains a value that indicates whether the XLANG schedule instance has finished executing
ModuleId	Contains the globally unique identifier (GUID) of the XML module associated with the current XLANG schedule instance
ModuleName	Contains the name of the XML module associated with the current XLANG schedule instance

(continued)

IWFWorkflowInstance Properties *(continued)*

NAME	DESCRIPTION
ParentInstanceID	Contains the globally unique identifier (GUID) assigned to the parent XLANG schedule instance of the current schedule instance
Port	Contains a IWFProxy reference to the named port. This is applicable only to COM-based port bindings

IWFWorkflowInstance Method

NAME	DESCRIPTION
WaitForCompletion	Blocks and doesn't return until the schedule instance that is referenced has completed

IWFProxy Properties

NAME	DESCRIPTION
FullyQualifiedName	Contains the fully qualified name of a COM-bound port
WorkflowInstance	Contains a reference to the current XLANG schedule instance

Index

Apress Titles

ISBN	PRICE	AUTHOR	TITLE
1-893115-73-9	$34.95	Abbott	Voice Enabling Web Applications: VoiceXML and Beyond
1-59059-061-9	$34.95	Allen	Bug Patterns in Java
1-893115-01-1	$39.95	Appleman	Dan Appleman's Win32 API Puzzle Book and Tutorial for Visual Basic Programmers
1-893115-23-2	$29.95	Appleman	How Computer Programming Works
1-893115-97-6	$39.95	Appleman	Moving to VB .NET: Strategies, Concepts, and Code
1-59059-023-6	$39.95	Baker	Adobe Acrobat 5: The Professional User's Guide
1-59059-039-2	$49.95	Barnaby	Distributed .NET Programming in C#
1-59059-068-6	$49.95	Barnaby	Distributed .NET Programming in VB .NET
1-59059-063-5	$29.95	Baum	Dave Baum's Definitive Guide to LEGO MINDSTORMS, Second Edition
1-893115-84-4	$29.95	Baum/Gasperi/Hempel/Villa	Extreme MINDSTORMS: An Advanced Guide to LEGO MINDSTORMS
1-893115-82-8	$59.95	Ben-Gan/Moreau	Advanced Transact-SQL for SQL Server 2000
1-893115-91-7	$39.95	Birmingham/Perry	Software Development on a Leash
1-893115-48-8	$29.95	Bischof	The .NET Languages: A Quick Translation Guide
1-59059-041-4	$49.95	Bock	CIL Programming: Under the Hood™ of .NET
1-59059-053-8	$44.95	Bock/Stromquist/Fischer/Smith	.NET Security
1-893115-67-4	$49.95	Borge	Managing Enterprise Systems with the Windows Script Host
1-59059-019-8	$49.95	Cagle	SVG Programming: The Graphical Web
1-893115-28-3	$44.95	Challa/Laksberg	Essential Guide to Managed Extensions for C++
1-893115-39-9	$44.95	Chand	A Programmer's Guide to ADO.NET in C#
1-59059-034-1	$59.99	Chen	BizTalk Server 2002 Design and Implementation
1-59059-015-5	$39.95	Clark	An Introduction to Object Oriented Programming with Visual Basic .NET
1-893115-44-5	$29.95	Cook	Robot Building for Beginners
1-893115-99-2	$39.95	Cornell/Morrison	Programming VB .NET: A Guide for Experienced Programmers
1-893115-72-0	$39.95	Curtin	Developing Trust: Online Privacy and Security
1-59059-014-7	$44.95	Drol	Object-Oriented Macromedia Flash MX
1-59059-008-2	$29.95	Duncan	The Career Programmer: Guerilla Tactics for an Imperfect World
1-59059-057-0	$29.99	Farkas/Govier	Use Your PC to Build an Incredible Home Theater System
1-893115-71-2	$39.95	Ferguson	Mobile .NET
1-893115-90-9	$49.95	Finsel	The Handbook for Reluctant Database Administrators
1-893115-42-9	$44.95	Foo/Lee	XML Programming Using the Microsoft XML Parser
1-59059-024-4	$49.95	Fraser	Real World ASP.NET: Building a Content Management System
1-893115-55-0	$34.95	Frenz	Visual Basic and Visual Basic .NET for Scientists and Engineers
1-59059-038-4	$49.95	Gibbons	.NET Development for Java Programmers
1-893115-85-2	$34.95	Gilmore	A Programmer's Introduction to PHP 4.0

ISBN	PRICE	AUTHOR	TITLE
1-893115-36-4	$34.95	Goodwill	Apache Jakarta-Tomcat
1-893115-17-8	$59.95	Gross	A Programmer's Introduction to Windows DNA
1-893115-62-3	$39.95	Gunnerson	A Programmer's Introduction to C#, Second Edition
1-59059-030-9	$49.95	Habibi/Patterson/ Camerlengo	The Sun Certified Java Developer Exam with J2SE 1.4
1-893115-30-5	$49.95	Harkins/Reid	SQL: Access to SQL Server
1-59059-009-0	$49.95	Harris/Macdonald	Moving to ASP.NET: Web Development with VB .NET
1-59059-091-0	$24.99	Hempel	LEGO Spybotics Secret Agent Training Manual
1-59059-006-6	$39.95	Hetland	Practical Python
1-893115-10-0	$34.95	Holub	Taming Java Threads
1-893115-04-6	$34.95	Hyman/Vaddadi	Mike and Phani's Essential C++ Techniques
1-893115-96-8	$59.95	Jorelid	J2EE FrontEnd Technologies: A Programmer's Guide to Servlets, JavaServer Pages, and Enterprise JavaBeans
1-59059-029-5	$39.99	Kampa/Bell	Unix Storage Management
1-893115-49-6	$39.95	Kilburn	Palm Programming in Basic
1-893115-50-X	$34.95	Knudsen	Wireless Java: Developing with Java 2, Micro Edition
1-893115-79-8	$49.95	Kofler	Definitive Guide to Excel VBA
1-893115-57-7	$39.95	Kofler	MySQL
1-893115-87-9	$39.95	Kurata	Doing Web Development: Client-Side Techniques
1-893115-75-5	$44.95	Kurniawan	Internet Programming with Visual Basic
1-893115-38-0	$24.95	Lafler	Power AOL: A Survival Guide
1-59059-066-X	$39.95	Lafler	Power SAS: A Survival Guide
1-59059-049-X	$54.99	Lakshman	Oracle9i PL/SQL: A Developer's Guide
1-893115-46-1	$36.95	Lathrop	Linux in Small Business: A Practical User's Guide
1-59059-045-7	$49.95	MacDonald	User Interfaces in C#: Windows Forms and Custom Controls
1-893115-19-4	$49.95	Macdonald	Serious ADO: Universal Data Access with Visual Basic
1-59059-044-9	$49.95	MacDonald	User Interfaces in VB .NET: Windows Forms and Custom Controls
1-893115-06-2	$39.95	Marquis/Smith	A Visual Basic 6.0 Programmer's Toolkit
1-893115-22-4	$27.95	McCarter	David McCarter's VB Tips and Techniques
1-59059-040-6	$49.99	Mitchell/Allison	Real-World SQL-DMO for SQL Server
1-59059-021-X	$34.95	Moore	Karl Moore's Visual Basic .NET: The Tutorials
1-893115-27-5	$44.95	Morrill	Tuning and Customizing a Linux System
1-893115-76-3	$49.95	Morrison	C++ For VB Programmers
1-59059-003-1	$44.95	Nakhimovsky/Meyers	XML Programming: Web Applications and Web Services with JSP and ASP
1-893115-80-1	$39.95	Newmarch	A Programmer's Guide to Jini Technology
1-893115-58-5	$49.95	Oellermann	Architecting Web Services
1-59059-020-1	$44.95	Patzer	JSP Examples and Best Practices
1-893115-81-X	$39.95	Pike	SQL Server: Common Problems, Tested Solutions
1-59059-017-1	$34.95	Rainwater	Herding Cats: A Primer for Programmers Who Lead Programmers
1-59059-025-2	$49.95	Rammer	Advanced .NET Remoting (C# Edition)
1-59059-062-7	$49.95	Rammer	Advanced .NET Remoting in VB .NET

ISBN	PRICE	AUTHOR	TITLE
1-59059-028-7	$39.95	Rischpater	Wireless Web Development, Second Edition
1-893115-93-3	$34.95	Rischpater	Wireless Web Development with PHP and WAP
1-893115-89-5	$59.95	Shemitz	Kylix: The Professional Developer's Guide and Reference
1-893115-40-2	$39.95	Sill	The qmail Handbook
1-893115-24-0	$49.95	Sinclair	From Access to SQL Server
1-59059-026-0	$49.95	Smith	Writing Add-ins for Visual Studio .NET
1-893115-94-1	$29.95	Spolsky	User Interface Design for Programmers
1-893115-53-4	$44.95	Sweeney	Visual Basic for Testers
1-59059-035-X	$59.95	Symmonds	GDI+ Programming in C# and VB .NET
1-59059-002-3	$44.95	Symmonds	Internationalization and Localization Using Microsoft .NET
1-59059-010-4	$54.95	Thomsen	Database Programming with C#
1-59059-032-5	$59.95	Thomsen	Database Programming with Visual Basic .NET, Second Edition
1-893115-65-8	$39.95	Tiffany	Pocket PC Database Development with eMbedded Visual Basic
1-59059-027-9	$59.95	Torkelson/Petersen/Torkelson	Programming the Web with Visual Basic .NET
1-59059-018-X	$34.95	Tregar	Writing Perl Modules for CPAN
1-893115-59-3	$59.95	Troelsen	C# and the .NET Platform
1-59059-011-2	$59.95	Troelsen	COM and .NET Interoperability
1-893115-26-7	$59.95	Troelsen	Visual Basic .NET and the .NET Platform: An Advanced Guide
1-893115-54-2	$49.95	Trueblood/Lovett	Data Mining and Statistical Analysis Using SQL
1-893115-68-2	$54.95	Vaughn	ADO.NET and ADO Examples and Best Practices for VB Programmers, Second Edition
1-59059-012-0	$49.95	Vaughn/Blackburn	ADO.NET Examples and Best Practices for C# Programmers
1-893115-83-6	$44.95	Wells	Code Centric: T-SQL Programming with Stored Procedures and Triggers
1-893115-95-X	$49.95	Welschenbach	Cryptography in C and C++
1-893115-05-4	$39.95	Williamson	Writing Cross-Browser Dynamic HTML
1-59059-060-0	$39.95	Wright	ADO.NET: From Novice to Pro, Visual Basic .NET Edition
1-893115-78-X	$49.95	Zukowski	Definitive Guide to Swing for Java 2, Second Edition
1-893115-92-5	$49.95	Zukowski	Java Collections
1-893115-98-4	$54.95	Zukowski	Learn Java with JBuilder 6

Available at bookstores nationwide or from Springer Verlag New York, Inc. at 1-800-777-4643; fax 1-212-533-3503. Contact us for more information at sales@apress.com.

apress™

books for professionals by professionals™

About Apress

Apress, located in Berkeley, CA, is a fast-growing, innovative publishing company devoted to meeting the needs of existing and potential programming professionals. Simply put, the "A" in Apress stands for *"The Author's Press"*™ and its books have *"The Expert's Voice"*™. Apress' unique approach to publishing grew out of conversations between its founders Gary Cornell and Dan Appleman, authors of numerous best-selling, highly regarded books for programming professionals. In 1998 they set out to create a publishing company that emphasized quality above all else. Gary and Dan's vision has resulted in the publication of over 50 titles by leading software professionals, all of which have *The Expert's Voice*™.

Do You Have What It Takes to Write for Apress?

Apress is rapidly expanding its publishing program. If you can write and refuse to compromise on the quality of your work, if you believe in doing more than rehashing existing documentation, and if you're looking for opportunities and rewards that go far beyond those offered by traditional publishing houses, we want to hear from you!

Consider these innovations that we offer all of our authors:

- **Top royalties with *no* hidden switch statements**
  Authors typically only receive half of their normal royalty rate on foreign sales. In contrast, Apress' royalty rate remains the same for both foreign and domestic sales.

- **A mechanism for authors to obtain equity in Apress**
  Unlike the software industry, where stock options are essential to motivate and retain software professionals, the publishing industry has adhered to an outdated compensation model based on royalties alone. In the spirit of most software companies, Apress reserves a significant portion of its equity for authors.

- **Serious treatment of the technical review process**
  Each Apress book has a technical reviewing team whose remuneration depends in part on the success of the book since they too receive royalties.

Moreover, through a partnership with Springer-Verlag, New York, Inc., one of the world's major publishing houses, Apress has significant venture capital behind it. Thus, we have the resources to produce the highest quality books *and* market them aggressively.

If you fit the model of the Apress author who can write a book that gives the "professional what he or she needs to know"™," then please contact one of our Editorial Directors, Dan Appleman (dan_appleman@apress.com), Gary Cornell (gary_cornell@apress.com), Jason Gilmore (jason_gilmore@apress.com), Simon Hayes (simon_hayes@apress.com), Karen Watterson (karen_watterson@apress.com), or John Zukowski (john_zukowski@apress.com) for more information.